Not-God

Not-God

A History Of Alcoholics Anonymous

Ernest Kurtz

HAZELDEN®

INFORMATION & EDUCATIONAL SERVICES

Grateful acknowledgment is made for permission to reprint the following:

Excerpts from *Bill W.* by Robert Thomsen. Harper & Row, Publishers, Inc. Copyright 1975 by Robert Thomsen. Reprinted by permission of the publishers.

Excerpts from *Alcoholics Anonymous*. Copyright 1939, 1955, 1976 by Alcoholics Anonymous World Services, Inc. Reprinted by permission of Alcoholics Anonymous World Services, Inc.

Excerpts from *Twelve Steps And Twelve Traditions*. Copyright 1952, 1953 by Alcoholics Anonymous World Services, Inc. Reprinted by permission of Alcoholics Anonymous World Services, Inc.

Excerpts from *Alcoholics Anonymous Comes of Age*. Copyright 1957 by Alcoholics Anonymous World Services, Inc. Reprinted by permission of Alcoholics Anonymous World Services, Inc.

The "A.A. Preamble," copyright © 1958 by the A.A. Grapevine, Inc. Reprinted by permission.

To
G.H.
with gratitude

About the Book

Not-God is a fascinating, fast-moving, and authoritative account of the discovery and development of the program and fellowship that we know today as Alcoholics Anonymous.

Easily readable, *Not-God* contains more anecdotes and excerpts from the diaries, correspondence, and occasional memoirs of A.A.'s early figures than are heard in a hundred A.A. meetings. Kurtz traces the interesting debts that A.A. owes to such persons and groups as the psychiatrist Carl Jung, American philosopher William James, Akron social matron Henrietta Seiberling, and John D. Rockefeller, Jr., as well as the Oxford Group of Frank Buchman, a few Irish-American Catholic priests, and fundamentalist religion.

Beginning with the well-known visit between the sober Ebby T. and the drunken Bill Wilson, Kurtz documents Wilson's spiritual awakening (or "hot flash" as the first fifty A.A.s called it), his desire to tell other alcoholics what he had discovered, and his ever-growing conviction that to stay sober he *must* work with other alcoholics.

The story relates the importance of the Oxford Group to the development of A.A., the painful writing of the Big Book, even the problems caused over the years by Wilson's unofficial status as "Head of A.A.," and the fight involving the A.A. Board of Trustees. All is told in the context of two important points: Wilson and the first recovered alcoholics were keenly aware of their own limitation as alcoholics, and—more important— they discovered a health and wholeness, a maturity, as sober individuals within the fellowship of A.A.

Ernest Kurtz was given full and complete access to the archives of the General Service Office of Alcoholics Anonymous in New York. His unhindered research, coupled with extensive interviews of surviving early members and friends of A.A., has resulted in an account with documented accuracy.

Not-God clearly details the slow but unswerving development of a program of recovery for alcoholics, and it carries the message that Alcoholics Anonymous as a program and fellowship has to give to the United States of America in the middle third of the twentieth century.

About the Author

Ernest Kurtz received his Ph.D. in the History of American Civilization from Harvard University in 1978 and came to the study of history after professional experience in both religion and psychology.

He is on the faculty of the Rutgers University Summer School of Alcohol Studies, and holds the title of Adjunct Research Scientist at the Center for Self-Help Research and Knowledge Dissemination at the University of Michigan, Ann Arbor.

"First of all we had to quit playing God."

Alcoholics Anonymous, p. 62

Contents

PREFACE AND ACKNOWLEDGMENTS xi

PART ONE: The History

              Introduction 3

    I   Beginnings: November 1934–June 1935
        The Limitations of the Drinking Alcoholic 7

   II First Growth: June 1935–November 1937
        The Limitations of the Sober Alcoholic 37

  III Independent Existence: November 1937–October
        1939 Finding Wholeness in Limitation 59

   IV Prelude to Maturity: October 1939–March 1941
        Needing Others — The Era of Publicity 83

    V Attaining Maturity: 1941–1955
        The Limitations of Alcoholics Anonymous........ 111

   VI Responsibilities of Maturity: 1955–1971
        Alcoholics Anonymous and the Wholeness
        of Limitation................................ 135

PART TWO: The Interpretation

              Introduction 157

   VII The Larger Context of American History 161

  VIII The Context of the History of Religious Ideas 175

   IX The Meaning and Significance of
        Alcoholics Anonymous....................... 199

APPENDIX A 231

APPENDIX B.. 251

NOTES 307

BIBLIOGRAPHY 409

BIBLIOGRAPHY INDEX 423

GENERAL INDEX 428

HAZELDEN INFORMATION AND EDUCATIONAL SERVICES is a division of the Hazelden Foundation, a not-for-profit organization. Since 1949, Hazelden has been a leader in promoting the dignity and treatment of people afflicted with the disease of chemical dependency.

The mission of the foundation is to improve the quality of life for individuals, families, and communities by providing a national continuum of information, education, and recovery services that are widely accessible; to advance the field through research and training; and to improve our quality and effectiveness through continuous improvement and innovation.

Stemming from that, the mission of this division is to provide quality information and support to people wherever they may be in their personal journey—from education and early intervention, through treatment and recovery, to personal and spiritual growth.

Although our treatment programs do not necessarily use everything Hazelden publishes, our bibliotherapeutic materials support our mission and the Twelve Step philosophy upon which it is based. We encourage your comments and feedback.

The headquarters of the Hazelden Foundation are in Center City, Minnesota. Additional treatment facilities are located in Chicago, Illinois; New York, New York; Plymouth, Minnesota; St. Paul, Minnesota; and West Palm Beach, Florida. At these sites, we provide a continuum of care for men and women of all ages. Our Plymouth facility is designed specifically for youth and families.

For more information on Hazelden, please call **1-800-257-7800**. Or you may access our World Wide Web site on the Internet at **http://www.hazelden.org**.

PREFACE
ACKNOWLEDGMENTS

It is always out of place to attempt to justify or to demonstrate the significance of a subject in the introduction to its study. If this statement could be intensified, that strengthening would apply preeminently to the subject of Alcoholics Anonymous. Similarly, simple acknowledgment rarely does justice to the depth and the breadth of the assistance enjoyed by any student in the pursuit of his or her subject. If this second observation can be enhanced, that heightening applies especially to this writer on this topic.

Professor Milton Maxwell and Professor George Gordon of the Trustees' Archives Committee of the General Service Board of Alcoholics Anonymous did more than introduce me to "official" A.A. They offered interest, encouragement, and tempered enthusiasm as well as the approval necessary for research in the primary sources. As the custodian of sensitive materials, the Trustees' Archives Committee bears great responsibility to the hundreds of thousands of members of Alcoholics Anonymous who have placed implicit trust in their professional judgment. Before the present project, never had any researcher been granted the access to materials that I requested as necessary to this endeavor. Yet, over several meetings I felt not so much screened as welcomed into a sharing of their responsibility. For such trust, I am grateful.

Beyond archival research, this study required immersion in the alcoholism literature and attendance at many meetings of Alcoholics Anonymous. My appreciation of Alcoholics Anonymous as "fellowship" as well as "program" was born at the latter, and for this I am especially grateful to six friends. They have insisted that their names remain completely unmentioned, and I accede to their wish. However I wish to

honor their contribution by the simple observation that there is but one
term adequate to describe their dedication to this project at its deepest
level — love. Their evident commitment to sobriety as honesty and their
patience with my early challenges to their beloved program in many
ways gave birth to the decision to pursue this project at this depth.

My research in the alcoholism literature, begun at the Center of Alcohol Studies of Rutgers University, was carried on most intensively at
the Hazelden Foundation in Center City, Minnesota. As a treatment
center for alcoholism and other chemical addictions as well as a research
center for problems of addiction and their treatment, Hazelden afforded the most helpful as well as a most congenial setting for my
research. I am grateful to the director of Hazelden, Dr. Daniel J. Anderson, to his staff, and especially to the late Sr. Mary Leo Kammeier,
C.S.J., of Hazelden's Research Department for their cheerful good will,
profound trust, and enthusiastic assistance.

The historical study of a subject of less than fifty years' existence
necessarily involves extensive research by interview. Especially the following people, significant in the early history of Alcoholics Anonymous,
gave generous and infallibly courteous help — at times in the face of
questioning that no doubt too often seemed impertinent: Lois Wilson,
Henrietta Seiberling, Marty Mann, Clarence S., Warren C., and Dick P.
I am deeply grateful to each of these kind individuals for their assistance,
honesty, and trust.

A very special acknowledgment must be reserved for Nell Wing,
long-time secretary to A.A. co-founder Bill Wilson and present archivist
of Alcoholics Anonymous. Her deep knowledge of the materials, her
generosity in sharing personal recollections, her faithful devotion to
assisting this project, her help with introductions and contacts, her
ready response to occasionally desperate requests for verification: all
these were exceeded by only one thing — her unfailing cheerfulness in
her dedication to service.

At this moment of history, the term "mentor" seems in danger of
destruction by cliché. Such a loss would be tragic, for the concept bears
a meaning that is profound. It has been my privilege and good fortune
to profit as person as well as student from the mentoring guidance of
two skilled historians, Professor Oscar Handlin and Professor William
R. Hutchison. Each labored tirelessly and far beyond ordinary responsibility to improve a style that was initially opaque. Each challenged assumptions and laid bare tortuous reasoning. Each encouraged or chas-
tised as one or the other impetus was needed; and each carefully shared
his own developing enthusiasm for the project as my ardor at times

waned in the labors of research and writing. To both, I am grateful: beyond the requirements of any academic relationship, these dedicated scholars have taught me that — and how — scholarship is humanizing.

In its final stages, this manuscript was read by Dr. Daniel J. Anderson, Dr. Sarah E. Williams, Professor Philip Natale, and Professor John J. Quinn. Their comments, offered from their deep knowledge of the field of alcoholism studies, of Alcoholics Anonymous, and of literary acceptability, led to many minor changes and one major revision. If this study has usefulness to workers in the alcoholism field, it is largely due to the informed suggestions of Dr. Anderson, who also guided the early stages of my research into the alcoholism literature. Dr. Williams at a critical moment facilitated my understanding more deeply an aspect of my subject that until our meeting had eluded me. Professor Natale, beyond encouraging this study in its earliest stages, shared the burden of late stylistic revision. Professor Quinn guided the revision of Part Two, offering substantial as well as stylistic guidance and the encouragement of his contagious enthusiasm for some of the larger ideas attempted in that interpretation. To each of them, I am grateful for much.

The staff of the Hazelden Press, especially Mr. John Burns who exercised final editorial responsibility, offered their skill, patience, and enthusiasm, rendering more enjoyable than tedious the task of turning a technical dissertation into a readable book. I am especially grateful to them for their willingness and care to make available to a wide variety of readers the scholarly apparatus that, on the topic of Alcoholics Anonymous, should interest many readers who are not themselves scholars.

Finally, especially for the beginning of several of the interpretive insights explored in Part Two, I am grateful to my sister, Mary Ann Kurtz, who at the time of this research was Research Instructor in Psychology, Department of Pediatrics, The Medical College of Pennsylvania. Beyond the requirements of siblinghood, she gave generously of her time and skilled insight in drawing on her knowledge of the psychological literature to direct my attention to and aid my exploration of valuable and productive ideas deriving from current research. Whatever contribution this study might make to psychological thinking on alcoholism is largely due to her generosity and patience in assisting this endeavor in the midst of her own continuing responsibilities.

Despite all this diligent assistance from mentors, readers, and others, I am aware that very probably some flaws of citation and infelicities of style remain: the responsibility for these is, of course, only my own.

14 July 1979   ERNEST KURTZ

PART ONE

The History

INTRODUCTION

The term *not-God* is the theme around which this history of Alcoholics Anonymous is recounted and its interpretation offered. The exact phrase appears nowhere in either the published literature of Alcoholics Anonymous or the primary sources used in this research, yet the two senses contained in this expression not only pervade the written documents but also lie at the heart of the A.A. fellowship and program.

"Not-God" means first "You are not God," the message of the A.A. program. As is clear from the epigraph on page vii — a pungent reminder drawn from the very heart of "How It Works," the key fifth chapter of the book *Alcoholics Anonymous* — the fundamental and first message of Alcoholics Anonymous to its members is that they are not infinite, not absolute, *not God*. Every alcoholic's problem had *first* been, according to this insight, claiming God-like powers, especially that of *control*. But the alcoholic at least, the message insists, is *not* in control, even of himself; and the first step towards recovery from alcoholism must be admission and acceptance of this fact that is so blatantly obvious to others but so tenaciously denied by the obsessive-compulsive drinker. Historically, it has been the concept of divinity, the notion of the deity, that includes the idea of absolute control. The program of Alcoholics Anonymous, then, teaches first and foremost that the alcoholic is *not* God. This insight rules each of the Twelve Suggested Steps, although it is appropriately most clear in the First: "We admitted we were powerless over alcohol — that our lives had become *unmanageable*" (emphasis added).

But Alcoholics Anonymous is *fellowship* as well as *program*, and thus there is a second side to its message of not-God-ness. Because the alcoholic is not God, not absolute, not infinite, he or she is essentially limited. Yet from this very limitation — from the alcoholic's *acceptance* of personal limitation — arises the beginning of healing and wholeness. It is this facet of the message of "not-God" that Alcoholics Anonymous as fellowship lives out. To be an alcoholic within Alcoholics Anonymous is not only to accept oneself as not God; it implies also affirmation of one's connectedness with other alcoholics. It is this connection that historically has provided for hundreds of thousands of people a way out of active alcoholism and the path into a life of health, happiness, and wholeness. The invitation to make such a connection with others and the awareness of the necessity of doing so arise from the alcoholic's very acceptance of limitation. Thus, this second message that affirms limitation is well conveyed by the hyphenated phrase, "not-God.

The form "not-God" further reminds that affirmation is rooted in negation, that the alcoholic's acceptance of self as human is founded in his rejection of any claim to be more than human. And the hyphen — a connecting mark — reminds of the need for connectedness with other alcoholics that A.A. as *fellowship* lives out and enables. The fulfilling of the implications of being not-God, the living out of the connectedness with others that comes about from the alcoholic's very limitation, is the story of Alcoholics Anonymous. It is this story, this history, that this book narrates.

"Not God," then, and "not-God": the alcoholic as essentially limited, but able to find a healing wholeness in the acceptance of this limitation. It is the author's hope that this distinction is less cute than memorable, for it is his conviction that this twofold message is one that not only the alcoholic but also modern mankind needs to hear and perhaps, then, even to heed.

Two further prefatory points, appropriate because of this book's origin as a doctoral dissertation. Part Two of the present study is an expansion of the final single chapter of the dissertation. That chapter was directed to scholars and assumed a comprehensive knowledge of interpretive themes in the history of ideas in America. In this expansion for a more general audience, I have at times chosen from among differing interpretations of some of these themes without detailing the historiographic reasoning underlying such choice. Scholarly readers interested in that historiographic process may consult the dissertation, which is available in the archives of Harvard University. The general reader will not suffer by not doing so.

Because of the diverse audiences this book hopes to reach and the widespread knowledge among members of Alcoholics Anonymous of many episodes in A.A. history, the dissertation's scholarly apparatus has in general been retained. The citation numerals within the text refer to the endnotes, which begin on page 308. A few notes that appeared in the dissertation as endnotes are so illuminating that they have been printed herein as footnotes. The general reader will not lose much by referring to those that remain as endnotes only occasionally, on points of special interest to that individual reader. I suggest, however, that readers making any extensive use of the endnotes not only check the "Index to Abbreviations" appearing on page 307, but also read first the brief bibliographical essay that begins on page 409.

I

Beginnings

NOVEMBER 1934–JUNE 1935

The Limitations of the Drinking Alcoholic

On a dank, cold afternoon in late November 1934, two men sat kitty-corner at the kitchen table of a brownstone house at 182 Clinton Street, Brooklyn, New York. The home, only partially heated, clearly had seen better days. In the hurriedly tidied kitchen hung the faintly sweet aroma of stale alcohol. On the white-oilcloth-covered table stood two glasses, a pitcher of pineapple juice, and a bottle of gin recently retrieved from its hiding place in the overhead tank of the toilet in the adjacent bathroom. The visitor, neatly groomed and bright-eyed, smiled in gentle but pained mirth as he surveyed the scene; his tall, thin, craggy-faced host laughed a bit too loudly, anxious less over his careless attire and the patches of whiskers on his quickly shaved face than at the announcement his friend, an old drinking-buddy, had just made.[1]

"No, thanks, I don't want any. I'm not drinking."
"No drink? Why not? Are you on the water wagon?"
"No, I don't mean that. I'm just not drinking today."
"'Not drinking today!' Ebby, what's gotten into you?"
"Well, I don't need it anymore: I've got religion."

The host's eyes and heart dropped. *Religion.* His mind wandered as his guest continued to speak. His first thought: "Good! That means more for me!" Now he did not need to worry about replenishing his supply should his wife return home before the visitor left. Although somewhat pleased with that realization, within his mind jarred a less happy awareness. As much as he had looked forward to swapping tales with an old pal, that happy prospect had now suddenly palled — "got religion" indeed! He knew that his friend had been a too-heavy drinker. "Had his alcoholic insanity become religious insanity?"[2]

7

Uninspiring and tawdry as that scene was, a profound significance and a deep irony lay buried within it. The significance: what was witnessed was the birth of the idea of Alcoholics Anonymous. The irony: the carefully groomed, dry, religion-spouting visitor, Edwin T. — nicknamed "Ebby" — would die three alcohol-sodden decades later, a virtual ward of charity; his cynical, moody, too loudly talking and laughing host — William Griffith Wilson — would after this one last binge never drink another drop of alcohol. As "Bill W.," he would give America and the world a program and a fellowship to which in time over one million people would offer allegiance as being for them literally life-saving.[3]

The birth of an idea: such moments of origin are always difficult to pinpoint, and Alcoholics Anonymous itself cherishes the memory of a different "founding moment." Yet here, in this kitchen, on that dark November afternoon, a seed was planted in Bill Wilson's own understanding that his alcohol-numbed brain could neither then drown nor later wash away — the seed that he eventually nurtured and cultivated into the core of the program and fellowship of Alcoholics Anonymous: "In the kinship of common suffering, *one alcoholic had been talking to another*."[4]

That such conversation could be helpful was an important idea. Ideas, of course, do not spring from nothingness. The origins and paths of the concepts that had led to this idea help to explain its development into the program and fellowship of Alcoholics Anonymous.

Sometime in 1931, another man, a young, talented, and wealthy financial wizard, had found himself on the verge of despair over his inability to control his drinking. Having attempted virtually every other "cure," he turned to one of the greatest medical and psychiatric talents of the time, traveling to Zurich, Switzerland, to place himself under the care of Dr. Carl Gustav Jung. For close to a year, Rowland H. worked with Jung, finally leaving treatment with boundless admiration for the physician and almost as much confidence in his new self.[5]

To his consternation, Rowland soon relapsed into intoxication. Certain that Jung was his last resort, he returned to Zurich and the psychiatrist's care. There followed, in Bill Wilson's words written to Dr. Jung in 1961, "the conversation between you [and Rowland] that was to become the first link in the chain of events that led to the founding of Alcoholics Anonymous." That conversation, in Wilson's and Jung's later memory, had made two points. "First of all, you frankly told him of his hopelessness, so far as any further medical or psychiatric treatment might be concerned." Second, in response to Rowland's frantic query whether there might be any *other* hope, Jung had spoken of "a spiritual or religious experience — in short, a genuine conversion," cautioning, however, "that while such experiences had sometimes brought recovery to alcoholics, they were . . . comparatively rare."[6]

Concerning the first point, Wilson wrote to Jung: "This candid and humble statement of yours was beyond doubt the first foundation stone upon which our society has since been built." In response to the second statement, which offered a slender thread of hope, Rowland had joined the Oxford Group, "an evangelical movement then at the height of its success in Europe." In recalling to Jung this channeling of his idea, Wilson — who was linked to Rowland H. through their mutual friend Ebby T. — stressed the Oxford Group's "large emphasis upon the principles of self-survey, confession, restitution, and the giving of oneself in service to others."[7]+

Within the Oxford Group, Rowland had found "the conversion experience that released him for the time being from his compulsion to drink." Returning to New York City, he joined and became active in the Oxford Group at its United States headquarters — the Calvary Episcopal Church of Rev. Dr. Samuel Shoemaker. Alcoholics had not been a primary interest of Oxford Group adherents in America or in Europe, but Rowland chose to devote to such sufferers his efforts at living out and promoting his own conversion experience. Thus, in August 1934, hearing that his old friend Ebby T. was threatened with commitment to an institution because of his drinking, Rowland H. intervened, and with his friend Cebra G., pledged for Ebby's parole, leading him to the Oxford Group and so to his first period of sobriety.[8]

For Ebby, indeed, did "get the message." Accepting that his only hope lay in a conversion experience, that such was the function of religion, and that the Oxford Group was the most famed and the most respecta-

---

+ The Oxford Group will be examined in detail in Chapter Two. It was a non-denominational, theologically conservative, evangelically styled attempt to recapture the impetus and spirit of what its members understood to be primitive Christianity. Begun as "The First Century Christian Fellowship" in 1908, its popularity under the name "Oxford Group" peaked in the late twenties and early thirties; after 1938 it was known as "Moral Re-Armament." Despite occasional confusing mis-use of the terms, the Oxford Group is to be distinguished from the "Oxford Movement": the latter was a late nineteenth-century, strongly liturgical movement within Anglo-Catholicism (the Anglican or Episcopalian Church) towards Roman Catholicism. The most prominent name associated with the Oxford *Movement* is that of John Henry Newman (1801–1890). A greater difference is difficult to imagine than that between Newman's thought on "the development of doctrine" and the dedication of Frank Buchman, who founded the Oxford Group, to recapturing "First Century Christianity."

ble evangelical expression of religion in America at that time, he joined and found in it "friendship and fellowship of a kind he had never known." Then, in a flush of confident enthusiasm, the hallmark of any experience of conversion, Ebby in turn sought out the most hopeless and most self-destructive drinker he knew — his old friend, Bill Wilson.[9]

The judgment and feeling were mutual. Wilson had long since marked Ebby an utterly hopeless case, even promising himself to stop drinking should he ever get as bad as *that*. As tough as things had been for Bill Wilson up to the day of that November 1934 visit, he had never been threatened with commitment to an institution . . . "well, hardly ever."[10]

William Griffith Wilson had been born, "fittingly enough" — his biographer noted — "in a small room behind the bar," on 26 November 1895, the first of the two children of Gilman and Emily Griffith Wilson. Yankees of Scots-Irish stock, Bill's parents had both grown up in East Dorset, Vermont, where he himself was born. In spite of their shared background, the Wilson's marriage was not happy, and one night in 1905 — after a long and largely silent evening buggy-ride with his puzzled but apprehensive son — Gilman Wilson deserted his family.[11]

Of this childhood trauma, one of his earliest recollections, Bill Wilson later nursed a memory and interpretation perhaps not unusual in such situations. "If only his parents had loved him more they wouldn't have separated. And this meant if he had been more lovable, it never would have happened. It always came around to that. It was, it *had* to be, his fault. He was the guilty one."[12]

Little evidence remains of how the lad interpreted his next separation — nor even, indeed, that it was necessarily traumatic at the time. His young mother, with characteristic Yankee realism, obtained a Vermont-quiet divorce and resolved to begin again. An exceptionally intelligent woman, she moved to Boston and launched herself on a brand-new career as an osteopathic physician, leaving Bill and his sister Dorothy in the care of their maternal grandparents.[13]

Fayette and Ella Griffith proved kindly as surrogate parents. Yet deep within young Bill Wilson ached a feeling of rejection — the more painful because, in his mind, it was deserved. Three incidents from these quiet years, a success, a discovery, and yet another failure, reveal the torment.

Grandpa Fayette tried hard to be a father to the boy, but he was a taciturn and introverted man, a too quiet person, like Bill's father, Gilly. Yet unlike Bill's father, Fayette was perceptive; recollecting, Bill felt that his grandfather was able to read his thoughts. One evening, Fayette intuitively marked the immense sense of determination beginning to form in the boy in response to the craving rooted in his felt-rejection. Almost casually, the grandfather thought aloud: "'I've been reading a good deal about Australia lately and no one seems to know why Australians are the only people in the world who are able to make a boomerang.'

"There was a pause, then Bill looked up into his eyes. 'The only people?'"[14]

And so young Bill set to work, reading library books, speaking with woodcutters, covering every available scrap of paper with diagrams, and finally sawing, carving, whittling, and throwing. Some six months later, the boy, in silence, led his grandfather to the church graveyard. Using a boomerang fashioned — the grandfather realized with chagrin — from a three-foot plank filched from the headboard of his bed, the boy threw, stood waiting, and succeeded. "I did it," Bill first whispered, then shouted. "Our Willie," his grandfather observed, "The very first American to do it. The number-one man."[15]

The "success": to be recognized and called a "number-one man." Whenever his proud grandfather reported the tale in Bill's hearing, "all the lights in the room seemed to come up higher. He was filled with a kind of power, and when they went on about his accomplishment, he could feel it growing, spreading through his body, as if some potent drug had been released." In later years Bill Wilson often harked back to that phrase, that quest. On the one hand, it was the story of his alcoholism; on the other, it was the source of Alcoholics Anonymous. A fitting irony: William Griffith Wilson's first "success" was the fashioning of a boomerang.[16]

The "discovery" was more complex. His biography reveals that young Bill Wilson had few if any peer friends, although Rutland — the town to which the Griffiths moved shortly after Emily's departure for Boston — was far from being the smallest town in Vermont. Bill's closest friend, from about 1908, was Mark Whalon, a university student ten years his senior. The two — boy and young man — passed much time together when Mark was home on vacation, the boy Bill reveling in his enthusiastic friend's quotations from Shakespeare and Burns, Ingersoll and Marx, Charles Darwin and William Graham Sumner.[17]

But ideas were not all that Bill Wilson imbibed during the times he spent with his friend. One dry but chilly afternoon, returning on Mark's delivery wagon from neighboring Danby, they stopped by a tavern. Bill quaffed hot cider, apparently non-alcoholic, but he also drank in something more — the atmosphere of a rural New England tavern late on a summer afternoon. That "atmosphere" was not primarily the physical aura of "the warm, friendly smell of wet sawdust, spilled beer and whiskey" — although he could lovingly recall this. But rather, it was an emotional and vivid memory of that afternoon, "his feeling of being at home, his feeling for the men." In later years, "sometimes he could think of nothing else. He wanted it again."[18]

On the surface of it, Wilson discovered the joy of friendly sociability, of feeling a belonging with others; more profoundly, he discovered the experience of "obsession-compulsion" — of "thinking of nothing else" and of "wanting it again" — ideas that later furnished him the key for his understanding of himself and his alcoholism. Bill had already revealed a kind of obsession in his work on the boomerang. On that earlier occasion, however, the compulsion to achieve had faded with recognition as "number-one man." Now, here, these deep feelings blended and persisted. Was it merely accidental, this discovery's association with alcohol? Bill Wilson spent the rest of his life finding, then teaching, his answer to that question.

His experience of "failure," which marked the end of Bill's childhood, was even more significant: it involved the joys and terrors of first love in the young adolescent life of one who had reason to feel unloved. In the fall of 1909, Bill Wilson began his secondary education as a weekday residential student at Burr and Burton Academy, a co-educational school. There he discovered — and was discovered by — Bertha Banford, "the prettiest, brightest and surely the most charming girl in the school. He fell in love, deeply, completely in love, and Bertha loved him." Bill and Bertha spoke deeply and shared much. They felt that their whole beings were attuned and understood their love as inevitable. Invited by Bertha's love, Bill for the first time in his life reached out to another — and, through her, he felt, even to all others.[19]

Then, one November morning while Bertha and her family were visiting in New York City, the usual daily chapel routine at Burr and Burton was broken. After the hymn, the headmaster stood to make an announcement. Reading from a yellow scrap of paper, he informed the students that "someone very dear to all of us, Bertha Banford, had died the night before following surgery at Fifth Avenue Hospital." For days, Bill Wilson was numb, struggling yet somehow also fearing to understand. The evening after Bertha's funeral service, standing in the cemetery next to the crypt that held her body in seeming mockery of his inability ever to hold it again, the suddenly aged Wilson achieved a revelation of "failure": "He knew now. . . . His need, his loving, didn't matter a good goddam. His wanting, his hunger and desire, meant nothing to the terrible ongoing forces of creation and he would never forget this truth which he saw and accepted that night."[20]

Wilson's formative years closed on this note of helplessness. For all his positive and affirming experiences in the following years — his World War I army career, his meeting of and eventual marriage to Lois Burnham, his Wall Street adventures through the 1920s — the feeling of helplessness never left the deep core of his being. Never, that is, with one exception: and in pursuit of that "exception" William Griffith Wilson — Vermont-born, socially-connected, retired Army officer, and Wall Street "flash" — attained the final qualification for becoming "Bill W., co-founder of Alcoholics Anonymous."

In the summer of 1917, some six months before his marriage to Lois Burnham and a full year before his brief war experience in France, the newly commissioned Second Lieutenant Wilson found himself stationed at Ford Rodman, Massachusetts. Wartime patriotism in those early months of American entrance into the Great War moved some of the well-to-do in the area to open their homes — mansions to one of Wilson's background — to "our brave boys in uniform." At one weekend entertainment, Bill discovered for the first time the feeling of loneliness in a crowded room. Awkward, ill-at-ease, he felt simultaneously ignored and conspicuous. As much for something to do with the gangling hands that hung from his six-foot three-inch frame as for any other reason, Bill took his first remembered drink of alcohol — a "Bronx cocktail" handed him by a "hearty but at the same time haughty . . . socialite" whose distracted attention as she pretended to chat with him immensely added to his "terrible feeling of inadequacy."[21]

The effect and therefore the meaning of that first drink of alcohol proved profound. More than a half-century later, Wilson recalled its details for his biographer, Robert Thomsen. The importance of this recollection, the depth of its significance for what Wilson later contributed to others' understanding of alcoholism, and the lack of other evidence require its quotation:

> Perhaps it took a little time, but it seemed to happen instantly. He could feel his body relaxing, a stiffness going out of his shoulders as he sensed the warm glow seeping through him into all the distant, forgotten corners of his being.
> . . . Soon he had the feeling that he wasn't the one being introduced but that people were being introduced to him; he wasn't joining groups, groups were forming around him. It was unbelievable. And at the sudden realization of how quickly

the world could change, he had to laugh and he couldn't stop laughing.

. . . It was a miracle. There was no other word. A miracle that was affecting him mentally, physically, and, as he would soon learn, spiritually too.

Still smiling, he looked at the people around him. These were not superior beings. They were friends. They liked him and he liked them.

. . . [As he later left,] at his back he could hear the whine of a saxophone, little waves of voices rising, falling, but now they in no way ran against the overwhelming joy he was feeling. His world was all around him, young and fresh and loving, and as he made his way down the drive he moved easily, gracefully, as though — he knew exactly how he felt — all his life he had been living in chains. Now he was free.[22]

From that moment, Wilson devoted a lifetime to recapturing that elusive — and ultimately illusive — sensation of freedom. The route, after his marriage to Lois Burnham and brief Army experience, led through "Wall Street, that famous shortcut to wealth and power — or poverty." During those years, Bill later recalled, "I was drinking to dream great dreams of greater power." He was still dreaming — and drinking — when the stock market crashed in 1929. Wilson "looked with disgust upon the bankrupt people who were then jumping from high buildings," but he himself "began sinking. . . . Finally I slid down into a state where I was not drinking to dream dreams of power; I was drinking to numb the pain, to forget."[23]

He soon had much to forget: two rare business opportunities squandered through drink; a night in jail; being too drunk to attend the funeral of Lois's mother, in whose home they lived. From 1930 through 1934 the details of Wilson's life gave almost too much texture to an over-used phrase: his life had become "an alcoholic hell."[24]

Through it all, Bill was watched over by two medical families. His sister Dorothy had married Dr. Leonard Strong, whom Bill liked and respected, once even accepting the physician's referral to a talented colleague who had prescribed "willpower." Lois's father, who left the Clinton Street homestead to her and Bill in 1933 when he remarried, was Dr. Clark Burnham. He attempted to tread the narrow line between concern for his son-in-law and non-interference in his daughter's marriage, leaning — perhaps wisely — more toward the second than toward the first.[25]

Through one of these family medical resources Wilson was introduced to the Charles B. Towns Hospital, a drying-out facility on Central Park West to which he was admitted four times in 1933–1934. It was apparently on the second of these visits that Bill first came under the care of Dr. William Duncan Silkworth. At their first meeting, Silkworth, later to be immortalized in A.A. lore as "the little doctor who loved drunks," provided Wilson with an understanding of his alcoholism, an understanding that offered some choice between founded hope and utter despair, but that left no chance for any vapid middle.[26]

According to Dr. Silkworth, Bill's alcoholism was an illness: one look at himself and that should be obvious, the physician pointed out. Wilson had become physically allergic to alcohol, the doctor went on, yet his mind remained obsessed with it, condemned to drink against any will of his own. Although Silkworth did not use the term, he also described to his patient the phenomenon of compulsion: given the physical allergy, once an alcoholic such as Bill ingested *any* alcohol — even one thin drink — he became totally unable to control further drinking. The first drink got the alcoholic drunk, whatever might be the case for "social drinkers" — those not afflicted with the physical allergy. A rather desperate picture: allergy, obsession, compulsion. But the doctor also held out a slim hope. They (Silkworth was including himself and always stressed his sharing in his patients' efforts, and theirs in his) had to accept the fact of physical allergy and the inevitability of alcoholic compulsion, but they could work together toward Bill's overcoming or at least living soberly with the obsession.[27]

Hardly a happy prognosis, yet it buoyed the painfully drunk Wilson, and this reaction itself was testimony to his alcoholic desperation. His new understanding and doubtless also the doctor's kindly interest temporarily sustained Bill, but to no apparent long-term avail. He began drinking again, and now, in order to purchase his alcohol, even stole the pitifully few bills he could find in Lois's purse. She had been maintaining her family home and supporting her drunken husband on a clerk's salary. When Bill was inevitably hospitalized again, Dr. Silkworth had seen enough. Wilson had proved unwilling or unable to use the only diagnosis and help that the doctor had to offer. His case was clearly hopeless, and Silkworth told Wilson just that. Downstairs, moments later, the doctor informed Lois of her choices: to have Bill locked up, to watch him go insane, or to let him die. From their experiences of the past five years, both Bill and Lois knew that the neuro-psychiatrist was right.[28]

And so, of course, alcoholic that he was, Wilson found hope in this very proclamation of hopelessness: knowing *this*, he surely would never drink again. Never lasted only the few weeks until Armistice Day. Having expounded — in a barroom — to his companion for the day his Silkworth-derived understanding of his alcoholism, Bill accepted the bartender's offer of a drink "on the house." After all, he had been in France sixteen years before. "My God!" his friend exclaimed. "Is it possible that you can take a drink after what you just told me? You must be crazy!" Wilson's response was brief, simple, and accurate: "I am."[29]

Thus began Bill Wilson's last binge, the one interrupted by the late November visit from his friend Ebby. During lucid intervals, Bill brooded morosely. The diagnosis was in, hopeless insanity, and surely he was validating it each time he reached for another drink to ease the pain or to nurse the self-pity from that awareness. Yes, he was hopeless. Only now, through the alcoholic haze, had come Ebby T., whom he — Bill Wilson — had labeled hopeless. After all, he himself had only been *threatened* with institutionalization; Ebby, Bill knew, had actually been *committed*. Yet here was Ebby, and Ebby was sober, and Ebby had just declined a drink with a smile.[30]

Confronted by that fact, Bill Wilson found hope. He was more aware, however, of confusion. The word *religion* troubled him deeply. "What a crusher that was — Ebby and religion! Maybe his alcoholic insanity had become religious insanity. It was an awful letdown. I had been educated at a wonderful engineering college where somehow I had gathered the impression that man was God."[31]

Of Bill's earlier exposure to religion, little is known — probably because there is little to know. Grandfather Fayette, the chief influence on the boy's life, was an Ingersoll-inclined transcendentalist. In response to his ideas, the young Bill Wilson had "left the church" at about age twelve — on "a matter of principle." Ironically, the "principle" involved concerned a required temperance pledge. Chapel was the custom at Burr and Burton; but Bill's recollections of his profound, under-the-stars conversations with Bertha Banford revealed that the young Wilson had no "religion" beyond an adolescent romanticism easily congruent with both his grandfather's Vermont vagueness and his friend Mark Whalon's adoring admiration of the power of the human mind. Here then, while Wilson sat drunk in his kitchen listening to Ebby T., at the moment of the conception of A.A.'s fundamental idea of "one alcoholic talking to another," was born the self-conscious wariness of "religion" that was so deeply to infuse the program and fellowship of Alcoholics Anonymous.[32+]

+   In Bill's earliest telling of his own story (*AA*, p. 9), the alcoholic author offered

Given his long history of alienation from formal religion, Bill knew that he would not tolerate being preached at. Yet his pain and confusion at this moment opened Wilson to *something*. Ebby was a friend. Indeed, Bill dimly felt as he began to listen, Ebby was proving his friendship by *not* urging this new-found "religion" upon him. Something else — something more significant to one mired in self-pity — was happening. As Wilson later recalled how that process that was to become Alcoholics Anonymous had begun: "In the kinship of common suffering, *one alcoholic had been talking to another.*"[33]

Ebby did go on to explain quietly some things about the Oxford Group: its non-denominational nature; the importance of taking stock of oneself, confessing one's defects, and the willingness to make restitution; that one could choose one's own concept of "God" — after using the term once, Bill noted, Ebby spoke instead of "another power" or a "higher power." Bill began to listen — a little. And just then, Ebby rose to leave, and Bill went back to his brooding. Bill Wilson knew deep in his heart that he couldn't accept this "getting religion"; yet Ebby — *hopeless* Ebby — was in fact sober, and this fact gnawed in Wilson's alcohol-soaked gut.[34]

A few days later, Ebby returned with a friend. Shep C. did not attract Bill. Shep seemed too "Ivy League," a "pantywaist socialite who'd probably gone wild one night on too many sherries at a Junior League cotillion." What could he possibly know about drinking? Ebby and Shep talked — incessantly, it seemed to Wilson. They spoke of serenity, of their new life and newly found sense of purpose; they talked of prayer, meditation, and especially the love of giving oneself in service. They finally left, and Bill's gagging changed from mental to physical; he'd been pouring himself stiffer and stiffer drinks while absorbing their onslaught.[35]

an even more vivid description of his feelings about religion on the occasion of that first visit from Ebby T.

The door opened and he stood there, fresh-skinned and glowing. There was something about his eye. He was inexplicably different. What had happened?

I pushed a drink across the table. He refused it. Disappointed but curious, I wondered what had got into the fellow. He wasn't himself. "Come, what's all this about?" I queried.

He looked straight at me. Simply, but smilingly, he said, "I've got religion."

I was aghast. So that was it — last summer an alcoholic crackpot; now, I suspected, a little cracked about religion. He had that starry-eyed look. Yes, the old boy was on fire all right. But bless his heart, let him rant! Besides, my gin would last longer than his preaching.

Decades later Wilson recalled the struggle within himself during that night and on the following day. His precise recollection expressed well the ambivalence to and wariness of religion that were later to abide so deeply at the core of Alcoholics Anonymous:

> Ebby and Shep C. were now asking him to give up the one attribute of which he was the most proud, the one quality that set a man above the animals — his inquiring, rational mind. And they wanted him to give this up for an illusion.
>
> Finally — and he knew he was pretty drunk by the time he reached this point — he had to look at the fact and admit it: what they were asking him to do represented weakness to him. How could a man so demean himself as to surrender the one thing in which he should have faith, his innate, inquiring mind?
>
> He was willing to concede religious comfort might be all right for some — for the old, the hopeless, for those who had passed beyond loving, beyond any hope of really living, but, by Christ, he was different.
>
> It might be the last arrogant gasp of alcoholic pride but, miserable and terrified as he was, he would not humble himself here. On this point he would go out swinging.[36]

Thus Bill decided the issue — or so he thought. Since he resolved it in favor of "his inquiring, rational mind," it struck him as only fair, the next morning, to undertake some inquiring, rational investigation — after all, that had been his Wall Street profession. If he wanted to learn the real souce of Ebby's sobriety, Bill Wilson must himself look into the Oxford Group at its headquarters, the old Calvary Church. To facilitate his investigation, of course, fortification was required, so Bill bar-hopped his way down Twenty-Third Street, for a time even forgetting his purpose and intended destination. Finally, dragging with him a Finnish fisherman whose vocation had reminded him of his own quest, Wilson arrived at the Calvary Church Bowery mission.[37]

There Bill found what he expected: "life's discards and the rejects of society." Upon seeing the drunken pilgrim, the door-greeter was about to eject him, until Ebby intervened, insisting that Bill could join the group in the meeting room if he first ate a large plate of beans and washed them down with a great deal of coffee. Even the greeter's rejection did not make Wilson conscious that some of those on whom he looked down might have seemed, to an objective observer, better off than he. Sitting in the last row in his alcoholic stupor, Bill mellowed as the coffee and food did their work. "Hell, these weren't bad fellows."

Why, they drank the way he did! And so when the leader, Tex, called for penitents to come forward and witness, Bill Wilson, showman, stepped forward. There was an audience in the hall. Wilson, who for five years had been mired in the isolation of alcoholic loneliness, surely could not let such an opportunity pass.[38]

The next day he felt like a fool, yet one fact struck him. On the way home from the mission, he had never even thought of stopping in a bar. For three days, days of internal struggle and bleak futility, Bill Wilson lay abed at home, unable to eat, drinking only enough to stave off the pain of withdrawal. He wanted to survive. But why? He knew himself doomed to the intolerable options of dependence on some spurious faith or an alcoholic death or incarceration in some institution. Bill felt paralysis of thought and will. Suddenly, on an impulse, with no clear plan beyond "more thinking," Wilson decided that he could think all this out more sharply if he were dried out. Acting on this "rational decision," he set off yet again to Towns Hospital and Dr. Silkworth, drinking four bottles of beer — the extent of Lois's credit at the neighborhood grocery — along the way.[39]

Dr. Silkworth was unenthusiastic about what little he could make of Wilson's ravings about a plan, but he gave Bill a bed. On the second day, Ebby stopped by. Only when asked by Bill for his "neat, pat formula," did he repeat it. "Realize you are licked, admit it, and get willing to turn your life over to the care of God." Wilson nodded, about all he could do, and Ebby left. Barely able to move, certainly unable to sleep, painfully suspended between full withdrawal symptoms and the sedation that was easing them, Bill Wilson tried to think.[40]

In the first formal telling of his story, Wilson slid quickly past what happened next. He had learned that recounting it injured rather than aided his credibility, and it certainly had not helped anyone else to "get the program." Yet, to him, it had happened, and he knew it, and eventually he had to set it down. Two decades later he did so, in the most detailed telling of his story, at the "Alcoholics Anonymous Comes of Age" Convention of 1955:

> My depression deepened unbearably and finally it seemed to me as though I were at the bottom of the pit. I still gagged badly on the notion of a Power greater than myself, but finally, just for the moment, the last vestige of my proud obstinacy was crushed. All at once I found myself crying out, "If there is a God, let Him show Himself! I am ready to do anything, anything!"
>
> Suddenly the room lit up with a great white light. I was

caught up into an ecstasy which there are no words to describe. It seemed to me, in the mind's eye, that I was on a mountain and that a wind not of air but of spirit was blowing. And then it burst upon me that I was a free man. Slowly the ecstasy subsided. I lay on the bed, but now for a time I was in another world, a new world of consciousness. All about me and through me there was a wonderful feeling of Presence, and I thought to myself, "So this is the God of the preachers!" A great peace stole over me and I thought, "No matter how wrong things seem to be, they are all right. Things are all right with God and His world."[41]

"A great peace. . . . Things are all right. . . ." But almost immediately the fears began again. Had not Silkworth warned him of alcoholic brain damage? Was this the evidence of it — a hallucination founded in his obsession with Ebby's sobriety? Hadn't he, after all, been doing strange things lately, like that foolish scene at the mission? Almost frantically, Wilson called a nurse and begged her to summon Dr. Silkworth. Let him decide, Bill thought. One way or the other — sobriety or an institution — this was it. Only, he had to know which.[42]

The doctor came, and Bill related everything that had happened, each detail he could remember. Then Wilson waited for his answer. Silkworth asked some questions first, "probing questions," and Bill strained to answer accurately. Finally the doctor sat back in the bedside chair, his brow furrowed. The suspenseful silence became too much for Bill Wilson. "Tell me," he pleaded, "was it real? Am I still . . . sane?" Silkworth hesitated a moment longer, the lower part of his face pursed. Finally he spoke: "Yes, my boy. You are sane. Perfectly sane, in my opinion." The physician continued briefly, speaking of "psychic upheaval" and "a conversion experience," but he quickly qualified the words by insisting that he was but "a simple man of science." Yet, Silkworth concluded, "Whatever it is you've got now, hang on to it. Hang on to it, boy. It is so much better than what you had only a couple of hours ago."[43]

The next day more light dawned. Bill could never remember exactly, but was inclined to think that Ebby, visiting again, brought him a copy of William James's *The Varieties of Religious Experience*. What Wilson got — or thought he got — from the book was to prove significant to the history of Alcoholics Anonymous:

> . . . Spiritual experiences, James thought, could have objective reality; almost like gifts from the blue, they could transform people. Some were sudden brilliant illuminations; others

came on very gradually. Some flowed out of religious chan-
nels; others did not. But nearly all had the great common
denominators of pain, suffering, calamity. Complete
hopelessness and deflation at depth were almost always required to make the recipient ready. The significance of all this
burst upon me. *Deflation at depth* — yes, that was *it*. Exactly that
had happened to me.[44]

This was the substance of what Wilson had come to understand; also
important was the meaning he found inherent in it, for this moment
was — taken together with his "spiritual experience" — the third of the
four founding moments of Alcoholics Anonymous. One-half of the core
idea — the necessity of spiritual conversion — had passed from Dr.
Carl Jung to Rowland. Clothed in Oxford Group practice, it had given
rise to its yet separate other half — the simultaneous transmission of
deflation and hope by "one alcoholic talking to another" — in the first
meeting between Bill and Ebby. Now, under the benign guidance of Dr.
Silkworth and the profound thought of William James, the two "halves"
joined in Wilson's mind to form an as yet only implicitly realized whole.

. . . *Deflation at depth*, yes, that was *it*. Exactly that had happened to me. Dr. Carl Jung had told an Oxford group friend
of Ebby's how hopeless his alcoholism was and Dr. Silkworth
had passed the same sentence upon me. Then Ebby, also an
alcoholic, had handed me the identical dose. On Dr.
Silkworth's say-so alone maybe I would never have completely
accepted the verdict, but when Ebby came along and one alcoholic began to talk to another, that had clinched it.

My thoughts began to race as I envisioned a chain reaction
among alcoholics, one carrying this message and these principles to the next. More than I could ever want anything else, I
now knew that I wanted to work with other alcoholics.[45]

The whole of what became Alcoholics Anonymous appeared in these
words — almost. The elements for the totality of Alcoholics Anonymous
seemed to be present, but perhaps this is apparent only in retrospect.
Until Wilson arrived at the explicit realization that whether or not he
wanted to, he *needed* to work with other alcoholics to maintain his own
sobriety, Alcoholics Anonymous was yet only coming into being.

Two intermingled themes brought Bill Wilson to the verge of the
ultimate, recognized founding moment: the hopelessness of the condition of the alcoholic, and the necessity of an experience of conversion.
Their sources were Silkworth and James.

Dr. William Duncan Silkworth, a Princeton graduate, had received his medical degree from New York University. In 1900 he began his internship at Bellevue Hospital, and the staff soon recognized that the young physician possessed a special talent very little prized. To even his own amazement, Silkworth found that he had a magic touch with drunks. In 1924, after completing specialty training in neuro-psychiatry, he became medical director of the Charles B. Towns Hospital in New York, a private facility specializing in alcoholism and drug addiction. Here his skill found full range and scope; yet, until Bill Wilson came along, the doctor estimated that the rate of real recoveries among the alcoholics with whom he worked had been "approximately only two percent."[46]

His experience — in his lifetime he treated well over fifty thousand alcoholics — convinced Dr. Silkworth of two things. One, "alcoholism is not just a vice or a habit. This is a compulsion, this is pathological craving, this is *disease!*" Two, in the science of medicine of the time, alcoholism was a hopeless disease — "an obsession of the mind that condemns one to drink and an allergy of the body that condemns one to die."[47]

A third idea probably followed upon Silkworth's experience with Wilson. In his published writings after 1937, "the little doctor who loved drunks" tended to stress less his theory of strict physical allergy (though he continued to hold and to teach it) and his suggestions for research in colloid biology. Rather, he turned his attention and emphasis to "recovery [as] possible only on a moral basis." Eventually, in "The Doctor's Opinion" essay that he submitted for use in the book *Alcoholics Anonymous*, Silkworth declared without qualification that "Unless [the alcoholic] can experience an entire psychic change there is very little hope of his recovery."[48]

Although Bill Wilson himself always remained wary of referring to alcoholism as a "disease" because he wished to avoid the medical controversy over the existence or non-existence of a specific "disease-entity," his usual terms "illness" or "malady" as well as his frequent comparison of alcoholism to "heart disease" bear witness to his acceptance of Silkworth's medical ideas. In later years, the widespread diffusion of "the disease concept of alcoholism" was largely due to Alcoholics Anonymous.[49] +

+ Wilson's most explicit treatment of his wariness over using the term "disease" occurred in *NCCA*, p. 20: "We have never called alcoholism a disease because, technically speaking, it is not a disease entity. For example, there is no such thing as heart disease. Instead there are many separate heart ailments, or combinations of them. It is something like that with alcoholism. Therefore we did not

The influence of William James upon Bill Wilson — and so upon Alcoholics Anonymous — was more complex. Reading James's *Varieties* profoundly affected Wilson. In fact, the American philosopher-psychologist was the only author cited in *Alcoholics Anonymous*, in a reference having more to do with "varieties" than with "religious experience": "The distinguished American psychologist, William James, in his book 'Varieties of Religious Experience,' indicates a multitude of ways in which men have discovered God. We have no desire to convince anyone that there is only one way by which faith can be acquired."[50]

Yet Wilson also seemed to attribute the phrase "deflation at depth" to William James. The problem: neither this expression nor the bare word *deflation* appears anywhere in *Varieties*. On the other hand, Wilson apparently did *not* note and certainly did *not* cite what *was* in James: the openness to explicit religion. Two examples, one minor, the second major. First, in one of the briefer footnotes in *Varieties*, James approvingly cited evidence that the only cure for "dipsomania" was "religiomania." Given the circumstances in which Bill Wilson, painfully sobering up founder of Alcoholics Anonymous, read this simultaneously profound and diffuse writing of James's Gifford Lectures, it is difficult to imagine that his eye did not pause for relaxation if not for refreshment at the scattered mentions of drinking and alcohol. Yet he never adverted to this clearly unwelcome idea — an idea that, bare weeks before, he had himself at first used to explain away Ebby on that first fateful visit. Second, if there is one key word as well as concept in *Varieties*, it is not "deflation" but "conversion." Yet this term, so suggestive in America of a certain style of religion, never passed Bill Wilson's lips or writing hand — at least not for publication — until many years later.[51]

Therefore, on the question of William James as — in Wilson's own words — "a founder of Alcoholics Anonymous," a hypothesis: consciously and even craftily in his own wariness of religion, Bill Wilson linked James's portrayal of "conversion" with what he had learned — directly from Dr. Silkworth and indirectly, *via* Rowland and Ebby, from Dr. Jung — of the necessity and role of hopelessness. Wilson's efforts over many years to give intellectual respectability to Alcoholics Anonymous sprang from his own deep need as well as from his perception of the needs of others. This underlined linkage with a major figure in American intellectual history was therefore eminently useful to him. He

wish to get in wrong with the medical profession by pronouncing alcoholism a disease entity. Therefore we always called it an illness, or a malady — a far safer term for us to use."

made pragmatic use of the pragmatist James — with all the helpful connotations of this to those looking for "results," for the "cash-value" of the idea of Alcoholics Anonymous.[52]

Less consciously, for he was not a deep thinker, but more explicitly in an almost careless way, Wilson, in the use he made of James, hit upon another deep thread of the American psyche — and one that also protected him and his program from seeming too religious. The pluralist James became eminently useful to the main theme of Alcoholics Anonymous. A large part of Wilson's wariness of religion lay in his horror of absolutes. Thinking "absolutely" about anything was, for Wilson, "alcoholic thinking." His — and A.A.'s — most frequent description of an alcoholic was "an all or nothing person." Thus, as part of its very origins and most fundamental understanding, Alcoholics Anonymous has committed itself to rejection of any claim to a role as "one and only." The pluralism of tolerating difference has remained as important and useful to Alcoholics Anonymous as its pragmatism. Especially in the early years of the fellowship, those who objected to the "religion of A.A." found their attention directed to the key phrase, "We have no monopoly on God." Later, when — using a derived sense — therapists of other persuasions objected to "the religion of A.A.," their attention was called to another virtual truism: "Upon therapy for the alcoholic himself, we surely have no monopoly."[53]

The utility to Alcoholics Anonymous of James's *Varieties* and its impact upon the fellowship/program, were thus profound. Each word of James's title served an important function, as confused as all this was in the mind of the hazily sobering Bill Wilson when he first made the philosopher's acquaintance. A deep resonance seems to have been sounded in Wilson's mind. Significantly, perceptive non-American students both of William James and of Alcoholics Anonymous have noted the peculiar "American-ness" of each.[54+]

At the time, of course, Wilson did not think of Silkworth and James as sources. Still awed by the sobriety of hopeless Ebby T., Bill considered Ebby's source the important one; so he associated himself with the Oxford Group and began a life-long friendship with the Rev. Dr. Samuel Shoemaker, rector of Calvary Episcopal Church and chief American publicist for the Group. Within the Oxford Group, Wilson's

---

+ "fellowship/program": members of A.A. consistently and vehemently resist references to "organization" or "doctrine": speaking of the membership or any external structure, they prefer the term, "fellowship"; referring to the ideas held, taught, or suggested by A.A. literature, they prefer the term, "program." This usage — and this distinction — is preserved throughout this study.

long alcohol-dulled drive to be a number-one man quickly reasserted itself, and he announced to his new associates that he was going to sober up all the drunks in the world.[55]

The Groupers were not impressed. Some of them had tried to work with alcoholics and their general experience had been the usual one of failure. Nevertheless they tolerated and even welcomed Wilson's efforts among them. In time, they felt, he would learn just how hopeless drunks were. At that point, they hoped, his drive and enthusiasm could be channeled into more constructive lines. They waited, seeking meanwhile to implant more deeply in Bill their principles and practices.[56]

Bill, of course, did not wait. Since he felt more at home with a small group of struggling alcoholics at a neighborhood cafeteria than he did at Oxford Group meetings, Wilson extended that contact. Some he brought back to Clinton Street to live with him and the long-suffering Lois; exactly why, he did not know. Yet a sense was developing: alcoholics struggling against their obsession with "booze" seemed to do better if they spent time talking with others engaged in the same struggle. They did not, of course, talk about booze — that, after all, was the obsession they were fighting. Their talk was of spiritual things: the Oxford Group principles of the necessity of conversion and restitution, or their efforts to attain the Group's "Four Absolutes" — absolute honesty, absolute purity, absolute unselfishness, and absolute love.[57]

They "seemed to do better." But better proved not good enough. All but Bill himself soon went out and got drunk. Lois Wilson, clerking now at Loeser's department store to support her husband's new enthusiasm, her home at times overrun by drunks, offered a gentle and fateful suggestion. She might understandably have urged Bill to heed his Oxford Group friends, to move closer to the Group and to its respectable efforts among the respectable people who were its special vocation. The daughter of Dr. Clark Burnham might surely have felt more comfortable among the habitués of Calvary Church than among the denizens of Stewart's cafeteria. But she did not feel that way for whatever reasons of background and temperament, nor did she prompt Bill in such a direction. As she saw her husband's mounting frustration over the failure of his efforts, Lois's suggestion was rather that on one of his visits to Towns Hospital, Bill express his concerns to Dr. Silkworth.[58]

One April day in 1935, Wilson did so. Silkworth, of course, might have offered the advice that Lois had not: "Look, Bill, Ebby and the Oxford Group have gotten you this far; why not get out of the driver's seat and do it their way? Who do you think you are, you barely-sobered-lush?" But he did not. Drawing upon his deep knowledge of alcoholism, the physician pointed Bill in precisely the opposite direction: "Look, Bill, you're having nothing but failure because you are preaching at these alcoholics." Silkworth pointed out the frightening aspect — especially to alcoholics — of the Oxford Group absolutes, the apparent weirdness and disconcerting nature of the "hot flash" conversion experience that Bill insisted on describing to each potential recruit. He reminded Wilson of what Bill himself had pointed out to him in William James and had told him of Dr. Jung's message to Rowland.

> "Bill [he told me], you've got the cart before the horse. You've got to deflate these people first. So give them the medical business, and give it to them hard. Pour it right into them about the obsession that condemns them to drink and the physical sensitivity or allergy of the body that condemns them to go mad or die if they keep on drinking. Coming from another alcoholic, one alcoholic talking to another, maybe that will crack those tough egos deep down. Only then can you begin to try out your other medicine, the ethical principles you have picked up from the Oxford Groups."[59]

Wilson needed time to think. Further, he faced yet another frustration. Family friends, of whom there remained precious few, had begun making snide comments about his "missionary endeavors." Lois's plight, they not too delicately suggested, had become worse since he had sobered. Previously she had had to support one drunk; now she was supporting a zealot and never even knew how many drunks she would be coming home to each day. Lois herself did not complain. Bill's sobriety was the most important thing in her life, the one thing she had always worked for. Bill knew this, but the remarks stung: a real man was not supported by his woman. Was it for such a life, after all, that he had gotten sober?[60]

So Bill Wilson began again to frequent Wall Street. In early May, a slim opportunity arose. A proxy fight in Akron, Ohio, required a small group of aggressive hagglers on the scene, and Bill jumped at this chance to demonstrate his skill. The proxy struggle proved brief and was resoundingly lost. Discouraged, the others left Akron, but Wilson's persistence — and the realization that he had no job to which to return — moved him to stay on in search of some last loophole.[61]

Any city can be a lonely place for a traveling man, and grimy Akron was no exception. On Saturday, 11 May, the day before Mother's Day, Wilson moped in the lobby of the Mayflower Hotel in downtown Akron.

He began to pace. At one end of his lobby track the bar gleamed dimly as it filled with late Saturday afternoon revelers. At the other, Bill noted with little interest, stood the hotel church directory. As Bill paced, the friendly buzz from the bar grew louder and began to impinge on his self-pitying consciousness. He thought about the proxy fight — his hoped-for return to Wall Street had fallen flat. He thought about Mother's Day — his mother had effectively deserted him thirty years before, and how would Lois understand his not returning to share the day with her? [62]

"God," he thought, "I am going to get drunk"; and in that thought began the final founding moment of Alcoholics Anonymous. For at that instant, Wilson panicked. Never before had he panicked at the thought of a drink. One idea rose out of all his recent intensive experience: "I *need* another alcoholic," and Bill Wilson turned on his heel, purposefully striding away from the bar and towards the church directory.

For an Oxford Group adherent and friend of Sam Shoemaker, the choice of a name from the directory proved simple: the listed Episcopalian minister was the Rev. Dr. Walter Tunks. Frantic, Bill called and poured out his tale, asking to be put in touch with any Oxford Groupers in Akron. Tunks furnished a list of ten names, and Wilson commenced calling. He had reached the last name on the list, that of Norman Sheppard, before he found someone who seemed to understand his concern and desperation. No, Sheppard told Bill, he himself was not an alcoholic, nor did he really know any alcoholics, but a friend of his, Mrs. Henrietta Seiberling, could perhaps prove more helpful. Desperately fearful, for from the phone booth Wilson could glimpse the bar and he had just caught himself thinking that perhaps a drink — just one — might make this last call easier, Bill tried her number. To the softly Southern voice which answered the phone, he gushed forth the beginning of his story: "I'm from the Oxford Group and I'm a rum hound from New York." [63]

Henrietta Seiberling, a Vassar College graduate and the daughter-in-law of the founder and one-time president of the Goodyear Rubber Company, was not an alcoholic. A deeply committed Oxford Group adherent, she had devoted the past two years of her young life to one project: sobering up Dr. Robert Holbrook Smith, a prominent Akron surgeon whose wife was her close friend. She had introduced the Smiths to the Oxford Group in Akron, a circle that had developed largely through the efforts of Harvey Firestone. Recently, in her private prayers, Mrs. Seiberling had received "guidance" concerning the alcoholic surgeon: "Bob must not touch one drop of alcohol." She had shared this with the doctor, but it had not done much good. "Henrietta," he had replied, "I don't understand this thing [alcoholism]. *Nobody* understands it." So it was that when Henrietta Seiberling heard Bill Wilson's frenzied voice and strange announcement over the phone, this cultured woman of faith was not put off. Her first thought ran, "This is manna from heaven," and she invited Bill to come by her home on the Seiberling estate.[64]+

Wilson went, told his story to Henrietta, and heard from her something about "Doctor Bob," as he was called in the Oxford Group. Dr. Bob, Bill was told, had tried all the medical cures and all the religious approaches, including the Oxford Group, yet somehow he couldn't stay sober. "Would you like to talk with him?" Henrietta asked. That, of course, was why Bill had come, and so the Smiths — Dr. Bob and his wife Anne — were invited to visit Henrietta Seiberling and her strange Oxford Group visitor from New York the next afternoon. "The next afternoon" because, although Henrietta called Anne with an immediate invitation upon hearing Bill's story, Dr. Smith was at that moment passed out under his dining-room table, as "potted" as the Mother's Day plant that he had just placed gingerly upon it.[65]

Promptly at five o'clock Sunday afternoon, the Smiths appeared at Henrietta Seiberling's door. Bill Wilson had passed most of the day meditating on the advice Dr. Silkworth had given him: "You've got to deflate these people first. So give them the medical business, and give it to them hard." Fine, Bill thought, but here he was, about to speak to a medical doctor. What could he, Bill Wilson, possibly tell him, *Doctor* Bob Smith?

One look at the twitching, trembling surgeon as they were introduced solved Bill's problem about what to say first. "You must be awfully thirsty, Bob. Say, let's talk a little while first — it won't take long." Moving off to a side room, Wilson began telling Smith the tale of his experiences with alcohol: the hopes, the promises, and the failure of both; the drinking

---

+ "Guidance" was to the Oxford Group a technical term. It referred to God's direction of one's life, and was usually explicitly sought in moments of silence after prayer. It was not necessarily understood as a "voice," although this was the usual understanding. The one who received "guidance" was usually certain that it was from God, but abuses of this understanding led the Oxford Group from the early 1930s to encourage "checking guidance": "sharing" with Group members the "guidance" received so that they could advise (under the influence of their own "guidance") whether or not the "guidance" seemed truly from God. In the mid- to late thirties, the Group moved toward establishing as the criterion for true "guidance" conformity with its "Four Absolutes" — absolute unselfishness, absolute honesty, absolute purity, and absolute love.

camaraderie in hotel rooms and the painful dryings-out; the loving devotion of his wife and how she had had to take a clerk's job to support his boozing. When he came to Dr. Silkworth's diagnosis of obsession, compulsion, and physical allergy, Bill "really laid it on." Then he told of Ebby's visit and his simple message: "Show me your faith and by my works I will show you mine."[66]

A tall, rigidly erect, stern-visaged man, Dr. Bob Smith studied Bill Wilson through his rimless glasses as he sat listening, fascinated. When the surgeon had agreed to visit Henrietta, he had extracted from his wife a promise that they would not stay longer than fifteen minutes. But now he wanted to hear more from this man. Yes, here was somebody who really knew how it was! This stranger from New York had "been there." He had felt the obsession of craving, the terrors of withdrawal, the self-hatred over failure — all the things that he himself, Dr. Robert Smith, had experienced and was experiencing even as he listened.

Something happened within Bob. He was an only child, and not until age thirty-six, after he had moved far down the road of alcoholic drinking, had he married. Dr. Bob Smith had become convinced of and had lived his life on the principle that no one else could really understand. He had had childhood friends, college buddies, respectful colleagues, a devoted wife, a circle of Oxford Group associates. None had ever heard Dr. Bob talk about himself. To them, it was his innate Vermont taciturnity — some of them at times joked about it among themselves. To him, it was the lonely pain of the deep conviction that no one else would or could ever understand — and it wasn't very funny, even — especially — when soaked in the treacherous balm of alcohol.[67]

But here was someone who did understand, or perhaps at least could. This stranger from New York didn't ask questions and didn't preach; he offered no "you must's" or even "let us's." He had simply told the dreary but fascinating facts about himself, about his own drinking. And now, as Wilson moved to stand up to end the conversation, he was actually thanking Dr. Smith for listening. "I called Henrietta because I needed another alcoholic. I needed you, Bob, probably a lot more than you'll ever need me. So, thanks a lot for hearing me out. I know now that I'm not going to take a drink, and I'm grateful to you." While he had been listening to Bill's story, Bob had occasionally nodded his head, muttering, "Yes, that's like me, that's just like me." Now he could bear the strain no longer. He'd listened to Bill's story, and now, by God, this "rum hound from New York" was going to listen to his. For the first time in his life, Dr. Bob Smith began to open his heart.[68]

Robert Holbrook Smith had been born on 8 August 1879, in St.

Johnsbury, Vermont. The only son of parents prominent in civic and church activities, Bob had been raised strictly, but he had also shown signs of revolt and rebellion from an early age. Perhaps for this reason, he had been especially popular with his peers. His first drink of alcohol, Smith recalled, had been at age nine, when he had found a jug hidden under some bushes. Even then, he had liked what it had done for him, "he liked the way it made him feel."[69]

After high school at St. Johnsbury Academy, Bob began his college career at Dartmouth. Liberated for the first time from his parents' supervision, young Smith put into practice a childhood vow. As a boy he had deeply resented enforced attendance at church, Sunday School, and Christian Endeavor. He had resolved that when finally free from parental domination, he would never again darken the doors of a church. It was a promise he had kept for forty years. Life at Dartmouth furnished other joys: he acquired campus fame as the school's champion beer-drinker. After graduation, Smith passed three years exploring the world of business. Yet he wanted to be a doctor, so eventually, Bob enrolled in the pre-medical program at the University of Michigan, where he was promptly elected to star membership in the school's drinking fraternity.

At Ann Arbor, something in him began to change. Certainly not his desire to drink: "that was stronger than ever." But Smith, who had boasted so often of never having a hangover, began to suffer morning-after shakes. Life became one binge after another. Bob quit school to dry out, then decided to return only to learn that the faculty entertained other ideas. He transferred to Rush Medical College in Chicago, but the binges continued. Yet, somehow, he managed to stay dry for two probationary quarters and so obtained his M.D. degree and even an especially attractive internship at the City Hospital in Akron, Ohio. For perhaps two years, the young Dr. Smith was so busy that he stayed dry. Then he developed "stomach trouble," and the drinking and the round of binges began again. At least a dozen times, he admitted himself to various sanitoria (Wilson noted the carefully proper plural), to no avail. Finally, his father sent another doctor to Akron, and a thoroughly frightened Dr. Bob Smith spent two months back in St. Johnsbury, silently crying himself to sleep in the bed in which he had been born.

Passage of the Eighteenth Amendment had brought hope. He couldn't drink if he couldn't get it. He soon learned the facts about the Great American Experiment, and some even less pleasant facts about himself. The government allowed doctors access to liquor for medical reasons. Dr. Bob, who had always held his profession a sacred trust, began to rummage through the telephone directory, picking out names at random and filling out the prescriptions that would get him a pint of whiskey. Smith developed two phobias, fear of not sleeping and fear of running out of liquor. His life became a squirrel cage: staying sober to earn enough money to get drunk, getting drunk to go to sleep, using sedatives to quiet the jitters, staying sober, earning money, getting drunk. . . .

For seventeen years this nightmarish existence had gone on, his wife Anne and their two children living in a shambles of broken promises. Unwilling to see their friends, they existed on bare necessities. Even in those bleak Depression years, fewer and fewer patients were willing to trust their bodies to a surgeon whose hands trembled. Bob was a proctologist, and he had seen the humor in but had not deeply appreciated a comment overheard one day at the hospital as the elevator door opened: "When you go to Doctor Smith, you really bet your ass!"[70]

Sometime in late 1932, Delphine Webber, a friend of the Smiths, called Henrietta Seiberling, one of the few members of Akron's elite rubber families who had stayed with the Oxford Group beyond Harvey Firestone's initial enthusiasm, to urge that "something has to be done about Dr. Smith — his drinking, you know." Henrietta had not known, but after praying for guidance, she called her friend Anne Smith and urged her — without mentioning the drinking problem — to bring Bob around to the Oxford Group meetings. When the time was right, Henrietta felt assured within herself, further "guidance" would direct her to further activity.[71]

Dr. Bob, guilty over the friendless life his drinking had forced upon his wife, accepted the invitation eagerly. When he learned that this new group had something of a spiritual nature, however, his initial enthusiasm flagged. Yet the surgeon found attractive the poise, health, and happiness of these new acquaintances. He sensed that they possessed something in which he did not share, and he resolved to examine it — as an objective student of religious philosophies. For the next two and one-half years Bob attended their meetings, joined in their practices — and continued to get drunk regularly. In fact, the Group did fascinate him. Religious philosophy had long been his hobby, and he had read much in the Scriptures, spiritual and devotional books, and the lives of the saints. Unfortunately, his own best ideas seemed to come only when he was well lubricated with alcohol, and invariably he forgot them by the next day.

Now, as he finished his story with these wry attempts at humor, watching to see if Bill "understood," something began to dawn on Dr.

Bob Smith. Slowly, at first, then with sudden clarity, *he* understood. Bill Wilson had been able to control his drinking problem by the very means — the Oxford Group — that Bob himself had been trying to use . . . but there was a difference. "The spiritual approach was as useless as any other if you soaked it up like a sponge and kept it to yourself." The purpose of life wasn't to "get," it was to "give": for all his dabbling in religion and philosophy, Dr. Smith had never before realized that simple and now obvious fact.[72]

By now it was nearing midnight, and Dr. Bob's thirst to give had overwhelmed his craving for alcohol. He invited Bill to return home with himself and his wife. So began three weeks of intensive Oxford Group living. Bill Wilson found himself in awe of Dr. Bob's "spiritual knowledge" and cherished the guidance of Anne Smith as each morning her pleasant voice read and interpreted the Christian Scriptures and Oxford Group devotional books. All Bob and Anne knew was that since Bill had moved in, the doctor had neither had a drink nor wanted one.[73]

Early in June, Dr. Smith raised a question. It was time for the annual medical convention, to be held that year in Atlantic City. Bob had been in the custom of attending and had hoped to do so this year, but Anne feared the separation from her and Bill, and so — in a way — did he. What did Bill think? On the one hand, Bill Wilson rarely answered questions directly, especially when it involved managing other people's lives. On the other hand, his opinion hardly ever lay deeply veiled under whatever added fact or further question he proposed for consideration. "Well, we have to learn to live in a world filled with alcohol. When do you think you might be ready to start practicing?"[74]

So Dr. Bob journeyed to Atlantic City, and nothing was heard of him for several days. Then one morning his office nurse called. She had picked up the doctor at the railroad station at four that morning: he was drunk. Anne and Bill fetched Bob home and put him to bed, learning in the process that he was scheduled to perform a vital operation three days later. Around the clock his wife and new friend sat up with Dr. Bob, tapering him off in order to minimize the effects of withdrawal. On the morning of the scheduled surgery, Bob awoke — shaking. "Bill," he said, "I'm going to go through with it." Wilson thought he was referring to the operation, but Smith waved him off. "No," he explained, "I mean this thing we've been talking about."[75]

Anne and Bill drove Bob to the hospital, Wilson handing the surgeon a bottle of beer as he alighted — to help steady his nerves and hand so that he could hold the scalpel. Leaving the doctor to do what he felt he had to do, they returned to the Smith home on Ardmore Avenue, and they waited. Many scenarios played in their minds, few of them happy. Noon passed, and the afternoon wore on: still no word from Dr. Bob. Had he been able to perform the surgery at all? If he had attempted it, what had happened? Had it perhaps been a success, and in a burst of celebratory relief, had Bob gone out and really tied one on? That last seemed their *best* hope. Finally, late in the afternoon, the telephone jangled. Was it Bob? Or the hospital? Or even the police? Perhaps only those who have lived with and loved an alcoholic can know the depths of intermingled hope and fear that conditioned the habitual response with which Anne Smith moved to answer the unnerving ring.[76]

It was Bob. The operation had gone well and had been completed quickly. Feeling the awful strain lifted, recalling what he had learned from his conversations with Bill, the doctor had left the hospital determined to begin living what he had absorbed from his acquaintance with the Oxford Group over the past two and one-half years. Visiting first his creditors and then others whom he had harmed by his behavior, Dr. Bob Smith had made his rounds: confessing to each what he knew of the honest reality of his condition, his illness; then promising and beginning to plan a practical program of restitution in each case.[77]

The date was the tenth of June. The outlined "Landmarks in A.A. History" recorded its full significance laconically: "1935, June 10: Dr. Bob has his last drink. Alcoholics Anonymous founded."[78]

The four "founding moments" in the history of the idea and the fellowship of Alcoholics Anonymous were: Dr. Carl Gustav Jung's 1931 conversation with Rowland H.; Ebby T.'s late November 1934 visit with Bill Wilson; Wilson's "spiritual experience" and discovery of William James in Towns Hospital in mid-December 1934; and the interaction between Wilson and Dr. Bob Smith through May and June 1935 which climaxed in the final and enshrined "founding moment" just recorded. Before examining what happened *to* this idea *in* this fellowship, how both evolved and were developed, how both matured and were spread, it is appropriate to examine more closely, carefully, and analytically the idea itself.

The fellowship — the organization — of Alcoholics Anonymous has consistently proclaimed the roots of its program to be twofold. A.A. saw itself as drawn from and bridging "medicine" and "religion," a claim of some historical soundness and larger strategic utility. Yet "medicine" and "religion" were extremely comprehensive terms, made specific in the light of history.[79]

The sources of A.A.'s core idea were complexly mingled in the four founding moments examined. Dr. Jung, for example, had spoken explicitly of "religious or spiritual experience" and "conversion," yet the *term* "deflation at depth" was drawn more from him than from William James. The James contribution was to reinforce and to clarify the *necessity* of spiritual experience/conversion, and especially to teach that its routes — and its roots — could be various.[80]

Similarly, a large reason for the Jungian stress on the necessity of conversion lay in the Zurich psychiatrist's understanding of the medical hopelessness of the condition of alcoholism. Yet Wilson proximately received this concept from Dr. Silkworth, conjoined with "the disease concept of alcoholism." That Wilson in his wariness of medical professionals avoided the term *disease*; that the idea of alcoholism as a disease had a long history; that the Silkworth specifics of "physical allergy" and "mental obsession" were generally rejected by later biochemical and psychiatric researchers: these points were irrelevant.[81]

These were "outside issues." The core idea of Alcoholics Anonymous was primarily the concept of the *hopelessness* of the condition of alcoholism. That most people in mid-twentieth century America found this hopelessness most understandable couched in terms of "disease," "illness," or "malady" derived from the historical context and revealed more about the culture than about Alcoholics Anonymous.[82]

The second aspect of the core A.A. idea was that *deflation* arose from this perception of hopelessness. In the developing argot of Alcoholics Anonymous, a language that moved always from the possibly mysterious to the sheerly vivid, the term *deflation* was replaced by *hitting bottom*.

Conversion, the third facet of the core A.A. idea, was a term avoided. Yet the profound reality of the concept was inescapable: "bottom" clearly implied that there was something else "higher." Most obviously, the conversion experience in Alcoholics Anonymous was from drinking to dryness. It was a turning from the condition of active alcoholism to a total life-style termed "sobriety." Most profoundly, it was a conversion from destructively total self-centeredness to the fourth aspect of the core idea: constructive, creative, and *fully human interaction* with others.

Alcoholics Anonymous thus offered a concept of the *alcoholic* rather than an understanding of *alcoholism*. The very title of its textbook, especially in its first misspelled form, *Alcoholic's Anonymous*, bore witness that direct concern was with the alcoholic rather than with alcoholism.[83]

And what was this core concept of the alcoholic? "Selfishness — self-centeredness! That, we think, is the root of our troubles. . . . The alcoholic is an extreme example of self-will run riot. . . ." The need to escape the private prison of the narrow self is one of the themes that undergirds and finds expression in all the great religions of mankind. That human life has meaning, ultimate meaning, only as lived for others — or for an-Other — seems one way of understanding the deep unity as well as the profound variety of the human experience termed "religious." Fundamental to all human existence seems the quest for self-transcendence.[84]

This idea was surely contained in the thought of Carl Jung and of William James, mediated to William Griffith Wilson and so to Alcoholics Anonymous by Ebby T., who was living it out in his visit to Bill. Verbally, Ebby brought the message of felt-deflation and the need for conversion; but just by being there, his very presence carrying this message proclaimed the further message that one must *do* — and do-for-others — in order to *be* sober. At the moment when Wilson realized that the meaning underlying his new unease, the source of what was driving him to examine the Oxford Group even cynically, was that "one alcoholic had been talking to another," the A.A. core idea began latent existence.[85]

To this idea, the elements of which were abundantly present to both of them, Bill Wilson and Dr. Bob Smith added a style, the proximate source of which was the April 1935 conversation between Wilson and Dr. Silkworth. Silkworth had told Wilson to stop talking about "absolutes" and his "spiritual experience" and instead "to deflate these people first, . . . give them the medical business, and give it to them hard." Through circumstances, Bill Wilson next approached with his message a medical man, and rather than preach medicine to a doctor, he further polished the Silkworth-suggested style. Wilson *told* hopelessness rather than preached conversion, and he *told* by using his own story, his own experience, the literal facts of his own life, rather than by offering abstract theory or even scientific facts.

Sitting in that side parlor of the Seiberling gatehouse on the evening of 12 May 1935, Bill presented to Dr. Bob four aspects of one core idea. Utterly hopeless, totally deflated, requiring conversion, and needing others, the drinking alcoholic was quite obviously not perfect, not absolute, *not God*.

Hardly a profound or original idea, but it was *how* Bill Wilson announced it that gave this message sufficient impetus to reach the alcohol-soaked head and heart of Dr. Bob Smith — albeit after a month's delay. Wilson said, in effect, *by his very presence*: "You, a drinking alcoholic, are not God, as I, a drinking alcoholic was not God. And I am not God even now, as a sober alcoholic. I still need others, but *now* I need them because I have something to give. Precisely *because* I accept my alcoholism, my weakness, my limitation, I have found that I have something to give — something to give *from* that very limitation. Thus I am also *not-God*: I am *some*one; I am one who finds that the invitation to wholeness, the opportunity for it, arises from the very weakness of my limitation. And for the alcoholic, Bob, that is the meaning of sobriety — and of life."

II

First Growth

JUNE 1935–NOVEMBER 1937

The Limitations of the Sober Alcoholic

To be not-God was to need others: to need them precisely in their weakness, from one's own weakness; to need them as they were — alcoholic — precisely because one was himself alcoholic. So important was this sense that two decades later Bill Wilson recorded that on the "next day" (11 June), Dr. Bob suggested that they both start working with other alcoholics. In fact, however, it was not until 28 June that Bill and Dr. Bob actually confronted Bill D., the first "man on the bed." Two days earlier, Bob had called a nurse-friend at Akron City Hospital and told her that he had "met a fellow from New York who had found a new cure for alcoholism." The nurse's first reaction was somewhat snide: "Is that so, Dr. Bob? You don't mean to tell me you've tried it on yourself!" Smith winced at this further, developing awareness of just how "secret" his drinking had been, but he answered with brief honesty, "Yes, I sure have." Relenting somewhat, the nurse told Dr. Bob that yes, she had on the floor "a real corker" who could not however be seen that day.[1]

Bill D., destined to become the third member of Alcoholics Anonymous, possessed the necessary credentials. A prominent attorney and former city councilman as well as former church deacon, he had just begun his eighth detoxification in six months by physically assaulting two nurses, leaving them with black eyes. Dr. Bob guessed that he and Bill Wilson would not have too difficult a time drawing this potential new recruit's attention to "hopelessness" and "bottom" . . . *if* he wanted to stop drinking.[2]

Bill D. did want to stop: he was ready for the message. He was also exquisitely ripe for the way in which the saving tidings would be delivered. On that Friday morning, he had been moved into a private room — unknown to him, at the initiative and expense of Dr. Bob. When, shortly, his wife appeared at the door, Bill D. became convinced that one of two things was about to happen: either he was going to die or she was going to leave him. Most crushing was the awareness that his wife's obvious happiness was unhelpful in deciding between these alternatives.[3]

"You are going to quit," she told him, relating how she had been "talking to a couple of fellows about drinking." Bill D. resented her talking to strangers about his drinking, and he told her so strongly. His wife waved aside his blustering protest about "loyalty" to him. She informed him that they, too, "were a couple of drunks." Bill relaxed. "That wasn't so bad, to tell it to another drunk," he afterwards reported. Mrs. D. had apparently had quite a conversation with Bill Wilson and Dr. Bob Smith, for she went on to tell her glassy-eyed husband that part of the plan these two drunks had for staying sober themselves was to tell their plan to another drunk: that was how *they* were going to stay sober. Years later, Bill D. reflected on the jumbled thoughts in his mind as his wife left and he began to lapse back into withdrawal stupor: "All the other people that had talked to me wanted to help *me*, and my pride prevented me from listening to them, and caused only resentment on my part, but I felt as if I would be a real stinker if I did not listen to a couple of fellows for a short time, if that would cure *them*."[4]

When Bill D. opened his eyes again, Wilson and Smith were standing at his bedside. The three began to chat, and the patient found himself unable to lie back and passively await their message. "Before very long we began to relate some incidents of our drinking, and, naturally, pretty soon, I realized both of them knew what they were talking about because you can see things and smell things when you're drunk, that you can't other times, and, if I had thought they didn't know what they were talking about, I wouldn't have been willing to talk to them at all."[5]

A true alcoholic, Bill D. — who had at first offered what was to become the usual protest: "But I'm different" — soon went to the opposite extreme, and at length Wilson had to interrupt. "Well, now, you've been talking a good long time, let me talk a minute or two." He and Bob probed again their new acquaintance's sense of hopelessness. Did he think he could get up and leave the hospital and not drink again, on his own? With seven recent failures of just such a resolution in less than six months under his ample belt, Bill D. harbored no illusions on that score. Wilson and Smith then stressed that they *had to* give their "program" to someone else if they were to stay sober, so was Bill D. really certain that he wanted it? Because if he did not, he was doing worse than wasting their time, he was endangering their sobriety. So they had to know, because if he did not want it, they were not going to stay and nag at him. For their own sakes, they would have to "be going and looking for someone else."[6]

Lying there, entranced by the clear-eyed enthusiasm of these two men even as they spoke of their hopelessness, Bill D. decided and declared that he "wanted the program." But when Wilson and Dr. Bob began to speak of "a spiritual approach" and a "Higher Power," he shook his head. "No, it's too late for me. I still believe in God all right, but I know mighty well that He doesn't believe in me any more." Bill Wilson and Dr. Smith appeared to their listener to hesitate. "Well," one of them asked, "maybe you'd like to think about it. Can we come back and see you tomorrow?"[7]

The co-founders of Alcoholics Anonymous did return the next day, and for several more visits. Finally, one morning they entered the room to find their first "pigeon" speaking excitedly with his wife.[+] He looked up and pointed to them, saying, "These are the fellows I was telling you about. They are the ones that know. They understand what this thing is all about." Bill D. went on to relate to all three how, during the previous night, "hope had dawned on him." He had had his "spiritual experience" and had grasped at the thread of faith, hope, and a muted charity: "If Bob and Bill can do it, I can do it. Maybe we can all do together what we could not do separately."[8]

Bill Wilson exulted. The saving message had been shared successfully a second time — Dr. Bob Smith was no fluke. Nor, apparently, need a suffering alcoholic necessarily be already familiar with Oxford Group principles. This fact especially lodged in Bill's mind. Grateful as he was to the Oxford Group and to their teaching, Bill's first experience at the Calvary Church mission still rankled. He could not yet put his finger on exactly what the difference was between the alcoholic and the non-alcoholic Oxford Group members of his acquaintance, but a deep instinct told him that there was something.[9]

Yet, uncomfortable as it might be at moments, especially to Bill, the Oxford Group was the only conceptual home Wilson and Smith had. More, although Bill did not realize it at the time, it was a womb which had still one further positive contribution to make to the yet unde-

---

+ "Pigeon" was the term used among members of A.A., especially in New York, to refer to prospects for their program. Its origin is lost in obscurity, but according to Lois Wilson, its use derived from A.A.'s earliest days and it was consistently understood as connoting affectionate care rather than as in any way derogatory. In Akron and Cleveland, it early became customary to refer to new prospects as "babies," understood with the same connotation.

veloped program that would become Alcoholics Anonymous. For the remainder of the summer of 1935, Bill Wilson stayed on in Akron, attending weekly Oxford Group meetings and living with Dr. Bob and Anne Smith in their Ardmore Avenue home. Wilson's financial support during this time came from his persistent if intermittent pursuit of the proxy fight that had brought him to Akron. Feeling that with proper legal assistance he could demonstrate that their defeat had been by fraud, Bill had obtained from his partners a small amount of money with which to pursue that thread of hope.[10]

Wilson and Smith directed their main efforts, however, at alcoholics. The quiet example of Anne Smith and almost daily visits from Henrietta Seiberling provided their spiritual nourishment and much religious education through the summer. Every morning, Anne, who for years had begun each day with the practice of a "quiet time" seeking "guidance," shared this practice with her husband and their visitor. Her "guided" Bible readings favored two themes: Paul to the Corinthians on love and the apostle James on the crucial importance of "works" if faith were to have meaning. Henrietta's visits led to further exploration of the same themes. Years later, Wilson looked fondly back on the summer of 1935 as the period in which Anne and Henrietta had provided him and Dr. Bob with their "infusion of spirituality."[11]

Progress in their work with alcoholics was not smooth. The Smiths took into their home a few who expressed an interest in "getting well." Once, when her husband and Bill had gone out to seek yet another potential client, Anne found herself chased around her kitchen by a crazed ex-drunk brandishing her own butcher knife in his demand for alcohol. On another occasion, with Bill and Bob at home, a prospect in search of booze shinnied down a gutter pipe and fled down the street with A.A.'s co-founders, after a delayed start, in hot pursuit — Bill on foot and Dr. Bob in his aged but beloved car. Anne Smith could understand and even accept such occurrences, but they proved somewhat less than welcome in the quiet, middle-class, residential neighborhood of Ardmore Avenue. The Smiths, able to retain their home only because of the depression-induced and Roosevelt-imposed mortgage moratorium, hardly relished such scenes. Gratefully then, they readily accepted the generous invitation of T. Henry and Clarace Williams to bring whatever alcoholics they could muster to the regular Wednesday evening Oxford Group meeting at the Williams home — a meeting which had had its origin largely in Henrietta Seiberling's much earlier effort to "do something" for Dr. Bob.[12]

At first, there were precious few alcoholics to bring. For all of Bill's and Bob's daily reinforcement with the Saint Jamesian idea of the importance of their "works," the second aspect of that term ("It works!" — a phrase later to be glorified as the chief and indeed the only claim of their program) had difficulty in blossoming beyond their own and Bill D.'s example. "It works!" was, of course, witnessed to by their own sobriety; but some of the goings-on at Ardmore Avenue as well as the blank stares and rejections which they most usually met when trying to convince new prospects, gave ample evidence that, for most others, it did not work easily.[13]

In 1944, Wilson blamed this early failure on the fact that "again came this tendency to preach, again this feeling that it had to be done in some particular way." A few years before, pondering the apparent greater success of Dr. Bob in Akron in comparison with his own New York efforts, Bill had proclaimed that the time had come to "stop pussyfooting about the spiritual." A happy and fruitful middle between the "tendency to preach" and "pussyfooting about the spiritual" was only laboriously worked out. In the summer of 1935, such a compromise was not even conceived, much less glimpsed. Then, imbued with the Oxford Group sense of imitating primitive Christianity, Wilson and Smith found hope in the gospel story that recounted how even after three years of preaching to the multitudes, Jesus of Nazareth had garnered but twelve close followers and that, later, even these had all but deserted him in his moment of crisis.[14]

A respite from this possible concern came in mid-July. Lois Wilson journeyed West to visit her husband and to meet his new friends. The gentle wife to whom Bill had preferred another alcoholic on Mother's Day was unable to be jealous of or to resent Bob and Anne Smith. Welcomed into their home, impressed with Dr. Bob's Vermont-manly affection for her husband, warmed to the core of her being by Anne's outgoing faith and love, delighted at her spouse's childlike joy in his sobriety, Lois gave her blessing to his efforts and enthusiasm. Her brief visit proved long enough to renew in her heart the first-married love and deep faith in her husband's abilities, the seeds of which had somehow survived the seventeen years of his destructive drinking. Certain more firmly than ever that her Bill was a great man, she returned to Brooklyn's Clinton Street determined to cooperate in every way possible. Sharing him with Bob and Anne was surely preferable to losing him to bottles of gin, and she sensed in him — even as a result of this sharing — a love for her which she had almost forgotten. Back at her job at Loeser's, Lois soon took up her new duties in her chosen field of interior decorating. So joyously at peace was she after years of mental turmoil worrying over Bill that her own creativity burst free. Lois wrote and found ready publication for an article on veneers as she serenely awaited her husband's return.[15]

She did not have long to wait. Early in September, Bill Wilson's proxy battle met another apparent defeat. His sponsors soured on the project's continuing costs, and Bill departed for New York. He left behind Dr. Bob and two other sober alcoholics. "Not very much to show for four months of intensive work," Bill meditated as his train rolled eastward; and he smiled wryly at the realization that this evaluation applied to both the frustration of his attempted re-entry to Wall Street and his and Bob's many failures with drinkers. But on the positive side, Wilson was now convinced of two things that he had held more as hopes than certainties when that train had carried him in the opposite direction four months earlier. He could stay sober — joyously sober — by working with other alcoholics; and whatever it was that he had, he could give — his sobriety could be shared.[16]

Bill and Dr. Bob had talked about these realizations as well as their frustration over their less than five percent success rate during their final moments together on the Akron station platform, as Wilson reached to explore with the surgeon for one last time before departure how he might proceed back in New York. Now, Bob's words echoed in his enthusiasm-turmoiled mind, restoring calm: "Bill, keep it simple."[17]

Back at 182 Clinton Street, Wilson shared his thoughts with Lois. The idea of attempting yet another return to Wall Street faded. Whether moved more by Bill's contagious enthusiasm or by her own joy and hope at seeing him so gloriously sober, Lois agreed that above all her husband must explore his developing ideas by continuing the work he had begun. Basking in his wife's continued devotion and still cherishing the warmth of the home Anne Smith had provided for Bob for so many years and into which she had welcomed him so readily, Bill conceived a new plan — one made possible by Lois's decision to give up her job at Loeser's. It was notorious that alcoholics felt unloved: an understandable fact, for few were so blatantly unlovable as the drinking alcoholic. If an alcoholic like them, not having the advantage of such loyal love as Lois and Anne had given him and Dr. Bob, were to "get the program," perhaps such an environment and atmosphere of home-like caring would be needed.[18]

And so the large old house at 182 Clinton Street opened again, but now with a new accent, to any alcoholics Bill Wilson could find for whom he might sense a glimmer of hope. Some degree of charity surely influenced this decision, but mainly it was inspired by the "inquiring, rational mind" of which Bill had been so proud when drinking. His self-consciousness of it did not desert him when he had sobered. "We thought we could feed our charges at low cost and pick up a lot of knowledge about alcoholism. As it turned out, we did not sober up a single one, but we *did* pick up a lot of knowledge." For six months, Bill and Lois carefully and lovingly "dry-nursed" a variety of alcoholics brought to Clinton Street from the Calvary Church mission. The results were nil. Once, Lois arrived home from her new efforts at independent interior decorating to find her husband trying to protect their own home's interior from being "decorated" by five rampaging drunks. On another occasion, she and Bill returned together from a brief vacation to find that the problem-drinking guest to whom they had entrusted their home had turned on the kitchen stove gas jets and committed suicide.[19]

From all this, Bill learned one very important thing which he later developed into one-half of his philosophy of life — or at least of alcoholism: "Lois and I continued to find that if we permitted alcoholics to become too dependent on us they were apt to stay drunk." Slowly, except for very special cases, the activities at Clinton Street were cut back to an open-house evening each Tuesday. Yet the idea that change of environment was needed persisted in a different form. From picking up alcoholics at the Calvary Church mission and bringing them to his home, Wilson shifted to seeking out likely prospects at Towns Hospital and taking them to the Oxford Group meetings at Sam Shoemaker's church. This new style and procedure involved an act of faith that meant much both to Bill and to the alcoholics whom he approached. Dr. Silkworth was risking his medical reputation and career in allowing Bill to roam the corridors of Towns. That a non-alcoholic, and a psychiatrist at that, could show such confidence in this new approach stiffened many spines when the going got rough, as well as immensely motivated many patients devoted to "the little doctor who loved drunks." He, the patients knew, was a medical man rather than a religious fanatic. And so at least some tolerated their initial discomfort among the Oxford Groupers and ignored their intuitive wariness of this strange enthusiast, Bill Wilson. Further, two of Wilson's Towns prospects soon achieved sobriety.[20]

Meanwhile, Bill's own role within the Oxford Group was becoming more ambiguous. Committed Groupers could not help but admire his enthusiasm. Let one of them even mention having received "guidance" about some apparently hopeless drunk, and Bill with his two newly sobered friends, Hank P. and Fitz M., would tear off in Hank's car, driving without complaint over to New Jersey or up into Westchester County. That was fine, the Groupers felt, but they soon discovered a problem. The difficulty arose because something happened, and because something else did not happen.[21]

The problem was that the objects of concern with whom Bill, Hank, and Fitz were successful began to attend the Oxford Group meetings, but clearly the Tuesday gatherings of the alcoholics at the Wilson home were far more important to them than anything occurring under the direct sponsorship of either the Group or Calvary Church. What did not happen seemed even more threatening. Not only the newcomers but also Bill himself limited their participation in the Group to attending meetings and seeking out other alcoholics. The Oxford Group self-consciously aimed to convert the world, and had chosen to achieve this by seeking out and converting the socially prominent who would then allow their prominence to help them "carry the message" to other potential leaders. The only thing in which Bill Wilson and his little coterie showed any interest, however, was seeking out hopeless alcoholics, prominent or not. Further, some of the "saved" alcoholics who still clung to remnants of careers in the world of business revealed extreme shyness about shouting their names and the fact of their salvation from the housetops.[22]

Slowly, as 1936 turned into 1937, the Calvary Church Oxford Group adjusted. Telling their experience — "sharing," as they called it, for "confession" and for "witness" — had from its beginning been an important part of Oxford Group practice. This telling of their experience the newly sober alcoholics had enthusiastically embraced. Clearly, they loved to tell their stories. But too often, according to Group standards, "They were giving views, not news of what God had done." Well, then, perhaps lengthened "quiet times" — the period spent in silent meditation listening for God's guiding voice — would help them appreciate the difference between "views" and "news." Further, the majority decided that the received "guidance" should not only be shared, but that the Group as group should "check" it. Wilson and his alcoholics seemed to pick and choose among the guidances offered. But if the *Group* could agree on what directives were clearly from God — by the criteria of the "four absolutes" of honesty, purity, unselfishness, and love — then perhaps they all could again function unitedly in seeking world conversion.[23]

The alcoholics responded by chafing under the changes. Increasingly, "Wilson's drunks" felt — and said — that the Tuesday evening meetings at Clinton Street did a lot more to keep them sober than the more strictly structured Calvary Church Oxford Group gatherings. With ever greater vociferousness, also, the more committed Groupers rejected the alcoholics' objection. The continuing small percentage of alcoholics to attain sobriety, they pointed out, proved the correctness of their own view. "Alcoholics just weren't worth all that trouble," and each week a few additional Groupers received guidance that Bill Wilson should abandon his efforts with drunks and turn instead more directly to the aims of the Group as a whole.[24]

Wilson himself became increasingly uncomfortable. He truly loved Sam Shoemaker, the kindly cleric who had introduced him to the Christian life and had helped him understand the meaning of adversity and apparent failure, prayer, and the unbounded goodness of a loving God. To separate himself from Sam would cut his spiritual taproot just when he was beginning to see that alcoholism was a "three-fold disease": physical, mental, *and spiritual*. Yet, more and more, his drunks were rebelling against the pressures imposed by the Oxford Group. "Absolutes, hell! I just want to stay sober today!" became an ever more frequent aside ever more raucously proclaimed as the newly sober began speaking about their newly found "salvation."[25]

The crisis came to a head in late spring 1937, while Sam Shoemaker was on vacation. One evening Bill discovered that alcoholics from the mission had been forbidden to come to Clinton Street, and soon it became loudly bandied about at the larger Oxford Group meetings that the Wilsons were not "really maximum." The phrase was strange to Bill and Lois, who found it upsetting. Finally, the "divergent work" of a "secret, ashamed sub-group" became the subject of a Sunday morning sermon at Calvary by the church's young associate pastor.[26]

All this, Bill decided, was just about enough. Wilson rearranged the ideas that had so far held him close to the Oxford Group. Yes, alcoholics still needed to believe in something greater than themselves. And it was still true that spiritual experiences of a blinding flash such as his own were rare. He accepted as true, too, that the spiritual side of alcoholism still had to be learned from others, and a spiritual way of life worked out with others. Yet more and more Bill discovered that new adherents could get sober by believing in each other and in the strength of *this* group. Men who had proven over and over again, by extremely painful experience, that they could not get sober on their own had somehow become more powerful when two or three of them worked together on their common problem. This, then, whatever it was that occurred among them, was what they could accept as a power greater than themselves. They did not need the Oxford Group.[27]

So the yet unnamed group of alcoholics struggling for sobriety separated from the Oxford Group. Later, in 1955 at the fellowship's twentieth anniversary and "Coming of Age" convention, Wilson set out to record carefully the exact nature of his and A.A.'s debt to the Oxford Group.

One circumstance of his address highlighted two concerns that impelled Bill to be as honest and as accurate as possible. He made his oral presentation with the Rev. Dr. Samuel Shoemaker and his close Jesuit friend, Fr. Edward Dowling, seated on the platform behind him. These two men of differing religious background personified Wilson's concerns. On the one hand, Wilson wished to acknowledge the Oxford Group contribution, thus not slighting Shoemaker's role in his own recovery. On the other hand, especially in this setting honoring him as co-founder of Alcoholics Anonymous, Bill felt the need to emphasize A.A.'s early and complete separation from the Oxford Group, thus not compromising the Roman Catholic principles of Dowling.[28]

The better to capture both the significance of this circumstance and the larger context of the problem, Bill Wilson's presentation on that occasion of his understanding of the relationship between Alcoholics Anonymous and the Oxford Group is offered at length and in his own words:

> The Oxford Groupers had clearly shown us what to do. And just as importantly, we had also learned from them *what not to do* as far as alcoholics were concerned. We had found that certain of their ideas and attitudes simply could not be sold to alcoholics. For example, drinkers would not take pressure in any form, excepting from John Barleycorn himself. They always had to be led, not pushed. They would not stand for the rather aggressive evangelism of the Oxford Group. And they would not accept the principle of "team guidance" for their own personal lives. It was too authoritarian for them. In other respects, too, we found we had to make haste slowly. When first contacted, most alcoholics just wanted to find sobriety, nothing else. They clung to their other defects, letting go only little by little. They simply did not want to get "too good too soon." The Oxford Groups' absolute concepts . . . were frequently too much for the drunks. These ideas had to be fed with teaspoons rather than by buckets.

> Besides, the Oxford Groups' "absolutes" were expressions peculiar to them. This was a terminology which might continue to identify us in the public mind with the Oxford Groupers, even though we had completely withdrawn from their fellowship.

There was yet another difficulty. Because of the stigma then attached to the condition, most alcoholics wanted to be anonymous. We were afraid also of developing erratic public characters who through broken anonymity, might get drunk in public and so destroy confidence in us. The Oxford Group, on the contrary, depended very much upon the use of prominent names — something that was doubtless all right for them but mighty hazardous for us. Our debt to them, nevertheless, was and is immense, and so the final breakaway was very painful.[29]

Clearly, the final clause was primarily for the ears of Sam Shoemaker. Shoemaker himself had broken with the Oxford Group in early 1941, but he remained deeply aware of the close and continuing dependence of the program of Alcoholics Anonymous upon the ideas and practices that he had impressed upon Bill Wilson. The realization that many newer A.A.s were ignorant of the similarity which their cherished program bore to primitive Christianity pained the committed cleric. He hoped that these, hearing of the connecting link when the name "Oxford Group" no longer fluttered the flags of controversy, would look into the matter and come to see.[30]

Earlier in Wilson's discourse, the phrase "the public mind" had brought a blissful smile to the lips of the genial Jesuit, "Puggy" Dowling. Looking out over the assembled conventioneers and recalling his experience at countless A.A. meetings across the country, Father Dowling guessed that approximately one-third of the members of Alcoholics Anonymous in 1955 were Roman Catholic. It had not always been so, he recalled with a muffled chuckle.

When the book *Alcoholics Anonymous* was ready for publication in 1939, the New York group had not contained a single Catholic. Dowling knew the story of that concern and its resolution when a new arrival, "fresh out of Greystone asylum," was quickly pressed into service. Morgan R. was not only Catholic but claimed friendship with an official in the New York Archdiocesan chancery. Hopefully, the fledgling group had invested subway fare that Morgan might carry the precious manuscript uptown to his friend for pre-publication scrutiny. His task had not been to seek official approval. A printed *imprimatur* would have spelled doom by labeling the book "religious." Rather, Morgan's errand had been to make sure that there was nothing in the work to which the Catholic Church might object. Bill Wilson had heard that the Catholic Church was about to condemn the Oxford Group, and conscious of how much "Oxford Group" was in his program, Wilson had feared to fall under the same condemnation. "Strange," Dowling mused. Bill ap-

parently had never even been acquainted with a Catholic until he himself had come wandering by the old Twenty-Fourth Street clubhouse on
a rainy night in 1940. The drolly inquisitive Jesuit whimsically wondered: in a free association test, would the most common first response
to "Irish" be "Catholic" or "alcoholic"? It would be close, he decided.
And now this Vermont Yankee was standing up there and equating
"Catholic Church" and "public mind"![31]

Wilson's careful analysis met the needs of 1955, but a greater historical distance allows deeper understanding of the origins of Alcoholics Anonymous in the Oxford Group. The Oxford Group, later
known as Moral Re-Armament, originated in the activities of Frank
Buchman, who had come to his own "spiritual experience" in 1908,
while traveling in Scotland. A sometime college chaplain, Buchman
sought to capture for his movement the aura surrounding universities
that produced world leaders and therefore occupied a pivotal place in
modern society. To achieve his mission of recalling the world to primitive Christianity, Buchman concentrated on the students and graduates
of such institutions. The association with Oxford, he deemed, could
facilitate acceptance and gain his message a respectful hearing.[32]

As Wilson stated often, strongly, and colorfully, the contributions of
the Oxford Group to Alcoholics Anonymous were twofold: positive and
negative. Among the positive contributions, direct and indirect, were
those having to do primarily with "tone" or "style," and those finding
expression in specific practices.[33]

In the first category of tone and style, three were noteworthy. First,
the Oxford Group cherished the informal setting of "house parties" or
"drawing-room conversations" which communicated non-verbally that
"religion" was a "joy," that pleasant "fellowship" was of its essence.
Second, members of the Oxford Group were not expected to leave their
own churches. The movement embraced no specific theological positions but sought only to assist in the practice of a truly Christian moral
life. Third, the Oxford Group focused on a "changed life" attained by
passing through "stages." The "changed life" was significant to A.A.
ideas because it provided a way of understanding sobriety as something
positive rather than the mere absence of alcohol or drunkenness.[+] Furthermore, in using the term, Buchman and the Oxford Group were
explicitly avoiding the more familiar word, "conversion." The *idea* of

+ The emphasis on Alcoholics Anonymous as a "life-changing" program, although reflected strongly in *AA* and *12&12*, was especially stressed in Akron,
Cleveland, and groups deriving from these two centers of A.A. activity.

"stages" contributed more to Bill Wilson's eventual program than the specific stages enumerated by Buchman — the "five C's" of Confidence, Confession, Conviction, Conversion (as *act*), and Continuance; but these also had direct impact on A.A. practice, especially as mingled with the "Five Procedures." [34]

A.A. practices directly and consciously derived from the Oxford Group also contained three items. The "Five Procedures" were (1) to give in to God; (2) to listen to God's directions; (3) to check guidance; (4) restitution; and (5) sharing — telling one's sins, itself sub-divided into "sharing for witness" or narration of how one's life had "changed," and "sharing for confession," to soothe guilt. [35]

The two other A.A. practices present in the Oxford Group were the insistence that its workers — and especially its founder — never be paid for the "soul-surgery" of aiding others to attain the "changed life"; and an emphasis on the obligation to engage in personal work with others in order to change the *helpers'* lives. [36]

The early members of Alcoholics Anonymous were aware of the impact of especially the last two Oxford Group principles on their fellowship. Other Oxford Group carry-overs, however, were more hidden, and few if any of the first generation of A.A.s seem to have been aware of their continuing impact even after formal separation. For example, neither Bill Wilson nor any other early A.A. had knowledge of Buchman's background, which pervaded the movement. Three profound influences played upon Frank Buchman, the Pennsylvania-born Lutheran minister who founded the Oxford Group: "the conservative Lutheran pietistic influence of his home and the Pennsylvania German people among whom he was brought up"; "the more traditional Protestant Evangelism," which shaped a life-long interest in the process of conversion; and "the American collegiate evangelism of the early twentieth century," which traced directly to Buchman's self-conscious identification with the great evangelist Dwight L. Moody. [37]

There were two further "tone-setting," indirect contributions of the Oxford Group to Alcoholics Anonymous: the Group's efforts were directed to the "up and outers" rather than to the down and out; and they operated under "six basic assumptions" (1) men are sinners; (2) men can be changed; (3) confession is prerequisite to change; (4) the changed soul has direct access to God; (5) the Age of Miracles has returned; and (6) those who have been 'changed' must 'change' others." [38]

In the final category of indirect or unconscious contributions to A.A. practice were the "undervaluation of intelligence" manifest in the love of slogans such as "Study men, not books," "Win your argument, lose your man," and "Give the *news*, not your views"; and the practice of "getting rid of guilt feelings" through the "discovery that others have been or are bedeviled by the same conflicts or problems." Such "discovery" became fundamental to the key practice of "story-telling" in Alcoholics Anonymous, although A.A. diverged in its insistence that as a result of such "sharing," lowered aim was to be accepted rather than increased accomplishment attempted. Except for this last point, the positive contributions of the Oxford Group to Alcoholics Anonymous were many, diverse, profound, and not always conscious.[39] +

The Oxford Group was a conscious attempt to return to primitive, fundamental Christianity. The briefest statement of the fundamental, primitive Christian message runs: "Jesus saves." The fundamental first message of Alcoholics Anonymous, proclaimed by the very presence of a former compulsive drunk standing sober, ran: "Something saves." "Salvation" as the message remained. Yet A.A.'s total omission of "Jesus," its toning down of even "God" to "a Higher Power" which could be the group itself, and its changing of the *verbal* first message into hopeless helplessness rather than salvation: these ideas and practices, adopted to avoid any "religious" association, were profound changes. Since these ideas and practices were consciously embraced to deny any Oxford Group implication, they indicate a negative contribution on the part of the Oxford Group. Wilson "learned from them *what not to do* as far as alcoholics were concerned."[40]

Four particular "negative contributions" merit consideration: Alcoholics Anonymous steadfastly and consistently rejected absolutes, avoided aggressive evangelism, embraced anonymity, and strove to avoid offending anyone who might need its program.

+ Of interest is the final question that the historian of the Oxford Group, Walter Houston Clark, asked of his material — and his answer to it: "whether the benefits of the Group may be enjoyed without its drawbacks." He continued: "Perhaps the best known modern illustration is the work done by Alcoholics Anonymous, where life-changing of a very effective nature is accomplished by methods fundamentally very similar to those of the Oxford Group. Both movements have accomplished results through religious emphases that have been possible by no other method. At its beginning, Alcoholics Anonymous owed something to the Group. Yet because of a more humble state of mind, a willingness to experiment and work with others, and strict avoidance of the objectionable type of publicity indulged in by the Oxford Group, A.A. has been publicly endorsed by leading medical men and most religious denominations including the Catholic. Alcoholics Anonymous has learned lessons from the Group, has appropriated what has seemed good and has discarded or reversed what has not been to its purpose."

Wilson's deepest problem with the Oxford Group concerned that movement's famous "Four Absolutes." A.A.'s co-founder pointed out that

> "the principles of honesty, purity, unselfishness and love are as much a goal of A.A. members and are as much practiced by them as by any other group of people, yet we found that when the word *absolute* was put in front of these attributes, they either turned people away by the hundreds or gave a temporary spiritual inflation resulting in collapse. The average alcoholic just couldn't stand the pace and got nowhere."

This explicit rejection of any claim even to an aim that was absolute became more significant to Alcoholics Anonymous than anything it derived more positively from the Oxford Group.[41]

The early and newly sober alcoholics felt discomfort with "the principle of aggressive evangelism so prominent as an Oxford Group attitude." Their early experience revealed to the New York alcoholics "that this principle, which may have been absolutely vital to the success of the Oxford Group, would seldom touch neurotics of our hue." The problem was twofold. Drinking alcoholics did not respond well to an aggressively evangelistic approach; and sober alcoholics who still held jobs justly feared the consequences of being publicized as "alcoholics." The promise of anonymity removed one obstacle which might have led prospects to fear even investigating the program.[42]

Painfully, some of the early adherents to the program of Alcoholics Anonymous learned that publicity brought the re-inflation of self-pride and thus endangered a sobriety rooted in the deflation of hopelessness. If they drank again, they lost their own sobriety and damaged the very credibility of their program. Bill Wilson summed up this reason for abandoning the aggressive evangelism of the Oxford Group: "Excessive personal publicity or prominence in the work was found to be bad. Alcoholics who talked too much on public platforms were likely to become inflated and get drunk again. Our principle of anonymity, so far as the general public is concerned, partly corrects this difficulty by preventing any individual receiving a lot of newspaper or magazine publicity, then collapsing and discrediting A.A." Thus a profound negative contribution of the Oxford Group was embodied in the fellowship's very name. They were "Alcoholics *Anonymous*."[43]

The final contribution emerged only very slowly and under one specific concern. Wilson always stressed the need for inclusiveness and tolerance in Alcoholics Anonymous, and explicitly expressed the fear that, "Were we to make any religious demands upon people I'm afraid many Catholics would feel they could not be interested." As late as the eve of the publication of the book *Alcoholics Anonymous* in 1939, A.A. in New York City had but one Catholic member, and he very recent, while Akron A.A. — still meeting side by side with if not within the Oxford Group — acknowledged none. By 1953, when he was about to begin work on the history of the fellowship which would be published as *Alcoholics Anonymous Comes of Age*, Wilson had attained sufficient distance to be more honest about one aspect of his concern over the Oxford Group connection. "The main reason" for omitting mention of the four absolutes, he wrote, "was possible trouble with the Catholic Church. . . . It seemed wise to omit any material that would identify us with the Oxford Group. Just at that juncture, the Pope had decreed that no Catholics could come to Oxford Group meetings. Therefore, if we used any of their words or phrases, the same sentence might fall on us." [44]

There is an interesting postscript. By mid-1947, Bill Wilson was taking instructions in the Catholic faith from Monsignor Fulton Sheen, to whom he had been introduced by Fulton and Grace Oursler. Wilson dropped his interest after about a year. The usual explanation for Wilson's not accepting Catholicism follows Bill's own as given in a letter of ten years later. He feared that his conversion to Catholicism might adversely affect Alcoholics Anonymous. [45]

From his correspondence at the time, however, a different — and more consistent — picture emerges. As attractive as Wilson found some aspects of Catholicism, especially the mystical ones, he simply could not stomach the idea of infallibility — not only the personal infallibility of the Pope, but the infallibility claimed for the effectiveness of sacraments in Catholic theology. "These excursions into the absolute are rather beyond me. Though no disbeliever in all miracles, I still can't picture God working like that." This particular concern linked to another one, and in its expression we approach close to the source of the protective instinct that led Alcoholics Anonymous to reject being apprehended as in any way a "religion." Wilson summed up his thoughts on his instruction experience in a 1948 letter to a close friend and continuing mentor: "The thing that still irks me about all organized religion is their claim how confoundedly right all of them are." [46]

Wilson had not spoken the Oxford Group "absolutes" at least partially because of concern for what the Catholic Church thought. Ironically but consistently, in time he turned from Catholic thought itself because of that tradition's own absolutes.

Meanwhile, Dr. Bob continued his efforts with alcoholics in Akron in close connection with the Oxford Group. The detailed narration of Bob E., who attained sobriety in February of 1937, furnishes a glimpse into the style and approach of the Akron branch of the yet unformed fellowship of Alcoholics Anonymous. The difference from the philosophy and methods evolving among the New York alcoholics both reveals a significant development and casts light on a continuing tension within Alcoholics Anonymous.[47]

A member of one of Akron's wealthiest families, Bob E., had drunk himself into total alienation from his father. One day early in 1937, Bob sat in his favorite bar, nursing both self-pity over his plight and the cheese sandwich and beer which he had just bought with thirty cents begged from a former business associate. His main life problem, he reflected, was whence would come his next meal — and drink. His meditation on this momentous concern was interrupted by the entrance into the bar of a former drinking companion, Paul S., whom he had not seen for some time. Instead of joining him or ordering a beer, Paul asked for a pack of cigarettes. "He was all dressed up, and I could tell by the looks of him that he hadn't been drinking. I knew he used to drink every day and I couldn't figure it out. I went up and said hello, figuring he'd be good for a beer, at least."[48]

Paul asked how his friend was, "and if I was still drinking."

"Not very much," Bob replied. "I don't have any money to drink on — no job." Ignoring the implicit plea, "Paul said he wasn't drinking and if I ever wanted to know anything more about how to quit, he would be glad to talk to me." Bob E. made an appointment for the next day, but kept it only a week later. Other friends — easier marks — had come in after Paul had left, and Bob had passed the intervening six days in a drunken stupor.[49]

"But I did show up at Paul's office a week later and he told me about this program of the alcoholic squadron of the Oxford Group and what it had done for Dr. Bob Smith, and if I would be willing to talk to Dr. Bob, . . . he would make arrangements for me to see him that noon." Fortified with a drink furnished by Paul on the way, Bob E. talked with Dr. Smith at his home for most of that afternoon. According to his memory, the doctor stressed "that I was chemically constituted differently from the average individual" and encouraged him to hospitalize himself. "He stayed away from the spiritual angle."[50]

Having one fear thus set to rest, for Bob E. had marked his friend Paul as a religious enthusiast, the man who was to become "A.A. Number Twelve" signed himself into Akron City Hospital. His physical withdrawal proved not difficult. By nine the next morning under the ministrations of Dr. Smith, Bob felt himself relatively clear-headed for his meeting with Paul. At least clear-headed enough to begin to wonder about this "new therapy," for over the next five days it seemed to consist simply of being visited by groups of two or three men. "None of them said anything about what I had to do — they just introduced themselves and started telling me their experiences." Bob E. listened carefully. He heard words such as "resentment" and "self-pity," and by the third day he began to feel refreshed after the visits — he knew not why. Beyond this ignorance of "why," Bob realized that neither did he know "how." His visitors told him nothing but their experience, with occasional allusions — especially by Joe D. — to a "day at a time" or a "twenty-four hour" way of living. But what else was there to it? Each time Bob tried to ask, his visitors simply again recounted their experiences — drunk and now sober.[51]

Over the fourth day, his visitors began also to listen; and when they finally heard Bob's story, it was told in the vocabulary they had subtly taught him. Finally on his fifth day in the hospital, his visitors having learned that Bob's background indicated an openness to Christian Science, his friend Paul returned to indoctrinate his new charge in "the spiritual side." According to Bob E.'s memory, "I was susceptible . . . and so he really laid it on thick. He got it over to me that drinking was simply a secondary proposition and was a form of release from whatever self-pity, resentment, imaginary weakness, so forth, and of course, he brought out the chemical reaction — the explanation that Dr. Smith gave from the medical standpoint — that all tied in."[52]

Bob E.'s last act before leaving the hospital was straight out of Oxford Group practice: he "made a surrender." On his knees at his bedside, Dr. Smith standing over him, Bob "shared completely — [it has] to be done with another person. Pray and share out loud. The act of surrender. . . . You couldn't attend a meeting unless you had gone through that. You couldn't just go to a meeting — you had to go through the program of surrender."[53]

Not all in Akron had been ready to make such a dramatic surrender — at least at first. A favorite story of the period concerned a nameless drunk who unwittingly bestowed upon the yet unnamed fellowship one of its temporary Akron nicknames, "the take-it-or-leave-it program." This worthy, having crawled back to Dr. Bob after what most of the others serenely assumed was one last binge, muttered to his first visitors during his second hospital stay: "Jeez — when you guys say 'Take it or leave it,' you mean it!" This experience and others similar to it, Bob E.

and other Akronites later testified, contributed for many years to come to the greater rigidity of A.A. groups stemming from Akron.[54]

But Bob E. readily "made surrender." Out of the hospital, still without employment as were most of the early Akron alcoholics, he fell readily and eagerly into his "new vocation of staying sober." One term which he had heard first from Dr. Smith and thereafter often from his visitors, Bob E. found himself beginning to live — "Christian fellowship." Daily, he and the other newly sober alcoholics met informally in each other's homes — or at least in the homes of those of their number fortunate enough still to have them. Freshly redeemed from their active alcoholism, few among these early alcoholics knew any real friends from "the old days." Families and employers in general remained mistrustful. The time recently devoted to drinking and oblivion hung heavily on their hands, and so they sought out each other. The first aim of this "sharing" may have been information about or experience with new prospects, but they soon found themselves sharing more deeply. Utilizing their well-known stories as the background for discussing their current hopes and fears, their joys and resentments, they began slowly and unconsciously to perfect their new vocabulary, and with it the new conceptual categories with which they were learning to understand life.[55]

On Saturdays they gathered informally at the home of "Mother G." — an Oxford Group matron whose son, sobered up by Wilson and Smith in 1935 and at age thirty-two their youngest member, seemed particularly unstable in his sobriety. The newly sober alcoholics stopped by to see Anne Smith even more frequently. Her warmth and overflowing motherliness readily embraced them all — perhaps the more so because her only son had that year left home for college. For whatever concerns they brought to her kitchen, Anne had no direct answers but she always found a relevant passage of the Bible to read with them. She herself was "'the sheltered place for people in trouble, a rod, a comforter," in her daughter-in-law's memory. Dr. Bob's sympathetic spouse especially favored readings about "love." When her large hands were too busy to hold the Bible or when the outpouring of disheartenment and confusion seemed to fluster even her for a moment, "Miss Annie" fell back on a simple Scriptural quotation that always seemed to her listeners to come more from her heart and eyes than from her lips and mouth: "God is Love." How it worked, her visitors did not know, but hearing those words from that woman always brought calm — and confidence that they would not drink that day.[56]

The formal "meetings" continued to be held each Wednesday evening at the large Westfield home of T. Henry and Clarace Williams, the alcoholics at times making up almost half the group as the year 1937 drew to a close. The sober alcoholics referred to themselves as "the alcoholic squadron of the Oxford Group." Whether the emphasis lay on the unity of the connecting word *of* or on the distinction implied by the two terms did not yet concern them. The expression furnished an important group identity. It was "the meeting" to which new prospects could be brought after they had "made surrender" (or even at times to "make surrender" in a small basement room before the meeting began); it was "the meeting" to which, by late 1937, a few Cleveland alcoholics whom Dr. Bob had sobered up began to return each week. It would appear in hindsight that most of their waking lives was a continuous A.A. meeting; in the perspective of history, their Wednesday night gatherings seem mainly an educational respite in their new crash-course socialization. But, of course, these awarenesses were not present to them at the time. The Akron alcoholics were conscious of owing much — indeed, *all* — to the Oxford Group; they relished their identification as its "alcoholic squadron." Thus, in November 1937, when Bill Wilson returned to Akron with news of the New Yorkers' departure from Oxford Group auspices, any tendency to pride in independence was blunted by concern over the withdrawal's implications.[57]

Wilson had come primarily to share this news, but with instinctive prudence he minified the significance of the separation. Focusing rather on the tidings that in the past six months some measure of success had begun to crown his efforts in New York, he concentrated attention on the meaning and implications of increasing numbers — something of which the Akronites were especially proud. Bill Wilson and Dr. Bob Smith paused privately for a moment's joint evaluation of two recent phenomena, the New Yorkers' independence and the Akronites' rapid growth.[58]

Most whom they had approached had neither stopped drinking nor shown any other interest in their ideas, yet there also had been some startling successes. Now, there was a hard-core group of over twenty very grim, last gasp cases who had by then been sober for almost two years. Counting all noses, Wilson and Smith realized that between the New York City and the Akron groups, over forty formerly destructive drinkers were now staying bone-dry a day at a time.[59]

The shared feeling of Wilson and Smith as they came to this realization was again that of being suffused in a brilliant flash of warming light. "Suddenly it burst upon us, — 'Something new has come into the world' — a new life and a science where there was none before. The question was: How do we transmit this experience?"[60]

Three possibilities were discussed, first by Bill and Bob, then among all the Akron alcoholics. Paid workers could serve as "missionaries"; there would be the construction and operation of a chain of hospitals specializing in the treatment of alcoholism — important both because most general hospitals were unwilling to offer any care to alcoholics and as the source of revenue to support the "missionaries"; and, above all, they needed to set down their experience and methods on paper as a guard against the garble and distortion deemed inevitable as soon as publicity came.[61]

Dr. Bob Smith, Wilson recorded, liked the idea of a book but was frankly dubious about paid missionaries and profit-making hospitals. Still, together they presented all three ideas to eighteen members of the Akron group. Supported by Dr. Bob, Bill strongly argued the *pros* of the proposed endeavors — and he did have to argue strongly. The initial overwhelming reaction of the group was to reject all three ideas: paying workers would diminish the effectiveness of their message; hospitals would appear to be, if not turn into, a "racket"; and Christ's apostles themselves, the Akronites anachronistically pointed out, had had no need of printed matter. But Wilson and Smith argued on. Finally, over the strenuous objections of a large minority, the Akronites hesitantly consented to go along with all three ideas.[62]

Thus, in November 1937, awareness of the larger implications of being not-God clearly did not yet permeate the still unnamed fellowship of Alcoholics Anonymous. To accept that the alcoholic, drinking or sober, was not God — that he was imperfect, flawed, less than absolute — had not been difficult. Such acceptance lay implicit in the avowal, "I am an alcoholic." But to accept further that the alcoholic, even joyously sober, was not-God — that one's very limitation issued in wholeness, that it implied affirmation more than denial, that the alcoholic could find strength albeit rooted in weakness, that being a sober alcoholic was a positive identity as well as a negative label: this required a deeper faith, a more profound insight. Thus the context was set for the contributions of the next two years. In both New York and Akron, events were soon to demonstrate that the highs and lows of sobriety could be as perilous to serenity as the ups and downs of alcoholic intoxication — that the acceptance of being "not-God" had to do with more than alcohol.

III

Independent Existence
NOVEMBER 1937–OCTOBER 1939
Finding Wholeness in Limitation

When Dr. Bob Smith had first attained sobriety and had embraced Bill Wilson's largely unformed ideas in June 1935, A.A.'s co-founders did not advert to their implicit debts to the influences of Carl Jung, William James, Dr. William Silkworth, and the Oxford Group. By November 1937, however, Wilson and Smith felt that they had a "program," and so they were able to think more explicitly about the ideas they had drawn from these diverse sources.[1]

These ideas remained understandings of *persons*/alcoholics rather than of any *thing*/alcoholism. The concept fundamental to Alcoholics Anonymous continued to be the pragmatic one of the *alcoholic* rather than any speculative reaching at some direct comprehension of *alcoholism*. Their tentative understanding of alcoholism as "an illness which only a spiritual experience will conquer" obviously described the alcoholic rather than analyzed the malady. The core perception of the drinking alcoholic's problem as "selfishness" likewise remained unchanged. Indeed, its further grasp at depth and the spelling out that followed from that grasp furnished the vehicle for Wilson and Smith to deepen their thinking about a "program." Within months, Bill, seeking to set forth in writing what they had agreed about "How It Works," baldly summed up his and Dr. Bob's understanding of the alcoholic's dire condition: "Selfishness — self-centeredness! That, we think, is the root of our troubles. . . . First of all we had to quit playing God. . . . The alcoholic is an extreme example of self-will run riot, though he usually doesn't think so."[2]

"Though he usually doesn't think so." If there be an example of intentional understatement in self-confessed extremist Bill Wilson's extensive writings, it lies concealed in that "usually." Especially in the unsuccessful phase of their efforts with drinking alcoholics, Bill and Bob had early and clearly isolated the obstacle inhibiting those who failed to grasp their ideas and so to attain sobriety — *denial*, denial fundamentally of being "an alcoholic." This denial, Wilson and Smith had learned from their failures as well as from their successes, tended to be expressed in especially two contrary insistences: the "claim to be able to drink like other people"; and the "exceptional thinking" that insisted that even though the problem-drinker's outward experience seemed to place him in the alcoholic camp, he was somehow "different" — an exception. The problem lay in the implications of "being different." Did *identity* flow from the ways one was like other people, or the ways in which one was unlike them? And to just which "other people" did one look in achieving identity, whether by likeness or unlikeness?[3]

The new program's first problem thus became the image it presented of "the real alcoholic." Slowly, from early 1938, Bill and Bob and their fellow admitted alcoholics progressively developed two ideas on which they had thus far relied only implicitly. These understandings concerned how the alcoholic "hit bottom" and the process by which a new-comer "identified" with admitted alcoholics. Neither the phrase *hitting bottom* nor the word *identifying* appeared in the literature of Alcoholics Anonymous for another fifteen years. When they finally did emerge, "hitting bottom" and "identifying" were terms that Alcoholics Anonymous immediately recognized as well summarizing how the program and fellowship had begun and worked — clear witness to the unconscious depth of the *concepts*.[4]

"The real alcoholic" continued to be understood as described by Dr. Silkworth. "At some stage of his drinking career he begins to lose all control of his liquor consumption, once he starts to drink." But "loss of control" could be and, of course, was denied even more easily than was "alcoholic behavior." Perhaps so, intuited the early A.A.s from their own abundant experience, but the denial was only external. Their own personal histories amply testified to the fact that, indeed, the greater the external denial, the more deeply and painfully clutched the internal confusion, fear, and dread — especially of the specter of insanity. At some deep level, however buried, they knew from their own experience that the drinking alcoholic *knew* that he was out of control. And so the external realization could come through the internal, and *hitting bottom* became understood not as loss of employment or family, not as "sleeping in the weeds," or even immediately as the felt inability to not drink, but as the sense of being "really licked" and hopeless in the terms, the concepts, and especially the *feelings* that Bob E.'s visitors had shared with him. As Bill Wilson summarized it in telling his own story: "No words can tell of the loneliness and despair I found in that bitter morass of self-pity." On another occasion, Wilson summarized explicitly what he and Dr. Smith had discovered: "You must always remember that 'hitting bottom' is the essence of getting hold of A.A. — really."[5][+]

A further problem immediately arose. If "hitting bottom" was such an *internal* phenomenon, how could anyone transmit to another this sobriety-inducing and so life-saving realization? Wilson's and Smith's answer was based on what they had learned at the time of their initial meeting with each other, and that answer's elaboration has already been glimpsed in the description of how Bob E.'s bedside visitors treated him. The telling of personal experience — *internal* personal experience — laid the foundation for saving identification. The antidote for the deep symptom of denial was *identification* marked by open and undemanding narration infused with profound honesty about personal weakness.

The process of identification was offered without any demand for reciprocity or for anything else. The sober alcoholic told his own story out of the conviction that such honesty was required only by and necessary only to his own sobriety. This example was evidence of the A.A. understanding that honesty was necessary to *get* sobriety. Rather than any direct attack upon the mechanisms of denial or the evidence of self-centeredness, the carrier of the program of Alcoholics Anonymous demonstrated literally and vividly the essential necessity of honesty to his own sobriety. This honesty basic to identification concerned precisely the speaker's weakness and vulnerability: he bared his internal torment while drinking — in this very act becoming further vulnerable — *now even to this listener.*[6]

The therapeutic power of this process of identification arose from the witness it gave, a witness to the healing potency of *the shared honesty of mutual vulnerability openly acknowledged.* The healing response to this invitation, this witness, lay in the act of surrender — the necessary foundation for "getting the program" of Alcoholics Anonymous. By November 1937, the outward manifestation of surrender had come a

+   The profound depth of this realization was perhaps best testified to in the theme chosen by A.A.'s co-founder on the occasion of his first published "Christmas Greeting to All Members":

> Nor can men and women of A.A. ever forget that *only through suffering* did they find enough humility to enter the portals of that New World. How privileged we are to understand so well the divine paradox that strength rises from weakness, that humiliation goes before resurrection: that pain is not only the price but the very touchstone of spiritual rebirth.

long way from Bill Wilson's tortured but private abdication of his "inquiring, rational mind." For Dr. Bob Smith, the act of surrender promised on the morning of that day ("I am going to go through with it") had been embodied in his post-operative activities of 10 June 1935. The surgeon, in his realistic economic fears so cravenly desirous of clinging to whatever tattered remnants endured of his medical reputation, had finally "let go" only when he sought out, confessed to, and promised restitution to those whom he had harmed throughout his years of alcoholic drinking. Perhaps because Dr. Bob's final surrender had come only as a dangerously delayed phenomenon, the Akron co-founder tended to make the explicit act of surrender a dramatic and required beginning. Surely Bob E.'s description of his "making surrender," a description virtually identical with those offered by other early Akron A.A.s, pointed in this direction.[7]

By November 1937, then, Bill Wilson and Dr. Bob Smith had come to some understanding of hitting bottom, identification, and the surrender resulting from the conjunction of these two key concepts and practices. As Wilson returned again from Akron to New York City, superficially the problem facing him with the yet unformed program of Alcoholics Anonymous concerned the proposed projects of hospitals, missionaries, and the book about which the Akronites had been so hesitant. More deeply he wondered, as his train's clickety-clack provided a soothing rhythmic background for his ponderings: if Dr. Bob's greater numerical success was due to the explicit, Oxford Group style "making surrender," how would his New Yorkers receive this intelligence? So recently and so self-consciously separated from the Oxford Group, harboring among their number at least one militant non-theist, acutely hostile to the very words *surrender* and *conversion* in their wariness of religion, they would hardly return readily to so religious a practice as kneeling to "make surrender." Was it possible to have both rapid numerical growth and openness to skeptics such as he himself had been if dramatic conversion experiences like his "hot flash" about which the New Yorkers warily joked were the exception rather than the rule?

Bill's head began to ache, and he rested his wearied brain on a more congenial Akron catch-phrase: he would just have to meet this perplexing problem, like that of the proposed projects, "a day at a time." Fortunately, handling the superficial problem would furnish the solution to the deeper one. The pragmatic philosophy of immediately treating people's behavior in preference to investigating directly underlying causes was beginning to penetrate the fellowship and program of Alcoholics Anonymous on more than one level.

Always one to accentuate the positive, Bill Wilson stepped off his train at Grand Central more buoyed by the slim Akron majority favoring the proposed projects than burdened by the awareness of deeper problems. Wilson did not realize it at the time, but this was the beginning of what would be for him a lifelong task within Alcoholics Anonymous. He had become "the man in the middle," and so his became the difficult role of mediating between different understandings of Alcoholics Anonymous by those who *were* Alcoholics Anonymous. For now, despite all his own vaunted "twin-engine drive" and promotional instincts, Bill found that his own zeal for the projects so grudgingly accepted by the Akronites was wildly surpassed by the enthusiasm of many of the New Yorkers, and especially by that of Hank P.

Wilson explained the concerns of the Akronites, who were — he had to point out often — a solid numerical majority of the new fellowship. But the New Yorkers, flushed with self-confidence, revealed no inclination to learn. They agreed that a book was the first appropriate and most important endeavor. Led by Hank and newcomer Jim B., most even seemed to feel that this project's most significant effect would be the education of the benighted Akronites.[8]

On one matter, Wilson saw the possibility of agreement. A major worry of the Akron alcoholics was the financial condition of Dr. Bob Smith: threatened with bankruptcy, he seemed certain to lose his home by foreclosure of its mortgage. Bound to Oxford Group principles as they were, the Akronites harbored no thought of selling their program or even of making a profit from the book which would set it forth, but they were convinced that such faithful, aggressive evangelism would, in God's providence, attract the support which the program and its cofounders needed. The New Yorkers shared a similar attitude toward "professionalism," as an incident earlier in the year had revealed.[9]

In mid-1937, the financial situation at 182 Clinton Street had become acute. Lois Wilson's income as an interior decorator was barely sufficient to support her husband and maintain their home. Its pitiful inadequacy, even without the added burden of live-in drunks most of whom made no contribution towards board, came home to Bill with the realization that some of the sober alcoholics who were coming each week to the Tuesday evening meetings were back on their feet financially and were earning good money back in the world of business. So it was that when Charlie Towns, the entrepreneur who ran Towns Hospital, one day met Wilson making corridor rounds in search of prospects, the proposition that he presented struck Bill as more than merely attractive.[10]

"'Look here, Bill,' said he, 'I've got a hunch that this A.A. business of yours is someday going to fill Madison Square Garden. . . . Look, Bill, don't you see you're getting the bad end of the deal? . . . All around you, these drunks are getting well and making money, but you're giving this work full-time, and still you're broke. It isn't fair.'"[11]

These sentiments uncannily summarized many of Wilson's own thoughts. But then Towns continued with a proposal that offered an opportunity to do something. "'Why don't you move your work in here? I'll give you an office, a decent drawing account, and a very healthy slice of the profits. What I propose is perfectly ethical. You can become a lay therapist, and more successful than anybody in the business.'" Bill later recorded that at this prospect he had been "bowled over." The Oxford Group-trained co-founder felt "a few twinges of conscience" over his rising, hopeful enthusiasm, but Towns's stress on "ethical" and his own guilt over the burden Lois had shouldered quickly relieved these.[12]

That very evening happened to be meeting night at 182 Clinton Street, and no sooner had the group assembled than Wilson burst into the story of his opportunity. As he explained its details and implications, however, Bill's ardor shifted to uneasy misgiving before the stolid impassivity of his hearers. "With waning enthusiasm, my story trailed off to the end. There was a long silence."[13]

Finally, a spokesman for the for once quiet group cleared his throat. "'We know how hard up you are, Bill . . . it bothers us a lot. . . . [But] don't you realize that you can never become a professional? . . . You tell us that Charlie's proposal is ethical. Sure, it's ethical. But what we've got won't run on ethics only; it has to be better. Sure, Charlie's idea is good, but it isn't good enough. This is a matter of life and death, Bill, and nothing but the very best will do.'"[14]

And so Bill Wilson, having heard for the first time the voice of what he would later term and praise as "the group conscience," had obeyed it and had politely declined Towns's generous offer. Now, some six months later, Bill knew that he need have no fear that any difference in attitude towards "professionalism" could jeopardize the tenuous unity between the New York and Akron contingents of the fellowship. If anything, he realized, this shared, Oxford Group-derived understanding might furnish the sound basis for cementing the threatened unity. Wilson adjusted his argument to meet the needs of the situation at hand. The special importance of a book, he pointed out, would be to demonstrate that the program was not the property of professionals, was not for sale.[15]

Given this sense and this concern, prior funding for publication was imperative. Since one advantage that the New Yorkers enjoyed from their very location as well as from the personal pasts of many of them was possible access to persons of wealth, Bill noted, their immediate responsibility was clear. They could more than pull their weight in the agreed-upon projects — even all three of them — by obtaining the funds necessary to implement them.[16]

The problem of obtaining money without strings attached became primary. The New York alcoholics drew up a list of wealthy prospects. In the alcoholics' hopeful expectation, the startling fact that they — sober — could approach potential donors who knew them to be hopeless drunks would provide the best proof possible of the worth of the program they were promoting. To their very real astonishment, then, they obtained neither one cent nor a single promise of support. "Some of the wealthy exhibited mild concern and sympathy, but they were not really interested. Almost unanimously they seemed to think that tuberculosis, cancer, and the Red Cross were better charity investments. Why should they try to revive a lot of down-and-out alcoholics who had brought their troubles upon themselves? In great dejection we finally saw that drunks as objects of large charity might never be a popular cause."[17]

Angry and depressed, Wilson vented his spleen to his brother-in-law, Dr. Leonard V. Strong, in a "diatribe about the stinginess and short-sightedness of the rich." Bill had chosen his listener well and perhaps craftily. Leonard Strong was a close friend of Willard Richardson, the deeply religious man who administered the private charities of John D. Rockefeller, Jr. After hearing out his wife's brother, the doctor called his well-placed friend, and the next day introduced Wilson to him in person.[18]

Richardson, an ordained minister, showed interest, and so a late December meeting was arranged, to be "held in Mr. Rockefeller's private board room." Besides Richardson, Bill Wilson and Leonard Strong, in attendance were to be: Albert Scott, Chairman of the Trustees of Riverside Church; Frank Amos, an advertising man close to Rockefeller; and A. LeRoy Chipman, an associate who looked after some of Rockefeller's personal affairs. Dr. William Silkworth, Dr. Bob Smith, and some of both the Akron and the New York alcoholics were also to attend.[19]

The meeting proved historic but began awkwardly. As the Rockefeller coterie waited to hear the presentation of the strangers who had attracted their attention by such a round-about route, the alcoholics for once sat mute — awed as much by the trappings of the room as by the wealth and power of their hosts. Finally, someone suggested that each alcoholic tell his story. The successive tales of misery, degradation, hopeless compulsion, and finally sober salvation made a deep impression. When the last alcoholic ended his pilgrim's tale, Albert Scott, who had chaired the meeting, stood up at the head of the table and exclaimed, "'Why, this is first century Christianity! What can we do to help?'" [20]

The longed-for and eagerly sought-after moment had come. Wilson spoke up, "going for broke." He mentioned the need for money, for paid workers, chains of hospitals, and especially literature, stressing the urgency as well as the worthiness of his appeal. Dr. Silkworth and the rest of the contingent — even those from Akron had been moved by Bill's plea and the proximity of assistance — enthusiastically seconded all the points made, noting with satisfaction nods of agreement among the assembled advisors to great wealth. But then Albert Scott spoke up with yet another question, one which followed up his earlier query from an unanticipated direction: "'Won't money spoil this thing?'" [21]

Discussion resumed along lines not very different from those first laid down in Akron a month before. Toward its end, agreement was reached that whatever the final decision, the enterprise — yet unnamed — surely needed *some* money. Frank Amos offered to investigate, proposing that his findings could then serve as the basis for a direct presentation to John D. Rockefeller, Jr. Wilson and Smith, still hopeful and enthusiastic, suggested that Amos look first at Akron — it was the older and larger group, and Dr. Bob's financial needs were the more pressing. [22]

Conflicting memories veil the outcome of this journey, the next step in the history of Alcoholics Anonymous. According to Henrietta Seiberling, she and others convinced Amos that money would indeed "spoil this thing," and he so reported to John D. Rockefeller, Jr., who agreed. In Bill Wilson's memory Amos returned from Akron as enthusiastic as were the New York alcoholics, and "he recommended that Mr. Rockefeller grant us $50,000 just as a starter." Wilson reported that "Uncle Dick" Richardson became just as enthusiastic, finding in this "conjunction of medicine, religion, and a great good work" something uniquely worthy of the Rockefeller beneficence. It was John D. himself, according to Wilson, who expressed again the concern of Albert Scott. On the basis that money would spoil any attempted living out of first-century Christianity, the world's richest man flatly refused to fund the enterprise. One concession, however, Rockefeller did make: $5,000 was placed in the treasury of Riverside Church to furnish necessary temporary assistance to Bill and Dr. Bob Smith.[23]

Bill Wilson had, at the time of these early 1938 events, come to his perception of the necessity of "deflation at depth" for the individual alcoholic. He had not yet extended this insight to the newly formed and yet unnamed group of non-drinking alcoholics that would become Alcoholics Anonymous. Sensing that Richardson, Amos, Chipman, and Strong were not in complete agreement with Rockefeller, Wilson sought further meetings with these four, hoping through them to continue soliciting other persons of wealth. From this beginning came — in the Spring of 1938 — the Alcoholic Foundation, which eventually evolved into the General Service Board of Alcoholics Anonymous. Among its first trustees were Richardson, Amos, Chipman, and Strong, and thus began the long and later troublesome tradition that made a majority of the organization's trustees non-alcoholics. In the circumstances of this origin was rooted another important development in the history of Alcoholics Anonymous. Because of the legal impossibility of defining "alcoholic," the group formalized itself under a simple trust agreement rather than by seeking any kind of legal charter.[24]

The Spring of 1938 was further significant, but not because of any success of the Foundation as its end had been conceived. The money-raising efforts "fizzled out. . . . It looked like the end of the line." But the idea of a book remained. Bill Wilson, whose writing experience had been confined to the company reports which he had submitted to Wall Street brokers during his 1920s personal heyday, found that he did not know how to begin a work of the scope contemplated. Weighed down by many grand ideas and hopes, he felt driven by a need to tell it *all*, and the impossibility of this for a time inhibited him from even beginning. Dr. Bob advised, as always, "Keep it simple." Trustees Frank Amos and LeRoy Chipman requested promotional literature for their fund-raising efforts; and in reply to Wilson's query about what they wanted, the non-alcoholic trustees pointed back to the fact that their own interest and enthusiasm had been awakened first by what they had heard at the December 1937 meeting — the stories of the assembled alcoholics.[25]

Wilson therefore produced what became the first two chapters of *Alcoholics Anonymous*: "Bill's Story" and "There Is A Solution." Whether these were drafts for a book or promotional literature was not quite clear to Bill. What became increasingly clear was that whether primarily because of the titillating view of the underside of human life afforded, or primarily because of the potential for identification, or primarily because a pragmatic people responded to and thrived upon experience, the main marketable commodity that any alcoholic had to offer was his story. Himself a product of all that pragmatism, Bill Wilson did not think in terms of "primarilies."[26]

A similar realization took place among the New York alcoholics. Their Oxford Group origins had acquainted them with the long religious and psychological tradition of the usefulness of confession. For the Oxford Group, this carried some connotation of "public" — although there was the distinction between "sharing for confession" which was private and "sharing for witness," which, of its nature, was public. A difference of opinion over this distinction, indeed, had been one factor in the New York alcoholics' departure from the Oxford Group, as had been the increased "group guidance" which Wilson found especially oppressive.[27]

But the separation from the Buchmanites having taken place, the alcoholics had to decide what was to be done at their own meetings. Aimed as this early experience was at potential adherents with whom some identification had to be established, the telling and re-telling of "stories" began un-self-consciously to develop into the practice that best embodied the core therapeutic process of what would soon become Alcoholics Anonymous. The book itself furthered this development.[28]

The remote internal pull to the publication of *Alcoholics Anonymous* was Bill's and Dr. Bob's November 1937 vision. The proximate external push came from an early fall 1938 meeting arranged by trustee Frank Amos between Bill Wilson and Eugene Exman, religious editor of Harper Brothers publishers. As attractive as Bill found the $1,500 advance promised him, the more promotionally-inclined New York spokesmen for the rapidly developing "group conscience" decided that the fellowship should own its own book, and further that if it had enough merit to prompt an advance from Harper's, the book could solve their financial problems and so show up the thus far unproductive Trustees and Foundation. The decision was made to form a stock company, and "Works Publishing, Inc." was born.[29]

In 1953, Works Publishing, Inc. would become A.A. Publishing, Inc., and finally, in 1959, A.A. World Services, Inc., but its original name bore a telling significance in the early history of Alcoholics Anonymous. According to most of the New York alcoholics at the time the name "Works Publishing" was chosen, "This name derived from a common expression, used in the group, 'It works.'" According to the early Akronites, the "Works" in "Works Publishing" reflected the St. James quotation that had played such a prominent part in the "infusion of spirituality" during that first summer of 1935. The book was to be the first of the

fellowship's "works" following out the Jamesian call to live faith externally — by works. Both interpretations were true — each in its own way.
Perhaps Wilson even consciously used the ambiguity inherent in the
word *Works*. It reflected the New Yorkers' fascination with and promotional stress on proven results; at the same time, it reassured the Akronites still hesitant about even this project. They would be encouraged
when they heard this echo of "Anne Smith's favorite quote." [30]

Meanwhile, through the final months of 1938 and into 1939, Bill
Wilson labored at writing. As he slowly roughed out the chapters, Wilson read them to the weekly meeting at his Clinton Street home and
sent them as well to Dr. Bob for comment by the Akronites. In New
York especially, there was heated discussion. Thus it was a not-very-
serene Bill Wilson who, after much hesitation and even stalling, finally
set out to put down in words the heart of the program through which
he and close to one hundred other alcoholics had achieved sobriety. [31]

Sprawling on his bed in an "anything but spiritual mood" one evening, Wilson poised his yellow pencil over the school tablet propped
before him. Quickly, lest he block, he scrawled the words "How It
Works" across the top of the page, then paused to meditate about the
six-step procedure which his associates at the previous meeting had
agreed pretty well summed up what they had learned from the Oxford
Group:

1. We admitted that we were licked, that we were powerless
   over alcohol.
2. We made an inventory of our defects or sins.
3. We confessed or shared our shortcomings with another
   person in confidence.
4. We made restitution to all those we had harmed by our
   drinking.
5. We tried to help other alcoholics, with no thought of reward in money or prestige.
6. We prayed to whatever God we thought there was for
   power to practice these precepts. [32]

Too preachy, too goody-goody, he winced; also too complex and even
unclear if one did not know the teachings of the Oxford Group. In any
event, it was certainly no way to begin *this* chapter, and — against his will
— the echo of "Oxford Group" reminded Bill again of the difference
between the Akron and New York approaches. His correspondence
and telephone conversations with Dr. Bob, and especially the surgeon's
increasing leadership in Akron, had somewhat soothed that difficulty,
but the problem remained unsolved. Quickly, before that thought could

overwhelm him, Wilson began to write, seeking to set down a theme of hope — something on which all could agree.[33]

"Rarely have we seen a person fail who has thoroughly followed our path." Bill's pencil began to fly over the paper, and his thoughts continued to flow as he wrote a paragraph beginning:

> Half measures will avail you nothing. You stand at the turning point. Throw yourself under God's protection and care with complete abandon.
>
> Now we think you can take it! Here are the steps we took — our program of recovery:
>
> We admitted we were powerless over alcohol — that our lives had become unmanageable.
>
> Came to believe that God could restore us to sanity.
>
> Made a decision to turn our wills and our lives over to the care of God.
>
> Made a searching and fearless moral inventory of ourselves.
>
> Admitted to God, to ourselves, and to another human being the exact nature of our wrongs.
>
> Were entirely ready to have God remove all these defects of character.
>
> Humbly on our knees asked Him to remove our shortcomings.
>
> Made a list of all persons we had harmed, and became willing to make amends to them all.
>
> Made direct amends to such people wherever possible, except when to do so would injure them or others.
>
> Continued to take personal inventory and when we were wrong promptly admitted it.
>
> Sought through prayer and meditation to improve our conscious contact with God, praying only for knowledge of His will for us and the power to carry that out.
>
> Having had a spiritual experience as the result of these steps, we tried to carry this message to alcoholics, and to practice these principles in all our affairs.[34]

Wilson paused. His intention had been to "break up into smaller pieces . . . our six chunks of truth . . . to be as clear and comprehensible as possible, [leaving] not a single loophole through which the rationalizing alcoholic could wriggle out." Almost idly, he began to number the new steps: "They added up to twelve. Somehow this number seemed significant. Without any special rhyme or reason I connected them with the twelve apostles. Feeling greatly relieved now, I commenced to reread the draft."[35]

Debate began almost immediately, as visitors arrived and Bill completed his first rereading aloud to them. Three points of view emerged. "Conservatives . . . thought that the book ought to be Christian in the doctrinal sense of the word and that it should say so"; "liberals" who "had no objection to the use of the word 'God' throughout the book, but . . . were dead set against any other theological proposition"; and the "radical left wing . . . the atheists and agnostics" who "wanted the word 'God' deleted from the book entirely. . . . They wanted a *psychological* book which would lure the alcoholic in. Once in, the prospect could take God or leave Him alone as he wished." Caught in this apparently inescapable cross fire, Wilson asked for a truce. Despairing of satisfying everyone, he finally secured temporary agreement that he would be the final judge of what the book would say.[36]

Wilson returned to his writing only to discover another problem. The most important parts of any book that sought to capture the attention and to change the habits of readers, he realized, were the beginning and the end. The beginning, after one false start, had posed no problem. His own story, after all, *was* the beginning of Alcoholics Anonymous. But how to conclude tortured him — briefly. Bill's first efforts proved invariably too "preachy" — a quality that over the years jarred many when they came to the conclusion of the substantive part of the book *Alcoholics Anonymous*, for neither Wilson nor A.A. ever did solve this problem:

> Abandon yourself to God as you understand God. Admit your faults to Him and to your fellows. Clear away the wreckage of your past. Give freely of what you find and join us. We shall be with you in the Fellowship of the Spirit, and you will surely meet some of us as you trudge the Road of Happy Destiny.
> May God bless you and keep you — until then.[37]

Such or a similar conclusion, Wilson felt understandably, might move a few readers to jump up and shout "Amen." It was hardly likely, experience had taught, to induce many to try the program. In that realization, however, gleamed the light of a solution. "Experience had taught" that what made the program work was the telling of their stories by now sober alcoholics. In the weeks during which Bill Wilson wrestled with the problem of how to conclude, he was reading what he had written to those who gathered at his home each Tuesday evening. From this practice and experience emerged the obvious solution of "the story or case history section" which not only concludes but comprises well over half the bulk of *Alcoholics Anonymous*. The main criticism that his hearers offered Wilson was that there was not enough "evidence in the form of living proof" that the program did indeed work. The decision to include a segment, "The Doctor's Opinion," in which Dr. Silkworth set forth his understanding of alcoholism and his endorsement of Alcoholics Anonymous was one step to meet this concern. But this piece, too, when submitted, ended by speaking of prayer and "mental uplift," and so it ultimately served as informal preface rather than substantive conclusion.[38]

Meanwhile, the telling of stories emerged in another, less direct, fashion as the best "evidence in the form of living proof" and — more — the very thing that made the program work. As the weeks of Bill's manuscript reading wore on, a division arose which seemed to threaten the unity of the New York group itself. The "oldtimers" who dated from 1936 and early 1937 shared Bill's enthusiasm for publication. They looked forward each week to hearing the work-in-progress and to discussing if not arguing over Bill's ideas and presentation. Those more recently arrived and savoring the glow of new sobriety longed to share this experience with their former drinking companions — and besides, they were being told that this, indeed, was the only way in which they could keep their own sobriety. But to bring some drunk quavering in the early stages of withdrawal, or even someone recently discharged from Towns Hospital and half-hopefully seeking the "new way of life" of which he had heard, all the way over to Brooklyn to hear arguments about a book "just didn't work." Nobody else was getting sober, and according to what they had been taught, their own sobriety was being endangered.[39]

And so story-telling took on two sharper functions: as a reinforcement for "Remember When," especially useful when the "when" experience wasn't vividly present to them in the person of some still-shaking sufferer; and as both the bait to attract and the means to convey the message that "this program works" to whatever suffering contacts they could "scoop," in their colorful term. Even after they had left the Oxford Group, the nameless members of the fledgling fellowship continued to receive word of mouth referrals and requests for help. They responded and each told his own story, but each also experienced the frustration of alcoholic exceptionalism. Whether the response was phrased, "But you're different" or "But I'm different," these "Twelfth Step calls" which attempted to carry the message even before the formulation of the Twelfth Step produced few new recruits. From this experience derived one specific of later A.A. practice: Twelfth Step calls were always to be made by at least two people. From this experience also came powerful impetus in a direction already marked out, the centrality of each drinker's story, especially at open meetings. Inclusion of a "story section" in *Alcoholics Anonymous* was, therefore, not a mere afterthought, but an experiential lesson learned in several diverse ways. While "How It Works" might contain the heart of the program, "How do you get it to work?" was a prior question, and one which could be laid hold of only by having the ex-drinkers tell their stories.[40]

Given the announced intention in each of the three editions of *Alcoholics Anonymous* to demonstrate through the story section the variety of people who had found sobriety in A.A., the limits to the diversity actually portrayed is instructive. In the first edition, eighteen of the twenty-eight stories were furnished by "Akronites who had substantial sobriety records for testimonial materials." At the time, of course, there were hardly enough "recovering alcoholics" to allow Wilson — and the others concerned with the breadth of the program — to choose among them. The problem was met by editing to accent different phases of the drinkers' common experience.[41]

For example: only thirteen of the twenty-eight stories indicated anything of childhood religious background, but of these, ten revealed very intensive training. Similarly, of the fifteen who mentioned education, eight clearly testified to college attendance, while the remaining seven stressed the fact that they did not even "finish school." Twelve — nine of these *not* having indicated early religious training — recalled their initial cynicism that any religious approach could help them.[42]

Social or economic class was less easily masked, for a common "bottom experience" was the loss of livelihood. Nineteen of the twenty-eight stories clearly revealed at least middle-class status: one doctor (Smith), three engineers, five in managerial or executive positions, two editors, six who owned their own businesses, plus a driver of Cadillacs who had supported "playgirls" and a woman who had frequented "teas" and "bridge parties."[43]

A special facet of the "bottom experience" of most alcoholics who successfully got the A.A. program was the painful awareness of dissonant behavior, that is, behavior under the influence of alcohol that clashed with ideals derived from social, educational, and religious background. Beyond being fired or losing their own businesses through drinking, five reported serious automobile accidents; eight, asylum hospitalization; and four, family break-ups. Also recounted were one suicide attempt, one case in which the drinker intentionally set fire to his own home, and instances of missing one's own engagement party, one's mother's funeral, and the birth of one's child.[44]

The almost perfectly typical story of Bill D., "A.A. Number Three," was not included. His "credentials," in fact the usual ones for "getting the program" in these early years, were apparently too blatant: highly respectable upper middle-class background, above average education, intensive youthful religious training which had since been rejected, and former social prominence recently nullified by such behavior as his assault on two nurses. Despite the omission of Bill D.'s story, Wilson and the others surely did wish to convey in their book the important point that such people could be alcoholics. The program of "Alcoholics Anonymous" would attract few customers as long as the term "alcoholic" evoked only the stereotyped image of a Skid-Row bum with a few days growth of beard, half-empty bottle of muscatel protruding from the torn pocket of his ragged, too large overcoat, as in baggy trousers and outworn shoes he rummaged through a trash-barrel in search of the newspapers that would furnish that night's mattress and blanket. In the future, however, an even more troublesome problem would arise. Granted that the respectable, middle-class types portrayed could be alcoholics, were such the only type able to profit from the therapy of Alcoholics Anonymous? This concern, only latent in 1939, provided one motive for expanding the story section in succeeding editions of the book, *Alcoholics Anonymous*.[45]

By the end of January 1939, Wilson was ready to rush the book to press. Then, mindful of the dual origins of the program, "someone sounded a note of caution: alcoholics could be awfully critical people. What if the book contained medical errors, or — worse — proved offensive to some religious faith?" So, four hundred multilith "loan copies" went out for evaluation. Comments were offered, but the most significant result occurred within the group itself.[46]

Wilson had written on the cover page of the multilith printing "*Alcoholic's Anonymous*" [*sic*] but many in New York — and more in Akron — found this unacceptable as a title. True, after leaving the Oxford Group in 1937, the New Yorkers had begun referring to themselves as a "nameless bunch of alcoholics," and by October 1938 some informally used the term "Alcoholics Anonymous." But from the time of the early 1938 financial endeavor, the search for a happy euphemism had led the non-drinking alcoholics to refer to themselves in writing as "The One Hundred Men Corporation," calling attention to the point that this was not a fluke enterprise — that the number of recoveries was substantial.[47]

A majority of the group in New York — and just about all in Akron — also felt it most important to transmit hope, and so the title *The Way Out* became very popular. For a time, Bill Wilson later confessed, he was attracted to this title because he contemplated expanding it to *The Way Out: The B. W. Movement.* Vigorously slapped down by the few on whom he tested the idea, however, Bill began leaning toward *Alcoholics Anonymous,* in time carrying most of the New Yorkers with him but totally failing to convince the Akronites. Finally, a New York oldtimer, visiting his family farm in Maryland, was asked to investigate titles in the Library of Congress. He responded by telegram: "Library of Congress has 25 books The Way Out 12 The Way . . . None Alcoholics Anonymous." All agreed that they deserved a better fate than being the thirteenth "The Way," much less the twenty-sixth "The Way Out," and thus the book — and eventually the society — received its name.[48]

The distributed multiliths returned, but the readers' comments produced few alterations in the final text. One striking and significant change came at the suggestion of a New Jersey psychiatrist, Dr. Howard. Most of the "we haves" and "we trieds" that many new readers found so attractive after years of being preached at and ordered to were originally "yous" and "musts." It was Dr. Howard who suggested that the insanity and death so vividly portrayed in the book as consequences of alcoholism were so persuasive that no further force was needed. Thus A.A.'s debt to the medical profession deepened.[49]

From "the world of religion," Dr. Harry Emerson Fosdick returned his copy without criticism, expressed deepest satisfaction with it, and sent a favorable review of the book which he encouraged A.A. to release as it wished. Morgan R., the group's first Catholic adherent, presented the manuscript to a friend on the New York Archdiocesan Committee on Publications. That committee, Morgan reported, "had nothing but the best to say of our efforts. From their point of view the book was perfectly all right as far as it went." A very few editorial suggestions understood as for improvement rather than as criticism were readily and gratefully incorporated, especially in the section treating of prayer and meditation. Only one change was requested: at the conclusion of Wilson's own story, he "had made a rhetorical flourish to the effect that 'we have found Heaven right here on this good old earth.'" The committee gently suggested changing "Heaven" to "Utopia": "'After all, we Catholics are promising folks something much better later on!'"[50]

This reminder of his tendency to extremes and grandiosity made it easier for Wilson to accept a final change now more insistently demanded by the "radicals" among the New York group. These few, led by Hank P. and Jim B., became adamant in pressing their concern that there was "too much God" in the Twelve Steps. Bill had learned the dangers of his tendency toward "too much" from Dr. Howard and from Morgan's Catholic contacts. He apparently also was aware that at least one Catholic priest in Cleveland, although happy to see his parishioners sober, had forbidden two of them to journey to Akron to participate in what was to him obviously a religious gathering not under Catholic auspices. And so, Wilson accepted the utility of compromise:

> . . . In Step Two we decided to describe God as a "Power greater than ourselves." In Steps Three and Eleven we inserted the words "God as we understand Him." From Step Seven we deleted the expression "on our knees." And, as a lead-in sentence to all the steps we wrote these words: "Here are the steps we took which are suggested as a Program of Recovery." A.A.'s Twelve Steps were to be *suggestions* only.[51]

Having argued over virtually everything else concerning their book's writing and publication, the newly sober alcoholics were hardly about to pass by in staid silence the one final opportunity for debate over their work: what price was to be charged for it? Stockholders Wilson and Hank P. argued for a price of $3.50. The book, in their view, was not only to spread the program, but to support its operations. Others, however, wondered — loudly — how many alcoholics needing the program would be able to spend that amount on a book in the spring of 1939. The prices they suggested ranged from $2.50 down to $1.00. Bill's telling of the tale had Hank finally winning out, but a touch of the Wilson humor appeared in the final compromise: "As a consolation to the contestants, we directed Mr. Blackwell to do the job on the thickest paper in his shop. The original volume proved to be so bulky that it became known as the 'Big Book.' Of course the idea was to convince the alcoholic that he was indeed getting his money's worth."[52]

If, after this happy outcome, Bill Wilson, alcoholic author, needed further deflation, he received it. A presumably promised and implicitly relied upon supportive article in *The Reader's Digest* did not come to be; the bank foreclosed the mortgage on the Clinton Street home, evicting Bill and Lois; all attempts through the summer of 1939 to obtain national magazine publicity for *Alcoholics Anonymous* failed; and despite a barrage of twenty thousand postcards unleashed upon every physician east of the Mississippi River and timed to coincide with the appearance of a New York alcoholic on nationwide radio, only two book orders materialized. Further, Hank began to manifest the first signs of his later paranoia, and the spreading suspicion that he had begun or would begin drinking again soon proved frighteningly accurate. Even Ebby —

the man who had brought to Bill Wilson the seed of what was to become Alcoholics Anonymous — had gone back to drinking and showed no sign of interest in stopping, even for "a day at a time." Through the hot summer of 1939, despite the fact that its program had finally been crystalized and published, the situation of Alcoholics Anonymous looked bleak indeed — and especially to its more inclined-to-enthusiasm and leaning-on-hope New York branch.[53]

Different yet related developments in Akron were as profoundly shaping the rapid evolution of the fellowship into Alcoholics Anonymous. Four significant occurrences are noteworthy, and all were separations: of the alcoholics within the Oxford Group; of the visiting Cleveland alcoholics from their Akron base; of Dr. Bob Smith's practice with alcoholics from Akron City Hospital; and finally of the newly self-conscious Alcoholics Anonymous from any Oxford Group association.

Almost immediately upon Bill Wilson's departure from Akron in November 1937, and probably related to the co-founders' conversations, the Akron surgeon began to invite the alcoholics attending each Wednesday's Oxford Group meeting at the Williams home to gather separately from the non-alcoholic Oxford Groupers after the regular session. The distinction between "closed meetings" (those for alcoholics only) and "open meetings" (those which non-alcoholics were welcome to attend) had not yet entered A.A. consciousness. Yet in New York at Clinton Street each week, after the "regular meeting" usually attended also by wives, alcoholics who wished to ask private questions about the program adjourned with Wilson to a smaller upstairs livingroom. The nature of the questions asked and the obvious utility of this practice in the all-important matter of honesty had no doubt led Bill to urge it upon Dr. Bob. In any case, by early 1938 the Akron alcoholics were meeting briefly but separately each week after the regular Oxford Group meeting.[54]

Early 1938 had also brought the first commuting Clevelanders to Akron each Wednesday evening. These men, after being sobered up by Dr. Bob at Akron City Hospital, had usually spent a few weeks in Akron — sharing the daily round of camaraderie that characterized these years. Eventually however they had to return to their families and — if lucky — their jobs in Cleveland, and when they did so, the loss of that intense feeling of fellowship proved painful. Thus began the practice of the Clevelanders making the seventy-five mile round-trip by car each Wednesday, a further testimony to the importance they attached to this meeting.[55]

Growth in Cleveland was at first very slow, but by early 1939, nine to twelve of that city's alcoholics were making the journey each week. At this point there emerged both a problem and an opportunity. The dynamo powering the Cleveland effort, Clarence S., was a zealous pigeon-pursuer, one who at times literally hauled his prospects off bar stools. Given the nature of Cleveland's population as well as Clarence's open-minded zeal, roughly half of the alcoholics making the weekly journey turned out to be practicing Roman Catholics. Some of these, when first approached by Clarence, had shied away from "the religion" they perceived in his message. But in the agony of their active alcoholism, in their desire "to do anything" to get sober, and on his assurance that the Akron gatherings were in no way a "religious service," they had agreed to give it a try.[56]

Those who did give it a try got sober. Furthermore, despite all Clarence's assurances, some of them began again to worry that what went on at the Williams's in Akron each week was "a Protestant religious service." They needled Clarence about this on the drive back to Cleveland each week, and eventually at least two of them carried their concerns to their parish priest — who promptly pronounced Catholic attendance at the Wednesday meetings a violation of Church law and so forbade his charges to attend.[57]

Meanwhile, the multilith draft of the text of *Alcoholic's Anonymous* had been circulating among the Akronites, and by mid-April of 1939 the first printed copies became available. Clarence at once borrowed from the title of the draft the name by which he began to refer to his group. This was not "the alcoholic squadron of the Oxford Group" but "Alcoholics Anonymous," apparently the first clear use of the term as a specific and exclusive name. The mere change of name did little to allay Catholic suspicion, but the availability of a written and published program afforded another option. At the Williams's home on Wednesday, 10 May 1939, Clarence — with the approval of his traveling companions — announced that this would be their last visit to the Akron meeting. On the next evening, interested *alcoholics* were invited to a new meeting to be held each week in Cleveland at the home of Abby G., the most recently sober of the visitors. This would be a meeting, Clarence declared, of "Alcoholics Anonymous."[58]

The Akronites — alcoholics and non-alcoholic Oxford Groupers — were shaken by this development, and the situation remained confused for the next three years. Clarence S. was an abrasive personality. Many expressed less than regret at his departure and predicted that there would soon be further problems in Cleveland. In this they proved correct, but the difficulties within Cleveland A.A. did not move any alcoholics to return to Akron or to renew connections with the Oxford Group. Yet the Clevelanders did continue to send their "really difficult cases" back to Dr. Bob in Akron for treatment. Some of these, after their release from the hospital, continued the practice of remaining in Akron for a time in order to absorb the intensive daily fellowship. Having developed strong bonds of affection and especially a sense of loyalty to T. Henry Williams, a few of these, even after they had returned to Cleveland and had joined a group there, continued to journey to Akron each week for the Wednesday meeting — even after, in late 1939, Dr. Smith and most of the Akron alcoholics had separated from the Oxford Group setting of the Williams's home. Only in 1942, under the impact of World War II gasoline rationing, did the visits of this significant minority cease.[59]

Meanwhile yet another unforeseen occurrence took on significance because of early A.A.'s wariness of Roman Catholic opinion. Dr. Bob Smith had treated his alcoholics, under varying diagnoses, at two hospitals — Akron City and Green Cross. Hospitals at the time were reluctant to admit alcoholics under *any* diagnosis, less over moral or treatment concerns than because of the blunt fact that alcoholics rarely paid their bills. In the spring of 1939, administrators at the Akron City and Green Cross Hospitals, noting that Dr. Smith's mysterious patients owed over five thousand dollars, began scrutinizing his admissions more carefully.[60]

Since 1934, Dr. Bob had been on the visiting staff of St. Thomas Hospital, a Catholic institution in Akron. Much of his practice there was in the emergency room, and he had often lamented over coffee with the gentle nun who was the hospital's admissions officer the ravages caused by alcohol-related accidents and fights. In the course of one such conversation, in the spring of 1939, A.A.'s medical co-founder confessed his own alcoholism to this nun, Sister Ignatia of the Sisters of Charity of Saint Augustine who staffed the facility. If the sister was surprised by this admission, she was less shocked by the request that followed it. "Sister, these people need medical treatment — *I know.* Do you think we could smuggle at least a couple who I'm sure I could help in here?"[61]

In later years both Sister Ignatia and Dr. Bob Smith relished a specific descriptive word and an ironic circumstance in describing the events of the next months. The sickly nun and the alcoholic surgeon cherished the thrill of "bootlegging" alcoholics into St. Thomas — most often under the diagnosis of "acute gastritis." And, to prevent discovery of their deception, they ensconced their patients who were in the most acute stages of withdrawal in the hospital's "flower room" — a nook previously used only for patients who had died and were awaiting removal to the morgue or funeral parlor.[62]

Soon, the nun saw some of the amazing results of Dr. Smith's ministrations and sought to learn more about his technique. Chatting with the endless stream of visitors who daily stopped by to visit her charges, Sister Ignatia learned of the Oxford Group connection and in this found another cause for possible concern if she were to ask the Sister Administrator openly to admit Dr. Smith's alcoholics. She took her problem to a young assistant pastor from the neighboring St. Martin's parish, a priest whose newly ordained zeal touched her heart and upon whom she was in the habit of calling when obvious alcoholics seemed in need of spiritual ministration.[63]

Father Vincent Haas listened quietly and carefully. Yes, it was wonderful what Dr. Smith was doing. He himself knew only frustration in his efforts at counseling alcoholics and their families — they just didn't seem to *hear* him. Yes, of course he would look in on one of "those meetings" — if Dr. Smith approved. So it was that one evening in early 1940 Father Haas trundled off to the King School where, by that time, the alcoholics were meeting. A profoundly spiritual man who saw the whole world through the prism of deep faith, the young priest found less "primitive Christianity" than "a movement just like the early Franciscans." Entranced, enthralled, and enthusiastic, he reported this perception and the warm welcome accorded him not only to Sister Ignatia but (at her urging) to her administrative superior, and Dr. Bob's St. Thomas practice found secure footing and sure support. The few Clevelanders who were visiting the King School each week of course carried this news back to their city and thus laid to rest the lingering bogey which still haunted some of that metropolis's more scrupulous Catholic alcoholics.[64]

Accidental circumstances had dictated that the first exposure of Father Haas was to "Alcoholics Anonymous" at the King School rather than to "the alcoholic squadron of the Oxford Group" at the Williams's home. Despite the departure of the Clevelanders, in the year 1939, "the alcoholic squadron of the Oxford Group increased in numbers and noise — until we took the place over." Bob E. gives the best account. "Instead of being the alcoholic squad of the Oxford Group, we were the main body there and we had the most to say and we were kind of running the thing." The committed Oxford Group members did not make this surrender easily. Bob E. says, "They had us in silence, listening for guidance half the time. . . . That's the way it started. That made the drunks very restless. We couldn't stand that — get the jitters, you know. As we increased in numbers and influence, that was almost cut out. They could see where their fundamentals were not being adhered to."[65]

Two further problems exacerbated the rapidly deteriorating situation. When the book *Alcoholics Anonymous* was published and distributed, some in the Oxford Group complained that the program was "being commercialized." These Groupers had no use for the alcoholics' pride in their literary venture. Also, not only were the alcoholics themselves feeling uncomfortably crowded sprawled across the floor and on thirty folding chairs in the Williams's livingroom, but Clarace Williams spoke to Henrietta Seiberling about her increasing anxiety over "what was happening" — to her home as well as to Oxford Group principles.[66]

Finally, in late October 1939, most of the alcoholics left the Williams's home and began meeting at the home of Dr. Bob and Anne Smith. The friendship among Henrietta Seiberling, Clarace Williams, and Anne Smith had seemed about to snap under the strain from the two factions in the Group. The most poignant yet apparently accurate memory recalled: "We pulled out rather suddenly. There were some hot conversations on the telephone; it was a 3-way thing between Clarace, Annie — the women decided it, as was usually the case in a thing like that. 'Hen' and Clarace and Annie decided right there and Doc went along with Annie. But we pulled out all of a sudden without any warning and so we had no place to go, so we held our meeting from October to December at Doc's house." The Smith home, however, soon also became overcrowded with "between seventy to eighty people in my small livingroom and diningroom." Before long, the alcoholics moved to the King School.[67]

For a time some of the Akron Oxford Group had difficulty accepting the separation. T. Henry Williams, of whom all factions always spoke most highly, finally shared some of his own pain and confusion with Bill and Lois Wilson. After apologizing for his delay in writing, he explained:

> Have been waiting trying to think through what to tell you and still do not know what to say. The boys are all free, white, and twenty-one. Therefore I have nothing to hold them here. Bob came over and insisted that the boys were not satisfied and felt we were unfriendly and insisted they meet elsewhere. He also insisted I make a statement telling them they were free to leave. . . . Do you think we would turn the boys out after

what it has meant to us? Our door is open and we love everyone of the boys and they will always be welcome.[68]

By late October 1939, Alcoholics Anonymous had come into a clear existence of its own. The book presenting its program had been published. Its final separation from Oxford Group sponsorship had been successfully completed. Most importantly, a new group flourished in a new city under the sole name "Alcoholics Anonymous," and without any direct impetus from either of A.A.'s co-founders.[69]

Yet there were also problems. Differences of opinion about publicizing the book as well as about financing the other projects persisted, especially in New York. Tensions and controversies over the Oxford Group connection smoldered, especially in Akron. And in Cleveland, there began to appear the first hints that the further development of Alcoholics Anonymous — both that desired and that feared — not only would continue, but would continue to be beyond the fellowship's own total control.

Sober as well as drunk, the members of Alcoholics Anonymous were learning they were limited and therefore needed others. But that need of others was also limited. Alcoholics Anonymous had been born — now it needed not only to grow but also to mature. Yet as was the case with the sobriety of its individual members, A.A.'s growth had to precede its maturity. In its growth as fellowship over the next two years, Alcoholics Anonymous honed its awareness of its style of needing others. By doing so, A.A. set the stage for its further development as program.

IV

Prelude to Maturity
OCTOBER 1939–MARCH 1941

Needing Others — The Era of Publicity

In both New York and Akron, the active presence of a strong personality who was accepted as "co-founder" shaped the development of Alcoholics Anonymous. Because of the respect in which Bill Wilson and Dr. Bob Smith were held, because in the minds of most of their cohorts these two men had brought them sobriety, A.A.'s growth in New York City and Akron waited upon them. But they were only two individuals; and although Wilson still harbored a zest for promotion, at least in comparison with Dr. Smith's habitual surgical preference for working carefully on one person at a time, Bill's own respect not only for Dr. Bob but also for the differences among his diverse coterie's preferences and for the tender sensibilities of newly sober alcoholics inhibited his promotional instinct.

The early Cleveland experience of Alcoholics Anonymous was different, at times weirdly so. Clarence S. arranged for the meeting of his fledgling group to take place each Thursday evening at Abby G.'s home even though Abby himself still languished in the Akron City Hospital. For five months, the Cleveland alcoholics met there in relative calm. Yet many sensed that this new style represented an act of faith. While there was general, fingers-crossed acceptance that the program could be "gotten" through the book rather than by informal transmission through the Oxford Group or by direct contact with Bill Wilson or Dr. Bob Smith, this was but theory and speculation. These were hopes rather than a reflection of Wilson's and Smith's actual experience, and thus Cleveland became the testing ground for what Alcoholics Anonymous was to be.[1]

The Clevelanders met and "Twelfth Stepped" drunks — alcoholics who were still drinking — but growth was slow, not least because of the tendency to ship "really difficult cases" off to Dr. Bob and his new practice at St. Thomas Hospital in Akron. Yet, like the early New York adherents, the Clevelanders were missionary-minded. They not only had a message to carry, they *had to* carry that message. Reinforced by the program as newly published in the Big Book, from the title of which they had seized their self-conscious identity, and acutely conscious of their traumatic separation from the Oxford Group, the early Cleveland A.A.s were especially aware that working with other alcoholics was essential to their own sobriety. Whether through greater effort or by happy chance, the Clevelanders early succeeded in obtaining the publicity that all members of the fellowship craved and strove to obtain. On 21 October 1939, Cleveland's most prestigious newspaper, the *Plain Dealer*, published the first of an editorially supported series of seven articles by reporter Elrick B. Davis. Both the articles and the editorials calmly and approvingly described Alcoholics Anonymous, emphasizing the reasonable hope this new society held out to otherwise hopeless drunks.[2]

The most coherent and therefore credible story of how this series came to be written and published tells that early in 1939, while the Clevelanders were still commuting to Akron, Dorothy S., Clarence's wife, aware of her husband's problems, uneasiness, and consequent plans, had sought out the city's most prominent minister, the Rev. Dr. Dilworth Lupton. Lupton, established and beloved pastor of Cleveland's First Unitarian Church, had himself failed in several efforts at helping Clarence to achieve sobriety. Dorothy, relying on the cleric's good humor as well as his civic prominence, hoped to obtain from him favorable publicity for the proposed endeavor to bring the "miracle" of Alcoholics Anonymous to Cleveland. The sympathetic minister heard her out graciously and patiently, readily sharing her joy in her husband's new-found sobriety. But he refused support without personal observation, and further declined even to visit a meeting in Akron, stating that "anything connected with the Oxford Groups" could not "enjoy lasting impact or success."[3]

Sometime in the late summer of 1939, the Stillman Avenue group now solidly established, Dorothy S. revisited the Rev. Dr. Lupton with the Big Book in hand and the names of Catholic members Joe D. and Bill S. as evidence that Alcoholics Anonymous was not the Oxford Group. The minister listened, read the book, came to a meeting, and was impressed. "He said 'Dorothy, you go back to the *Plain Dealer*. You tell these people that I'm going to preach on A.A.' It was enough for publicity as he was one of the really big Protestant ministers in Cleveland and he was interested in all of the civic affairs. What he said was good copy. We got hold of . . . a reporter for the *Plain Dealer*." [4]

Where and how Elrick Davis entered the picture must remain unanswered. Clarence, surely not publicity-shy, claimed to have found him on a bar stool in obvious need of the A.A. program, a claim about which the Cleveland originator became especially adamant when it developed that some of the alcoholics — fearing for their anonymity — objected to the presence of a newspaperman at their meetings. In any case, Davis attended meetings and finally in late October published his series — a glowing report that carefully preserved Clarence's and all others' anonymity.

In the memory of Alcoholics Anonymous, this Davis publicity led to an influx of members, which addition, in turn, touched off the brisk multiplication of A.A. groups in Cleveland and vicinity; but this memory is not totally accurate. The number of those interested and attracted did increase substantially, and a split into three groups did develop in the weeks following the *Plain Dealer* series. But the split had less to do with greater numbers than with the Cleveland members' disagreement with Clarence S. over the publicity itself and so over the fellowship's yet uncertain understanding of anonymity. Indirectly, the publicity deriving from the Davis series and from a follow-up sermon by Dilworth Lupton on 26 November 1939 — a sermon reprinted in pamphlet form and widely distributed — furnished the occasion for further favorable newspaper treatment into 1940. This, in turn, set the stage for the next episode of Cleveland-based publicity for Alcoholics Anonymous: a celebrity event that in Cleveland at least marked A.A.'s breakthrough to rapid growth with all its attendant problems and opportunities. [5]

This next publicity was totally unsolicited, and its impact reached far beyond the Lake Erie metropolis just then beginning to flaunt itself as "the best location in the nation." In a Chicago hotel news conference of 16 April 1940, Rollie Hemsley, erratic star catcher for the Cleveland Indians baseball team, announced that his past eccentric behavior on and off the diamond had been due to "booze," that he was an alcoholic who had now been dry for one year "with the help of and through Alcoholics Anonymous." [6]

In 1940, the revival of economic activity and the ostrich-like American attitude to the European war combined to focus the attention and enthusiasm of very many middle-class Americans on the world of spectator sports, and in 1940 professional baseball ruled triumphant among spectator sports in America. Further, the attention of the baseball world focused — through late 1939 and early 1940 — upon a quintessentially American, raw-boned, eighteen-year-old Cleveland pitcher who could throw a baseball at speeds approaching one hundred miles an hour: Robert William Andrew Feller.[7]

Most sportswriters played Feller up as a gawky, talented farm boy of amazing ability who needed mature guidance and handling if he were to reach his full potential. A nation of fans would willingly have become the proxy parents of Bob Feller, and there was intense interest in the man assigned that role in actuality. Cleveland Indian manager Oscar Vitt wisely understood that he could not undertake this task himself without endangering his relationship with the rest of the team, so he and Great Lakes shipping magnate Alva Bradley, the team's owner, sought out and hired an experienced catcher, Rollie Hemsley. Hemsley was considered "experienced" largely because he had played for three teams and in both leagues. Vitt and Bradley either did not know or chose to ignore that Hemsley's shuttling about was due to the simple fact that wherever he played, the catcher's bizarre behavior soon revealed him to be the team drunk.[8]

According to Alcoholics Anonymous legend, some time in 1939, Bradley — who had heard of Dr. Bob Smith's Akron activity with hopeless drunks — "offered two hundred thousand if we could dry [Hemsley] up, a great amount of money, and Doc told him he couldn't buy it." Yet, as Bob E. relates, Dr. Bob did promise to try to help. "We picked a squad of six to work with him. I was one of the six"; and although Bradley "couldn't buy it," one member of the "squad" moved from the gutters of Cleveland to an executive position in the Bradley firm almost as rapidly as Feller's fastball traveled between the mound and home plate. Somehow catcher Hemsley "got the program. He became one of the staunchest members we ever had, [setting] a terrific example for the children all over the country." That example was strengthened in 1940 as Bob Feller reached an apparent peak. For with the calm modesty that was one of his hallmarks, the boyish sports hero attributed much of his success to the wisdom, handling, and fatherly care of the "ex-alcoholic" Rollie Hemsley.[9]

The impact of the Hemsley publicity contributed far more to Alcoholics Anonymous than his service as "a terrific example for the children." Early Cleveland A.A. had been especially cautious concerning anonymity, and on the matter of A.A.'s relationship to the Oxford Group, its members, despite their eagerness for publicity, remained even secretive. Cleveland was not New York or Akron. In New York, the very size of the city and variety of employment opportunities helped the newly sober alcoholics shed some of the consequences of their drinking histories. In much smaller Akron, the close-knit establishment's familiarity with Oxford Group practices could even ease a former drinker's re-entry into that city's business community. But in Cleveland, fears over the economic effects of being known as an ex-drunk were realistic: personal anonymity had been to the Clevelanders an especially cherished protection.

Group anonymity carried even to secretiveness had also been deemed important as the specter of its Oxford Group origins rose to haunt Cleveland A.A. even in the midst of the Hemsley publicity. On the one hand, Cleveland members feared that advertising the Oxford Group source would alienate respectable supporters such as Lupton and render Catholic participation in Alcoholics Anonymous impossible. On the other hand, fears arose from a concern that explicitly denying A.A.'s Oxford Group roots might provoke those who were Group-inclined to attempt a take-over and make a clear return to Group orthodoxy. Both misgivings had especially pressed after the internal fracas over Clarence's role in the Elrick Davis affair.[10]

Through the summer of 1940, the wake of the Hemsley publicity proved not only unthreatening but uniquely beneficial. Despite an uncautious and even erroneous mention of the Oxford Group in one newspaper story, Hemsley's example contributed to the sobering of the father of a strategically located and respected Catholic priest. Father N.'s gratitude resulted in the staff of at least one Catholic hospital welcoming Alcoholics Anonymous within its institution. Within Cleveland A.A., some who were more seriously committed to *all* the Oxford Group principles moved off to begin their own group. But the new group saw itself as an expression of Alcoholics Anonymous rather than as a return to the Buchmanites who by now were calling themselves "Moral Re-Armament." Thus the actual results of the Hemsley publicity soothed diverse anxieties for all A.A.s. Later in 1940, Wilson could and would approve even the use of pictures in the Jack Alexander *Saturday Evening Post* story, but for which concession the story might not have been carried in that pictorially-oriented magazine. More ambiguously, the foundation was laid for the later breaking of anonymity "for the sake of the good of others" by Marty Mann — the next occasion on which Alcoholics Anonymous would face the necessity of re-thinking its understanding of its name.[11]

Yet despite the importance of these events in Cleveland to A.A.'s membership growth and confrontation with anonymity, the heart of the Cleveland contribution to Alcoholics Anonymous only accidentally had to do with numbers or publicity. Fundamental to the program of Alcoholics Anonymous from its moment of self-conscious origin had been "working with others." The factors that ultimately shaped this awareness for all A.A.s lay embedded in the Cleveland experience that flowed from the Davis and Hemsley events. Most significantly, the membership influx generated by these events came in the context of special wariness over anonymity and about the Oxford Group connection.

In this precise context, three characteristics that were distinctively to mark the fellowship and program of Alcoholics Anonymous developed. Like everything else in A.A., their workings-out were pragmatic; yet how these characteristics evolved revealed much about the core of Alcoholics Anonymous. Because of the tensions over anonymity and the Oxford Group relationship, but related also to the quick increase in membership and the peculiar geography of Cleveland and environs, groups quickly split up and split off. The passage of time and later developments veiled particular causes in individual cases in the memories of Cleveland "oldtimers," but as the groups split and grew, each of the four listed factors were operative — often in confused combination.[12]

Perhaps because of the very confusion over how each group got started, the early Clevelanders found it useful to rotate leadership — even for the simple functions of selecting speakers, choosing discussion topics, and putting those who requested information or help in touch with currently active members. Six months became the usual term on a committee, one of whose members dropped off and was replaced each month, and membership on which was determined only by seniority within the group. Everyone thus had an equal opportunity to hold office, the criterion being sobriety rather than the popularity rewarded by election. Responsibility to the program became more important than pleasing any individual, faction, or group: no one could be kept either in or out of this modest and shared role. And insofar as the sobriety of all was deemed due to faithful practice of the A.A. program, the program received first loyalty. Thus the ideals of "trusted servants" and "principles before personalities" became enshrined and safeguarded in practice.[13] +

+ The phrases "trusted servants" and "principles before personalities" are from the Twelve Traditions of Alcoholics Anonymous, to be treated in Chapter Five.

Again several factors — some peculiar to the Cleveland situation of the early 1940s, and others inherent although latent at the time in Alcoholics Anonymous — combined to produce the unique A.A. phenomenon of "sponsorship." The factors peculiar to Cleveland were rapid numerical increase, brisk fission into new groups, the divergent understandings of the program of Alcoholics Anonymous that arose from differing attitudes to anonymity, and the members' differing attitudes to Oxford Group ideas and principles. The core A.A. ideas mediated from latency into practical expression were the importance of "identification" as the main, if not the sole route, to "getting the program"; the deep sense that "this simple program" could be "gotten by anybody," but that the "anybodys" concerned were very different in accidental ways; and a profound awareness concerning sobriety that "you keep it only by giving it away," an especially impelling conviction of the need for "working with others."[14]

And so, "sponsorship" came into practice. The official Alcoholics Anonymous pamphlet entitled *Sponsorship* began in typical A.A. style: "What Is Sponsorship?" a question answered by an historical narration of Bill Wilson's contacts with Ebby T. and Dr. Bob Smith in 1934–1935. Only after this story was an analytical description of sponsorship offered. "Essentially, the process of sponsorship is this: An alcoholic who has made some progress in the recovery program shares that experience on a continuous, individual basis with another alcoholic who is attempting to attain or maintain sobriety through A.A."[15]

"Shares." The Oxford Group-derived term at first shunned by Alcoholics Anonymous was reinstated at the very heart of the continuity of the A.A. program. The ready, easy, open-housed "fellowship" of A.A. — especially as it had bloomed in Akron — could not be maintained as Alcoholics Anonymous grew and expanded; nor could the life-style of "communal living" which pre-1942 Cleveland alcoholics cherished in recollection of their earliest days in the program. To the east, New Yorkers and groups derived from New York experimented briefly with "A.A. clubhouses" — a trace of which long remained in the ever-full coffee urn surrounded by overstuffed chairs at A.A.'s central offices in larger cities. But clubhouses in general did not work out nor did the primitive feeling of "fellowship" survive.[16]

At a most profound level, then, early Cleveland Alcoholics Anonymous — largely enabled by its very self-conscious, explicit rejection of the Oxford Group connection — reached back into the womb from which it and all A.A. had issued to seize for its own practice the means that transmitted the continually evolving key to life as a member of Alcoholics Anonymous: the achievement of honesty and identification by "sharing."

The first national publicity given Alcoholics Anonymous had preceded that in the Cleveland *Plain Dealer*, but it had not produced a similar effect. In the summer of 1939, Fulton Oursler, editor of *Liberty* magazine, had agreed to a proposal by feature-writer Morris Markey for an article on Alcoholics Anonymous. The piece appeared in the 30 September 1939 issue under the somewhat unwelcome title, "Alcoholics and God." Although they desired publicity, most members of Alcoholics Anonymous — wary of being labeled a "religious" group — winced at both this heading and the article's content. The title and Markey's almost cravenly apologetic insistence that "the root of this new discovery is religion," explained for many of the new fellowship's members the failure of the coverage to attract many to their program. Markey's failure to grasp or to present adequately the experience and sense of "bottom," and especially the way in which he did present the alcoholics' need to work with other alcoholics, proved unlikely to make the program attractive to Americans.[17]

Markey highlighted the image of required zeal that the group had been so careful to avoid: "Every member of the group — which is to say every person who has been saved — is under the obligation to carry on the work, to save other men." The *Liberty* treatment offered an analysis of the success of the program that was ill-designed to render it desirable: "Their psychological necessity to drink was being changed to a psychological necessity to rescue their fellow victims. . . ." Alcoholics Anonymous as organization needed other people, and at this time needed some of them for publicity; but with all the good will in the world this kind was less than adequately helpful.[18]

Especially galling was the fact that the *Liberty* treatment was the second failure of nationwide publicity. Earlier in the summer of 1939, the irrepressible Morgan R., the vibrant, red-headed Irishman who, a few months before, had used his acquaintance with an official of the Archdiocesan chancery to mediate between Alcoholics Anonymous and the Catholic Church, remembered still another well-placed friend, and triumphantly reported that the popular radio journalist Gabriel Heatter was willing to interview him on his nationwide broadcast.[19]

The group was ambivalent — agog but also aghast. Alcoholics Anonymous needed public attention: the Big Book had just been published but had not been noticed. Surely Morgan's story on the air might evoke interest — and sales. On the other hand, "My God . . . *Morgan?*" With some recent fiascos in mind, the group had reason for concern. "What if the lately released asylum inmate should be drunk on the day of the broadcast?" Using one A.A.'s membership in the Downtown Athletic Club, they conducted the grumbling Morgan into captivity. For almost a week, members took turns sitting up with him around the clock, never letting him out of their sight. Morgan stayed sober, the broadcast took place, but book orders did not flood in.[20]

Morgan's sobriety sustained the re-inflation of personal (but anonymous) national publicity; whether Alcoholics Anonymous itself could survive the subsequent deflation was another question. Hank P., "brandishing his pad of [virtually worthless] Works Publishing certificates," had extracted from recruits new to the fellowship five hundred dollars with which "to send a shower of postal cards to all physicians east of the Mississippi River," calling their attention to the importance of the broadcast and including a return order-card for the book *Alcoholics Anonymous*.[21]

So confident were the New York alcoholics after what they felt was the smashing success of Morgan's radio appearance that "by a great effort of self-restraint" they stayed away from the post office "for three whole days." That brief eternity later, armed with "a couple of suitcases to bring home some part of the great influx," they went to the neighborhood post office. They found exactly twelve cards. This was surely discouraging, but perhaps their alcoholism had prepared the sober alcoholics for what came next, because it got worse. Of the twelve replies, "some ribbed us unmercifully. Others, evidently inscribed by medics in their cups, were totally illegible." Their painfully scrounged five-hundred-dollar investment and complicated efforts to ensure Morgan's sobriety had netted a grand total of two orders for the book.[22]

As the late summer of 1939 passed into autumn, reviewer notice of the Big Book increased. Unfortunately, most of the reviews appeared in the denominational religious press. The Fosdick review had been submitted, "as a matter of first choice," to the *New York Herald-Tribune*, but this respected, large-circulation newspaper proved uninterested. Percy Hutchison of the *New York Times* had reviewed the book favorably — devoting more attention to "psychology" than to "religion" — in June of 1939. Yet nothing more came of this till after the *Plain Dealer* notice, when the *Washington Post* referred back to the *Times*-Hutchison review as evidence of the new phenomenon's seriousness and credibil-

ity. This fortunate coverage probably helped prepare the public to receive sympathetically the splash of new publicity from the soon-to-come
Rockefeller dinner and Hemsley notoriety.[23+]

At the first 1940 meeting of the trustees of the floundering Foundation, Willard Richardson appeared beaming with ill-concealed mysterious enthusiasm. After the regular business, of which there was precious
little, had been settled, Richardson revealed that John D. Rockefeller,
Jr., had indicated that he thought the time had come to offer the struggling fellowship encouragement and impetus. Rockefeller had proposed a dinner meeting to which he would invite several hundred of his
friends and business associates. First-hand exposure to the program
would offer these men of wealth and power the opportunity "to get in
on the ground floor" of a worthy enterprise.[24]

Eagerly, Wilson scanned the list of four hundred proposed names.
He found "a veritable constellation of New York's prominent and wealthy." Certain from all his own experience that what his program most
needed was financial support, Bill noted approvingly "that their total
financial worth might easily be a billion dollars," and he left the trustees'
meeting in high spirits to engineer his side of the preparations: priming
the alcoholics invited for the significance of the event and the opportunity of the occasion.[25]

+   The most unsympathetic review was an unsigned one in the *Journal of Nervous and Mental Diseases* in September 1940: "As a youth we attended many
'experience' meetings more as an onlooker than as a participant. We never could
work ourselves up into a lather and burst forth in soupy bubbly phrases about
our intimate states of feeling. That was our own business rather than something
to brag about to the neighbors. Neither then nor now do we lean to the autobiographical, save occasionally by allusion to point a moral or adorn a tale, as the
ancient adage puts it.

"This big, big book, *i.e.*, big in words, is a rambling sort of camp-meeting
confession of experiences, told in the form of biographies of various alcoholics
who had been to a certain institution and have provisionally recovered, chiefly
under the influence of the 'big brothers of the spirit.' Of the inner meaning of
alcoholism there is hardly a word. It is all the surface material.

"Inasmuch as the alcoholic, speaking generally, lives in a wishfulfilling infantile regression to the omnipotency delusional state, perhaps he is best handled
for the time being at least by regressive mass psychological methods, in which, as
is realized, religious fervors belong, hence the religious trend of the book. Billy
Sunday and similar orators had their successes, but we think the methods of
Forel and Bleuler infinitely superior."

Hardly more favorable, but less impassioned, was the review accorded by the
Journal of the American Medical Association on 14 October 1939: "This book is a
curious combination of organizing propaganda and religious exhortation. . . .
The one valid thing in the book is the recognition of the seriousness of addiction
to alcohol. Other than this, the book has no scientific merit or interest."

On the evening of 8 February 1940 the dinner party gathered at the Union Club in New York City, "a club," Wilson noted almost smugly, "even more conservative than the Union League itself." Some seventy-five of the invited four hundred were present. During the mingling before dinner, the non-alcoholics were cheerfully supplied their customary cocktails, while the alcoholics nursed the sweetness of the thrill of thus so casually witnessing that they were not anti-alcohol, that their scheme was not to dry up the world. Strategically, Wilson had arranged that the tables be small and that at each was seated one of his sober alcoholics. Though the best was yet to come, especially from the point of view of the non-alcoholic guests, the seating too proved to be a masterstroke: "At one table sat our hero, Morgan, as impeccably dressed as a collar-ad boy. One gray-haired banker inquired, 'Mr. R., what institution are you with?' Morgan grinned and replied, 'Well, sir, I am not with any institution at the moment. Nine months ago, however, I was a patient in Greystone asylum.' The interest at that table took a sharp upturn."[26]

After the dinner ("squab on toast. For a bunch of ex-drunks, we were doing remarkably well"), Bill and Dr. Bob spoke, recounting their stories. Then, to underline the seriousness and worthiness of the project, they were followed by "Dr. Harry Emerson Fosdick, representing religion, and Dr. Foster Kennedy, the world-renowned neurologist, . . . for medicine." John D. Rockefeller, Jr., had been taken suddenly ill, so his son Nelson served as host. Finally it came his turn to speak, in his father's name. To the alcoholics present, the suspense was almost unbearable as young Nelson went through the formalities of reviewing his father's interest in this new enterprise. Breathlessly, they awaited "the climax — the matter of money."[27]

Nelson Rockefeller obliged. "Gentlemen," he concluded to the guests representing almost inconceivable wealth, "you can all see that this is a work of good will. Its power lies in the fact that one member carries the good message to the next, without any thought of financial income or reward. Therefore it is our belief that Alcoholics Anonymous should be self-supporting so far as money is concerned. It needs only our good will."[28]

The non-alcoholics clapped lustily at the content if not the style of this peroration, rising to express their agreement with and appreciation of the Rockefeller perspicacity. In a stunned disbelief which masked their shattering disappointment, the alcoholics went through the motions of joining in the applause. The dinner over, a fresh cordiality infusing the final handshakes and goodbyes, the guests began to leave. Ruefully, their puzzlement muffling their frustration, Wilson, Smith, and the precisely proper alcoholics watched "the whole billion dollars' worth of them [walk] out the door." [29]

In the week following the dinner, John D. Rockefeller, Jr., expressed interest in sending transcripts of the talks and copies of the Big Book to all who had been invited. Alcoholics Anonymous sold the books to Rockefeller — "and we let him have them at a whopping discount, too: one dollar each." In an accompanying letter, the world's richest man "reiterated his high confidence in Alcoholics Anonymous, the satisfaction he had in knowing that many of his friends had witnessed the start of a movement of such great promise, and his deep conviction that our society ought to be self-supporting." He went on to say, however, that a little temporary assistance was needed, and that he was giving $1,000 to the new group: an amount — it might be noted — just balancing his $2.50 discount on four hundred books. Yet the money was important, and from those who heard a hint in the Rockefeller letter and gift of the book, A.A. realized an additional $2,000. [30]

More important than the money, however, as the alcoholics began to realize in the weeks following the dinner, was the resulting publicity. Despite the curiosity of the press, no reporters had been allowed at the dinner. This was understandable, for Rockefeller was taking no chances. "Had any of us alcoholics turned up stewed," Bill Wilson realized, "the whole affair would have collapsed ignominiously." But as soon as all had gone well, Alcoholics Anonymous was put in touch with the firm of Ivy Lee, the Rockefeller publicity consultants. Together, they drafted a statement to the press. Marked by the Ivy Lee touch, the ensuing publicity was widespread and generally favorable, despite some lurid treatments such as the New York *Daily Mirror's*: "John D. Dines Toss-Pots." Requests for help and orders for the Big Book "poured in, and the awful letdown which had followed the departure of the dinner guests was now forgotten." [31]

The Rockefeller dinner — its hopes, their shattering, and the final resolution of both — might serve as a blueprint for this whole period. The newly sober alcoholics, especially in New York, were slowly coming to the discovery that "putting the cork in the bottle" was not the whole story. As their experience unfolded, they coined two phrases — appropriately ugly phrases — to describe and interpret what they observed happening around them and to them. "Alcoholic grandiosity," they discovered, could also characterize a "dry drunk." And insofar as this marked a retraction of "surrender," forgetfulness of "bottom," the attempt again to take over control of their lives and wills, it gave warning of, if not a return to active alcoholism, at least a kind of dry hangover that could render sobriety itself almost too painful to bear.[32]

Bill Wilson, with his cherished drive to be a "number-one man" and his vaunted "twin-engine propulsion," himself provided an almost too accurate living out of this problem. The Pietist message, "Let go and let God," which was in time to infuse the "A.A. Way of Life," pushed only slowly and with great and painful strains into his consciousness, mainly through the experiences of this "era of publicity." The return to drinking of promoter Hank, who had been his first New York success, and of Bill's friend Ebby, whom the co-founder revered as his sponsor, weighed against Wilson's confidence in and hopes for Alcoholics Anonymous. The loss of the Clinton Street home, the early failures to obtain publicity for the Big Book, the frustrations of fund-raising and especially of the hopes cherished for the Rockefeller connection, all these muted his joy and enthusiasm over the slowly increasing number of hopeless drunks attaining sobriety.

As always, Wilson avoided the obvious theological term for what was emerging as the "original sin" of even sober alcoholics: *pride*. Yet a foundation was being laid for the discovery and awareness that the First Cause of an alcoholic's difficulties — drunk *or* sober — was an appropriately unique specification of the "self-centeredness" that lay at the "root of our troubles." It was what Wilson and the years would call "alcoholic grandiosity."[33]

Concerning his own greatest manifestation of grandiosity, even in his 1955 history purporting to detail "the full story" of Alcoholics Anonymous, Bill Wilson could bring himself only to hint. When the Rollie Hemsley story — complete with full name and pictures — broke in the newspapers in April of 1940, it provided the first challenge on a national level to the fellowship's still evolving understanding of its principle of anonymity. For a moment, as some within the New York group even at the time realized, A.A.'s co-founder found himself in a predicament. Anonymity was indeed becoming more deeply understood as a first principle, but also emerging as a fundamental guideline was A.A.'s sense that it was "fellowship" rather than organization — the acceptance that, beyond the "twin ogres of madness and death," Alcoholics Anonymous possessed no central authority capable of imposing discipline.[34]

To the astonishment of virtually all in New York, Bill escaped the dilemma by grasping both its horns. Inwardly, he still cherished the warm glow of the Rockefeller contact which had honored him as virtual sole founder and the copious praise of the post-dinner publicity. Hence, he responded to the Hemsley notoriety by taking to the road, courting the press in every city he visited, giving out interviews and encouraging pictures.[35]

In several cities, especially at the beginning, the local membership of Alcoholics Anonymous, mostly new adherents who had been attracted by the Hemsley publicity, relished and encouraged his efforts. But not for long. Soon many of these newcomers were celebrating their newly found social acceptance by toasting their success — and that, of course, did not "work." Older members began to close ranks; they pointed out to Bill the dangers in his new approach. For a time, at summer's end, Wilson argued with them in defense of his new activity. Rapidly, however, there unfolded a three-phase phenomenon which would be named only at its end. Bill, one oldtimer eventually told him to his face, "had better watch himself because he was sure as hell acting like a man on a *dry drunk*." [36]

Its stages had been easy to spot — by oldtimers from the outside at the time, by Wilson himself in hindsight. First had come his "exceptional thinking." Bill had forgotten why he had sought out Dr. Bob that first time — for his own sake. He might by gratuitous accident of history be "co-founder," but before that and after that he was also and more deeply "just another drunk trying to stay sober." Thinking he was "different" led in only one direction — straight to another drink, and so, inevitably, to another drunk.[37]

Second, at least briefly, Bill thrived on the dissension and controversy that his new mode of acting provoked. A journey by Hank to Akron and Cleveland was interpreted as proof of Hank's "problem" — not entirely inaccurate, for Hank was drinking and in his tales attacked Wilson viciously. But Bill relished the "challenge" in this. It became a test of "loyalty," and he cherished the realization that Dr. Bob and Anne Smith had had nothing to do with Hank and had expressed openly their disbelief of his stories. What Bill was doing in this matter was clear to some who remembered more of "How It Works" than did its author. There, Wilson had written: "Resentment is the 'number one' offender. It destroys more alcoholics than anything else." Patently, many oldtimers realized, Bill was setting himself up for some grand-daddy resentments.[38]

Third, and here the term "dry drunk" proved frighteningly accurate, what had gone up had to come down. Almost overnight, as the winter of 1940 broke, Wilson plunged into the depths of despair. Of what use were all his efforts? They had gotten mostly criticism. Many people were sober, but many also were drinking again. In Cleveland, some were calling for his exclusion from Alcoholics Anonymous and even accusing him of financial trickery — this the result of the activities of the first New York alcoholic *he* had saved. A spiritually bedraggled Bill Wilson cut back his travels and returned to the Twenty-Fourth Street clubhouse where he was now living. The retreat did him little good. Mainly, it was just a reminder of others' ingratitude, a reminder that his own house had been lost despite Lois's heroic efforts. His two upstairs rooms struck him as tinier and more drab than ever, but in them Bill sat and thought. What was the meaning of the events and emotions of the past few months? How was one who had written the key words, "Made a decision to turn our will and our lives over to the care of God," to understand them? [39]

In time, Bill Wilson not only remembered but enlarged upon what he had written of "resentment." In time, too, he suggested that the "inventory" of the Fourth Step of his program be conducted according to the outline of "the Seven Deadly Sins" — and "pride," of course, headed that list. These realizations came only slowly and painfully over the years.

But now, in 1940, something very special happened: an occurrence that not only sowed the seeds for much of that later development, but that also helped to consolidate Bill's own growth in sobriety over the preceding six years into the maturity that would characterize his thought for the rest of his life. [40]

Whenever Wilson in later years looked back on this next significant happening in his own and A.A.'s life, he waxed uncharacteristically poetic. In his mind, it had been the gift of a very special providence, and Bill strove to fit his language and imagery to the elegance of that understanding. Anyone who would understand Wilson must gain an appreciation of what this moment meant in the life of the blunt, direct man who wrote the stylistically spare text of the book *Alcoholics Anonymous* — and of just how Bill Wilson habitually recalled that moment.

It would seem that on a chill, rain-pelting early winter evening in late 1940, as Wilson almost tangibly felt himself being wrapped ever more tightly in a gloomy pall of spiritual darkness, he sat forlorn in the sparsely furnished clubhouse rooms in which he and Lois were then living. Disconsolate, his former way of escape — alcohol — forever denied, Wilson nursed his many shattered hopes and recent stinging disappointments in self-pitying and frustrating reverie. Just then, when he was at the very nadir of that abyss, a veritable gleam of light came literally knocking at his door, as Bill's morose meditations were suddenly interrupted by the building's janitor. Someone downstairs wanted to see

Wilson. For the first time in his sober life Bill was about to say no when force of habit led him instead to wave his hand in tired acquiescence. Any interruption was to be welcomed, and besides, perhaps what he needed was to work with yet another drunk, although lately every success was bringing even more frustration than had all the failures earlier.

Hesitantly, the uninvited caller shuffled into the room, and Bill sensed in dismay that this bundled, partially crippled man wasn't even an alcoholic. Probably just some bum looking for a hand-out, Wilson guessed to himself, until the stranger's raincoat came unbuttoned and revealed the Roman collar around his neck. Father Edward Dowling introduced himself as a Jesuit priest from St. Louis who, as editor of a Catholic publication, was interested in the parallels he had intuited between the Twelve Steps of Alcoholics Anonymous and the Exercises of St. Ignatius, the spiritual discipline of his Jesuit order. That he showed delight rather than disappointment when Wilson wearily confessed ignorance of the Exercises at once endeared the diminutive cleric to Bill.[41]

Dowling shuffled across the room and sat down in the shabbier of the room's two decrepit chairs, balancing his cane across his knee. As they began to converse, Bill noted that his visitor's round face seemed to gather in all the light in the room and then reflect it directly at him. The priest wasted little time on small-talk. His very tone of voice pulled Wilson out of himself, but it soon became clear that Dowling was ready to do more than merely listen. That evening "Father Ed" began sharing with Wilson an understanding of the spiritual life that then and subsequently seemed always to speak to Bill's condition — if this Quaker phrase can be appropriate for conversations between a troubled former agnostic and a saintly member of the Roman church's elite society. Not since his earliest days in the Oxford Group had Wilson felt himself in the loving presence of such a receptive listener. Then, Bill had unburdened himself especially to Ebby. But it was only now, as this evening with Father Dowling wore on, that the man who had written A.A.'s Fifth Step came to feel that he himself was finally "taking his Fifth."+ He told Dowling not only what he had done and had left undone — he went on

+ Long before the Congressional hearings chaired by Senator Joseph McCarthy attached a different popular connotation to the expression, alcoholics — who had ample experience with the bottling habits of distilleries — found a special drollness in the fact that an important part of the program of Alcoholics Anonymous required them to "take the Fifth." The reference, of course, was to the Fifth Step of the A.A. program: "Admitted to God, to ourselves and to another human being the exact nature of our wrongs."

to share with his new sponsor the thoughts and feelings behind those actions and omissions. He told of his high hopes and plans, and spoke also about his anger, despair, and mounting frustrations. The Jesuit listened and quoted Matthew: "Blessed are they who do hunger and thirst." God's chosen, he pointed out, were always distinguished by their yearnings, their restlessness, their thirst.[42]

In pain, Bill asked if there was ever to be any satisfaction. The priest almost snapped back: "Never. Never any." He continued in a gentler tone, describing as "divine dissatisfaction" that which would keep Wilson going, always reaching out for unattainable goals, for only by so reaching would he attain what — hidden from him — were God's goals. This acceptance that his dissatisfaction, that his very "thirst," could be divine was one of Dowling's great gifts to Bill Wilson and through him to Alcoholics Anonymous. Another was to prove less happy from the Jesuit's own point of view. Bill spoke of his own difficulties in prayer and his continuing problem in conveying the meaning of his "spiritual experience" to other alcoholics. There was a move afoot within the fellowship just then, he told Dowling, to change that phrase in the Twelfth Step to "spiritual awakening" — it seemed to Bill an attempt to mask rather than to clarify the role of the divine in the alcoholic's salvation. Tartly, Father Ed offered a succinct response: "If you can name it, it's not God." Years later, Wilson would paraphrase the expression back to Dowling as a partial explanation of his difficulties in accepting the Catholic faith.[43+]

But at this moment Wilson cherished the consolation his new friend's words brought. The priest continued, his clear eyes sparkling as he sensed his effect on the now relaxed figure slouched in the other chair. With characteristic gentleness, Dowling pointed out what should have been obvious — that from which, indeed, he had intuited a link between the Exercises of Ignatius and the program of Alcoholics Anonymous. Bill's own prayer had been answered, had it not? He himself was sober. If God was choosing to use him to offer a program for sobriety to others, this was a great and glorious "fringe benefit." Who was he to demand "more" of what was already a gratuitous gift? To seek more, yes. That was inevitable, for it was the seeking of the God who had made him — and made him sober — for Himself. But to demand?

+   According to a letter from Ruth H. (Wilson's secretary) to Dr. Bob Smith, 11 February 1941, the addition of an Appendix titled "Spiritual Experience" to the second printing of *A.A.* was designed "to try to dispel somewhat the idea many seem to get that in order to recover, or stay sober at all, it is necessary to have a sudden illuminating spiritual experience."

Dowling shook his head with a sad smile, and Bill realized with sudden clarity that for all he had confessed in his Fifth Step recital, being demanding had been and would always be his main spiritual problem, the chief threat to his sobriety. Shortly, Dowling left, and Bill Wilson, cherishing this new self-awareness, for the first time in months slept peacefully and soundly.[44]

As the year 1941 began, Alcoholics Anonymous continued its slow expansion. In more than one sense, its growth was the work of sales-men.[+] A good percentage of those newly sober had worked in sales, and as they regained the confidence of their employers, many were again sent on the road. Strange cities and lonely hotel rooms often brought back the old fears, so in new places they sought out alcoholics to whom they could give their program in order to keep themselves sober. From Akron and Cleveland they traveled, finding willing hearers in Minneapolis, Milwaukee, and St. Louis; from New York, the message was carried to Boston, Miami, and points in between. Even with the Big Book available, the pattern of sending "really difficult cases" back to Dr. Bob's new practice in Akron continued. On the East coast, such were sent to New York and Wilson's hard core of sober alcoholics, although Bill himself — with less publicity now — continued to travel to larger cities when informed that they contained however small a group of interested and effort-inclined drunks.[45]

The winter of 1940–41 had brought a second at first misunderstood visitor to the Alcoholics Anonymous clubhouse on Twenty-Fourth Street. Jack Alexander was a writer who prided himself on his cynicism and who wore this trademark on his sleeve. Fresh from a major exposé of the New Jersey rackets, he had been summoned by *Saturday Evening Post* owner Judge Curtis Bok. Two of Bok's good friends, medical doctors, had recently begun singing the praises of something called "Alcoholics Anonymous." Would Alexander care to do a story for the *Post*? No strings were attached. The curious judge wanted the truth, and Alexander had demonstrated his ability to ferret out that elusive commodity. The reporter at first hesitated, but word that his proposed

+ Despite the statement in A.A.'s Eleventh Tradition that "Our publication relations policy is based on attraction rather than promotion," the reminscences available and those interviewed from early Akron and Cleveland all strongly testify that in the early days, at least in their area, "selling the program" was a work of promotion rather than mere attraction. A.A.'s Twelve Traditions, of course, were formulated only in 1946 — *cf.* just below and in Chapter Five — and partially in response to what were seen as some abuses of such an understanding.

quarry had connections with both religion and Rockefeller whetted his curiosity and honed his cynicism. The meetings he attended in Philadelphia proved frustrating. At them, he found apparently intelligent men who answered his questions about their activity by explaining only, "The Big Book says . . ."; and his promise to respect their anonymity unless he could find good reason to do otherwise closed off the obvious routes of inquiry.[46]

That Bill Wilson, the supposed author of the Big Book, seemed revered by some as a still-living saint especially stimulated the journalist's curiosity. Alexander traveled to Manhattan to see for himself. In New York, the writer was first taken aback by the fact that despite his reputation for cynical exposé he was greeted with enthusiasm. Then he reflected that if these self-confessed con-artists really had confidence in their con, of course they would welcome the public exposure that he could afford, and he resolved all the more to get to the bottom of Alcoholics Anonymous.[47]

Wilson himself struck Alexander as either incredibly naive or a bit stupid. He not only spoke openly of his alcoholism in the past, but in explaining his concerns about the publicity which he readily acknowledged the group desired, this "co-founder" stressed his recent errors of grandiosity and suggested that he and the reporter bundle off to the hick town of Akron so that Dr. Bob might receive adequate attention. Then, Wilson added, they ought to go on to Cleveland so that Alexander could observe the different ways in which Alcoholics Anonymous had developed.[48]

For the rest of his life, the journalist remained a close friend of Bill Wilson and of Alcoholics Anonymous, even accepting for his later articles on the fellowship editorial supervision from Wilson, something he never accepted from anyone else on any other topic. Occasionally, in his correspondence with Wilson, Alexander referred to his initial skepticism about A.A. If Bill Wilson's or Dr. Bob's conversion marked the beginning of Alcoholics Anonymous, its nationwide diffusion was due in the first instance to a similar experience on the part of Jack Alexander.[49]

Under the impact of Alexander's glowing story in the *Saturday Evening Post* of 1 March 1941, membership in Alcoholics Anonymous began a rapid, nation-wide growth. In the last ten months of 1941, membership quadrupled from 2,000 to 8,000, and one of the visions of the Big Book finally came true. Suddenly it was no longer possible to send sober alcoholics experienced in the program to visit all those expressing interest. In the countless nooks and crannies of an America mobilizing for war, the program would have to be "gotten by the book." And significantly, an ever-increasing chain of correspondence developed, as many ordering the Big Book from its New York distribution center appended requests for further detailed information.[50]

The first "mail-order" group had formed in early 1940 in Little Rock, Arkansas, deriving initial impetus from the Morris Markey story in *Liberty*. Others had followed the mail-only style of origin through 1940, and the pace had picked up after the Rockefeller dinner publicity, but these groups had still been few enough in number so that eventually some traveling "oldtimer" from New York or Akron-Cleveland had been able to look in on them in response to the initial request for literature. So long as this method of visitation remained usual, Alcoholics Anonymous retained two characteristics which the Alexander-inspired deluge shattered. In the first place, there remained two self-conscious "centers" of Alcoholics Anonymous, and — although word of the difference was not much spread — those who visited both noticed the greater "spiritual" emphasis of the Akronites who retained the Oxford Group "Four Absolutes" even after their 1939 separation from the Buchmanites. In the second place, Akron and New York as self-conscious centers retained a hold on their derived groups. There tended to be but one group in each city, and periodic pilgrimages were made to Akron or New York to "touch base." Chicago, for example, embraced the practice of at least a pair of members visiting Akron every two months.[51+]

The membership flood that came as a response to the 1941 *Post* story changed all this. The Big Book rather than travelers became the main means of spreading the message, and since New York was its publishing and distribution center, Bill Wilson and the people around him became the nerve center of Alcoholics Anonymous. From the letters that poured in, and from Wilson's generally pragmatic and largely off-the-cuff responses to them, began to emerge the "Twelve Traditions of Alcoholics Anonymous." Thus, New York rather than Akron or Cleveland became "the center" of Alcoholics Anonymous in the minds of most members.[52]

In turning this corner, Bill Wilson and A.A. relied on principles drawn from self-awareness of their own history: the primacy of experience; anonymity as a two-sided protection; an emerging sense of "limited control"; and wariness of the possible dangers inherent in the exercise of authority, and even in the fact of organization itself.

+   For the perdurance of stress on "the spiritual" in Akron and Cleveland, *cf.* Appendix A.

The very name of the Alcoholics Anonymous publishing venture was a reminder of the program's first principle and sole claim: "It works." Their personal backgrounds had tended to ensure that the early newly sober members of Alcoholics Anonymous had attempted other forms of treatment for their alcoholism. The most striking feature of Alcoholics Anonymous, to them, was that "it worked": this became the basic theme of the message that they carried to still-suffering alcoholics. Superficially the message was one of deflation, bottom, and the hopelessness of the active drinker's present condition. More profoundly, a saving hope was extended by their very presence.[53]

Bill Wilson and Dr. Bob Smith, with their own histories of treatment, early found that even drinking alcoholics tended to be fascinated with their sobriety, that an invariable question inevitably came: "How does it work?" Aptly, then, Wilson chose to title the fifth chapter of the Big Book, the one setting forth the steps of the program of Alcoholics Anonymous, "How It Works." But this chapter, reflecting all that Bill and Dr. Bob had learned, offered not analysis but witness — the witness of their experience. The structure and style of this whole chapter in no way examined origin or causation — of alcoholism or of its cure. The simple format was "This is what we did," a sharing of experience, drinking and sober.[54]

From the beginning, Wilson and Smith openly showed willingness to accept in their program changes based on successful experience equal to or greater than their own. As for listening to arguments — no matter how cogent — not based on experience, Bill and Bob knew well that legendarily alcoholics were reputed to be the greatest of rationalizers, a tendency Wilson in time castigated as "this odd trait of mind and emotion, this perverse wish to hide a bad motive underneath a good one. . . ." Smith's chief contribution to Alcoholics Anonymous, his frequent reminder and cherished last words to Bill, embodied the same wariness of argument, analysis, and explanation: "Keep It Simple."[55]

Alcoholics Anonymous had found only grief in attempts at argument over or explanation of its simple, basic message. The first and lasting testimony of its own experience was to the primacy of experience. Thus, as Bill Wilson embarked in 1941 on his long career of writing letters in answer to questions about the fellowship and its program, a certain style readily and naturally emerged. Rarely were answers offered on principle. The deductive mind and approach were foreign to him. Rather, Wilson shared experiences — his own and, as time went on, what he knew of the experience of others. Each letter followed a well-defined if largely unconscious pattern: (1) if I understand correctly, your problem/concern is similar to . . .; (2) this is what was done on that occasion; (3) this is how it worked out; (4) a statement to the effect: "But of course you need not follow my understanding; all I can do is tell you what has seemed to work in the past, and I hope that your own continuing experience will help all of us to understand both this problem and A.A. itself still better."[56]

Experience, then, was the first principle. It is doubtful that the world has ever seen a more consistent living-out of the pragmatism that so many have thought characterizes American culture.

Yet "experience" as first principle could lead to other principles, and even to inflexible norms. This possibility posed a special problem for Alcoholics Anonymous with its inherent sense of being not-God, its sense of limitation. Thus the qualified degree of rigidity with which A.A. internalized three further principles derived from experience sheds light both on the fellowship itself and on its embodiment and expression of "American pragmatism."

If there was one absolute rigidity in the *program* of Alcoholics Anonymous, it was the admonition to its adherents, "Don't drink." This absolute statement sprang from the concept of what it meant to be an alcoholic. If there was one absolute rigidity in the *fellowship*, it was contained in the second word of its name — Anonymous.[+] This principle was founded upon two-faceted experience. The first was of the need for protection, both of the individual alcoholic himself from economic sanction and of the fellowship from the possible failings of its members. When later experience revealed that these concerns need not always be relevant or even that, in certain circumstances, they might yield to other considerations for the good of A.A. or of the individual alcoholic, still further experience revealed a second and deeper reason for anonymity. As "grandiosity" came to be understood as the greatest danger to all alcoholics, drunk or sober, willing acceptance of the limitations imposed by anonymity came by experience to be seen as the surest witness, especially to self, of "true sobriety."[57]

The same experience was displayed on a larger scale. Early on, Alcoholics Anonymous had eagerly sought and even abjectly craved publicity. Then came the *Saturday Evening Post* article. This public notice had been welcomed, but what first turned Jack Alexander's cynicism into an impressed admiration which he transmitted to his readers was understood by Wilson and by Alcoholics Anonymous to be the percep-

+ The concept of "absolute" will be explored more fully and directly in Appendix A, *cf.* below, pp. 242ff.

tion that "these men were not out to get publicity for themselves." That they had finally allowed photographs only reluctantly, under *Post* pressure, and on the condition that faces not be recognizable, this was understandable for the majority of the membership, but in Wilson's and Smith's application of the same stricture to themselves, Alexander found impressive testimony to their altruistic dedication. These men were primarily interested in others, something unusual in the journalist's experience. Thus Alcoholics Anonymous, the fellowship itself, was set on the productive path of shunning organizational and institutional as well as personal grandiosity — an attitude that Wilson would attempt to hone and to sharpen as continuing experience unfolded.[58]

This awareness that experience did continue to unfold lay at the root of yet another principle, one destined to become a key to the "A.A. Way of Life." This key was the concept of *limited control*. Openness to continuing experience implied the avoidance of any closing off that might exclude new experience. Thus any control·by even past experiences was limited. The wariness of "absolutes" that Alcoholics Anonymous revealed in its separation from the Oxford Group led with paradoxical inevitability to a philosophy of no absolutes but one — that there are no absolutes.[59]

"Limited control." One of the first pragmatic discoveries of Wilson and Smith, and one clearly inspired by the "primitive Christianity" approach of the Oxford Group, had been that — even using Silkworth's understanding of alcoholism — to require "don't drink ever again" was unrealistic. It was unrealistic because it was too difficult, and therefore, it frightened away some who needed the program. Or it was unrealistic because it was too facile for others whose paths to alcoholic bottom were strewn with broken pledges. In either case, it didn't work. So Bill and Dr. Bob began to present their idea as the "Twenty-Four Hour Program," the "Day at a Time Program."[60]

"You can do something, but not everything" became the basic message of Alcoholics Anonymous to alcoholics, drinking or sober. This message served simultaneously both to protect against grandiosity and to affirm the sense of individual worthwhileness so especially important to the drinking alcoholic mired in self-hatred over his failure to achieve absolute control over his drinking. Further, this sense of limited control soon became the message of Alcoholics Anonymous to itself. Already in the Big Book Wilson had written, "We have no monopoly on God," and now, in the period under examination, explicit expression of its obvious corollary quickly emerged: "We have no monopoly on the treatment of alcoholics." Both messages continued to develop and to deepen in meaning.[61]

The clearest statement of this sense of limited control, for the individual as well as for the fellowship, came in the statement and history of A.A.'s membership requirement. Set forth first in the "Foreword" to *Alcoholics Anonymous*, it ran: "The only requirement for membership is an honest desire to stop drinking." There was no imposition of nor even request for any action, not even the negative one of not drinking alcohol. No one who presented himself or herself as wishing help could ever be challenged on the right to be there. The fundamental for A.A. membership could thus never be under the control of any other person. Nor need it — nor could it — even be under the complete control of the alcoholic, for the "honest desire to stop drinking" could surely co-exist with a desire to drink — something to which many even long sober alcoholics could readily testify.[62]

Yet asking even this limited control proved in A.A.'s continuing experience to be asking too much. The qualification "honest" or "sincere" was dropped in 1949, at the time of the first publication of the "short form" of the A.A. Traditions. The official explanation revealed A.A.'s continuing openness to learn from continuing experience:

> As A.A. has matured, it has been increasingly recognized that it is nearly impossible to determine what constitutes an "honest" desire to stop drinking, as opposed to other forms in which the desire might be expressed. It was also noted that some who may be interested in the program might be confused by the phrase "honest desire." Thus . . . the descriptive adjective has been dropped.[63]

But the deepest living out of the sense of limited control in Alcoholics Anonymous occurred on a more complex level. The tension between Akron and New York A.A. was partially resolved by the publication of *Alcoholics Anonymous*, the withdrawal of Akron A.A. from the Oxford Group, and the deluge of correspondence and new members after the *Saturday Evening Post* publicity. Yet other tensions remained, and as Bill Wilson meditated on the reports of travelers as well as on his own experiences of different styles of Alcoholics Anonymous, the basic rebelliousness of all alcoholics, drinking or sober, forcefully and repeatedly came home to him. Two directions lay open: to move to greater and more rigid organization, structure, and central authority; or to choose the route of always allowing and even cooperating with the greatest openness and lack of central authority possible. Despite his drive to power and need to be "number-one man," Wilson seems never to have seriously considered the first alternative. His early experience, especially his visiting of various newly formed groups between 1939 and 1941, had taught him — and so Alcoholics Anonymous — an important lesson.

Cherished within Alcoholics Anonymous as expressing this lesson was the fellowship's famed "Rule Number 62." Some time in early 1940, the program succeeded in sobering up an alcoholic possessed by a promotional drive greater even than Wilson's. This worthy, in his enthusiasm, drew up comprehensive plans for three separate corporations to spread the message — a club, a clinic, and a loan office. He submitted his blueprint, outlined in sixty-one rules, regulations, and by-laws, to A.A.'s New York headquarters, requesting a "super-charter."[64]

Wilson replied in his usual format: "Even less grandiose schemes of a like character failed everywhere before . . . [but your] very autonomous group [of course has] a right to . . . ignore our warnings." It did, and the result, as anticipated, "was like a boiler explosion in a clapboard factory." In time, the furor quieted, and eventually the chastened promoter wrote again to New York. His letter said basically, "Well, you folks at Headquarters were right and I was wrong," but with it he enclosed a card which he had already mailed to every A.A. group in the United States. Designed and folded like a golf score card, it had printed on its outside: "Group [the location] — Alcoholics Anonymous: Rule No. 62." When the card was opened, a single pungent sentence met the eye: "Don't take yourself too damned seriously."[65]

Under Wilson's influence, Alcoholics Anonymous clung to this commitment that within it there was to be no central authority and therefore only the most minimal of organized structures. Not always, however, did humor such as that over "Rule No. 62" highlight the humility in its self-restraint. Over the years many outside the fellowship but favorably disposed toward it pressed Wilson and Alcoholics Anonymous to develop differently. Dr. Harry M. Tiebout, A.A.'s first psychiatric friend, saw in the renunciation of authority an abdication of responsibility, and accused both Alcoholics Anonymous and its co-founder of "immaturity" because of their careful avoidance of formalized governance. The Jesuit moralist Father John Ford, a friend to whom Bill often turned for help in clarifying his own thought after their meeting at Yale in 1943, consistently assailed A.A.'s "anarchy," warning darkly of its consequent deviations and the dilution of the A.A. program sure to ensue.[66]

Wilson's replies to such criticism were consistently simple. Alcoholics

Anonymous could afford its "almost anarchistic . . . structure that actually invites deviation, knowing in advance that it will fail, [because] we have the coercives of continuous drunkenness, insanity, and death." The reasoning underlying this insight was plain. Experience taught that the drinking alcoholic faced three choices: abstinence, insanity, or death. Alcoholics Anonymous had proven itself, by further experience, certainly the best and often the only means to abstinence. A.A. thus had, without *any* organization, sufficient authority and an adequate disciplinarian.[67]

"For our group purpose there is but one ultimate authority — a loving God. . . ." Bill and A.A. never forgot this idea formalized in the fellowship's Second Tradition. The disciplinarian was "John Barleycorn." "Because the penalty for enough deviation is drunkenness and the penalty for drunkenness is insanity or death, we think that this is sufficient. We don't have to supplement God's work of correction. . . . We can simply leave the job to John Barleycorn. . . ." "Great suffering and great love are A.A.'s disciplinarians; we need no others."[68]

Other anti-authoritarian and anti-organizational fellowships have been inspired by a similar vision. The "primitive Christianity" which so many saw Alcoholics Anonymous reflecting had itself, indeed, been such. Earlier attempts to effect a return to the primitive had suffered a predictable fate. Surprisingly, given his background, Bill Wilson was aware of this problem. Especially as he observed the continuing development of the Oxford Group and watched his friend Sam Shoemaker in 1941 follow him out of it because of that cleric's disapproval of Frank Buchman's increasing personal dominance, Wilson's first concern became the pitfall often inherent in personal charisma. Further, for all his drive to be a "number-one man," the experiences of 1940 had taught Wilson to be wary of his own grandiosity or of anything that might feed it.[69]

Wilson's problem, then, became to find a safe course for the fellowship of Alcoholics Anonymous between the twin dangers of organizational overload and personal charisma. Hazily at first, he attempted more and more to utilize whatever organizational structure was at hand to insulate A.A. as a whole from his own person and personality. More and more as time went on, Bill withdrew from prominence and leadership. Yet at each step, the long-lived co-founder also confronted the hazards of organizational development that loomed from the other side.[70]

Thus, happy as he was in the spring of 1941 over the success of the fellowship's growth through magazine publicity and the book *Alcoholics Anonymous*, the troubling experiences to which he was exposed as new adherents ever more frequently petitioned for guidance led Wilson to embark upon a new endeavor: the clear and explicit formulation of what experience had taught and was continuing to teach the fellowship. The appropriate quest had emerged as one for limited control. The sober alcoholic was clearly not-God as well as not God: the sober alcoholic was made whole by acceptance of his limitation. The same, then, had to be true of A.A. as an association of alcoholics. It could claim neither more nor less. Alcoholics Anonymous was human, not God: it was essentially limited. But A.A. was also humanizing, for it existed in service to sobriety. In accepting this limited responsibility, Alcoholics Anonymous was also not-God, was made whole precisely by its acceptance of limitation. Any who forgot this risked their own sobriety and, indeed, jeopardized the fellowship's existence.

V

Attaining Maturity
1941–1955

The Limitations of Alcoholics Anonymous

After 1941, Alcoholics Anonymous turned its attention to the problems inherent in the burgeoning growth of its fellowship, problems that at times seemed to threaten its program. In each of the three five-year periods that followed, A.A. worked through one particular facet of the problematic realization that it itself was limited, but that its very strength flowed from acceptance of this weakness. Under Wilson's guidance over these fifteen years, the fellowship of Alcoholics Anonymous learned to apply its program to itself. And for this fellowship of alcoholics, that process proved no easier than it had been for its individual alcoholic members.[1]

From 1941 through 1945, the primary concern was how to share effectively the rapidly accumulating wisdom of experience without establishing a central authority, the very existence of which might stifle further experience and greater wisdom. The solution devised was the explicit formulation and proclamation of "The Twelve Traditions of Alcoholics Anonymous" and the beginning of the exemplary living out of these traditions. The example was essential because A.A. soon confronted two new problems: necessary development of its understanding of the concept of "hitting bottom" and the increasing use in the larger society of psychoactive drugs other than alcohol.

Perhaps because of the Traditions' focus upon the *fellowship* of Alcoholics Anonymous, the decade from 1945 to 1955 was characterized by discovery of a not particularly welcome implication of one of its maxims. Alcoholics Anonymous — and especially Bill Wilson — learned that if indeed, on the one hand, in every "problem" lay hidden an "opportunity," so, on the other hand, could large opportunities and even apparent successes at first disguise but then reveal ominous problems. Between 1945 and 1950, the happy opportunity of increased social acceptance inclined Wilson and others to think of Alcoholics Anonymous more as *adequate* to its task than as *limited* in its mission. A problem arose when the focus on adequacy led some to forget that this sufficiency itself sprang from limitation — that precisely as "fellowship," A.A. was first *community* rather than even diluted organization.

But Alcoholics Anonymous and Wilson learned from the unwelcome results of social acceptance and first strivings to organizational autonomy. Between 1950 and 1955, "Bill W." as sole surviving co-founder turned his attention back to the roots of the A.A. program, analytically as well as historically. Both the opportunity and the problem surfaced in the presentation to Alcoholics Anonymous by the American Public Health Association of its 1951 Lasker Award for "a great venture in social pioneering which forged a new instrument for social action; a new therapy based on the kinship of common suffering; one having vast potential for the myriad other ills of mankind."[2]

The tribute contained a subtle but severe threat to the sense of wholeness in limitation to which Wilson had begun to retreat. In largely unconscious response to this threat, influenced also by what had been learned from the problem-opportunities of the previous five years, Bill Wilson and Alcoholics Anonymous devoted the half-decade between 1951 and 1955 to a self-conscious quest for the "Coming of Age" of the fellowship, with attention directed to whatever was deemed immature and alienating in the group's experience more than to its strengths or possible extension of its competence. Bill set out to write a second book. In it, he portrayed and explained Alcoholics Anonymous as "a way of life" to be ever open-ended and so to be ever more deeply grasped. On the tenuous organizational level, meanwhile, Wilson pushed step by step the changes that would give Alcoholics Anonymous the qualities of a mature, democratic society: representation, election, and — ultimately — responsibility.

Mid-1941 found Alcoholics Anonymous moving its offices uptown to a location near Grand Central Station. Wilson and his helpers welcomed not only the additional space but also the opportunity to be of more ready and handy service to the many travelers who came to New York City. Slowly, listening to a variety of stoppers-by, Wilson and the people assisting him "began to see Alcoholics Anonymous as a vision for the whole world."[3]

The fellowship's growth continued by almost geometric progression.

The two thousand members, largely in the northeastern United States, who had witnessed the *Saturday Evening Post* publicity in 1941 had by 1945 grown to over fifteen thousand. Most were American citizens, but because of wartime circumstances, a small percentage of their number were scattered around the globe. Especially in Anglo-Saxon cultures, these "loners" began to find native alcoholics ready and eager to hear their message.[4]

As the membership increased, so proportionately grew the correspondence directed to the New York City office. Most of the letters requested literature or information about other local anonymous alcoholics, but many also contained questions of procedure, practice, and on occasion, theory. Doggedly, Wilson devoted hours on end to answering these queries: "If I understand correctly, your problem sounds similar to. . . . On that occasion, these good people, now years sober, tried. . . . Of course, it is for you and your group to work this out: I can only relate to you what we seem to have learned from past experience. Perhaps you and your group will choose to follow this, but whether you do or not, please let us know how it comes out."[5]

The "Twelve Traditions of Alcoholics Anonymous" emerged directly from this correspondence. By 1945, some of the questions had become noticeably repetitious, which suggested that "all this mass of experience might be codified into a set of principles which could offer tested solutions to all our problems of living and working together and of relating our society to the world outside." Such matters as "membership, group autonomy, singleness of purpose, nonendorsement of other enterprises, professionalism, public controversy, and anonymity in its several aspects" certainly seemed settled by consistent — and at times painful — experience. Yet Wilson hesitated. He feared loss of the personal touch that also added to his own and A.A.'s larger reservoir of experience. Slowly, however, writer's cramp, the scantness of staff assistance, and the repetitive nature of some concerns won out. Stressing that "a code of traditions could not, of course, ever become rule or law [,] but might serve as a guide for our Trustees, Headquarters people, and especially for groups with growing pains," Wilson first published "Twelve Suggested Points for A.A. Tradition" in the fellowship's recently inaugurated journal, *The A.A. Grapevine*, in April of 1946.[6]

This first publication was in a "long form." Its text was soon reduced, more closely and memorably to parallel the precisely two hundred words of the Twelve Steps which comprised the constitution of the A.A. program. In this now hallowed "short form," the Twelve Traditions of Alcoholics Anonymous read:

One: Our common welfare should come first; personal re-
         covery depends upon A.A. unity.

Two: For our group purpose there is but one ultimate
         authority — a loving God as He may express Himself
         in our group conscience. Our leaders are but trusted
         servants; they do not govern.

Three: The only requirement for A.A. membership is a de-
         sire to stop drinking.

Four: Each group should be autonomous, except in matters
         affecting other groups or A.A. as a whole.

Five: Each group has but one primary purpose — to carry
         its message to the alcoholic who still suffers.

Six: An A.A. group ought never endorse, finance, or lend
         the A.A. name to any related facility or outside enter-
         prise, lest problems of money, property, and prestige
         divert us from our primary purpose.

Seven: Every A.A. group ought to be fully self-supporting,
         declining outside contributions.

Eight: Alcoholics Anonymous should remain forever non-
         professional, but our service centers may employ
         special workers.

Nine: A.A., as such, ought never to be organized; but we
         may create service boards or committees directly re-
         sponsible to those they serve.

Ten: Alcoholics Anonymous has no opinion on outside
         issues; hence the A.A. name ought never to be drawn
         into public controversy.

Eleven: Our public relations policy is based on attraction
         rather than promotion; we need always maintain per-
         sonal anonymity at the level of press, radio, and films.

Twelve: Anonymity is the spiritual foundation of all our
         Traditions, ever reminding us to place principles be-
         fore personalities.[7]

These twelve traditions served the fellowship of Alcoholics Anonymous well, perhaps because two of the major problems the organization
faced were being resolved at the very time of their formulation.

In the earliest history of A.A., those who sobered up and "got the
program" had tended to be "grim and utterly hopeless cases, almost
without exception." Such had been the type of alcoholics sought out by
the earliest members: people who, they thought, could readily identify
with the degradation they themselves felt. Further, "the experience of
bottom" had fostered such selectivity. Felt-degradation was rooted in a
perceived falling from ideals — and usually quite high ideals in the days

of the Oxford Group connection and the religious press publicity. The common explanation offered for anyone's failure to grasp the program of Alcoholics Anonymous ran, "He hasn't reached bottom yet"; and thus those primarily seeking "success" in their Twelfth Step work had tended to search out their "pigeons" literally in the gutter.[8]

The aftereffects of the *Saturday Evening Post* story began to change this. "Now younger folks began to appear. Lots of people turned up who still had jobs and homes and health and even good social standing. These in their turn were able to persuade others like themselves of the need for A.A." The concepts of "bottom," however, and of "surrender" and "conversion" remained. The idea of *limited control* both clarified and was clarified by this development: "bottom" could be raised, but the *necessity* of the bottom experience perdured. As Wilson himself continued his explanation:

> Of course it was necessary for these types of newcomers to hit bottom emotionally. But we found that they did not have to hit every possible bottom there was in order to admit that they were licked. We began to develop a conscious technique of "raising the bottom" and hitting them with it.[9]

The "conscious technique" developed was the stark portrayal of the early symptoms of alcoholism as these were understood by Alcoholics Anonymous, joined with a dreadful stress on the inevitability of the "progression" of these symptoms. The safeguarding of the A.A. vision, the acceptance of "not-God," was meanwhile guaranteed by the now-formalizing Third Tradition: to seek out Alcoholics Anonymous would ever imply the desire to stop drinking *plus* felt inability to do so without assistance and support. To approach Alcoholics Anonymous was necessarily to proclaim publicly, "I need help." This proclamation lay at the root of "the only requirement for membership."[10]

"With my *drinking* [of alcohol]" was of course implicitly understood as subjoined to the "I need help," according to the Third, Fifth, and Tenth Traditions of Alcoholics Anonymous. The question of "other problems" remained latent through most of this period, and was finally resolved only laboriously over the next twenty-five years. Yet as early as the autumn of 1945, Bill Wilson took notice in two *A.A. Grapevine* articles of what in time became a seductive invitation to extend the scope of the program of Alcoholics Anonymous. "Evidence on the Sleeping Pill Menace" and "Those 'Goof Balls'" treated the "Pill Problem" as it affected alcoholics. As awareness of the parallels and especially of the mutually enhancing relationship between alcohol and more esoteric mood-changing chemicals deepened, A.A. experienced pulls from both within and without its own membership to include in its program all "mood-altering drugs," and in its fellowship all those apparently addicted to them.[11]

The invitation was attractive, for the understanding of the taking of psychoactive drugs as "chewing your booze" — and so inevitably a step to the drinking of actual "booze" — came more and more to be verified by the sad, painful, and at times fatal experience of too literally fundamentalist members. Further, many *individuals* accepted the invitation. Expanding the notion of alcoholism to a concept of "chemical dependency," they began to apply the precise program of Alcoholics Anonymous to other chemical addictions. By the 1960s, this practice provided a pathway for A.A. ideas to infuse treatment techniques aimed at an astounding diversity of problems and people in the larger culture for whom alcoholism, strictly speaking, was only a very remote bogey.[12]

But Alcoholics Anonymous itself, faithful to its traditions, remained aloof. Generously, the fellowship shared its ideas and literature with any who found them helpful. More cautiously, it declined to accept responsibility for other ideas and literature that reached further than the precise problem of alcoholism. A.A.'s final formulation of its stance on "chemical dependency" occurred only after 1955, but the Traditions hammered out in the experience of the early 1940s rendered that ultimate posture inevitable.[13]

Helpful to this process of resolution was the fellowship's discovery of an aptly guiding larger history. On the front page of the August 1945 *A.A. Grapevine*, Bill Wilson — two months before his first calling of attention to the "Pill Problem" and eight months before the formal publication of the Twelve Traditions — offered under the title "Modesty One Plank for Good Public Relations" his understanding of the then just century-old history of the Washingtonian movement. A.A.'s co-founder began by praising the phenomenon, to which his attention had been called by a member-submitted article in the previous *Grapevine*, for its success in motivating "about 100,000 alcoholics who were helping each other stay sober." His pointed lament was "that today the influence of this good work has so completely disappeared that few of us had ever heard of it."[14]

Always one to point a moral and here explicitly conscious of seeking support for the Traditions he was formulating, Wilson listed four flaws that had led to the demise of the Washingtonians: "Overdone self-advertising — exhibitionism"; "Couldn't learn from others and became competitive, instead of cooperative with other organizations in their field"; "The original strong and simple group purpose [the reclamation of drunkards] was thus [by prohibition zealotry] dissipated in fruitless controversy and divergent aims"; and "Refusal to stick to their original purpose and so refrain from fighting anybody."[15]

The lessons drawn by Wilson were many-sided. Yet buried within them lay but one essential principle: "[A.A. must] make everlastingly certain that we always shall be strong enough and single-purposed enough from within, to relate ourselves rightly to the world without." This simple equation of strength with singleness of purpose guided Alcoholics Anonymous through perilous cross pressures in the following twenty-five years. Wilson concluded his article with the exhortation: "May we always be willing to learn from experience!" A.A.'s ability to learn from the experience of others as well as from its own development was tested in many ways over these twenty-five years.[16]

Other final stances, apparently ultimate but far less inevitable, required as long to be hammered out. The first hints of the medical profession's acceptance of Alcoholics Anonymous as a respectable therapy occurred in 1943 and 1944. Within an eighteen-month period, Bill Wilson addressed: at the invitation of the Mental Hygiene Commission of the State of Maryland, the Neuropsychiatric Section of the Baltimore City Medical Society meeting at Johns Hopkins University; through the good offices of A.A.'s Rockefeller-connected friend Dr. Foster Kennedy, the Section on Neurology and Psychiatry of the Medical Society of the State of New York; and at the urging of Dr. E. M. Jellinek, the experts newly assembled at Yale University's Summer School of Alcohol Studies.[17]

A.A.'s pride in its ideas and its founder momentarily swelled only to be immediately deflated. Such acceptance, the fellowship and its co-founder quickly learned, threatened its just then budding principles of anonymity and of non-involvement in outside enterprises. In 1944 came the first faint hint of the potential major problem. Within a month of Wilson's presentation before the Medical Society of the State of New York, Towns Hospital began advertising the claim: "Our outstanding contribution to the medical profession is Alcoholics Anonymous." With gingerly tact, Bill protested in his own name this distortion of history as he understood it; and he breathed a sigh of relief when the current director of Towns, Dr. John Bullard, agreed that such publicity was inappropriate.[18]

The aftermath of the Yale experience proved more difficult to contain. In January 1944, inspired largely by the efforts and connections of Marty Mann, Dr. E. M. Jellinek, America's premier researcher into alcoholism, joined with Dr. Howard W. Haggard, outstanding medical authority on alcoholism, and Dr. Selden D. Bacon, leading sociological investigator of alcohol-related problems, to announce the "Yale Plan for Alcohol Studies," "Yale Plan Clinics for the Treatment of Alcoholism," and the formation of the "National Committee for Education on Alcoholism." Behind each endeavor — research, treatment, and public education — lay the desire to bring "to the forefront two momentous discoveries about alcoholism: *FIRST* that alcoholism is a *sickness*, not a moral delinquency. *SECOND* that when this is properly recognized *the hitherto hopeless alcoholic can be completely rehabilitated.*"[19]

Carefully side-stepping the wet-dry controversy, the Yale group even flirted with accepting funds from both the alcoholic beverage industry and militant temperance advocates. Such support seemed at first a veritable *coup*. Each side, convinced of the truth of its own stand, was confident of enlisting Yale's prestige for its own point of view. The New Haven group soon discerned the danger to its credibility in such financial dependence and drew back, but the problem of funding remained.[20]

Finances, however, were not the only problem. The educators also feared being mistaken for the kind of ivy-covered ivory tower academics whom drinkers such as Bill Wilson habitually scorned — "pantywaist[s]" whose nearest exposure to alcoholism had been going "wild one night on too many sherries at a Junior League cotillion." The surest way to demonstrate that they really knew about real alcoholism was clearly to advertise a "*real* alcoholic." Such had been Mann's idea in the first place, and she herself became "Exhibit A," a move that involved anonymity. Despite the subtle distinction between proclaiming oneself an alcoholic and revealing oneself to be a member of Alcoholics Anonymous, almost everyone at that time understood that only members of Alcoholics Anonymous possessed enough comfort about their "disease" to label themselves publicly "alcoholic."[21+]

Bill Wilson and most A.A.s realized this. Yet inspired by their zeal to teach the truth and to reach still other alcoholics by following out the mandate of the Twelfth Step of their program, most not only accepted Mann's activities as "for the greater good," but "William Wilson" and

---

+ Some who gained a measure of control over their problem-drinking, or even achieved total abstinence, by the use of other treatment modalities, at times in this period advertised themselves as "ex-alcoholics." Only A.A. members professed that their fundamental condition remained unchanged, that they continued to be "alcoholics."

"Robert Smith, M.D.," became members of the Advisory Board of the N.C.E.A., their names (but not their relationship to Alcoholics Anonymous) thus appearing on its letterhead. Marty Mann, meanwhile, embarked on a nationwide tour telling her story to newspapers and eventually readily acknowledging membership in Alcoholics Anonymous. She had shed her anonymity, the "lady ex-lush" explained to reporters puzzled at the apparent contradiction, "for the sake of others." [22+]

The ice was thin indeed. No one feared that Marty might drink again, although Dr. Tiebout, who had been her therapist and had introduced her to A.A., expressed to Wilson at least ambivalent concern about "re-inflation." Yet it was not from this direction that trouble directly struck. To "expand its staff and multiply its facilities," the N.C.E.A. in 1946 launched a large-scale public appeal for funds. The solicitation not only carried the names of Wilson and Smith on its letterhead and in its substance implied a relationship with "*Alcoholics Anonymous*" (thus emphasized), but it also was mailed to some A.A. groups. As one of A.A.'s trustees observed in a letter to Bill Wilson, who was absent from New York at this time: "If this letter should ever go out to the A.A. mailing list quoting A.A. throughout and soliciting funds on a letterhead that carries both your name and Bob Smith's as sponsors, no little hell would be popping." [23]

The observation proved perceptive. Within hours the New York office of Alcoholics Anonymous was flooded with calls and wires of question and protest, and two days later the office staff telegraphed Wilson: "A.A. can split if Marty carries your backing." Quickly, Bill wired back to Dr. Bob and the office. His telegram began by lamenting, "What a situation," and went on for four pages as Bill carefully acknowledged his error in allowing such a use of his name. Three days later, just a week after it all began, the Alcoholic Foundation released a terse statement dissociating itself from the solicitation and noting that "Alcoholics Anonymous looks with disfavor on the unauthorized use of its name in any fund-raising activity." [24]

All this took place while Wilson himself was traveling in the Far West. His journey had two purposes. It was an extended vacation at the low point of the depression that haunted him through most of this decade,

+ "lady ex-lush": a delightful but apparently apocryphal tale, cherished especially among female members of A.A. of a certain class background, concerns Ms. Mann's vehement protest to a careless editor who had captioned her picture: "ex-lady lush." Marty is reported to have wired: "I am still a lady — goddammit!"

and it provided an opportunity to discuss with producer Hal Wallis a proposed major motion picture feature about Alcoholics Anonymous, another mark of social acceptance accorded A.A. in this period.[25]

Early in 1944, a Hollywood producer had sought the help of Alcoholics Anonymous with the intention of devising a feature movie that would dramatize A.A.'s understanding of alcoholism. This project was first sidetracked and then abandoned when the Charles Jackson best-seller, *The Lost Weekend*, was made into a motion picture accomplishing just that. Through 1945 especially, in the wake of the popularity of *The Lost Weekend*, Alcoholics Anonymous received helpful publicity from newsreel coverage and opportunities to carry its message through radio features and even regular programming. The most helpful general publicity came in 1951, when *Fortune* magazine offered an article about Alcoholics Anonymous that the fellowship informally adopted and for well over a decade reprinted and distributed as an effective brief description of its program.[26]

Not all magazine publicity was so favorable. In 1946, *True Confessions* ran a lead feature titled: "Let Me Tell You About the Miraculous Redemption of a Confirmed Drunkard." Although overtly positive, this treatment was lurid in details and implication. The nether depths of such journalism were reached in 1954, when *Confidential* magazine offered an "exposé" of "Alcoholics Anonymous: No Booze BUT PLENTY OF BABES!" Interestingly, A.A.'s internal response was less outrage than a philosophical "Well, *we* realize it isn't true, in general; but who knows? Maybe it will move some who need the program to investigate, and these — if they give it a chance — just might get what they need instead of what they want!"[27]

The mid-1940s witnessed another significant development in the unfolding history of Alcoholics Anonymous, although this growth occurred first in the continuing personal maturation of Bill Wilson. In 1946, as a part of the aftermath of the Mann-N.C.E.A. affair, Wilson attained another insight, one that proximately lifted Bill from the nadir of his depression. This new realization perfectly complemented his decade-earlier intuition of the dangers of excessive dependency: "I suddenly realized the extent to which I have been trying to dominate . . . others; also the extent to which I have been indulging in fruitless self-accusation . . . everything swinging in the direction of *control* of something or somebody." This insight was very healthy for Wilson, and it eventually proved very productive for Alcoholics Anonymous. But from 1945 to 1950, Bill had to struggle to make it operative in his own life within the A.A. fellowship. Only then could he share its wealth with his fellow alcoholics by publishing the deeper understanding of the A.A. program to which this insight had led him.[28]

That Alcoholics Anonymous itself was not God, Wilson seemed acutely aware. As he wrote to a complaining correspondent, "Alcoholics Anonymous is a terribly imperfect society because it is made up of very imperfect people. We are all dedicated to a perfect ideal of which, because we are very human and very sick, we often fall short. I know because I constantly fall short myself." Institutionally as well as personally, Bill Wilson found many occasions to proclaim: "We're Not Perfect Yet"; ". . . we are approaching maturity. . . . It is clear we cannot forever be immune from the pressures that are tearing modern society apart." [29]

On 1 November 1945, Wilson submitted to A.A.'s Trustees a proposal, "Concerning the Future of the Alcoholic Foundation." After praising the contributions of the non-alcoholic trustees, the co-founder suggested that "we . . . begin to evolve the ultimate set-up [of A.A.] now." Pointing out, not accurately given the circumstances, that "functionally I am letting go," Bill urged the same course of action upon the trustees. "Facing [the] paradox of spiritual principle [,] should they [not] let go of their temporal power to increase their own spiritual influence?" [30]

Bill Wilson was here striving for acceptance of Alcoholics Anonymous as "a new kind of human society," one that lived out in daily practice the realization that "our group strength seems to stem from our individual and ever potential weakness." Perhaps spurred on by political science hobbyist Father Edward Dowling's comment to his initial proposal — "A.A. has proved that democracy is therapy" — Bill sought to overcome the ancient political and organizational problem of the separation of authority from responsibility. As fellowship rather than organization, Alcoholics Anonymous disclaimed authority. Yet its program seemed to require that precisely as fellowship, Alcoholics Anonymous serve as a model of responsibility for its members. Faced with a flurry of trustee resignations as he pushed his vision in 1948 and momentarily disheartened by Dr. Bob Smith's 1949 initial refusal to support his concept of A.A. "maturity," Wilson retreated to re-think — to re-think in terms of "spiritual" as the proper modifier of "maturity," of "*spiritual* responsibility" as well as of the questions of "authority" and "money" on which his proposals had thus far concentrated.[31]

Bill was not to begin writing out the results until 1952, when the concepts he revised led Alcoholics Anonymous to the solution of its fellowship-organization difficulties. Wilson achieved this solution by returning again within himself to draw from the one thing upon which ultimately all of his ideas and activities were based: his understanding of alcoholism, and especially his experience of this "malady" in himself. For if to be a sober alcoholic was to find the wholeness of one's being in the acceptance of limitation and therefore to need others who also accepted their limitation, then Alcoholics Anonymous as fellowship and program of mutual need was first *community* rather than organization. The *fellowship itself* had need of its program, for it also was made whole only by its explicit acceptance of its own limitations.[32]

The culmination of public medical acceptance of the therapy of Alcoholics Anonymous also came in this period. In 1949, Wilson was invited to address the annual convention of the American Psychiatric Association at its convention in Montreal. The chief medical question concerning alcoholism was the legitimacy of the claim that it was a "disease." To Wilson, alcoholism, of course, was such. But there was more to the issue, and, importantly for Alcoholics Anonymous, Bill had learned as well as taught, from psychiatric critics as well as from his own experience.[33+]

The significance of understanding alcoholism as "illness," "malady," *or* "disease" rather than as "*symptom*" was profound. Alcoholics Anonymous, regarding the controversy as an "outside issue," did not directly enter the debate. Yet insofar as the disagreement more deeply concerned the meaning of human life, Alcoholics Anonymous as an expression of "spiritual" ideas had something to contribute.[34]

Medical men understood that the debate was neither an idle pastime nor merely a product of the academic mind. "'If . . . alcoholism is regarded as a symptom, then the treatment program is designed to cure the underlying disease': [whereas, regarding] addictive drinking itself as an illness [leads to directing efforts] toward 'the break-up of the sequence of activities involved in addictive drinking.'" The premier example of this latter approach was Alcoholics Anonymous. Yet as the

---

+ The circumstances of Wilson's invitation to speak at Montreal are related in detail in Tiebout (Greenwich, CT) to Wilson, 18 November 1948; *cf.* also Dr. Frank C. (Charlottesville, VA) to Wilson, 30 December 1948: it is clear that many in the A.P.A. were unenthusiastic about Wilson's appearance. Wilson offered cute witness to this in an oft-told anecdote describing how a past-president of the A.P.A. had after his talk noted that "outside of the few A.A.'s in the room, and myself, I do not think a single one of my colleagues believed a word of your explanation." Bill expressed surprise, for he had been applauded. ". . . the old man replied, 'Well, Mr. Wilson, you A.A.'s have a hundred thousand recoveries and we in the psychiatric profession have only a few. They were applauding the *results*, much more than the *message*.'" (Wilson to Dr. John G., 9 October 1967, italics Wilson's).

medical debate over alcoholism unfolded, a subtle change in its understanding of alcoholism was taking place within Alcoholics Anonymous, and especially within the mind of Bill Wilson.[35]

The change was one of addition rather than of substitution. Wilson and his followers never wavered in the understanding that their alcoholic "illness," "malady," or "disease" was to be confronted directly. Their aim continued to be "the break-up of the sequence of activities involved in addictive drinking" — in A.A. parlance: "not taking the first drink, one day at a time." But *sobriety* as understood in A.A. carried a further corollary implication.[36]

Confronted with the problems and concerns of "living sober," aware from often tragic experience of the special danger to alcoholics of such personality pitfalls as grandiosity, resentments, and the tendencies to dominance over or excessive dependence upon others, old-time members began to formulate a significant three-faceted distinction. "Active alcoholism" was the condition of the obsessive-compulsive drinker who continued to imbibe alcohol. From this situation, *two* others were to be distinguished. The first was that of the "merely dry" former obsessive-compulsive drinker who "put the cork in the bottle" yet continued to "think alcoholically"; i.e., to entertain grandiose plans and expectations, to nurse feelings of resentment, etc. In "true sobriety" or "serenity," one embraced a new "way of life"; i.e., abandoned grandiosity, resentments, and other claims to be "special," and became aware that one's only true dependence was on the "Higher Power" — that the *whole* program of the Twelve Steps of Alcoholics Anonymous was to be utilized in *all* aspects of daily life.[37]

The "merely dry" or "dry drunk" state was precarious, whether as an intermediate stage between "active alcoholism" and "true sobriety," or as simply a falling away from "true sobriety." A person in this dry but alcoholic condition suffered much or all of the torment formerly soothed in some way by alcohol, but the accustomed painkiller was no longer an available option, and the fact that "active alcoholism" had been overcome inhibited any perception of "bottom" that could lead to the "surrender" required for "conversion" to "true sobriety." It was a purgatory worse than hell, for one suffered the torment under the illusion that this was heaven; further, from this alcoholic limbo one passed more usually to the hell of active alcoholism than to the heaven of true sobriety.[38]

This developing understanding of three rather than two choices permeated the self-understanding of the members of Alcoholics Anonymous more and more deeply in the early 1950s. It explained not only themselves but the successes and failures of others. A newer and somewhat muted two-fold distinction began to emerge: that between "living sober" and "thinking and living alcoholically" — the latter whether actually drinking alcohol or not. Such an understanding of "the A.A. Way of Life" had, of course, been implicit in its Oxford Group origins, but only in 1967 did this precise phrase become enshrined in the title of a collection of Bill Wilson's writings. In this earlier period, A.A.'s surviving co-founder turned to the task of setting it forth clearly in terms more familiar both to his own mind and to his followers in Alcoholics Anonymous.[39]

In 1950, Wilson began to withdraw from active leadership in the ever increasing enterprises of the fellowship's New York office, declaring his desire to devote concentrated time to several writing projects. Bill began formal work on the philosophically most important of these only in 1952, but he clearly based it on his experiences between 1946 and 1950. The treatise emerged in 1953 as *Twelve Steps and Twelve Traditions*. This book set forth Wilson's deepest understanding of the "A.A. Way of Life." It was A.A.'s New Testament — bringing to fruition the original revelation of the Big Book, *Alcoholics Anonymous*.[40]

Influenced by the events surrounding him, Bill Wilson began and ended his portrayal of A.A.'s Twelve Steps as "a way of life" by stressing the continuing necessity of the total deflation of even a raised "bottom" and the persistence in even the "recovering alcoholic" of childishness, immature grandiosity, and infantile defiance. Between these themes and derived from them, Wilson located an ancient motif. The key to the A.A. Way of Life was — simply — "humility."[41]

Humility. The key to the A.A. program, "the step that separates the men from the boys," was presented — perhaps surprisingly — as Step Six: "Were entirely ready to have God remove all these defects of character." The point was that not only can "*I*" not directly achieve this removal, but even before an-Other can, "*my*" main "activity" can be only the apparently most passive one of readiness, openness. Wilson's explicit exploration of the meaning of humility bracketed his indirect treatment of it in the Sixth Step. Although "often misunderstood, . . . genuine humility" was presented simply and classically in Step Five as "realism . . . , straight thinking, solid honesty." Especially as "first . . . consist[ing] of recognizing our deficiencies," "actual humility" eased "the old pains of anxious apartness." Thus Step Five which exemplified it "was the beginning of true kinship with man and God."[42]

In Step Seven, where "the attainment of greater humility" was presented as "the foundation principle of each of A.A.'s Twelve Steps," Wilson expanded his favorite understanding of the *glory* of the alcoholic condition as residing in its clear and personal demonstration of the fundamental truth that strength comes out of weakness. Three key elements rapidly tumbled forth from this stark realization of the essence of the condition of the recovering alcoholic: 1) the character and role of "instincts"; 2) the exact nature of the danger in "demand"; and 3) the special pitfall for the alcoholic of the contradictory two-pronged quest for both "dependence" and "independence." [43]

In his discussions of instincts, Bill Wilson usually listed the basic human passionate cravings as "security, sex, and society." Wary more of repetition than alliteration, he at times substituted "to eat, to reproduce, to be somebody" or "money, romance, companionship and prestige" when describing how "the unnatural act [of] pour[ing] so much alcohol into themselves that they destroy their lives" led alcoholics to turn these "basic natural desires" into destructively "distorted drives." The co-founder accepted human nature as his experience had taught him his was: the basic "instincts" were neither good nor bad — they simply *were*. [44]

What distorted these drives, perverted these passions, was *demand*. "We have been making unreasonable demands upon ourselves, upon others, and upon God." The danger in demand was two-edged. "Either we insist upon dominating the people we know, or we depend upon them far too much." "Either we . . . tried to play God and dominate those about us, or we . . . insisted on being overdependent on them." Each demand denied limitation, whether of oneself or of some other. For essentially limited creatures, then, any demand was doomed to frustration. [45]

To escape the snare of demand, Wilson proposed a profoundly simple solution. *Proper* dependence was the only true *independence*. In the "spiritual program" of Alcoholics Anonymous proper dependence was first upon God. "The more we become willing to depend upon a higher Power, the more independent we actually are. Therefore dependence, as A.A. practices it, is really a means of gaining true independence of the spirit." But even if secondarily, *proper* dependence was also immediately upon others: "Going it alone in spiritual matters is dangerous." As the Fifth, Eighth, Ninth, and Twelfth Steps imposed as well as testified, "salvation" in Alcoholics Anonymous consisted in "emerging from isolation" to the "feeling of being at one with God and man," to "the sense of *belonging*, [the awareness that] we no longer live in a completely hostile world. We are no longer lost and frightened and purposeless." [46]

The route traversed in the A.A. Way of Life led from destructive dependence upon the chemical alcohol to a dependence proper to God and appropriate upon others; from honesty regarding instincts to a rejoicing in the strength arising from weakness; from the self-hating confusion of the "bottom" to identity derived essentially from accepting the wholeness of the limitation of one's being. Only under this realization came the "spiritual awakening" in which was founded "the joy of living [that] is the theme" of A.A.'s Twelve Steps. That spiritual awakening was "a new state of consciousness and being." It meant acceptance by the A.A. member that "he has been transformed, because he has laid hold of a source of strength which, in one way or another, he had hitherto denied himself." [47]

In practice, this theory came from Wilson's reflection on his own experience, as virtually all the co-founder's correspondence made clear. In practice also, this theory shaped the history of the fellowship for the next twenty years. That history marked the process by which Alcoholics Anonymous itself achieved the "true maturity of responsibility." [48]

For if the careful formulation of its "way of life" was the introverted, *program*-developing accomplishment of Alcoholics Anonymous — *via* Bill Wilson — during the early 1950s, the extroverted, *fellowship*-developing task of A.A. was its self-conscious effort at "Coming of Age" — again, under the at times prickly goading as well as the statesmanlike leadership of its surviving co-founder. The two developments were related. As medical — and especially psychiatric — investigation and thought proceeded through the "disease" debate focusing especially upon "dependency," one trait especially became isolated as characteristic of alcoholism and the alcoholic: the specific over-dependency of immaturity. [49]

The diagnosis was one with which Bill Wilson himself could readily identify — up to a point. In the mid-1940s, Wilson had sought out Dr. Harry M. Tiebout and had entered upon a regimen of psychotherapy. Dr. Tiebout, a psychiatrist specializing in the treatment of alcoholics, from early on had supported Alcoholics Anonymous and had referred to the fellowship its first successful female member, Marty Mann. Throughout his long and distinguished career, the Connecticut psychiatrist published a series of perceptive analyses of alcoholism and of the therapeutic dynamic inherent in the program of Alcoholics Anonymous. Tiebout came to this comprehension largely through his knowledge of Bill Wilson, and his diagnostic understanding was both profound and simple. Drawing upon a phrase attributed to Freud, the psychiatrist pointed out to A.A.'s co-founder that both in his active alcoholism and in his current sobriety he had been trying to live out the infantilely grandiose demands of "His Majesty the Baby."[50]

Wilson accepted the diagnosis; indeed, he incorporated it and developed his understanding of its implications in *Twelve Steps and Twelve Traditions.* But somehow it stuck in Wilson's craw that even "truly sober" alcoholics be thought essentially "immature." His correspondence with Tiebout especially was studded with both acknowledgments and denials of this ambivalence, perhaps most strikingly on one occasion in 1951 when — responding to a letter from the doctor accusing him of immaturity in historical distortion — Bill dashed off a heated response which he later directed not be mailed: "This shows more ego than Harry! *Don't Send!*" In himself at least, Wilson always readily found traces at least of "His Majesty the Baby."[51]

But for Alcoholics Anonymous Bill refused to accept so reductively degrading an understanding. Another consideration moved Wilson and the oldtimers around him. A new twist in the post-war age of consumer advertising portrayed the drinking of alcohol as the "grown-up" thing to do. The push to "maturity" and "adulthood" was on from many directions, reflected in clothing styles, entertainment breakthroughs, and a myriad of other cultural pressures. Alcoholics Anonymous could not combat directly an advertising industry that presented the drinking of alcohol as the hallmark of maturity, but it could and did launch an attempt to demonstrate in its own existence that abstinence from alcohol was not in itself a sign of immaturity.[52]

In Bill Wilson's understanding, the chief characteristic of maturity was responsibility. From 1950, Wilson turned his attention to demonstrating that sober alcoholics could be responsible — for themselves as well as for other, drinking alcoholics. His second chosen mode of achieving this demonstration was to effect obvious and advertised change in the structure of the fellowship.[53]

This was the "second chosen mode" because Wilson had found himself caught in a quandary, and his initial attempt to circumvent it had fallen almost disastrously flat and been almost fatally counterproductive. The quandary was that as necessary to the needs of that time as had been the Alcoholic Foundation with its majority of nonalcoholic trustees in the spring of 1938, its original money-raising function had been unnecessary since 1945. In that latter year, Alcoholics Anonymous adopted its tradition of "no outside contributions" and signally informed the 1940 Rockefeller dinner guests that their assistance not only was no longer needed but even would no longer be accepted. Yet the Foundation with its Trustees had continued in existence. As a source and reservoir of good will, they mediated between Alcoholics Anonymous and the community at large. Explicitly composed of a majority of non-alcoholics, the Trustees and Foundation were the most visible witness to the fellowship's respectability. Such dependence upon non-alcoholics was to Wilson a denial of responsibility and evidence of immaturity. But the Foundation and its trustees could not simply be shed. These men had given much, and most had become close personal friends. Appropriate gratitude, Wilson knew, was also a responsibility of and a witness to maturity.[54]

Faced with these problems, Wilson labeled the fifteenth anniversary convention of Alcoholics Anonymous which met in Cleveland in 1950 "A.A.'s Coming of Age party." Prior to the meeting, he used the pages of the *A.A. Grapevine* to exhort delegates to seize this "chance to prove that we *have* reached a stage of maturity. . . !" Intriguingly, this was done under the title rubric: "May Humility Be the Keynote!" Afterwards, Bill's and others' reports of this meeting were sprinkled with examples of and attestations to "maturity"; for example, by an anonymous cab-driver who rejoiced that at *this* convention he had not had to wrestle with drunks; and by *Cleveland Press* editor Louis Selzer, who testified that in his field, at least, A.A. was very needed and welcome. Despite all this patent flackery, the matter proved hardly settled.[55]

Dr. Tiebout, for example, wrote reminding Wilson that loud proclamations of "maturity" were the surest evidence of its opposite. The psychiatrist questioned further whether, given the self-embraced and self-defining "anarchy" of Alcoholics Anonymous, the fellowship could ever hope to be mature, and he cited as further evidence its prolonged "fence straddling" about support of Marty Mann's N.C.E.A. Wilson's reply attempted conciliation. On the N.C.E.A., he explained again A.A.'s "policy toward all outside enterprises"; on "anarchy," Bill conceded the point, but called attention to A.A. as "tightly, and paradoxically, bound together by a common interest." Before closing with an astute request for his former therapist's guidance in these matters, Wilson acknowledged that while "in some respects A.A. has doubtless grown up . . . in many others it hasn't, and may never," asking almost plaintively, "Is it necessarily pessimistic to face the possibility that our Society may never be very mature?"[56]

With his letter to Tiebout, Bill enclosed the manuscript of his coming *Grapevine* article, "Your Third Legacy: . . . a proposal to form "The General Service Conference of Alcoholics Anonymous' — a small body of State and Provincial A.A. Delegates meeting yearly, who could assume direct responsibility for the guidance of the A.A. General Service Headquarters at New York City." The proposing article offered six considerations as impelling to the change. The first four merit *verbatim* recording:

> Let's face these facts:
> First — Dr. Bob and Bill are perishable, they can't last forever.
> Second — Their friends, the Trustees, are almost unknown to the A.A. movement.
> Third — In future years our Trustees couldn't possibly function without direct guidance from A.A. itself. . . .
> Fourth — *Alcoholics Anonymous* is out of its infancy. Grown up, adult now, it has full right and the plain duty to take direct responsibility for its own Headquarters.[57]

Upon this proposal, rather than the conciliatory letter accompanying it, the psychiatrist pounced: "The note of bestowal is, I am afraid, going to irritate some people. . . . I hear a note which is a bit Rotarian in its emphasis [and therefore] likely to feed the collective ego a considerable amount of fodder." The doctor went on to demolish the idea of a General Service Conference: "Any body which meets once a year and only once a year without intervening committee work and responsibility is likely to end up the essence of futility." Afraid of thus opening the door to continued dependence upon some "benevolent despot . . . whose feeling of need to keep in touch with the grass roots is completely nil," Tiebout did offer one positive suggestion: "Set up . . . a parliamentary body, just as the House of Delegates of the American Medical Association."[58]

Wilson's response revealed stiffened spine and clearer thinking about the uniqueness of Alcoholics Anonymous. Stressing how members of A.A. were "impersonally and severely disciplined from without," he rejected the earlier charge of "continuous chaos," and — naming two autocratic former presidents of the A.M.A. about whom Tiebout had apparently complained — pointed out that "I'm pretty sure we shall never see a [name] or a [name] for long, if at all. Here egocentricity works in our favor — the drunks won't obey them or have them."[59]

In response to Bill's "Third Legacy" call, the first General Service Conference of Alcoholics Anonymous met in New York City in April 1951, its Wilson-chosen theme, "Not to Govern but to Serve." Throughout the proceedings, the thirty-seven elected delegates were reminded of their limitations — that, for example, they "represented no more than half the territory covered by A.A." Yet they also were reminded of the exact nature of their privilege. They were to accept "full present and future responsibility for the General Services of Alcoholics Anonymous," i.e., especially, "the A.A. Book, *The A.A. Grapevine*, and the diverse functions of the Alcoholics Anonymous General Offices."[60]

A report on this first meeting of the General Service Conference of Alcoholics Anonymous in the June 1951 *A.A. Grapevine* again roused the ire of Dr. Harry Tiebout. The psychiatrist wrote Wilson an accusing letter, "pointing out the dangers of historical distortion, egotism, and damaging ingratitude." His special objection was that Bill had unjustly ignored the role of A.A.'s non-alcoholic friends in saving Works Publishing, Inc., in its troubled early days. This particularly irked the doctor because he himself had been an open-pursed purchaser of the apparently worthless stock.[61]

In rejoinder, Wilson acknowledged that some clarity had indeed been lacking in his brief description of that episode of history, but Bill went on to deny vigorously any intentional "historical distortion" in the interests of making Alcoholics Anonymous appear "self-sufficient" and so more maturely independent than had actually been the case in its early days. He pointed out, in obvious high dudgeon, that "in the past year we've tremendously spread information concerning the vital roles played by Silkworth, Tiebout, Dowling, Fosdick, Rockefeller, Richardson, Alexander and a dozen others."[62]

The underlying argument between Tiebout and Wilson clearly concerned "maturity" — its meaning, and the accuracy of any claim by Alcoholics Anonymous to it, in the past or in the present. The psychiatrist was asking: "How can a person, or a group of persons, who achieve first identity by proclaiming, 'I am an alcoholic' — i.e., 'I am obsessively-compulsively inclined to addictive dependency' — and whose greatest danger is the claim to 'self-sufficiency' ever claim maturity? Is not that very claim rather the best proof of *immaturity* — the denial of the reality of dependence?" The co-founder heard the questions. In the next four years he attempted to search out the answers. Themes of the succeeding meetings of A.A.'s General Service Conference bear out this interpretation. In 1952, the theme "Progress" was chosen, and the gathering's keynote was set by Bernard B. Smith, non-alcoholic Chairman of the Board of Trustees of the Alcoholic Foundation: "We here must dedicate ourselves to insure that there is never any government in the hearts of Alcoholics Anonymous." The 1953 theme was "We Are Standing on the Threshold of Maturity," in the words of Wilson who that year delivered the keynote address himself. "But," as the *Grapevine*'s "Final Report" itself immediately tacked on, "he was quick to add: 'No one can say in truth that we are really mature yet. The process of maturing will go on as long as we last.'"[63]

Yet the effort to cross that threshold of maturity continued. The theme of the 1954 General Service Conference, "Confidence and Responsibility," set up the 1955 twentieth anniversary convention as truly marking the "Coming of Age" of Alcoholics Anonymous — this time demonstrated rather than merely proclaimed as had been the case in Cleveland five years earlier. The conflicting pressures within and upon Bill Wilson over this endeavor were clear in much of his correspondence. As one writer — eight-and-a-half-years sober — gently rebuked Wilson, striking a sympathetic chord in the co-founder's own heart: "To my way of feeling A.A. is, and always will be, two drunks talking at the kitchen table over a cup of coffee." Bill's response revealed how he had resolved this apparent problem in his own mind: "God knows I believe in keeping A.A. simple. But you can make a thing too simple. So simple in fact that it soon gets complicated." Wilson listed some of the examples of "plain irresponsibility" that had arisen from the members' sense of separation from the Trustees of the Alcoholic Foundation. Moved by this perception, in October 1954, Bill pushed through the transformation of the Alcoholic Foundation into the "General Service Board of Alcoholics Anonymous." Yet the renamed entity remained the same in composition: a majority of the Board were non-alcoholic, and selection continued to be essentially from within, although the elective process was slightly opened and formalized.[64]

Thus, by the time of its twentieth anniversary gathering at St. Louis in July of 1955, Bill Wilson and Alcoholics Anonymous felt that they had sound basis to label this convention the demonstrative living out of A.A.'s "Coming of Age." Three convention events earmarked this significance: the fellowship's acceptance, grasp, and setting forth of its own history — as recalled and understood by William Griffith Wilson; the presentation of the program and fellowship of Alcoholics Anonymous in a new and revised edition of its virtually sacred "Big Book"; and the formal handing over to the membership, as represented by the General Service Conference, of the "Three Legacies of Alcoholics Anonymous . . . Recovery, Unity, and Service."[65]

To acknowledge, to accept, and to forgive one's parents — both what they gave and what they did not give, both one's dependence upon them and one's independence of them — is the ultimate hallmark of maturity: a perception as valid for institutions as for individuals. Bill Wilson and Alcoholics Anonymous accomplished this in 1955 in acknowledging and accepting their history.[66]

One motive impelling Wilson to write *Twelve Steps and Twelve Traditions* had been the realization that the original text of the "Big Book," *Alcoholics Anonymous*, had become "frozen" — too "sacred" for even its principal author's taste. Yet because of the phenomenal success of the original edition, Wilson and virtually all others were wary of change. The modification in one of the early printings that had substituted "spiritual awakening" for "spiritual experience" in the Twelfth Step was made more consistent in other scattered references, and the words *disease, cure,* and *ex-alcoholic* were more carefully avoided, the first generally replaced by "illness" and the second and third by circumlocutions adverting to the persistence of the condition.[67]

Otherwise, the stated "main purpose" of this first revision of *Alcoholics Anonymous* was "to bring the story section up-to-date, to portray more adequately a cross section of those who found help. In general, one important purpose [was] to show that low-bottom drunks are not the only ones who can be helped." Accordingly, the thirty-seven stories of the second edition were arranged under three headings: thirteen "Pioneers of A.A." whose stories were retained from the first edition; twelve "high-bottom" alcoholics whose stories were presented under the heading, "They Stopped in Time"; and twelve "low-bottom" alcoholics whose tales were headed, "They Almost Lost All."[68]

These stories and their sources revealed that twenty years after its founding, for all its efforts at and claims to universality, Alcoholics Anonymous had not yet become a microcosm of American society or even of American alcoholics. By city, eight of the story-tellers were from Akron-Cleveland and thirteen from New York; otherwise only Chicago and Los Angeles with two story-tellers each were represented more than once in the collection. The second edition stories described eleven women and twenty-six men, a not significant distortion of A.A.'s roughly one to four female-male ratio in 1955. The distortion that was allowed, indeed, sprang from the editors' conviction that women were under-represented in Alcoholics Anonymous partially because the historical circumstances of the book's first edition had led to it not furnishing sufficient models with which they might identify. Occupationally, the analytic breakdown by the second edition's editors tended to understate employment status. The "patent expert," for example, had been a powerful attorney on the national legislative scene and in 1955 was generally recognized as an outstanding authority in his own and three neighboring states. Similarly, the "upholsterer" owned his own fairly large firm even though he continued to work as a craftsman; and the "accountant" held a position of great responsibility in a large national firm.[69]

Impressions revealed a similar picture. In one of his few passing references to his own attendance at A.A. meetings, Wilson remarked that on successive evenings he had "rubbed shoulders" with a "fur-clad countess" and a diminutive, self-effacing man "who turned out to be a former driver for Al Capone." The claim was clearly to universality, but the impression of both sociologists and casual observers was that most regulars at meetings had hit the rocks of alcoholism from one of two related directions: the frustration of efforts at upward mobility — preeminently a lower middle class affliction; or the pains of perceived downward mobility — a torment of especially the children of the upper middle classes who had not successfully internalized the values (or the luck) of their forebears.[70]

"Oldtimers" related an interesting change. In their perception, Alcoholics Anonymous in 1955 no longer had so many "low-bottom drunks" among its members. In fact, general A.A. membership had moved from those falling from upper middle-class status to those striving to transcend lower middle-class circumstances. The very rich and the very poor were avidly welcomed at A.A. meetings, largely because they "proved" the universality of "the disease." Only they usually did not last long within the fellowship. For all the welcome, the sense that they were making others uncomfortable eventually made them also uncomfortable.[71]

If, then, universality across class lines of actual membership is accepted as a criterion of the "maturity" of Alcoholics Anonymous, the fellowship's composition in 1955 still left quite a bit to be desired. Whether more in reflection of its Oxford Group origins or as a corollary of how its key concept of "the experience of bottom" had come to be understood, the active membership of Alcoholics Anonymous was skewed to the middle classes and, more significantly, especially to those among the middle classes whose background or aspirations were above the median of even this modal population.

But, thanks in large measure to Wilson's propagandizing efforts, the main foundation of the maturity claimed by Alcoholics Anonymous in 1955 lay in the fellowship's acceptance of responsibility — through its indirectly elected General Service Board — for "the Three Legacies of Recovery, Unity, and Service." The transfer of this responsibility by Bill Wilson was accomplished with significant qualifications. Wilson clearly reminded his followers that although their fellowship "has come of age, . . . [this] expression does not mean that we have grown up, for that is a lifetime, if not an eternal, process." Moreover, while praising provisions that "the authority for service [is] spread over many rotating members of [the] Conference" to minimize "the tendency to worship people," Bill realized that his own role would always be special. Therefore he attempted to delimit it precisely. He would "help in a pinch" but would "no longer continuously act for, or try to protect the movement from itself." Wilson ran on a continuation of this point to a conclusion that was far more than a mere after-thought: "Neither will the Trustees, nor indeed can they, praise God."[72]

In 1955 Bill Wilson praised God that neither he nor its trustees could save Alcoholics Anonymous — even from itself. Yet one problem of "salvation" remained. Like the individual alcoholic, Alcoholics Anonymous itself was not God. This evident fact, all connected with A.A. — especially its trustees — clearly accepted in 1955. But the transition from accepting not being God to embracing its limitation as the source of its wholeness was to prove as difficult for Alcoholics Anonymous itself — and especially for its trustees — as it had been for the fellowship's individual members. That not being God implied being not-God was a difficult lesson to learn. Yet the acceptance that A.A. was made whole by its very limitations was necessary to both the fellowship and the program, and so to it — with strategic but largely unconscious acumen — Wilson turned his attention and efforts in the years after 1955.

VI

Responsibilities of Maturity
1955–1971

Alcoholics Anonymous and the Wholeness of Limitation

Bill Wilson withdrew from formal leadership within Alcoholics Anonymous at the climactic moment of the fellowship's "Coming of Age" convention on 3 July 1955; he died on 24 January 1971. In the years between, the fellowship faced and attempted to solve the organizational problem created by its founder's longevity. A.A. thrived over these years because the continuing presence of the charismatic authority of its co-founder served powerfully to reinforce its qualities of openness, simplicity, and tolerance. So long as "Bill W." lived, even his remote presence inhibited the development of any organizational bureaucracy that could stifle A.A.'s original vision and zeal under a haze of self-serving process. But Alcoholics Anonymous also suffered because that same presence impeded the development of any kind of truly autonomous, self-renewing authority. Despite the acceptance of its "Legacies" by A.A.'s General Service Conference, a society shy of even the term *leadership* was hard pressed to locate the source of its authority when the essentially charismatic prestige of original vision was withdrawn from "official" service.

Yet Alcoholics Anonymous did establish limited independence from Wilson as he diverted his attention to other areas whither it could not follow. Further, A.A. received, largely involuntarily, its co-founder's final legacy — the "responsibility" of changing the trustee majority from non-alcoholic to alcoholic. Most importantly, Alcoholics Anonymous finally achieved clear and definitive acceptance of its fundamental limitation, of its profound not-God-ness. The fellowship attained this ultimate acceptance largely by following Wilson's insistent even if "unofficial" example, as A.A. finally resolved its relationship to "other problems" and to the use of psychoactive chemicals other than alcohol.[1]

"A.A. isn't fool-proof, and never can be." Some of the more timorous among A.A.'s trustees felt that after 1955 Bill Wilson himself had set out to disprove at least one sense of this axiom. They — and he — carefully shielded from public scrutiny three areas among the co-founder's many activities. Each could have been seen as related to A.A.'s direct confrontation with alcoholism. That they were not so understood revealed the fellowship's sense of its own limitations. The three areas were Wilson's interest in spiritualism, his experimentation with LSD, and his promotion of the Vitamin B-3 therapy.[2]

Evidence of the reality of "the spiritual" fascinated Bill Wilson. His conviction that he had incontrovertible personal evidence of individual human conscious life lasting beyond physical death profoundly influenced Bill's adult faith, at least from the mid-1940s. After 1948, drawn through friendship with philosopher-mystic Gerald Heard into the ambit of the later-life interests of Aldous Huxley, Wilson experimented with and eventually claimed some power over spiritualistic phenomena. So profound was Bill's immersion in this area that he at times confused the terms "spiritualism" and "spirituality."[3]

Yet despite his conviction that he had evidence for the reality of "the spiritual" and so — in his logic — of the actual existence of a "higher Power," Wilson chose not to share, much less to proclaim or to impose, this foundation for faith either with, to, or upon Alcoholics Anonymous. The fellowship through its trustees heartily and gratefully accepted its co-founder's silence on so potentially controversial a topic. Only guardedly did Bill share the insights of his experiences in this realm with a few trusted friends, for he apparently believed that the faith required for salvation from alcoholism had to be just that — faith, and so by definition based on the intellectual "bottom experience" of insufficient evidence. Such, after all, had been his own "spiritual experience," despite all his certitude concerning it.[4]

Wilson's two other outside interests related more directly to treatment for alcoholism, and therefore, their relationship to Alcoholics Anonymous was even more ambiguous. Perhaps bridging the understandings of alcoholism as "spiritual disease" and as "mental (or psychological) disease" arched a line of research and experimentation that approached apparent fruition only in the late 1950s with the synthesis of lysergic acid diethylamide — the psychoactive chemical popularly known as LSD. The most common theory underlying the therapeutic use of LSD ran that the alcoholic was seeking to induce chemically the experience of transcendence but using the wrong chemical to that end. If a more appropriate chemical could evoke the experience of transcendence, it was hypothesized by serious medical experimenters, the obsession with and compulsion to ingest increasing doses of alcohol could be allayed. The alcoholic would come to see the drinking of alcohol as inappropriate to his transcendence, and therefore would give up his drinking. The closeness of this understanding to the Jungian insight and Dr. Jung's own experiments in this area added to its attractiveness to Wilson and to some of his medical friends who agreed with his intuition of the three-fold nature of the alcoholic sickness. If the human psychological quest for spiritual transcendence could be satisfied by a physical chemical, a three-fold unity of treatment/cure would balance the felt-unity of the "three-fold disease" with an elegance appealing to the scientific mind.[5][+]

Little is known concerning Wilson's personal experimentation with LSD beyond the fact that it certainly occurred. Whatever its effects upon him, there is no evidence that he ever thought his alcoholism "cured" in the sense that he could again drink alcohol safely. His main interest was in the possible usefulness of the LSD experience as an aid for those who otherwise could not "get the [A.A.] program." More and more in his later years, Bill Wilson realized that many who approached Alcoholics Anonymous turned away unhelped, and many more never even approached it. Wilson's main efforts outside A.A. in the final fifteen years of his life were attempts to remove the mental or psychological and physical obstacles that impeded some persons from openness to the spiritual.[6]

More clearly and explicitly aimed at this goal than his interest in LSD was Bill Wilson's final pursuit, "the Vitamin B-3 therapy." The two medical researchers with whom Wilson explored the LSD experience, Doctors Abram Hoffer and Humphrey Osmond, had discovered in their work with schizophrenics that massive doses of vitamin B-3 — also known as niacin or nicotinic acid — seemed to be of special help to those of their patients who were also alcoholics. Bill became so involved in this final interest of his long lifetime that he established a separate mailing address from which to spread information about this therapy, especially among physicians in Alcoholics Anonymous, urging upon them research efforts to verify the treatment's utility. Further, Wilson's enthusiasm for this treatment was so great that he is reputed to have said,

---

+ By "transcendence" in this paragraph is meant "outside or beyond the limits of ordinary self." No implication is intended that such "transcendence" touched directly the divine — except in an understanding that "the divine" *is* "that beyond the limits of the ordinary self." Wilson's understanding of a personalized God/Higher Power clearly went beyond such an understanding.

near the end of his life, that if his name were to go down in history as having made any contribution to mankind, he suspected that it would more likely be for his promotion of the B-3 therapy than for his role in the creation of Alcoholics Anonymous — a strong and surprising statement indeed.[7]

Because of his promotional efforts among A.A. physicians, Bill's involvement with the B-3 therapy became a threat to Alcoholics Anonymous with its tradition of "no opinion on outside issues." At the trustees' suggestion, Wilson moved the work to his home and then — with the co-operation of one physician-friend and still under pressure from his trustees — still further from identification with himself, to an Oyster Bay mailing address. On the one occasion when the question of Bill's involvement with the B-3 therapy was raised at a meeting of the General Service Conference of Alcoholics Anonymous, the proffered answer was succinct and definitive:

> Q.: Can you discuss the subject of Bill and Niacin in any detail?
> A.: Such a discussion has no place at this Conference, since it has nothing to do with A.A. The General Service Board is on record as recognizing that niacin has nothing to do with the A.A. program. Bill concurs in this.[8]

Bill Wilson's concern for those who seemed unable to "get the program" was the constant thread uniting the three aspects of his personal history that some feared might adversely affect Alcoholics Anonymous. In these instances, this concern verged so closely to "opinions on outside issues" — and so to the danger of being "drawn into public controversy" — that both Wilson and Alcoholics Anonymous carefully segregated such explorations from the A.A. name and from even erroneous hint of A.A. connection. In two other areas, however, the problems and solutions were not so clear-cut. The image of Alcoholics Anonymous held by those outside the fellowship and the problems of potential adherents who because of "other problems" seemed unable to grasp or even to approach the "simple program" of Alcoholics Anonymous continued to exercise the ingenuity of this fellowship so aware on the one hand of its dedication to "the Legacies of Recovery, Unity, and Service," and on the other hand of its own profound and essential limitations.

From almost the closing moment of the 1955 Coming of Age convention, Wilson — despite his overt withdrawal from A.A. leadership — undertook to promote a change in the ratio among the trustees of Alcoholics Anonymous from a majority of non-alcoholics to one of recovering alcoholics. The intertwining of this endeavor with expansion of the theme of "responsibility" was clear in his correspondence. In these letters, Bill's first concern was to include in A.A.'s responsibility those who remained outside its fellowship but were in obvious need of its program. More and more, however, perhaps because of the objectivity that retirement afforded, Bill moved to emphasize A.A.'s responsibility to sufferers from alcoholism who rejected its program because they found membership in its fellowship unattractive or even repulsive. Wilson apparently intuited that the "immaturity" diagnosis of alcoholics, which in this period some were extending into a critique of Alcoholics Anonymous itself, inhibited many who needed the program from approaching it. The most devastating criticism of those who are sensitive to their immaturity, after all, is to label their very efforts at maturity but further manifestations of their immaturity. Thus the stress Wilson placed upon "responsibility" as a characteristic of maturity furthered his aim of achieving the change in the trustee ratio. More deeply, however, the ratio change served the co-founder's lofty but limited concept of responsibility.[9]

Wilson's letters between 1955 and 1960 reveal him pulling back from a style of ratio change advocacy that at times seemed to some to threaten the independence that Alcoholics Anonymous had achieved from him at its Coming of Age convention. Over most of these five years, Bill relied upon the fellowship's elected delegates to each year's General Service Conference to carry forward and to implement his vision of responsibility. The 1954 General Service Conference theme had been "Confidence and Responsibility." A subtle shift of emphasis followed the 1955 lull during which, on the eve of A.A.'s most significant convention, its General Service Conference meditated on the theme "Awareness" (of the implications of the impending changes). In 1956, A.A.'s chosen representatives assembled under the theme "Confidence in Stability" — an apparent marshaling of a sense of direction as the fellowship confronted and internalized Wilson's changed role in their midst. By 1957, however, some of the delegates themselves caught Bill's earlier vision. Gathering to discuss the problems of "Stability and Responsibility without Complacency," they announced a secondary theme that echoed not only Wilson's earlier hopes for fellowship self-direction but also his enduring fear of organizational imposition. Their theme was "The Need for Authority Equal to Responsibility." Under the impact of this problem-recognizing motif, Wilson further subdued his advocacy of the ratio change. "At the forthcoming Confer-

ence I am having nothing to say whatever about the Trustee ratio. . . .
I really did quit at St. Louis and meant to."[10]

After the General Service Conference of 1959, however, Bill Wilson
again found himself torn by pressures that, while in conflict as to means,
were directed to the same end — the maturity of Alcoholics Anonymous.

> Nobody wishes to quit the "papa" business any more eagerly
> than I do. A.A. needs to stand on its own feet, that's the pri-
> mary thing. . . . What am I supposed to do? Am I supposed
> to transfer the remainder of my leadership to a Board in which
> I cannot have full confidence? I haven't the slightest ambition
> to be the Great White Father of A.A., I am fully fed up with
> it. . . . [But at St. Louis] I . . . agreed to turn over full re-
> sponsibility to the groups. . . . So, when they still refuse to
> name a majority of their own membership to run their own
> affairs, I wonder if they are really doing this. It looks to me
> rather that they were consulting their fears rather than their
> trust. . . ."[11]

And so Wilson, clearly by 1961, entered the lists again, now even
more strongly and explicitly stressing the responsibilities of "Responsibility" itself. A late 1961 letter to Bill from Dr. Tiebout, a letter in which
the Connecticut psychiatrist promised to vote against Wilson's proposed
trustee ratio change, offered — in the reason Tiebout gave for his stand
— the clear reason why Wilson felt it necessary to push his project:
"Most [A.A.s] are not impressed by the need to grow up." If this reason
itself proved not sufficiently stinging to his former client, the doctor
concluded by reminding Bill of something he had been telling him for
almost twenty years: "Incidentally, may I again stress what I noted in
passing [!]: I am not very much moved by the emphasis on growing up.
Most adolescents are very conscious of having grown up. The trouble is
that they do not know that they still have a lot to learn."[12]

The battle continued, intermittently but at times bitterly, over the
next four years. As it progressed, Wilson increasingly urged A.A.'s
trustees to ponder the meanings of "responsibility," especially that of
Alcoholics Anonymous to those outside its fellowship who had apparent
need of its program. By late 1964, Dr. Tiebout came sufficiently around
to Bill's way of thinking to vote for the ratio change. In his letter of
thanks to the psychiatrist, Wilson stressed that he himself "continued to
be ever more interested in the psychological implications of the change.
[For] in considerable part, progress seems to be measured by the
movement from irresponsibility toward responsibility." A similarly

motivated letter to another trustee-supporter drove home the same point. After reviewing his concept of "leadership," Wilson summarized: "The word 'responsibility' is the keynote of every democracy, and of Alcoholics Anonymous also. Nearly every A.A. principle asks us to become more responsible, as individuals, as areas, and as a whole."[13]

Yet the question and concern continued to gnaw. A final exchange of letters between Tiebout and Wilson rehearsed the points at issue. Despite his own recent vote, Bill's former therapist rebuked:

> You state that the continuation of the non-alcoholic majority at the top "would be a standing confession of our weakness and irresponsibility." I simply disagree with that observation. . . .
>
> I was not impressed by this coming-of-age bit. Every adolescent glories in his sense of being grown-up but he still has a lot to learn before he is really mature. . . . The mature person has no reason to assert his independence; he is comfortable in the realization that he does not have to go it alone in life.
>
> Your continued stress on A.A.'s need to assert independence strikes me as lamentable. I wish you would stop reminding A.A.'s that they need to grow up. That can start some very screwy thinking.[14]

The ex-patient replied in concepts likely learned in his own therapy:

> Almost any experienced A.A. would heartily agree that we are immature adolescents, and he would include himself. To outgrow some of these traits and thereby enable us to better deal with adult responsibility has always been a chief aim — sobriety being only the starting point.
>
> Since "coming of age" seems a pretty important turning point in the life of an individual, we have assumed this would be the case for A.A. as a whole — hence "St. Louis, 1955." To most of us this meant the assumption of full responsibility for the management of our own affairs. At the time we were careful to note that we *had not* "grown up" — we simply proposed to go on our own, minus the former guardianship of the old-timers.
>
> . . . It is notable that each of these [elided] projects encountered heavy resistance from our "protectors" — a Board of Trustees composed of "old-timers" and nonalcoholics. The nub of their view always was that our instability and immaturity would preclude success.
>
> For ten years now we have seen much the same phenomenon respecting the implications of the ratio business. . . . The underlying, though not spoken, argument was the same: it was

"immaturity" and, surprisingly, I find this inference in your letter.

When I look at such events and ask to what extent these developments — over Trustee protests — were powered by childish rebellion on the one hand, and by legitimate aspiration on the other, I can't estimate. I can only report that the net result of these forces has been in the direction of increased A.A. responsibility, despite the fears of our protectors on the Board.[15]

In the early summer of 1965, exultantly flexing its sense of internationalism by meeting in Toronto, Ontario, the Thirtieth Anniversary Convention of Alcoholics Anonymous accepted as its keynote "The Declaration." That declaration embodied Wilson's decade-long vision of A.A.'s ultimate responsibility. In accepting it, each member of Alcoholics Anonymous pledged: . . . "I Am Responsible. When anyone, anywhere, reaches out for help, I want the hand of A.A. always to be there. And for that: I am responsible." Bill Wilson himself, his insatiable thirst now directed to alcoholics rather than alcohol, had set up this theme, having used his keynote address at that year's General Service Conference to warn against a too complacent focus on international diffusion and increasing numbers. His pointed challenge began, "What happened to the six hundred thousand who approached [A.A.] and left?" and the co-founder went on to estimate that the program and fellowship had "reached less than ten per cent" of those needing its help.[16]

Under the impact of this continuing stress on "Responsibility," the long sought change in A.A.'s trustee ratio finally occurred in 1966. The terse but emotion-laden words of the published "Landmarks in A.A. History" read, "1966: Change in ratio of Trustees of the General Service Board to provide for a two-thirds majority of alcoholic members, the historic occasion on which the A.A. Fellowship accepts top responsibility for the future conduct of all its affairs."[17]

Wilson's concern through these efforts and events did not arise only from the long-standing psychiatric critique of the emotional immaturity of Alcoholics Anonymous. In the three years previous, this criticism had three times burst the bonds of the sedate professional journals in which to that point it had been buried. Articles in *Harpers, The Nation*, and — the unkindest cut — even the *Saturday Evening Post*, had strongly and sharply flayed Alcoholics Anonymous over both supposed developments within its fellowship and the philosophy underlying its program. Such criticism came to the attention not of professionals but of the public-at-large who perhaps needed the program's therapy but could now rationalize the refusal to seek it.[18]

Thus, the concept of "Responsibility" became relevant. Anything about A.A. that discouraged investigation of or openness to its program by those in need of its therapy was clearly a manifestation of irresponsibility and so a testimony to "immaturity." Alcoholics Anonymous itself, of course, faithful to its Tenth Tradition concerning "public controversy" even over itself, did not offer public defense or openly enter the fray. Indeed, Wilson advised those protesting the cavalier treatment of their beloved fellowship to heed not only its Tenth Tradition but the possible grains of truth in the criticism itself:

> Probably the Cain article kept some people away from A.A. Maybe some will stay sick longer, and maybe a few will die because of it.
>
> But so far as we folks who are in the fold are concerned, I think it a rather good experience. In all the years this is the first thorough-going criticism our Fellowship ever had. So the practice of absorbing stuff like that in good humor should be of value.
>
> Despite its petulant and biased nature, the piece did contain some half-truths. It certainly applied to some A.A.'s at some places at some times! Therefore it should help us take heed of these natural tendencies.[19]

The three articles were the work of two authors, Arthur Cain and Jerome Ellison, but the foundation for them and the climate of opinion for their diffusion were the product of a slightly earlier, book length, semi-popular presentation by a distinguished psychiatrist and a sociologist. Dr. Morris E. Chafetz and Harold W. Demone, Jr., in 1962 published *Alcoholism and Society*. The chapter examining "Alcoholics Anonymous" reviewed the Steps and Traditions of the program and fellowship perceptively and in general sympathetically, calling attention especially to the fact that A.A.'s success testified to the defects of other, more classically medical, treatments. In conclusion, Chafetz and Demone reviewed approvingly but not scathingly the usual psychiatric critique of Alcoholics Anonymous. Among the "social and psychological mechanisms" that made A.A. work were that it furnished "a gratifying maternal reunion symbol . . . [for] the surroundings of the anonymous mass are comforting and secure"; Alcoholics Anonymous required of its members "compulsive, almost vengeful attention to the A.A. way of life [thus utilizing constructively] the mechanism of compulsion"; it "point[ed] the road back to our middle class way of life . . . perhaps the

essence of A.A. derived as it is from our dominant 'Protestant Ethic'";
"most striking" were "the sect-like or cult-like aspects of A.A."[20]

All this had been heard before and even acknowledged, especially by
Wilson, as possibly even usefully true. The same might be said of the
foundation on which Chafetz based his final and most devastating criticism, for to note that "the conscious turning toward God or emotional
giving to others requires a certain sense of being a person" may be
understood as simply a slightly different formulation of the sense that
had led Wilson to his LSD and vitamin B-3 explorations. But the final
critique itself, the one patently picked up by Cain and Ellison, was less
acceptable to and surely directly threatening of A.A.'s self-image. "In
our opinion, A.A. is really not interested in alcoholics in general, but
only as they relate to A.A. itself."[21]

Arthur Cain, in two articles in 1963 (*Harper's*) and 1965 (*Saturday
Evening Post*), offered less restrained criticism. In an opening paragraph
that reflected the pomposity he found in Alcoholics Anonymous, the
Columbia-trained psychologist flayed "a movement which is becoming
one of America's most fanatical religious cults: 'A.A.'" Cain expatiated
on his "religious" critique by accusing Alcoholics Anonymous of being
"anti-science," "intolerant," "dogmatic," and even of having its own
"Holy Grail ('the actual coffee pot Anne used to make the first A.A.
coffee')" and more. "The cake and coffee served after meetings are just
refreshments, not the body and blood of Jesus Christ."[22]+

Any at all sympathetic to Alcoholics Anonymous could readily turn a
deaf ear to such an assault as being itself wildly intemperate. Indeed,
Bill Wilson — even as he complained that the charges were "garish" —
suggested that in them might lurk "half-truths" from which A.A. members could learn. But Cain's deeper criticism was more telling and
harder for A.A. to swallow. His fundamental call was for "sobriety in
Alcoholics Anonymous without slavery to it." As he picked up and
summarized his theme in his 1965 *Post* "Speaking Out" contribution:
"A.A. has become a dogmatic cult whose chapters too often turn sobriety into slavery to A.A. Because of its narrow outlook, Alcoholics
Anonymous prevents thousands from ever being cured. Moreover A.A.

+ The photograph of "the actual coffee pot . . ." that appears in *AACA* (following p. 114) might be accepted as justifying the "Holy Grail" reference. Despite attendance at hundreds of A.A. meetings in the course of this research, I
am at a loss to suggest the possible basis for any sense of Eucharist in the stale
cheese, dry crackers, and invariably either too strong or too weak coffee served,
except perhaps to the most mystically inclined — which Cain clearly is not.

has retarded scientific research into one of America's most serious health problems."[23]

The key to one aspect of the Cain critique lay hidden in the first verb in the just-quoted passage, "has become." It was the key also to what Alcoholics Anonymous felt to be the sharper-than-a-serpent's-tooth attack of Jerome Ellison in 1964, "Alcoholics Anonymous: Dangers of Success." The *Nation* writer directed his assault at the "Headquarters" of Alcoholics Anonymous, castigating it as "rich in its own right," run by "self-styled experts" in service to an "ultraconservative board of trustees" and in its "affluence and short-sighted conservatism" offering "tacit endorsement to racial segregation" and preserving "the A.A. 'Big Book' [despite its having] an out-of-date, early-century, historical sound." Ellison reserved his praise for "the rank and file [which] teems with exciting, relevant, informed and up-to-the-minute experience" in much the same way that Cain had harked back to a golden past and urged that "Alcoholics Anonymous should return to its original purpose of being a much-needed first aid station" in his insistence that "sobriety in itself is not a way of life. It is simply the absence of intoxication."[24]

A.A.'s late sixties stress on "responsibility" and change in the trustee ratio at least indirectly spoke to these criticisms. A historian may be more direct, finding more than a little anomaly in a critic of the "religion" of Alcoholics Anonymous basing his assault on an appeal to a largely imaginary Golden Age in the past; also in a scolder of a Headquarters as short-sightedly conservative and so separated from its grass roots, citing as his only two specific examples matters clearly due more to "rank and file" practice than to organizational imposition. For all the truth in the criticisms offered by Cain and Ellison, the continuing history of Alcoholics Anonymous at least to the time of Bill Wilson's death contradicted their fundamental thrust.

"Responsibility" declared and the trustee ratio change effected, Bill Wilson's last years — in many ways A.A.'s first years — were quiet. More and more wracked by the emphysema that would eventually kill him, his public appearances became fewer, and even his letter writing diminished to a comparative trickle. At the Thirty-Fifth Anniversary Convention of Alcoholics Anonymous in Miami Beach in 1970, Bill was brought before the conventioneers in a wheelchair to receive their tribute in a standing ovation. Within seven months he would be dead, but now he "reached up, gripped the lectern with both hands, and in one smooth motion hauled himself to his full six-foot-three height" to address briefly those gathered. The keynote of the convention was its

"Declaration of Unity," and to this Bill Wilson gave hearty and appropriate blessing. "This we owe to A.A.'s future: to place our common welfare first; to keep our Fellowship united. For on A.A. unity depend our lives and the lives of those to come."[25]

It was a significant theme: a reminder of limitation. For twenty-five years, a consistent and ultimately momentous problem had harassed A.A. and Bill Wilson: how to maintain the *unity* of Alcoholics Anonymous? A.A.'s unity was rooted in and sprang from its singleness of purpose — helping the alcoholic. Two corollaries flowed from this identity of unity with singleness of purpose. First, Alcoholics Anonymous restricted its endeavors to the one problem shared by all alcoholics — their alcoholism. Second, because all alcoholics shared the problem of alcoholism, any claim to "specialness" — to *difference* from other alcoholics — threatened their sobriety. At depth, as A.A.'s insight of the centrality of the need for the alcoholic to "quit playing God" made clear, it was the claim to specialness that was "the root of [the alcoholic's] troubles." The program of Alcoholics Anonymous worked because it deflated the alcoholic's claim to specialness. Yet precisely because its program worked, A.A.'s very success in time gave rise to a new manifestation of the problem of specialness. This outcome was not surprising, for also fundamental to A.A.'s insight was the perception that even sober alcoholics continued to be *alcoholics*. The problem of A.A.'s success, then, became how to maintain its unity when because of its success some who continued to consider themselves "special" exerted constant pressure either to narrow the gateway to their particular expression of A.A. or to claim wider competence for the program and fellowship as a whole. The threat to the basic Alcoholics Anonymous principle that identified its unity and its singleness of purpose had come, over the years, in two ways: as a challenge to the adequacy of the fellowship's claim to be "Anonymous"; and as a constant tug to expand its understanding of "Alcoholics."[26]

An early and constant concern had been the inclination of some members of Alcoholics Anonymous to form "special groups."[+] The more general A.A. attitude was summed up in the title of the fellowship's 1976 pamphlet, "Do You Think You're *Different?*"[27]

Alcoholics Anonymous by its very name promised anonymity. A common reminder was often spoken at the end of meetings. "This has

+ By "special groups" (more recently called "special-purpose groups") are meant groups claiming to be "Alcoholics Anonymous" but restricted in attendance according to some shared factor in the lives of their members other than their alcoholism.

been a typical meeting of Alcoholics Anonymous. We remind you that we are 'Alcoholics Anonymous,' and ask that you remember from to-night what you have heard and not whom you have seen." Yet some oc-cupations and professions were from the beginning especially fearful of the perils of broken anonymity. Periodically, groups of physicians, cler-gy, and police indicated a desire to meet separately. The main considera-tion was that assured protection of anonymity would help potential newcomers. Through such "special groups," requisite identification could more easily take place, and they would remove a barrier to ac-ceptance of Alcoholics Anonymous — the fear of professional ostracism or of diminished occupational effectiveness.[28]

Another main impetus for "special groups" came from the same con-cern with the wary potential newcomer but sprang also from some perception of the religion inherent in Alcoholics Anonymous. Some within A.A. who shared a particular religious tradition at times indi-cated anxiety that their religious peers mistrusted the program's close-ness to religion. Further, these believed that they could explore the "spiritual depths" of the A.A. way of life more deeply with others who shared their religious convictions.[29]

Given the Alcoholics Anonymous definition of an A.A. group — "Traditionally two or more alcoholics meeting together for purposes of sobriety may consider themselves an A.A. group," — there seemed no intrinsic barrier to such "special groups." Yet Alcoholics Anonymous did not grant such gatherings recognition as A.A. groups. An "official" A.A. group was one listed in some publication, national, regional, or local; and A.A.'s New York General Service Office and its local Central Service Offices listed only those groups to which access was totally open, i.e., those that applied the traditional sole criterion for membership of "a desire to stop drinking." Any other restriction indicated to Alcoholics Anonymous that such was not an A.A. group.[30+]

Further, in a fairly short time, virtually all members of Alcoholics

+ Recently, at least in large metropolitan areas, some A.A. meetings are listed in official "Meeting Lists" as "Women's" or "Gay." I have no way of reconciling this with what is said in this paragraph, beyond noting: (1) such did not exist before 1971, when this narrative essentially stops; (2) such meetings tend to be indistinguishable from many other A.A. small group meetings that also seem to verge as much to group therapy as to be "A.A."; (3) none which I attended *excluded* "visitors" — rather, the visitor was told that he would be "more comfort-able" at "a regular A.A. meeting" but was allowed to remain if such were not readily available; (4) the *AAGV* 34:5 (October 1977) contained five articles treat-ing, in general critically, of "special-purpose groups" (pp. 6–18), calling this "an issue of moment in A.A."

Anonymous became so imbued with the philosophy and spirit of the program that they themselves insisted that such "special groups" were "not really A.A." Such gatherings convened usually for the indicated purpose of making easier investigation by the separately self-conscious potential members described. Members of Alcoholics Anonymous present at these "meetings," however, insisted that such gatherings were "not really A.A."; and they especially stressed the importance of "identification with and through feelings" rather than according to externals. Once the wary newcomer found others who shared his or her "specialness" as well as "drinking problem," these others began shepherding the novice to "regular, real" meetings of Alcoholics Anonymous.[31]

The essential point was that saying, "I am an alcoholic doctor, or minister, or policeman, or Catholic, or Jew, or Humanist, or *anything* was in no way equivalent to the crucial acceptance of "bottom" inherent in "I am an alcoholic — Period." The self-consciously professional and religious were usually marked as "getting the program" when they could speak without indicating what they did to earn a living, or how, specifically, they related to their "Higher Power" beyond the fundamental acceptance of the "Power greater than ourselves" of the Second Step of the program of Alcoholics Anonymous.

A more sensitive facet of the "special group" question arose from the long-standing American practice of segregation by color. Alcoholics Anonymous was harshly criticized on this score, and legend held that Bill Wilson, a Vermont Yankee, private-school graduate who had inhabited the world of Wall Street, was discomfited by black people.[32] +

Wilson did engage in correspondence on this question. Complainants of both sides appealed to him. His suggestions — as always, he rarely proposed "answers" — contained two themes. First, obey the law; do not make A.A. too odd for any community — "we are outcast enough

+   The phenomenon referred to here is more usually described as "racial segregation." Three considerations impel to my preference for the phrase "segregation by color": 1) "color" is the more exact term — "race" cannot be seen; 2) recent anthropological thought cautions against thinking in terms of "race" on the grounds both that it is theoretically inadequate and that it too readily can feed discriminatory bigotry; 3) the not-God theme that I find inherent in the philosophy of Alcoholics Anonymous essentially implies that there is but one "race" — the *human* race — and that all members of it are first and fundamentally equal in their shared not-God-ness. I regret if my choice here offends, but I hope these considerations plus the discussion to follow in Chapter Nine will add to the solution rather than to the problem of one of the tragedies of our time. If I have judged wrongly, forgive me: I too am human, and so not God.

already"; and "live the program" — "take your own inventory," not that of others. Second, however, he responded here in exactly the same way as to any question of "special groups" or exclusionary practice. Alcoholics Anonymous would never print "whites only" or "blacks only" in a listing of meetings, but if the community understood such from the listed meeting place, well, that was reality — part of "the things I cannot change." Those excluded, given the A.A. understanding of its history and tradition, were perhaps by this very fact being invited by their Higher Power to form a needed new group. This last could be and has been viewed as cowardly evasion as applied to the question at hand; yet such judgment seems eminently rash as well as profoundly unhistorical, given the broad range of problems for which this faith-rooted solution was suggested and Bill Wilson's acceptance of his own — and A.A.'s — limitations.[33]

But "special groups" concerned over anonymity or even over the very special problem of segregation by color were not the only nor even the major problem posed by the sense of "special" to which some in Alcoholics Anonymous clung. A more profound threat to the fellowship's understanding of itself arose from the tendency of some members who had problems other than alcoholism to expand the scope of "their program" to others with whom they shared *only* that "other problem." Efforts to form groups called "Alcoholics Anonymous" that would treat *both* problems were especially great among those whose "other problems" involved psychoactive drugs other than alcohol — the "Pill Problem" to which Bill Wilson and Alcoholics Anonymous had adverted as early as 1945. One aspect of the solution here was the development of the concept of "chemical dependency" and of treatment for it outside of Alcoholics Anonymous even if often by A.A. members.[34]

More ticklish was the problem of members with other problems who sought to restrict their "A.A." to those like themselves; i.e., alcoholics *also* addicted to "pills." Beginning in the late 1950s and through the 1960s, Bill Wilson and Alcoholics Anonymous wrestled with this question. Significantly, on this fundamentally philosophical rather than organizational problem, the fellowship turned implicitly, instinctively, and apparently without awareness of any inconsistency to its "retired" cofounder for guidance. Resolutely, Wilson in many letters and one key article drew from two principles one significant and revealing practical conclusion.[35]

The first principle: since in order to be "Alcoholics Anonymous" a group must be "of alcoholics" and "seeking sobriety, . . . it has . . . been learned that *there is no possible way to make nonalcoholics into A.A.*

members"; "a group [even] of A.A.s dedicated to a special purpose [other than sobriety] . . . is not an A.A. group." The second principle: "as individuals we ought to carry our A.A. knowledge and experience into other areas. . . . All of us want the widest use of A.A. principles and practice to be the privilege of anyone who wishes to try." The practical conclusion: *"But not under straight A.A. auspices."* [36]

In every letter as well as in his "Problems Other Than Alcohol" article, Wilson drove home two points. Alcoholics Anonymous had limitations: *therefore*, the name *Alcoholics Anonymous* was to be restricted to alcoholics seeking sobriety. [37]

Such conjunction of A.A.'s concern to protect the exclusiveness of its *name* with insistence that A.A.'s essential *unity* derived from and was even identical with its acceptance of its own limitation bore a profound significance. Alcoholics Anonymous here applied to itself as fellowship the stricture of not-God-ness that its program imposed upon its members. Thus, under the guidance of its co-founder, Alcoholics Anonymous witnessed in its very being that the acceptance of limitation begot a saving wholeness. [38]

The sense that a saving strength arises from the acceptance of weakness is a profoundly religious insight. A.A.'s own intuition of this was clear, and, surprisingly, most clear in a choice the fellowship made about *not* protecting its name long before the problem of "other problems" began to pinch. Early in 1951, seeking "to protect its name," the newly-formed General Service Conference of Alcoholics Anonymous investigated the wisdom of seeking legal incorporation through a Congressional charter similar to that held by the American Red Cross. The Committee assigned this exploratory task recommended against such incorporation. The last two of the nine reasons given for this decision established the point:

8. We believe that "spiritual faith" and a "way of life" cannot be incorporated.
9. A.A. can and will survive so long as it remains a spiritual faith and a way of life open to all men and women who suffer from alcoholism. [39]

The prime witness of the name "Alcoholics Anonymous" lay in its declaration of weakness and limitation. An "alcoholic" was one who could not control his or her drinking, and anonymity served as an effective reminder of the vulnerability of this condition. This very proclamation of weakness, the source of the fellowship's only but glorious "success," demonstrated as first truth that strength comes from weakness, ability from impotence, identity from limitation.[40]

The A.A. member who lived the program in the fellowship discovered that the precise factor in his life that provided the basis for his sharing in the salvation of sobriety was individual weakness. Members shared identically that which was the First Step toward their salvation — the acceptance of personal weakness and of the limitation imposed by their powerlessness over alcohol. Thus Alcoholics Anonymous solved the paradoxical challenge of the alcoholic's sense of being "different" in a way that allowed, opened to, and indeed even enforced a joyous pluralism. A unity of identity founded in shared weakness could not be threatened — on the contrary, could only be enriched — by "differences"; for "difference" became by definition "good" when its basis was identical identifying weakness.[41]

Thus Alcoholics Anonymous unraveled the "But I'm Different" denial that had haunted it from the first words of Bill D., "A.A. Number 3." The program proclaimed the telling truth: "*Yes*, you are different, only not in the limitation that identifies you with others identically limited, but in whatever strength in you arises from that weakness. Acknowledge that you share our weakness that we may also share in each other's strength — it is the necessary first step." The anonymous alcoholic within Alcoholics Anonymous achieved identity by positive reference — identification — with weakness. Then and only then could individuating identity by the negative reference of felt-difference beneficially take place. The sense of "But I'm Different" thus became a source of social living rather than the alienating fear it had been in the tortured life of the drinking alcoholic.[42]

The fundamental flaw that all observers consistently noted in the drinking alcoholic was "defective socialization." The underlying dynamic as invariably pointed out in Alcoholics Anonymous was its process of "socialization." How *this* "worked" was A.A.'s inculcation in its members of both the theory and the practice of joyous pluralism as the key to relationships among those self-consciously not-God.[43]

"Joyous pluralism." The concept and its living out infused Alcoholics Anonymous from its moment of origin and throughout its history. Implicit in "sources" as diverse as William James and the Oxford Group, Ebby T. and Doctors Carl Jung and William Silkworth, it blossomed in the first meeting between William Griffith Wilson and Dr. Robert Holbrook Smith — "two men who in other circumstances would never have spent ten seconds together." Beyond their Vermont background, the rigidly reserved and socially self-conscious surgeon and his fawningly promotional new acquaintance in 1935 shared absolutely nothing — except their alcoholism. Yet from this meeting and this sharing — and their results — sprang an enduring mutual respect: a respect for precisely what each in his "difference" could offer the other and through the other, many others.[44]

The continuing history of Alcoholics Anonymous demonstrated and validated this profound insight. In New York, the influence of the deeply religious Fitz M. offset the tugs on the developing program of the militantly agnostic Hank P. and the erratic Jim B. In Akron-Cleveland, the abrasive personality of Clarence S. balanced the pull of the sweetly dispositioned T. Henry Williams and the spiritually dedicated Henrietta Seiberling. Outside influences impinged, and were absorbed, similarly — whether the critical cynicism of Jack Alexander or the gentle profundity of Father Edward Dowling. A.A.'s claim of Wilson and Smith as "co-founders" rested not so much on their very real participation in these tensions as on the tiny part of each of them that remained above the struggles and saw the differences for what they proved to be in A.A. history: richly fruitful rather than harmfully destructive — and so "good."

This perception, this sense, flowed vividly through Bill Wilson's two favorite images. "In my Father's house there are many mansions" meant to Wilson that *difference* was *good*. Recalling and relating to this awareness a childhood memory — "My grandfather used to have a saying, 'It takes all kinds of folks to make a world'" — Bill found and proclaimed it not only foolish but impossible for himself or for Alcoholics Anonymous ever to forget that "one *can't* be all things to all men." Wilson's cherished image of "Pilgrim's Progress" carried the same message: limitation, and because of it, the need for others. If all were "pilgrims," then no one had "arrived." "Progress" upwards — as "progression" downwards — if possible, was also necessary.[45]

For all their thinking in terms of "salvation," neither Bill Wilson nor Dr. Bob Smith nor Alcoholics Anonymous as such ever fell into the treacherous trap such an understanding could lay — the oppressive burden of obligation to impose vision and the consequent intolerance that often ensnared those conscious of possessing "saving truth." "In the early days of A.A. I spent a lot of time trying to get people to agree with me, to practice A.A. principles as I did, and so forth. For so long as I did this . . . A.A. grew very slowly." Quickly although painfully Wilson early noted, "Nor have we ever had the slightest success in insisting upon some particular form of salvation. Nevertheless we can bring people within the reach of salvation — that is, of the salvation *they* choose." [46]

Fundamental to this understanding was Wilson's own sense of limitation — and sense of humor. As the co-founder urged his followers in one early plea for "openness" in Alcoholics Anonymous, "The way our 'worthy' alcoholics have sometimes tried to judge the 'less worthy' is, as we look back on it, rather comical. Imagine, if you can, one alcoholic judging another!" Late in his career Wilson explicitly rejoiced "[A.A.] works for people with very *differing* views — that is *good!*" Very early in his public career, Bill in sly quotation of Dr. Bob had sagely informed those gathered under the august auspices of Yale University to hear their and A.A.'s "secret": "As someone well put it, 'Honesty gets us sober but tolerance keeps us sober.'" [47]

Two decades later, William Griffith Wilson drove home the same point and a deeper one in replying to a correspondent who, upset at some of the "goings-on" in Alcoholics Anonymous, had sought to enlist the co-founder's support for his own vision — "in many ways attractive" — of "what A.A. should be": "It seems absolutely necessary for most of us to get over the idea that man is God." [48]

PART TWO

The Interpretation

INTRODUCTION

"A.A. is an utter simplicity which encases a complete mystery."
(Wilson to J.L.K., 1943)

Part One has considered in detail the history of Alcoholics Anonymous — the story of the origins and development of the ideas conveyed within the fellowship.

A historical phenomenon may be likened to a plant or a flower. Each blossom possesses its own distinctive quality, but its beauty — and especially an observer's appreciation of its uniqueness — is strongly influenced by two circumstances: the background against which it is seen and the nature of the environment in which it has grown. The historian calls the first the "historical context" and refers to the second as the "climate of opinion."

The historical narrative of Part One examined what may be called the "soil of opinion," primarily the Oxford Group, out of which Alcoholics Anonymous grew and blossomed. It also noted and analyzed other nutrients: the ideas of Dr. Jung and William James, for example. The story revealed especially the primary role of the early members' own personal experience in sustaining and shaping their program's growth.

There are several preliminary points to be noted as we turn to examine the larger contexts from which Alcoholics Anonymous came to be. To the historian, the study of history is never reductionist: it never implies downgrading any phenomenon to "nothing but." Yet the discipline of history imposes the obligation to attempt some interpretation, at least of *meaning*.

The "meaning" of Alcoholics Anonymous to the individual sober member of the fellowship is, of course, first and foremost that through its program he attained sobriety. There is perhaps no greater meaning possible, even if Alcoholics Anonymous had saved but one life rather than the over one million to which its members point. But "meaning" is also a social and cultural phenomenon. The first task of Part Two is to explore *this* meaning: what Alcoholics Anonymous says about and to its culture.

This examination of meaning in context has also a second function, one more precisely historical but not for that any less significant. That Alcoholics Anonymous did not drop from the sky fully formed is by now clear from the historical narrative which examined the influences upon A.A. of Dr. Silkworth and Dr. Jung, of William James and the Oxford Group, of the particular experiences of founding members as diverse as Bill Wilson, Dr. Bob Smith, Fitz M., Jim B., and Clarence S. of Cleveland. Yet passed by within the narrative except for a note was an intriguing congruence that, while it had no significantly direct influence upon Alcoholics Anonymous, will surely interest later historians.

Alcoholics Anonymous was not the only therapy for alcoholics that flourished in its time. Other approaches to treating alcoholism, although they derived from sources very different from the influences that impinged upon A.A., used similar methods and even incorporated some of the same ideas that a forgetfulness of history leads later thinkers to associate exclusively with Alcoholics Anonymous. In particular, the approach of Richard R. Peabody, as developed by Francis Chambers and popularized especially by the talented writer Jim Bishop, not only preceded in time Wilson's own sobriety but was well into the 1950s accepted and endorsed by many doctors and clergy much more enthusiastically than was Alcoholics Anonymous. Why did Alcoholics Anonymous take root and over time flourish so spectacularly while such other, similar approaches soon languished into the demise all too usual for "new approaches" to the treatment of alcoholism? The analysis of context that follows in Part Two will, I believe, answer this question at least for the present generation of historians.[1]

Three cautions must preface this Introduction to Part Two. These concern the sources of evidence and the questions of idealization and advocacy.

The history narrated in Part One focused upon Bill Wilson and the General Service Office of Alcoholics Anonymous in New York City. "Real A.A.," a reproach might remind, "is the grass roots, the individual groups." I heartily agree. Yet, all members of Alcoholics Anonymous cherish their "Big Book," and most over the years revealed deep interest in Bill Wilson's other thoughts and writings. It was to "Bill W." in New York that most A.A. members throughout the country turned with their problems so long as the co-founder lived, and the *ideas* that are Alcoholics Anonymous nowhere else appear in writing whether published or unpublished with the aura that surrounds Wilson's contributions.[2]

Nevertheless, because Alcoholics Anonymous is fellowship as well as program, Part Two attempts to balance the concentration of Part One on A.A. literature and documents. The generalizations that follow, especially in Chapters Eight and Nine, derive first from actual attendance at a variety of A.A. meetings. Because Alcoholics Anonymous is anonymous, these are uncitable; and therefore, when appropriate, such citations as are offered are to printed or written sources. Yet it should be kept in mind that the development of analysis that follows is based less on the perusal of documents than on approaching Alcoholics Anonymous — albeit critically — on its own terms, as fellowship.

The second caution is that the total, over-all picture of Alcoholics Anonymous detailed in Part Two presents a somewhat idealized vision. Not all A.A. members and not every A.A. group can be adduced as evidence for any of the facets of Alcoholics Anonymous here described, and the total description probably fits no individual A.A. group exactly. Individuals and groups of any kind rarely live up to all their ideals, nor are all implications that are clearly present in a philosophy always lived out in practice even by those who enthusiastically embrace that philosophy. Yet what follows describes not merely an ideal. Most of the A.A. groups observed and most of the A.A. members met *did* reflect in daily life and practice a living out of the ideas presented. There are exceptions, but they are by and large just that — exceptions, if what actually occurs within almost any A.A. group at virtually any A.A. meeting be carefully and open-mindedly observed.

Finally, because of the nature of the data on which Part Two is based and the type of interpretation that it attempts, a caution is in order against reading exposition as advocacy. Having found in the historical study of Alcoholics Anonymous a coherent world view — the vision of fundamental human not-God-ness — I have tried to define and to explain that implicit but over-all philosophy as clearly as possible. This is any writer's obligation to his subject, and it implies two corollaries. First, as has been noted above in another connection, no one A.A. meeting or A.A. group or item of A.A. literature will evidence all the points treated — and I do not mean to imply that they *should* do so. Second, the congruity of the A.A. world view with, or its deviation from, my own philosophy and values are not meant to be argued in this book. Neither such congruity nor such deviation has provided either a criterion for inclusion or a guide to interpretation.

The task of interpretation to which Part Two addresses itself is divided into three parts in the three chapters that follow. Chapter Seven establishes and describes the larger context and meaning of American history in which Alcoholics Anonymous came into existence and developed. After an opening discussion of the meanings of "spiritual" and "religious" as these terms were understood by early A.A. members, Chapter Eight explores the larger history of specifically religious ideas as they are reflected by Alcoholics Anonymous, with special attention to American expressions of them. The final chapter examines the precise significance of Alcoholics Anonymous within these contexts, striving first to define and then to interpret the message proclaimed by Alcoholics Anonymous to its larger culture.

It is the writer's hope that the message of Alcoholics Anonymous — "not-God" — is clearly defined, examined, analyzed, and enabled to be heard by this book. Only the book's readers can make it come to pass that this message — if appropriate — be heeded.

VII

The Larger Context of
American History

So long as its founding members — especially the charismatic Bill
Wilson — lived, Alcoholics Anonymous was in the process of formation.
Even after their deaths, development as well as growth continued.
Sheer time and proven effectiveness have enshrined A.A.'s Twelve
Steps and Twelve Traditions, but the essentially unorganized nature of
the fellowship works against any absolute rigidities. However dogmatic
or inclined to absolutism any A.A. group may become, any two or three
alcoholics who disagree with such a turn may depart and by meeting for
the purpose of sobriety form their own, new, A.A. group. So Alcoholics
Anonymous grew and so will it continue, despite complex problems
such as those of "other problems" and "special groups." [1]

Yet even among those who prize such essential openness, some stages
of formation are more significant than others. By its very sensitivity to
and definition of its "Coming of Age," Alcoholics Anonymous itself
carefully marked off the years that in the fellowship's own awareness
were the most formative. Those years, from 1935 to 1955, saw A.A.'s
program for both alcoholics and itself hammered out and set forth in
the fellowship's formulation of its Twelve Steps and Twelve Traditions
and the publication of its key books, *Alcoholics Anonymous* and *Twelve
Steps and Twelve Traditions*. During those first twenty years, A.A. membership grew from two to 133,000 and attained international diffusion.
These phenomena in themselves offered adequate evidence that further growth and development would be significantly different. Signally,
as one of the most important acts of its coming of age, Alcoholics
Anonymous in 1955 accepted itself as a historical entity and thus as
formed enough to *have* a history. [2]

The twenty years from 1935 to 1955 span three decades. "The thir-

ties," "the forties," and "the fifties" are our customary categories, however tortured their interpretation must at times be because the obstinate
realities of history rarely present themselves in such neat packages.Yet
for our purpose here, the three decades that embraced Alcoholics
Anonymous in its self-consciously formative stage offer interpretive as
well as convenient labels, especially in popular memory and understanding.[3]

The 1930s were the "Depression Decade." As some of its alcoholics at
decade's depth reached their realization of personal "bottom," the culture reckoned its own deflation "Great," both as Crash and Depression.
At their bottom of Crash and Depression, Americans struggled to understand these phenomena in order to rise from them. In their understanding of how their plight had occurred, many arrived at insights
similar to those of their alcoholic compatriots. They looked back on the
decade of the twenties as a false and artificial "high," deeming that their
downfall had come about because of high-flying speculation — because
of blithe forgetfulness if not denial that paper wealth was not real
wealth. The people of the thirties also revolted against the 1920s as a
decade of privacies. Some harkened readily to leaders who offered
them a sense of unity, if only against so largely mythical a common
enemy as "Wall Street." Others sought new bases for more practical
unions in enthusiasms as diverse as the C.I.O. and the Civilian Conservation Corps, the bonus march and Townsend Clubs. Internationally,
however, Americans of the 1930s clung to their imagined isolationism
— or thought they did.[4]

In the 1940s, this last isolationism gave way to a temporarily repressed but deeply craved dedication as the attack on Pearl Harbor
brought home the war that ended the Depression. This new crusade
aimed not to "make the world safe for democracy" but, at least in a
hindsight aware of Nazi atrocities, to preserve a world safe for humanity. The war was won, but how victory came posed new threats. The
strange coalition between capitalist and socialist nations, the absolute
demand for unconditional surrender, and the awesome dawning of the
atomic age brought triumph, but the triumph was tainted first by unrealistic expectations and then, inevitably, by newer and deeper fears.[5]

Strange paradoxes marked the decade of the fifties. Americans
moved within its brief span from almost paranoid fears over internal
subversion to a life-style of denial masked by complacency. A revival of
interest in religion — or at least in the churches — issued not in profound theology nor even in revived interest in the social gospel, but in
deeper complacency. Sociologists observed this first, and their specialty

briefly threatened to unseat psychology as the religion of the un-churched who found comfort in understanding such a turning to faith as an ethnic rather than a spiritual phenomenon.[6]

Despite a root assumption that international confrontation would bring about all-or-nothing apocalypse, the 1950s also witnessed at least the dawning of a new realization. The experience of Korea, coming so soon after a victory of unconditional surrender forced by nuclear holocaust, prompted at least a few to accept that at least at times, at least some goals — and means — could be "limited." It was a sense that was to expand in the decades that followed. But at first its acceptance was stunted, as the majority of Americans so freshly conscious of both the necessity and the precariousness of freedom were reminded of the perverse uses to which the concept of limits could be put. The U.S. Supreme Court's 1954 decision that racial equality could *not* be limited issued an implicit challenge to engage in profound re-thinking about both equality and limitation. Most Americans, caught in the web of denial spun by racial chauvinism, fears of nuclear cataclysm, and suspicion of Communist intrigue, declined the invitation.[7]

Most people long continued to refuse it, but meanwhile at least the alcoholic Americans who in greater and greater numbers were joining Alcoholics Anonymous were learning *something* — on a more personal but not therefore less profound level — above the treachery of denial, the reality of limitation, the true basis of equality, and the addictive nature of any attempt to rationalize away these realizations — by drinking or any other means.

Our historical sketch has but glimpsed only America. Alcoholics Anonymous claims, and to some extent enjoys, worldwide diffusion. Yet in more than one sense both the A.A. fellowship and its program are profoundly "American." Two of these senses are relevant to our discussion here: the origins of Alcoholics Anonymous and the usual understanding of America.

Bill Wilson, in reflecting on how Alcoholics Anonymous had begun, often and fondly stated that "it all started in a consulting-room in far off Zurich, Switzerland." The role in A.A. history of Dr. Carl Gustav Jung — the great psychiatrist's admission of his own helplessness to cure Rowland's alcoholism and the advice that flowed from that acceptance — was, of course, important. Yet it was only remotely so, as Wilson exerted hindsight in striving both to understand and to undergird his own insights. Far more obvious and more proximate were the American foundations of the fellowship and its program.[8]

Despite its name, the Oxford Group was an American phenomenon. At heart, Frank Buchman remained throughout his life an American collegiate evangelist. A sophisticated sort of Dwight Lyman Moody, he preached conversion to those whose understanding of religion, he felt, verged too closely to that of H. L. Mencken. Both Buchman's seizing upon the name "Oxford Group" and his constant reaching for larger international impact can be understood as springing from his eagerness to avoid the charge of American provincialism. Some Oxford Group insights, derived as they were from Buchman's Pennsylvania Pietist background, stretched beyond the mainstream of early twentieth-century American religious thought, but the Oxford Group's own general unawareness of this only further marked it as "American."[9]

Only late in his career and under the specific influence of increasing psychological sophistication did Bill Wilson reach back to establish a connection between Alcoholics Anonymous and Dr. Carl Jung. Earlier, for many years and in appropriately diverse ways, A.A.'s co-founder and early members launched their claim to intellectual respectability from their real relationship with the thought of William James. The Harvard philosopher-psychologist's book *The Varieties of Religious Experience* had in fact influenced Wilson at a critical moment, and early members of Alcoholics Anonymous habitually recommended this book to any who complained of difficulty with "the spiritual side" of their program. William James, whose name will be forever associated with "pluralism" and "pragmatism," possessed adequate Americanness to pass on this quality to any who followed his thought — and to pass it on especially to those whose largest link with his philosophy lay precisely in their application of pragmatic pluralism to religious insight.[10]

In addition to these American-rooted origins, the early growth and spread of Alcoholics Anonymous could hardly have been more "American," however diversely and often confusingly that abused adjective be used. Traveling salesmen riding the rails in search of prospects; the early-sought tie to John D. Rockefeller, Jr., and through him the connection with Ivy Lee and Harry Emerson Fosdick; reliance upon *The Reader's Digest* and successful publicity in *The Saturday Evening Post*; the co-opting of journalists and popularizers such as Jack Alexander, Philip Wylie, and Paul deKruif: in a score of ways, Alcoholics Anonymous was at least by association as American as baseball, apple pie, hot dogs, and the Fourth of July.[11]

Clearly then, Alcoholics Anonymous was an occurrence first in the history of ideas and their implementation in America. But what, beyond geography, is "America"? It would be foolhardy to claim to answer where so many have stumbled, but most people readily agree, even if variously, that one meaning of "America" is "modern." And A.A., with very little notice, has uniquely confronted the problem of the modern even as it has shown the way to sobriety to a million men and women.[12]

The United States has been hailed as "the first new nation," with reference less to its economic system than to its pattern of economic growth. Attention to America as model of the modern emphasizes the nation's political example of democracy and especially American dedication to that hallmark of modernity, secularization. Whether the ideas that compose the only unifying Americanism possible in a population so diverse and a space so vast derive from John Locke or from the Scottish Common Sense Realists, the United States is the one political entity founded as *new* in the age of the Enlightenment out of commitment to the living out of Enlightenment insights. Whether the modern era began in 1609 or in 1789, with Copernicus and Galileo or with the writings of the French Encyclopedists and the philosophies of Descartes and Kant, American development as the pattern of the modern has so entered modern assumptions that modern minds seem bereft of analytic power if deprived of this model. A later generation may escape the model, but the unfolding equation "Enlightenment=American=Development=Modern" must suffice for us. It is the framework within which one can best understand the second key facet of the Americanness of Alcoholics Anonymous.[13]

The deeper meaning of the Enlightenment-Modern approach — its own development — has become clear especially in the twentieth century, which advertises its self-consciousness of modernity in its very claim to be "post-modern."

Both the key starting-point and the goal of the Enlightenment, expressed in one word, was *autonomy* — the essential independence of each human individual. Every person, as rational, was to use his own reason to set and to achieve his own goals. Reason rather than authority guided to both truth and happiness. The centrality of autonomy, of individual independence, and of personal responsibility only for and to oneself may be seen in two key Enlightenment thrusts that followed from that insight's own commanding metaphor of growth to become the dominant assumptions of all modern thought. The first was the exercise and extension of rationalization and control as the purpose of human life; the second was the embrace of ultimate relativism as the necessary corollary of accepting as ultimate the human-as-autonomous.[14]

The Enlightenment's enthronement of human autonomy sprang from a two-edged revolt that aimed to protect the truly human from debasing encroachment by other humans. Enlightenment thinkers labored mightily to attain for mankind *freedom*. First and foremost in this endeavor, they cast off as superstition all sense of mysteriously hidden forces beyond human understanding and control. To man belonged the responsibility as well as the right to determine and to shape human destiny. Second, but as part of this same commitment, the leading minds of the Enlightenment rejected all human claims to embrace or to represent any Absolute.[15]

Given the definition of human freedom as individual autonomy, the Enlightenment was a success and its modernity has ever more triumphed. But the very victory of the modern has proved ironically hollow if one of the responsibilities of attained human freedom is service to human happiness. The irony is most poignantly revealed, and its relevance to Alcoholics Anonymous most clearly seen, in one key, pivotal Enlightenment idea — a new understanding born in that age that has boomeranged to generate almost infinite unhappiness: "Man is by nature insatiable, and it is the will of his maker that he should be so."[16]

That human freedom meant insatiable craving was only the first irony, for other incongruities were intermingled with the Enlightenment insight. Because Enlightenment thinkers proposed to break all chains of superstition, they claimed to abolish all intelligent belief in and claims for mysteriously hidden forces beyond human rationalization and control. Yet a bare century after the triumph of the French Revolution had irreversibly established the path of modernity, something unexpected occurred, eluding Enlightenment assumptions about rationalization and control. The new insatiability of the quest for rationalization and control began to discover or create its own esoteric secrets and its own recondite mysteries — if not so evidently its own profound absolutes. Subtly and in newly secularized garb, an ancient intuition revived and a classic paradox regained command: that which was most real was least tangible.[17]

The triumphs of rationalization and control, especially in an era moving simultaneously and self-consciously toward increased equality and greater democracy, soon revealed themselves as paradoxical indeed. The scourge of sickness offers a good example. Less and less was sickness understood in its ancient sense, as a form of admonition or punishment by a Hidden God or an ultimate reality. In that former understanding, any person enjoyed at least some hope of control insofar as he could conform himself to ultimate reality. Now the triumph of modernity proclaimed illness to be the product of mysterious entities called germs and viruses, visible if at all only to skilled eyes assisted by long training and by special and costly microscopes. And all people yielded more and more of any sense of control over their own lives to a new priesthood of medicine, with its acolytes of technology, prelates of public health, and hierarchies of hospital administration.[18]

An example. Symbolically, in a space of less than eighteen months, Roentgen's discovery of the "x-ray" and Freud's first published claim for the determinism of the "*un*conscious" joined to proclaim the ultimate result of "enlightened" methods of investigation. The most importantly real things could not by definition be "seen" — at least not by "ordinary" men. Descartes's criterion of the "clear and distinct" thus became the hallmark of falsehood rather than the guarantee of truth. Soon Planck and Heisenberg, representatives of the model modern science of physics, came along to pick up — and throw away — any lingering loose scraps of the ultimate certainty that the Enlightenment quest had set out to realize. Such direct correlation of ultimate hiddenness with ultimate reality was hardly what Enlightenment thinkers had in mind when they set their definition of "modern."[19]

Another paradoxical irony: the Enlightenment definition of the human as autonomous gave birth to another ever more flourishing characteristic of modernity — a sense of crisis concerning human identity. This paradox is not unrelated to the first, for running parallel to the modern tendency to locate ultimate reality as hidden within has been the democratic era's inclination to seek identity as something bestowed from without. This search for identity was pursued in two ways: one, by devoting increasing attention to what an individual *does* or *makes* as defining the *being* of the self; two, by expanding the sense that one is defined by others — a person is as he or she is treated; to be human is to shape one's being according to the expectations and responses of others.[20]

Post-Enlightenment man professes devotion to openness and fundamental faith in the possibilities of change. Yet it seems less from these commitments than from an unthinking relativism which denies the concept of essence that modern thinkers derive their understanding of the meaning of human. Post-Enlightenment thought tends to interpret products as producing their producer. "Mr. Carpenter," for example, is not *one* who saws, hammers, and joins; he is *the carpenter*, who chooses recreations, educates his children, and even shares love *as a carpenter*. Moderns tend to dismiss *persons who think* by sheer labeling of the assumed source of their thought: "Oh yes, well, of course, he's a police-man, a psychologist, a professor, a property owner," or whatever.

Further and as a corollary of that same relativism, post-Enlightenment man tries to analyze relationships among persons as a series of transient *roles* rather than as rooted in any enduring *identity*. "Are you speaking now as my friend or as my stockbroker?" "He used to be my doctor, now he's my friend," tells little if anything about *who he* is. Lacking such an anchor as *identity*, even the metaphor of growth — which implies a goal — has been overcome by the terminology of flux, and a welter of attention to externally determined "stages" and nebulous "process" has all but demolished any concept of *personhood*. But perhaps children raised through "The Terrible Twos" were inevitably destined to agonize over their "Trying Twenties" on the way to "Catch-30" and "The Age 40 Crucible," their only goal "Renewal." [21]

Roles and process, essentially transient and variable, offer scant basis for stability and so little sense of self-as-person. Ever increasingly, moderns feel their humanity precarious. From two very different directions, the two classic critiques of twentieth-century man-in-society have attempted to speak to this point.

The Marxist insight, albeit "modern," offered a profound criticism of modernity. Marxist thought located the *meaning* of "being human" in what humans make or produce, thus embracing modernity's sense of ultimate power and so of absolute autonomy. But in the Marxist challenge of capitalism's separation of the worker from the products of his labor lies a deeper protest: even if humans "make" reality, human beings themselves can never *become* products, commodities. What one does or makes can never *become* what one is. [22]

The relationship between *being* and *doing* also exercised the ingenuity of existentialist philosophers, and their investigation of modernity's understanding of it carried to a deeper disjunction. For thinkers such as Jean-Paul Sartre and especially Martin Heidegger, the truth of human existence as Being-in-the-world had been lost. The Cartesian *cogito* with its futile quest for absolute objectivity was the final wedge that split man and his world irrevocably asunder. Dissatisfied further with role as ultimate, these philosophers and their hybrid offspring attempted to quench the thirst for identity-as-human by directing sole attention to sheer be-ing and very is-ness — to use the tortured language that the modern age imposed upon their very efforts to confront it. [23]

Existentialist thinkers, searching from the depths of the twentieth century, sought to specify for their time the Enlightenment insight that "human" meant *free*. They found only a paltry and pathetic shadow of the Enlightenment vision of human autonomy. For Sartre, the ultimate freedom was to say, "No!" Heidegger found freedom — and so authenticity — in the embrace of human finitude. Can it surprise that the historical moment bracketed by *Sein und Zeit* and *L'être et le néant* gave birth to the Alcoholics Anonymous of "not the first drink," "one day at a time," and "not-God?" Significantly, existentialist insights, at times directly but most often in garbled form, infuse virtually all popular psychotherapies of the later twentieth century. "Who am I really?" and "Why do I feel so empty?" are the questions most psychotherapists hear most consistently even if usually only implicitly. Despite Marxist and existentialist insight, therapeutic training has taught most modern therapists to follow one of two approaches. If they practice as depth psychologists, they focus client attention on the hidden reality within. If they operate as behavior therapists, they help the client change his doings and makings. Most often, in either case, the client's presenting questions remain unanswered. "Success" in therapy seems to mean repressing the questions as "meaningless" — strange therapy indeed for an age committed to rationalization and control.[24]

Fittingly, our examination of the Enlightenment-modern ironies of the hidden as real and identity as requiring search have brought us to the psychotherapist's office, for the twentieth century is pre-eminently the Age of Psychology. Its vaunted claim has been acknowledged as "The Triumph of the Therapeutic" — but in the saddest irony of all by a careful scholar who reminded, correctly, that the goal of therapy is not healing wholeness but "understanding." "Religion," Philip Rieff cautioned, "is where therapy leads when it takes on hope."[25]

If so, if *religion* is where therapy leads when it takes on hope, then effort expended to understand Alcoholics Anonymous as a religious expression of American hope in the therapeutic twentieth century is a worthy historical endeavor.

The twentieth century began in America with the "Progressive Era" — a self-conscious quickening of hope in the possibilities of extending rationalization and control in service to human happiness and fulfillment. The era's philosophers and economists agreed in identifying "doing" and "making" with *being* — that is, with being "American." Its psychologists built on a controlling assumption that understood imitation and socialization as the root of as well as the route to mature adulthood as an American. The Progressives consequently sought to apply rationalization and control, so successful in the technological and economic spheres, to the political and psychological lives of their fellow citizens. They instituted manipulative reforms such as proportional representation and city-manager government, hailing them as especially progressive in cities swollen by immigrants needing to be *made* "American." The movement called "Americanization" reflects this. An earlier generation of immigrants had enjoyed the privilege of *becoming* American. The Progressives wrested this privilege from a later immigrant generation's grasp, and made "Americanization" the onerous task of native-born Americanizers. Meanwhile still others devised "improvements" such as assembly-line production and advertising for mass consumption. Despite the premonitions of a few that this effort to extend rationalization and control to humans themselves was essentially flawed, despite suspicions that the insatiability inherent in the twin goals of efficiency and democracy led them to become at some point contradictory rather than complementary, most saw the grandest of goals as capable of achievement — and soon. The Progressives were certain that American culture stood poised on the threshold of the fulfillment of modernity.[26]

It did not cross that threshold. The idealism invigorated by American intervention in World War I broke down in the aftermath of the contagious cynicism of Versailles, and a population accustomed to the deflationary economy of the late nineteenth century found it impossible to comprehend, much less to cope with, the inflationary underside of their very modernity. Pained and confused, Americans retreated, internationally into isolationism and domestically into privacies. Even the abundance was for most illusory. At the height of the twenties' "boom," over sixty per cent of American wage earners supported their families on less than the income required for a minimum standard of decent living.[27]

Still, in the twenties, some roared and some soared until the Crash of 1929. The thirties brought depression to all, and new attempts at community for almost all. In the forties, surprise attack led to a war that ended in hollow triumph as new fears emerged. Then, in the 1950s, there was Korea with its hint of limitation; and there flourished a curious mixture of suspicion and complacency rendered tolerable only by denial that it existed. The decade of the sixties brought in every way too much for even the insatiable. There were the enthusiastic idealisms of Camelot and the New Frontier, the confidence-shattering violence of assassinations, and an increasing mistrust of government not unrelated to increasing immersion in an increasingly unpopular war.[28]

A sense of limitation was clearly and distinctly born. A "consumer movement" arose and soon sired offspring that made earlier concerns for conservation look amateurish. Adversarial relationships began to displace the presumption of even the existence of a "common good" as groups of newly self-conscious underdogs of every variety sought to impose their own definition of "equality." "Doing good" itself became suspect as the sixties turned into the seventies, and the spectacle of a virtually impeached vice-president, then president, shattered lingering altruisms. Dedication to rationalization and control had led, paradoxically, to the sense that, in human affairs at least, the only rational understanding was that there could be no effective control over all the contingencies and complexities so newly and carefully made understandable.[29]

Twentieth-century American history is the story of four paradoxes of modernity that loomed ever more as contradictions plaguing first Americans, then all moderns. Increasingly, the very triumphs of rationalization and control seemed to reveal only the final impossibility of any ultimate rationalization and control. The thirst and quest for more rationalization and control, however, increased even as each success at them came to be perceived as increasingly empty. The fundamental modern endeavor, the very *identity* of modernity in modernity's own terms, revealed itself as inherently addictive: the striving always harder for the ever more that always satisfied ever less.

Similarly the tension pulled ever more taut between understanding ultimate reality as hidden within and seeking personal identity that would relate one truly to others outside. The very terms "meaning" and "real" came to be reduced more and more to unreal and meaningless nonsense as the feeling of hollowness within and the sense of artificiality without impelled to an ever more desperately urgent quest for "the natural" in everything from foods to fuels, clothing styles to life-styles, art to medicine. Identity — the sense of *self* as "real" — became through the twentieth century an ever more rapidly receding goal apparently ever less capable of achievement.[30]

The third paradox lay entwined in the confusion engendered when moderns were confronted by limitation. The corollary of both the prior dilemmas of rationalization and control and lost identity, it too became an ever more painfully pinching contradiction. When the inherent and insatiable demand for *more* met ultimately inevitable frustration, whither could moderns retreat? An age that had extended "either-or" to "all or nothing" understood pause and compromise only in terms of utter defeat and total withdrawal. Whether applied to the "doing good" of social justice or to the carefully wrought gains of technological expertise, necessarily acknowledged limitation seemed ever more able to issue only the denial of *any* goods or goals. Moderns equated *limited* ability with *inability*, and typically extended their frustration over the immediate lack of practical and technical means to an ultimate negation of social and moral goals.[31]

At the beginning of the nineteenth century, the English Luddites had smashed the knitting machines on which they blamed their unemployment and poor wages. Now, toward the end of the twentieth century, a petulant insistence that if they couldn't have it *all*, they didn't want *any*, drove many self-consciously post-modern social theorists to demolish their intellectual and spiritual heritage. Appalled by this new and more terrifying Ludditism, other thinkers lamented "narcissism" or prescribed "caring." Clearly, the sense of limitation had itself to be limited; but *how* in a culture habituated to denial of the very concept of limitation?[32]

Finally, the paradox of Progressivism that had arisen as harbinger in the very first decade of the twentieth century had eventually to be faced. How was the understanding that modernity meant rationalization and control to be applied to human beings themselves? The Progressives, naively idealistic reformers, assumed that ever-increasing individual liberty and ever-greater social equality were infinitely complementary. Having set as parallel goals in human affairs the ever greater growth of both efficiency and democracy, they presumed harmony between efficiency as interchangeability and democracy as equality. But it did not work out that way, even over the very brief span of the Progressive Era itself. Especially in an America so richly diverse, people rebelled against the equation of equality with being identical. They did not find in such equality the *freedom* that being "American" promised. But what then did the freedom to be fully human mean? If human equality could not mandate human interchangeability, if identical sameness was no true basis for human relationships, how and on what deep basis could humans relate to each other as equal?[33]

These four quandaries, at heart deep paradoxes, crescendoed in contradiction and pinched more and more tightly through the years of the twentieth century. As inherent in the rich concept of "modern," they grew first and pinched most painfully in the United States of America, the first modern society. The deep and increasing sense of them must, then, be the contextual framework for an understanding of any phenomenon in the intellectual history of the American twentieth century. They thus form the foundation for our deeper understanding of Alcoholics Anonymous.

But Alcoholics Anonymous itself was an occurrence in the intellectual history of the American twentieth century. Not surprisingly, then, its fellowship and program did not merely find in these paradoxes a context. The problems were also A.A.'s own, and as both fellowship and program it spoke to them. The dual message of Alcoholics Anonymous — its proclamation that the human as "not God" was limited but that the human as "not-God" could find wholeness in this very limitation — offered at least a suggestion for the resolution of each dilemma.

Since either claiming absolute control or denying any ability to control seemed equally dehumanizing, Alcoholics Anonymous sought to locate a human control that was appropriate. Because to be human was neither simply *to be* nor merely to be what one *did*, A.A. tried to find a basis on which identity as human could be founded. Because "no man is an island" but others could threaten by their very otherness, A.A. further sought an appropriate basis for human relationships. And, especially, since to be human was to sense limitation, Alcoholics Anonymous worked to establish how that very sense of limitation could itself be limited.

The value of studying Alcoholics Anonymous within an explicit awareness of these paradoxes is twofold. First, for many and diverse reasons, A.A. offered both its diagnosis of the paradoxes and its suggested remedy for their apparent contradictions largely unconsciously. It thus avoided the ideological entrapment that has ensnared so many more loyally orthodox and therefore self-conscious approaches to these problems. Second, Alcoholics Anonymous was both deeply immersed in its culture and at the same time able to stand outside of that culture. Why this was possible and how it was true is the analytic task of the next chapter, which will explore the specific source from which the fellowship drew and will examine the precise foundation on which its program built its diagnosis of and prescription for the paradoxes of modernity: A.A.'s participation in a far larger source and longer skein of cultural and critical insight — the history of religious ideas.

VIII

The Context of the History of Religious Ideas

A familiar A.A. cliché describes the fellowship's program as "spiritual rather than religious," and members of Alcoholics Anonymous tend to enforce this distinction vigorously upon both those who comment on their program and themselves at A.A. meetings. This deep and real concern over its image as "spiritual" bears vivid witness to A.A.'s authentic modernity, especially as a religious phenomenon. The mistrust of religious claims that matured in the Enlightenment has so deepened and spread that, in the twentieth century, secularization has become the hallmark of modernity. Over those same two centuries between the Enlightenment and the present, however, the reaction of Romanticism against Enlightenment rationalism has also become culturally internalized and effectively stylized. Thus, in yet another paradox, moderns readily accept "feeling" even as they resolutely reject "belief" as a wellspring of personal action, at least so long as it does not intrude upon the autonomy of others.

The "Power greater than ourselves" of the "spiritual program" of Alcoholics Anonymous well fits this modern category. Faithful to the pragmatic criterion of truth, most members of Alcoholics Anonymous come to an understanding of their God through His *felt* rather than believed effect in their lives. Their knowledge of their sobriety is not an act of blind faith: it is the embrace of a lived reality. Yet, like the object of faith, that feeling of sobriety is unseen. Insofar as it is perceptible, it is known best if not only by its possessor.[1]

As the historical narrative of Part One has detailed, Alcoholics Anonymous came to its wariness of "the religious" but acceptance of "the spiritual" under the impact of diverse influences that operated both from within and from outside the fellowship. The Oxford Group, A.A.'s proximate parent, was ardently non-denominational although specifically Christian. Alcoholics Anonymous learned from the experience of the Oxford Group both the advantages of independence from the organized religion of the churches and the disadvantages of too militant criticism of those churches. The fellowship perceived its problem as two-sided: it had to remain attractive to the temperamentally non-religious while it avoided giving offense to the personally religious. The experience of Alcoholics Anonymous led it to solve this dual concern by projecting itself as "spiritual rather than religious," thus avoiding confrontation with the polarizing term *churchy* hidden within the concept of religion.[2]

Long before 1935, most alcoholics had had more than their fill of pious admonitions to be good and moralistic adjurations to be responsible. Most often, at least into the 1920s, as the larger history of the misnamed American temperance movement bears out, these overtly solicitous attempts to help had come under clerical auspices. The early experience of Alcoholics Anonymous and especially the stories in the first edition of its "Big Book" testified clearly that most alcoholics who tried such "religion" found it wanting. As sick as they sensed themselves to be, they were most sick of being preached at, and preaching seemed to most the main function of religion in America.[3]

Yet from the early time when Albert Scott, Frank Amos, and John D. Rockefeller, Jr., detected in the new-born Alcoholics Anonymous the "primitive Christianity" that characterized the Oxford Group's self-image, the understanding of A.A.'s own fellowship and program as fundamentally religious lurked never far from this society of sober alcoholics, even as it moved ever further from its Oxford Group connection. This appraisal united the descriptions of ministers of religion sympathetic to Alcoholics Anonymous and of at least one observer (Arthur Cain), clearly unfriendly to the fellowship and apparently hostile to all religion. It permeated the interpretations of a French journalist, an English sociologist, and a respected American psychiatrist. Over the years, other careful students — among them diverse sociologists, psychologists, and anthropologists — have as clearly and consistently intuited the key to the program and the fellowship of Alcoholics Anonymous somehow to be "religion." For all the problems inherent in the connotations of the term, such diverse unanimity cannot be ignored simply because of A.A.'s own insistence that it is "a spiritual rather than a religious program."[4]

Members of Alcoholics Anonymous sensed the problem, as the attempted distinction between "spiritual" and "religious" testifies. But their often expressed disappointment with the churches reveals that — in more common usage — the more proper distinction lies between "spiritual" *or* "religious" and "churchy." "We are only operating a spiritual kindergarten," Bill Wilson often claimed, but he never hesitated to speak on that basis "about faith . . . and the bearing it has in my case on the question of whether we humans live in a universe that adds up to a sense of justice and love. . . ." Wilson insisted that "good theology ought to ask every man's question: Do I live in a rational universe under a just and loving God, or do I not?" He pointed out that "theology doesn't seem to answer this any more." And so, despite the fact that this quest seemed to be precisely what "many A.A.'s . . . seek in churches, . . . in all probability, the churches will not supply the answers for a good many of us."[5]

A.A.'s disappointment with organized churches and their theology was rooted in more vivid experience. "The record of the missions who had tried to salvage alcoholics through a complete Christian teaching . . ." did not impress Wilson, who thought that "some of these theological propositions were tremendous obstacles [to sobriety]." By contrast, "The spiritual worked." Hundreds, if not thousands, had suggested that the program of Alcoholics Anonymous would work better without the religion. "In almost every case," Wilson reported, "they haven't had much luck."[6]

Sensitivity to both the non-religious within the fellowship and the professionally religious outside of it led Alcoholics Anonymous to resist identification as an expression of religion. The plea within was for "open-mindedness." It infused A.A. from Dr. Bob Smith's stress on "tolerance" to the final substantive paragraph of the Big Book's appendix, "Spiritual Experience": "We find that no one need have difficulty with the spirituality of the program. *Willingness, honesty, and open-mindedness are the essentials of recovery. But these are indispensable.*"[7]

The other concern was over those professionally religious. Mindful of the sad experience of the Washingtonian movement, which had anticipated many of the ideas of Alcoholics Anonymous, the fellowship was especially wary of seeming to have "opinions on outside issues" that were patently the claimed competence of the clergy. Bill Wilson, like Dr. Carl Jung and Aldous Huxley, had intuited a religious component in alcoholism itself: this was why the spiritual approach of Alcoholics Anonymous "worked."

> More than most people I think alcoholics want to know who they are, what life is all about, and whether they have a Divine

origin and an appointed destiny, and live in a system of cosmic justice and love. . . .

It is perfectly true, too, that alcoholics find in A.A. . . . a great deal more of what they glimpsed and felt while trying to grope their way toward God in alcohol. A.A. has of course seized this advantage. . . .

If, however, we were to publicly claim that the alcoholic's desire to drink had a heavy component of religious motivation, . . . the average clergyman would see red and the average psychiatrist would call this arrant nonsense. Since we require the cooperation of those professions, and because they are our chief source of new members, there wouldn't be too much sense in doing this wide-spread. . . .

And so, Alcoholics Anonymous had to be "a spiritual rather than a religious program," but truly an expression of *religious* insight.[8]

The fundamental religious *or* spiritual insight is that there *is* a "God," which is to say that man is *not* God. The human condition is not perfect, but somehow humans are called to perfection. Religious language has classically expressed this by describing humanity as existing in a state of *sin* and therefore in need of *salvation*. A familiar phrasing of this ancient perception and feeling is Augustine's: "Our hearts are restless until they rest in Thee."[9]

Augustine's "Thee" is of necessity outside the self, a power greater than the self. It offers salvation from the essential limitations of the self, whether this state of limitation — "sin" — be understood as depravity or as deprivation. Because limited, the human condition itself is, in the classic sense, tragic. In the craving for and consequent claim to more than is possible or given abides the essential "tragic flaw" of all tragic characters. The human situation of need — of needing specifically *other*, whether that "other" be an-Other, an-other, or others — has inspired all religion, most love, and much art. From these points of view at least, the history of human existence is the story of the human quest for human fulfillment.[10]

In that quest, the fulfillment sought is first *of* the human, but precisely as "human" it implies also a facet of fulfillment *by* the human. Every religious insight strives to embrace and to affirm both aspects. It speaks both to the sense that perfection can be found only beyond the human, at least beyond the individual self, and to the awareness that an essential part of being human consists in the self's cooperation in, seeking of, or at least openness to that fulfillment of self and others.

According to which of these two aspects is emphasized, religious insights group themselves into two styles. These styles need not — and do not — contradict each other. The history of religious thought, indeed, may be understood as the effort to strike a creative balance between them.

The first of these emphases concentrates upon the separation of the human individual from the fulfilling Other. Attentive first to the lack of freedom imposed by human limitation, it finds a source of awe and a reminder of humility in the possibility of salvation from humanity's essential alienation. This first style thus stresses "salvation" as from outside the self, and because of its root perception of awe and sense of humility is well-termed "Pietist." When it joyfully announces its sense and proclaims its perception as "good news," the style of this emphasis is also called "Evangelical."

The second emphasis, on the contrary, is impressed first by human participation in the Other. Aware first of the human potential to transcend *some* limitations, it finds a source of hope and a spur to responsible action in its sense of human freedom to fashion human destiny. The second style thus stresses human participation in human salvation, and, because of its profound respect for human possibility, rejoices in the name "Humanist." Because of its faith in human freedom, this style is also well-termed "Liberal."

Both these approaches have shaped religious thought in America, and both appear in the fellowship and program of Alcoholics Anonymous. In American history, however, it is the second — the Humanistic and Liberal tradition — that has generally held sway, especially in the twentieth century and among those wary of the claims to certitude and encroachments upon liberty of both organized religion and unorganized religious enthusiasms. In Alcoholics Anonymous, it is the other — the Evangelical and Pietist — sense that infuses and dominates. The reason for this is historical, but not merely historical. The Oxford Group, out of which Alcoholics Anonymous sprang, shared deeply in the Evangelical Pietist insight. But the Group also, and precisely as American, allowed its liberal optimism about human potential to overwhelm its specifically Pietist sense. This may be seen in the "aggressive evangelism" that characterized the Oxford Group approach and led directly to the departure from it of Wilson's early sober alcoholics.[11+]

+   The heart of Evangelicalism consists in the *announcement* of salvation as *gift* from God. By "Pietist" is meant the religious intuition struck first by man's *need* for salvation, by the transcendently *other* goodness and power of the divine. There has been, I contend, no adequate expression of this Evangelical Pietist

More significant to A.A.'s own specifically Evangelical Pietist religious intuition was the climate of opinion in which the fellowship was born and grew. By an almost too happy historical coincidence, the self-defined seed of Alcoholics Anonymous — Ebby's visit to the Clinton Street home of the then-drinking Bill Wilson — was planted in November 1934.

The year 1934 has been called, in the history of religion in America, *annus mirabilis*, "that wondrous year." It marked the blossoming in the United States of the age of neo-orthodoxy. This "new-old" theology strongly reasserted the omnipotence and otherness of a sovereign God. It merged a deep aversion to all emphasis on human strengths with a profound objection to any stress upon merely human sufficiency, and so expressed "protest against the prevailing tendency to glorify man and all his works." Neo-orthodox thinkers were diverse. Their essential consensus lay not in specific doctrines, but "in a sense of urgency and a demand for moral and intellectual humility." The "finitude of all things human must not be ignored," they said; "the tragic sense of life must be apprehended." Neo-orthodoxy's sense of hope "rested on faith in the God who was beyond, beneath, and above all human possibilities."[12]

Thus, both its proximate origins and its historical context exposed Alcoholics Anonymous to the Evangelical Pietist style of religious insight. But exposure is not determination. Other phenomena shared the neo-orthodox context, and the Oxford Group itself strayed still furthur from its Pietist root in its second re-incarnation as "Moral Re-Armament" in the late thirties. The core of A.A.'s insight into the meaning of "human" resided not in the fellowship's historical context nor in its program's proximate origins but in its early members' experience of their own alcoholism. The very heart of the Pietist insight lies in its sense of being brought low — of essential humiliation in one's very being. Especially in the context of the assumptions of the modern age concerning rationalization and control, few if any had more reason justly to feel thus brought low than did the alcoholic.[13]

In the America of the mid-twentieth century, the transfer of social authority from revealed religions to moralizing psychologies rendered the self-pitying plight of the drinking alcoholic even more desperate. The churches had castigated the "sin of alcoholism," promising salva-

insight in the mainstream of American thought since the death of Jonathan Edwards in 1758. The special affinity of Alcoholics Anonymous for this Pietist sense is testified to by several phenomena: for example, the continuing use among especially mid-Western A.A.s of Oxford Group devotional books; the popularity among especially West Coast A.A.s of the writings of Meister Eckhart.

tion through moral regeneration. The psychologists "understood" the "immaturity of the alcoholic" and offered the mature adulthood of diminished latent homosexual oral-fixation as the reward for acknowledging these perversions. Ironically then, more alcoholics experienced being brought low under the ministrations of psychiatrically amateurish friends than under the fulminations of religious professionals. Unfortunately, continuing modern experience taught that neither species of humiliation in itself cured many alcoholics.[14]

Given, then, A.A.'s Oxford Group background, the neo-orthodox climate of opinion in which Alcoholics Anonymous came into being, and the manifold sources from which any self-conscious alcoholic could derive the sense of being brought low, the deep extent to which the Evangelical Pietist insight infuses and dominates the A.A. program hardly surprises. Yet neither should the Humanistic and Liberal facets of Alcoholics Anonymous astonish. In the first place, A.A. was also American, and it is the Humanistic and Liberal insight that most deeply infuses all thought throughout the history of the United States, *the* Enlightenment nation. Further, granting the Evangelical Pietism of A.A.'s immediate parent and context, it was to the thought of William James that members of Alcoholics Anonymous early and consistently turned whenever they self-consciously sought to understand themselves and their program in terms of intellectual context and content.[15]

In James they found not only a vehicle for understanding and teaching the importance of their "spiritual experience," but also profoundly Humanistic and Liberal routes to and justifications of their fundamental Evangelical Pietist insight. Their embrace of James as pragmatist enabled A.A.'s shaping generation to accept and proclaim as a facet of their own experience what their neo-orthodox contemporaries scorned and castigated as a "psychologism" on which no worthy saving faith could be based. Following James as pluralist promoted the open-mindedness that early Alcoholics Anonymous intuited to be not only essential to their fellowship's growth but also as lying at the heart of their program itself. The pluralistic insight fostered their welcoming of differences among alcoholic insights as well as alcoholic styles; it shaped their dedication to "tolerance" as *active* virtue with curative effect; and in reinforcing their wariness of any monistic claim to absolutes of any sort, it guided the fellowship itself through treacherous hazards in its unfolding history.[16]

Thus the Humanism and Liberalism of Alcoholics Anonymous, for all the program's Evangelically Pietist core, are neither mere accidental after-thoughts nor overflow effusions of some affinity with mind-cure religious philosophies. Mind-cure explanations of Alcoholics Anonymous fail not least because, in the A.A. understanding, there is no "cure" for alcoholism or for the alcoholic. A.A.'s fundamental impetus derives from an opposite, more ancient insight, one that interprets the dis-ease of pain and illness not as less real because merely mental, but as more than merely real because an aspect of human reality itself. The after-thought understanding ignores the extent to which Alcoholics Anonymous is truly "American" — the program from its beginning was so totally immersed in and infused by the intellectual culture so well-reflected by William James that the fellowship readily found itself in this quintessentially American philosopher's thought.[17]

Any expression of religious ideas invites examination under two headings. What was believed? And how was this faith exemplified and conveyed? For Alcoholics Anonymous, the deep answers are clear in the Steps of its program. For the sake of insight into the larger historical context, however, the analysis that follows is carried on in terms and concepts more classically familiar in the history of religious ideas in America. In these terms and concepts, the fundamental impulse revealed by and lived out within Alcoholics Anonymous will be found to be that of a uniquely American expression of Evangelical Pietism.

The substantive faith set forth in especially the first three Steps of Alcoholics Anonymous was in *salvation* attained through a *conversion*, the pre-condition of which was the act of *surrender*.

In the First Step of the program Alcoholics Anonymous, "We admitted we were powerless over alcohol — that our lives had become unmanageable," the individual alcoholic gave up any claim to absolute control over anything. This surrender was made vivid by its style. The alcoholic admitted absolutely *no* control over alcohol, more offering this fact as evidence than claiming it as cause of the unmanageability of his life. The admission of the First Step marked acceptance that "bottom" had been hit. It also echoed a deeper admission — the irony of "original sin" as described by the Book of Genesis. In the Garden of Eden, Adam and Eve had sinned by reaching for more than had been given. They ate of the forbidden fruit because the serpent promised that eating it would make them "as Gods." Their punishment was loss of the garden they had been given. The alcoholic, in drinking, had sought inappropriate control over reality — more than was granted to human finitude. The promise of alcohol was likewise one of Godlike control: alcoholic drinking sought to control how outside reality impinged upon the alcoholic as well as his own moods, feelings, and emotions. As in the mythic parallel, the penalty for such abuse was the loss of any ability to use properly: reaching for more than had been given resulted in the loss of even that which had been given. To this understanding, the alcoholic surrendered by the very admission: "I am an alcoholic."[18]

Alcoholics Anonymous carefully avoided the term *conversion*. It came freighted with religious rather than spiritual connotations. Yet keen observers of the fellowship and its program consistently noted that successful affiliation with them depended upon the capacity of the individual to experience "a conversion with its attendant emotional components." Dr. Harry M. Tiebout, premier psychiatric analyst of Alcoholics Anonymous, was even more blunt: he titled his paper suggesting what A.A. might teach psychiatry, "Conversion as a Psychological Phenomenon."[19]

In its understanding of the conversion process, Alcoholics Anonymous unconsciously reflected a larger religious tradition that had been exemplified most strikingly in an earlier age of American "Revivals." Exactly a century to the month before Bill Wilson's spiritual awakening in Towns Hospital, another belated great awakener had in the same city set forth his definitive understanding of "What a Revival of Religion Is." Charles Grandison Finney listed the "stages" of a "revival" as "conviction of sin, . . . a deep repentance, a breaking down of the heart, . . . [and] reformation [of life.]" One hundred and twenty-seven years later, Dr. Tiebout, in his most mature exposition of his understanding of "Alcoholics Anonymous — An Experiment of Nature," recognized "four elements . . . as playing an essential role" in the A.A. program: "hitting bottom, surrender, ego reduction, and maintenance of humility." Earlier, Tiebout had carefully analyzed "The Act of Surrender in the Therapeutic Process" that was the working of Alcoholics Anonymous, in concepts if not terms clearly reminiscent of classic American revivalism. He wrote, "The specific part of the personality which must surrender is the inflated ego . . . the carry-over of infantile traits into adult life . . . a feeling of omnipotence. . . ."[20]

Whether presented as "serenity" or as attained adult life, the sobriety promised by Alcoholics Anonymous to its adherents was clearly *salvation*. As with "conversion," the general popular fear — especially in the aftermath of the failure of national Prohibition — of reformed drunks as crusading, anti-booze zealots, and A.A.'s own wariness of religion, led the fellowship to abstain from the use of a term so culturally loaded with pejorative connotation as was "salvation" in mid-twentieth-century America. Yet "sobriety," especially when it came to be distinguished from "merely dry" and expanded into "way of life," was clearly the A.A.

equivalent of classic religious salvation. And it was, classically, salvation or justification *by faith.*[21]

But the program's First Step faith affirmed belief not in the *fact of* salvation but in the *need for* it. Indeed, *the fact* of salvation was never witnessed to directly in the Twelve Steps of Alcoholics Anonymous; after the Second Step extended faith to the *possibility* of salvation, each succeeding Step testified to human rather than to divine activity. Subtly, however, at the beginning of the last of that list of "Steps," an assumption appeared: the twofold activity of the Twelfth Step — "to carry this message" and "to practice these principles" — *assumed* "Having had a spiritual awakening. . . ." Salvation was *needed*, and from outside the self; salvation was *possible*, but by a Power greater than the self. At this point Alcoholics Anonymous borrowed a special sensitivity to human psychology, via William James, from earlier but different American expressions of religious insight. Indeed it had been from this very psychological sensitivity that Bill Wilson had learned the importance of the ancient religious insights. Salvation was required, in the classic religious understanding of a new life; and this salvation came from outside the self. But salvation was explicitly apprehended, laid hold of, made operative, by *human* activity.

The human activity mandated/suggested by the Third through the Eleventh Steps of the A.A. program best reveals the integrity within Alcoholics Anonymous of the Evangelical Pietist and the Humanistic Liberal religious insights. This activity is *human*, and it is *freely* engaged in by the A.A. member: thus Alcoholics Anonymous manifests the Humanistic and Liberal emphasis that marks it as a typically American religious phenomenon. But this human activity, freely engaged in, which leads to the salvation of sobriety, consists essentially in a continuing elaboration and amplification of the initial act of *surrender*. Thus, Alcoholics Anonymous remains true to its core Evangelical Pietist insight. According to this insight, which can be expressed in either religious or secular form, the human activity most fundamentally essential to the attainment of "salvation" is *accepting reality.*+

What does "accepting reality" mean within the spiritual program of Alcoholics Anonymous? The explicit theism of Alcoholics Anonymous

---

+ A respectful parody of the A.A. program, a paraphrase heard often at meetings directed at newcomers, may help clarify the point. Based on the first three words of the Second Step, the parody runs: "We came, we came to, we came to believe." Human activity, that is, comes first; but the specific human activity that leads to sobriety is the alcoholic's surrender to the fact that he or she needs Alcoholics Anonymous.

witnessed clearly that its founders believed that the fundamental reality was "God." Over the first forty years of its history, most who approached Alcoholics Anonymous as "atheists or agnostic" in time came to believe in the reality of a personal divinity, usually in a Christian understanding. But not all. Especially fascinating to Dr. Tiebout as well as to Wilson was the success of Alcoholics Anonymous among Buddhists in southeast Asia. And among those "unconventional in belief," more and more remained both sober and unconventional through the A.A. program and within the A.A. fellowship in later years.[22]

In some of A.A.'s more explicitly religiously inclined derivations, the confrontation with self by way of honesty about self with others that is outlined in Steps Four through Ten led to an understanding of the fundamental therapeutic dynamic of "The Answer to Addiction" as "devotion to truth." At root, Alcoholics Anonymous presented a simultaneously very modern and very ancient religious perception. The embrace of not-God-ness led easily to the acknowledgments: "Accept reality, for reality affirms you"; "Be devoted to truth, and the truth will set you free." Whether or not to capitalize "reality" or "truth" was left by A.A., with cautious strategic wisdom, to the individual believer.[23]

The program of Alcoholics Anonymous, especially in its first three Steps, thus deeply shared in and clearly reflected the Evangelically Pietist insight. The salvation of sobriety — the restoration of the sanity of appropriate contact with reality and truth — resulted from the active interest and free gift of a Higher Power. But A.A. also manifested more than a trace of a sense that at first glance might appear to highlight the Humanistic in its belief that human cooperation with the divine saving activity could be useful and was even necessary. In addition to "raising the bottom," the fellowship attempted to "work up" a kind of individual revival in its insistence, to those having difficulty with its program, that they should "bring the body." "Thirty meetings in thirty days" was its standard prescription for newcomers. This maxim asked for investment and commitment, but it also expressed a faith that if one brought the body, the mind would follow.

Another frequent injunction more explicitly pointed up both the humanistic tinge of A.A.'s faith in human nature and the specific source of this faith in the thought of William James. Practices such as attendance at meetings, the inventory Steps of its program, and asking for help even if one did not believe, were urged under the mandate: "Act yourself into a new way of thinking rather than trying to think yourself into a new way of acting." The suggested sequence echoed the classically American understanding of the psychology of the emotions and of the impact of habit upon the will that had been articulated by James in 1884. Under this maxim as well as those earlier noted lay a perception that was at the same time both deeply American and profoundly Pietist. Expose yourself to "the truth," and "the experience" will come! Participate in the external occurrence, and the spiritual experience will be added unto it! [24]

How its substantive faith in a salvation attained through a conversion rooted in surrender was daily realized and conveyed in the fellowship of Alcoholics Anonymous further clarifies A.A.'s place in the history of religious ideas in America. Three facets of this living out merit attention: the mode of Word and Witness by which A.A.'s message was conveyed; and both the anti-professional bias and the style of anti-intellectualism implicit in this mode.

Alcoholics Anonymous transmitted its not-God core intuition exclusively by Word and Witness. The fellowship's faith in the efficacy of the telling by stories about personal experience was rooted in its memory of Bill Wilson's first call on Dr. Bob Smith. This faith in Word and Witness was also itself witnessed to by the "story section" of its hallowed book, *Alcoholics Anonymous*. Carrying the message by Word and Witness marked in the first place an acceptance and corollary of limited control. The core A.A. philosophy allowed no place for any attempt at the triumphal imposition of the salvation of sobriety. In the accumulated experience of Alcoholics Anonymous, fewer than one in five to whom "this message" was proclaimed responded by showing any willingness to attend even one A.A. meeting with a serious intention of getting and staying sober. A style of transmitting salvation better designed to drive home even the sober alcoholic's limited control would be difficult to devise. [25]

Three further facets of the reliance upon Word and Witness still more sharply clarify the place of Alcoholics Anonymous in the history of American religious thought: its implication for the classic problem of mediation; the insight such reliance offers into the deeper significance of attendance at A.A. meetings; and the light it casts on Twelfth Step work.

A representative figure in *both* American Evangelicalism and the Liberal Era in Protestant Thought, Henry Ward Beecher, provides a clue to the first point. On 22 September 1861, this most popular preacher of that era delivered his considered thoughts on the essence of the Christian message, "Preaching Christ." Within this sermon, Beecher moved quickly to his main point. Central to Christian preaching was the "*crucified* Savior, . . . the power [over the sinner's] heart of a broken Christ":

> But when divine and infinite things are brought before the mind, some things are more apt to stimulate men than others.

Those views which impress the mind with its own weakness, and want, and imperfection, and guilt, and dreadful danger, are very apt to be influential. The impression of these things upon the mind is the result of preaching Christ crucified.[26]

The preacher, to move his hearers, vividly recounted the effects of human sin upon the person of Christ. He pointed to Calvary and said, "This is what sin did to Him." On Twelfth Step calls and at meetings of Alcoholics Anonymous, each speaker, to move his hearers, vividly recounted the effects of his alcoholic drinking upon himself — his degrading "bottom" of "weakness, and want, and imperfection, and guilt, and dreadful danger." He pointed to himself and said, "This is what 'booze' did to me." The witness to "resurrection" was as parallel and as profound.[27]

Any expression of religion that wrestles with the problem of the divine as both transcendently other and immanently saving has need of a "mediator," a *proximate* "savior" to communicate salvation from divinity to humankind. The tendency of some to regard the A.A. program (so often referred to by speakers as "this God-given program") as "the savior" lay behind much of the fellowship's continued wariness of the Christian churches, albeit unconsciously.[28]

Obvious parallels to attendance at A.A. meetings and Twelfth Step work are church-going and missionary endeavor. The member of Alcoholics Anonymous "goes to meeting" for his or her own sake, for help, because of weakness rather than as any proclamation of goodness or strength. For all the fact of actual sobriety, the witness is primarily to fault and frailty rather than to any claimed righteousness. Some churches have tried to claim the same dynamic, to present church attendance as a confession of sinfulness and thus a testimony of depravity. Rarely have they succeeded in achieving this, nor likely can they, given the assumptions of American society about the "goodness" of church-going. The culture does not hear the confession, "I am a sinner," as threatening or disgusting. It does so apprehend the admission, "I am an alcoholic."[29]

The Alcoholics Anonymous parallel to missionary activity, "carrying this message to other alcoholics" in "Twelfth Step work," is more complex — and more revealing. The individual A.A. member always remains acutely aware that "faith alone does not save him." He has to act, to do something. He must *carry* his message to others. "Mere belief in right principle and sound tradition cannot make a Group a going concern." The individual member and the A.A. group itself had to engage in missionary works of Word and Witness; but the efficacy of the works lay in their effect on the *worker*, rather than in any external result.[30]

By the dawn of the twentieth century, most American religion had been so infiltrated by the secular sense of progress that the heated debate and denominational in-fighting over missionary endeavor was carried on largely in terms of results. An earlier intuition had been lost. Formerly, there had been a sense that the main efficacy of Witness was to be found in its effect in the life of the one giving it, but by the 1890s a nation oriented to results and progress no longer tolerated nor even grasped this key facet of an earlier Evangelical witness. An important aspect of the pragmatism that evaluated according to results had been lost, and the pragmatic philosophy of those oriented to *doing* was itself stunted by such sole focus on results outside the do-er. Here, then, Alcoholics Anonymous blended its Pietist insight and its American intuition to proclaim by example a message singularly appropriate to its time: looking also to subjective results could richly enhance the overall appraisal of objective actions. Results within the one who acted were also *results*.[31]

The A.A. program's substantive insight was that "salvation" is attained through conversion and by surrender. The A.A. fellowship's mode of conveying this insight was its style of Word and Witness. Both reflected the core idea of Alcoholics Anonymous that the acceptance of limitation begot wholeness. Two further characteristics, A.A.'s anti-professionalism and anti-intellectualism, can perhaps be appreciated only in this precise context, for they were corollaries of that core concept. Yet the anti-professionalism and anti-intellectualism of Alcoholics Anonymous are also important because they clarify the fellowship's participation in the larger, respectable, intellectual history of ideas with which human beings have attempted to grapple with the meaning of human existence.[+]

+ Some have suggested that rather than "anti-intellectualism," a more proper term here would be "wariness of intellectualization." Many psychiatric thinkers understand "intellectualization" as a mechanism of defense by which a person avoids confronting a reality by instead analyzing it, thus establishing a certain distance that denies involvement. Alcoholics Anonymous is surely also wary of such "intellectualization," and A.A.'s cautions concerning "rationalization" can be understood in this way — but not completely. Precisely because it is a phenomenon in the history of religious ideas, Alcoholics Anonymous also manifests *anti-intellectualism* in the philosophically technical sense of that term that will be explored here.

My understanding of "anti-professionalism" and "anti-intellectualism" here and in the following paragraphs follows essentially that of Richard Hofstadter, *Anti-Intellectualism in American Life* (New York: Random-Vintage, 1966); for

Although more ancient than such labeling may seem to imply, anti-professionalism and anti-intellectualism are characteristically both American and Pietist. These characteristics issue from a profound respect for individual human worth, but for this worth as *limited*. From such an understanding flows not only immense reverence for "the common man" and vast trust in "ordinary people" but also consequent wariness of any "expert" claim to be more than ordinary, to be less limited than the common man.[32]

The Eighth Tradition of Alcoholics Anonymous reads: "Alcoholics Anonymous should remain forever non-professional. . . ." The roots of "this hard but healthy doctrine," beyond the Oxford Group practice and understanding that there was to be no charge for "soul-surgery," lay in the 1937 experience of Bill Wilson with the attitudes of his New York alcoholics concerning the Towns Hospital job offer. "Sure," one of them had said, "It's ethical. But what we've got won't run on ethics only: it has to be better." The rejection of any personal profit from the carrying of so saving a message as Alcoholics Anonymous offers profoundly echoes the ancient Pietist rejection of "bought grace" as "cheap grace."[33]

The historical problem for Alcoholics Anonymous has been not so much the professionalization of its own endeavors, but how to harmonize these endeavors with those of the professions. Over the years, A.A.'s intuitive wariness of professional claims tended to burgeon under the impact of the ever increasing number of adherents who approached the fellowship from a new style of "bottom." Having exhausted their financial and emotional resources in pursuit of a cure for their alcoholism from psychiatry and organized religion, these came to Alcoholics Anonymous in the desperation of "proven" hopelessness only to find relatively easy and comparatively cheap sobriety. Often, they then tended to denigrate all those who had "failed" them in the past. Because such resentful criticism posed both a political threat to the fellowship and a psychological danger to its program, Bill Wilson felt obliged to meet it head-on. In countless letters and in a 1957-series of

"anti-professionalism" *cf.* especially Part IV, "The Practical Culture," pp. 233–296. For those who find objectionable application of these terms to Alcoholics Anonymous, a point and a caution: *Read* Hofstadter's treatment of "The Evangelical Spirit" and "The Religion of the Heart" with awareness of the historical context in which it was written (early 1960s). *Hear* Hofstadter's own caution against careless extrapolation of his point: ". . . I have found it desirable to discuss the anti-intellectual implications and the anti-intellectual consequences of some educational theories of John Dewey; but it would be absurd and impertinent to say, on this account, that Dewey was *an* anti-intellectual" (p. 22).

articles in the *A.A. Grapevine*, Wilson developed the theme, "Let's Be Friendly With Our Friends." He took pains to call attention to both the past contributions and the present usefulness to Alcoholics Anonymous of psychiatry, medicine, religion, and "workers on the alcoholism front."[34]

Overt attention to the root problem remained scant, however, until Alcoholics Anonymous achieved some security in its sense of maturity. The revival of the concern, in the mid-1960s, revealed that the problem not only had continued but indeed had increased in both breadth and depth. Further, it remained extremely sensitive for A.A. members, for when the theme was again picked up, it was by two close friends of the fellowship who were not themselves members. Their comments were benign, and, with their official aura, were intended to quell controversy over "professional relations" and "problems of cooperation." Yet from deep within the intuitively religious heart of Alcoholics Anonymous came a formally unofficial cry of profound lamentation that made several points vividly revealing of both the core anti-professionalism of Alcoholics Anonymous and the specifically Pietist root of that trait.[35]

A recovering alcoholic halfway-house counselor bemoaned "The Death of a Philosophy." He noted that while "the symptoms of alcoholism . . . anxiety, hostility, depression, loneliness, fear . . . can be counter-acted with love, care, trust, and empathy," they could also be alleviated by "chemical agents." The problem was that "absolutely nothing in a doctor's training" prepared him to deal with "'Soul Sickness.'" Going on to attack the whole concept of "scientific credentials" as "unrealistic and stupid," the pained para-professional struck an ancient theme. "Using government criteria — Jesus Christ, Peter and Paul would all be unemployed today (especially Jesus, inasmuch as there is some question as to his literacy.)" Psychology could offer only "tools and methods . . . a poor substitute for the A.A. philosophy." The writer's concluding point witnessed clearly to the deep source of his concern:

> What ever happened to 12 Step work? . . . The twelfth step doesn't say, "Having had a spiritual awakening as a result of these Steps, I will henceforth take every alcoholic to the county detox center and turn him over to someone else for 72 hours. . . ."[36]

The root concern was clear. If professionals denied the competence of A.A. members for "12 Step work," or — worse — if such work were abdicated by Alcoholics Anonymous to professionals, what happened to the program? What happened to the fellowship itself, to which "carrying the message" was so essential? What to do when ordinary people prefer the "cheap grace" offered by experts has been a constant and characteristic problem for expressions of Evangelically Pietist religion.[37]

Another constant trait of both the Evangelical tradition in America and all Pietism has been anti-intellectualism. Undergirding much of A.A.'s anti-professionalism lay an implicit, albeit not universally held, truism. The Alcoholics Anonymous restatement of the doctrine of the priesthood of all believers (and *only* believers) ran, "Only an alcoholic can understand/help another alcoholic."[38+]

At the very heart of all the experience of Alcoholics Anonymous lay *experience*. To be shared, something first had to be possessed. "You can keep it only by giving it away," but "You have to have it before you can give it." What was being talked about was "new life" — the heart of the "born again" or "twice-born" understanding inherent in all Evangelical religion.[39]

"Getting the program" in Alcoholics Anonymous paralleled the Evangelical sense of "getting religion." Experience, in this understanding, was in essence ineffable. Such experience could be only witnessed to, not put into words. Reasoning, on the contrary, was necessarily verbal — the logical progress of argument. A.A.'s own experience consistently testified that "rationalization" — defined as "this odd trait of mind and emotion, this perverse wish to hide a bad motive underneath a good one" — was "our ancient enemy." It led only to drinking again.[40]

For these and other reasons, there inhered in Alcoholics Anonymous

+ It is this writer's impressionistic conclusion, after careful listening to many A.A. speakers in a variety of settings and interviews with both alcoholic and non-alcoholic — volunteer as well as professional — workers in the alcoholism field, that deep acceptance of this "truism" is more widespread than open avowal of it might suggest. As might be expected, there does seem to be some negative correlation between acceptance of it and level of formal education. The root insight behind the truism is the same as that which underlies A.A.'s ancillary program for families and friends of alcoholics, Al-Anon. Al-Anon's "First Step" is the same as A.A.'s: "We admitted we were powerless over alcohol — that our lives had become unmanageable." The conviction is that until the potential helper admits *his or her own* powerlessness over the alcoholic's drinking of alcohol, no help is possible. Acceptance of "Only an alcoholic can help an alcoholic" arises from the belief that, in general, only a self-admitted alcoholic is prepared to make such an admission. Yet as is clear from the very existence of Al-Anon and its relationship to A.A., it is not deeply held that a non-alcoholic cannot make such an admission — at least under A.A. tutelage.

a deep anti-intellectualism. A.A. experience taught that if sufferers from alcoholism not cured by "experts" were to have any chance at "getting the program," the fellowship had to proclaim the simple truth learned from its experience: sobriety came through witness, not by reasoning. If the historically mediated Evangelical and Pietist intuitions concerning human limitation, the style of certitude, the loveliness-to-God of the lowly, the necessity of surrender, and the abdication of "control" were to be experienced more than understood, then this message proved pragmatically useful. It has never been the style of any expression of this ancient vision to be shy about what followed from its insight that "salvation" required *surrender*.[41+]

The words *surrender, conversion, salvation*; *word* and *witness*; *anti-professionalism* and *anti-intellectualism* point out one contribution of Alcoholics Anonymous to modern America and the twentieth century. A.A. preserved and re-introduced concepts that had become lost or perverted through the accretions of history. Sad and at times tragic associations of some of these terms had led the terms and therefore also their concepts to be ignored, abandoned, or perhaps worst of all, twisted beyond recognition. But the loss of these concepts that for centuries had enabled men better to understand and make sense of their experience was itself a sad and tragic deprivation. By its mere rescuing of these concepts, Alcoholics Anonymous rendered a significant contribution to modernity itself.

Both the style of this rescue and the pragmatic use to which the retrieved concepts were put also merit attention as considerable contributions. Largely because the primary and only direct concern of Alcoholics Anonymous was with the suffering alcoholic, A.A. as a phenomenon of a psychological age reached for psychological terms and understandings in its effort to communicate clearly. Psychological terminology is notoriously slippery, not least because the very popular-

+ Sight of the wellsprings of this insight became lost not so much within A.A. as in the more secularized therapies derived, often unawarely, from it. The roots of such manifestations of apparently rootless anti-intellectualisms as Encounter marathons and EST, of the whole touchie-feelie fad in group dynamics, may be found in the Evangelically Pietist perception of reality mediated to them by Alcoholics Anonymous. Concerning this mediation, the most perceptive treatment does not advert explicitly to A.A.: Thomas C. Oden, "The New Pietism," *Journal of Humanistic Psychology* 12: 24–24 (1972); adverting to A.A. less insightfully but more thoroughly is Nathan Hurwitz, "Peer Self-Help Psychotherapy Groups," in P. M. Roman and H. M. Trice (eds.), *The Sociology of Psychotherapy* (New York: Jason Aronson, 1974), pp. 84–138.

ity of the psychological approach leads to careless use — and so to abuse — of its categories. The mistaking of labeling for diagnosis is a special pitfall of any popular science. It threatens more and damages most when popular understanding too casually appropriates, then extends precise, technical terminology.[42]

In its role as bridge-builder between ancient religious insight and modern psychological understanding, Alcoholics Anonymous avoided this snare by its insistent reliance on the simplest possible language as the most effective way of grasping its essentially simple program. The fellowship's literature, most notably the "Big Book" and *Twelve Steps and Twelve Traditions*, accepted and used ordinary words in their common meaning. Over the years some have felt it psychologically unfashionable to speak in terms of "instincts" and "moods" rather than of "drives" and "complexes"; yet by this freezing of vocabulary — no matter how time-bound or imprecise later critics may find it — all members of Alcoholics Anonymous were enabled to communicate with each other across lines of time, social class, and educational background.[+]

Denial, after all, had been earmarked by Alcoholics Anonymous to be the characteristic symptom and deep core of alcoholism. The clever use of language in service to denial has throughout history subverted true communication and so fostered alienation and the separations of mistrust. The true communication of experience by "the language of the heart" was essential to Alcoholics Anonymous. By "keeping it simple" in an area all too often marked by terminological obfuscation, the program of Alcoholics Anonymous offered assistance in confronting denials to its adherents — and even, to modern culture, an invitation to examine its own not dissimilar problem.[43]

Most members of Alcoholics Anonymous remained unconscious of any larger significance in their style of keeping it simple. They were even less aware of the possible grander utility to a culture struggling with limitations of such maxims as "One Day at a Time" or "First Things First" — ancient concepts rescued and restored to experience by the A.A. program. This was appropriate, for an essential component of sobriety as the wholeness of accepted limitation was careful vigilance against any tendency to think in terms of "larger" or "grander." Yet the utility was there — implicitly inherent in their program even if explicitly

---

+   This was one criticism of Jerome Ellison: *cf.* above, p. 145. The criticism ignores or forgets that the "Keep It Simple" stress in A.A. originated with Dr. Bob Smith, early A.A.'s most educated and only medically knowledgeable member, and one whose earlier experience within the Oxford Group surely convinced him of its importance. *Cf.* above, p. 32 and note #72 to it.

ignored in their practice. The rescued insights, precisely because they were ancient, afforded a perspective on modern society. They furnished a set of tools apt for offering constructive criticism of modernity's very understanding of *modern*.[44]

The problem of critical perspective is itself an ancient one. Here, narrowly, the problem of any criticism and a problem of all religion fuse. How are criticism and religion to relate to their culture? On the one hand, in order to be heard and still more to be heeded, any expression of criticism or religion must give evidence of its participation in its culture. It must bear witness that it is truly *in* its time. On the other hand, in order to fulfill the critical responsibility of offering perspective on, and the religious function of passing judgment upon, any criticism or religion must also in some way stand apart from its culture — or at least seem to do so. It must be seen as not totally *of* its time.

In restoring concepts such as "surrender," "conversion," "salvation," and "limitation" without insistence on these terms, Alcoholics Anonymous achieved the critical stance necessary to any expression of religion. A.A. stood both immersed within and anchored outside of its immediate cultural context. The critique it was thus enabled to give is the topic of the next chapter, but its understanding may be facilitated by careful consideration of the two most obvious term-concept anomalies in the program and fellowship of Alcoholics Anonymous. The first — "spiritual rather than religious" — has been the topic of this chapter; the second is contained in the very name of the fellowship — "Alcoholics Anonymous."

For its own members at least, Alcoholics Anonymous rendered acceptable and even embraceable two terms that modernity had laden with pejorative meaning as well as implication — "spiritual" and "alcoholic." Yet at the same time, by counterpoising the term "spiritual" to "religious" and by insisting upon and promising anonymity as a necessary condition qualifying "alcoholic," A.A. itself accepted and embraced key assumptions of the modernity which it even thus transcended.

It is significant and noteworthy that even within Alcoholics Anonymous, given its origins and the nature of its insights, the modern prejudice against "religion" remains. At times, indeed, this bias against religion seems more intense than it does in more fashionably "modern" settings. But the related concept and its simple term "spiritual" have been rescued, inviting at least thoughtful listeners to engage in that careful distinguishing that is the hallmark of intelligence. By opposing "spiritual" to "religious," Alcoholics Anonymous achieved a contemporary *coup*: in accepting the modern derogatory connotation of the word "religious," A.A. clothed the word "spiritual" with acceptability. To render the spiritual acceptable in modern times is no small achievement.

The more subtle associations as well as the direct meanings of the word *alcoholic* posed a similar problem — and one of which early A.A.s were explicitly conscious, as the shifting of terms in succeeding editions of the book *Alcoholics Anonymous* testifies. Only slowly did A.A. members achieve any degree of comfort in calling themselves "alcoholic." In time, the term even took on a positive connotation for some of them, especially as distinguished from *drunk* or *problem drinker*. Yet culturally the stigma remained. For many in the larger society, the implications of the label *alcoholic* did shift; but it was at best dubious whether those changes were for the better, at least from the point of view of that society's self-defined alcoholics.[45]

Under the impact of A.A. publicity and National Council For Education on Alcoholism propaganda in the mid-1940s, many Americans found it increasingly difficult to retain the classic stereotype of the alcoholic as skid-row bum, unkempt eyesore, and unemployable social tragedy. The stereotype shifted, especially as applied to those who proclaimed their alcoholism publicly. The new image, not completely undeserved, was of the alcoholic as non-drinking zealous bore, determined to detail over and over again, to those unable to escape, the story of his salvation from "booze." In the 1950s, after A.A.'s understanding of anonymity had expanded sufficiently to inhibit such displays, at least among its own members, the stereotype shifted again. And again, the change was hardly favorable to the alcoholic, as popularization of a vast body of less than careful research into "the alcoholic personality" issued in the understanding that the term *alcoholic* labeled its now even more pathetically pitiable subject as an "immaturely dependent deficient personality."[46]

Such shifts in meaning were inevitable and proved even helpful to Alcoholics Anonymous. The first change in the cultural understanding of *alcoholic* — from skid-row bum to over-zealous bore — cast new light on the fellowship's understanding of anonymity. Alcoholics Anonymous alcoholics needed anonymity as a reminder that they were not God, that they needed to avoid pride, that it was dangerous to attempt to impose *anything* on *anybody*. The formulation of A.A.'s Twelve Traditions enshrined this newer understanding and more profound acceptance of the fellowship's own social vulnerability.[47]

The second change in a psychological age's comprehension of *alcoholic* — from pushy bore to dependent personality — recalled A.A. to its original understanding of the purpose of anonymity. It reminded that newer interpretations of something as basic as anonymity did not cast out old understandings, but built upon the foundation of initial intuition. Significantly also, the new stigma adhered to the fellowship's members precisely as members of Alcoholics Anonymous rather than merely as alcoholics. Some in the larger society came to see "having to go to those meetings" a more degrading disgrace than alcoholic intoxication itself. Reproach thus subtly shifted from alcoholism, which it was thought a "real man" could conquer, to A.A. membership, which was seen as capitulation to the weaker side of one's personality. Painfully but opportunely, A.A.s were reminded again of their not-God-ness in recovery: when they shared honestly, they became mutually vulnerable. They might openly acknowledge this at their meetings, but they relied on each other's respect for anonymity to shield their vulnerability in the larger society where the lack of any sense of shared weakness prevented such honesty from becoming truly mutual and thus healing.[48]

For the larger society, then, A.A.'s name summarized its message. Especially as a religious phenomenon, there was a special anomaly in the chosen rather than imposed name bearing such connotations as did "Alcoholics Anonymous." Most religious groups in Western history, from "Christians" through "Protestants" to "Puritans," "Dunkers," and "Quakers," have had their names imposed from outside, as derogatory. A.A. chose its own name, albeit accidentally and surely without thought of such implications. The fellowship's early members did not understand the conjoined terms as necessarily pejorative. Indeed, to them, being "A.A.s" witnessed to their actual sobriety. Accepting the designation *alcoholic* both alerted to their availability and summed up the program's First Step admission of powerlessness. The promise of anonymity counteracted the fear of some who might suspect their need for the program yet hesitate to approach it because of possible social consequences.[49]

Yet for most outside Alcoholics Anonymous, both terms in its name continued to imply disgrace, even if with shifting emphases. The understanding that being alcoholic was a continuing condition, redeemable only by continuing dependence on an essentially tenuous salvation from outside, highlighted A.A.'s Pietist insight that was so alien to habitual American thought: to be human was first to be not God, to be other than omnipotent or absolutely autonomous. The word *alcoholic* proclaimed that there was "sin," and that it was the enduring state of at least this portion of humankind. This state of "sin" consisted in essential separation from ultimate reality, and the most destructive act of "sin" was denial of the actuality of this separation from ultimate reality. Such denial led to self-destruction through increasing self-centeredness, because ultimate alienation afflicted those who acted as if they were themselves ultimate reality.

Most twentieth-century Americans did not want to hear such a message. Following ancient tradition, they tended to slay — modernly, by subtle social ostracism — the messenger who brought such "bad news."

But Alcoholics Anonymous was itself American, and therefore it was Evangelical in its Pietism. A.A. understood its message to be not the "bad news" that salvation was necessary, but the "good news" that salvation was available. The fellowship proclaimed the basis of that redemption's availability in the second half of its name, "Anonymous." The proclamation concerned a sharing union with others in a mutual acceptance rooted in weakness rather than strength. That alcoholics within the A.A. fellowship were anonymous contained a subtle and religious irony. Despite all their deceptions and denials, actively drinking alcoholics were rarely anonymous. Significant others, at least, knew all too well of their desperate condition, no matter how uncomprehending that knowledge. Anonymity, then, in the sense that others would not know of one's vulnerability to alcohol, came only with membership in Alcoholics Anonymous and consequent sobriety. To the alcoholic who grasped this, his anonymity to those outside A.A. was a delicious irony indeed.

Within Alcoholics Anonymous, the promise of anonymity made possible the acceptance of oneself as limited. Sharing this acceptance with others who were similarly limited — the price of admission, so to speak — in turn made possible acceptance of self *and those others* as not-God, as men and women made whole by the acceptance of limitation. This realization that sharable strength arose precisely out of acknowledged weakness enabled this new strength in its turn to enrich both self and others in a relationship of truly mutual giving and receiving — each undertaken as the only way of accomplishing the other. Mutual honesty about shared vulnerability followed from acceptance of self and others as other-than-perfect. It led in its turn to the shared honesty of mutual vulnerability that enabled at least a reaching toward ultimate reality and the touching of ultimate reality at least in human relationships.

From this sense of sharing, this sense of participation in ultimate reality in and through others, sprang a profound realization of alcoholic equality. And from this awareness of equality flowed a liberating sense of true freedom. Among others who openly acknowledged their not-God-ness, there was neither need nor inclination for any alcoholic to play God. Each alcoholic could simply be — be who he was and what he was, limited, and so able both to exult in the strengths that arose from his own weakness, and at the same time to be enriched by the different strengths that flowed from others who could not threaten because they shared the same weakness.

Anonymity testified to this shared equality and its consequent freedom. Those outside the fellowship, the culture in general, saw in anonymity only a witness to the weakness of shame and fear. The members of Alcoholics Anonymous, however, saw beyond that. In testifying to their acceptance of equality in vulnerability, anonymity reminded them of their freedom to be themselves.

In thus teaching and living out the insights that knowing the truth makes free and that great love accepts vulnerability, Alcoholics Anonymous unconsciously witnessed to its incorporation of the first century Christian vision that had inspired its Oxford Group parent. Because the witness was unconscious, A.A.'s members could insist that their program and fellowship were "spiritual rather than religious." Yet the nature of these insights concerning truth and freedom, love and vulnerability, was such that even in secular and modern garb they firmly located Alcoholics Anonymous as a significant phenomenon in the history of religious ideas in twentieth-century America.[50]

IX

The Meaning and Significance of Alcoholics Anonymous

The other claimed root of Alcoholics Anonymous was medicine. Roughly parallel to A.A.'s historical concern over "religion" and "the spiritual" ran the consistent problem posed for the fellowship by its understanding of alcoholism as in some way "disease." Bill Wilson and others sensitive to this problem attempted to finesse it in two ways. First, they generally avoided the quasi-technical term *disease*, using in its stead some synonym such as "malady." Second, they stressed "the threefold nature" of alcoholism — physical, mental, and spiritual; indeed, they based the whole rationale of their program upon this latter understanding.[1]

If the word *disease* presented a problem, it was not first and foremost A.A.'s problem. As Dr. E. M. Jellinek observed in discussing the cliché that "alcoholism is a disease," acceptance of this truism was fine, and just about everyone agreed with it. The difficulty arose, Jellinek pointed out, because there existed no agreement about just what "alcoholism" was, nor any real consensus even among doctors about just what constituted "disease." Given such confusion, it was fortunate for the serenity of Alcoholics Anonymous that it treated the problem of alcoholism as disease as an "outside issue." A.A. thus on principle escaped direct confrontation with the problem as the fellowship itself lived out its Tenth Tradition.[2][+]

The present study is not bound by that Tradition, but entering the controversial discussion over alcoholism as disease would be at least as

+ The Tenth Tradition of Alcoholics Anonymous: "Alcoholics Anonymous has no opinions on outside issues, hence the A.A. name ought never to be drawn into public controversy."

unhelpful to its purpose as public controversy over the question would be to A.A.'s mission. For one thing, Jellinek's acute observation is, if anything, even truer today. Two decades of continuing, sophisticated medical research and psychological investigation have revealed complexities rather than produced any agreed-upon understanding. Further, neither disease as entity nor "dis-ease" as concept furnishes the most helpful category for the task of historical analysis at hand. Rather, one clear intuition arises from the historical narration and contextual analysis that have been presented: especially as religious in its inspiration, the Alcoholics Anonymous understanding of alcoholism begs for exploration within the insight that disease can also be metaphor.[3]

Finding in understandings of disease either a conscious or an unconscious metaphor is not a new idea. The concept is an ancient one, and also one intriguingly revived in twentieth-century cultural analysis.[4]

In antiquity, the Bible portrayed leprosy as a metaphor for sin. The disease of leprosy — a noisome rotting of the flesh — aroused disgust in others, and their horror was accentuated because the malady was thought to be highly contagious. Thus lepers were segregated from the society of the healthy. The image, then, both reminded that sin was a disgusting evil and reinforced awareness of its social nature: even sin that was apparently merely personal threatened others and therefore alienated from society as well as from God. Finally and most strikingly, the power to cure leprosy — like the power to forgive sin — was seen as a divine attribute.[5]

The nineteenth and especially the twentieth centuries have witnessed a rebirth of the use of disease as metaphor, albeit the figure has become subtler and more extended. At the beginning of the twentieth century, and specifically in America, the Progressive Era found its disease-metaphor in the "white death" of tuberculosis. A self-consciously expanding economy feared stiflings from within, as critical thinkers worried over the implications of monopolistic enterprise and ever denser city slums. Although usually unconsciously and sometimes even erroneously used, the image of tuberculosis helped some Progressive reformers to face up to the apparent paradox in the new economy: it seemed to produce vigor and beauty even as it sapped both enterprise and the city by smothering their essence from within. The plaint pathetically described by Robert Hunter — "Breath, breath, give me breath" — symbolized the cry of the small entrepreneur even more poignantly than it recorded the dying words of a young man in a New York tenement.[6]

More recently, the self-consciously post-modern era so aware of the perils of untrammeled growth has discovered its disease-metaphor in the malignancy of cancer. It is still too early to grasp all the ramifications of cancer as metaphor. Two of the image's socially relevant insights would seem to concern the dangers of uncontrolled growth and the fear that fatal contamination can be induced by the minutely accidental — by unintended and even unknown by-products. But such metaphorical wisdom comes at a terrible cost, a price paid by the actual victims of the actual disease, for metaphor too easily veils a process by which fear of the disease becomes loathing of the diseased. Susan Sontag has well analyzed and brilliantly protested this process and price for victims of cancer. Significantly, one hint that alcoholism and cancer may be related — *as metaphors* — stems from the awareness that alcoholism as metaphor imposed a similar stigma. As even less conscious metaphor, it may further have exacted an even greater price.[7]

Before exploring the relationship between the metaphors of cancer and alcoholism, and what it might tell moderns about modernity, an essential *caveat* must be stated and even flourished. As the examples of leprosy, tuberculosis, and cancer so vividly attest, to posit any specific illness as an age's disease-metaphor in absolutely no way denies the objective reality of the disease so used. An important and significant point about disease-metaphors, indeed, arises precisely because they are most often drawn from and rooted in a society's uncomprehending terror in the face of its direst malady. The sad irony is that the metaphor, especially as unconscious, serves to deepen the incomprehension and to increase the terror even as it illuminates the culture. The actual victims of the actual disease used as metaphor thus become their culture's double losers — victims of both the disease and the metaphor. Leprosy, tuberculosis, and cancer are "real" diseases; the use in what follows of alcoholism as disease-metaphor intends neither to deny nor to affirm the objective reality of alcoholism as a disease. The analysis to follow derives from two plain facts: "alcoholism is a disease" has become a generally accepted cliché in the America of the second half of the twentieth century, and that first fact is generally attributed to the impact upon the culture of Alcoholics Anonymous.[8]

The importance of what has been carefully explained concerning the use of disease as metaphor, the peril as well as the promise of this mode of analysis, derives from the intuition that the uses of alcoholism and of cancer as disease-metaphors are connected. Each reveals modern concerns over the very meaning of modernity. The disease-metaphor of alcoholism, however, precedes that of cancer in both historical and logical sequence. Alcoholism-as-metaphor deals with the subjective consciousness of moderns, while cancer-as-metaphor discloses the objective implications of modernity. The metaphor of alcoholism lays bare modernity's internal process; that of cancer laments its external results.

Understanding alcoholism as a metaphor for the subjective condition of modernity illuminates the modern era's discomfort and therefore dis-ease when confronted by an apparent paradox of the human condition — the *meaning* of human as limited but frustrated by this limitation. By applying the insights gleaned in Chapter Eight to the historical context glimpsed in Chapter Seven, what follows attempts to penetrate this veiled metaphor. It explores the subjective sense of "being modern" by applying to this modern sensibility the classic Evangelical Pietist intuition conveyed within Alcoholics Anonymous. This ancient insight suggests that humankind exists in a state of being that is essentially limited, and that transcendence of this limitation requires first acceptance of it, then the embrace of salvation from it as coming only from outside the individual self.[9]

The analytic insight that finds in alcoholism a metaphor suggests that three facets of the Alcoholics Anonymous understanding of alcoholism merit special study: alcoholism as threefold disease, as obsessive-compulsive addiction, and as distorted dependency. Further, because this insight proposes alcoholism as specifically the disease-metaphor for the *subjective condition* of modernity, the exploration of each of these three aspects of A.A.'s understanding begins with a reminder that Alcoholics Anonymous itself never treats directly of *alcoholism*, but rather directs its attention to the *alcoholic* — the subject of the disease.[10]

Although the phrase appears nowhere so succinctly in A.A. literature, immersion in that literature makes it clear that an understanding common among members of Alcoholics Anonymous and often detailed at A.A. meetings infuses the very heart of their program: "alcoholism is a threefold disease — physical, mental, and spiritual." The clear message is that there is a unity in human life, ill or healthy. The parts of the human experience are so interconnected that to suffer disturbance in one is to suffer dislocation in all; and in recovery, all must be attended to if any is to be healed.[11]

The most common diagnosis of the source of modern malaise describes that cause as "alienation" and *anomie* — the feeling of separation and the despairing loneliness of a deeply sensed isolation which, because there are no norms, denies the very possibility of meaning. Critics of modernity have also called attention to its monstrosity, its characteristic of disproportionate growth. The vision of society as organic especially points up such discrepancies as those between "haves" and "have-nots"; and modern individuals seem divided into the distinct categories of those who think but can't feel, those who feel but don't think, and those who act and so have time for neither thinking nor feeling. All these situations cause pain, as the recognition of the twentieth century as "The Age of Psychology" — and especially of psychotherapy — testifies.[12]

In presenting alcoholism as threefold disease, Alcoholics Anonymous both speaks to this modern pain and sharpens these critiques of the modern situation. The pinch of alienation, A.A. suggests, comes less from man's separation from the product of his labor than from modernity's claim and attempt to separate three aspects of human life and experience that are in reality essentially conjoined — the physical, the mental, and the spiritual. The A.A. insight insists first that body, mind, and spirit are so intimately related within each individual that what affects one influences the others. The headache that impedes concentration is not merely physical, nor can the guilt that issues in such a headache be deemed merely spiritual. The thinking that denies guilt into repression, or that expresses its brilliance in devising rationalizations that will inevitably lead to more such hangover mornings, is also "sick."

The message of this insight is that the self is complex, and that in order to live comfortably with self as well as with others, both self and others must be accepted as complex. The *total* experience of *each* human being comprises at least these three dimensions: physical, mental, and spiritual. These are evidently related to each other, and as evidently bespeak also a larger relatedness. If one is to live a fully human life among human others, as well as if one is to live with oneself as fully human, there must be sensitivity to each of these three components in both self and others. In the absence of such sensitivity, alienation occurs — a felt-separation the pangs of which are both two-sided and twofold as they mutually reinforce each other. This destructive mutuality arises because feeling divided within oneself both results in and is intensified by feeling separated from others, while at the same time the felt-separation from others both reinforces and is furthered by deliberate dissection of the self. Feeling "messed up" leads to distance from others, as others' distance encourages "feeling messed up."

That which would attempt to heal such alienation clearly must speak also to this destructive reciprocity, for false separation within the self and destructive separation between selves are mutually related. Just as "a sound mind" and "a sound body" — according to the ancient adage — promote each other's soundness, the healthy self both helps and is helped by healthy others. Because Alcoholics Anonymous offers itself to the recovering alcoholic as *both* fellowship and program, it suggests by this very understanding of itself that these twin aspects of human experience can beget a twofoldness of mutualities that are healingly related. As program, A.A. teaches that the physical, mental, and spiritual components of each alcoholic's individual life are mutually connected. To injure one is to harm the others, and to treat one healthfully is to promote the well-being of all three and so of the whole organism. But A.A. is also fellowship, and as such it teaches that it is with others rather than as individual that one treats self healthfully. Thus the mutuality among alcoholics within the A.A. fellowship reinforces the threefold recovery of each alcoholic, and the ongoing recovery of each alcoholic in turn promotes healthy mutuality within the fellowship.

Few can ignore that the drinking alcoholic destroys himself physically and impairs his mental faculties. Many have also stressed moral degradation, but one effect of the Alcoholics Anonymous understanding of the alcoholic has been to shift this last emphasis to "the spiritual." The heart of the alcoholic malady, A.A. teaches, is *spiritual disease*. It is the spiritual in the trilogy of "physical, mental, and spiritual" that wastes first in the progression into alcoholism and is restored last in recovery from it. The spiritual is the key to the A.A. program, as befits the understanding of a phenomenon in the history of religious ideas. The spiritual also provides the linchpin of Alcoholics Anonymous as fellowship, as exploration of the implications inherent in A.A.'s understanding of alcoholism as obsessive-compulsive addiction and as distorted dependency will clarify.[13]

———————————

A.A.'s presentation of alcoholism as "obsession-compulsion" reflects its borrowing from Dr. Silkworth's diagnosis of Bill Wilson. This understanding describes more than explains the alcoholic's insatiable quest for *more* and unrelenting pursuit of *again*. Bill, like countless alcoholics before him, described to the doctor his fixation of being able to "think of nothing else," and how he was driven to seek to recapture again that glowing feeling of warmth that his early drinking had brought. At least until he had first heard Ebby's message, that fixation (obsession) and that drive (compulsion) had been the story of Wilson's adult life. The psychiatrist's main contribution here was to give A.A.'s co-founder labels for an experience that every true alcoholic knew all too well but rarely was able to describe so succinctly.[14]

The other alcoholics to whom Wilson carried Silkworth's diagnosis as a way of introducing Ebby's message identified readily with it. Bill's description of obsession-compulsion hit home, and so it helped these early adherents of Alcoholics Anonymous to admit hopelessness and thus to make the surrender that sobriety within A.A. required. Because "it worked," they in their turn described rather than attempted to explain when they later approached their own "pigeons," and it is in this way that the first message of Alcoholics Anonymous has been consistently carried. Founded in experience, A.A. has little use for philosophizing. Yet there are philosophical and even theological ideas contained in A.A.'s portrayal of obsession-compulsion, and those who would understand at depth its message of not-God-ness might well explore them.

The first of these ideas has to do with the concept of infinity. The infinite is the unbounded, the unlimited, the immeasurable, *the* absolute. In the history of human thought, the infinite has been identified with the divine. To be infinite is, in a word, to be God. To be human, according to the ancient religious insight expressed by Alcoholics Anonymous, is precisely to be not infinite, and so not God, but to yearn for just such unlimited fulfillment. The human thus longs — thirsts — to transcend the limitations of being human. In the phrase set forth by Saint Augustine as the theme of his classic confession: "Our hearts are restless until they rest in Thee."[15]

The alcoholic soul readily identifies with this quest. According to the insight underlying A.A.'s "spiritual program," it was this thirst for transcendence that expressed itself in the alcoholic's addictive, obsessive-compulsive drinking. The thirst for transcendence had been perverted into a thirst for alcohol. Some members of Alcoholics Anonymous have indeed guessed that it was the intuitive perception of precisely this perversion that inspired "good people's" special disgust for alcoholism. Especially in A.A.'s early years, members often remarked on the dual sense of the word *spirit*: the alcoholic's problem had been, in one formulation of the insight, confusing "spirits" with "the spiritual." Bill Wilson at times observed to trusted correspondents that the alcoholic seemed to be an especially sensitive person, one haunted by a particularly pressing need for transcendence. That, he and others suggested, was why the spiritual program of Alcoholics Anonymous worked. It spoke to the need for transcendence by offering the alcoholic real contact with the really spiritual.[16]

The first message of that real contact was that the alcoholic himself was not, and could not be, God. Not-God-ness was taught first, of course, by bringing home to the drinking alcoholic his dire helplessness — his powerlessness over alcohol and the unmanageability of his life. But once this had been demonstrated, and the alcoholic had accepted its truth, A.A. occasionally faced a different problem with its newly sober member. At times, in the very flush of new sobriety, a formerly destructive drinker would adduce precisely this success to press another claim that threatened to deny not-God-ness: yes, he was not God, but that was all right because there was no God — no absolute — anyway. This equivalent denial of *any* ultimate reality of course still implied the ultimate self-centeredness that Alcoholics Anonymous had diagnosed as "the root" of the alcoholic's problem. Because of this, A.A. had to meet its challenge directly.

The Alcoholics Anonymous response was simple. A.A. argued neither theology nor philosophy, but rather pointed to a simple fact in the drinker's experience that effectively embodied a deeply philosophical and psychological truth — a fact that even by its very dissonance with traditional formulations eloquently made the key point. The alcoholic had been unable to stop his alcoholic drinking, the obsessive-compulsive acting out of his alcoholism, on his own, by himself. Yet within Alcoholics Anonymous he had achieved this success. Indeed, even before he himself had attained sobriety, the drinking alcoholic had been impressed by this group of men and women, former alcoholic drinkers, who had succeeded where he could not. All right, then, the first steps to sobriety did not require classic belief in a traditional "God"; but they did require that the alcoholic accept his not-God-ness by acknowledging *some* "Power greater" than himself. The A.A. group itself, clearly, was such a "Higher Power." Its members had achieved what he could not, and in that admission lay the true core of the alcoholic's acceptance of not-God-ness: there was *some* Higher Power; there did actually exist a Power greater than his own. In time, perhaps, he would come to accept what those who made up *this* "Power greater" accepted as *their* "Higher Power."[17]

Such acknowledgment was surely attenuated infinity and but small transcendence, yet it made the point. By drawing on his own proximate and vivid experience, it drove home the individual alcoholic's personal limitation and so pointed to getting out of, beyond, the mere self as holding the only hope for "salvation" — at least from active alcoholism. The very existence of the A.A. group as successfully sober not only taught but insistently riveted attention on these two truths: the individual alcoholic was hopelessly limited, and he could transcend that limitation only by reaching beyond himself to others. This was the essential message of not-God-ness that broke the drinking alcoholic's obsession-compulsion with merely finite and all too immanent and readily available alcohol.

Alcoholics Anonymous thus shifted attention from the material — even if "spirits" — to the spiritual that truly satisfied the spirit. The lesson involved also a shift of attention from quantity to quality. Both of these changes derived from A.A.'s understanding of the fundamental nature of alcoholism as "obsession-compulsion." Because the alcoholic's striving was for the infinite, for transcendence, it could not be satisfied by pursuit of the material. The material was necessarily finite, measurable, limited. Of the material there could always be "more," and so concentration on the material when the real quest was for the spiritual was doomed to frustration. By stressing that it presented a "spiritual program" for "quality sobriety," Alcoholics Anonymous changed the drinking alcoholic's fixation and drive to imbibe ever more alcohol to a dedication to seeking the *quality* of *the spiritual* in his life. Unlike the material, of which there could always be "more," the spiritual was inherently qualitative. The spiritual could admit of degrees, perhaps, but spiritual phenomena were essentially either-or. Despite all the styles of living discernible, one is either alive or dead. The alcoholic, at least, is either drunk or sober, even if both states allow for degrees all too easily noticeable. More classically, in the theological understanding that informed A.A.'s insight, one is either saved or damned.

As is evident from the examples, even in these clear cases of either-or, there is a tendency in the human mind that imposes some perception of degrees, of shadings. One reason for A.A.'s almost instinctive avoidance of the Oxford Group's "Four Absolutes" lay in the insight derived from its early experience that encouraging this perception led to a different kind of obsession-compulsion, one that, allowed entrance into the alcoholic's thinking, led in its turn to alcoholic drinking once again. But with the specter of a possible "absolute spirituality" removed as a reachable or possible goal against which to measure, the alcoholic was enabled and encouraged to concentrate on the either-or, to focus attention upon enhancing quality rather than increasing quantity. The difference may be subtle, but the experience of Alcoholics Anonymous insisted that it was real, and the practice of Alcoholics Anonymous as both fellowship and program was designed to teach that difference.[18]

A.A.'s emphasis that it is a "spiritual program" for "quality sobriety" works to offset the danger that even the sober alcoholic might think in quantitative terms of *increasing* sobriety rather than from the qualitative concept of *growing* in it. As adherents of a "fellowship," members of Alcoholics Anonymous judge the success of their groups not by the numbers who attend but by the serenity of the sobriety of those who attend. "Serenity," as spiritual, is inherently unquantifiable. Nor does the program of Alcoholics Anonymous, as "spiritual," admit of quantitative comparisons. Despite the recognized importance of taking the Twelve Steps and attending meetings, A.A. members do not "measure" sobriety by the number of times they have been through the former or by how frequently or for how long they have practiced the latter. No Step is ever *perfectly* taken, Wilson stressed in and after writing *Twelve Steps and Twelve Traditions*; and the wisdom of A.A. has taught that meeting attendance can be *too* frequent. "You didn't get sober to go to meetings," enthusiasts are often cautioned; and any who are perceived to brag over the frequency or faithfulness of their meeting attendance are usually less than gently reminded that such grandiose fanaticism smacks of the "dry drunk" syndrome.[19]

In a similar vein, speakers at A.A. meetings, especially those who themselves in fact have long-term sobriety, are wont to remind their hearers — and themselves — that "whoever got up earliest this morning is the 'most sober' person in this room: this is a day-at-a-time program." There are no recorded instances of members of Alcoholics Anonymous pushing back the alarm clock before they go to bed in order that they may be the "most sober" at the next day's meeting.

"Obsession-compulsion," as presented by Alcoholics Anonymous, arose from seeking to grasp the infinite by pursuit or piling up of the limited, from the effort to attain the spiritual by means of the material. But the infinite, as qualitative and spiritual, was not *additive*; that is, it could not be attained by the adding up of *any* quantity of limited experiences. Rather, the demanding quest to lay hold of the essentially unlimited by pursuit of the inherently finite became *addictive* — doomed to the frustration of self-defeat. Happiness, A.A. taught, was not attained by *having more*; nor, its witness testified at every meeting, could peace be found in material things.

Alcoholic experience taught Alcoholics Anonymous that the root of the alcoholic's addiction to alcohol lay essentially in his misunderstanding and denial of the spiritual. The active alcoholic was attempting to attain the spiritual, the unlimited, by means of the material. He was trying to achieve a *quality* of living by the mere adding up of quantities of or experiences with alcohol. This insatiable craving for "more" and "again," a veritable addiction to addition that was indeed an addiction to addiction itself, contained its own perverse ironies. The first was that the addictive drinking of *more* alcohol became progressively *less* fulfilling.[20]

The perception of this irony further impelled Alcoholics Anonymous to present itself as a "spiritual program" for "quality sobriety." From the beginning, Alcoholics Anonymous intuited that a deep root of addiction lay in the denial of the reality of the spiritual. It is only in the realm of the spiritual, as Western thought has understood it, that transcendence — going beyond — is not achieved by mere addition, that quality is not improved by the mere increase of quantity. The reality of the spiritual — that something could be real without being tangible — was indeed A.A.'s first and only advertisement. It was not the number of drinks left undrunk but "living the program" that constituted the evident sobriety of its members.

Also related to the spiritual was A.A.'s intuition and use of the second irony inherent in the phenomenon of alcoholism, the irony that linked its presentation of the threefold disease of alcoholism as "obsession-compulsion" and as distorted dependency. In searching for fulfillment as qualitatively human — a spiritual search — but seeking this fulfillment in increasing quantities of alcohol, the drinker trapped himself in a contradiction. The drinking alcoholic demanded a *control* that was inappropriate and so impossible. This demand for control involved a claim to the absolute; it strove to reach beyond the limits of human finiteness. The alcoholic attempted to achieve by the drinking of alcohol what reality would give only by living as fully human. Reality does not grant to humans *absolute* control over moods and feelings; emotions are meant to be *responses* to reality, and mainly to realities outside the self. *Absolute control* over emotion, in the sense of absolutely autonomous self-determination of moods and feelings, involved a claim to unlimitedness, and so a claim beyond any human.[21]

This striving demand for such absolute control led, with all the perverse irony characteristic of deeply religious thought, to its very opposite — absolute *dependence* upon a most finite and tenuous limited creature, spiritous liquids. The First Step of the A.A. program pointed out to the alcoholic this frustrating irony. His refusal to accept dependence upon ultimate reality — the refusal implicit in the claim to inordinate control — had led to a perverted dependency upon the virtually unreal.

A.A. proposed and indeed operated on the assumption that this denial of dependence upon ultimate reality was at root a denial of the reality of the spiritual. It was this denial of the spiritual that A.A. found underlying all the other denials so characteristic as to be pathognomonic of alcoholism. The alcoholic's first denial was of the reality of his finiteness: by "playing God," he denied that he was not God. In his solipsistic claim to be the ultimate reality ("self-centeredness"), the alcoholic falsely limited his acceptance of what *was* "reality." The self-centered alcoholic accepted as *real* only that which was subject to his own rationalization and control. This limitation of "the real" cut off the alcoholic from "the spiritual," from that by definition beyond human manipulation. The use of the chemical ethyl alcohol for its mood-changing effects marked the alcoholic's insistence upon absolute control over faculties that related him to reality outside himself. Such an insistence was an abuse that resulted in lack of ability to use properly. Emotions controlled absolutely by the self eventually no longer related the self to outside reality, and so perversely issued in lack of control of even the self. Reality comprised of only the controllable effectively excluded not only "the spiritual" but also other human beings insofar as they participated in the spiritual. Thus the alcoholic imposed upon himself the alienation and isolation characteristic of alcoholism.[22]

The alienation that resulted from the alcoholic's denial of dependence upon spiritual reality led to a more demeaning dependence upon the material substance alcohol and the unreality that it provided. This process ironically led, in an ever-tightening vicious circle, to even more alienating denials. The alcoholic's first denial of his own limitation as finitely dependent, his denial that there could be reality beyond his rationalization and control, ended in his absolute dependence upon the very means of control that he had chosen precisely because it was supposedly controllable — his drinking of alcohol. This new dependence, of course, was even more vociferously denied; and thus the alcoholic cut himself off from those who would help him by calling attention to his dire plight. Those who cared for the alcoholic *had to* separate themselves from him: in order to preserve their own sanity, they had to extricate themselves from the alcoholic's ever-expanding web of denials. The alcoholic's initial denial of limited dependence upon spiritual reality was revealed as intrinsically and ironically perverse when it issued in an absolute dependence upon alcohol that progressively destroyed his relationships with other human beings. The chosen means of control itself eluded control, and other people — the desired objects of control — abandoned the alcoholic, taking their reality with them.[23]+

+   Helping those who are affected by an alcoholic's drinking is the chosen task of Al-Anon. Al-Anon bases its approach on the Twelve Steps of Alcoholics Anonymous. It is not a part of A.A., but understands its own chief founder to be Lois Wilson, Bill Wilson's wife.

If somehow, at this point, the alcoholic could be brought to glimpse the reality of his situation — if somehow the alcoholic could be given an insight into the spiritual unreality of his life by breaking through his denial and bringing him face to face with the absolute nature of his dependence upon alcohol — then the alcoholic "hit bottom." He became able to make the admission of powerlessness and unmanageability that was the necessary First Step to his recovery of real human personhood. It was at this point that Alcoholics Anonymous sought to reach the drinking alcoholic, and this role that the fellowship and its program played in the alcoholic's life.[24]

A.A.'s prescription for alcoholism diagnosed as the denial of *any* dependence in its claim to *absolute* control flowed from its deep awareness of the human as not-God and therefore limited. The human as not-God needed to accept limitation and further to find wholeness in that very limitation. Because he was not God, not absolute, the alcoholic had to embrace and live the realization that *all* absolutes escaped him: the absolute of control because it was beyond him; the absolute of dependence because it was beneath him. The prescription, then, was to accept *limited* control and to acknowledge *limited* dependence.

The alcoholic's *absolute* lack of absolute control was driven home by A.A.'s insistence on his absolute powerlessness over alcohol. The admitted alcoholic could not imbibe even one drink, for it was the first drink that got the alcoholic drunk in the sense that the first drink by an admitted alcoholic signaled the denial of essential limitation that reintroduced the claim to be God.[+]

The second part of A.A.'s recommended remedy for alcoholism treated the denial of "the spiritual" inherent in the alcoholic's denial of *any* dependence — his restriction of "the real" to that which was under his own rationalization and control. For the alcoholic to become "not-God" — able to give to and to receive from others — required accepting the *reality* of others. Since they as human were not subject to absolute rationalization and control, these others participated in "the spiritual," and thus attested to its reality. Those not God regained reality by entering into relationships with others who comfortably accepted that same limitation. In such relationships, the conscious mutuality of those who cherished their not-God-ness precluded demands for any rationalization and control of others who also accepted precisely that same limitation as the foundation of their positive identity.

+ Stressing this psychological and spiritual aspect is not intended to imply that A.A. ignores the physiological component of alcoholism in its emphasis on "not taking the first drink."

In the simple language of Alcoholics Anonymous, this twofold prescription is epitomized in a reminder usually spoken at the conclusion
of A.A. meetings: "And whatever else, remember: don't take the first
drink and keep coming to meetings." "Don't take the first drink" reminds that the alcoholic is not God. It signals the importance of accepting limitation. "Keep coming to meetings" speaks to the alcoholic as
not-God. It alerts to the *wholeness* to be found in limitation. Since to be
human is to be limited, wholeness as human is always unfinished
process rather than ever achieved condition. The phrase reminds also
that this process involves giving to and receiving from others who also
accept this truth and strive to live it in relationships of true mutuality.

A.A.'s two-sided message of not-God-ness — of the necessity of accepting limitation and of the wholeness of that accepted limitation — is
revealed clearly in its twin prescription of limited control and limited
dependence. Both control and dependence were limited because the
alcoholic was both not God and not-God. Limited control arises more
clearly from not being God, and limited dependence from being not-
God, but the two are inextricably intertwined — as they must be from
the evident fact that the drinking alcoholic's effort at absolute control
and denial of any dependence were in service to and mutually reinforced each other. The image of the drinking alcoholic seeking human
warmth by reaching for a bottle may clarify the point. In Alcoholics
Anonymous, the truly sober alcoholic both seeks and reaches for *others*,
rather than for a bottle *or* for warmth.

The acceptance that both control and dependence are limited, and
the sense that wholeness as human flowed from this dual acceptance of
limitation, were so centrally important to Alcoholics Anonymous that its
program and fellowship sought to instill these fundamental lessons in
many ways. Historically, its message of limited control has been reinforced most evidently by A.A.'s resolute rejection of any claim to any
absolute and by its inherent anti-perfectionism. Because these aspects of
Alcoholics Anonymous border on complex current controversy, their
direct treatment in this book has been put off to an Appendix at its
conclusion. Only at that point can all the diverse threads needed for fair
evaluation be gathered together and woven into a coherent explanation. Here, it should suffice to remind of the obvious in A.A. history and
literature.

A large reason for the departure of Alcoholics Anonymous from the
Oxford Group lay in the Group's insistence upon "The Four Absolutes." Bill Wilson and the first New York A.A.s found in this emphasis
a special threat to alcoholics with their tendency to be "all-or-nothing

people." Its Oxford Group experience early and definitively taught Alcoholics Anonymous the dangers of "going broke on this sort of perfection — trying to get too good by Thursday," in one of Wilson's favorite expressions.[25]

The A.A. program as set forth in the book *Alcoholics Anonymous* enshrined this understanding. At the very climax of its explanation of "How It Works," the Big Book offered as suggested goal the most that Alcoholics Anonymous claimed or promised: "spiritual progress rather than spiritual perfection." That very description of "How It Works" had opened, after lengthy discussion among A.A.'s early members, with a reminder even to themselves of the necessity "to avoid anything that would look like a claim of a 100% result": "*Rarely* have we seen a person fail who has thoroughly followed our path." The central importance of limited control also strongly influenced the fellowship's anti-professionalism and anti-intellectualism. Both phenomena derived from the sense that the human is limited, and each reminded of and opened to this fundamental intuition's corollary of the need for others in relationships of true mutuality.[26]

Such awareness of the need for others, however, can itself be treacherous, and from this realization flows the corollary of limited control — limited dependence. Forgetting that even others who are needed are themselves also limited can lead to a denial of *their* not-God-ness, and from such denial can then spring the unreasonable demand of excessive dependence upon them. In many ways, problems concerning dependence continued to haunt Alcoholics Anonymous long into its history and its members well into their sobriety. A.A.'s confrontation of the paradox of limited dependence in its portrayal of alcoholism as distorted dependence thus illuminates both Alcoholics Anonymous as therapy and alcoholism as metaphor.

Alcoholics Anonymous achieved its awareness of the dangers of excessive dependence honestly. Co-founder Bill Wilson's self-knowledge as an alcoholic led him relatively early in his sobriety to keep in careful check his tendency to dominate. With his tendency to dependence and with the manifold and insidious forms in which this trait could reveal itself, Bill had more, greater, and longer-lasting problems. One major insight came in 1947, rescuing Wilson from his depression of that mid-decade. In a letter in which he discussed his withdrawal from Dr. Tiebout's generally Freudian treatment and his own recent interest in the thought of Dr. Carl Jung, Bill broke off his generally abstract analysis to utter as heartfelt cry the insight that would in developed form undergird his whole approach to Alcoholics Anonymous as "Way of Life": "Highly satisfactory as it is to live one's life for others, it cannot be anything but disastrous to live one's life for others as those others think it should be lived. One has, for better or worse, to choose his own life."[27]

Six years later, as Wilson was putting the finishing touches on his final re-working of the synthesis of the A.A. Way of Life in *Twelve Steps and Twelve Traditions*, the alcoholic author in back-to-back letters to friends laid out clearly his personal understanding and his final resolution of his own history of "dependence":

> I know that my underlying difficulty from which all others stem and are merely symptomatic, is that inner insistence which demands that I either be absolutely dependent upon someone, or else dominate them. The latter being merely the reverse side of the coin whose main face is "absolute dependence." Since I have begun to pray that God may release me from absolute dependence on anybody, anything, or any set of circumstances, I have begun to do so much better that it amounts to a second conversion experience.[28]

> I am beginning to see that all my troubles have their root in a habitual and absolute dependence upon my personal prestige, security, and romantic attachment. When these things go wrong, there is depression. Now this absolute dependence upon people and situations for emotional security is, I think, the immense and devastating fallacy that makes us miserable. This craving for such dependencies, this utter dependence upon people and situations, can only lead to conflict. Both on the surface and at depth. We are making demands on circumstances and people that are bound to fail us. The only safe and sure channel of absolute dependence is upon God himself.[29]

The alcoholic's dependence upon anything but God was limited. Yet the tendency to seek ever more dependence upon creatures would always press, even within Alcoholics Anonymous. A.A. is, after all, a fellowship of *alcoholics* — of those who insatiably quest for *more*. What follows will explore A.A.'s awareness of this danger and how the fellowship confronted this reality under two headings: an examination of what actually happens at meetings of Alcoholics Anonymous, and an analysis of A.A.'s implicit response to the charges that were leveled against it of fostering immature dependency.

The typical meeting of Alcoholics Anonymous is a model of the living out of the *shared honesty of mutual vulnerability openly acknowledged* that the historical narrative has pointed out to be the essential dynamic of A.A. therapy. Because the honesty is shared, and because it expresses a vulnerability that is mutual, the dependence involved in this relationship is inherently and essentially limited. Each speaker at every meeting of Alcoholics Anonymous introduces himself or herself (usually by first name only) and immediately adds, "and I am an alcoholic." Except at "Beginners" or "Inquiry" meetings, this affirmation is the foundation on which the right to speak is based. Its acceptance witnesses to "the desire to stop drinking" that is "the only requirement for membership."[30]

Except in small discussion groups where the members already know each other's stories, it is then customary for the speaker to "qualify." He or she tells the story of a life disrupted by alcohol: how drinking for the effects of alcohol began, to what it led, how the alcoholic found A.A., and both the joys and the difficulties of personal growth in sobriety. Some stories are mainly of triumphal witness; others concentrate on the problems of living soberly; all *both* offer hope *and* ask for help.

But these stories and even the discussion that contains them at Discussion or Step meetings do not best reveal the very heart of Alcoholics Anonymous. Grasping this requires, appropriately, something extra of the person who would penetrate to the core of the fellowship and its program. He must "come early and stay late." It is in this free gift of self and time that one best discovers the true dynamic of A.A. meetings, for the *mutuality* that underlies and characterizes every A.A. conversation stands most clearly revealed then. Every A.A. conversation — every meeting of two or three for the purpose of sobriety — begins with one of two usually implicit introductions: "I think you can help me" or "I think I can help you." At times these are made explicit after formal meetings in such words as "Thank you for what you said — it helped me" and "Did what I said seem helpful?"; but whether implicit or explicit, the essence of A.A. therapy remains clear. Each recovering alcoholic member of Alcoholics Anonymous is kept constantly aware, at every meeting, that he has *both* something to give *and* something to receive from his fellow alcoholics. The lesson instilled has two points: that one is dependent on others, for both giving and getting; and that this dependence is *limited*, for the presenting quality of each other — the one sure thing known about him and the certain reason why he is there — is that *he* is limited and is present precisely for help in accepting that limitation.

Such acceptance and embrace of even limited dependence within Alcoholics Anonymous has been sharply criticized in a culture and an age that self-consciously defines its modernity precisely in terms of its claimed autonomy and independence. The language of a psychological age tends to construct this criticism of Alcoholics Anonymous around the concept and term *maturity*, but the criticism as well as A.A.'s response to it involves more deeply the meaning of *dependence*. Consistently over time and by widely diverse observers, the essence of alcoholism has been intuited to consist in dependence. For the modern mind, the cure for dependence is independence. According to modern thought, the alcoholic must conquer his dependence upon alcohol rather than merely transfer that dependence to some other object — whether that new object be different oral gratification, a transcendent Higher Power, or other sick alcoholics. To the modern understanding, "full maturity" means *absolute, total* independence; and for the modern understanding, of course, only *full* maturity is satisfactory. The modern mind, inhabited by its Nietzschean will, pushes always for the *absolute*. The not-absolute, the less than full, cannot quench the thirst of modernity, and so the demand for "total" tends to inhere in whatever moderns quest. Quest, indeed, necessarily becomes demand in the context of modernity, and it is precisely this facet of the modern criticism of itself that Alcoholics Anonymous in its turn most acutely criticizes, in the understanding of alcoholism as a disease-metaphor for modernity.[31]

The Alcoholics Anonymous understanding, although "modern" in its use of twentieth-century insight, remains infused by its ancient Pietist root. A.A. embraces and incorporates the insight of modern psychology that interprets the alcoholic's dependence upon the chemical alcohol as in service to his infantile quest for grandiose omnipotence, although A.A. literature simplifies the concept by calling it "playing God." Given this insight, however, Alcoholics Anonymous proposes as the remedy for alcoholism thus understood not the elimination of dependence but its shift to its proper object. Human dependence, A.A. proposes, is not to be denied. The problem of the alcoholic lies not in the *fact* of dependence, but in its *distortion*. According to the A.A. vision, to be human *is* to be dependent, but upon ultimate reality outside the self rather than upon alcohol inside oneself. Accepted ultimate dependence is the essence of the experience of bottom. It is both the cause and the result of surrender, both the inspiration to and the term of conversion. Accepted ultimate dependence is, in a word, salvation, at least for the alcoholic.[32]

The implicit response of Alcoholics Anonymous to the accusation that it panders to immaturity by fostering dependence consists in the insistence that to be human *is* to be — existentially — an infant, that is, *ultimately* immature. The problem of being human lies not in dependence, but in the denial of dependence through the claim to omnipotence. The problem of the alcoholic is not "infantilism," but the collision between the contradictory claims of existential and psychological infancy, the dissonance inherent in the quest for total omnipotence launched from a situation of total dependence. The program of Alcoholics Anonymous resolves this intolerable tension by conscious and explicit choice of one side and rejection of the other. True to its deeply religious insight, A.A. requires the abdication of *all* claim to omnipotence while willingly and even enthusiastically embracing *total* dependence on an omnipotent ultimate reality.[33]

In the modern demand for absolute independence, in the modern denial of absolutely all human dependence, Alcoholics Anonymous locates the era's root misapprehension of the meaing of "human." A.A.'s message proclaims the *integrity* of dependence, if this dependence be upon an ultimate absolute outside the control of human experience. The human as not-God, the fellowship announces by its own example, derives wholeness from limitation — if limitation is rightly, *wholly* understood.[+]

Alcoholics Anonymous locates its deeper diagnostic understanding of the dis-ease of modernity as illuminated by the metaphor of alcoholism in the demand for domination, for *absolute* rationalization and control. Frustration of this modern demand for absolute control is inevitable, for the quest for such rationalization and control is intrinsically insatiable — doomed by its very nature as absolute to an ever emptier and ever more destructive craving for "more" and "again." In a burst of insight that unites "the religious" and "the medical" far more profoundly than the fellowship ever realized in its self-conscious reference to these twin roots, Alcoholics Anonymous points out that the "modern" quest is, on the one hand, the claim to infinity, the blasphemous equation of self with God; and on the other hand, the ultimate manifestation of the immaturity of which the culture accuses the fellowship itself. It is

---

+   Some who approach Alcoholics Anonymous at times complain that acceptance of its philosophy and especially of this dependence will turn them into "doormats." The usual response to this within A.A., one that also points up the advantage of accepting A.A.'s "spiritual approach," is to point out a sentence on p. 83 of *AA.*: "As God's people, we stand on our own feet, we don't crawl before anyone." Most A.A. members claim that accepting their ultimate dependence upon God, and therefore themselves "as God's people," not only frees them from the toadying that characterizes the guilt-ridden drinking alcoholic, but also gives them a freedom to be themselves that even non-alcoholics without such an anchor of faith often lack.

the infant, after all, who perceives and insists upon all reality being an extension of the self.[34]

Alcoholics Anonymous thus reintroduces into modernity the concept of "sin." After Heisenberg, the claim to possess the absolute is as much scientific sacrilege as it is religious blasphemy; and the accusation of infantilism is, in the post-Freudian era, the ultimate diagnostic epithet. In a stunning reversal of assumptions that derives from its own experience and practice, Alcoholics Anonymous not only suggests that alcoholism itself is not sinful, but indicts the modern society that would implicitly call it such by the manipulation of psychological terms of the real "sin" — denying the *meaning* of the *human*. To be truly human, the fellowship insists through its program, even the modern human must accept that he is not-God as *affirmation* as well as not God in appropriate surrender of all claim to any absolute.[35]

The need of others that Alcoholics Anonymous teaches to be essential and fulfilling of the human in and of its very being *is* "dependence." The dependence implied by and accepted in the Second and Third Steps of the A.A. program is clearly first dependence upon ultimate reality — "God as we understand Him" or as "Power greater than ourselves." But the dependence of the admitted alcoholic does not stop here. Other human beings, and especially the A.A. group, are also understood as *needed*. Individualistic as the program of the Twelve Steps may seem at first glance, it reveals on closer examination another facet as well. The implied subject in each Step is "We": indeed, in the earliest version of the Steps, the "We" was explicitly stated in each. Not vainly nor merely rhetorically, then, does Alcoholics Anonymous insist that it is "fellowship." A.A.'s fundamental creedal statement of not-God-ness expresses limitation, and this limitation in turn — if accepted — implies *need*, for it is of the essence of being human to quest beyond individual limitation. The Steps make clear that this need is two-faceted even if its aspects may not require actual separation. The need is for *both* a "Power greater" *and* for other alcoholics with whom to utter that first "We" and then to take all the other Steps.[36]

The essence of not-God-ness is revealed to be needing others, and needing them in a mutuality that accepts that *every* human being needs others both to give to and to receive from. *Need* is not, within Alcoholics Anonymous, a dirty word. The inability to say "I need" — the *denial* of need — was what characterized the drinking alcoholic, who denied with special vehemence his very need for alcohol. A.A. began the restoration of the active alcoholic to sanity by enabling him to say, "I need." Admitting the *need* for alcohol — and so implicitly for transcendence — was the First Step toward recovery. Accepting the need for others as the *real* route to transcendence was the rest of the A.A. program — and the foundation of the A.A. fellowship. It is this enthusiastic embrace of the continuing reality of each not-God needing others that distinguishes Alcoholics Anonymous from the other therapies, in other respects similar, that in its time have briefly flourished only to quickly pass away and soon be forgotten.[37] +

Alcoholics Anonymous clearly proposes the need for others as an essential component of the alcoholic's not-God-ness. The fact that most criticism leveled against Alcoholics Anonymous has been aimed at precisely this aspect of its message alerts to the possible larger significance of the insight. It is all too human to attack most sharply that which threatens most acutely, and the instinct of the modern mind here is accurate. If Alcoholics Anonymous has a contribution to make to modernity, that potential contribution will best be located by a careful analysis of the specific need for others that A.A. teaches by its practice.[38]

The style as well as the content of A.A.'s invitation to live out the need for others is clear. The invitation is founded in the individual alcoholic's sure awareness that if he, as an alcoholic, is not-God, then neither is any other member of Alcoholics Anonymous "God." From the beginning, an essential aspect of the story-telling format that carried the A.A. message lay in the admonition: "Identify, Don't Compare." This injunction reminds the alcoholic to be especially attentive to his similarities with other alcoholics and their experience rather than concentrating on contrasts, searching for differences that might hinder shared and saving identification. "Identify, Don't Compare" encapsulates the pro-

+ The precise difference between Alcoholics Anonymous and these other therapies may be conceptualized variously, but the essential point will always be found to reside in their attitude to "dependence." Therapies other than A.A. were inherently "modern" in the sense explored in Chapter Seven: they aimed essentially to lead clients to responsible personal *autonomy*. The A.A. insight, deriving from the fellowship's historical rejection of absolutes and consistent dedication to not-God-ness, focused attention not on autonomy but upon the essential limitation of the human experience. A.A. did teach the alcoholic that he is *someone*, but it proposed this insight in a way that accented both concepts within that one word. The acceptance and affirmation of *some*-ness closed the door to any claim of being *either* "all" or "nothing." The embrace and cherishing of *one*-ness opened to the joyous pluralism of the shared honesty of mutual vulnerability that will be analyzed just below as the essential therapeutic dynamic of Alcoholics Anonymous.

Although the authors cited do not speak explicitly to this point, the interested reader will find useful to understanding it the materials cited in end-notes #31–36 to the treatment above, as well as the discussion that follows here.

gram's understanding of both alcoholism and its treatment. The sin of the active alcoholic had been to *identify* with "God," an endeavor reinforced by his tendency to *compare* (contrast) with other humans. The A.A. prescription cures this penchant. It suggests that differences among alcoholics are superficial and to be valued as *enriching* of the individual's vicarious experience and so of his identification as alcoholic. That one relates on the deepest and most helpful level to other alcoholics from weakness, from limitation, from one's own alcoholism, teaches and implements the message that human strength is rooted in human weakness. It inculcates by practice the awareness that one gives of oneself most effectively not from the overflowing richness of superfluous abundance, but from the yawning emptiness of acutely felt defect. If it be a function of authentic religion both to make comprehensible the human experience of suffering and to open human sufferers to each other in a healing way, Alcoholics Anonymous qualifies well.[39]

For want of a more available term, this welcoming with enthusiasm of the sense of the reality of needing others in enriching mutuality may be called "joyous pluralism." The word "pluralism" unfortunately limps; this is inevitable, for it signals how deeply this concept speaks to modernity's problem. The modern age does not even have a word for the essence of what Alcoholics Anonymous suggests and offers as remedy for the dis-ease described by the metaphor of alcoholism. We must, then, half-borrow and half-construct a new term. "Joyous pluralism" denotes the idea that those who accept themselves as limited and who find in their very limitation the glimmer of wholeness as well as an invitation to that wholeness can welcome *difference as good* — as fundamentally enriching rather than threatening, enhancing rather than diminishing.[40]

Appropriating the term "pluralism" is meant to distinguish this acceptance from both absolutisms and relativism. In baldest caricature and within the framework of philosophical and theological concepts most appropriate here, absolutisms claim that *something finite* can adequately grasp ultimate reality, while relativism asserts that there is *no ultimate* reality. The first assumption and fundamental assertion of the pluralistic point of view is that there *is* an ultimate reality, but that it lies *utterly beyond* the self and so cannot be totally comprehended by any finite entity. The finite may and indeed does participate in ultimate reality, but it cannot comprehend it — totally embrace or claim possession of that ultimate reality. The first intuition of pluralism is that the only absolute in the human experience is that no human experience can be absolute. Immediately derived from this flows the acceptance that since every human experience participates in the ultimate of being not-absolute, all human experience can enrich all other human experience.

Yet all that is but abstract philosophical musing. Pluralism is best seen in its pragmatic effects. The pluralistic insight issues in a "tolerance" that *actively welcomes* difference. The sense of incompleteness shared leads to ready acceptance that the partial completenesses of others complement rather than destroy, enrich rather than diminish, one's own partiality. And since in the pluralistic assumption others share this sense and this acceptance, one's own partiality — limitation — can be embraced as of value, cherished rather than regretted, lived rather than concealed. These implications of the philosophy of joyous pluralism are evident at meetings of Alcoholics Anonymous. Joyous pluralism invites to and enables the true opening to others in honest mutuality that takes place at these meetings. The assumptive acceptance that each alcoholic is present out of need both to give and to get issues in the sense that each person is enriched rather than diminished by the participation of every other. In the realm of "the spiritual," there exists no sense that "the good" is limited. Like the religionist's "salvation," the A.A. member's sobriety becomes richer rather than poorer as more share in it.[41]

Can such "joyous pluralism" exist outside of Alcoholics Anonymous? How far can even A.A.'s attenuated sense of "the spiritual" be extended without destroying it? The problems of the modern age, after all, hardly spring from agitation over the difficulties of sharing in "the spiritual" — or so it would seem. The question is a difficult one; and to claim insight here for Alcoholics Anonymous, even within the understanding of alcoholism as disease-metaphor, may seem to claim too much. Yet given even the possibility that that metaphor might contain wisdom rather than be mere figure of speech, A.A.'s presentation of pluralism hardly allows settling for less than an effort to unfold and explore this insight. Often, at meetings of Alcoholics Anonymous, some member will voice the wistful thought: "If only the world was like an A.A. meeting." That eventuality is surely unlikely and probably impossible, but exploring the sense from which this fancy derives may somewhat facilitate the contribution that Alcoholics Anonymous may be able to offer to its culture — the modern America of the twentieth century.

Our historical analysis has discovered the core dynamic of Alcoholics Anonymous to be "the shared honesty of mutual vulnerability openly acknowledged." But there is a step necessarily prior to this honest sharing in vulnerable mutuality. The individual alcoholic's first contact with

Alcoholics Anonymous takes place within the context of at least exploratory readiness to admit in a relationship of *mutual honesty* the *vulnerability he shares* with other alcoholics. One first attends an A.A. meeting, that is to say, only if at least wondering about "a drinking problem," and with at least some confidence that others one might meet there share at least the same wondering. This openness, however small, to mutual honesty *about* shared vulnerability necessarily precedes the capacity to participate in the shared honesty *of* mutual vulnerability, especially as openly acknowledged. Awareness of this sequence highlights an important point about A.A. therapy and points up what is perhaps A.A.'s most specific contribution to the modern dilemma concerning limits: the acceptance of a philosophy of pluralism such as A.A.'s — the capacity to accept difference as enriching rather than threatening and the ability to flourish within the context of the shared honesty of mutual vulnerability openly acknowledged — requires that the *basis of sharing be weakness rather than strength.*[42]

That strength arises precisely from weakness is the ancient and first fundamental religious insight. It is also precisely the insight to which, among the myriad of phenomena that dot the historical landscape of America in the twentieth century, Alcoholics Anonymous best if not also alone witnesses with a clarity and simplicity that render its wisdom readily, easily, and vividly understandable by all and accessible to all.[43]

Alcoholics Anonymous derived from its experience with alcoholics the insight that ultimate disaster occurs when there is denial of the essential limitation of *the human.* The first and therefore most dangerous denial is not that resources or *things* are limited, but that the human itself is essentially limited. If "sin" be understood as that which is essentially destructive of the human, Alcoholics Anonymous points out that the sin of modernity consists not primarily in any denial that resources are limited but first in the claim that the human is ultimate and so, unlimited — the claim to be "God" inherent in "self-centeredness."

The essential vulnerability of alcoholic and non-alcoholic humans alike is to that "self-centeredness" that A.A. proposes as "the root of our troubles." The acceptance that self-centeredness *is* vulnerability and that both the self-centeredness and the vulnerability are *shared* must precede any open acknowledgement of sharing honestly in the *mutuality* of this vulnerability. The barely dry alcoholic summoning up the courage to attend his first A.A. meeting reminds himself over and over again that both his vulnerability to alcohol and his hopes that he might transcend this vulnerability can be safely acknowledged there because anyone he might meet at that meeting admits that same vulnerability and that same hope simply by being there. So also, one who would live the joyously pluralistic philosophy of the shared honesty of mutual vulnerability needs first to grasp that because others share his vulnerability to self-centeredness, *their* hope of transcending *this* vulnerability lies in the mutual honesty of each acknowledging together that self-centeredness is weakness rather than strength. This is to say, in an unfashionable but understandable vocabulary, that acknowledging and accepting both self and others as "sinners" who need each other in their very "sinfulness" are necessary to attain the "salvation" of being *fully* "human." Only mutually honest acceptance that each is self-centered and that this shared quality is vulnerability — weakness rather than strength — only such acceptance can issue in the shared honesty of mutual vulnerability that becomes mutually healing.

Within Alcoholics Anonymous, this passage from mutual honesty *about* shared vulnerability to the shared honesty *of* mutual vulnerability is facilitated by the awareness of the necessity of anonymity. Most A.A.s cherish the irony of the realization that, except for those closest to them who were injured by their destructive drinking, modern American society more readily accepts them as occasionally drunk than as members of Alcoholics Anonymous. Society better tolerated their vulnerability to alcohol when they were drinking than when they are sober, and so their proximate vulnerability has been transfered from alcohol to the fact of their A.A. membership. But this first vulnerability of A.A.s to each other, the fact that they know each other to be members of Alcoholics Anonymous, is only the first step to and foundation for what takes place within A.A. meetings as the members grow in sobriety. Painfully, at first, their honesty grows, and with it their vulnerability as they share more of themselves with others to whom they are bound at first only by their mutual vulnerability to alcohol and to public opinion. They soon sense, however, that as their honesty and thus their vulnerability increase, so grows their sense of being healed, of being made whole-as-human. The experience of Alcoholics Anonymous testifies that the fulfilling sense that all need each other both to receive from and to give to is the reward inherent in the acceptance that the healing wholeness of salvation from self-centeredness comes from the shared honesty of mutual vulnerability openly acknowledged. It is no small reward, especially in an age when the expansion of "me" and "more" as the watchwords of modernity seem to jeopardize all human community.[44]

Whether or not to acknowledge that self-centeredness — "playing God" — is the ultimate vulnerability remains a decision for those moderns who are not A.A.s to make for themselves. The example of Alcoholics Anonymous, however, demonstrates the benefits of such acknowledgement and of its consequent acceptance that this ultimate vulnerability is mutual as well as shared. The most obvious benefit is that, while living in such acceptance of mutual vulnerability to self-centeredness is limiting, *by it the sense of limitation is itself limited.* An era that preens itself as "post-modern" especially needs this limitation of the sense of limitation. The Age of Limits is post-modern only in the sense that it acknowledges the existence of limits. The Age of Limits remains mired in the modern trap of pushing always and only for "more" and "again," its inherent insatiability rendering it unable to limit even its own dawning sense of limits.[45]

The insight that weakness necessarily precedes strength and strength arises precisely out of weakness can check this spiral of insatiability. Alcoholics Anonymous broke the pejorative progression of the concept "alcoholic," at least for those who acknowledged this limitation and embraced it as the foundation of their sobriety. A.A. achieved this by demonstrating that once not being God is accepted, the not-God-ness of relatedness to others follows an upward, ever-open progression in sobriety. The acknowledgment of essential need to receive from others does not lead within Alcoholics Anonymous to infinitely increasing need to receive, but rather begets the ability to give. Acknowledging and accepting need removes the coercive power and insatiability that need imposes when denied. The recognition and acceptance of *both* self and others as not-God, and so mutually needful, mitigates imposition and demand. Awareness of this *mutuality* of needing others gives rise to a special kind of dialectic that sets limits to *both* the conviction that self is limited *and* the awareness of others as limited. The shared, honest acceptance that limitation, and specifically vulnerability to self-centeredness, is mutual, limits the very sense of vulnerability — the limitation of self-centeredness — from which it arises: this is the heart of the fellowship of Alcoholics Anonymous.

Within that fellowship, following an A.A. maxim, this insight is utilized rather than analyzed. It is therefore more easily described than explained. But the program of Alcoholics Anonymous conveys the same insight; and, because that program is explained in A.A. literature, a less abstract and therefore perhaps more effective statement of the insight may be found there.

Because of its role as bridge between ancient religious insight and modern psychological age, the A.A. program from both historical circumstance and practical necessity employed the simplest concepts: its language had to be readily understandable by all. Further, as a child of the popular thought of his age, Bill Wilson carried on most of his own "psychological thinking" in popular terms. He thus clothed the A.A. understanding of human psychology in terms of "instincts" and "moods." Concerning both, the basic quest in Alcoholics Anonymous was to be for balance, for some middle course or happy medium. Attention was directed to the *excesses* of acting out or of denial as harmful. "The charting of a safe path between these extremes" thus became the life task of both the fellowship and the individual sober alcoholic, a life task essential because of the "characteristic intemperance" of alcoholics.[46]

Although the precise terms varied according to time and circumstance, the basic human instincts were presented by Wilson as the inherent human quests for "sex, security, and society." These instincts were not to be escaped, repressed, or denied; rather, recovery from alcoholism was characterized by their proper and appropriate use as opposed to the improprieties of the drinking days. They needed to be "tempered and redirected," for active alcoholism had turned these "natural instincts" into "distorted drives"; the task of sobriety was to understand and implement their "true purpose and direction." In other words, these basic instincts, as human, were also to be accepted and affirmed — but like "the human," as *limited*.[47]

Related to instincts were moods; and the bridge connecting the two in the A.A. analysis of human psychology is especially noteworthy in the understanding that alcoholism can be a metaphor for the dis-ease of modernity. The literature of Alcoholics Anonymous delineated as moods four that are readily reducible to two: elation, often expressed as grandiosity; and depression, which as often found outlet in resentments or unjustified anger. Wilson's apparently unconscious fondness for alliteration triumphing yet again, he declared the bridge between the "instincts" of sex, security, and society, and the "moods" of elation and depression to be "the unjustified demand for domination or dependency."

"Demand" was the basic bugbear, for demand denied limitation. Insofar as satisfaction of the instincts required the cooperation of others, demand — which to Wilson involved a quest for the absolute — demeaned and distorted others by treating them as either more or less than they were in reality. No single "other" could satisfy the absolute in any demand, and so a relationship of demand inevitably degenerated into either an attempt to dominate that destroyed the other's humanity (and also one's own), or a craven dependence that denied one's own humanity (and also the other's). In moods of elation and grandiosity, the inclination was to dominate — to demand by imposition sex, security, and society. In tempers of depression and resentment, one tended toward a demeaning dependency: through abdication of the human-as-limited to demand some *absolute* satisfaction of one or more of the same basic instincts.[48]

In each case, the root flaw lay in the demand for absolutes — in the denial of essential limitation. The instincts for sex, security, and society endured, requiring *some* satisfaction; the moods of elation and depression continued their inexorable swing; and *some* domination or dependence would always infuse any human relationship. "Sin" occurred only when any of these went beyond limits, became intemperate, turned into a demand that denied the essential not-God-ness of either self or others.

What the A.A. program had to say about control and dependence was also profound in its disarming simplicity. Control and dependence existed, but they were limited; and in the denial of *either* of these plain facts lay the deep source of distortion in both human relationships and man himself. The claim to the absolute was thus again revealed as the root evil. The absolute insisted upon, of course, could be either positive or negative. Trouble arose from claiming *either* all *or* no control, pretending either total or no dependence; for to be human was *both* to possess *and* to be limited in *both* control *and* dependence. To deny any of these plain facts was to deny the others; and, quite literally, in the experience of Wilson's alcoholics, in the wake of such denial all hells broke loose — for both self and others.[49]

These insights — that accepted limitation affirmed, that the root flaw in human experience lay in demand, and that the possibilities of human control were less than infinite — were not unique to Alcoholics Anonymous, even in twentieth-century America. Indeed A.A.'s own history foreshadowed an interesting convergence in the larger cultural context. The first international diffusion of Alcoholics Anonymous occurred under the impact of World War II. A.A. members in the military services carried their message to other cultures as they sought out other alcoholics in their own quest for continuing sobriety. At first, as sociologists readily noted and the history detailed in *Alcoholics Anonymous Comes of Age* testifies, the Alcoholics Anonymous message found attentive and interested new adherents mainly in Anglo-Saxon cultures: English, Australian, and Scandinavian alcoholics readily embraced the A.A. program. But in the mid-1950s a new development and direction began to unfold. Especially in Southeast Asia, more and more of those chemically addicted whose religious tradition was Buddhist also and increasingly welcomed and undertook to live the program of Alcoholics Anonymous. This development fascinated Dr. Harry Tiebout as well as Bill Wilson, and it led to deeper and more productive analyses in the psychiatrist's later papers on Alcoholics Anonymous.[50]

In the late 1960s, elements of American culture itself discovered the religious insights of Buddhism and other Eastern religions. What was first appropriated from Buddhist thought and most clearly attractive to felt American needs were those elements that taught calm acceptance of human limitation and the sanctity of a life lived without demand. This phenomenon calls attention to a special even if thusfar largely only potential contribution of Alcoholics Anonymous to the American context.[51]

American acceptance of the limiting insights of Buddhist thought is itself sharply limited. Its Oriental associations render Buddhism unhelpfully mysterious to most Americans, who tend to see that faith as alien to their own experience and indeed as seized upon precisely by those somehow "un-American." Americans are self-consciously proud of their American-ness, and for most that "American-ness" includes at least a marginal affinity for classic Western thought and especially for the Judaeo-Christian tradition. An important contribution of Alcoholics Anonymous thus might arise from its very American-ness and its deep Christianity as these characteristics of the fellowship and its program have been pointed out and analyzed in Chapters Seven and Eight. If a philosophy accepting not only limitation but the wholeness of that limitation is ever to be made effectively available to the vast majority of ordinary Americans, this will likely have to be achieved by a source as pragmatically American yet deeply Christian as Alcoholics Anonymous.

The spreading diversity of A.A.'s appeal reflected in the increasing variety of its membership testifies, in the late 1970s, that this need not be A.A.'s only contribution. The philosophy of joyous pluralism implicit in the practice of Alcoholics Anonymous allows and even invites more. But it is, of course, precisely of pulls and pushes to *more* that that same philosophy is inherently wary. Different individual A.A. members may carry the A.A. message in different ways to still more different other sufferers, but the categories of the fellowship's experience remain anchored in its program's literature. That literature, from historical circumstance as well as out of pragmatic necessity, first and foremost kept it simple. Within the plain, Christian, Western vocabulary natural to it, even A.A.'s simplest message of "not-God" was difficult enough to inculcate. Yet indirectly, the need to teach that same message led Alcoholics Anonymous to provide two services from which other thinkers may profit. Within the context of the history of ideas in America, Alcoholics Anonymous pointed the way to avoiding a fundamental philosophical pitfall and itself restored as basic a philosophical concept.[52]

The acceptance of limitation, and the consequent embrace of the wholeness of that limitation, constituted the philosophical heart of Alcoholics Anonymous. A.A.'s core concept of not-God seems to leave absolutely *no* opening for *any* absolute. Yet there is — and quite necessarily is, if A.A. is to avoid falling into the very trap of the relativistic modernism to which it speaks — one absolute even in Alcoholics Anonymous. Superficially, this is the absolute of "absolutely no alcohol"; but within the fellowship, even "absolutely no alcohol" is limited in two ways. First, in the twenty-four hour, day at a time, A.A. program, its members do not think in terms of "absolutely" or "never." Each lives this day, *this* twenty-four hours, without alcohol. Second and more important, even within "this day" the limited absolute of no alcohol is achieved not absolutely, by self, but with and by the help of others — the Higher Power and/or Alcoholics Anonymous.[53]

More profoundly, the one absolute that allows Alcoholics Anonymous to avoid the trap of ultimate relativism is the absoluteness of the one certainty: "I am not God"; that is, "I am not absolute." An absolute of "not absolute" may be paradox, but it opens the way to escaping the contradiction inherent in the "absolute relativism" in which much modern thought remains mired. For the fundamentally religious intuition of Alcoholics Anonymous, that the absolute of not-absolute is paradox even witnesses to its truth. In the perennial philosophy expressed by Alcoholics Anonymous, the simple paradox of not-God appropriately reflects the mysterious simplicity of "God."[54]

Although for very valid historical reasons the word itself was carefully avoided, the concept embracing the root virtue that Alcoholics Anonymous proclaims and seeks to inculcate is *temperance*. "Temperance" is hardly a novel prescription for drunks, but the term and even the concept had become perverted in the historical context out of which A.A. came to be. Alcoholics Anonymous presented as achievable ideals "emotional sobriety" and "serenity." What these and their other synonyms suggested and prescribed was, however, in more classic terms, "temperance." A.A. rendered vivid and striking this prescription of the temperance of balance, of the middle between extremes, by applying it not to the drinking of alcohol, but to the challenges of human life: the instincts of sex, security, and society; the moods of elation and depression; the interpersonal relationships of power over and dependence upon. In this way, Alcoholics Anonymous avoided its culture's earlier tragic error of becoming intemperate about temperance.[55]

"Alcoholics," Bill Wilson often reminded, "are all or nothing people." Recovery from alcoholism, then — as disease or as metaphor — meant quite simply for Alcoholics Anonymous the living of a *life* of temperance: the acceptance that, in *reality*, one was *neither* all *nor* nothing. A more recent thinker, imbued with the philosophy of Alcoholics Anonymous, has formulated this principle — and more — in an arresting insight derived from years of experience treating alcoholics: "The problem of the alcoholic is not that he thinks 'I am a worm'; nor even that he thinks 'I am very special.' The problem of the alcoholic is that he nurses the thought, 'I am a very special worm.'" To read the literature of modernity is to suspect that the term "modern man" begs to be substituted for the word "alcoholic" in that insight.[56]

A human theology of *not-absolute*, a human psychology of *temperance*: is it only a religious intuition that can regard these as witness to deep and saving truth? Or might Alcoholics Anonymous be understood not only as the bearer of an ancient religious vision but also as harbinger of and witness to the "End of Absolutes" and as provider of a significant metaphor and a sense of historical continuity to the "Age of Limits"? Serving as harbinger and witness, furnishing metaphors and testifying to continuities: these also are profound contributions to social and intellectual history.[57]

For the historian, of course, the question is how and why the perennial philosophy incarnated by Alcoholics Anonymous obtained its particular social diffusion at the precise moment of history when it did. The America of the thirties looked backwards in disillusionment on the twenties, which were themselves disillusioned with the Progressives who in their turn had been disillusioned with yet earlier absolutes. The America of the thirties was the America of failed Prohibition and the Great Depression. The America of the thirties itself evolved into as disheartening decades: the forties' horrors of World War II, the fifties' anxiety over Communism, and thereafter ever increasing fears of loss of control. In that America, all sense of *temperance* in its classic meaning had been lost. The term became indelibly besmirched by its association with the abortive Eighteenth Amendment. The concept also, in reaction against those fifteen years of "noble experiment," went as much down the drain as had the spirits destroyed by Volstead Act agents. It is tragically ironic that the same socially traumatic decade-and-a-half witnessed both the final slaying of the respectability of "temperance" and the most destructive drinking of those who would become the first generation of Alcoholics Anonymous.

More happily ironic seems the realization that the message of Alcoholics Anonymous — the not-God-ness of all human endeavor — may be heard as a gentle call for the restoration to the modern human and specifically the American experience of precisely the virtue of temperance. The perennial philosophy understands temperance as a "cardinal virtue." Etymologically, then, temperance is a hinge. It may be the hinge virtue that allows opening the door to a new, long-delayed age, to a "modernity" unafflicted by Enlightenment arrogance and post-Enlightenment obfuscation. To perform this function, however, the cardinal virtue of temperance had to be rescued from the trash-heap of history. Alcoholics Anonymous attempted that rescue. That it cost so many so much to retrieve for modern American society so little — the bare concept of temperance — provides profound comment on both the felt loss of absolutes and the increasing sense of limitation that marked the history of American civilization in the middle third of the twentieth century.

APPENDIX A

ALCOHOLICS ANONYMOUS AND "ABSOLUTES": "THE SPIRITUAL" AS GROWTH OR PERFECTION

The complex history of Alcoholics Anonymous and especially its origins in the Oxford Group gave rise to continuing tensions within the fellowship. At times, these spilled over into its program. Awareness of such strains led A.A. to emphasize, from the 1946 formulation of its "First Tradition" to the theme of its thirty-fifth anniversary convention and beyond, that its essential *unity* consisted in its singleness of purpose — helping the alcoholic.[1]

Yet the tensions existed and even endure. These differences arise from within Alcoholics Anonymous and indeed are promoted by alcoholics who specially cherish their membership and affiliation as "A.A.s"; thus they less attack the fellowship and its program than attempt to shape them according to particular inclinations and preferences. Since these implicit critiques of A.A. arising from within A.A. often seek to justify their points of view by an appeal to the history of Alcoholics Anonymous, it is fitting that the present endeavor attempt to place the critiques themselves in historical perspective.

A second motive also impels to this effort: one style of the criticisms, the pull to what with some justice may be termed "the right," may seem by its very existence within A.A. to threaten the theme that has been proposed as central to Alcoholics Anonymous, the not-God-ness of the wholeness of accepted limitation. After the briefest examination of the opposing tendency, a review that will content itself with noting this critique's very different relationship to the not-God theme, this Appendix will seek to meet this implicit challenge directly. The whole point has been remanded to this Appendix because its resolution in depth requires understanding the significance to Alcoholics Anonymous of its attitude to "difference" and especially its ambivalence to "the spiritual"

— concepts fully clear only after the reader has absorbed all that has gone before.

_____

The implicit critiques are well characterized "tensions" because they strain from two opposite directions. Labeling these is difficult, for virtually all names applicable imply evaluation at least by connotation. Descriptively, the two poles are that urged by those especially wary of explicit theistic religion and that argued by those who derive from their conviction of the centrality of "the spiritual" in the A.A. program the insistence that explicitly religious values — and specifically those of the Oxford Group — be accepted and adhered to by all "true" A.A. members. For convenience but without any intended implication of value-judgment, in what follows, the term "left" will be used for the first tendency, and the name "right" for the second.

Historically, these positions and this tension are rooted in the differences between Akron and New York City in the early days of Alcoholics Anonymous. More recently, however, the clearest written expressions of the "left" point of view have come from Cambridge, England, and Minneapolis, Minnesota, despite the fact that this approach seems most common in the large metropolitan centers of East Coast America.

Throughout the latter half of 1963, Denys W., an aggressively self-defined "Scientific Humanist" writing from Cambridge, England, bombarded Wilson and A.A.'s General Service Office with proposals for a re-thinking of Alcoholics Anonymous and a revision of the Twelve Steps designed to make the fellowship and its program more attractive to and more acceptable by committed humanists. Denys's letters make clear that he was motivated by the same concerns that had led the "radicals" of an earlier time to urge dilution of the Big Book's explicitly Christian ideas. Anticipating the objection that any demand for such further attenuation as he proposed would be slight, Denys drew on World Health Organization figures to point out — in blazing capital letters — that even a less than one per cent increase in the number of alcoholics helped would be significant: "½% really means, in ENGLAND AND WALES ALONE — FOUR HUNDRED AND THIRTY chronic alcoholics. . . ." He further and strongly agreed with his radical predecessors that "responsibility" itself required such an effort, and "that ONLY A.A. can extend its reach to alcoholics who at present, are BEYOND ITS INFLUENCE" — thus unwittingly touching on what was an especially sore point for Wilson at just this time.[2]

To expound his ideas, Denys submitted a draft for a proposed official

A.A. pamphlet to be aimed at militant non-believers. This draft contained five basic ideas: (1) stress upon faith in and hope of RECOVERY; (2) the chief obstacle to RECOVERY was "False Pride"; (3) the way to remove this obstacle was to learn "True Pride" — portrayed as that taken in A.A. membership; (4) the main secondary hindrance to RECOVERY was "the conviction of abnormality"; and (5) "sanity" came through the realization that this "abnormality" was not "true abnormality," but, in A.A., "a simple statement of fact." In conclusion Denys offered a rewording of the Twelve Steps designed to render them more acceptable by "Scientific Humanists," a faith he explained as " . . . a practical and positive alternative . . . the transcendent of all religions. It is simplicity itself (keep it simple) — it teaches that Man matters." The main change set forth in the draft substituted for the phrase "God as we understand Him" in the Third Step, "the advancement of human dignity and human worth."[3]

The shallowness of this critique, at least for the theme of "not-God," barely requires comment. A hypostatized "RECOVERY," "False Pride" as keeping alienated from "RECOVERY," "True Pride" as the acceptance of limitation in A.A. and as "a simple statement of fact": such ideas were hardly revolutionary of Alcoholics Anonymous, unless revolutions be located in words rather than ideas — leaving aside the perhaps deeper question whether revolutions be best instituted by ideas or by actions.

Jon R. Weinberg, Ph.D., Clinical Assistant Professor of Psychiatry at the University of Minnesota, in 1975 published through the Hazelden Foundation *A.A.: An Interpretation For the Nonbeliever.* Weinberg directed his pamphlet to professionals, stating explicitly that his ideas "should in no way be construed as reflecting any A.A. position." Calling his own viewpoint "secular and psychological," the Minnesota psychologist wove his interpretation around the suggestion that, since "the word 'God' [in Steps Three and Eleven] is followed by the only italicized words in the steps — '*as we understood Him*'":

> The author proposes that God may be best understood by many as an *appropriate higher power which we consult for advice,* and turning over our will and lives means *following the advice.* With regard to the specific problem of alcoholism, the appropriate higher power may be considered the A.A. program itself. . . . The common element is the humility involved in allowing selected other people, or a set of principles, or a traditional deity to guide our actions, as opposed to grandiosely assuming that we are the wisest authority on all matters.[4]

Here again, clearly, neither Alcoholics Anonymous nor the theme "not-God" as expressing its essence are threatened. The sense of individual human subordination, and of such subordination as essential reality, is evident. That the health of sobriety flows from this acceptance is a patent statement of the wholeness of accepted limitation.

The more significant threat to Alcoholics Anonymous and specifically to its theme of not-God-ness comes from the "right" — the heirs, often literal but at times only spiritual, of early Akron A.A. This position, which some would term "fundamentalist A.A.," finds several expressions. For purposes of analysis, what follows delineates and explores three of these as most significant in both philosophical and practical impact on the larger fellowship of Alcoholics Anonymous. These are: (1) "A.A. of Akron" and the distribution of a pamphlet titled "The Four Absolutes" by the Cleveland District Office of Alcoholics Anonymous; (2) an approach somewhat common in southern and mid-western A.A. but best expressed by the fellowship's longest sober, currently active member, Clarence S.; and (3) the "Survivors Program" promoted by "The Church of the Way" through its treatment program, East Ridge, and its literature, *24 Magazine* and the book, *The Answer to Addiction*. Perhaps unsurprisingly, the last and most extreme of these "right" positions will be seen to arch full circle to a connection with one expression of the extreme "left" position, Synanon, which in its heyday offered its own telling critique of their common direct parent, Alcoholics Anonymous.

At the 1975 Fortieth Anniversary Convention of Alcoholics Anonymous held in Denver, Colorado, some members attending received a private invitation to participate in one or more meetings of "A.A. of Akron." Those without such an invitation and unaccompanied by someone having one were not admitted to these meetings — if they could find them. Within the meetings, although in many ways the story-telling format reminded readily of "ordinary" A.A. meetings, a special kind of lamentation was expressed in virtually every presentation. Almost univocally, speakers bemoaned not the ravages of alcoholism but the declension of "so-called Alcoholics Anonymous" from the pristine purity of its original principles, and most specifically from adherence to the "Four Absolutes" and "Five C's" of the Oxford Group.[5]

Both before and after 1975, at some meetings of Alcoholics Anonymous, a member would quote from one of four pamphlets — "A Manual for Alcoholics Anonymous," "A Guide to the Twelve Steps of Alcoholics Anonymous," "Spiritual Milestones in Alcoholics Anonymous," "Second Reader for Alcoholics Anonymous." Almost always, a challenge was raised: "But that's not 'Conference-approved literature,' is it?" It was not, nor did it pretend to be, despite the words "Alcoholics Anonymous" in each title. These pamphlets, each informed, were published by "A.A. of Akron," and available directly from a New Jersey post office box number.[6]

The differences between the "A.A. of Akron" approach and that of more ordinary Alcoholics Anonymous are evident in each pamphlet. The "Manual," for example, offers as its "definition of an Alcoholics Anonymous . . . an alcoholic who, through application of and *adherence to rules laid down by the organization,* has completely foresworn the use of any and all alcoholic beverages. The moment he wittingly drinks so much as a drop of beer, wine, spirits, or any other alcoholic drink he automatically loses all status as a member of Alcoholics Anonymous."[7]

"Spiritual Milestones" offers "a simple, step-by-step religious guide" to supplement "the Ten Commandments and Twelve Steps":

1. Eliminate sin from our lives.
2. Develop humility.
3. Constantly pray to God for guidance.
4. Practice charity.
5. Meditate frequently on our newly found blessings, giving honest thanks for them.
6. Take God into our confidence in all our acts.
7. Seek the companionship of others who are seeking a spiritual life.[8]

"Second Reader" bluntly asserts that "a fully rounded life is divided into four classifications, all of them being equal: WORK, PLAY, LOVE, AND RELIGION. Translating into terms of the alcoholic, we substitute ALCOHOLICS ANONYMOUS for RELIGION."[9]

In its explanation of the "Four Absolutes," after acknowledging that they "were borrowed from the Oxford Group Movement" and "are not a formal part of our A.A. philosophy of life," the Cleveland pamphlet proposes that while "The Twelve Steps represent our philosophy[,] the Absolutes represent our objectives in self-help, and the means to attain them." Yet its concluding reminder is that: "The real value is in our striving for these Absolutes. It is a never-ending journey, and our joy and happiness must come each step of the way, not at the end because it is endless."[10]

Thus, both "A.A. of Akron" and the Cleveland District Office's promotion of "The Four Absolutes" are less challenges to any understanding of the core proclamation of Alcoholics Anonymous as "not-God" than reinforcement of this very message from the "more spiritual" point of view that permeated Akron and Cleveland A.A. from their origins. One portrayal of Akron's formalized "surrender" has been offered in Chapter Two, and another will follow shortly. From early Cleveland, despite the dominance of the Oxford Group-rejecting personality of Clarence S., note the following two descriptions. The first is by Warren C., who was "Twelve-Stepped" by Clarence himself in July 1939; the second, by Dick P., who contacted A.A. as a result of the Hemsley publicity.[11]

Clarence felt the Oxford Group had no regard for "the ordinary drunk" and was too religious — "Bible-waving," he used to say, and they were. But his main concern was to keep A.A. open for Catholics. I'd really messed up when I was drinking — the whole thing was bad companionship [and it got worse when I was drunk]. Well, "surrender" was based on the four absolutes — it meant throw away your old lifestyle, *change* your lifestyle — that's all. Clarence gave me a copy of this manuscript of the Big Book — we had to read it, then, *before* we could go to a meeting. In order to go to a meeting, you had to qualify — your sponsor judged whether you were sincere or not, and Clarence insisted two things were necessary: you had to want A.A. above everything else in the world, and you had to know something about it. No, Clarence didn't make me kneel down — he didn't have to — God, I wanted the program! I had to — it didn't come easy — it doesn't come easy; and well, in the early days especially, the companionship was so important — the new, sober friends — we had to be *sure*. Yeah, we were "fixing" other drunks, but only because we had to fix ourselves, so we made sure everybody wanted what we wanted. Now that might sound harsh, or it might sound like "humility" — all I know is we wanted to be sober, and we were scared, and so we did what we were told. That was "surrender": you did what your sponsor told you to do. No arguments, no questions, you *did* it, or you got drunk again, so by God we did it!

I wasn't working in 'forty — was living in a flophouse with just one extra pair of pants to my name. So Tom V. showed me this newspaper story and gave me the number. Three days later, Harry R. came to see me — right into the flophouse. He asked for me by name, then he started right in in front of the others: "Are you a drunkard?" And he talked about the allergy and the first drink. He asked me if I could stop drinking, lying, mooching for a week. I said, "How?" and he told me I had to get down on my knees and ask God to help me. He said if I didn't want to do it right there with all the other bums — he said that, "*other* bums" — watching, I could go into the john in the corner to kneel down, but to leave the door open so *he* could see me. Well, I did, and he wrote the address of the Orchard Grove group and told me if I could kneel down every morning, and not take a drink, and kneel down every night to thank God, and didn't lie or mooch, then I could come to the meeting. By God, a week later I did, and I felt something I never felt before — surrounded by clean, wholesome, friendly people. The raffle seller took me home that night, and he gave me a bag of donuts, and so I forgot and started to mooch — told him I only had one other pair of trousers. God, he jumped all over me! "Mex," he said, "you want too much: you only have to do three things to get everything you want, because everything you want is being sober: Don't ever take a drink again — if you do, Mex, slit your throat, you'd be better off. And don't ever miss your meeting; and anytime you're asked to do something in A.A. *do it* — never say 'No' to A.A." And, God, I got scared, but I did those three things, and here I am.

The point: The difference in the way those deriving from Akron and Cleveland lived their Alcoholics Anonymous lies not so much in any specific clinging to "absolutes," but in the greater emphasis on "the spiritual" and especially "surrender" that derived from historical circumstance. In New York, Bill Wilson was influenced especially by the pressure of those who feared "too much religion" — they, and he, had been such. Meanwhile Dr. Bob and his Akron-Cleveland followers and even Clarence S. found themselves threatened and pressured especially by those who felt that in separating from the Oxford Group they had jettisoned "the spiritual" altogether.

For those in Akron-Cleveland so conditioned, clinging to "the Four Absolutes" did not contradict "not-God," for there were "four absolutes" only because at root there was but One Absolute — the God who was ultimate reality. The four as the One remained beyond human control: as always to be striven for, they reinforced the core sense of not-God-ness. To Dr. Bob Smith, "those four absolutes" were "the only yardsticks we had in the early days." As he said of "absolute love," "I don't think any of us will ever get it. . . ." The key, for Dr. Bob Smith as for "A.A. of Akron" and Cleveland's "Four Absolutes," lay not in the absoluteness of rigidity that they historically had special reason to fear, but in the not-God-ness of "simplicity" and "tolerance" that they also, because of their history, implemented in their own "different" way.[12]

Clarence S., formerly of Cleveland but at the time of this writing residing in Florida between extensive jaunts to serve those who respect him as the longest continuously sober member of Alcoholics Anonymous, offers in his presentations an interpretation of Alcoholics Anonymous that currently seems to be in a moment of cultural ascendency. It may well be termed an approach from the "right," although of course that term is used in its religious rather than political or economic sense.[13]

Openly theistic and a conservative Christian by any objective norm, Clarence explicitly takes as his text explaining Alcoholics Anonymous the words of Paul in Second Corinthians, Chapter Five, verse seventeen: "Therefore, if any man be in Christ he is a new creature. Old things are passed away. Behold all things are become new." The key to his understanding and presentation of A.A. is that it is first and foremost "a life-changing program," "a program that teaches us how to live," and so "not a sobriety program but a living program." Also central to Clarence's appreciation of Alcoholics Anonymous, as *fellowship* as well as program, is his insistence that "alcoholics are different from people": they are a "Chosen People." The alcoholic is a "type," and "it is a privilege to be an alcoholic." He presents the "whole [A.A.] program" as derived from "two sources in the Bible: the Sermon on the Mount and Saint James on faith without works being dead and the healing ministry." "Carrying this message to other alcoholics *is* our ministry," says Clarence, stressing that "every alcoholic can have a terrific effect on another human being."

Especially in his larger public presentations, Clarence S. offers a clear framework for positive thinking to the alcoholic mired in self-hatred. Yet he also proclaims his A.A. to be "a very tough program." In order truly to "get A.A.," one must "qualify" as Clarence himself did: one must say that he is "willing to do *anything*" to achieve sobriety, and the first "anything" is blind, absolute obedience to one's sponsor. This specification of Wilson's "deflation at depth" clearly equates with "the act of surrender" that Dr. Harry Tiebout analyzed as the core of "the therapeutic process" not only in Alcoholics Anonymous but in *any* psychotherapy. Indeed, despite its clothing in classic and explicitly religious language, and for all Clarence's carefully expressed wariness of psychiatrists and psychiatry, his appreciation of Alcoholics Anonymous seems identical to that of the self-consciously secular Tiebout. The

Pietist insight that one must "let go" in order to "be" to say nothing of to "have" need not always be affirmed in a directly Pietist vocabulary, but this message is surely clearest in that language.[14]

The Cleveland-rooted longest member speaks "Absolutes," stressing "Absolute Honesty." He would change the word "Rarely" at the beginning of "How It Works" to "Never," and relishes describing to appreciative audiences with all his abundant rhetorical skill how Dr. Bob Smith, "my sponsor," treated his initial lack of faith in early 1938:

These birds came into the hospital and visited me every day. They were smiling and laughing — it was a long time since I'd had anything to laugh about. They told me their stories, and then at the end they told me they "had the answer," and then they up and left. They never told me *what* "the answer" was: they just told me they had it and then hightailed it out of there.

Finally this day Doc comes in and as usual sits down on the end of the bed and asks me what I think of all this. I tell him it's just wonderful. I mean all these guys who don't know me from a bale of hay coming in and visiting me and telling me their stories. "Only," I tell Doc, "I'm puzzled about just one thing." And he says in his abrupt way, "And what's *that*?" So I say, "Well, they all tell me they have the answer to my drinking problem and then they leave. What are you going to do to me? How do I get 'fixed'?"

Doc says, "Young fellow, you're kind of young yet, and we don't know if you've had enough." My God! "Enough!" Well, I finally convinced him I'd had "enough," and he says to me, "Well, okay, young fellow. I'll give you the answer to this: do you believe in God?"

Now that's the last thing I expected to hear from a doctor. Well, I was too smart to try to answer that, so I say: "What does *that* have to do with it?"

"Young fellow, that has *everything* to do with it: *do you or do you not believe in God?*" Now notice: Doc doesn't say, "Do you believe in *a* God?" He says, "Do you believe in *God*?"

Well, now I'm getting scared that they're not going to fix me, so I come up with: "Well, I guess I do." Doc almost shouts: "There's no guessing about it — you do or you don't." So finally I say, "Well, yes I do believe in God." And Doc says, "Well, now then, that's fine, young fellow; now we can get somewhere."

And then he says, "Get down out of that bed and get on your knees." Well, I remember that he's a rectal surgeon, so I say; "For *what*?" And Doc says: "You're going to pray"; and I say, "*Who's* going to pray?" and he says, "*You're* going to pray."

Well! I tell him: "I don't know anything about praying"; and he says, "I don't suppose you do, but you get down there, and I'll pray, and you can repeat it after me — that'll do for *this* time."

And so Clarence, "on that cold, concrete floor, in my shortie nightgown," got down on his knees and got the A.A. program a year before it was first called by that name.

It is in this context that the continuing significance of Clarence S. in the history of Alcoholics Anonymous seems best grasped. "No one does *anything*," Clarence states with emphasis, "unless he hurts pretty badly. But then, you have to take a stand: because if you don't take a stand, you're liable to fall for anything."

The emphasis that Clarence and others like him place on "absolute honesty" and on the words "entirely" and "all" in A.A.'s Twelve Steps thus in no way implies rejection of "not-God" as the central theme of Alcoholics Anonymous. As has been explored in Chapter Eight, the first step of surrender — so essential to the Pietist process — is the rejection of *any* claim to an absolute in oneself. The one absolute of admitting absolutely "I am not God" may be a mysterious paradox in the acceptance of not-God-ness, but it appears a contradiction only to those whose claim to absolute relativism seems itself at least as great a contradiction.[15]

The apparent challenge to "not-God" posed by the Survivors Program promulgated by The Church of The Way is substantially similar but historically different. Exploring this viewpoint in context should clarify and deepen both appreciation of the centrality of the theme of the wholeness of accepted limitation to Alcoholics Anonymous itself and the special threat that is posed for Alcoholics Anonymous by pulls from the religious "right" even if not by the Survivors Program itself.[16]

This program — "The Way" — consists of "The Twelve Steps," which are the Twelve Steps of Alcoholics Anonymous with the words "over alcohol" omitted from the First, and in the Twelfth, "other alcoholics" changed to "others," and "The Four Absolutes":

1. Absolute honesty — non-lying to oneself or others; fidelity to the truth in thought, word, and actions.
2. Absolute purity — purity of mind, purity of body, purity of the emotions, purity of heart, sexual purity.
3. Absolute Unselfishness — seeking what is right and true in every situation above what I want.
4. Absolute love — loving God with all your heart, all your

soul, all your mind, and all your strength, and your neighbor as yourself.[17]

It is of interest and significance that A.A. members who are adherents of the Church of The Way and its Survivors Program and the most extreme critics of Alcoholics Anonymous from the religious "right," virtually echo the critique leveled against A.A. by Synanon. Synanon, while perhaps in the categories of some sociologists itself a glaring expression of "religious" righteousness, understands itself and has been culturally regarded as a manifestation of therapeutic radicalism. The founder of Synanon, Charles E. Dederick, in 1958 turned his incorporated A.A. club, which he "found limiting," into what would become that confrontational creation of slurred speech, Synanon.

> "We were building something new and different. Although I will always be grateful to A.A. for helping me personally, Synanon has nothing to do with A.A., any more than a rowboat compares with an airplane. . . . We emphasize self-reliance rather than dependence on a higher being."
>
> Synanon emphasizes *self-help*, with a focus on individual self-reliance. This attitude reflects one of the major areas of contrast between Synanon and Alcoholics Anonymous. The latter builds upon man's reliance on a higher being. Synanon's emphasis is upon the individual's self help and "actualization."[18]

The comparison of "airplane" to "rowboat" also infuses the attitude of adherents of the Survivors Program toward Alcoholics Anonymous. Further, despite strong claims — advanced with special vehemence after late 1970s developments within Synanon itself — that "The Survivors Program" originated from a return to the Oxford Group roots of Alcoholics Anonymous rather than from any Synanon connection, a large inspiration to and some of the formalization of this "return" derived proximately from informal contact with Daytop, one of many Synanon offshoots.[19]

The critique that some adherents of "The Way" have offered of Alcoholics Anonymous bears significance also because it reveals the dangers of even unintentional historical distortion supposedly in service to "absolute truth."

> There is much that AA could learn from Synanon. Wherever AA has grown weak and ineffective — and many AA groups suffer from complacency and conventionality — it has done so because the truth has been dishonored. Many AAs will argue that life can be compartmentalized. It is not necessary,

they say, to try to correct *all* one's character defects, just the drinking. Synanon's demonstration of the enormous power released by dealing with the truth as it concerns *one's whole life* ought to have been, and could have been, a stimulus to reform within AA, a return to the original sense of AA's Twelve Steps, which clearly point to moral reform in *all* areas of one's life. Bill Wilson said that he built the four absolutes of the Oxford Group — absolute truth, absolute love, absolute unselfishness, and absolute purity — into the Sixth and Seventh Steps of the Program.[20]

What is said of "many AA groups" and "many AAs" may be correct, but the leap from this value-judgment to locating the source of realistic "reform within AA" through a postulated "original sense of AA's Twelve Steps" to "'the four absolutes of the Oxford Group'" at best unintentionally ignores or unconsciously distorts the actual historical development of Alcoholics Anonymous. The quotation of Bill Wilson is accurate. Yet lifted so starkly from context, it misconstrues and distorts the deeper problem with "absolutes" with which Wilson was concerned. Sensitivity to this more profound difficulty more directly and even self-consciously infuses the approach of Alcoholics Anonymous than this criticism adverts. Exploring the precise problem in historical context may clarify this study's presentation of the A.A. fellowship and its program under the title, "not-God."[21]

It is significant that, when Wilson himself felt pressured about A.A.'s omission of the Oxford Group "Four Absolutes," he consistently responded from historical context. The fellowship's early experience and awareness of its own history had taught it two relevant and related things: the problem with the specific term "absolute" and the special danger to alcoholics of the quest for perfection. As Bill replied to one curious and challenging correspondent:

> . . . As you so well understand, we drunks are all-or-nothing people.
>
> In the old days of the Oxford Groups, they were forever talking about the Four Absolutes — Honesty, Purity, Unselfishness, and Love. There we saw people going broke on this sort of perfection — trying to get too good by Thursday.
>
> . . . There is another factor, too, which perhaps you have overlooked.
>
> Absolutes in themselves are not necessarily destructive. Every sound theological system contains them. When we say that our destiny is to grow in the likeness and image of God, we are stating a healthy relation between a relative and an abso-

lute state of affairs. Therefore when writing the Twelve Steps, it was necessary to include some sort of absolute value or else they wouldn't have been theologically sound. . . . That could have been unfortunate. However, we couldn't make them as promising and as misleading as we found them in the Oxford Group emphasis. So in Steps Six and Seven, and *in the use of the word God, we did include them.*[22]

Wilson's stress on alcoholics as "all or nothing people," on "going broke on . . . trying to get too good by Thursday," and on the need for "taking the middle course" infused and pervaded not only this one letter but his every response to any challenge concerning A.A.'s omission of "absolutes." How this emphasis permeated and was lived out in Alcoholics Anonymous informs much about "not-God" as the fundamental message of the fellowship and its program. Appropriately, this emphasis is best explored by a study of the paradoxes of A.A. experience.

The core paradox confronted most newcomers to Alcoholics Anonymous at the first meeting at which they were sober enough really to listen. On the one hand, the key initial intuition of A.A. — quoted from the Big Book — proclaimed that "Selfishness — self-centeredness" lay at "the root of our troubles." Yet, almost simultaneously, the newcomer heard emphasized an equally key A.A. slogan epigram: "This is a selfish program."[23]

In time, with increasing sobriety and deeper immersion into the A.A. program, the member attained awareness of the resolution of the apparent paradox. Like the "instincts" deftly analyzed in *Twelve Steps and Twelve Traditions*, selfishness was recognized as a given of the human condition and so to be honestly accepted rather than dangerously denied. But also like the instincts, selfishness could be directed and tempered — applied to its proper object with the help of another of the program's maxims: "First Things First."[24]

On several occasions, Bill Wilson labored to clarify and to drive home a necessary distinction in the alcoholic's selfishness. ". . . It seems to me that the primary object of any human being is to grow, that being the nature of all living things. Therefore he is bound to have a huge self-interest." Another correspondent complained directly that he had been "disturbed to hear some A.A. speakers say, 'A.A. is a selfish program.'" The co-founder's response was eventually published in *The A.A. Way of Life*:

> I can see why you are disturbed. . . . The word "selfish" ordinarily implies that one is acquisitive, demanding, and

thoughtless of the welfare of others. Of course, the A.A. way of life does not at all imply such undesirable traits.

What do these speakers mean? Well, any theologian will tell you that the salvation of his own soul is the highest vocation that a man can have. Without salvation — however we may define this — he will have little or nothing. For us in A.A. there is even more urgency.

If we cannot or will not achieve sobriety, then we become truly lost, right in the here and now. We are of no value to anyone, including ourselves, until we find salvation from alcohol. Therefore, our own recovery and spiritual growth have to come first — a right and necessary kind of self-concern.

Implicitly, Wilson was distinguishing between self-centeredness and self-esteem. The key to the answer, insofar as "answer" could be given to "paradox," lay not so much in the bare concept of *growth*, but in that emphasis's necessary implication of continuing essential imperfection: there is *always* danger of becoming "truly lost."[25]

The fellowship's continuing experience verified what its earliest consciousness had taught: "we alcoholics are all or nothing people"; "the drive for glory, . . . [having] to be perfect, outstanding," remained the most treacherous trait of even the sober alcoholic's "neurotic disease." The suggestion of the A.A. program, then, as well as its promise, was "spiritual progress rather than spiritual perfection": "We are not saints. The point is, that we are willing to grow along spiritual lines." This promise with its implicit admonition came at the conclusion of the Big Book's listing of the "Twelve Steps suggested as a program of recovery." And appropriately so: consistently and indeed inevitably, given the nature of their "disease," anonymous alcoholics wrote to Wilson "Dear Bill" letters lamenting their inability to practice the A.A. program "perfectly." As consistently and inevitably, given the nature of his insight, the co-founder fired back tempering responses.[26]

The nature and style of these replies further clarify A.A.'s resolution of the paradox inherent in the only absolute of "not-God" being absolute acceptance of self as not God and so not absolute. The very possibility of "progress" taught continuing imperfection, and caution against implying otherwise inspired Wilson's every response.

Many found the quandary incorporated into the very heart of the fellowship's presentation of itself in its textbook, *Alcoholics Anonymous*. The very first word of the key Fifth Chapter of the Big Book — the chapter titled "How It Works," the first part of which was read at the beginning of many meetings — encapsulated the problem: "Rarely have we seen a person fail who has thoroughly followed our path." Often someone raised the question: "In light of the 'thoroughly,' why the 'Rarely'?" The query was of course frequently carried to Wilson's desk. In time, his answer became standardized but nevertheless revealing:

> Concerning your comment about the use of the word "rarely" in Chapter Five of the Big Book. My recollection is that we did give this a considerable thought at the time of writing. I think the main reason for the use of the word "rarely" was to avoid anything that would look like a claim of a 100% result.[27]

To a member who had complained that since "a decision is a decision," meetings that explored the Steps need not re-hash the first three, Wilson suggested a different understanding of "decision" — "Most A.A.'s, I think, feel that decisions have to be repeatedly taken for the reason that we are apt to fall down on the original ones." Another sober alcoholic offered a similar criticism concerning "surrender": it was either present or not, so why keep talking about it, especially to sober A.A.s? Launching from his favorite images of "Pilgrim's Progress" and "our Father's many mansions," Bill responded by summarizing his philosophical and psychological understandings in two brief sentences: "Such is the nature of the human being that I doubt *any* 100% conformity or surrender is possible — the *only perfection is in God Himself. All the rest is relative.*"[28]

Because of Wilson's charismatic status within their fellowship, many alcoholic members felt driven by their faith in A.A. to demand perfection of its co-founder. As had Dr. Bob in his "Last Major Talk," Wilson reminded most who complained that although the Twelve Steps could be understood — "in their absolute sense" — as directing towards perfection, they were only "*counsels* of perfection that no one will ever attain — at least in this life." Bill himself felt that many early failures in Alcoholics Anonymous had been due to his forgetfulness of precisely that fact. "In my early A.A. years I used to demand perfection or bust of myself and even more of those around me." Accordingly, he resisted vigorously — whether the request for his own perfection came as demand or as counsel.[29]

Faced with demand, Bill exposed his continuing vulnerability:

> That you seem disillusioned with me personally may be a new and painful experience for you. But actually since the beginning of A.A. many members have had like experiences. Most of their pain has been caused, not only by my several

shortcomings, but by their own insistence in placing me, a drunk trying to get along like other folks, upon a completely illusory pedestal — a station which no fallible person could possibly occupy.

I'm sure that a little inquiry can convince you that I have never held myself out to anybody, either as a saint nor a superman. I have repeatedly and truthfully said that A.A. is full of people who have made more spiritual progress than I ever have, or can; that in some areas of living I have made some gains, that in others I have stood still, and that in still other ways, I may even have retrograded.[30]

Evaluating counsel, Wilson was more philosophical:

To me, Jim, your present advice seems to be of the absolute variety. It is actually a counsel of perfection. So far as it goes, that's all to the good. But perfection is only *one kind* of reality. Perhaps you are overlooking the other kind — the *relative reality* of the world we live in. For any real progress, I think we have to keep a keen eye on both. That is why the Big Book emphasizes spiritual progress rather than spiritual perfection.

. . . As a practical matter, isn't it a fact that we can go broke on perfectionism, just about as fast as we can on egotism?[31]

"Spiritual progress rather than spiritual perfection" implied continuing spiritual imperfection. It also meant looking to effort rather than to results. The Third Step of the A.A. program expressed and accepted the Pauline vision that no matter who "watered," it was God who gave the growth. As Wilson summarized this perception for two distraught correspondents:

This guilt business is a sort of pride in reverse. So you simply accept yourself as you are and try to work for better things. Your success is not to be measured by the results of your effort, it is only measured by trying to do something.[32]

You shouldn't be disturbed that you can't practice A.A. perfectly — who can! If you report progress that's all you can expect of yourself and all that anyone can expect of you. So don't worry about that so much — just keep trying.[33]

"Don't worry" is surely the most useless and often the most counterproductive advice possible. But to suggest exchanging as the *object* of concern results outside individual control for personal effort appropriate to the responsibility of not-God-ness over the years brought at least some peace to Bill Wilson's correspondents . . . and to countless other members of Alcoholics Anonymous.

Appendix A

Thus whatever may be challenged in the abandonment of the quest for explicit absolutes by Alcoholics Anonymous, the significance of that apostasy becomes clear only in the context of Bill Wilson's — and A.A.'s — awareness of the history of both the fellowship and its program as lived by its individual members. Early on, the term had smacked too much of the Oxford Group and so was relinquished out of concern for "Catholic opinion." Later, increasing experience with the pitfalls of even sobriety led to the conviction that the alcoholic's inherent idealism and this trait's correlative quest for *personal* perfection required essential emphasis on the uniqueness of "God" as absolute.

This Absolute was of course to be sought: such was the thrust of the conversion that led to salvation. But that this Absolute was Other, that *the* Absolute could never in any way be any aspect of the self: the heart of this message justifies its encapsulation as "not-God."

Within American history, a last gasp of Evangelical Pietism — of the intuition that salvation was both necessary and available, and therefore of the wholeness of accepted limitation — flourished briefly in the early nineteenth century. It may have been a re-awakening of the Edwardsean insight prompted by primarily political events between the War of 1812 and the Jacksonian triumph of 1828. It may have been the first effervescence of "Freedom's Ferment" in the insecurely self-confident new nation. It may even have been a hang-over from Cane Ridge, the Second Great Awakening, and frontier Methodism. Its deep source is difficult to determine, because this final flush of the Pietist insight was but a spark, a quickly passing glimmer now almost completely buried in the available evidence.[34]

For this bare insight was soon swallowed up in the relentless march of that strange anomaly, Evangelical Liberalism, across nineteenth-century American religious thought. An insecurely hopeful nation heard in the message of Evangelical revivalists not the Pietism inspiring awe, but the promise of human perfection; and the announcement of human self-perfectibility began its baneful blight of American theological insight. The perversions of late nineteenth-century — and even later — paranoid, ethnocentric revivalism were monstrosities only remotely: they flowed naturally from their proximate parent, an Evangelical Perfectionism that in its pre-millennial demand for all-at-once-ness had long since forgotten that "human" and "humility" shared the same root.

Appendix A

The doom of all true Pietism has been perfectionism. Perhaps, indeed probably, the Pietist perception — essentially Laius-like — sires its own Oedipal destroyer, but such theorizing need not concern us here. Within familiar Western history from the time of the Radical Reformation, the *fact* is inescapable. William Griffith Wilson and other early A.A. members saw it taking place within the Oxford Group, and so they left those auspices. Alcoholics Anonymous itself has found and continues to embrace this tension within itself. Its spiritualizers in every A.A. generation cry for a return to a largely imaginary pristine purity. Insofar as their pressure helps Alcoholics Anonymous retain its Pietist perception of the wholeness of accepted limitation against those pulling from the other direction and promoting merely human — *individual* — self-salvation, that influence is benign, positive, and preserving. But insofar as their demands become absolute, insofar as they ignore the other side of A.A.'s insight — its dedication to pluralistic tolerance and deep sense of responsibility to broaden rather than to narrow the gate to salvation — to this extent they themselves embark upon the path of destroying Alcoholics Anonymous as herald of not-God-ness.

The early members of Alcoholics Anonymous — whether Akron Oxford Groupers or New York agnostics — rejected "religion" precisely because, to them, religion seemed to claim to have all the answers but clearly had offered no workable solution to their drinking problem. They incorporated this rejection of any claim to even the possibility of knowing any absolute other than that of not-God-ness into the heart of their pragmatic program. Those who would claim to find within Alcoholics Anonymous a new absolute are thus not the most loyal to its insight but the most destructive of it.

So it has apparently always been in the history of religious insight. One reason, although a minor one, why this direct treatment of "absolutes" has been remanded to this Appendix thus appears to bring this study of the history of Alcoholics Anonymous to a final, fitting conclusion.

Over the period of the writer's research, one especially serious question was repeatedly asked by both old-timers interviewed and others with whom observations were shared. Perhaps this question was at least partially inspired by the brazenness of an attempt to write the "history" of a still vigorously living phenomenon, but it was nevertheless a serious question always seriously asked: "How long will Alcoholics Anonymous last? Might it change so that it will no longer be Alcoholics Anonymous?"

To pretend to be able to answer directly would be to claim the mantle of prophet rather than that of historian; but for all those who so queried, I can now offer explicitly at least the intuition that their very questions as well as this research have suggested. Alcoholics Anonymous shall survive so long as its message remains that of the not-God-ness of the wholeness of accepted limitation; and this itself shall endure so long as A.A.'s spiritualizers and its liberals — its "right" and its "left" — maintain in mutual respect the creative tension that arises from their willingness to participate even with others of so different assumptions and temperaments in the *shared honesty of mutual vulnerability openly acknowledged*.

Alcoholics Anonymous will live, in other words, so long as it *is* "Alcoholics Anonymous": "an utter simplicity which encases a complete mystery" that no one claims *perfectly* to understand.

APPENDIX B

FULLNESS OF TIME
1971–1987
OLD BOUNDARIES AND NEW LIMITATIONS

The fifteen years following the death of A.A.'s longer-lived co-founder proved no less eventful than any similar period in the fellowship's earlier history. For his appearance at the thirty-fifth anniversary gathering of Alcoholics Anonymous in Miami Beach in July 1970, Bill W. was flown from his Bedford Hills home in a specially chartered, medically equipped airplane. His emphysema made it necessary for oxygen to be constantly available. Although he was not yet attended around the clock by nurses, someone stayed with Bill at all times, especially after he began hallucinating shortly after his Miami arrival. In an irony perhaps of special interest to alcoholics, as he himself commented at the time, Bill's main hallucination was of constantly speaking on the telephone. Despite this new complication, Wilson's sense of humor remained unimpaired, and his lanky frame seemed frail only when no stranger was present. As always, the company of others invigorated Bill, and this was never more evident than during the Miami Beach gathering.[1]

For three days, the assembled conventioneers awaited Bill's presence to receive their recognition. Although they had heard of the dire state of his health, most anticipated at least an appearance. Yet hope for it waned as the long weekend drew to a close with former trustee chairman Bernard B. Smith substituting for the co-founder at Wilson's scheduled appearances. One who was there described what happened on Sunday morning:

> [Bill] was too ill to take his scheduled part in any other
> convention event, but now, unannounced, on Sunday morn-
> ing, he was wheeled up from the back of the stage in a wheel-
> chair, attached with tubes to an oxygen tank. Wearing a

ridiculous bright-orange, host-committee blazer, he heaved his angular body to his feet and grasped the podium — and all pandemonium broke loose. I thought the thunderous applause and cheering would never stop, tears streaming down every cheek. Finally, in a firm voice, like his old self, Bill spoke a few gracious sentences about the huge crowd, the outpouring of love, and the many overseas members there, ending (as I remember) with these words: "As I look out over the crowd, I know that Alcoholics Anonymous will live a thousand years — if it is God's will."[2]

Bill's other "gracious sentences" had touched on A.A. unity, an apt final legacy that perhaps reflected a final concern.[3] Six months later, at 11:30 P.M. on Sunday, January 24, 1971, at the Miami Heart Institute in Miami Beach, Florida, William Griffith Wilson died. Suddenly both his hopes and others' fears could finally find free scope. So long guided by the presence of its charismatic co-founder, how would the A.A. fellowship adapt to his absence?

The week following Bill's death, a group of about fifteen attended a private ceremony held at the Wilsons' Stepping Stones home in Bedford Hills, New York. The local Methodist minister conducted the service, with Bill's former secretary Nell Wing playing the hymns on the piano. Bill's body, meanwhile, remained in Miami Beach, the frozen Vermont earth preventing final interment until spring. Months later, on Saturday, the eighth of May, Wilson's remains were finally laid to rest in a casket fashioned of Vermont maple, buried on an East Dorset hillside overlooking the valley where as a boy he had fashioned a bomerang, quaffed cider with Mark Whalon, and lamented the death of Bertha Banford. A simple stone marked his grave. It read: William G. Wilson 1895–1971. As he and Dr. Bob had decided over two decades before, no mention was made of Alcoholics Anonymous.[4]

Bill's death did not pass unnoticed, by either A.A.'s membership or the larger world. *The New York Times* accorded Wilson a front-page obituary, complete with picture, identifying him as "a co-founder of Alcoholics Anonymous."[5] As delegates at the April 1971 General Service Conference were informed in response to a question, after a member's death anonymity need be observed only if that was the member's expressed wish and his family's continuing desire. In Bill's case, the final use of his full name "was neither an accident nor a hasty decision.... [His] anonymity simply *could not* be kept. In this sense, then, the decision was, in effect, a bowing to the inevitable."[6]

No less than other humans, alcoholics need to grieve and to celebrate. Perhaps more than most individuals, A.A. members crave also
to express gratitude. And so, although hesitantly, a Bill W. "Memorial
Fund" was established by A.A. World Services to receive but not to
solicit donations.[7] More pragmatically from an A.A. point of view, the
date February 14, 1971, was suggested as a day for members throughout the world to hold services honoring the memory of Bill W.[8]

Despite uneven press coverage and unevenly planned events, individuals assembled in each of the fifty states and in at least sixteen other
nations. At each gathering, gratitude overwhelmed sorrow, and confidence in A.A.'s stability muted both hopes and fears. The insight uniting those themes concerned Bill's own humanity. " 'He was not a tin
god,' " the Associated Press reported, "Marty M. reminded the
2,000 who turned out for services at The Cathedral of St. John the
Divine in New York. 'He was a man among us.' "[9]

Bill's intention, from as far back as the late forties, had been that
A.A.'s annual General Service Conference would be his and Dr. Bob's
successor. Grateful as he remained to A.A.'s trustees, respectful as he
was of the skills brought by those who worked in the General Service
Office of Alcoholics Anonymous World Services, Wilson from the beginning had insisted that the membership run its own affairs. The
1955 Coming of Age convention, Bill's decade-long urging of the
change in A.A.'s trustee ratio, the fellowship's 1965 embrace of the "I
Am Responsible" Declaration: each had served the same goal of assur-
ing the continuity of Alcoholics Anonymous by investing its members
with proximate authority.

The years that followed would unfold the success of those efforts.
But already in April 1971, at the first gathering of A.A.'s General Service Conference in Wilson's absence, Conference Coordinator Waneta
N. spoke for the delegates in reminding those assembled of the continuity they represented:

> Our co-founder, Bill, left us on January 24, 1971, to con-
> tinue his spiritual journey; since that time there seems to
> have been some unspoken questions about A.A.'s future. We
> need have no fear as a resolution offered by Bill and adopted
> at the 20th Anniversary Convention of A.A. in 1955 states:
> **"This resolution authorizes the General Service Conference
> to act for Alcoholics Anonymous and become the successor
> to its co-founders."** It is important to remember that the

purpose of the General Service Conference is to assume the responsibility of leadership for the founders of Alcoholics Anonymous.[10]

In telling A.A.'s story up to the time of Bill W.'s death, the co-founder's writings — and especially his correspondence — structured the narration. With Wilson gone, that framework changes, the *Final Report* of each year's meeting of A.A.'s General Service Conference becoming the primary source for investigating the historical development of Alcoholics Anonymous.[11] The necessary shift from the co-founder's thoughts to the delegate-members' actions preserves a kind of continuity, for it best allows telling the ongoing story of Alcoholics Anonymous not as institution or organization but as the *fellowship* that the "A.A. Preamble" portrays it to be.[+]

Yet this change of focus also opens a new ambiguity. As A.A.'s Second Tradition reminds: "For our group purpose there is but one ultimate authority — a loving God as he may express Himself in our group conscience. Our leaders are but trusted servants; they do not govern." No more than Bill W. did does A.A.'s General Service Conference possess authority to rule. The authority of each year's *Conference Proceedings and Final Reports*, which afford the chronological spine of this chapter's discussion, thus merits a moment's examination. For purposes of the present story, it seems apt to compare the authority of the Conference documents with that of Bill's correspondence.

Wilson's writings carried weight because, as co-founder, he shared not only his own experience but that of A.A. as a whole insofar as he knew it. No one else had been there from the very beginning. Yet Bill remained conscious that as an individual he needed to be guided by the group conscience. Despite the A.A. fellowship's increasing distance

---

+ "Alcoholics Anonymous is a fellowship of men and women who share their experience, strength and hope with each other that they may solve their common problem and help others to recover from alcoholism.

The only requirement for membership is a desire to stop drinking. There are no dues or fees for A.A. membership; we are self-supporting through our own contributions. A.A. is not allied with any sect, denomination, politics, organization or institution; does not wish to engage in any controversy, neither endorses nor opposes any causes. Our primary purpose is to stay sober and help other alcoholics to achieve sobriety."

First formulated by an *A.A. Grapevine* editor in 1946, this Preamble usually appears on p. 3 of each issue of the *Grapevine* and is customarily read at the beginning of all A.A. meetings. (*Cf. Final Report of the 1974 General Service Conference*, p. 18.)

from members' memories of its Oxford Group origins, the ancient spiritual concept of guidance or direction remained firmly entrenched not only in the practice of sponsorship but also in the frequently recalled "group conscience." In this sense, then, each year's General Service Conference meeting possessed greater authority than had Wilson's letters: he had reflected A.A.'s group conscience; the Conference came closer to constituting it, at least for the moment of its meeting.[12]

In another sense, however, the authority of each year's Conference lacked the consistency that in general did inform Bill's writings. No Conference can bind its successors. Although respectful of past Conference decisions, each year's delegates have felt free to rescind as well as to affirm previous Conference Advisory Actions. Such an approach enjoys the manifest advantages of allowing ready adaptation to changing circumstances, but it at times suffers the drawback of at least apparent inconsistency.[13]

But consistency can be a dubious goal for a fellowship such as Alcoholics Anonymous. A.A. throughout its history has been not a political entity that makes decisions but individual members who meet in a wide variety of groups trying to live a spiritual way of life. As the constant turnings to actual experience attest, not Advisory Actions but actual practice defines A.A.'s story. Yet the storyteller confronts two realities. First, individuals and groups rarely leave records, but Conferences do. Second, as Alcoholics Anonymous grew and spread, geographical variations in practice increased. More and more, then, the best vantage point for viewing the actual practice of *all* A.A. groups became each year's meeting of the General Service Conference.

Within the fellowship as a whole, many concerns — problems that contained opportunities — carried across the watershed of Bill Wilson's death. The problem of "other problems" continued and even expanded, but in ways that more enriched the fellowship than threatened its program. Similarly, Wilson's constant concern about those unreached by Alcoholics Anonymous found continued expression under a new heading, as people became more concerned with various minorities, and through a new outlet, as a new kind of professional emerged in the field of alcoholism treatment. Not unrelatedly, both interest in those unhelped and the influence of professionals gave impetus to the formation of "special groups," and that concept came to be more clearly defined. Finally, the continued emphasis upon A.A. unity as founded in and guaranteed by the fellowship's single-purposed focus on alcoholism more and more evidenced A.A.'s uniqueness, especially in the wake of the spring 1987 decision of the National Council on Alcoholism to extend its mission to include "other drugs."[14]

Continuous as were these concerns, the overarching theme that had characterized the story of Alcoholics Anonymous from its very beginning remained even more consistent: how the fellowship maintained its unity in the face of ever-increasing diversity. The motif of pluralism established at Bill's first meeting with Dr. Bob attained full richness only after the co-founders' departure. Pluralism involves the capacity to experience oneness in such a way that differences are perceived as enriching rather than threatening. Pluralism rejoices in the realization that differences can serve a higher unity, so long as disagreements are not contested disagreeably. The openness to difference assumes "fellow-feeling" — the sense of shared and mutual vulnerability that is the foundation of any true fellowship. As the first generation of Alcoholics Anonymous knew and attempted to capture in their appropriation of that word, "fellowship" implied finding strength in a oneness that derived from accepting weakness.

But "difference" itself means different things. The most obvious difference, as A.A.'s story continues, was that between the situation of the fellowship with and without the presence of its esteemed co-founder. The next layer of difference can be sub-divided into two related topics: how increasing length of sobriety, increasing numbers of those long-sober, and increasing social enlightenment about alcoholism revealed different styles of living A.A.'s fundamental Twelve-Step program; and how new and different drugs and a widening concept of addiction and chemical dependency raised at least apparently different questions concerning "other problems."

The pluralistic theme of unity amid diversity thus frames this chapter no less than it shaped A.A.'s earlier story. How did Alcoholics Anonymous maintain unity in the midst of increasing differences both within the fellowship and in its cultural context? How did Alcoholics Anonymous adapt to increasing difference while preserving the unity of its Twelve Steps and Twelve Traditions? A preliminary answer may be found in the Twelve Concepts, but before turning to their examination, here is a brief outline of the sub-themes and topics to be treated in what follows.

The theme of pluralism is best explored under the headings of growth and communication that furnished the motifs of the 1971 General Service Conference. Under *growth* falls examination first of its fact, then of its implications. One implication of A.A.'s growth and its changing role within society involved communication needs. A.A. *communication* was both internal and external. The former addressed service, anonymity, and self-support; the latter aimed to carry A.A.'s message not only to alcoholics as yet unreached by the fellowship but also to the professionals who were increasingly involved with both actively drinking and soberly recovering alcoholics. Moreover, A.A.'s most recent history suggests that both growth and communication have led to renewed attention to spirituality, in a context replete with potential for both triumph and tragedy.

As that brief outline hints, many of the differences that concerned Alcoholics Anonymous involved the fellowship's "Third Legacy of Service." Pursuing that clue leads to the discovery that A.A. practice suggests a way of understanding how the fellowship's General Service Conference has over the past sixteen years lived out its responsibility both as Bill W.'s successor and as microcosm reflecting what actually occurs in individual groups and in the practice of the program by individual members. Following the sequence of attention that guided A.A.'s co-founder during his lifetime, the fellowship's internal development may be divided into three periods. The first would run from the beginnings until about 1950: the period of the Twelve Steps being practiced, accepted, and confirmed in the lives of both its members and the fellowship itself. The second spans the era from the fellowship's coming of age in the early fifties to Bill's death in 1971. This was the period in which the Twelve Traditions were finally internalized and tested in A.A. practice. Finally, although Bill W. wrote the Twelve Concepts for World Service in 1959 and witnessed their embrace in 1962, the era of the Concepts truly began only after his death. As of this writing, it is an epoch that still runs.[15]

The sequence of Steps–Traditions–Concepts that guided A.A.'s history also shapes its story, for it parallels the unfolding of the fellowship's three legacies of Recovery–Unity–Service. Especially the ever-increasing number of members who worked in service saw the relationship among Steps–Traditions–Concepts as paralleling the relationship that existed among the Steps themselves. Trying to work them separately, although perhaps a necessary beginning, in the long run just did not work. No more than one could make amends without taking personal inventory could one labor effectively in service if not working one's program. Conversely, just as each Step seemed to pull its practitioner into the Step following, so did the practice of the Steps and guidance by the Traditions lead one to the Concepts of Service. "Service is gratitude in action," runs one reminder. As Bill W. realized at the very beginning, and as the telephone calls that led to his first meeting with Dr. Bob S. attested, the Twelfth Step — carrying the message — was both guardian and springboard: guardian of individual sobriety and springboard to the A.A. way of life.

Bill designed the Twelve Concepts to guide change. Two continuing changes in the larger culture, Wilson foresaw, would especially require ongoing development within Alcoholics Anonymous: growth and communication. Someone who had lived through the advents of radio and television recognized that means and styles of communication rarely remain fixed. And the co-founder who had witnessed A.A.'s growth from two individuals to 8211 groups composed of 151,606 individuals (in 1959) surely suspected that A.A.'s growth would continue and that its expansion would involve as great changes as had the fellowship's earlier flowering.[16+]

The first General Service Conference of Alcoholics Anonymous to meet without the presence of Bill W. assembled in April of 1971. Sessions were held at the Hotel New Yorker for the last time, the delegates in 1972 returning to the Hotel Roosevelt, where they have since remained except for a 1977 visit to the Statler-Hilton.[17]

The theme of the Twenty-first General Service Conference — "Communication: Key to A.A. Growth" — aptly summarized the two threads that would bind the unity of the next fifteen years of A.A.'s history. Through these years, A.A. grew, and both opportunities and

---

+ The themes of A.A.'s annual General Service Conferences suggest an initial outline for the developments that followed in the years under consideration:

1971: Communication: Key to A.A. Growth
1972: Our Primary Purpose
1973: Responsibility — Our Expression of Gratitude
1974: Understanding and Cooperation — Inside and Outside A.A.
1975: Unity: Through Love and Service
1976: Sponsorship — Our Privilege and Responsibility
1977: The A.A. Group — Where It Begins
1978: The Member and the Group — Recovery Through Service
1979: The Legacies: *Our* Heritage and *My* Responsibility
1980: Participation: The Key to Recovery
1981: A.A. Takes Its Inventory
1982: The Traditions — Our Way of Unity
1983: Anonymity — Our Spiritual Foundation
1984: Gratitude — The Language of the Heart
1985: Golden Moments of Reflection
1986: A.A.'s Future — Our Responsibility
1987: The Seventh Tradition — A Turning Point

problems attended that increase. Changes occurring in larger culture as well as the fellowship's own growth combined to require innovations in how A.A. communicated its message not only to its own members and to "alcoholics who still suffer" but to the ever-increasing number of professionals who offered service to both.

Delegates began the 1971 General Service Conference by marking the death not only of Bill W., but of long-time A.A. trustee Bernard B. Smith.[18] For the fellowship to lose two such leaders in less than seven months seemed gratuitously cruel. Yet after honoring the memories of Wilson and Smith, the delegates did not linger in their grief but turned smartly to present concerns. Three large topics framed the agenda not only of this twenty-first Conference but of the next decade and a half of A.A.'s history: communication with active alcoholics, relationship with professionals, and the composition of A.A. groups.

The delegates' first chore was to explore ways of carrying A.A.'s message to still-suffering alcoholics. A recent survey revealed that over 50 percent of the general American public regarded A.A. members as "weak," "unhappy," and "neurotic."[19] Such attitudes challenged not only A.A.'s future growth but also its present spirituality.

A second concern involved A.A.'s ongoing relationship with professionals. This was hardly a new topic: in reviewing the Conferences' history in 1977, General Service Board chairman Dr. John L. Norris recalled "much concern about 'outside agencies'" as a 1959 theme.[20] Concern had in fact dawned as early as 1946, with the flap over funding for the nascent National Conference for Education on Alcoholism.[21] But the 1971 Conference addressed with a new urgency the sub-theme borrowed from Bill's series of *Grapevine* articles "Let's Be Friendly With Our Friends." As the delegates at the Conference learned from a report on the federal Alcoholic Counseling and Recovery Program Act, government attention to alcoholism and the provision of federal money for its treatment would irrevocably change the world in which Alcoholics Anonymous operated.[22] True to its Tradition of avoiding "outside controversy," Alcoholics Anonymous had no opinion on funds or programs, federal or otherwise. But also within that Tradition, a two-sided concern emerged.

First, how would the "outside professionals," whose number was sure to burgeon, relate to Alcoholics Anonymous? Would they reject its non-professional approach? Or would they expect too much of the fellowship and its program? By 1974, a substantive solution began to be devised, but its elements had not yet emerged in 1971. Second came the concern about A.A. members who themselves became professionals in what would rapidly become the "alcoholism treatment industry." Outside professionals who recognized Alcoholics Anonymous as essential to recovery wisely sought to involve in their treatment programs those they initially termed "A.A. counselors."[23] A chief responsibility of these counselors was to help those treated to understand the nature of recovery and the place of Alcoholics Anonymous in it. But was this not "selling the Twelfth Step"? Did such terms as "A.A. counselor" and even "two-hatter" cohere well with the fellowship's Traditions? These concerns, too, would be worked out over the next decade, but the delegates who for the first time were conscious of standing in the place of A.A.'s revered co-founder could not yet glimpse their ultimate solution.

A related consideration connected the concern about professionals with the desire to reach still-suffering alcoholics. Trustee John R. reminded of Bill W.'s insistence that Alcoholics Anonymous had "No Monopoly on Recovery."[24] Some of the fellowship's more enthusiastic adherents were reputed to claim that theirs was the "one and only" way. Henceforth, in the new world sure to follow government attention, the delegates realized, such an attitude, carelessly expressed, could betray the fellowship's purpose. The highest concept of professionalism suggested that true professionals were intolerant of only one thing: intolerance. But if they did not attend A.A. meetings, professionals would have no way of knowing A.A.'s pluralism, the wide variety of recoveries detailed in the stories told at meetings, or A.A. spirituality, "the spirituality of not having all the answers."[25]

Its very nature saddled Alcoholics Anonymous with a problem rarely directly confronted. A.A.'s Steps and Traditions combine with the fellowship's practice of anonymity to issue in an ironic reality: those who best practice them speak least dogmatically about them. The anonymity tradition attempted to forestall the difficulty, but those most loudly public about their A.A. opinions were by that very fact least qualified to speak for Alcoholics Anonymous. Communicating this truth would remain a prime task as A.A.'s story continued to unfold.

The Twenty-first General Service Conference's final concern involved changes in group composition. A.A.'s second survey was to be taken that year, and in affirming the need for such data, delegates addressed a perceived "generation gap" and lamented an increasingly noticeable trend for groups and meetings that had begun in inner-city areas to leave their neighborhood of origin.[26] Both tendencies boded ill for the fellowship's future. Similar afflictions had in the 1960s grievously wounded much of mainstream American religion. Emerging youth and slum subcultures threatened pluralism by denying unity. Were events outrunning the fellowship's ability to adapt? Would A.A. have to change its program in order to adapt?

Discussion convinced participants that there existed no generation gap in Alcoholics Anonymous, that at least so far as A.A. was concerned, the phrase represented a slogan rather than a reality.[27] In the terms in which the problem had been formulated, this perception was accurate. But the cliché "generation gap" served to obscure what would soon emerge as the real problem/opportunity: the increasing numbers of individuals who approached Alcoholics Anonymous bringing a problem not with alcohol but with other mood-altering chemicals. This soon proved a topic that would have its own story over the succeeding decade and a half.

The concern about groups and meetings leaving slum areas bore witness to the realities of the fellowship's social composition. Although relatively few members came from skid row, those who did thus originate soon — and happily — escaped that background. Returning for meetings could afford a beneficial "Remember When." But again ironically, as more and more slum dwellers turned to more and more potent drugs, such returning became increasingly unsafe. A.A.'s inner-city exodus was not unlike that of the churches. Members left with at least a twinge of guilt and frustration, with the sense that their inability to remain and flourish implied a kind of judgment on themselves. Here, A.A.'s single-minded focus on alcoholism helped. At times, settings that hosted meetings of Alcoholics Anonymous became the new home of groups of Narcotics Anonymous.[28]

Although only implicit at the 1971 Conference, the conjunction of the concerns to carry the A.A. message to alcoholics who still suffered and to serve areas being abandoned revealed the dawn of what would become one growing preoccupation over the following decade and a half — the difficulties that inhered in reaching various kinds of minorities. At the fellowship's earliest dawn in both New York and Cleveland, concern about Catholics shaped its presentation of the Alcoholics Anonymous program. The mid-fifties had witnessed tribulations over *de facto* segregation by color. Sensitivity to those factors that inhibited women's A.A. participation hallmarked the 1960s. As the seventies unfolded, changes in cultural reality and attitudes suggested the need to find ways of carrying the message to two new minorities — the increasingly numerous Hispanic alcoholics and the increasingly visible handicapped ones, especially those burdened by hidden deficiency in literacy.[29]

As late as 1975, efforts to make available Spanish-language literature sprang more from concern to carry the message into the countries of Latin America than from awareness of a need to serve the
increasing numbers of Hispanic Americans migrating into the United
States. Old biases shaped the earliest stages of that effort. Legends of
Hispanic *macho* attitudes suggested to some the necessity of downplay-
ing the concept of surrender. Others emphasized the need to recruit
male members first, lest sobriety seem to be only for the weak. Reality
— both the exigencies of producing the Spanish-language literature
and the continuing sharing of "experience, strength and hope" by
Spanish-speaking members — soon rectified the biases. As with all
other earlier groups at first perceived as somehow "different," Spanish-speaking alcoholics soon came to be accepted as *first* alcoholic.[30]

The transition was not so easily achieved for a less traditional
minority. Although the first comic-book style publication, "What Happened to Joe," was conceived in 1966 and produced in 1967, calls for
further ways of reaching non-readers continued at virtually every
General Service Conference meeting. By the late seventies, cassette
tapes of A.A. literature originally intended for the blind began being
aimed also at those who could not read. Yet an early 1987 report that
the prison population of one southern state was "24 percent illiterate"
suggested to the General Service Office staff the need to do still more.
Partially because so many of them experience their inability as something shameful, the illiterate form an undervocal minority in an increasingly raucous context. Although Alcoholics Anonymous is to
some extent a program "of the book," its practice of story-telling, reliance on identification, and existence through meetings and groups
well situate the fellowship to reach those handicapped in literacy. Impressions suggest that this began occurring more frequently in the late
1980s, with results yet to be determined.[31]

From an A.A. point of view, the 1970s in some ways resembled the
1940s: during both decades, the fellowship's task was to establish an
independent identity after losing connection with a shaping force. In
the forties, Alcoholics Anonymous had voluntarily left the formative
womb of the Oxford Group; now, in the seventies, its midwife had
departed.[32] Just as, in the 1940s, members discarded such remnants of
their Oxford Group connection as "the five C's," so now in the early
seventies, enduring affection for their co-founder did not inhibit
G.S.C. delegates from shedding aspects of Bill Wilson's continuing

presence.[33] The standard of "principles before personalities" implied that shrines were inappropriate, an interpretation supported by both co-founders' much earlier decision concerning their final resting places. Thus it was that the 1972 General Service Conference followed previous practice and declined to accept the gift of Bill W.'s Bedford Hills home, Stepping Stones. The same Conference had, "after discussion," "voiced the unanimous opinion that A.A. groups should not be named after an A.A. member or non-alcoholic, living or deceased."[34]

On a related matter, the 1972 General Service Conference temporized. By April when the Conference met, A.A. members had contributed some $36,000 to the "Bill W. Memorial Fund" that demand had seemed to require establishing fourteen months earlier. Delegates deferred decision on a motion to transfer the money to A.A.'s General Fund. In 1973, the transfer of $39,755 was accepted and completed.[35]

Except for the topics of Stepping Stones and the Memorial Fund, the 1972 and 1973 General Service Conference reports were surprisingly silent about Bill W. Save for trustee Ralph A.'s reference to Wilson's 1950 observation that the General Service Conference assured "that Alcoholics Anonymous was at last safe — *even from me!*" no speakers directly quoted A.A.'s longer-lived co-founder and the author of all of the fellowship's literature.[36] It was almost as if the delegates needed to demonstrate to themselves that they could take Bill's place. Finally, that confidence having been successfully achieved over the intervening two years, the 1974 Conference heard a taped reproduction of Bill's 1955 St. Louis talk — the presentation in which he had most clearly summarized his hopes that A.A.'s General Service Conference would serve as its co-founders' successor. Bill's recorded address immediately followed the Conference's keynote, an appropriate placement that seemed to hint that sufficient autonomy had been achieved for it now to be safe to acknowledge his necessarily continuing influence.[37]

The years between 1971 and 1974 also saw the initial shaping of the post-Wilson outcome perhaps most important for A.A.'s long-range future. In the absence of its strong-minded co-founder, how would Alcoholics Anonymous preserve its pluralism, the openness to difference that a conviction of unity invited? Inevitably, a kind of unity was lost with the death of so central a figure. How compensate for that deficit? An annual meeting of delegates, one-half of them newly chosen each year, seemed ill fitted for such a task. In diverse ways, members of Alcoholics Anonymous differ. A.A.'s vision indeed paraphrases Tolstoy: all drinking alcoholics are alike; each sober alcoholic develops a sobriety that is unique. Much of A.A.'s history up to the time of Bill's death involved the acceptance, the embrace, and the practice of locating "the joy of living" in that discovery.

But how balance the unity required for recovery with the diversity that flowed from that same recovery? Sober alcoholics come in different sizes and shapes, backgrounds and colors, as well as languages and cultures and levels of education and employment: not surprisingly, they tend to develop many different ways of interpreting and practicing A.A.'s simple program. How conceive the Second Step's "power greater than ourselves"? What should be the format and frequency of meetings? These and a hundred other questions needed to be addressed by individuals and individual groups, but could not be answered for A.A. as a whole. But how preserve that line, and adjust it if necessary, in the absence of the one who had drawn and so long guarded it?

The preliminary answer followed Wilson's practice of opting for the airing of differences. The 1971 delegates furthered General Service Conference openness by making specific provision for unhurried "gripe sessions" at the Conference itself.[38] That practice and the continued custom of the open-ended "Ask-It Basket" worked well at such gatherings but had little impact on the generality of A.A. groups and meetings. By 1974, the Canadian regional trustee chosen to deliver the Conference keynote implored:

> When we say, "Let's Be Friendly With Our Friends," why not start with each other?
>
> Squabbles are going on in our Fellowship, within groups, among A.A.'s in and out of the field of alcoholism, between area committees and central offices. They aren't cooperating; they are downright competitive.
>
> Honest differences of opinion should coexist in A.A. But when our disagreements stand in the way of our primary purpose, we are in trouble. . . .
>
> I suppose it is a miracle there isn't *more* controversy inside A.A. Does anyone deny we were at one time pretty argumentative, full of booze and boozy logic? Now we have to love each other or else, damn it![39]

Matt N.'s logic hinted A.A.'s solution: just as unity ensured recovery, service guaranteed unity. The following year's silver anniversary General Service Conference thus met aptly under the theme: "Unity:

Through Love and Service."⁴⁰ "Unity," of course, did not mean uniformity. Jack M., editor of *The A.A. Grapevine*, suggested one benefit of "squabbles" in his report to the 1975 General Service Conference. Answering his own topic-question, "Can the *Grapevine* avoid controversy?" Jack pointed out that A.A.'s Tradition referred to "outside controversy." "A magazine would be terribly bland if there was never *any* controversy. In A.A., there are as many opinions as there are alcoholics. We welcome diverse points of view."⁴¹

Declarations and themes may guide practice; they rarely shape an entity so informally construed as is Alcoholics Anonymous. In the years that followed, a kind of dialogue emerged between A.A.'s New York General Service Office and its grass-roots membership. As the ultimate coordinators of activities as diverse as publishing Conference-approved literature and serving as a clearinghouse connecting Loner members, arranging international conventions and regional forums, and dealing with anonymity breaks, G.S.O. represented an extension of Bill W.'s operational leadership. Members curious or troubled about goings-on in A.A. once wrote to Bill. After 1971, many of them wrote to G.S.O., the operational arm of Alcoholics Anonymous World Services, Inc.

In their efforts to serve A.A. unity, G.S.O. staff quickly found themselves serving the same anomalous function as had Bill Wilson. The chief responsibility of the guardian of unity was to assure openness to and tolerance of diversity. Grass-roots A.A. groups, composed as they were of alcoholics, had from the time of Clarence S.'s 1939 removal from Akron to Cleveland tended to want "New York" both, on the one hand, to leave them alone and, on the other hand, to confirm that their particular way of holding meetings or whatever was the "right" way, the "real A.A." way. Literally thousands of Bill W.'s letters walked the tightrope of gently explaining that *each* A.A. group was autonomous, that the role of General Service was neither to confirm nor to condemn but only to serve as a clearinghouse so that the experience of all groups could be available to each group.

At times over the years since Bill W.'s death, that continuing dialogue nevertheless also seemed to reflect a kind of fear on the part of G.S.O. staff and perhaps an increase of rigidity among at least some A.A. members. As earlier generations of letter-writers had expected of Bill, some correspondents demanded too much. The November 1971 *A.A. Grapevine*, for example, in the same issue that began running the series of Wilson's articles explaining A.A.'s "Twelve Concepts for World Service," reprinted a *Box 4-5-9* reminder that "G.S.O. Is No Censor." As the piece plaintively protested:

It is not GSO's function to tell people in or out of AA what they can or cannot do. And a very good thing, too! Put a bunch of alkies into a position where they could start dictating to anyone, and they would all be drunk within six months.[42]

Despite that awareness, or perhaps because of that concern, the effort to avoid offending has tended to issue in blandness. Recognizing that no individual could possibly replace Bill Wilson, those charged with carrying on his activities so eschewed even the semblance of such an attempt that the result has frequently been a form-letter approach that inevitably seems devoid of character. Letters not composed by individuals tend to lack human spark, and so to move from the reading of Bill's letters to the perusal of G.S.O. correspondence is to confront the reality that Alcoholics Anonymous has not proved immune to the insight that defines a camel as a horse designed by a committee.

No group can ever replace any individual, and the General Service Office of Alcoholics Anonymous has maintained Wilson's commitment to pluralism — the awareness that A.A. unity involves a diversity that keeps the fellowship's doors open to the wide variety of alcoholics who need its program. In the mid-eighties, this commitment found expression in two memorable forms.

The 1983 Conference's keynote speaker — again, a Canadian trustee — addressed the topic under the title "Salvation from self":

> . . . there appears to be developing within our Society a rigidity, a perceived need for law and order, a determination to enforce the Traditions to the letter, without any elasticity. If that attitude became widespread, the Fellowship could not function.[43]

Three years later, retiring G.S.O. senior advisor Bob P. — director and trustee for six years, office general manager for a decade and chief writer of A.A.'s forthcoming extension of its own history since the publication of *Alcoholics Anonymous Comes of Age* — gave what 1986's *Final Report* termed "a powerful and inspiring closing talk" titled "Our greatest danger: rigidity." His words merit quoting at length:

> If you were to ask me what is the greatest danger facing A.A. today, I would have to answer the growing *rigidity* — the

increasing demand for absolute answers to nit-picking questions; pressure for GSO to "enforce" our Traditions; screening alcoholics at closed meetings; prohibiting non-Conference approved literature, i.e., "banning books"; laying more and more rules on groups and members. And in this trend toward rigidity, we are drifting farther and farther away from our co-founders. Bill, in particular, must be spinning in his grave, for he was perhaps the most permissive person I ever met. One of his favorite sayings was "Every group has the right to be wrong."[44]

Bob P.'s words likely fell on receptive ears. Five days previous, the delegates had addressed the question Are we becoming too rigid? in workshops on "Letting go of old ideas."[45] More than most A.A.s, delegates to the General Service Conference had the responsibility as well as the opportunity to recognize the need for both unity and diversity within Alcoholics Anonymous. Conscious of themselves reflecting the hammered-out consensus of their regions, the conferees during the brief week of their meeting discovered how diverse were the points of view they represented in their shared pursuit of A.A. goals and protection of A.A. principles.

Each year's General Service Conference in its own way rediscovered both the perils and the promise of pluralism — rediscoveries made necessary by the chief reality confronted by Alcoholics Anonymous between 1971 and 1987, the simple and obvious fact of growth. Profound problems inhere in quantifying increase in any anonymous entity as loosely organized as is Alcoholics Anonymous. Yet because A.A.'s method of establishing membership has remained the same, comparative figures demand credence even if absolute numbers might be challenged.[46]

Three perspectives are available. Between 1971 and 1987 the number of A.A. groups increased from 16,459 to 73,192; the number of A.A. members, from 311,450 to 1,556,316; and the number of individual copies of the book *Alcoholics Anonymous* sold in the previous year from 69,104 to 816,200.[47]

Of the data available, Big Book sales afford the most reliable indicator because the numbers derive from actual transactions. As such, these figures shed further light. It required thirty-four years, from 1939 to 1973, for total sales to reach one million.[48] The two-million mark was attained only five years later in 1978, three million in 1981, and four and five million each a scant two years later, in 1983 and 1985. The six million mark was passed in early 1987, and at the present rate, another million copies will be sold every fifteen months.[49] The sales record also indicates that A.A.'s greatest burst of growth occurred between 1971 and 1975, a period during which sales increased each year by over 20 percent. Until the 1986 publication of the paperback *Alcoholics Anonymous*, 1979 was the only other year to show a greater than 20 percent increase.

A.A.'s international spread merits special notice. Bill Wilson's terminal illness prevented his taking the one last trip he had hoped to enjoy, a tour of Alcoholics Anonymous west of California. Within a year after Bill's death, however, his widow, Lois, embarked on that round-the-world effort, spending two and a half months visiting A.A. and Al-Anon groups in South Africa, Australia, New Zealand, Hong Kong, Japan, and Hawaii.[50] Between that 1971 visit and 1987, A.A. Overseas grew from 66,632 members in 3,559 groups to 30,868 groups embracing 698,271 adherents in 107 countries. Present trends suggest that no later than 1989, Overseas membership will surpass membership within the United States.[51]

Especially within the United States, A.A.'s growth involved more than numerical increase. Cultural changes, some of them partially influenced by the fellowship's increasing popularity, shaped the direction and therefore the substance of its growth. Increasing sensitivity to various kinds of disability, an extension and even explosion of interest in varieties of popular psychotherapies, the increasing use of recreational drugs other than alcohol, and a diversely manifested broadening and intensifying thirst for "the spiritual": to each, Alcoholics Anonymous contributed, and by each was its development framed.

Both the civil rights and the economic opportunity legislation of 1964 — as amended, interpreted, and supplemented by the Alcoholism Rehabilitation Act of 1968, the Comprehensive Alcohol Abuse and Alcoholism Prevention, Treatment, and Rehabilitation ("Hughes") Act passed in December of 1970, and the Rehabilitation Act of 1973, especially as interpreted by Attorney General Griffin Bell in April 1977 and clarified by PL 95-602 in October of 1978 — together, changed the options available for alcoholism treatment and also moved public practice, if not always attitudes, toward understanding alcoholism as a disability meriting the same consideration as other handicaps.[52]

A.A.'s role in this spate of legislative attention, although officially minimal in accordance with the fellowship's Traditions, was substantial in that most who testified for and shaped the legislation were themselves, or were influenced by, A.A. members. These members acted as individuals, but their individual thinking was shaped by the Alcoholics Anonymous way of life.[53] In another area, not unrelated to the sudden availability of massive funding for those who treated alcoholism and apparently connected disabilities, there was more confusion. Many outside and even some within the fellowship showed signs of confusing the spiritual way of life that was the A.A. program with the dawning proliferation of "self-help" uplift therapies that the late-twentieth-century entrepreneurial mind found so profitable.

Popular therapies of the mind-cure and "positive thinking" variety have been a staple of American history for well over a century.[54] Rather than subverting their popularity, the advent of the depth psychologies ironically afforded practitioners and enthusiasts new scope. By the late 1960s, for reasons linked to the period's sense that religious faiths had failed, a boom in such therapies began. The contemporaneous turning to other chemical ecstasies — from the unprescribed use of prescribed medications to experimentation with marijuana, LSD, heroin, and cocaine — was not unrelated to either the therapies of "feeling good" or the implicitly spiritual quest for transcendent experience. Astute commentators readily recognized the "narcissism" that underlay both the drugs and the therapies, but only the most acutely psychoanalytic realized that Alcoholics Anonymous, far from being a manifestation or cause of the craze, afforded perhaps the only cure for both the fads and the malaise underlying them.[55]

Throughout this period, then, Alcoholics Anonymous grew not only in size but in influence. Although members tended to deny the fellowship's political and social power, its reality was the necessary result of A.A.'s numerical expansion conjoined with the respect that it increasingly won from professionals and politicians. Much of that respect derived from the fellowship's steadfast faithfulness to its Traditions of non-involvement, avoiding controversy, and having "no opinion on outside issues." That, of course, was the ideal: at times individual members, and on at least one notable occasion A.A.'s non-alcoholic trustee-chairman, forgot or found it momentarily impossible to be that self-abnegating. At other times, a kind of ambivalence can be detected in A.A.'s eschewing even the appearance of an influence that realistically could not be gainsaid. Three developments merit brief discussion under this heading: how A.A.'s influence was exercised, members' ambivalence about some of the results of the program's increasing acceptance, and the fellowship's response to the criticisms that increased visibility and power inevitably spawned. Each sheds light on A.A.'s continuing maturation.

As alcoholism became a respectable malady in the larger society, A.A.'s place in that society necessarily changed. Although the Twelve Concepts served to shape more sharply the style of the fellowship's "trusted servants," it remained the task of the Twelve Traditions to guide members in the everyday contacts that defined the less formal role of Alcoholics Anonymous. In these efforts, the National Council on Alcoholism proved of invaluable help. Dedicated to education in the widest sense, N.C.A. could do what A.A. could not: publicly seek to guide public perception and policy. That N.C.A., under Marty Mann, was imbued and guided by the Alcoholics Anonymous philosophy was accepted by most as a happy coincidence.

Largely, but at times ambiguously, due to the efforts of the National Council on Alcoholism, a series of 1960s legal decisions led to the decriminalization of alcoholism and its recognition as the nation's fourth largest public health problem.[56] Subsequently, a division of the National Institute of Mental Health addressed itself to alcoholism, pointing the way toward greater direct federal involvement in treatment and research. Treatment pioneers, celebrities, and at least one recovering political figure combined to spearhead an effort that culminated in the Comprehensive Alcohol Abuse and Alcoholism Prevention, Treatment, and Rehabilitation Act of 1970. The popularly named "Hughes Act" established a separate agency, the National Institute of Alcohol Abuse and Alcoholism (NIAAA), to direct federal efforts, thus giving the rapidly proliferating alcoholism constituency a firm voice in public health planning and research programs.[57]

The legislation had not emerged out of a vacuum, but it was enacted without input by Alcoholics Anonymous *as* "Alcoholics Anonymous." A.A.'s impact was nevertheless real and significant, for in a fellowship such as Alcoholics Anonymous, the individual members *are* Alcoholics Anonymous. Many A.A.s, generally very anonymously, had participated mightily in shaping both the content and the direction of the legislation. Despite a myriad of possible pitfalls, the vast majority remained anchored in their Twelve Traditions. Many, indeed, discovered the Traditions' value under the impact of these events, and it became more common in some parts of the country for "Step Meeting" groups also to hold at least one "Tradition Meeting" a month.[58] Yet more important for the present story was an impact of these changes on local Alcoholics Anonymous groups: the need to contend with sometimes vast numbers of not always "bottomed out" newcomers.[59]

Even before A.A.'s 1974 survey revealed the increasing percentage of members coming to the fellowship by way of treatment, delegates at the 1973 General Service Conference recommended that "The General Service Office of Alcoholics Anonymous, as well as the members of the fellowship, cooperate with agencies dealing with alcoholism — welcoming referrals . . . and keeping in mind as our primary purpose the welfare of the alcoholic and his recovery."[60] Five years later, negative as well as positive impacts were being noted. Among factors that had "worked to encourage A.A. growth in the past five to seven years," G.S.O.'s chief of staff noted:

> Perhaps the most significant has been the proliferation of rehabilitation programs and treatment centers. Adding to the momentum have been court programs for drunk-driving offenders, industrial programs for employees, and armed services alcoholism programs. With growth have come growing pains. Groups in the vicinity of treatment centers have been inundated with busloads of patients. Young people bring with them other addictions, explicit language, and free discussion of sex. Court-referred drunk-driving offenders want attendance slips signed. These and a thousand other problems have strained A.A. unity and rocked the serenity of many an old-timer.[61]

Concluding with the observation, "The continuing miracle is that A.A. weathers every storm and flourishes," Bob P. suggested that the reason for that miracle could be found in A.A.'s Traditions, service structure, and simplicity. All three continued to be challenged by "the profanity problem," a mere speck on 1973's horizon. Over the next decade and beyond, expressions of concern multiplied, local Central Service Offices increasingly tendered reminders, and a special ten-page treatment in the January 1987 *A.A. Grapevine* attested to the continuing liveliness of the concern. The majority opinion of the fourteen *Grapevine* contributors reflected two earlier General Service Conference answers to Ask-It Basket questions:

> (1976) Q. What can be done about the use of four-letter words by our group?
> A. Our program clearly states that if you live the program in every area of your life, every area of your life will improve.
> (1979) Q. In the past when you went to an A.A. meeting,

vulgar language was not allowed. Now when people come from treatment, vulgar language seems the common thing. Is this the "new way," and how could it be corrected?

A. Experience seems to indicate that this problem eventually solves itself as new members grow in the program. It was pointed out that alcoholics should be allowed to say anything necessary to express themselves.[62]

Outside criticisms of Alcoholics Anonymous increased after the 1976 publication of the popularly named "Rand Report," an NIAAA-funded preliminary report of research that seemed to suggest that at least some individuals diagnosed as alcoholics could learn to control their intake of alcohol.[63] True to its Traditions, and relying also on the certainty that the National Council on Alcoholism was better equipped to evaluate the NIAAA study, A.A.'s "trusted servants" declined comment — with one noticeable exception. The nonalcoholic chairman of A.A.'s Board of Trustees, Dr. John L. Norris, contacted by a journalist for comment, was interpreted as "repudiating" the report.[64] Immediately on the story's publication, Dr. Norris sought to clarify that he had spoken as a physician who had long personal experience as a pioneer in industrial alcoholism programs rather than as any sort of spokesman for Alcoholics Anonymous. Few A.A. members or others became upset. As similar flaps would demonstrate in succeeding years, few researchers who found "controlled drinking" a viable treatment goal attempted to enlist members of Alcoholics Anonymous in their way of thinking, and A.A. members who chose to comment on that goal tended to limit their expression of concern to how the adduced evidence might affect alcoholics new to recovery.[65]

Although informal because exercised through the private choices of its individual members who worked in the alcoholism field, A.A.'s clout was nevertheless substantial — or so it seemed to some non-members whose work generally involved research rather than treatment. In March and July 1979, a significant scholarly debate graced the pages of the usually sedate *Journal of Studies on Alcohol*, fomented by Robert E. Tournier's article "Alcoholics Anonymous as Treatment and as Ideology." The thrust of Tournier's piece is well captured by its *Summary* abstract: "It is proposed that Alcoholics Anonymous's continued domination of the alcoholism treatment field has fettered innovation, precluded early intervention and limited treatment strategies."[66]

That A.A. required no extensive defense was clear from several of the "Comments" published in the same issue as Tournier's original article. The ensuing discussion resulted in general agreement that Alcoholics Anonymous was lay rather than scientific and that although some A.A. members were intolerant and closed-minded, the presence of far larger numbers of adherents to the A.A. "ideology" who were open-minded and tolerant indicated that factors other than membership in Alcoholics Anonymous might better explain the disparity. The term *ideology* of course rankled, but by the 1980s at least some A.A.s were well practiced in humoring the scholarly penchant for substituting academic precision for spiritual concepts such as "way of life."

Yet the discussion did suggest points that some members of the fellowship and some G.S.O. trusted servants took to heart. Criticisms of A.A.'s "middle-class" orientation were not new, but these now gave impetus to reminders encouraging members to carry the message to low income, less educated alcoholics. A.A. World Services intensified its effort to produce pictorial literature using very simple language, and recent changes in A.A.'s committees on Public Information and Cooperation with the Professional Community seemed ratified.[67]

Although a direct line cannot be traced, those changes surely flowed in part from the information being garnered by Alcoholics Anonymous from the triennial surveys of its membership that the fellowship began taking in 1968. At the time of the first survey, Dr. John L. Norris, chairman of A.A.'s General Service Board, noted that it was undertaken for two primary reasons: "(1) it will enable the A.A. fellowship to furnish more accurate and scientific data about A.A. and its effectiveness to the growing numbers of professionals — doctors, psychiatrists, social workers, law enforcement officials and others — who are working today in the field of alcoholism; (2) it will provide those of us in A.A. with more information about ourselves and what brought us to A.A. so that we might work even more effectively in carrying the A.A. message to those who still suffer."[68]

In 1975 and 1978, Dr. Norris first promulgated the results of the previous year's surveys to international professional groups. By 1977, however, a shift may be discerned from the prime purpose listed by Norris a decade earlier. At that year's General Service Conference, the chairman of the Trustees' Public Information Committee, Walter M., "stated the three-fold purpose of the 1977 survey: (a) to update the findings of previous surveys . . . and note changes in the composition of the typical A.A. meeting; (b) to provide the public with a realistic appraisal of the effectiveness of A.A. in arresting the disease of alcoholism; (c) to develop a new understanding of the characteristics of the typical member attending an A.A. meeting."[69] The following year, Professor Milton Maxwell succeeded Dr. John Norris as the chairman of A.A.'s trustees, and the surveys from 1980 on have been first reported not to professionals but to A.A. members via *Box 4-5-9*.

The seven surveys conducted between 1968 and 1986 revealed four definite trends. First, between 1968 and 1983, the proportion of women in Alcoholics Anonymous moved from less than one in four to more than one in three. Second, the percentage of those under age thirty meanwhile tripled, from less than 7 percent to more than 20 percent. Third, although a question about dual addiction, dependence on some chemical in addition to alcohol, was added only in 1977, by 1983 the percentage responding affirmatively had almost doubled, from 16 percent to 31 percent. In 1977, 14 percent of the males reported dual addiction, 28 percent of the females; by 1986, those figures had reached 35 percent for the men and 45 percent for the women, for an overall total of 38 percent. Fourth, and finally, the source of referral — how a member came to attend his or her first A.A. meeting — significantly changed. The number of those answering "another A.A. member" declined from 55 percent in 1968 to 37 percent in 1983; those responding "physicians" diminished over the same span from 16 percent to 7 percent. Those replying "counselor" or "treatment center" had meanwhile reached 33 percent by 1980. Although dropping to 31 percent in 1983, this figure rebounded to over 35 percent in 1986, indicating a vast increase from the less than 8 percent total of those answering "counseling agencies" (4%), "hospitals" (2%), "psychologists" (1%), and "social workers" (0.4%) in 1968.[70]

Comparison of a preliminary impression of the 1986 results with trend indications from 1977 to 1983 confirms that the three factors other than dual addiction are stabilizing at the percentages noted. Women continue to comprise one-third of newcomers; young people (under age 30), between one-fifth and one-fourth. The number of those who attribute first A.A. attendance to an A.A. member meanwhile remains a few percentage points above one-third, while those attending via treatment and counseling have attained almost the same fraction.[71] However useful this type of data may be or not be to social scientists and professionals, most A.A. members who are cognizant of the information find in it affirmation of past practice and encouragement to continue their traditional Twelfth-Stepping even in a changed and changing world.+

+ Just before the 1987 Conference, several delegates raised the subject of surveys, indicating a feeling of grass-roots A.A. that the General Service Office was

A time-framing snapshot of the year 1975 affords a useful transition from the topic of A.A.'s *growth* and its corollaries to an examination of how that growth and the changing world influenced A.A. *communication* in the years between 1971 and 1987. Anniversaries celebrate both permanence and change, both unity and diversity, and 1975 witnessed both the silver anniversary meeting of the General Service Conference and A.A.'s fortieth birthday gathering — the first international convention held since Bill W.'s death. Each marked a milestone in the fellowship's ongoing story.

The April 1975 meeting of A.A.'s General Service Conference directed attention to the topics of sponsorship, literature, and members of Alcoholics Anonymous employed in alcoholism treatment programs. One decision of this gathering bequeathed to its 1976 successor the theme, "Sponsorship: Our Privilege and Our Responsibility." The practice of sponsoring had originated in earliest Cleveland A.A. to meet the challenge of the burst of growth that had followed the publicity accorded the baseball player Rollie Hemsley. An incursus both similar and dissimilar motivated the renewed interest thirty-six years later. As the later surveys would demonstrate, more and more individuals were approaching the fellowship not at the invitation of someone already a member but from a program of treatment. These newcomers tended to bring not only a much more sophisticated knowledge of

conducting too many surveys. "They feel like they're being surveyed to death," commented John B., G.S.O. general manager.

It is useful to distinguish between the triennial surveys seeking data, as those here being treated, and the surveys sent out asking questions in order to determine the group conscience. This practice began in earnest after the 1986 General Service Conference when the groups were polled on the questions of whether Alcoholics Anonymous should publish a softcover edition of the Big Book or a meditation book.

Apparently led by West Coast attendees, delegates to the 1987 General Service Conference reported a general feeling that surveys are not an effective way of measuring the group conscience. For one thing, there did not seem to be enough time for an adequate response: publication of the softcover Big Book was announced while some groups were still filling out their survey. But there was also expressed the feeling that this is not a proper way to determine the group conscience because there is no give or take discussion, therefore no real "*group* conscience." Traditionally in A.A., "group conscience" has not been the same as taking a vote. (*Cf. Box 4-5-9* 33:2, 3 [April/May and June/July 1987], especially p. 3 of the latter, reporting on a discussion of the topic "Use of Surveys in Making Conference Decisions.")

the malady of alcoholism but also more background in the psychological than in the spiritual dimensions of recovery. They needed a different kind of guidance than had earlier generations of recruits, and both 1975's and 1976's delegates explored suggestions on how members could shape traditional sponsorship to meet that need.[72]

The topic of literature celebrated success but also raised hints of what would become a source of concern in the later 1980s. Overall literature sales increased in 1975 by more than 50 percent over 1974 — a rate three times as great as the growth in membership. Those who approached Alcoholics Anonymous by way of treatment clearly tended to be readers. Most treatment centers, in fact, dispensed A.A. publications to their clients. And in that reality lay the yet unperceived seeds of a future problem. In two short years, 15 percent of A.A. literature would be sold to non-A.A. buyers. By late 1986, that figure would approach 50 percent, and both A.A. members and G.S.O. staff were questioning whether such selling of literature outside the fellowship at a profit violated A.A.'s Traditions of non-affiliation and self-support.[73]

The final large 1975 General Service Conference topic concerned A.A. members who worked in the treatment programs that were in so many ways impinging upon Alcoholics Anonymous and shaping its growth. How was the principle of "cooperation without affiliation," formulated in the late 1940s and urged again in 1959 and 1972, working? Fairly well, the delegates agreed, again rejecting the term "two-hatters" for members employed in treatment as an earlier Conference had repudiated "A.A. counselors."[74]

The centerpiece at the Fortieth Anniversary International Convention of Alcoholics Anonymous held in Denver, Colorado, in July of 1975 was a gleaming, stainless steel, six-hundred-gallon coffee urn that dispensed the warm brown brew through fifty spigots. At this "Whip Inflation Now" juncture in American history, whether because of economic conditions or inspired by the convention theme of "Let It Begin With Me" or because of the location, the Denver gathering witnessed the greatest leap in attendance: from about 11,000 in 1970 at Miami Beach, to 1975's total registration of 19,300. Rivaling the coffee urn, a "monster replica" of the Big Book, 28 feet by 14 feet by 3 feet, filled center stage in Currigan Hall, where the largest meetings were held.

Convention activities ran each day from July 4 through 6, from 8:00 A.M. to 2:00 A.M. Paralleling the A.A. proceedings, Al-Anon and Alateen held their own conventions offering full schedules of events. One participant described a memorable highlight:

> . . . the alkathon "drum and dance meeting" presented by Indian A.A. groups. Between talks, the huge drum spoke in tribute to the Higher Power that the leader chose to call the Great Spirit, and A.A.s in the regalia of many tribes went on to the Arena floor to dance — but not alone. They reached out their hands, and soon white A.A.s and black A.A.s were on the floor with them.[75]

As that vignette attests, communication need not always be verbal. Within Alcoholics Anonymous, indeed, even within the central practice of story-telling, the most essential kind of communication, that aspect of it which less provides information than invites identification is always somehow more than merely verbal.

Perhaps because he hoped to write one last book that explored "practicing these principles in all our affairs," after completing *Alcoholics Anonymous Comes of Age* in 1957, Bill W. became intensely interested in just that kind of A.A. communication. His contribution to the *A.A. Grapevine*'s publication celebrating the fellowship's twenty-fifth anniversary, *A.A. Today*, was titled "The Language of the Heart." A year earlier, the co-founder had explored the same territory in a *Grapevine* article that reminded, "A.A. Communication Can Cross All Barriers."[76]

Bill's interest does not surprise. Always a profound participant in his age and acutely sensitive to what was going on at the group level, Wilson was responding both to the needs engendered by the fellowship's growth and to the climate of opinion that embraced Marshall McLuhan and spawned a new era of critical theory. Communication was in the air, and the context of a decade that ran from Kennedy to Nixon, embracing both assassinations and the landing of men on the moon, assured that the topic of communication would be linked with profound awareness of the possibility and even the likelihood of change. In 1970 and again in 1976, delegates to A.A.'s General Service Conference were reminded that Alcoholics Anonymous had a procedure for changing even the Twelve Traditions and Twelve Steps, should such need arise.[77]

But A.A.'s immediate communication concerns were far more mundane. Any institution faces the challenges of maintaining integral identity while adjusting to changes in its context, but neither the fellowship's own growth nor the changes wrought by treatment programs, neither wider use of mind- and mood-altering chemicals other than alcohol nor changing demographics, suggested any need to change the substance of the A.A. program. The 1971 General Service Conference helpfully divided practical concerns into two obvious parts: internal communication within the fellowship and external communication with individuals and groups who do not belong to Alcoholics Anonymous. What follows will explore each in turn, under the first treating developments concerning anonymity, self-support, and *The A.A. Grapevine*; under the second surveying A.A.'s outreach both to still-suffering active alcoholics and to various kinds of professionals.

In addressing both those within and those outside its fellowship, Alcoholics Anonymous always recognized the need for two different types of communication: that aiming to furnish information and that hoping to invite identification. A.A. literature served both needs, and the kinds of literature distributed revealed another two-sided demand within the fellowship. Some members sought help in carrying the message of recovery, while others looked for assistance in continuing personal growth in recovery. The two needs are complementary rather than mutually exclusive, but the first more directly involves service.

Living out the mandate of service, encapsulated in the Twelfth Step and the Fifth Tradition, led over these years to two particular problems. The first, anonymity, was largely resolved even before the beginning of our period, although new technologies and the changing cultural context required specification of that solution. On the second matter, the question of how the service function of Alcoholics Anonymous and specifically the fellowship's New York General Service Office would implement the Seventh Tradition's mandate of self-support, a solution began to be glimpsed only at the 1987 thirty-seventh meeting of A.A.'s General Service Conference, which for the first time in its history chose a theme related to finances: "The Seventh Tradition — A Turning Point."[78]

In one sense, the greatest threat to A.A.'s tradition of anonymity derives from the fellowship's own success. Because of increasing knowledge, but especially because of the sober lives lived by individual members of Alcoholics Anonymous and their acceptance of identification as "alcoholic," alcoholism has become to some small extent a respectable condition — at least for those who accept the A.A. philosophy. A.A.'s Tradition of anonymity, meanwhile, continues to apply not to whether or not one is an alcoholic but to one's membership in Alcoholics Anonymous. Those outside the fellowship, however, whether or not they themselves agree with A.A.'s understanding of alcoholism, have come to realize that anyone who comfortably acknowledges being alcoholic is almost certainly an A.A. member. Those who are not members of Alcoholics Anonymous do not serenely identify themselves as "alcoholic."

Over the years, A.A. practice has simply accepted this reality. There has been no movement toward expanding the scope of the anonymity Tradition, which remains confined to the fact of A.A. membership. The only recent interpretation concerned the use of audiotapes and videotapes, especially since the advent of cassettes. Delegates to the 1974 General Service Conference suggested, "At A.A. meetings [tape recordings] should not be made without permission of the people speaking," recommending further that tapes made at meetings be lent or offered to groups outside A.A. "only if the individuals whose speeches are recorded have also protected their anonymity by using first names only." Because videotapes do not afford the same opportunity, the visual equivalent of "first name only," their use has been seen as a violation of anonymity and therefore not accepted.[79]

The question of taping recalled to attention an issue thought to be earlier settled — the matter of anonymity *within* the A.A. fellowship. One 1971 General Service Conference workshop had warned against its increase, suggesting that within Alcoholics Anonymous the use of full names not only did not violate anonymity but instead enabled effective communication.[80] Practices differed over the years that followed, geography being the main apparent determinant. Individuals accustomed to attending "open" meetings and groups that welcomed many newcomers tended, for reasons of consistency and calming, to stick with "first names only" even within closed meetings. Groups self-consciously "oldtimer" or claiming derivation from Akron-Cleveland tended to use full names proudly. Visitors rarely questioned either practice, generally accepting local custom as yet a further manifestation of the diversity for which sobriety frees.

Despite these resolutions, anonymity remained a potentially difficult topic. The mid-1980s saw the appearance of several books that told of the A.A. experience of relatively prominent individuals, and the difficulties dogging the "Creating a Sober World" project hinted that anonymity safeguarded not only the ideal of "principles before personalities" but also the ultimately practical necessity of valuing established principles more than transient projects. Some members felt that anonymity breaks were increasing, but impressions derived from sheer quantity can mislead, as data presented at the 1982 General Service Conference suggested. Delegates that year heard presentations on "a hot topic throughout A.A. history": "Anonymity Breaks — How Are We Handling Them?" Discussion offered data: "Some members are under the impression that anonymity is being broken at the public level more and more. Factually, over the past fifteen years, about one member in 5,000 has had his or her anonymity broken. Despite our apprehension, our wonderful Eleventh Tradition seems as respected today as in the past."[81]

Communicating the implications of A.A.'s Seventh Tradition of self-support was more difficult. Awareness of the need emerged more slowly, and the question of support for A.A.'s New York General Office remained intertwined with the tension between Akron and New York, the fellowship's twin foundation locales, as well as with the "us against them," urban northeast *versus* the rest of the country thinking so pervasive in the history of the United States. In 1972, for example, General Service Conference delegates raised questions about using the money in the Bill Wilson Memorial Fund "toward the purchase of a permanent location for the General Service Office–Grapevine Office" and about the possibility of limiting costs by moving the Alcoholics Anonymous World Service offices out of New York City; 1978 brought a similar suggestion. On both occasions, the questions were summarily answered and the deeper concern ignored or brushed aside — perhaps the reason why, in mid-1987, events hint that the suggestion will soon surface again, with perhaps different results. The 1972 response was instructive in a different way: "It is traditional not to own properties. One reason is that this could commit future generations of A.A.s to indebtedness which they might not be able to support as the years pass."[82]

The tradition "not to own properties" reflected Bill W.'s concern that each A.A. generation reaffirm financially the commitment to carry the message of Alcoholics Anonymous through "general service" activities distinct from individual Twelfth-Step work and individual group availability. From the very beginning of A.A. history, member contributions consistently fell short of meeting that need. The early stock certificates in "World Publishing, Inc.," the carefully measured John D. Rockefeller contribution: repaying each had been made possible mainly by profits from the selling of the book *Alcoholics Anonymous*. Throughout his own service, Bill W. had not received a salary but had subsisted on the royalties from his writings — later, *Twelve Steps and Twelve Traditions* and *Alcoholics Anonymous Comes of Age* as well as the A.A. Big Book.[83]

After Bill's death, 1973 witnessed G.S.O. suggesting "a penny a day" annual contribution per member from individual groups to Alcoholics Anonymous World Services — the first increase in the three dollars per year originally suggested in 1961 and reaffirmed by the 1963 and 1969 General Service Conference. In 1975, G.S.O. recommended a "60-30-10" percentage split of the monies collected in the basket at A.A. meetings. Also over the years, inflation led to increasing the dollar amount of allowable individual contributions, from $100 to $200 in 1967, $500 in 1984, and $1,000 in 1986.[84]

But none of these schemes or projects changed the reality of A.A. World Service's ultimate dependence on revenues derived from literature sales. The problem that arose by the late seventies and that reached crisis proportions by the late eighties has already been introduced: selling literature outside Alcoholics Anonymous at a profit was seen as "increasingly violating" the Tradition of self-support. For A.A. to balance its budget by such sales to treatment centers seemed also, less directly, to jeopardize the Tradition of non-affiliation.[85]

The problem had arisen almost unnoticed, but nevertheless suddenly, around 1977. At that year's twenty-seventh meeting of the General Service Conference, the question was first raised in the Ask-It-Basket session: "Does the large amount of literature sold to outside agencies conflict with our Tradition of being self-supporting?" The concern was brushed aside: "Sales to everyone outside A.A. combined are less than 5% of our total sales."[86] At the 1978 Conference, a delegate questioned sales figures without adverting to the self-support concern. By this time, one brief year later, the answer had changed substantially: "About 15% [of A.A. literature is sold to non-A.A. buyers]. One facility alone buys 10%."[87]

A decade later — as Alcoholics Anonymous prepared to confront this apparent challenge to its Tradition of self-support by choosing as the theme of its Thirty-seventh General Service Conference the topic "The Seventh Tradition: A Turning Point" — the percentage of literature sales outside A.A. has increased to just short of 50 percent, with one large treatment facility accounting for two-thirds of that figure. Meanwhile, a late-1986 appeal to groups for greater contribution support sparked several rejections for, among other things, the "slickness" of the kit supporting it.[88]

The complaints about the appeal echoed the experience of eleven years earlier, when Dr. Norris's proposal for "regional service meetings" that would allow the General Service Board closer contact with A.A.'s grass roots was interpreted as "New York trying to dominate." But others saw a deeper danger: "dependency on publishing income to cover the shortfall of group contributions . . . threatens a very basic element in Alcoholics Anonymous — that we are self-supporting and unaffiliated because of group contributions."[89] A late 1986 article in *Box 4-5-9* spelled out the precise peril: it involved "The Power of the Purse."

> . . . what difference does it make whether support comes from the groups or A.A. publishing income? According to Concept One, "The final authority and ultimate responsibility in A.A. rests with the groups." If the groups are interested in keeping it that way, their power to guide and direct the General Service Board and the General Service Office is through contributions — "the power of the purse." If the percentage of income from contributions continues to decline while income from literature sales increase, then the groups are giving up control and relinquishing responsibility.[90]

Although not an insoluble problem, concern over self-support had been present from the unwilled beginning of that tradition in the Rockefeller refusal of 1938 — a point often recalled as representatives searched for solutions in 1986. By the spring of 1987, the pressure had been relieved, and a resolution seemed at hand. As the General Service Conference "Early Bird" edition of *Box 4-5-9* reported:

> A.A.W.S. mounted a vigorous campaign of communication to the Fellowship, and already there is indication of a heartening response.
> . . . The 37th Conference noted with gratitude that the Fellowship had responded with increases of from 30% to 50% in contributions from last year's levels for the past five months. It was noted that a continuation of this trend for the next year and a half would bring the Fellowship essentially to a level of self-support from which the rates of increase enjoyed in the past, in proportion to the growth of the Fellowship, would suffice.[91]

As general manager John B. put it in a private conversation: "The members' spirituality has allowed them to see the necessity of increased support, and that same spirituality has led them to respond generously."[92]

A smaller, related concern that also peaked in 1986–87 had a briefer but nevertheless substantial history. This lesser problem also found less of a solution. Since 1945, A.A.'s chief means of internal communication has been *The A.A. Grapevine*. At the pivotal 1971 General Service Conference, *Grapevine* editor Jack M. painted an attractive but measured vision of the journal's role, skirting internal controversy by noting how occasional pieces that reflected A.A.'s diversity sparked greater reader participation.[93]

The *Grapevine*'s problems had not begun with Bill Wilson's death. Indeed, the magazine's status and future had been one of the cofounder's chief concerns as he withdrew from active management of Alcoholics Anonymous in the early sixties. Bill shared his hopes for the *Grapevine* in his 1960 correspondence with Dr. Jack Norris, letters that in many ways summarized the legacies of his retirement. Noting that the journal "has sometimes been looked upon as a profligate and troublesome stepchild, having not too much use or merit," Wilson reiterated points he had previously made to the A.A.W.S. board:

> [The *Grapevine*] is a chief means of communication between us — with the newcomer and to an increasing number of older readers. It is a mirror in which we view current progress and experience. It is a text to some, and is more and more used by closed meetings.... It is a source of news, and sometimes a forum for debate.... So the GV is not a luxury. To AA as a whole, it is really a necessity.[94]

Grapevine history in many ways encapsulates the story of the A.A. fellowship as a whole, affording a keen summary of the problems that Alcoholics Anonymous has faced over time. As managing editor Paula C. put it in 1975, "Our magazine both records and makes A.A. history!"[95]

Despite editor Jack M.'s insistence at the same Conference that if the *Grapevine* did not reflect "the kind of controversies that occur within A.A. it would be a dull magazine," the *A.A. Grapevine* since Bill's death and especially since Jack M.'s retirement generally tended to avoid any topic that might displease any of the membership. Although its monthly "gray pages" continued to report goings-on outside Alcoholics Anonymous and thus afforded a useful broadening of perspective, the pages of the magazine proper included fewer pieces by non-alcoholics and carefully eschewed all but the blandest treatments of "the spiritual." In earlier years, contributions by A.A.'s friends such as Rev. Sam Shoemaker and Dr. Harry Tiebout had helped members see themselves from different perspectives, and even awkward attempts to delve into spirituality's depths usefully kept vivid the wealth of ways in which that essential need might be explored. In the mid-1980s, the *Grapevine's* editors seemed most aware of the polarizations that characterized American society. In such an environment, outsiders tended to be suspected of having hidden agendas, and it seemed impossible to treat of the spiritual without treading on someone's theological toes.[96]

Despite those difficulties, the *Grapevine* responded with alacrity and sensitivity to changes in A.A. demographics. Improved artwork attracted younger readers, and carefully crafted articles treated the specific concerns that affect women. Evidence suggests that members of these groups called such issues to each other's attention. But the orientation toward newcomers came at a cost. Renewals by individual subscribers consistently under-performed the rates of comparable journals, and evidence also indicates that relatively few members with more than five years of continuous sobriety regularly rely on *The Grapevine*. Readers' words of praise cluster around such responses as "keeps it simple," "back to basics," and the like; negative responses converge around "Doesn't seem to help much with spiritual growth" and "Just keeps saying the same thing over and over again." Whatever the value of such criticisms, the stark reality is that *A.A. Grapevine* circulation has remained flat or even declined in the period under consideration.[97]

Because of the growth of the fellowship's international membership and the recent increasing concern over those handicapped in literacy, it seems fairest to compare *Grapevine* circulation with sales of the English-language *Alcoholics Anonymous*. In 1971, the *Grapevine* circulation of 59,-175 represented 85.6 percent of Big Book sales for that year; the December 1986 circulation high point of 126,967, 15.6 percent. Confronted with that reality, the 1987 General Service Conference Advisory Actions urged that the *Grapevine* Corporate Board accept its responsibility to resolve the journal's "serious management problems." Still a "stepchild" in mid-1987, the *A.A. Grapevine's* future appeared as murky and bleak as it had when Bill Wilson involved himself in its 1960 plight. But knowledge of that earlier history encouraged many who loved the *Grapevine* to hope for better days. Staff turned to new projects, and at least some readers began thinking more seriously of writing for the journal rather than criticizing it.[98]

Communicating with those outside its fellowship presented Alcoholics Anonymous with another task the two sides of which were not unrelated. First and most obvious came the Twelfth-Step requirement to carry the message to alcoholics outside the fellowship. Next, but in its own way as important, flowed the continuing necessity of informing new generations of the ever-increasing variety of professionals about what Alcoholics Anonymous could and could not do.

Each need was itself many-sided. Most observers reported alcoholic non-members to be far more heterogeneous than A.A. adherents.[99] In the mid-seventies, some previously under-represented alcoholics began approaching Alcoholics Anonymous in greater numbers. Their advent refuted earlier criticisms but also raised new difficulties.

Professionals similarly afforded a constantly moving target for A.A.'s outreach efforts. Especially "the new profession" — alcoholism counselors, many of whom were A.A. members — posed both opportunities and problems for the fellowship's traditional understanding of itself. But other professions also raised risks. Celebrities and politicians, media experts and government officials, afforded previously un-dreamed-of opportunities for carrying the message. The proliferation of professionals involved in alcoholism treatment settings continued. Renewed attention to drunk-driving laws, sparked by such groups as Mothers Against Drunk Driving, moved more judges to sentence offenders to A.A. attendance.[100]

In the late 1970s and early 1980s, A.A.'s concern to carry its message to categories of alcoholics previously unreached sparked some brief local controversies. The misunderstanding surfaced in events surrounding the 1975 international convention, when some speakers and programs incautiously referred to French-speaking Canadians as a "minority." This did not sit well with the Quebecois. In the next few years, again responding to criticisms that they had not carried the A.A. message to other groups such as blacks or Hispanics, some local Central Services and Intergroup offices replicated the insensitivity.[101] Finally, at the 1982 General Service Conference, the Public Information Committee report attempted clarification. "The word 'minority' is used only in regard to groups of alcoholics conspicuous by their absence from A.A., depending on the community. In some areas, for example, they might be young people or senior citizens; in other communities, blacks, Hispanics, Native Americans, or women."[102]

One subtle but significant shift in A.A.'s minority sensitivity occurred in 1986. Emphasis moved from "young people" to "the elderly." As a key manifestation of the change put it in introducing the question, "How Can A.A. Reach Out to the Elderly?": "As young people in A.A. have pointed out, alcoholism is not an age, it's a disease. But just as young A.A.s have problems unique to their time of life, so do the elderly.''[103] The young, in general, readily accepted that alcoholism was an illness, and this acceptance paved the way for their enthusiastic participation in Alcoholics Anonymous. More of those past mid-life had a problem with the disease concept. Earlier ways of thinking thus tended to lock those over a certain age more deeply in denial, for acknowledging the shame of alcoholism seemed to involve the abdication of a final shred of dignity. Impressions suggest that this group thus benefited most from the publicity accorded some celebrity alcoholics of their own generation. Some A.A. oldtimers meanwhile relished the irony of now being deemed "too old" for the program for which they had once been judged "too young." As this is being written, it appears that many A.A. groups are beginning to devote increased attention to outreach to new groups of the elderly.[104]

Those handicapped in literacy composed another obvious, non-local minority in the sense of that term suggested by the 1982 Public Information Committee report. Because the illiterate are generally also the poor, their absence reflected a fact that discomfited some thoughtful A.A.s: the fellowship's social composition tended to be narrowly middle class. The advent of celebrities had extended the upper end of the spectrum, although superficially so, given the realities of economic class structure. But the Alcoholics Anonymous understanding of the universality of the alcoholic malady seemed to require more.[105]

In the ebullient early sixties, some had been of two minds on this topic, as the National Council on Alcoholism stance in the Powell case attested. National NCA refused involvement as *amicus curiae*, fearing that such an extension of decriminalization would reinforce the stereotype of the skid-row alcoholic. Within A.A. itself, meanwhile, most members' conviction that alcoholism was the cause of future problems rather than the result of previous ones moved them to carry even more meetings to inner-city detoxification settings.[106]

Late 1986 witnessed A.A.'s General Service Board picking up the topic in a calmer atmosphere. Wariness of offending reminded of the need for sensitivity, but signs emerged that A.A.'s trustees had learned from members' practice. In unanimously urging greater efforts to reach those underrepresented in Alcoholics Anonymous, the Board report concluded by quoting: "A black respondent put it succinctly: 'Don't be snowed by "I'm different." We're all different, our disease is our alikeness — it makes us unique.' "[107]

Throughout its history, Alcoholics Anonymous has dealt with the clinging to the sense of being "different," the claim to some kind of "unique" condition that sets one off from other alcoholics, primarily under the heading of "other problems." The fellowship confronted four types of "other problems" during these years, although none of them for the first time: other chemicals, other disorders, special groups, and family groups.

The group conscience of individual A.A. groups was not always consistent, especially concerning those addicted to chemicals other than alcohol. In general, the resolution foreshadowed in the 1940s and worked out in the 1960s held: alcoholics also addicted to other chemicals were welcomed at A.A. meetings so long as they spoke mainly about alcohol. Those who did not consider themselves alcoholics were referred to Narcotics Anonymous. Over time, this division inclined some who considered themselves both alcoholics and addicts and who wished at meetings to discuss both problems to form "dual-purpose groups." The 1973 General Service Conference ratified the A.A. World Service practice of neither listing such groups in A.A. directories nor accepting contributions from them. Dual-purpose groups were not recognized as A.A. groups — an understanding strongly reaffirmed in the 1979 General Service Conference discussion of "A and P" — alcohol and pills — groups.[108]

Although 1979 Conference approval of the pamphlet "Problems Other Than Alcohol" seemed to settle the matter, many 1983 delegates nevertheless indicated that their "biggest problem" was still "addicts who attend closed [A.A.] meetings" — a situation that seemed not at all changed since 1972.[109] And the 1987 General Service Conference saw fit to adopt Advisory Actions making available for reading at the beginning of A.A. meetings service pieces emphasizing "singleness of purpose."[110] But perhaps the most telling evidence that this remains an unsettled issue was the action of the 1987 General Service Conference in choosing "Our Singleness of Purpose — Key to Unity" as the theme for 1988's General Service Conference meeting.

Because of A.A.'s ready generosity in allowing its Twelve Steps to be borrowed and adapted, groups designed to help those who suffer other obsessive-compulsive disorders went their own way with a minimum of confusion. Gamblers, overeaters, and sex addicts, although at times occasioning raised eyebrows, lived A.A.'s Twelve-Step program without intruding upon its strictly alcoholic fellowship. Individuals who found themselves eligible for more than one of these or any of the over one hundred other groups that used the Twelve Steps generally found it possible to attend meetings of both groups without blurring the distinction between their disabilities.[111]

"Special groups" of those who were primarily A.A. members posed a different problem. By definition, an Alcoholics Anonymous group is open to all alcoholics.[112] Some groups, however, as well as some meetings, in the 1970s began listing themselves as "men's" or "women's" or "gay," for example. The 1974 General Service Conference affirmed that all A.A. groups that so wished should be listed in A.A. directories, an acceptance applied explicitly to "gay groups" at that time and reaffirmed by the 1977 General Service Conference. Delegates in 1979 explored historically the distinction between "special *composition* and special purpose" groups, clarifying also the difference between a *group*, which traditionally had to be open to all A.A.s, and a "meeting," which could cater to some special interest.[113] All A.A. groups and meetings serve the *purpose* of sobriety, although some meetings are attended primarily by those with some particular shared interest, such as sobriety for women or sobriety within a gay life-style. Although not a pressing issue, the topic's consistent reappearance among the Ask-It Basket questions suggests that clarity on the issue of "special groups" yet eludes many members.[114]

By the mid-1980s, that issue pressed hardest in the particular area of family groups. As early as January 1971, *The A.A. Grapevine* reported on "Family Discussion Groups," describing a particular open meeting format. By the time of the 1972 General Service Conference, concern over the listing of family *groups* led A.A. World Services no longer to list them in the Alcoholics Anonymous World Directory. As the *Final Report* noted: "It is suggested that the word 'family' not be used in the name of an A.A. group; if A.A.s and their non-alcoholic mates wish to meet together on a regular basis, it is suggested they consider these gatherings 'meetings' and not A.A. groups." One reason for that decision and A.A.'s refusal to list "family groups" in its World Directory derived from "discussion of the problem last fall with Al-Anon, who felt that the word 'family,' long identified with their fellowship, should not be used in the name of A.A. groups."[115]

Although at times disruptive of Al-Anon meetings in some areas, individuals styling themselves "children of alcoholics" or "adult children of alcoholics" have thus far posed little threat to Alcoholics Anonymous itself. Reports of A.A. members who attend both A.C.O.A. and A.A. meetings suggest that the former's psychological emphasis can usefully complement the latter's spiritual approach, at least for those sufficiently grounded in the spiritual to be able to recognize that difference.[116]

The difference between the psychological and the spiritual underlies another contrast important not only for distinguishing between Alcoholics Anonymous and such more recent groups as A.C.O.A. but also because it clarifies varying expressions of a constant reality within A.A.'s story: the difference between A.A.'s resolute non-professionalism and the multitudinous styles of professionally guided group therapy increasingly available to the variously disabled. The most reputable pushers of A.C.O.A. insights caution about the need for professional guidance. Indeed, unlike groups such as Overeaters, Gamblers, and Sex Addicts Anonymous, A.C.O.A. originated as a professional concept.[117]

In a summary so brief it verges on caricature, the psychological approach focuses on *push* forces ("drives," "conditioning"); the spiritual attends to *pull* forces ("meaning," "virtue"). Focusing on what one *can* do, the social scientific style aims to effect change. Rooted in the admission of creatureliness, of powerlessness and unmanageability, spirituality emphasizes becoming willing and then humbly asking to be changed. Most practitioners of healing in fields related to alcoholism acknowledge the need for both the psychological and the spiritual, recognizing them to be complementary rather than in conflict. But the different emphases lead to diverse approaches and, at times, to styles difficult to harmonize. Reflecting a tension as ancient as culture itself, those who view themselves primarily as masters of hard-earned knowledge and those who find their first identity as recipients of the gift of wisdom tend to view each other warily. Academics and artists usually respect, but rarely understand, each other.[118]

Yet from the time of Doctors Silkworth, Kennedy, and Tiebout, A.A.'s success attracted professional attention. Increasingly over the years, that attention merged into respect. Setbacks to that process, such as Margaret Bean's scathing analysis reducing Alcoholics Anonymous to ignorantly sick dependence and the Tournier critique of "ideology," were offset by Bean's later revision of her interpretation and by the insights suggested by her Harvard colleagues John Mack and Edward Khantzian. George Vaillant's continuing work was meanwhile ratifying empirically much of what had been impressionistic A.A. lore.[119]

Three landmarks in the evolving relationship between professionals and members of Alcoholics Anonymous occurred during the period between 1971 and 1987. The first was the 1971 General Service Conference, at which a G.S.O. representative succinctly stated A.A.'s fundamental, historical point: Alcoholics Anonymous has a "program that works for most of those who want it. The 'pro' can *help* the alcoholic want it." Also in 1971, a committee on professional relations was created, distinct from the Public Information Committee. In 1974, its name was changed to the C.P.C. Committee — Committee on Cooperation with the Professional Community.[120]

The late 1970s and especially the international convention of 1980 marked the second milestone, as new data combined with earlier perceptions to ratify an emerging synthesis. The 1977 General Service Conference formalized recognition of alcoholism treatment centers by replacing its Institutions Committee with separate Correctional Facilities and Treatment Facilities committees. Also noteworthy at the twenty-seventh Conference was Dr. John L. Norris's reminder that A.A.'s basic stance on "outside agencies" had been set forth as far back as 1954, when "the idea of cooperation without affiliation was outlined."[121]

A.A.'s forty-fifth birthday celebration at its 1980 New Orleans convention signaled acceptance of those understandings by a dual emphasis. From early publicity through the actual convention itself, greater than usual attention was focused on the participation of non-A.A. speakers and on the variety of A.A. members. The twenty-two non-A.A. presenters included "judges, physicians, psychiatrists, clergymen, educators, prison officials, media specialists, government officials, a labor leader, an industrialist and alcoholism agency officials."[122] Meanwhile, workshops were scheduled for gay members and for young people as well as for doctors, lawyers, and women.

Although the hot, muggy atmosphere of New Orleans over the Fourth of July weekend somewhat muted the conventioneers' enthusiasm, most found ways of living up to the convention theme, "The Joy of Living." Walking tours and riverboat trips invited conversational mingling, the culturally diverse city's graciousness nicely complementing A.A. informality. New Orleans witnessed the first archives presentation of the filmstrip "Markings on the Journey," which then and in later years brought tears to the eyes and a lump to the throats of viewers sensitive to history. On the Fourth of July itself, the presentation of the first copy of the Italian edition of the A.A. Big Book, the "eleventh in an ever-growing collection of authorized foreign-language Big Books," highlighted an impressive ceremony in the Louisiana Superdome.[123]

If the discussions and workshops held at both the Thirtieth General Service Conference and the 1980 International Convention did not make sufficiently clear the usefulness to Alcoholics Anonymous of its traditional "cooperation without affiliation" relationship with professionals, the 1980 survey results, reported in late 1981 but brought before the General Service Conference only in 1982, filled the gap by supplying the third and final milestone. For the first time in that year, virtually as many newcomers reported being referred to Alcoholics Anonymous by "treatment" or "counselor" as by "an A.A. member." As the 1982 General Service Conference *Final Report* acknowledged in a special presentation, treatment facilities had become "our largest source of new members."[124]

The separate workbooks published in the early eighties confirmed the continuing importance of professionals to Alcoholics Anonymous: Public Information in 1981, Cooperation with the Professional Community in 1982, and both Corrections and Treatment Facilities workbooks in 1985. At the 1986 General Service Conference, a workshop asking "Are We Being Friendly With Our Friends?" replied, "Resoundingly . . . Yes." Nineteen eighty-seven's delegates indeed scented the possibility of a very different danger, recommending as a workshop topic for the 1988 "Our Singleness of Purpose — Key to Unity" Conference: "Are We Being *Too* Friendly With Our Friends?" Meanwhile A.A.'s alertness to the needs of its relationship with professionals continued to be evidenced by "About A.A. — A Newsletter for Professional Men and Women."[125]

Within the process of establishing a comfortable stance toward "outside professionals," Alcoholics Anonymous also moved — although not without continuing ambivalence — toward a consistent position on A.A. members who themselves work as professionals in the alcoholism field. Naming them came first. At the 1970 General Service Conference, "A motion was made and carried that the Twentieth General Service Conference go on record as opposing the use of the title 'A.A. Counselor.'" In both 1973 and 1974, questions from the floor casually referred to such members as "two-hatters," but the 1975 General Service Conference reported a "consensus reached on terminology" that recommended that the term "two-hatter" should be phased out of Conference-approved literature and replaced by "AA members employed in the alcoholism field."[126]

The problem of naming solved, the 1976 General Service Conference offered specific recommendations for A.A. workers in the field: "adequate training; three to five years of good, stable sobriety; sponsor who does *not* work in the alcoholism field." Suggestions were also tendered "to alleviate some of the problems involved in people coming to A.A. from treatment centers, courts/A.S.A.P. programs, etc.":

(a) Establish greater communication between the referral sources and local A.A. groups; (b) Recognize the necessity of meeting the new member where he presently is, listen to him, try to determine what he really knows about the A.A. program; (c) See that specific programs are set up for sponsoring people from treatment centers into local A.A. groups.[127]

Earlier Advisory Actions had precluded other alternatives. The 1965 General Service Conference had advised against members setting up transitional facilities using A.A. names such as "Twelve Step House": "Since these ventures are separate from the Fellowship, it is advisable that they operate under names which do not link them to A.A."[128] Two years later, in 1967, the Conference "approved a position paper on rehabilitation centers to the effect that such rehabs, rest homes and hospitals are *not* part of A.A., and therefore are not responsible for adhering to the Traditions of A.A."[129] To a 1967 query that challenged the confusion that might arise if A.A. members "become expert in the alcoholism field," "the consensus was that an individual A.A. working in these programs can educate both the agency and A.A."[130]

The two-sided nature of that education manifested itself in different ways on different levels. At the grass-roots group plane, those newly arrived from treatment and those experienced in A.A. recovery tended to get along quite well so long as the former did not numerically overwhelm the group in too short a time. What went on at higher levels proved more problematic. As one acute observer put it:

Between 1970 and 1986, the service structure of A.A. became more organized. Various committees were added at the level of trustees and throughout the area structure. The most notable increase was in the committees for Public Information, Cooperation with the Professional Community, Correctional, and especially Treatment Facilities. This development raises questions: Has A.A. become too organized? Does this increased structure place more emphasis on itself than it does on carrying the message?[131]

Such questions appropriately introduce the conclusion to this necessarily incomplete story. Not only because Alcoholics Anonymous still thrives, but also because even if the fellowship itself should cease to exist, the impact of its program would continue, A.A.'s whole story cannot be told in the foreseeable future. Yet it is clear that any interim summary, any attempt at a concluding snapshot of Alcoholics Anonymous embarked on its second fifty years, must be framed within the two-sidedness that has shaped the fellowship and its program and its story from the very beginning. A.A. suggests to its members that their stories reveal that they can be *both* "sober" and "alcoholic." Earlier chapters attempted to capture the unfolding of that insight by exploring the implications of the key Big Book sentences, "First of all, we had to quit playing God. It didn't work."[132]

The acceptance of not-God-ness, the embrace of being both-and that the Twelve-Step program inculcates in A.A. members, applies also to the A.A. fellowship itself. Nowhere is this clearer than in the enduring yet creative tension between the necessity of unity and the need for diversity. A.A.'s pluralism reflects the core of its spirituality — "the spirituality of not having all the answers."[133] For despite the apparent successes of explosive growth and broadening respect, despite the heady triumphs of a golden anniversary that saw the ceremonial presentation of the five-millionth copy of its Big Book, despite an outreach opportunity that seems on the verge of carrying A.A.'s spiritual message to nations guided by Marxist-Leninist thought, each high bore with it also a low. Members of Alcoholics Anonymous, because they are alcoholic, found nothing surprising in that. But as the fellowship continues to seek the wisdom that will allow it to distinguish between the realities that it can and those it cannot change, its members have increasingly turned to their own story, the story of Alcoholics Anonymous, for guidance in discerning both serenity and courage. And in that quest that itself is the continuation of A.A.'s story, recent history shows promise of proving as helpful as ancient annals in shaping the changes required by continuing growth and by still newer means of communicating essential identification.

Bill Wilson's 1971 death reminded Alcoholics Anonymous how fragile were its ties with its past. While some scurried to establish archives and to record the memories of still-living oldtimers, others in A.A.'s service structure hit upon the idea of making each November's issue of *The A.A. Grapevine* not only a reminder of "Gratitude Month" in accordance with the American Thanksgiving celebration, but also a "Classic Grapevine" issue carrying articles devoted to A.A. history and reprints of pieces from the journal's early years.[134]

"Classic Grapevine" began appearing in November 1972. At the same time, led by two trustees with academic ties, others sought to bring to fruition Bill W.'s intention of establishing the formal archives of Alcoholics Anonymous. A.A.'s co-founder had well prepared the ground: his correspondence was almost wholly preserved, as were the results of his research for the book *Alcoholics Anonymous Comes of Age.*[135] Bill dropped by his new corner office at 468 Park Avenue South, to which Alcoholics Anonymous World Service moved in April of 1970, only a few times, but on one of those laborious visits, he suggested how and where the archives could be begun. Mindful of Wilson's hopes, A.A.'s trustees formed an archives committee in 1973. Its chairman, George G., explained the archives' function to the 1974 General Service Conference: "The main purpose of the archival library is to keep the record straight, so that myth does not predominate over fact regarding the history of our Fellowship. The library can give A.A. a sense of its own past and the opportunity to study it."[136]

With Nell Wing, Bill's long-time secretary, serving as custodian, A.A.'s archives formally opened on November 3, 1975, with a brief ceremony in which Bill's widow, Lois, took part. The New York archives soon began serving many, but before tracing that outcome, it merits notice that especially in the 1980s, A.A.'s archivists have encouraged local and regional service offices to erect local archives preserving their own history. The 1981 distribution of a forty-four-page "Handbook For Setting Up An Alcoholics Anonymous Archival Repository" has been supplemented by annual publication of "Markings: Your Archives Interchange." At the time of its 1987 General Service Conference meeting, the fellowship rejoiced in over sixty such local area repositories, and new ones were being established at the rate of about six a year.[137]

Although some of the local archives are of more antiquarian than historical interest, the preservation of local newspaper stories and memoirs generally supplements such enshrined tokens as an early printing of the first edition of the book *Alcoholics Anonymous* or a souvenir coffee pot. Early meeting lists or even membership or Twelfth-Step call lists sometimes allow tracing how groups spread, and an occasional annotated copy of the Big Book or of *Twelve Steps and Twelve Traditions* invites appraising continuity of interpretation. In the later 1980s, local historians were only beginning to mine such treasures.

The Alcoholics Anonymous General Service archives have from their origins served both in-house and outside explorers of A.A.'s story. The fruits of that research began to appear in 1979, with the publication of the original, dissertation version of this book. Even within that process, however, my research was aided by that of Niles P., who was gathering additional primary data as he worked on the book that Alcoholics Anonymous published in 1980, *Dr. Bob and the Good Oldtimers*. Contemporaneous with that project, A.A.'s archives co-operated with research for Al-Anon's 1979 publication of the book *Lois Remembers*.[138]

Scholarly interest in Alcoholics Anonymous has been more than merely historical, and non-historians have not always needed the archives. Trustee Milton Maxwell's book, *The A.A. Experience*, drew on them; Mary Catherine Taylor based her anthropology dissertation on participant-observation and interviews. Until the late seventies, most serious scholars had ignored both alcoholism and Alcoholics Anonymous. Occasional exceptions — Bales, Bacon, Keller — "proved" the rule in the proper sense of that term: they stood outside the scholarly mainstream. Then Madsen, Taylor, Blumberg, Leach and Norris, Kurtz, Robinson, Rudy, and Denzin, as well as Bean, Mack, Khantzian, and Vaillant, presented their findings, and other as yet unpublished studies await polishing. Although less rigorous observers still sometimes confused Alcoholics Anonymous with the intellectually fuzzy, pop-therapeutic fads that perennially sprout on the American landscape, those mindful of the fellowship's history and its program's grounding in the mainstream tradition of Western spirituality have been more and more heard and heeded.[139]

Within the fellowship, members attended mainly to Conference-approved literature.[140] After the mixed reception accorded Robert Thomsen's *Bill W.* in 1975, A.A. hoped to publish paired biographies of its co-founders under the fellowship's own auspices. Because of a dearth of archival material from Dr. Bob, who died in 1950 and had not been in the habit of writing letters, and also as a pledge to non-New Yorkers that the co-founders' and A.A.'s history would receive balanced treatment, work began first on the Dr. Bob book. Its writer's bad health and untimely death pushed that work to early publication in 1980. *Dr. Bob and the Good Oldtimers* had a rough-hewn quality, telling its story more anecdotally than narratively. Until its pairing with the new biography of Bill W. at A.A.'s 1985 convention, sales proved disappointing.[141]

The Wilson biography was further delayed when that writing assignment had to be shifted for a second time. Finally, in late 1984, in more than ample time for its distribution to precede A.A.'s fiftieth birthday celebration, *Pass It On* appeared. Blending simple style with narrative comprehensiveness, the book became an immediate popular success within the fellowship. Meanwhile, an outpouring of meditation books by treatment-center publishers stimulated recurrent suggestions of the need for a Conference-approved daily reflection book, and a 1986 survey confirmed that members approved such an undertaking. The 1987 General Service Conference thus advised "development of a daily reflections book based on individual A.A.'s (including Bill W.'s) sharing based on the Traditions and Steps, and that a progress report be submitted to the 1988 Conference Literature Committee."[142] Of more likely proximate appearance is yet another book filling in A.A.'s history — a kind of *"Alcoholics Anonymous Comes of Age,* volume 2," picking up where Wilson's 1957 work left off. Given the trustees' and delegates' wariness of interpretation as well as its writer's announced intentions, the book will be comprehensive and anecdotal.[143]

The reception of the filmstrip "Markings on the Journey," first shown at the 1980 New Orleans convention, alerted A.A.'s trusted servants to the members' desire to know more of the story of Alcoholics Anonymous, their own story. As befits golden anniversary celebrations, much attention to the historical also infused A.A.'s 1985 Montreal gathering. Unsurprisingly, then, attention was turned to ways of making more such material available to the fellowship. One result, in addition to the ventures already described, was the 1986 General Service Conference's conditional approval of a project designed to bring to the membership, in book form, at least a substantial number of the 156 articles that Bill W. wrote over the years for the *A.A. Grapevine.*[144]

In its turn to the historical, as always, Alcoholics Anonymous reflected not only its own development but the era in which it flourished. From diverse directions, interest in narrative, a fascination with storytelling, had been reborn in the late 1970s and rekindled into flame in the 1980s. Philosophers and theologians, literary critics and historians, even psychologists in a turn to qualitative research — each examined, theorized about, and attempted to utilize story. Alcoholics Anonymous, meanwhile, lived story and lived by story, thus affording a rare laboratory for the illustration and testing of theory.[145]

Because the concept of "sober alcoholic" lies at the core of the A.A. program, Alcoholics Anonymous most vividly reflects its own philosophy by embracing, as fellowship, its own being both-and. The fellowship's current story affords many such opportunities. Like the individual alcoholic, Alcoholics Anonymous experiences both ups and downs, and both have been as clear as ever in its most recent history.

The 1985 Montreal International Convention, A.A.'s well-publicized golden anniversary celebration, was an "up," except perhaps for some of the several hundreds who could not find rooms. Despite comprehensive advance preparations, every hotel room within eighty miles of Montreal was booked. Some conventioneers counted themselves lucky to locate accommodations in Burlington, Vermont. Those who found themselves without a room either left early or scrounged space on the floors of rooms of friends. Few chose to sleep in parks or other public places — an observation sedately offered by a reporter apparently surprised that alcoholics would not choose the environment stereotypically associated with them.[146]

In general, from the television news shows through the news magazines to the local newspapers, media coverage was comprehensive, occasionally insightful, always respectful, and surprisingly subdued. The more than 44,000 conventioneers, representing fifty-four countries, participated in meetings from nine each morning to after one the next — with a few hundred "early birds" also arranging 6:00 A.M. meetings each day. An ambivalence that combined "mixed feelings of awe and a sense of 'down home'" framed the opening flag and closing candle ceremonies. Thoughts of history and emotions of fulfillment spilled over each other especially at the Friday night "introduction of historic figures" — the moment of Lois Wilson's appearance and when the five-millionth copy of the book *Alcoholics Anonymous* was presented to Ruth Hock Crecelius, who as Bill's and Hank P.'s secretary had "typed the original manuscript."[147]

Many found both humor and honor in the House of Seagram paying tribute to Alcoholics Anonymous by lowering the three flags adorning its Montreal headquarters to half-staff for the duration of the A.A. convention.[148] For the thousands who attended, the Sunday morning "Spiritual Meeting" seemed to tap the deepest roots of their sense of "the spiritual." Overall, the centrality of A.A.'s own story suffused the whole convention and became permanently enshrined in the "Family Album and Souvenir," *Fifty Years With Gratitude*, which in its reproduction of over a hundred newspaper clippings and old photographs recalled their history to A.A.s and A.A.s to their history.

Perhaps of greater ultimate significance than the 1985 anniversary convention in the story of Alcoholics Anonymous as it will be written fifty years from now was a very different project that began in December of the same year. From at least two distinct directions — one officially public, the other resolutely private — individuals became involved in ventures designed to carry the A.A. message to the Soviet Union. Alcoholics Anonymous had existed in Poland since 1959, four

Poles making a memorable appearance at the Montreal convention.[149] The fellowship had begun there informally and initially without official notice, much less sanction. Political problems plagued Polish A.A., as attested by the Polish National Service Board delegates' inability to attend the 1986 Ninth World Service Meeting in Guatemala City and the public letter sent to them by that gathering.[150]

The Russian initiatives were different. The first, a joint project of the National Council on World Affairs and the American-Soviet Dialogue on Common Problems, involved visits between American alcoholism experts and members of the Russian Temperance Promotion Society, a prohibition group.[151] Three American experts, who were not identified with Alcoholics Anonymous, first visited Russia in August of 1986. Earlier, in April, and later, in October, other individuals specifically (but not officially) identified as A.A. members visited the Soviet Union, somewhat under the auspices of a totally different project styling itself "Creating A Sober World." According to one participant's report, "questions ranged from what we meant by 'higher power' to who had paid our way and, 'What do you mean by unstructured and no leaders?' "[152]

Many difficulties dogged the participants in both ventures, but a door had been opened. Although the Russian experts' 1987 return visit was postponed from April to May and involved stops in Washington, D.C., Cleveland and Akron, Ohio, southern California, and Minneapolis–Saint Paul rather than New York City, A.A. and Al-Anon representatives did make presentations at the Washington stop. Some who knew of the venture shied away, fearing political implications. Others dreaded more that the push of some American alcoholism entrepreneurs to get on the Russian bandwagon would jeopardize the small beginnings so slowly accomplished. A.A.'s official non-involvement plus the way of thinking inherent in its program's way of life meanwhile seemed likely to prove all the more effective a way, in such circumstances, of carrying its message in the long run. That promise seemed closer to fulfillment in late 1987, when a G.S.O. staff member joined the group of alcoholism experts on their second Russian visit.[153]

Both the Montreal convention and the "Creating A Sober World" initiative had their "down" sides — the logistical confusion of the former and the more seriously disruptive jockeying for prestige and advantage in the latter. Of more significance for A.A.'s story, however, were two other 1985 occurrences. Both were rooted in A.A. history: they flowed, albeit diversely, from the Akron–New York differences that went back to the fellowship's earliest origins. Just before the 1985 convention, Alcoholics Anonymous discovered that the copyright to the first and second editions of the book *Alcoholics Anonymous* had expired without being renewed. Over the same months, a group styling itself "The Founders Foundation" announced purchase of the Ardmore Avenue building that had been the home of Dr. Bob Smith and its intention to turn that house into a shrine.

"The Big Book Problem," as it quickly came to be called, raised two important concerns: the integrity of the A.A. program and the threat that loss of literature income would pose to the financial stability of A.A. World Services. The second concern had its own two aspects: A.A.W.S. had a responsibility both "to protect an important source of revenue to the fellowship and to fulfill our obligation to Lois Wilson and her estate." A 1963 agreement between A.A.W.S. and co-founder William Griffith Wilson had stipulated reciprocal obligations after Bill's retirement, making provision to pay Wilson's royalties to Lois after his death. Copyright loss thus jeopardized A.A.W.S. legally as well as financially.[154]

As always in such legal matters, the details of the copyright problem verge on the arcane. The best brief summary is Tom J.'s as he reported to the 1986 General Service Conference:

> The copyright on the first edition of the Big Book lapsed in 1967, and the copyright on the new material in the second edition lapsed in 1983 — both because of a failure to renew them in a timely fashion. There was a mistaken belief that registering the copyright on the second edition in 1956 served to revive the copyright on the first edition; the misconception continued, with respect to the second edition, when the third edition was copyrighted in 1976.[155]

G.S.O.'s Services Director went on to detail the anxieties aroused by this turn of events — and a further complication:

> The news of the copyright loss generated several immediate concerns: What would happen if every major publisher produced its own version of the Big Book in direct competition with A.A.W.S., Inc.? Also, what would happen to A.A.'s unique message of recovery and spiritual growth, as defined in the book *Alcoholics Anonymous*? How might we prevent distortion or even simple erosion of our message without copyright protection?
>
> While still recovering from the first shocking news, the

other shoe fell: Initial reports, quickly supported by hard evidence, confirmed that an outfit called C.T.M., Inc., intended to produce replicas of the first edition of *Alcoholics Anonymous* for $25 a copy. The A.A. General Service Board, the
A.A.W.S. board, and G.S.O. took a number of actions demanded by the situation.[156]

On August 26, 1985, Alcoholics Anonymous World Services and
Lois B. Wilson signed an agreement holding each other blameless for
the copyright loss and protecting the rights of both parties. Meanwhile, as word of the C.T.M. effort spread through the fellowship,
members disturbed by its "distasteful promotion" declined to support
the venture by buying its book. The G.S.O. staff had apparently not
realized it at first, but the main market for A.A. literature was and
would always be A.A. members.

Perhaps because of their deeper immersion in the world of competitive business, treatment-center executives recognized that reality more
readily. Because of that awareness and because also of their commitment to Alcoholics Anonymous as a program of recovery for the patients they treated, treatment-center publishers such as Hazelden and
Comp-Care, although technically capable of producing the A.A. Big
Book at less cost than could A.A. itself (because of the fellowship's
royalty commitment), recognized the folly of such a course of action.
New discount structures were negotiated both within the fellowship
and between A.A.W.S. and others who distributed A.A. literature, but
by mid-1986 it had become clear that no one could make money trying
to sell A.A. literature that did not flow from Alcoholics Anonymous
itself. World Services' main concern had been met: "The main purpose of A.A.W.S. in respect to the Big Book is to provide it in nearly
its present form . . . to recovering alcoholics without losing money."[157]

Early in the flap, shortly after the 1985 convention but before the
resolution with Lois Wilson and one of the larger treatment centers,
even as an IRS auditor was routinely examining the fellowship's 1963
royalty agreement with Bill Wilson, some members suggested, and
some G.S.O. staff pursued, seeking a special congressional act to re-
store the Alcoholics Anonymous copyright. Individuals met with congressional committee members, but the idea was abandoned —
apparently in part because of a U.S. district court decision declaring
unconstitutional a similar act passed to protect the literature of a religious group, but also because several of those involved were uncom-

fortable with the alcoholic familiarity of such an attempt to claim "special" status.[158]

Thus it developed, as 1986 turned into 1987, that what sociologist and non-alcoholic trustee Joan Jackson had reported at the 1986 General Service Conference as her reading of the will of the A.A. membership came to pass:

> Above all, members' comments revealed that they felt our actions in response to the loss of the Big Book copyright should be such that this chapter should "become another positive story in the history of Alcoholics Anonymous."[159]

The most proximate positive result, as the context of Jackson's remarks suggested, was the late-1986 publication of a paperback version, the twenty-fourth printing, of the third edition of the book *Alcoholics Anonymous*. Delegates to the 1986 General Service Conference approved a questionnaire on that project and authorized A.A.W.S. to produce such a book if the General Service Board so interpreted the results. The 1986 Conference also rejected the idea of producing a fourth edition of the Big Book, "because the story section is still up-to-date," and advised inquiry into a project until then consistently tabled — determining "the need for a daily reflection book."[160]

In the midst of the fiftieth anniversary and Big Book copyright flurries, few in A.A.'s New York Service Office much adverted to the "Founders Foundation" and its purchase of Dr. Bob and Anne Smith's former home. Historical purists winced at the claims that 855 Ardmore Avenue was "The Birthplace of our Fellowship" and that it housed "the Bible Anne Smith read from for the first Meeting for Bill and Bob"; but historical purity was not a chief concern of the project's "promoters" — a term A. Wesley P. emphasized in his letter announcing the endeavor and soliciting funds to enable more fund solicitation.[161]

As had so many things in previous A.A. history, the Founders Foundation project stemmed from the lingering fault line that had in some ways endured, differentiating Akron-oriented and New York-based A.A. from as early as 1937. As Alcoholics Anonymous grew, the geography spread. Today, what may be termed "Akron-style A.A." embraces much of central and western Florida and the coastal Carolinas, large areas around Houston and Galveston, Texas, virtually the whole state of Arizona, about a 60 percent patchwork of southern California, the southwest side of Chicago (but not that city's far suburbs except on the northern edge), an irregular ring around Detroit, as well as an uneven pattern embracing mainly the west side of Cleveland and especially the west-side suburbs of that city, as well as most of Ohio to the east, but not to the south, of Akron itself.

Akron-style A.A. is of course A.A.: "The only requirement for membership is a desire to stop drinking" is a tradition adhered to even if the Traditions themselves are sometimes criticized and one gathers the feeling that the "desire" had better be well implemented. One recognizes Akron-oriented A.A. by that greater rigor, by emphasis that what the Big Book terms "the Steps we took, which are suggested as a program of recovery," are more than *suggested*, by the use of such literature as the pamphlets put out by "A.A. of Akron" (at the time of this writing, from a post office box in South Carolina), by more explicitly Christian talk about "the spiritual," by the preference for Dr. Bob over Bill W. whenever the topic of "co-founders" comes up, and by the feeling that Alcoholics Anonymous has been in decline at least since the death of Bill Wilson and probably since the death of Dr. Bob Smith, and that the main cause is "those New Yorkers." Rarely, in other words, is A.A.'s 1930s origin more plainly visible than when New York-oriented and Akron-inclined members explain how they differ one from the other, even as both defend each other's right to be different, so long as a member does not drink, attends meetings, and works the Twelve Steps.[162]

And so we return to the motif of difference within the theme of unity, for as this narrative has often illustrated, the convergence of that motif and that theme define the story of Alcoholics Anonymous. A non-event best frames that closing discussion: A.A.'s Nobel Peace Prize.

In early 1986, rumors were rife that the Nobel Peace Prize committee was prepared to nominate Alcoholics Anonymous for that honor, if assured that A.A. would accept. Discussions, all unofficial, canvassed every option except a simple yes. The chief precedent adduced was Bill Wilson's far from parallel refusal of the Yale honorary degree in 1954. Apparently because Alcoholics Anonymous hesitated, the matter was dropped. Those who had coveted the honor saw that outcome as another casualty of A.A. World Services' hesitancy to do anything to which some members might object. Others found tradition vindicated and cherished this quiet reminder of fellowship humility.[163]

For reasons not entirely clear, the 1986 General Service Conference held a "brief 'What's On Your Mind?' sharing session" rather than the traditional, more open and lengthy "Ask-It Basket" — a strange change at a conference at which the fellowship's retiring top servant decried "rigidity."[164] Although the problems associated with the Big Book copyright loss seemed substantially resolved, many among both delegates and G.S.O. staff prepared warily for the 1987 meeting of A.A.'s General Service Conference, which less surprisingly in these circumstances also omitted the Ask-It Basket. The issue of self-support, always touchy, came framed by grass-roots questions challenging group-conscience surveys and the administration of the *A.A. Grapevine*. The old animus between Akron and New York, between coast and heartland, lived on, demonstrating more than anything else the lasting influence of its own origins on the fellowship of Alcoholics Anonymous.

Yet the 1987 Conference, as we have seen topically throughout this chapter, lived up to its responsibilities and moved toward measured resolutions of the problems at hand. To an outside observer of A.A.'s General Service Conferences since Bill Wilson's death, the pattern seems simple: a complacent New York office provokes delegate orneriness; troubled, puzzled, fearful staff members seem on the other hand to inspire Conference responsibility.

In other words, Alcoholics Anonymous continues to be what Bill W. once termed it: "an utter simplicity which encases a complete mystery."[165]

Since the publication of the earlier version of the present book in 1979 (which did not include Appendix B), I have had many occasions to travel and to speak with both members and scholars on topics related to the history of Alcoholics Anonymous. Consistently, echoing questions have arisen: What next? Won't Alcoholics Anonymous change because of greater acceptance of alcoholism as an illness, or because people know more about all drug addictions? Hasn't Alcoholics Anonymous already changed from what it was for its first twenty years?

The questions echoed because they repeat queries gently tendered by many oldtimer interviewees during my initial research. Having reminded those generous individuals that a historian is not a prophet, I nevertheless promised to attempt an answer at the conclusion of my study. That promise was kept on the concluding pages of Appendix A, published in 1979:

> Alcoholics Anonymous shall survive so long as its message remains that of the not-God-ness of the wholeness of accepted limitation; and this itself shall endure so long as A.A.'s spiritualizers and its liberals — its "right" and its "left" —

maintain in mutual respect the creative tension that arises from their willingness to participate even with others of so different assumptions in the *shared honesty of mutual vulnerability openly acknowledged.*

Alcoholics Anonymous will live, in other words, so long as it is "Alcoholics Anonymous": "an utter simplicity which encases a complete mystery" that no one claims *perfectly* to understand.[166]

Today, almost ten years of additional research and observation of the fellowship and program of Alcoholics Anonymous suggest that that answer holds: it does not require revision, but perhaps it could benefit from a slight expansion.

A.A.'s story reveals over and over again that the key to A.A. life and growth is the tolerance that flows from humility. Humility — the acceptance that, although sober, they remain alcoholic — keeps members honest and keeps them coming to meetings: thus they grow in sobriety. The individual member's humility and consequent tolerance and the A.A. group's tolerance and consequent growth are mutually related: each promotes the other.

A new yet also not-new challenge faces Alcoholics Anonymous as these words are written. In early 1987, G.S.O.'s trusted servants gingerly explored precedents for answering a singular request: could there be "special interest" groups of A.A.s diagnosed as having AIDS? A new disease — and therefore a new disease metaphor — had seized American consciousness. As had alcoholics for so many decades, sufferers from acquired immune deficiency syndrome bore the stigma of moral degeneracy. And for at least the moment, fear of contagion led the AIDS victim to be even more stigmatized than the alcoholic.

Staff approached the question as A.A. has consistently resolved all questions of "special interest groups": so long as the group was of alcoholics, meeting without other affiliation for the purpose of their sobriety, and so long as the group would accept any alcoholics who wished to join it for that purpose, it could call itself and be listed as "Alcoholics Anonymous." A.A.'s Twelve Steps, Twelve Traditions, and Twelve Concepts, as interpreted by each year's meeting of the General Service Conference of Alcoholics Anonymous, continue to guide the fellowship.

As time unfolds, A.A.'s story reveals ever more clearly the simplicity of that process. From the very beginning, the Twelve Steps have been both the foundation and the apex of the Alcoholics Anonymous way of life. As A.A. began to grow in the mid-1940s, the Twelve Traditions emerged to safeguard and to apply within A.A. group life the principles of the Steps. The years that immediately followed Bill W.'s death confirmed their centrality. The fellowship discovered the pivotal role of service's Twelve Concepts more slowly. Although Bill penned the Concepts in 1959 and saw them accepted in 1962, although the *A.A. Grapevine* ran a series of articles on them beginning in November of 1971, even today most A.A. members look blank when the Twelve Concepts are mentioned. Some hope that the recent concern over the self-support Tradition might awaken interest in the legacy of Service: few things focus an alcoholic's mind so well as the ever-difficult relationship between money and "the spiritual."[167]

Meanwhile, Alcoholics Anonymous remains, as always, not Conference nor office but fellowship. And so when questions arise about A.A.'s future, although there rarely is the time to offer all these details or to establish the context of the answer, it does seem worthwhile to try to capture at least that reality:

> Whenever, wherever, one alcoholic meets another alcoholic and sees in that person first and foremost *not* that he or she is male or female, or black or white, or Baptist or Catholic or Jew, or gay or straight, or *whatever*, but sees rather another alcoholic to whom he or she *must* reach out for the sake of his or her own sobriety — so long, in other words, as one alcoholic recognizes in another alcoholic first and foremost that he or she *is* alcoholic and that therefore *both* of them need each other — there will be not only *an* Alcoholics Anonymous, but there will be *the* Alcoholics Anonymous that you and I love so much and respect so deeply.[168]

For the deeper answer is that alcoholics, once they have tasted sobriety, become addicted to it and therefore to Alcoholics Anonymous — to the way of life encapsulated in the Twelve Steps and protected by the Twelve Traditions and extended through the Twelve Concepts. It is conceivable, I suppose, because all institutions degenerate, that individuals who call themselves "Alcoholics Anonymous" might some day ignore service, violate tradition, and scorn the Steps — or worse, accord them only lip service. But should that happen, I am sure that somewhere, perhaps under a battered bridge or in a dingy alcove, perhaps even in an atmosphere free of cigarette smoke and lacking coffee, some alcoholic who is trying to stay sober will sidle up to some other alcoholic who may even be drinking and say: "Psst, buddy. You must be awfully thirsty, but let me tell you how it was with me when I used to need a drink . . ." And in that moment an A.A. meeting will begin, and the story of Alcoholics Anonymous will continue.

"Our stories disclose in a general way what we used to be like, what happened, and what we are like now." So long as they do, Alcoholics Anonymous lives. For A.A.'s story is one of those stories that will never end so long as there are human beings who discover, however painfully, having tried to play God, that they are not-God — that they can be *both* "sober" and "alcoholic," both whole and flawed.

NOTES

KEY TO ABBREVIATIONS

The following abbreviations are used in the Notes. They are explained more fully in "Notes on Primary Sources" at the conclusion of the Bibliography.

AA: Alcoholics Anonymous, 2nd ed.

AACA: Alcoholics Anonymous Comes of Age

AAGV: The A.A. Grapevine

ABSI: As Bill Sees It

Amos, "History": Frank Amos, "History of the Alcoholic movement up to the formation of The Alcoholic Foundation on August 11th, 1938"

"Basic Concepts": Wilson, "Basic Concepts of Alcoholics Anonymous"

"Beginnings," [Wilson], "Alcoholics Anonymous: Beginnings and Growth"

CAAAL: The Classified Abstract Archive of the Alcohol Literature

"Co-Founder": [Wilson], "Alcoholics Anonymous as Seen by W.G.W., a co-founder"

"Fellowship": [Wilson], "The Fellowship of Alcoholics Anonymous"

HS: Henrietta Seiberling

HS, "Origins": Henrietta Seiberling, "Origins of Alcoholics Anonymous"

int: interview

JSA: Journal of Studies on Alcohol (before 1975, the citation is to *QJSA* and the reference to *The Quarterly Journal of Studies on Alcohol*)

Jim B., "Evolution": Jim B., "The Evolution of Alcoholics Anonymous"

LM: [Wilson], "Talk at LeMoyne College, Syracuse, New York"

"Memo": [Wilson], "Memorandum to Our Writing Team, subject: Historical Time Table"

NCCA: [Wilson], "Clergy Conference: talk to the Annual Convention of the National Clergy Conference on Alcoholism"

NCEA: The National Committee for Education on Alcoholism; later, NCA: The National Council on Alcoholism

NW: Nell Wing

NW, "Outline": Nell Wing, "Outline of A.A. History"

NW, "Pre-History": Nell Wing, "Pre-A.A. History"

OG: The Oxford Group (for introductory explanation, *cf.* page 9; for in depth treatment, *cf.* pp. 43–52.

QJSA: cf. JSA, above.

"Review": [Wilson], "Bill's Review of the Movement"

"Rockland": [Wilson], "Transcription of Presentation to Board Meeting, Rockland State Hospital, 14 December 1939"

"Society": [Wilson], "The Society of Alcoholics Anonymous"

Thomsen: Robert Thomsen, *Bill W.*

tr.: transcript of tape recording or tape recording

12&12: Twelve Steps and Twelve Traditions

VRE: William James, *The Varieties of Religious Experience*

I   1934–1935

1   The opening story is reconstructed from *AACA,* pp. 58–59; *AA,* pp. 9–13; Wilson, *LM;* Wilson, *NCCA,* pp. 9–10; Ebby's tr., pp. 12–13; the physical description and details of the setting are from Lois Wilson, interview of 7 April 1977.

2   The final quotation is from *AACA,* p. 58.

3   Regarding Ebby's sobriety history, letters of Ebby to Wilson: 24 November 1940 (Keswick), 19 November 1942 (Philadelphia), 12 November 1948 (New York), ? November 1949 (Dublin, NH), ? March 1952 (Spring Valley, NY), ? December 1952 (Katonah, NY) — the last three from drying-out facilities. *Cf.* also: Wilson to John T., 27 December 1948; Wilson to Emma D., 21 April 1950; Wilson to Jack T., 3 October 1950; also Nell Wing, interview, 4 April 1977, and Ruth H. tr. Despite his continued drinking, Wilson always regarded Ebby as his "sponsor." This regard is a profound witness to the central importance of "carrying the message" in Alcoholics Anonymous. This point is most strikingly clear in Wilson, "Review."

"over one million": the best treatment of membership figures for A.A. is Barry Leach and John L. Norris, "Factors in the Development of Alcoholics Anonymous (A.A.)," in Benjamin Kissin and Henri Begleiter (eds.), *Treatment and Rehabilitation of the Chronic Alcoholic* (New York: Plenum Press, 1977), pp. 443–507; *cf.* also John L. Norris, "Alcoholics Anonymous and Other Self-Help Groups," in Ralph E. Tarter and A. Arthur Sugerman (eds.), *Alcoholism: Interdisciplinary Approaches to an Enduring Problem* (Reading, MA: Addison-Wesley, 1976), p. 764: "We believe the figure of 896,700 active members to be conservative. This does not include those who have recovered in A.A. and are no longer attending meetings." Nor, of course, does it include those who died between 1935 and 1976.

4   *AACA,* p. vii; p. 59 (italics Wilson's).

5   Ebby's tr., pp. 9–11; obituary of Rowland H., *New York Times,* 22 December 1945 — from which I take the spelling "Row*land*": Wilson and those following him habitually omitted the "w".

6   Wilson to Jung, 23 January 1961; Jung's reply (Zurich), 30 January 1961, accepted Wilson's portrayal of "our conversation" as "adequately reported." This correspondence was published twice in slightly edited form in *AAGV,* in January of 1963 and 1968. *Cf.* also NW, "Pre-History"; Wilson, tr., p. 98; Wilson, *LM:* "I suppose it really began in far off Zurich . . ."; Wilson to Margarita L., 14 January 1946: "So, you see, I could claim to be a lineal descendant from Dr. Jung." Margarita L. had been a student of Jung: *cf.* Dr. Harry Tiebout (Greenwich, CT) to Dr. Ralph B., 15 November 1945; Wilson to Della C., 6 March 1947. She was Wilson's most proximate continuing contact with Jung's thought.

7   Wilson to Jung, 23 January 1961.

8   Wilson, tr., p. 115: In August 1934, a small Oxford Group contingent was vacationing at the H. summer home near Bennington, VT. One of the number, Cebra G., learned that his father, a judge in Manchester, was about to commit Ebby to Brattleboro Asylum. He and another visitor, Shep C., decided with Rowland to make Ebby a "project." *Cf.* also: Ebby, tr., p. 12; NW, "Pre-History."

9   Ebby, tr., pp. 12–13; *cf.* Wilson, tr., p. 117.

10   *AA*, p. 9; *AACA*, p. 58.

11   Thomsen, p. 15; — on my use of the Thomsen biography, *cf.* p. 340 in the Bibliography; for the background of Bill's parents, *ibid.*, pp. 12–14. The significance of the "desertion evening" in Wilson's mind is witnessed by the fact that Thomsen made its description his opening chapter, pp. 3–11.

12   Thomsen, p. 28 (italics Thomsen's).

13   Thomsen, pp. 17–21. Wilson's relationship with his mother, and hers with him, always remained constrained: *cf.*, e.g., two of her letters to him: 24 November 1940 and 22 November 1953. Bill had been born at Thanksgiving time, and his mother's straining to transmit acceptance in these annual epistles is striking; e.g., Emily Wilson Strobell (San Diego, CA) to Wilson, 24 November 1940: "Now many children are not wanted, as perhaps you may know, and so it may be of some pleasure to you to know that you were not in the unwanted class." *Cf.* also Wilson to Fred B., 20 May 1946: "Neither Dorothy [his sister] nor I have ever stood in quite the right relation to Mother in spite of our best efforts to do so." Wilson mentions the "great disgrace and great stigma" attached to his parents' divorce as leading him to feel "that I didn't belong, I was somehow different": *LM*, [p. 2].

14   Thomsen, pp. 30, 34.

15   Thomsen, pp. 30–31, 34–36.

16   Thomsen, p. 38.

17   Thomsen, pp. 43–44. Neither Wilson nor Thomsen mentions Darwin or Sumner by name, but their description of the ideas bandied by Whalon make clear the impact of these thinkers.

18   Thomsen, pp. 49–51.

19   Burr and Burton: Thomsen, pp. 52–53; the Bertha Banford story is detailed by Thomsen, pp. 56–63. Wilson first told this, somewhat condensed, in *LM*, [p. 3]; he abbreviated it much more drastically in *AACA*, p. 54.

20   Thomsen, p. 63.

21   Thomsen, pp. 104–106.

22   Thomsen, pp. 106–108; *cf.* also pp. 162–163.

23 *AACA*, p. 55.

24 Thomsen, pp. 169–174.

25 Thomsen, p. 160; Lois Wilson, interview, 7 April 1977.

26 Wilson recalled the referral to Towns Hospital as by Dr. Strong, *cf.*, *AA*, p. 7. Thomsen follows this from the taped recollections. Lois Wilson, interviewed 7 April 1977, said that she first obtained the reference to Towns from her father, Dr. Burnham. If Lois mentioned this to Bill or to Dr. Strong, the memories need not conflict.

"four times": Thomsen, p. 191. Wilson habitually indicated *three* stays at Towns as a patient, and does so in tr. at this point. The hospital records, except for photostats of Bill's final two admissions in September and December 1934 have been lost. I incline to agree with Thomsen here: Bill seems to elide his June and September 1934 hospitalizations, and the page reference to his first admission on the September admission photostat seems to imply a late 1933 date for his first admission. Yet Dr. Silkworth, *AA*, p. xxiii, indicates three stays, adding to the confusion, as does Thomsen in placing his *third* admission in July of 1934 (p. 194). The solution to this quandry, given the destruction of the hospital records, would seem forever veiled. In Thomsen's almost despairing summary of the tapes at this point: "In fact, [Wilson's] memories of the entire period from '33 until about the end of '34, were totally disordered." (pp. 192–193). Thus, whether the conversation between Silkworth and Wilson narrated below took place in June or September (or even July) must remain unknown in the obscurity of "mid-summer 1934" — *AACA*, p. 52, despite the fact that on p. 56, *idem*, Wilson says "September." My own considered preference is for late June.

27 Dr. Silkworth's understanding of alcoholism, as offered to Wilson on this occasion, will be analyzed below, pp. 21–22 with fuller citations. Here, *cf.* Thomsen, pp. 191, 194–195.

28 Thomsen, p. 193; *AACA*, p. 52. "on a clerk's salary"; *cf.* notes #26, above, on the problem of timing, and #58, below, for Lois's employment history.

As a doctor who received his training in the pre-Freudian era, Silkworth was most properly a specialist in neuropsychiatry; *cf.* also note #46, below.

29 *AACA*, p. 57.

30 The sources cited in note #8, above, make clear that although Ebby's commitment had been formalized, it had not been actually executed before his friends intervened.

31 *AACA*, p. 58. Wilson's "wonderful engineering college" was Norwich, the Vermont military academy to which he had repaired in 1914 after having failed almost every subject of the Massachusetts Institute of Technology entrance exam. The wonders of the memory of alcoholic grandiosity! — *cf.* Thomsen, p. 72.

32 Bill's grandfather: Thomsen, pp. 31–34; *AA*, p. 10; "leaving the church": Wilson, NCCA, pp. 3–4; *AA*, p. 10; Wilson to Herb B., 3 June 1968. The "self-conscious wariness of 'religion'" is most clearly illustrated within A.A. by the insistently reiterated claim: "This is a spiritual, not a religious, program." That exact phrase appears nowhere in the literature, and its origin eluded discovery, yet it is pervasive. The concept as fundamental is best witnessed by the "We

Agnostics" chapter of *AA*, pp. 44–57; its importance (to A.A.) and motive, by *AA*, p. 93, where the concern is presented as the first caution about "Working With Others." Its significance will be examined in detail in Part Two, especially within Chapter Eight, below.

33   *AACA*; p. 59 (italics Wilson's).

34   *Cf. AA*, p. 12; *LM*, [p. 5]; NCCA, p. 10.

35   Thomsen, pp. 211–212.

36   Thomsen, pp. 213–214; on the Wilson tape, the word "different" at the end of the second-last paragraph of this quotation from Thomsen is heavily stressed, and there is a touch of sarcasm in Bill's voice. Clearly, the word should be italicized.

37   Thomsen, p. 214; *AACA*, p. 59; Lois Wilson, interview of 7 April 1977.

38   Thomsen, pp. 215–216; *AACA*, pp. 59–60.

39   Thomsen, pp. 216, 219; *AACA*, pp. 60–62. A confusion about timing exists here: in the foregoing narrative, I have preserved — because of no specific reason to change — the time intervals indicated in Thomsen and the other sources: "two days later," "the next day," etc. Yet since Ebby's first visit was in late November (probably between the 26th and the 30th) and Wilson's final Towns Hospital admission began indisputably (from hospital records) at 2:30 PM on 11 December, there is an unexplained hiatus. Best conjecture would place it between Ebby's first visit and Bill's trip to the Calvary Mission: Lois Wilson (interview of 7 April 1977) recalled Ebby visiting several times, once even staying for dinner, before Bill set off on his "investigation."

40   *Cf. AACA*, pp. 62–63; Thomsen, p. 221.

41   *AACA*, p. 63; *cf.* Thomsen, pp. 222–224; *AA*, pp. 12–13. Wilson's most succinct later understanding of this experience appears in a letter to Marjorie W., 3 April 1958: "What I really meant was this: I was catapulted into a spiritual experience, which gave me the capability of feeling the presence of God, His love, and His omnipotence. And, most of all, His personal availability to me."

42   *AACA*, p. 63; Thomsen, p. 224; *LM*, [p. 6].

43   Thomsen, p. 224; *cf. AACA*, p. 63; description of Silkworth's facial mannerisms from Lois Wilson, interview of 7 April 1977.

44   *AACA*, p. 64 (italics Wilson's).

45   *AACA*, p. 64 (italics Wilson's).

46   Biographical information on Silkworth is drawn from *The National Cyclopedia of American Biography* (New York: James T. White Co., 1954), vol. 39, p. 299; obituary, *NYT*, 23 March 1951; A.A. archive copy of his "Application for Appointment to the Courtesy Staff of the Knickerbocker Hospital," filled out in Silkworth's hand and dated 28 April 1945; and the *AAGV* obituary tribute, "The Little Doctor Who Loved Drunks," *AAGV* 7:12 (May 1951), 2–8.

47   *AAGV. op. cit.*, 7; "A Doctor's Opinion," *AA*, p. xxvii. That Wilson received these ideas from, and attributed them to, Silkworth, is clear from Wilson, tr., and all the printed sources; also with somewhat greater detail and analysis from

Wilson to Howard C., 4 January 1956; to Helen C., 9 April 1962; to Bert B., 19 October 1965; *cf.* also "After Twenty-Five Years — by Bill," *AAGV* 16:10 (March 1960), 22.

48   *AA*, p. xxvii; *AAGV*, "The Little Doctor," 7; W. D. Silkworth, "Alcoholism as a Manifestation of Allergy," *Medical Record* (New York), 145: 249–251 (1937); *cf.* also W. D. Silkworth, "A New Approach to Psychotherapy in Chronic Alcoholism," *The Journal-Lancet* (Minneapolis) 59: 312–314 (1939); William D. Silkworth, "A Highly Successful Approach to the Alcoholic Problem," *Medical Record* (New York), 154: 105–110 (1941).

49   The classic and perhaps still most authoritative treatment of the idea that alcoholism is a disease is E. M. Jellinek, *The Disease Concept of Alcoholism* (New Haven: College and University Press, 1960); the most overtly historical treatment, although undertaken and carried out from a sociological point of view, is A. E. Wilkerson, *A History of the Concept of Alcoholism as a Disease*, unpublished dissertation, University of Pennsylvania, 1966, University Microfilms #67:188; the most recent review of the concept and literature is Mark Keller, "The Disease Concept of Alcoholism Revisited," *JSA* 37: 1694–1717 (1976); but *cf.* also Bruce Holley Johnson, *The Alcoholic Movement in America: A Study in Cultural Innovation* (unpublished dissertation, The University of Illinois at Urbana-Champaign, 1973), for a sociological study of shifts in cultural understanding of the concept of alcoholism. The continuing complexity of medical thought on this question, and perhaps the unconscious profundity of Wilson's "heart disease" analogy, may be gathered from perusal of the research reported in Kissin-Begleiter and Tarter-Sugerman, *cf.* note #3 above: and even more deeply from the first four volumes of the series of which the Kissin-Begleiter cited is vol. 5.

50   *AA*, p. 28.

51   William James, *The Varieties of Religious Experience* (New York: Mentor, 1958), p. 213. Lecture 9 is titled "Conversion," Lecture 10, "Conversion-concluded." As difficult as it is to prove a negative, I am certain that the word "deflation" does not occur in *VRE*; likewise that only most slowly, warily, and late was Wilson able to speak with any comfort of "conversion." On this latter, he was more at ease with his New York alcoholics' joking over his "hot flash" than with any more exact reference to his "conversion experience" — interview with Lois Wilson, 7 April 1977; interview with Marty Mann, 15 November 1977. Wilson did speak openly of his "experience of conversion" in his 1939 Rockland State Hospital presentation: I suspect this might be why this first public talk to a group of doctors was so assiduously ignored by Wilson and therefore by those following him.

52   Wilson, tr., p. 133: "By nightfall, this Harvard professor, long in his grave had, without anyone knowing it, become a founder of Alcoholics Anonymous"; *cf.* also the analysis following, tr., pp. 133–134. Wilson frequently and avidly recommended *VRE* to correspondents telling of difficulty with the A.A. program or concern over their "spiritual experience": *cf.*, e.g., Wilson to Marion R., 21 January 1952; to Paul H., 28 October 1954; to Mel B., 2 July 1956; to Ed. B., 28 July 1958. *VRE* heads the list of six titles of "Spiritual Reading Bill and early A.A.'s found helpful" (Box 31, Folder 19.2, A.A. archives). Jim B., "Evolution," p. 3, notes about the writing of *AA*: "Bill probably got most of his ideas from one of these books, James' 'Varieties of Religious Experiences' [sic]." Two recent interpretations of James may deepen the understanding of the thoughtful reader concerning the affinity of his ideas for the insight of Alcoholics Anonymous; *cf.* John E. Smith, *Purpose and Thought: The Meaning of Pragmatism* (New Haven: Yale, 1978), especially within chapters 3 and 6; William Barrett, *The Illusion of Technique* (New York: Anchor-Doubleday, 1978), especially pp. 253–294.

53 On the one occasion when he was asked, by a Fordham University philosophy professor, to explain more exactly his use of James, Wilson answered cautiously and defensively, but in terms that support my interpretation: "While I cannot pinpoint the particular part of the 'Varieties' I vividly remember that in general the experiences described, whatever their variety, did often arise out of conditions of complete hopelessness — exactly my own just prior to the illumination." Wilson to Rev. Robert J. Roth, S.J., 12 November 1965; *cf.* Robert J. Roth, "William James and Alcoholics Anonymous," *America* 113: 48–50 (1965).

The quotations are from *AA*, p. 95; p. xxi (foreword to 2nd ed., 1955).

54 For a sensitive interpretation of William James's personal history that the reader aware of Wilson's personal history may find especially provocative, *cf.* Cushing Strout, "The Pluralistic Identity of William James," *American Quarterly* 23: 135–152 (1971).

For non-American advertences to A.A. revealing this point, *cf.* R. Bircher, "'A.A.' Alcoholics Anonymous oder das Budnis der 'Namenloser Trinker'" ("'A.A.' Alcoholics Anonymous or the alliance of nameless drinkers"), *Wendepunkt*, Zurich, 23: 214–220 (1946);

G. Mouchot, "Alcoholics Anonymous. Lettre de'Angleterre" ("Alcoholics Anonymous. A Letter from England"), *Concurs medical* 76: 1863–1864 (1954);

P. Bensoussan and E. M. Villiaumey, "Le movement 'alcooliques anonymes,' structure et dynamique; essai d'adaptation aux malades en cure de desintoxication" ("The Alcoholics Anonymous movement, its structure and dynamics; attempted adaptation to patients during detoxification treatment"), *Annales medical-psychologiques*, 114: 280–289 (1956);

Joseph Kessel, *Avec les Alcooliques Anonymes* (Paris: Libraire Gallinard, 1960), U.S. ed. titled *The Road Back*, trans. Frances Partridge (New York: Knopf, 1962);

P. Borghes and E. Medaglini, "A proposita di una forma di psicoterpia di gruppo nell alcoolismo cronico; considerazioni critichi su l'Alcoholics Anonymous" ("Concerning a type of group therapy in chronic alcoholism: critical observations on Alcoholics Anonymous"), *Rass. Stud. psichiat.*, 54: 79–92 (1965);

R. K. Jones, "Sectarian Characteristics of Alcoholics Anonymous," *Sociology* (Oxford), 4: 181–195 (1970).

55 *AACA*, p. 65; Thomsen, pp. 232–233; "A Fragment of History — by Bill," *AAGV* 10:2 (July 1953), 6–9. For the depth of Shoemaker's friendship with Wilson, *cf.* his speech at A.A.'s 1955 "Coming of Age" convention, reprinted in *AACA*, pp. 261–271. Shoemaker's role in the Oxford Group will be treated in Chapter Two. On Wilson's deep sense of the OG as a source of Alcoholics Anonymous, *cf.* Wilson to Charles P., 1 July 1938. This witness is specially significant because it comes from the time when Wilson had just painfully split his nascent New York group from its OG connection.

56 *AACA*, p. 65; Thomsen, pp. 232–233. The interpretation in this paragraph is based on my own investigation of the Oxford Group — *cf.* citations in Chapter Two — and on interviews with Lois Wilson (7 April 1977) and Henrietta Seiberling (6 April 1977).

57 Thomsen, pp. 232–233; Lois Wilson, interviews of 16 November 1976 and 7 April 1977. Whether Bill started bringing alcoholics home to Clinton Street now or only after his late 1935 return from Akron is veiled by conflicting memories, including Wilson's own. I follow Thomsen in finding the practice beginning in very early 1935. Although Lois Wilson "tends to think" it was only later when answering to this directly, some of her own recollections of circumstances indicate otherwise — interviews cited. The "neighborhood cafeteria" was Stewart's, in the neighborhood of the Calvary Church Mission rather than Bill's at Clinton Street.

58 That "all but Bill himself got drunk" is clearest from Wilson, "Memo," where he delineates the history of those who later sobered up again and finally did "get the program" — because some did, other commentators have been confused about the total nature of the failure here.

Wilson always referred to Lois's job as "at Macy's" or "clerking in a department store." Lois left Macy's in March of 1934. When she returned to work in September of 1934, it was at Loeser's, also a department store, but one which now promised her work "as an interior decorator" after a probationary period in draperies. That Bill felt demeaned by his wife working is understandable, but this has led others such as Thomsen to place misguided emphasis on Lois's "having to work." Whether or not she was at this time about to give up on Bill (and she denies this), Lois cherished the idea of a career in interior decorating as creative and fulfilling. After leaving Loeser's in 1936, she did some such work on her own, and her present home bears witness to her talent and ability in this field. (Lois Wilson, interviews of 16 November 1976 and 7 April 1977).

The hypothetical alternative explored in this paragraph was gently probed by this writer with Lois: beyond the wryly smiling statement: "Well, I didn't have much use for the Oxford Group: I didn't think I needed 'conversion,'" Lois declined to speak further of her thoughts at this time (*idem*).

59 AACA, pp. 67–68; *cf.* "A Fragment of History — by Bill," *AAGV* 10:2 (July 1953), 6–9; Thomsen, pp. 233–234.

60 Lois Wilson, interview of 7 April 1977; *cf. AACA*, p. 65; Thomsen, p. 234.

61 *AACA*, p. 65; Thomsen, p. 235.

62 The incident, the narration of which begins here, is the self-consciously supreme moment of A.A. history — often lengthily and romantically described. The basic narration is Wilson's in *AACA*, pp. 65–70; Thomsen, using all the Wilson sources, covers the ground on pp. 235–240. My retelling is based directly on the sources used by Wilson and Thomsen, supplemented by the Seiberling sources and interview memories of Dr. Smith described and evaluated in the "Notes on Sources."

Citations will be offered here and in the following paragraphs only to support my addition to or changes of the Wilson-Thomsen narrations.

For Bill's frame of mind, an obvious source often overlooked: *AA*, p. 154.

Except for Lois herself, there remains no witness who could offer testimony on the quality of her and Bill's marriage during the difficult years up to

1935. Yet Lois's memories do have some documentation, and the present research enjoyed access to some of that documentation — *cf.* Bibliography, below, p. 417. Based on these sources, and also what Lois told me (interview of 24 January 1979) was to appear in her autobiography, *Lois Remembers*, which is scheduled for publication in mid-1979, and because of questions asked by readers of the earlier version of the present book, it seems appropriate to add here a few words about the state of the Wilsons' marriage in 1935.

Lois insists that she never thought of leaving Bill. Indeed, despite his drinking, Lois felt for the first fifteen years of their marriage that it was her contribution to the relationship that was deficient. Both Lois and Bill wanted children, but doctors discovered after two ectopic pregnancies that Lois suffered from a congenital defect that prevented her from ever bearing a child. Lois was grateful for, but at times worried about, Bill's continuing acceptance of and love for her despite this disappointment. It seems clear that some coolness did develop between the Wilsons in the early 1930s, but it is even more clear that both strove mightily to make their marriage work — except for Bill's drinking and the episodes that followed from it. After Bill attained sobriety, the Wilsons' marriage improved — briefly. Soon new tensions developed, and it is the description of these — and their resolution — that Lois's autobiography is expected to explore. Many of Bill's published writings as well as his letters offer hints about his understanding of the problems in his marriage. Some of these will be noted, as appropriate, in the narration and notes that follow.

63 Henrietta Seiberling, "Origins," [p. 3]. Wilson and others, especially Mrs. Seiberling, stress the "coincidence" and "Providence" in Bill's choosing Tunks, especially because it was a Presbyterian minister in Akron who most actively supported and championed the OG. (According to Mrs. S., interview of 6 April 1976, he was on Tunks's list, but was "too busy preparing his sermon to speak with Bill.") Given Bill's dearth of experience with organized religion and his new friendship with Sam Shoemaker, I find his choice logical.

The consistent Wilson-Thomsen version is that Mrs. Seiberling's was the tenth name on the list. I choose to follow the HS version, especially because she herself — a Presbyterian — barely knew Dr. Tunks: "Origins," [p. 3].

The final quotation is from *ibid.*, the "from New York" added later orally by HS and inscribed in the A.A. archive copy by Nell Wing; also added orally to this writer, interview of 6 April 1976.

64 Mrs. Seiberling's background from interview cited; her efforts with Dr. Smith, *ibid.*, and HS, "Origins," [pp. 1–2]. Mrs. Seiberling's *memory* of Bill's physical appearance at their first meeting may aid in understanding some of the tensions which over the years marked the relationship between the Oxford Group and Alcoholics Anonymous as it came into being: "Bill stood hunched over, and was dressed in ill-fitting and unmatched clothes. He laughed too loudly and showed too many teeth even when talking. He had this mannerism of rubbing his hands together and a simpering smile — a regular Uriah Heep." It is Mrs. S's conviction that she "polished" Bill, and clearly her belief that only through her efforts did Wilson — and A.A. — achieve "class." (Interview of 6 April 1976).

65 According to Dr. Bob's telling of his story, *AA*, p. 179: "The day before Mothers Day . . . I came home plastered, carrying a big potted plant which I set down on the table and forthwith went upstairs and passed out." Admittedly, I here prefer the more colorful detail as related by Mrs. Seiberling on the basis of later conversation with Anne Smith as precisely "more colorful." (Interview cited; *cf.* also Sue G., tr.).

66   The direct quotations are from Wilson's recounting of Dr. Bob Smith's story on the occasion of the latter's death: "Dr. Bob," *AAGV* 7:7 (January 1951), 22. According to Mrs. Seiberling, the Smiths had been invited to dinner and the four did dine first; this is reflected by Wilson in *AACA*, p. 67, although "[Bob] did not eat." Bob's description of the meeting in his own story, *AA*, p. 179, seems to belie this — as does his emphasis in "Last Major Talk" that he had extracted from his wife a promise that they would stay only "fifteen minutes," and Wilson's stress in the earlier sources on "immediately on seeing." This writer's guess is that Mrs. Seiberling would not have invited Sunday afternoon guests to arrive at five o'clock unless they were to dine. Perhaps, then, Wilson's in *AACA* is the most accurate memory; I have not reflected this in the narrative here because of the emphasis in A.A.'s self-consciousness of its own history on the *immediacy* of identification between Bill and Bob. I suspect that at the beginning of the dinner, perhaps even before they sat, Bill noted Bob's discomfort at facing in his condition a fully laden table and suggested that they adjourn privately — an hypothesis which also fits well with Mrs. Seiberling's opinion of Wilson's deficiencies in "class."

67   There are but two printed sources for Dr. Bob's story: his own telling of it in *AA*, pp. 171–192; and the *AAGV* detailed obituary cited in the previous note, 10–44. Beyond what is available by inference from "Last Major Talk," these sources have been supplemented by (1) the taped memories of Dr. Bob's son, Robert R. Smith, as reported to me by Nell Wing and Niles P.; (2) interviews with Dr. Russell Smith, a cousin of Dr. Bob, 12 and 13 June 1977; (3) conversations with Niles P., who at the time was working on a biography of Dr. Bob, 5 April, 27 August, and 14 November 1977; (4) interview with Anne C., who knew Dr. Bob before 1935 and after her own entrance into A.A. in 1948 was cherished among Akron-area A.A.s as "Dr. Bob's girl," 7 September 1977; (5) Sue G. tr.: Sue G. was the adopted daughter of Dr. Bob and Anne Smith.

68   Bill's stress on his felt-need of Dr. Bob at this moment is clear less from Dr. Bob's story than from Wilson's many retellings of the tale: *cf.* especially "Fellowship," p. 465; *LM*, [p. 8]; "Society," p. 8 tr.; also *AACA*, p. 70. The quotation of Dr. Bob is from *AACA*, p. 68; the exact quotation of Wilson is my construction from the sources just listed — *cf.* also Thomsen, pp. 237–238.

69   "Dr. Bob," 13; the details narrated in the paragraphs to follow derive from the printed sources cited above, notes #66 and 67. As these are brief and easily followed, I shall offer specific citation only when some other source is also used or I have employed direct quotation.

One correction: "Dr. Bob," 17, gives as Smith's final medical school "Brush University"; according to Niles P. and Dr. Russell Smith, and confirmed by Dr. Bob's *Akron Beacon-Journal* obituary (17 November 1950), it was Rush Medical College in Chicago.

70   The mildly scatological memory is indirectly from Dr. Russell Smith, from family lore. I, of course, have no way of knowing for certain that Dr. Bob recounted this incident to Bill on this occasion; however, such an attempt at humor would well fit what I know of his personality and the "reaching to be understood" amply verified in the other sources and to which this narrative turns again in the second paragraph hence. For Dr. Bob's sense of humor, *cf.* Ruth H., tr., and especially Virginia M., tr.

According to Henrietta Seiberling, interview of 6 April 1977, Dr. Bob had been dismissed from the staff of Akron City Hospital in 1934. According to Dr. Russell Smith and Niles P. (June and August 1977 interviews cited), this was not so, although his privileges may have been in jeopardy. I incline to accept this latter opinion and research rather than Mrs. Seiberling's strongly held memory: neither Wilson nor Smith recount or allude to such an occurrence, for all their eagerness to portray the depths of "alcoholic bottom." Further, the 1938 examination of Akron A.A. by Frank Amos, intended to be carefully critical and based on interviews with many prominent Akronites including the chairman of the board of ACH, makes no mention of either such disgrace or subsequent reinstatement — a point which it seems would surely have been used by Amos in his ultimate enthusiastic effort to portray A.A.'s many "salvagings." — Attachment, dated 23 February 1938, to Frank Amos (New York) to J. D. Rockefeller, Jr. of the same date: "Notes on Akron, Ohio Survey."

71 The information in this paragraph is basically from Henrietta Seiberling, "Origins" and interview cited. It seems fairly certain that Dr. Bob in 1932 had in no way realized that others were concerned about his drinking, nor that even in 1935 he was aware that such concern had led to his invitation to join the OG. This interpretation, and the reference to Bob's guilt that begins the next paragraph, are supported by Sue G., tr.

72 "Dr. Bob," 22; this point is especially clear in "Last Major Talk," *cf.* especially p. 5: "I had done all these things that these good people told me to do. Everyone of them. And I thought very faithfully and sincerely but I still continued to overindulge. But the one thing that they hadn't told me was the one thing that Bill had, the instructions to attempt to be helpful to somebody else."

Yet: those who remember the OG more favorably than most A.A. members, and my own study of the OG (*cf.* note #33 to Chapter Two, p. 323, below), indicate that, unless the Akron OG was a glaring exception (which is a real possibility, given its origin and composition), Smith's final point here was due less to the Groupers not saying this than to Bob's not hearing it. This last, indeed, seems very likely, and the hypothesis is strengthened by two observations. First, Smith's subsequent four years within the OG, and the esteem in which he was held by OG adherents even after he left the Group in 1939, indicate that after this first meeting with Wilson, Bob moved closer to rather than away from the OG. Second, that this insight was available within the OG but was heard by Smith only when it was presented by Wilson (who, be it noted, was here consciously working from OG principles), points up and makes understandable Wilson's and Smith's early emphasis upon the special *identification* possible between alcoholics. On this latter, *cf.* pp. 60-61, below.

73 Wilson did not return home with the Smiths that evening. Mrs. Seiberling had arranged for him to stay at the Portage Country Club, and Bill did so for several more days. The exact chronology remains obscured by conflicting memories rooted in the continuing disagreement between the OG-inclined and most other A.A.s about the role of the OG in the genesis of A.A. and so over the relative importance of the roles of Wilson, Smith, and Seiberling at this moment.

It is certain that Bill stayed at the Country Club for a time; it seems as certain from all the sources considered and evaluated together, that Bob and Anne Smith were anxious to welcome Bill into their home as soon as possible.

74   *AACA*, p. 70: I have slightly varied Bill's exact words there in order to highlight his characteristic question-answering style — a style abundantly witnessed to in all his correspondence. This style is treated more directly in Chapter Four, below, pp. 103–104. In "Last Major Talk," p. 4, Smith wryly stressed his "terrific thirst for knowledge" in telling of this incident.

75   *AACA*, p. 71. Sue G., tr., again adds colorful details — for example, the plying of Dr. Bob with tomatoes, sauerkraut, and Karo syrup.

76   *Ibid.*; *cf.* also, beyond Wilson, tr., Smith, "Last Major Talk," p. 4.

77   *AACA*, p. 71.

78   *AACA*, p. vii.

79   The point concerning A.A.'s self-conscious sources should be clear from the text by this time; yet, should further explicit citation be desired, *cf.*:
Wilson, "Fellowship," where he expands at length on the sentence in his outline in his letter to Paul D., 4 August 1943: "An attempt will then be made to show some of these common denominators of psychiatry and religion . . .";
Wilson, "Basic Concepts": "A.A. is a synthetic concept — a synthetic gadget, as it were, drawing upon the resources of medicine, psychiatry, religion, and our own experience of drinking and recovery."
Wilson, "Co-founder": "Therefore it is now clear that Alcoholics Anonymous is a synthetic construct which draws upon three sources, namely: medical science, religion and its own peculiar experience."
Wilson, "Beginnings": "Certainly nobody invented Alcoholics Anonymous. A.A. is a synthesis of principles and attitudes which came to us from medicine and religion."
That others outside of A.A. share this understanding is also clear; *cf.*, e.g.,
R. Bircher (note #54, above): "The founders of A.A. learned through experience that psychiatry and religion meet in their field." (Translation from CAAAL #4791);
C. N. Davis, "Alcoholics Anonymous," *Archives of Neurological Psychiatry*, Chicago 57: 516–518 (1947): "A.A. employs a composite of many fundamental principles of medicine, psychiatry, religion";
cf., also note #4 to Chapter Eight;
The earliest name referring to "the program of Alcoholics Anonymous" before either of these terms was in use was "moral psychology": *cf.* Silkworth, *AA*, p. xxv; Bob E., tr., p. 4; Warren C., interview of 8 September 1977;
Finally, the only definition of alcoholism in the book *AA*: "an illness which only a spiritual experience will conquer." — p. 44.

80   On "deflation at depth" as from Dr. Jung, my reading of the sources was confirmed by Fred W., interview of 20 November 1976. Mr. W., a prominent Philadelphian, was a correspondent of Wilson's and had spent a considerable time in treatment under Jung.

81   On Dr. Silkworth as the source here, *cf.* notes #46–48 above; on the history of the understanding of alcoholism as "disease," *cf.* note #49 above.

82   The Tenth Tradition of Alcoholics Anonymous reads: "Alcoholics

Anonymous has no opinions on outside issues, hence the A.A. name ought never to be drawn into public controversy." The "Twelve Traditions of Alcoholics Anonymous" are treated in Chapter Four, below, pp. 113–114. For a discussion of the Tenth Tradition, *cf. AACA.* pp. 123–128; *12&12,* pp. 180–183. For the early stress on the essential centrality of hopelessness and "incurability," *cf.* Wilson to Smith, 15 July 1938.

83   The "misspelling" occurred in the multilith draft distributed for comment before publication, a copy of which is in the A.A. archives. The whole approach of *AA*, most clear in Chapter 2, "There Is A Solution" and Chapter 3, "More About Alcoholism," is the description of "the real alcoholic" (p. 21) so that the reader may decide whether or not "I am one of them too" (p. 29).

84   *AA*, p. 62. (Citations for the larger thoughts in this paragraph will appear in Chapters Eight and Nine.)

85   That Wilson at the time focused on this aspect of Ebby's visit is clear not only from his stress on *"one alcoholic talking to another"* in *AACA*, p. 59 (italics Wilson's); but also and even more clearly from Wilson, "Society," pp. 2–3 of the draft. For the evolving centrality of this idea between Ebby's visit to Bill and Bill's meeting with Dr. Bob, *cf.* also "After Twenty-Five Years — by Bill," *AAGV* 16:10 (March 1960), 27; Wilson's remarks in the news story, "Epic Gathering Marks Tenth Anniversary," *AAGV* 2:2 (July 1945), 6; Wilson in his 1943 Yale talk outlined in the letter to Paul D. of 4 August 1943. Dr. Smith's perception of this infuses "Last Major Talk." The striking nature of this emphasis to those in early contact with A.A. is attested to by Ruth H., tr., and Marty Mann, tr. and interview of 15 November 1977.

II   1935–1937

1   *AACA*, p. 71; *cf. AA*, p. 184, Bill D's story as it appeared in the second edition, for the date; a later date is also implied in *AA*, p. 156; Thomsen, p. 243, follows *AACA* uncritically: "The next morning. . . ."

The nurse's conversation: *AACA*, p. 71; *LM*; *AA*, p. 156.

Perhaps because Wilson in *LM* (and apparently orally elsewhere) mistakenly implied so, it is often assumed that Bill D. was the first alcoholic approached by Wilson and Smith. A too regularly overlooked aside, *AACA*, p. 72, belies this misconception; this aside, it might also be noted, indicates a date much closer to 28 June than to 11 June. Further, Anne C. of Akron, interview of 7 September 1977, offered the name — of Ed R. — of the alcoholic reputed in Akron tradition to have "missed the chance to see 'A.A. #3.'" A neighbor of the Smith's (Sue G., tr.), he was not hospitalized; thus Bill D. accurately remains "the first man on the bed." Edgar R. (Youngstown, OH) to Wilson, 8 February 1957 bears this out and offers his own memory of the circumstances and sequence. According to Mr. R., he was approached *before* Dr. Smith's Atlantic City "slip," lived at the Smiths with Bill and Bob for a time, and accompanied A.A.'s co-founders on their first hospital visit to Bill D. In his own summary: "My own distinction is that I was the first one in Akron NOT to make the grade" (emphasis R.'s).

2   For Bill D.'s background, his story, *AA*, pp. 182–192; *cf.* also *AACA*, p. 72, *AA*, pp. 156–158. "Eight times in six months": *AA*, pp. 156 and 184; Wilson, *AACA*, p. 72 and *LM*, says "six times in four months" — of course compatible.

3   The private room: *LM*; *AA*, pp. 157, 184 — the latter also for Bill D.'s thoughts; at Dr. Smith's expense: according to Henrietta D. (Bill D.'s wife), tr.

4 *AA*, pp. 184–185 (italics Bill D.'s).

5 *AA*, p. 185.

6 *AA*, pp. 185–186; the "But I'm different" *verbatim: LM*.

7 *AACA*, p. 72; *cf. AA*, p. 186.

8 *AA*, pp. 187–190. Wilson, *AACA*, p. 72, here as earlier says, "The next day," implying after the initial visit: the circumstances of both narrations incline me to accept Bill D.'s memory, *AA*, p. 189: "in the next two or three days. . . ."

9 No citation is available for Wilson's state of mind here, although it is hinted at in *LM*. My interpretation also rests on: (1) the history yet to unfold; (2) Ernie G., tr. — Ernie was the only other Akron alcoholic to achieve sobriety in this period (but *cf.* note #16 below): a lukewarm Grouper, he spoke to Wilson about this concern; (3) Henrietta Seiberling, interview of 6 April 1977, supporting (4) HS, "Origins," [p. 6], on Wilson (and here also Smith) "in the early days [saying] 'Henrietta, I don't think we should talk too much about religion or God.'"

10 Wilson, tr.; Lois Wilson, interview of 7 April 1977; Thomsen, p. 249, obfuscates with "there had been no further developments in Bill's proxy fight."

11 "Dr. Bob" [explicit eulogy tribute — "by Bill" — distinct from the following], *AAGV* 7:8 (January 1951), 4; "Dr. Bob," *AAGV* 7:8 (January 1951), 22; Obituary of Anne Smith, *AAGV* 7:1 (June 1950), 3–4; Wilson tr.: "We much favored the Apostle James. The definition of love in Corinthians also played a great part in our discussions." *Cf.* Smith, "Last Major Talk," pp. 8–9, also Sue G., tr., and Virginia M. tr.

12 There is disagreement among Bob E., tr., Dr. Bob's son's taped memories, and Wilson, tr., on whether alcoholics lived with the Smiths. I choose to follow the latter two sources for this period (Bob E. was not yet around); this understanding is confirmed by Edgar R. (Youngstown, OH) to Wilson, 8 February 1957, and by the interview interpretations of Niles P. The incidents narrated are from Wilson, tr.; the role of the Williamses is also treated in *AACA*, pp. 75–76, Bob E., tr., William V., tr., Eve G., tr., and HS, interview of 6 April 1977; on the Smiths' financial condition, *cf.* J. C. W., tr., Sue G., tr., and also Smith (Akron) to Hank P., 15 September 1939, and to Wilson, 23 April 1940.

13 For discussion of the number sobered, *cf.* note #16 below. This ultimate "number sobered" does not, of course, mean that some others were not, at least briefly, brought to the OG meeting.

14 Wilson, "Fellowship," p. 466; "pussyfooting about the spiritual" from Wilson to Clarence S., 8 January 1940; evidence that this was stressed in this period is offered by Ruth H. [Wilson's secretary] to A.J.M., 17 August 1940; *cf.* also Wilson to Larry J., 27 June 1940: this letter contains Wilson's suggestions to an Akronite who, having moved to Houston, was in the process of establishing A.A. in Texas. Since Larry J. was himself a protege of Clarence S. (Clarence to writer, 9 September 1977) and this was the first occasion Wilson had, after the publication of *AA*, to explain A.A. in depth in writing, reference to this letter here and later is especially significant.

15 Lois Wilson, interview of 7 April 1977; *cf.* Thomsen, p. 249. This writer was struck in his interviews of 6 and 7 April 1977, that both Lois and Henrietta

Seiberling stressed that Anne Smith's role in the beginning of A.A. has been much underrated. HS, who considers Anne with herself one of the "four co-founders" of A.A., emphasized especially Anne's "motherliness," "homeyness" [*sic* from "Origins"] and "the atmosphere and environment she provided which substituted for what the boys used to get at the saloon." Lois enlarged especially on "warmth" and "motherliness," also "the security and confidence she gave everyone who talked to her."

The correspondence between Bill and Lois from the summer of 1935 remains closed. The feelings here recorded are based, beyond the interview cited, on NW's report of that correspondence, *cf.* also note #62 to Chapter One, p. 258, above. Lois's article was published in *House Beautiful*, 16 October 1935.

16   Wilson, tr.; interview with Lois Wilson, 7 April 1977. The number of alcoholics sobered is variously reported: *AACA*, p. 73, seems to imply four; Thomsen, p. 249, says "five, possibly six," but it is unclear whether he includes Wilson and Smith. Part of the difficulty here as in New York is that some who were first approached in this period did continue drinking but eventually returned and "got the program." The situation is especially complicated because Ernie G.ʼ had at least one such slip, and since he was at this time courting and eventually married Dr. Bob's daughter, Sue, his relationship to A.A. was somewhat special. If there be a valid distinction between one — or even more — "slip[s]" by an alcoholic who remained "close to the program" and a lapse of years actually drinking, then only Bill D. and Ernie G. "got the program" in the summer of 1935. Niles P., interview of 27 August 1977 and private communication of 3 January 1978, says "two or three": his definites are also Bill D. and Ernie G. Our impression is that Phil S. — also at times mentioned as dating from this period — was approached only in early September; thus I choose to stand with "two other sober alcoholics" in my projection of Wilson's thoughts in this paragraph. *Cf.* also Sue G., tr., and Wilson to Charles P., 1 July 1938.

17   For "Keep it simple" as Smith's favorite phrase and in the minds of most his greatest contribution to A.A., *cf. AACA*, p. 9; as his last message to A.A., "Dr. Bob," *AAGV*, 43; as his last words to Wilson, *AACA*, p. 214. "Simple" pervades *AA: cf.*, e.g., pp. 14, 27, 28, 46, 50, 52, 57, 62. . . .

18   Wilson would, throughout the rest of his life, be at times involved in various business and financial enterprises, too complicated even to mention in the present study. (NW, interview of 5 April 1977); *cf.* Wilson to Ned F., 11 July 1940, which reveals the problem: his wariness of being or seeming a "professional [alcoholic]." The problem of "professionalism" would haunt Bill over the next two decades: it will be alluded to in the notes at appropriate points. It is clear, however, that from this point — the end of 1935, he had begun to determine to devote the main portion of his time and life to work with alcoholics. The ambiguities inherent in this problem come through most clearly, for this early period, in Ruth H., tr.; *cf.* also especially Smith (Akron) to Hank P., 15 September 1939, and Ruth H. (New York) to Clarence S., 16 July 1940.

On Lois's employment history, *cf.* Chapter One, note #58; Lois began to separate herself from Loeser's in December, 1935; she finally quit 22 March 1936, still — however — doing some independent work as an interior decorator — interview of 7 April 1977.

The alcoholic as unlovely and self-pitying over this is a theme which pervades *AA*: *cf.*, e.g., p. 16; *cf.* also Wilson to Larry J., 27 June 1940, and to Al C., 6 May 1942, in which Bill analyzes the reasons for the failure of the endeavor described here and in the following paragraphs.

The "change of environment" idea also permeated Dr. Bob Smith's approach: *cf.* two informal histories of the alcoholic ward at St. Thomas Hospital by Sister Ignatia (concerning which and whom *cf.* pp. 79–80, below) — files of Rosary Hall, St. Vincent Charity Hospital, Cleveland, Ohio; also, "The Operation of the A.A. Ward," a fourteen topic treatment establishing procedure on the basis of past experience.

19   *AACA*, pp. 73–74; *cf.* also p. 11.

20   *AACA*, p. 74; Thomsen, p. 252; Wilson to Larry J., 27 June 1940, and to Al C., 6 May 1942. That Wilson learned more than the dangers of excessive dependency is hinted at in an early letter: "The first 8 or 10 cases never got anywhere, and there have been lots since. . . . We had a lot of conceit knocked out of us." Wilson to R.F., 15 July 1938. For Silkworth, *AACA*, p. 74; "The Little Doctor Who Loved Drunks," *AAGV* 7:12 (May 1951), 5, 7.

21   *AACA*, p. 74; Thomsen, pp. 250–252.

22   *Ibid.*; for the OG, *cf.* below, note #33. Wilson offered the best summary in "Memo," p. 21: "The Oxford Group wanted to save the world, and I only wanted to save the drunks."

23   HS, "Origins" [p. 5]; *AACA*, pp. 74–75; Thomsen, p. 256, *cf.* also note #33 below.

24   *AACA*, pp. 74–75; Thomsen, p. 256.

25   *Ibid.*; the direct quotation is my projected construction from these and the other Wilson sources, especially tr. and *LM*.

26   *AACA*, pp. 74–75; Thomsen, pp. 256; interviews with Lois Wilson, 16 November 1976 and 7 April 1977. The direct quotations are *via* Thomsen, p. 256.

27   *AACA*, pp. 74–75; Thomsen, pp. 255–256, clearly reflects the *tone* of Wilson, tr.

28   Wilson's analysis was published in *AACA*. pp. 74–75 — its essence is quoted just below in the text; his most detailed analysis occurred in a letter to McGhee B., 30 October 1940: this letter was made available to Jack Alexander under the condition "not to be quoted" (archive copy), a reflection of the continuing tenderness of this issue in early 1941. *Cf.* also Wilson to Elmer ?, 8 October 1943. Supplementing these "official" sources, I rely also on Ebby T., tr.; Clarence S. to writer, 9 September 1977; and interviews with Anne C. and Warren C., 7 and 8 September 1977.

Thomsen treats the matter scantily, pp. 261–262; the best previous authoritative analysis, beyond Wilson's, is Irving Peter Gellman, *The Sober Alcoholic* (New Haven: College and University Press, 1964), *passim*, but *cf.* especially pp. 160 ff. Gellman stumbles here as in his whole analysis from a too Procrustean effort to fit A.A. into Nottingham's sociological paradigm of "a religion."

For the description of the 1955 convention here and in the following paragraphs, I am grateful to John C. Ford, S.J., interview of 12 April 1977.

29 *AACA*, pp. 74–75 (italics Wilson's).

30 *Cf.* Helen Smith Shoemaker, *I Stand By the Door: The Life of Samuel Shoemaker* (New York: Harper & Row, 1967), and especially Samuel M. Shoemaker, "The Spiritual Angle," *AAGV* 26:1 (June 1969), 29–33, reprinted from the *AAGV* of October, 1955, pagination unavailable. A hint of this concern, and of Shoemaker's own disillusionment with the OG and especially with Frank Buchman, may be found in Shoemaker (New York) to Wilson, 27 June 1949, to be quoted below, Chapter Four, note #69.

31 Interview with John C. Ford, S.J., 12 April 1977. Father Ford disclaims having been a close friend of "Puggy" Dowling, but he did share this occasion with him. Ford himself is a significant figure in the history of A.A.: America's leading Roman Catholic moral theologian in the 1950s and a frequent writer on the moral problems of alcoholism and alcoholics, Ford met Wilson at Yale in 1943 and mailed A.A.'s co-founder a copy of his paper, "Depth Psychology, Morality, and Alcoholism," in 1951. Wilson apparently was impressed with Ford as a writer, for he sought the Jesuit's editorial assistance for both *12&12* and *AACA*. Ford offered extensive editorial and some theological comments on both texts; his main concern — "too explicit MRA attitudes" — echoed Wilson's own — "Catholic opinion"; interview cited and the extensive file of Wilson-Ford correspondence in the A.A. archives. My reading of Dowling's mind in this paragraph is based on my sense of him derived from these sources and the Wilson-Dowling correspondence.

Dowling's role will be treated below, Chapter Four, pp. 97–100.

The Morgan R. story appears in *AACA*, pp. 168–169, and will be treated below, p. 75.

32 For Buchman's background and this understanding of the name OG, *cf.* Walter Houston Clark, *The Oxford Group: Its History and Significance* (New York: Bookman Associates, 1951), pp. 117–122.

33 Wilson on the OG: *cf.* note #28 above; also Wilson to Jack Alexander, 13 December 1949, where the separation is noted as "the first" of the "turning points" in A.A.'s history; also Wilson to Howard C. (a writer who asked Bill's help for his own analysis of A.A.), 4 January 1956 and 15 November 1960.

Wilson often indicated that "A.A. should always give full credit to its several well-springs of inspiration and . . . should always consider these people among the founders of our Society." This quotation, from a letter to Sister F., 29 January 1952, is especially interesting because of Wilson's reference in it to "the turmoil caused Christian Science by the Quimby Letters." Christian Science and especially the Quimby Letters, which raised serious questions about Mary Baker Eddy's claim to originality, apparently fascinated Wilson: he did not want A.A. to stumble into the same pitfall. On Bill's interest in Christian Science, Wilson, tr., indicates that he had looked into the faith for possible help with his drinking in the early 1930's; one reason for his rejection of it was that the Quimby letters disillusioned his "inquiring, rational mind." This point was clarified in an interview with Lois Wilson, 7 September 1978.

My analysis of the Oxford Group is based on the following sources:

Hadley Cantril, *The Psychology of Social Movements* (Huntington, NY: Robert E. Krieger, 1941), pp. 144–168;

Charles Samuel Braden, *These Also Believe* (New York: MacMillan, 1951), pp. 403–420;

Walter Houston Clark, *The Oxford Group: Its History and Significance* (New York: Bookman Associates, 1951) — this is the definitive scholarly treatment of the OG, and I rely on it heavily in my analysis;

Allan W. Eister, *Drawing-Room Conversion* (Durham, NC: Duke University Press, 1950) — a sociological study of the movement;

What Is The Oxford Group?, fwd. L.W. Grensted (London: Oxford University Press, 1933);

Samuel Shoemaker, Jr., *The Conversion of the Church* (New York: Fleming H. Revell, 1932): Shoemaker was the chief publicist for the OG from 1930 to 1941. Calvary Episcopal Church, of which he was the rector, was the U.S. center of the OG. — Braden, pp. 412–413; Eister, pp. 37–38; Clark, pp. 54, 80; Cantril, who uses Shoemaker as his prime source, pp. 145, 148, 150, 152–153, 165, *Cf.* also Helen Smith Shoemaker, *I Stand By the Door: The Life of Samuel Shoemaker* (New York: Harper & Row, 1967), especially pp. 90–94.

Sir Arnold Lunn, *Enigma: A Study of Moral Re-Armament* (London: Longmans & Green, 1957) — used especially for attitude of the Catholic Church to the OG;

Rachel Crothers, *Susan and God* (New York: Random House, 1938) — this was a play which opened at the Plymouth Theater, New York City, 7 October 1937; it is a satire on the OG and according to Professor George Gordon, who has interviewed many A.A. oldtimers, was very popular among early New York A.A.s.

An earlier version of my treatment of the Oxford Group was read and criticized by Mr. Bryan Hamlin and Rev. Harry J. Almond, present-day members of Moral Re-Armament. Although unable to follow all their suggestions, I have incorporated into my understanding and the treatment of the Oxford Group here two books recommended by them as illuminating its history: Theophil Spoerri, *Dynamic out of Silence: Frank Buchman's relevance today* (London: Grosvenor Books, 1976), and H. A. Walther, *Soul-Surgery: Some Thoughts on Incisive Personal Work* (Oxford: at the University Press by John Johnson, 1940), 6th ed. — the first ed. was published in 1919.

34   The "Five C's": Clark, p. 28.

35   The "Five Procedures": Cantril, pp. 148–151.

36   Distaste for the idea as well as the term "soul-surgery" was the main reason Henrietta Seiberling, though remaining self-consciously an Oxford Grouper, separated herself from some manifestations of the Group. In her view, A.A. at the time was more true to OG principles than those who retained the OG name; interview of 6 April 1977. Lois Wilson revealed special distaste at the mention of this term, interview of 7 April 1977.

37   Clark, pp. 117–122.

38   The "six basic assumptions": Cantril, pp. 147–148.

39   Clark, pp. 238–239, 253–254.

40   *AACA*, p. 74 (italics Wilson's); the pervasiveness of this understanding within A.A. is attested to by a letter from M.R.B. [A.A.'s general secretary at the time] (New York) to John H., 13 January 1949: ". . . the early members say that the greatest contribution the Oxford Group made to Alcoholics Anonymous was to show what would not work for alcoholics."

41   Wilson to McGhee B., 30 October 1940; the same idea was strongly expressed to C.H.M., 15 June 1953, and to Howard C., 15 November 1960; *cf.* also *12&12*, pp. 69-70.

Concerning this "rejection of absolutes" and the continuing use of "The Four Absolutes" in, e.g., Cleveland A.A., *cf.* Appendix A.

42   Wilson to McGhee B., 30 October 1940. Anonymity will be treated more deeply, with further citations, in Chapter Four, pp. 104–105.

43   Wilson to McGhee B., 30 October 1940.

44   *Ibid.*; Wilson to C.H.M., 15 June 1953; according to John C. Ford, S.J., interview of 12 April 1977, as well as my reading of the Lunn book cited in note #33, no such papal decree existed, although there was strong Catholic suspicion of the OG. For the possible source of the misunderstanding by Wilson, *cf.* below, p. 78.

45   Wilson to Father O., 1 December 1947; to Maria I., 31 December 1949; to Joe D., 8 October 1957.

46   Wilson to Margarita L., 14 July 1947; to Clem M., 8 April 1948; to Father Dowling, Wilson wrote (24 September 1947): "It is ever so hard to believe that any human beings, no matter who, are able to be infallible about anything." The context makes it clear that he is here agitated as much about theologians on the sacraments as about the personal infallibility of the Pope.

47   Beyond the tr. of Bob E., information on Akron in this era is drawn from HS, "Origins"; "Dr. Bob," *AAGV* 7:1 (June 1950), 3–4; Amos, "History"; trs. of T. Henry Williams, Ernie G., J.D.H., Sue G., Virginia M., and William V., all of Akron; also interviews with Niles P., 5 April, 27 August and 14 November 1977, with Anne C., 7 September 1977, and with Clarence S., 5 and 6 October 1978.

48   Bob E., tr., p. 2.

49   *Ibid.*, pp. 2–3.

50   *Ibid.*, pp. 3–4.

51   *Ibid.*, pp. 4–6; "A.A. Number Twelve" is not in the tr., but Nell Wing testifies that it is in the introductory comments on the tape; this was "hazily" verified by Anne C., interview cited, and is also the understanding of Niles P.

Although Wilson in the Bill D., "A.A. Number 3," story had Dr. Bob use the phrase "a day at a time," general and especially Akron A.A. lore attribute this expression as also "twenty-four hour program" to Joe D., "The European Drinker" of *AA*, pp. 230–237. The idea, if not these phrases, was familiar to the OG in its self-conscious "primitive Christian" focus on "daily bread." — HS, interview of 6 April 1977; Nell Wing, letter to writer, 6 December 1976. *Cf.* also Thomsen, p. 248; trs., of William V. and J.D.H.; interview with Anne C.

This technique and style was also described in detail by Clarence S., interview of 5 October 1978, cf. pp. 239–240, below.

52   Bob E., tr., pp. 6–8.

53   *Ibid.*, pp. 8–9.

54   Ed B., tr., Dan K., tr.; *cf.* also Norm Y., tr., and Oscar W., tr. That kneeling to pray and thus to make surrender also took place in New York in this era, but not so rigidly, is clear from Ruth H., tr., and William R. (East Orange, NJ) to Wilson, 26 January 1957: this letter is especially valuable for the insight it offers into the relationship between the practice of kneeling and the OG connection.

55   Bob E., tr., pp. 9–10; Ernie G., tr.; Henrietta Seiberling, interview of 6 April 1977.

56   Bob E., tr., p. 13; Ernie G., tr. The description of Anne Smith is from Bob E., tr., pp. 12–13; Sue G., tr.; Virginia M., tr.; tapes of Mr. and Mrs. Robert R. Smith as reported by NW; interviews with Dr. Russell Smith of 12 and 13 June 1977, and with Anne C., 7 September 1977; *cf.* also note #15 above, and Sr. Ignatia as cited in note #18 above.

57   *Cf.* sources cited in note #47 above. Wilson remembered and recorded this visit as occuring in November: *AACA*, p. 76; and it has been thus enshrined in A.A.'s historical memory — e.g., "Landmarks," *AACA*, p. vii. According to information available from Lois Wilson's diaries, the visit described here would seem to have taken place towards the end of July 1937. It seems possible that Bill wrote "November" because he confused this visit with another that he made — this time by car, with Lois — in mid-October. The question of exact timing is significant to only one historical point — *cf.* note #18 to Chapter Three. Although the meeting described here in the text certainly occurred earlier than November, the pervasiveness and enshrined quality of this historical memory within A.A. have led me to retain "November 1937" here and in a few later references in the text and chapter headings.

   Some claim (Niles P., based on his interviews, reported to the writer in a private communication, 3 January 1978) that the "making surrender" described in mid-paragraph took place "in an upstairs room." My own evaluation of the sources and my interviews lead me to judge that "small basement room" is more likely correct. I suspect that the "upstairs room" reflects and derives from the popularity of the devotional/inspirational book *The Upper Room* among the early OG-connected members of A.A.: interview with HS, 15 November 1976; *cf.* Dorothy M., tr.

58   The primary *occasion* for Wilson's visit at this time was the failure of another Wall Street venture; *cf. AACA*, p. 76 and, more accurate here, Thomsen, p. 266.

   Wilson always referred to the history of A.A. up to this November 1937, meeting as "the period of flying blind," e.g., *AACA*, p. 76.

   Wilson's focus on the positive, especially the increasing number of Akron successes, is most clear from his correspondence *not* seeking financial support over the next year; *cf.*, e.g., to Dr. Esther R., 10 August 1938.

59   *AACA*, pp. 76, 144; Thomsen, pp. 266–267.

60   Wilson, *LM*; *cf. AACA* and Thomsen, *loc. cit.*

61   *AACA*, pp. 144–145.

62   *AACA*, p. 145; *cf.* Thomsen, pp. 269–270; also "The Book Is Born — by Bill," *AAGV* 2:5 (October 1945), 2, 6, which offers more details of the discussion; also "Lack of Money Proved A.A. Boon — by Bill," *AAGV* 4:1 (June 1947), 3; "Dr. Bob" [eulogy], *AAGV* 7:8 (January 1951), 8.

III   1937–1939

1   On "November," *cf.* note #57 to Chapter Two, above. There is no transcript of this or any other meeting between Wilson and Smith. The centrality of the event in Wilson's mind — "the end of the period of flying blind" (repeated at *AACA*, pp. 76 and 144) — alerts to its felt-significance. As to *what* was discussed, the changes and new ideas that rapidly became clear and implemented over the next year must have originated somewhere. Surely the contents of the book setting forth the program, the only project about which Smith shared Wilson's enthusiasm, were discussed. In the sparse Wilson-Smith correspondence, these ideas are buried under more urgent discussion of the external events to be described below, *cf.* especially Wilson to Smith of ? June, 15 July, 22 September, 3 November, and 9 November 1938 — cover letters for the chapters of *AA* Bill was sending to Dr. Bob over these months. I believe this fact in itself supports my interpretation of the key ideas examined in this section having been worked out at this time, although I make no claim that Wilson and Smith discussed the ideas in these terms or so abstractly. Yet, this is one of the rare occasions on which Dr. Bob's thoughts are also available: *cf.* his recollection of them in "Epic Gathering Marks Tenth Anniversary," *AAGV* 2:2 (July 1945), 6, a recollection which well supports my interpretation, as does the veiled and passing reference to this meeting, *A.A.* pp. 159–161; *cf.* also Wilson, "Review." On the dearth of written evidence on how Wilson and Smith developed their ideas, *cf.* [Sr. Ignatia], "St. Thomas Hospital" p. 3: "While Bill lived in New York, . . . he and Dr. Bob talked over the phone every few days to keep in touch with what was happening. Bill and Dr. Bob often seemed to be twins — both from New England, both tall, and both with the same thoughts."

2   *AA*, pp. 44, 62; *cf.* Wilson, "Fellowship," p. 462: ". . . the drinking of alcohol is a sort of spiritual release. Is it not true that the great fault of all individuals is abnormal self-concern?" The proximity of this understanding to the ideas of Carl Jung and William James is beyond adequate citation. It was the key to Wilson's link with Margarita L. and Fred W. (*cf.* Chapter One, notes #6 and 80); for James. *cf.* the context of his note quoted above, Chapter One, p. 23, and note #51.

3   Bill D.'s first response, as recalled by Wilson at *LM*, was; "But I'm different"; several of Wilson's early letters to those lamenting lack of success in working with others stress the same theme: *cf.* especially to Larry J., 27 June 1940; to Fitz M., 16 August 1940; Ruth H. [Wilson's and A.A.'s secretary](New York) to A.M. 17 August 1940. Wilson's continued focus on the "sense of being different" as a cause of problems is clear in much of his correspondence to those who wrote him of their troubles; e.g., to Peter M., 23 February 1955: "Perhaps one thing that bothers you is the feeling that your case is somehow much different and much worse than other people's." For the theme's significance to Dr. Bob, *cf.* beyond "Last Major Talk," Sue G., tr. On Wilson's attitude to how his own sense of "being different" was related to his alcoholism, *cf.* in Chapter One, p. 18, and especially note #36 to that quotation.

4   *AA*, pp. 21, 30, 62; *cf.* especially p. 30, the opening of Chapter 3: "More About Alcoholism": "Most of us have been unwilling to admit that we were real alcoholics. No one likes to think that he is bodily and mentally different from his fellows. . . . The delusion that we are like other people . . . has to be smashed."

It is impossible to date with any exactness the shift from "deflation" to "bottom" or the beginning of the common use of the term "identification." The term "bottom" seems to come out of the period of self-consciousness about its "raising" — *cf.* Chapter Five, below. The idea of "identification" is clear in *AA*'s description of "the real alcoholic" (the same Chapter 3 of *AA*) and, as *key*, in Wilson, "Rockland," where Bill sets forth as the first "elemental principle . . . of our work" that "the man on the bed feels he is one of us. [This is the] strong bridge [over which] we begin to introduce our ideas." The importance of this as the key perception of Dr. Bob Smith is stressed by Leach and Norris, "Factors in the Development. . . , in Kissin and Begleiter, p. 456. The explicit emergence came in *12&12*.

5   *AA*, p. 21; *cf. 12&12*, p. 22. *AA*, pp. 42, 8; Wilson to Ray H., 25 April 1961; *cf.* also *AA*, pp. 92, 116, 141; the quotation in the footnote is from "Greetings on our Tenth Christmas — to All Members," mimeo copy in A.A. archives, 1944 "Alcoholic Foundation" file (italics Wilson's).

The point in this paragraph is clearly the key in all the early trs.; *cf.* especially that of Marty Mann: as self-consciously the first woman to "get the program" and later nationally prominent in the alcoholism field, Ms. Mann's experience was often used as paradigmatic *re* the "sense of being different": *cf.* Wilson, "Fellowship," p. 461. This interpretation was explored in depth with and confirmed by Marty Mann, interview of 15 November 1977.

6   This concept was most usually treated in early A.A. under the heading of "honesty," with much harking back to the OG insistence on "absolute honesty" by those less consistent than Wilson in abhorring "absolutes": *cf.* Ebby T., T., tr., p. 12. For Wilson's stress on "honesty," *cf.* especially "Rockland," where in the discussion following his presentation several doctors pointed out that this was the equivalent of their "mental catharsis." This understanding of how A.A. works also becomes central to the writings of Dr. Harry M. Tiebout, a friend of Wilson's from 1939, and his personal therapist in the mid-1940's: Marty Mann, tr., and especially interview of 15 November 1977. *Cf.* Chapter Eight, below, for treatment and citations.

7   On "surrender," *cf.* Chapter Eight, below. Although so blatantly "religious" a description was of course veiled in these stories, 12 of the 26 stories in the first edition of *AA* (and 10 of the 16 from Akron) witness to such an expression of surrender. (The numbers 26 and 16 here because I am not counting Dr. Bob and "An Alcoholic's Wife.") The point is made vividly clear by a comparison of Clarence S's description of his hospitalization as recounted in the Appendix, p. 239, below, with his story as it appeared in *AA*, pp. 297–303. That it was the former style that was carried over to Cleveland A.A. is witnessed by the descriptions of Dick P. and Warren C., interviews of 8 September 1977, also quoted in the Appendix, pp. 236–237.

8   *AACA*, p. 146; Thomsen, p. 273; Nell Wing, interview of 5 April 1977, reporting the memories of Ruth H., who was secretary to Wilson and Hank P. from early 1938. Wilson to Smith, ? June 1938, testifies that "a lot of people . . . had got quite afire" about the book. Jim B., "Evolution," pp. 2–3, unconsciously reveals himself as leading this attitude from the time of his January 1938, arrival.

9   For Dr. Bob's financial condition: *AACA*, p. 149; interview with Henrietta Seiberling, 6 April 1977; also the sources cited in note #12 to Chapter Two, p.

320, above. Virtually all the sparse Smith correspondence through the mid-1940's bears witness to his financial plight: *cf.*, e.g., Smith (Akron) to Hank P., 15 September 1939; *cf.* also Wilson to Clarence S., 23 April 1940. For the Akronites' attitude to the book, HS, interview cited; trs. of Bob E., Dorothy M., and Sue G.

10 Wilson's financial condition: *AACA*. pp. 99–100; Thomsen, p. 257. Clarence S., annotated copy of *AACA* sent to this writer, p. 100, claims of the Towns Hospital story which follows here: "This is B.S." According to Clarence, *he* had received such an offer in Cleveland, and Wilson in *AACA* untruthfully "switches the story to be his experience!" Supporting Wilson's accuracy are Ruth H., tr. and — more tellingly — Wilson to Frank Amos, 26 September 1938, which mentions the incident as known to Amos. Lois Wilson's diary places the occurrence in December of 1936: *cf. Lois Remembers*, p. 197. I follow in the text here Wilson's telling of this event in *AACA*: despite some slight inconsistencies and its aura of incredible coincidences, the other sources indicate that it is substantially correct.

11 *AACA*, p. 100; *cf.* Thomsen, pp. 257–258. Towns, in early 1937, almost certainly did not say "A.A.": *cf.* discussion of the name below, pp. 74–75.

12 *AACA*, p. 100; *cf.* Thomsen, pp. 257–258.

13 *AACA*, p. 101; *cf.* Thomsen, pp. 258–260.

14 *Ibid.*

15 The projection of Wilson's thoughts here and in the next paragraph is based on subsequent events and my general sense of him rather than on any specific source.

16 For the background of the New York alcoholics, *cf.* stories in *AA*, 1st ed.; Hank P., e.g., had been a regional sales manager for Standard Oil.

17 *AACA*, pp. 146–147; *cf.* Thomsen, p. 273.

18 *AACA*, p. 147; *cf.* Thomsen, pp. 273–274. A.A. legend has it that Strong and Richardson had courted the same girl: Strong lost (and married Bill's sister). The evidence of Lois Wilson's diary (cited in note #57 to Chapter Two) solves what would otherwise be a problem of chronology here. Dr. Strong's letter introducing Wilson to Richardson is dated 26 October 1937, and the meeting described in the next paragraph is proposed in a letter from Richardson (New York) to Strong, 10 November 1937. Some who were aware of this timing and uncritically accepting of Wilson's "November" on *AACA*, p. 76, have on this evidence accused Wilson of dishonesty and promotional over-zeal. The real problem clearly is Wilson's atrocious memory for dates.

19 *AACA*, p. 148; Thomsen, pp. 274–275.

20 *Ibid.*

21 *AACA*, pp. 148–149; Thomsen, p. 275.

22 *AACA*, p. 149; Thomsen, p. 275.

23 *AACA*, pp. 150–151; interview with Henrietta Seiberling, 6 April 1977; *cf.* also "Lack of Money Proved A.A. Boon — by Bill," *AAGV* 4:1 (June 1947), 3, 13; Amos, "History."
     Richardson (New York) to Rockefeller, 23 February 1938, seems to support the Seiberling version: Richardson's proposal is that Rockefeller aid with

$5,000 for two years. The attachment, "Notes on Akron, Ohio Survey by Frank Amos," makes the same recommendation. Yet Rockefeller's practice, as I understand it, was to discuss orally and then have letters confirming consensus written — this point as hearsay to me is noted to explain my refusal to decide here. Rockefeller's agreement so to aid, in a letter to Richardson of 17 March 1938, offers as his chief consideration for his decision his general policy on charity rather than any perception of "money ruining . . . first century Christianity."

Henrietta Seiberling, interview of 6 April 1977, claimed that her impact on and guidance of Amos was responsible for his favorable report, her interpretation based on the "class" point noted above, Chapter One, note #64. I doubt it, although Amos does stress the "quality" of those "salvaged," and this point had no doubt been emphasized to him by Mrs. Seiberling. The style of Wilson's appeals for funds at this time indirectly reflects the "quality" point: he stressed in his presentations the worth of such "salvagings" to business; *cf.*, e.g., Wilson to Charles P., 1 July 1938; Wilson to Dr. Esther R., ? June or July 1938; also, recalling those efforts, Carlton S. (New York) to Wilson, 6 March 1957.

24 *AACA*, pp. 151–152. The actual "Trust Indenture" is dated 5 August 1938; Amos, "History," refers in his title to "the formation of The Alcoholic Foundation on 11 August 1938." I here preserve "Spring" from *AACA*, p. 151, as the time when the decision was made to begin work to form the Foundation. On *AACA*, p. 152, Wilson dates the actual Foundation as from "May, 1938": erroneous, and another example of his lack of memory for dates. The first clear expression of many ideas eventually incorporated into the Foundation appears in Hank P. (New York) to Frank Amos, 16 March 1938.

25 *AACA*, p. 153; *cf.* Thomsen, pp. 277–278. Jim B., "Evolution," p. 3, dates the beginning of writing as "in June 1938": slightly erroneous, but intriguing witness to his insistence on his own impact on the book; he was the group's chief "radical" arguing against "too much God" in the book — *cf.* below, pp. 71 and 75–76; also Wilson to Jim S., 28 February 1955.

Wilson's 1920s activity was best described by Thomsen, pp. 148–159; supplementary light on this and the beginnings of the writing was offered by Lois Wilson, interview of 16 November 1976; *cf. AACA*, pp. 153–154; *LM*; Thomsen, pp. 278–279; what may be inferred of Dr. Smith's letter from Wilson to Smith, ? June 1938, also, for color and detail, Ruth H., tr.

26 Wilson's earliest drafts have been lost. In the "promotional stage" of the material, the ultimate Chapter 2, "There Is A Solution," preceded the ultimate Chapter 1, "Bill's Story." — A.A. archives, inclusion with Frank Amos (New York) to Albert Scott, 24 June 1938. The sense of the stories as "the heart of the book" as well as a witness to this arrangement appears in Wilson to Smith, ? June 1938; *cf.* also below, pp. 71–73.

27 *Cf.* above, pp. 44–45.

28 Interview with Lois Wilson, 16 November 1976; Bob E., tr., p. 22; *cf.* also pp. 71–73, below.

29 *AACA*, pp. 153–157; *cf.* Thomsen, pp. 279–280.

30 NW, "Outline"; *AACA*, p. ix; Jim B., "Evolution," p. 4; interview with Henrietta Seiberling, 6 April 1977; "Anne Smith's favorite quote" according to Ruth H., reported by NW, letter to writer of 6 December 1976.

31 *AACA*, p. 159; Wilson to Smith, ? June, 15 July, 7 August, 27 September, and 3 November 1938; Jim B., "Evolution," pp. 4–5, offers the best description of "these chapters, as completed, [being] raked and mauled over. . . ." Much A.A. myth surrounds the composition of the Twelve Steps: I find Wilson's telling in *AACA*, followed here, scrupulously accurate. Its greatest external support, to me, is Dr. Bob's telling of his role in their writing, "Last Major Talk," pp. 10–11: "I didn't write the Twelve Steps. I had nothing to do with the writing of them. I think probably I had something to do with them indirectly, because after this June 10th episode, Bill came to live at our house and stayed for about three months and there was hardly a night in that three months that we didn't sit up until two and three o'clock discussing these things. And it would be hard for me to conceive that something wasn't said at or during these nightly discussions around our kitchen table that influenced the actual writing of the Twelve Steps." *Cf.* also Virginia M., tr., reflecting the Akron sense, and Ruth H., tr., for a convincingly detailed description of the writing and editing processes.

32 *AACA*, pp. 160–161. A.A. legend has it that these six steps derived directly from the OG: this is simply wrong. *Cf.* sources cited in Chapter Two, note #33; Henrietta Seiberling, who — if anyone — *would want* to claim so, interview of 6 April 1977; extensively annotated copy of Anne Smith's OG "workbook" in A.A. archives. These six "steps" summarize what the early A.A.s had plucked from diverse OG sources. That this exact formulation of these six "steps" was contrived by Wilson only as he set out to record the history in *AACA* seems clearest from the differences between them and the "six points" noted by Wilson in "Review" as "learned from the Oxford Groups."

33 Wilson's conscious wrestling with the problem of making what he wrote acceptable to both his New York alcoholics and the Akronites, who were still tied to the OG, is clear in his letters to Dr. Bob Smith — *cf.* citations in note #1, above. It seems that it was Wilson's reliance on Smith here that brought Bill explicitly to view Dr. Bob as "co-founder" of A.A. — Smith's leadership among the Akron alcoholics, and his role in enabling the acceptance of the book by all, were crucially important and indeed essential at that point. Others in New York — Hank P., for example — did not yet share Wilson's awareness of the centrality of Smith: *cf.* Chapter Four, note #31, p. 286.

34 *AA*, pp. 71–72 (1st ed.), with the final changes to be treated below, p. 76, returned to their original form. Here also, the original draft has been lost. Insofar as I have been able with the help of NW to reconstruct from the earliest available drafts and comments the *original* form of the Twelve Steps, there were slight differences in the following six (the italics mark the differences):

     3. . . . over to the care *and direction* of God. (I also suspect that the word *surrender* originally appeared in this Step.)
     6. Were entirely *willing that* God remove. . . .
     7. . . . shortcomings — *holding nothing back.*
     8. Made a *complete* list. . . .
     11. [the word "conscious" is omitted]
     12. Having had a spiritual experience as the result of *this course of action*, we tried to carry this message to *others, especially* alcoholics, and. . . .

35 *AACA*, p. 161.

36   *AACA*, pp. 161–164.

37   *AA*, p. 164.

38   *AACA*, p. 164; "The Doctor's Opinion" appears in *AA*, pp. xxiii–xxx (2nd ed.); in the 1st ed., it comprised pp. 1–9. Dr. Esther R. (Baltimore) to Wilson, 18 July 1938, suggested concerning Bill's early draft of the first two chapters that although she found "the presentation of the material . . . gripping," and that "what you say carries the conviction of truth, . . . I think you should get a No. 1 physician who has a wide knowledge of the alcoholic's medical and social problems to write an introduction."

39   Interview with Lois Wilson, 16 November 1976; for the Akron situation, Bob E., tr., p. 22. Also Ruth H.'s description of these early meetings as recorded by NW and reported to writer in a letter of 6 December 1976.

40   In New York, only one speaker and Wilson spoke formally at each of these early meetings. Knowledgeable New Yorkers — e.g., NW and Professor George Gordon reporting on interviews of Ruth H. and Marty Mann — claim that the practice of many speakers at the same meeting originated in Akron. However, Anne C., Warren C., and Dick P. — interviews of 7 and 8 September 1977 — denied this, pointing out that even then in Akron and Cleveland what are now called "one-speaker discussion meetings" were by far the most common type of A.A. meeting. It seems likely that the practice of having many speakers and no formal discussion at A.A. meetings originated as a carry-over from Twelfth-Step practice with individuals. On "Twelfth Step calls," which informal A.A. tradition insisted always be made by more than one member, each A.A. told his story to the not-yet-sober object of their concern, in an effort to facilitate identification. Exactly when and where first occurred the transition that made this into a meeting-format is impossible to determine, although a good guess would seem to be that it took place spontaneously, in different places, as A.A. entered the phase of its growth described at the beginning of Chapter Five, below.

41   *AACA*, p. 164; for the "intention to portray variety" in the 2nd ed., Tom P. (New York) to writer, 15 December 1976; *cf.* also below, Chapter Five; for the 3rd ed., interview with Bob H., one of its editors, 15 November 1976.
   On the actual variety among members of A.A., *cf.*:
   M. M. Murphy, "Values Stressed by Two Social Class Levels at Meetings of Alcoholics Anonymous," *QJSA* 14: 576–585 (1953);
   R. H. Seiden, "An Experimental Test of the Assumption that Members of Alcoholics Anonymous are Representative Alcoholics," thesis, Denver University, reported by CAAAL #8400;
   H. M. Trice, "Sociological Factors in Association with A.A.," *Journal of Criminal Law and Criminology* 48: 378–386 (1957);
   G. Edwards, C. Hensman, A Hawker, and V. Williamson, "Who Goes to Alcoholics Anonymous?" *Lancet* 2 (n.s.): 382–384 (1966);
   Beyond the detailed information offered by Leach and Norris, "Factors," in Kissin and Begleiter, the most recent analysis from more critical points of view may be synthesized from four other contributions in Kissin-Begleiter;
   B. Kissin, "Theory and Practice in the Treatment of Alcoholism," pp. 40–41;
   A. Beigel and Stuart Ghertner, "Toward a Social Model," pp. 215–219;
   D. R. Doroff, "Group Psychotherapy in Alcoholism," pp. 237–240;

F. Baekeland, "Evaluation of Treatment Methods in Chronic Alcoholism," pp. 402–408.

Wilson recalled often, e.g., to Jay ?, 13 April 1965: "For the first 15 years of A.A. we had hardly any young people at all. We were equally slow in making progress either on Skid Row or Park Avenue."

For A.A.'s self-consciousness of this problem at this time, *cf.* Wilson to Charles P., 1 July 1938; also the information sought on a questionnaire sent to members in late 1938 — apparently in the hope of finding more variety for the stories: "age; occupational history; educational history; age serious drinking started; age uncontrolled drinking started; years uncontrolled drinking; when drinking, how long did sprees last; average time between sprees last two years drinking; how strong was religious background as a child; what was religious history after leaving childhood home; number of hospitalizations; effects of hospitalizations; number and effects of physicians and psychiatrists; number of jobs lost through drinking; marital results of drinking; during drinking, were any religious approaches made and what were the results and your attitudes towards." Important here, of course, are the assumptions in the questions asked and the other possible questions unasked.

For early Cleveland, I asked Warren C., interview of 8 September 1977, if he could recall the occupations of the members listed on a record in his possession of the names of the charter members of that city's second group, a group which from circumstances contained no one also in the Oxford Group. After noting that "almost all were unemployed at the time we got them, but just about all went back to what they had been doing," he recalled: "newspaper distributor, commercial artist, sales and promotion, clothing salesman, family income, advertising, accountant, traffic manager, sales manager, railroad brakeman, farmer, typewriter repair, office supplies, clothing sales, hortoculturalist."

42 The "story-section" of the 1st ed. ran pp. 183–390.

43 "Cadillacs" and "playgirls," p. 194; "teas" and "bridge parties," p. 219 (1st ed.).

44 Strangely, inexplicably, and incredibly, writer Jack Alexander in a later recollection of his 1940–1941 investigation of A.A. claimed that after observing A.A. in Philadelphia, New York City, and Akron, it was in Cleveland that he first saw the movement's universality. That by itself makes sense, but hear his explanation: "In Akron it had been mostly factory workers. In Cleveland there were lawyers, accountants, and other professional men, in addition to laborers." *AAGV* 1:12 (May 1945), 1, 8. All other evidence, oral and written, testifies that the Oxford Group-tied early Akronites were hardly "mostly factory workers."

45 Bill D.'s story appeared in the 2nd ed., pp. 182–192: according to Anne C., interview of 7 September 1977, it was not in the 1st ed. "because he was too humble"; letter of Tom P. to writer and interview with Bob H., as above, #41.

46 *AACA*, pp. 164–165; the direct quotation is reconstructed from *AACA*, p. 164, and *LM*. Ruth H., tr., details this concern.

47 *AACA*, p. 165;

Wilson to Smith, ? June 1938: "By the way, you might all be thinking up a good title. Nearly everyone agrees that we should *sign* the volume Alcoholics Anonymous. Titles such as *Haven, One Hundred Men, Comes the Dawn,* etc. have been suggested." (emphasis added).

A form-letter of introduction, "To Whom It May Concern," by Albert L. Scott (New York), 1 July 1938, lays heavy stress on "a fellowship of 100 ex-alcoholics who have recovered";

Frank Amos (n.p.) to Albert Scott, 4 October 1938, refers to Wilson and Smith as "leaders of the 'Alcoholic Squadron'" and makes reference to the proposed book as titled, "One Hundred Men";

Jim B., "Evolution," p. 4, testifies that "about the middle of October [1938] the manuscript of the book was finished . . . the name of the book at this time was '100 Men'";

Wilson to Frank Amos, 4 January 1939, refers to the proposed book as "One Hundred Men." Amos, in a memo to Rockefeller dated 6 January 1939 and apparently inspired by this Wilson letter, titles his memo, "Alcoholics Anonymous";

An early draft which seems intermediary between the fund-raising and book stages of the first two chapters of *AA*, dated 7 January 1939, is headed: "Memorandum — Final Draft — 100 Men Corp.";

Dating from late January or early February 1939, is a pamphlet proposal headed: "Alcoholics Anonymous"; yet it begins: "It is proposed to form — 'THE 100 MEN CORPORATION': Purpose: to publish the book — '100 Men'";

After the date of the telegram cited in the following note, all references to the book call it "Alcoholics Anonymous."

48   Telegram from Fitz M. (Washington) to Henry P., 11 February 1939; "The B.W. Movement" idea: *AACA*, pp. 165–166; *cf.* also "A Tradition Born of Our Anonymity — by Bill" *AAGV*, 2:8 (January 1946), 2–10;

On the significance of the title of the book for the name of the fellowship, *cf.*, beyond note #47, above, p. 78, below.

A.A. lore attributes the first use of the name "Alcoholics Anonymous" to Joe W.: NW, interview of 14 November 1977, responding to the writer's question *re* a parenthesized insert in Ruth H., tr.

49   *AACA*, pp. 168–169; *cf.* Ruth H., tr., Virginia M., tr., Jim B., "Evolution," p. 4, reports *re* Dr. Howard: "He became greatly interested and enthusiastic, but was highly critical of . . . entirely too much 'Oxfordism' and that it was too demanding." It would be nice to be able to determine whether it was Dr. Howard or Jim B. himself who linked the suggested stylistic changes with "Oxfordism"; since Dr. Howard's correspondence has been lost, this is impossible. My own reading of the multilith draft in question, for what it is worth, inclines me to suspect that this is Jim B.'s projection: such would surely be in character.

50   *AACA*, pp. 168–169 (italics Wilson's); the history of reviews of the book, including Fosdick's, is treated in Chapter Four, *cf* especially pp. 91–92 and note #23.

51   *AACA*, p. 167; Ruth H., tr., offers color and detail; concerning the Cleveland occurrence, *cf.* p. 78, below.

52   *AACA*, p. 170; the problem of Wilson as "professional" reappears here: the only income Bill ever received "from A.A." was his royalties on his writings, especially *AA* and *12;12*. (Until his death in 1950, Dr. Smith received a part of the royalties for *A.A.*) Those who objected to such "professionalism" consistently pushed for a cheaper — and in later years, paperback — edition of *AA*. Those who stressed that "A.A. has to stand on its own financial feet" as consistently — and more successfully — opposed such moves. Citations are unavailable because the Trustee Minutes remain closed, but reflections of the debate may be found in the "Final Report of the __th General Service Conference of Alcoholics Anonymous" for almost every year after 1955.

The early beginnings and heat of this controversy may best be followed in the Clarence S. correspondence: *cf.*, Clarence S. (Cleveland) to L. V. Harrison, 27 April, 21 July 1944, and an undated letter between the two just cited. Further comments by Clarence on the topic are available in the marginated copy of *AACA* sent by him to the writer; also in a tape recording I hold of an interview with him, 6 October 1978.

53 *AACA*, pp. 171–179; *cf.* also "Book Publication Proved Discouraging Venture — by Bill," *AAGV* 4:2 (July 1947), 3.

54 "Dr. Bob," *AAGV* 7:8 (January 1951), 26; the New York practice from the recollections of Marty Mann, tr. and interview of 15 November 1977; "wives": in both New York and Akron at this point, the alcoholics approaching the program were all male.

According to some (Henrietta Seiberling, Clarence S.), these separate gatherings were not "meetings" but private sessions in which any newcomers who had not yet "made surrender" then did so. However: according to Bob E.'s own testimony — useful here because he is among the "some" indicated — "making surrender" was a *pre-requisite* for meeting attendance, and the phenomenon here under analysis clearly took place *after* the OG meeting *each week* once it began. Doubtless the distinction was not so clear-cut as I make it in the text: little was in this period. It seems to me clear, however, that a significant and self-conscious separation did take place at this time, in this way.

55 Trs. of Dorothy M., Lloyd T., Dave T., J.T.C., Joseph K., Bob E., p. 20; interview with Clarence S., 20 August 1977, and Clarence S. to writer, 9 September 1977.

56 Clarence S. is the main source here and for much that follows; beyond the other trs. cited in the preceding note, his version is supplemented by Dorothy M., tr. Dorothy M. was in 1939 the wife of Clarence S. Her tr. is of a 1954 interview by Wilson, and thus especially useful in sorting out the discrepancies between the Wilson and the Clarence S. versions of A.A. history. Also extremely helpful was Warren C., interviews of 7 and 8 September 1977. Warren came into A.A. as Clarence's pigeon in mid-1939. He has remained above the disputes between Clarence and A.A.'s New York General Service Office, and he was recommended by Clarence as "the best source for the real story." I found Warren knowledgeable and of trustworthy memory: in cases of otherwise unresolvable contradictions, I have tended to follow his recollections.

57 Much of the Catholic lore surrounding these events is courtesy of John C. Ford, S.J., interview of 12 April 1977; *cf.* also Clarence S. to writer, 9 September 1977; Warren C., interviews of 7 and 8 September 1977. It seems a reasonable assumption that Wilson's misunderstanding *re* papal condemnation of the OG was rooted in awareness of this occurrence in Cleveland.

58 Dorothy M., tr.; Clarence S., tr. Clarence offered vivid and colorful details of the Akron meeting of 10 May and the Cleveland meeting of 11 May in a letter to the writer of 9 September 1977.

59 Dorothy M., tr.; Clarence S., tr.; *cf.* also trs. of T. Henry Williams and

Lloyd T. According to Clarence S. (letter to writer of 9 September 1977, interview of 22 October 1977), the "fussbudgets" among the Oxford Groupers "were very unhappy with me (really some were damned nasty). . . . If I [thought] that was a riot [his Akron announcement of the Cleveland meeting], you should have witnessed next Thursday nite at Cleveland at our first meeting. That whole bunch from Akron and other places descended upon us and tried to break up our meeting — one guy . . . was going to whip me!" The harassment continued through the summer and into autumn, and Clarence at times later claimed that it was the reason for the split into the Orchard Grove and Borton groups in November of 1939. Warren C., interview of 7 September 1977, testified to the continuing but diminishing "bother." The history of the matter to 1942 is too complicated as well as inconsequential (once personalities are left aside) to detail here: my evaluation of its significance appears within note #1 to Chapter Four, below.

60 "Dr. Bob," 23; Bob E., tr.; NW, "Outline"; *LM*; "Another Fragment of History — by Bill"; *AAGV* 10:9 (February 1954); Dr. Russell Smith, interviews of 12 and 13 June 1977. The matter of hospital use in Akron and Cleveland is the most complicated and I believe essentially insoluble problem in the history of Alcoholics Anonymous. While insisting that the history narrated in the text here is substantially correct, I offer in this and the following note some hint of the complexities involved. Frank Amos, "Notes on Akron, Ohio Survey," attached to Amos (New York) to Albert Scott, 23 February 1938, reported of his interview with Judge B., the Chairman of the Board of Akron City Hospital: "His Board, he said, was proud to give Smith fullest privileges in handling alcoholics at City Hospital." I have difficulty in accepting this and suspect that Amos misunderstood B. or that one of them was less than fully accurate. Beyond the sources just cited, the tr. of Dr. Smith's nurse at this time, Emma K., and the detailed research of Niles P. into Smith's biography belie such a claim.

61 Sr. Ignatia, tr.; "For Sister Ignatia — by Bill," *AAGV* 22:3 (August 1966), 2–9; Sister Ignatia, "Care and Treatment of Alcoholics," *AAGV* 25:1 (June 1969), 5–8: this last is based on an interview given by Sister Ignatia in 1951; *cf.* also *AACA*, p. 7. Because Clarence S. denies Wilson's and Bob E.'s accuracy concerning these events, it is important to note that reliance here and in the following paragraphs is also upon two brief informal histories (undated) of St. Thomas Hospital by Sr. Ignatia, and also upon her letters (Cleveland) to Wilson of 13 March and 3 April 1957: in the letters she is replying to Bill querying her about Clarence's objections to the history recorded in *AACA*. These materials are in the files of Rosary Hall, the alcoholic ward of St. Vincent's Charity Hospital, Cleveland, Ohio, of which Sr. Ignatia was in charge from 1952 until her death in 1966. Further, the source suggested by Clarence "for the real story," Sister Victorine, who was Sr. Ignatia's predecessor and successor at St. Vincent's, in interviews of 8 September and 23 December 1977, verified the details of Sr. Ignatia's histories, contradicting Clarence on several points. An anonymously-authored (but not by Sr. Ignatia) "History of A.A. Activities at St. Vincent's Charity Hospital, Cleveland, Ohio," [1953] further confirms the narration here and the final sentence three paragraphs hence. *Yet:* one of Clarence's claims is that Wilson inflated the St. Thomas Hospital and Sr. Ignatia roles in order to curry Catholic favor (interviews cited and marginated copy of *AACA*). Thus it may be wise not to accept these sources without noting the following points: (1) Clarence was hospitalizing patients in Cleveland in early June of 1939 — Clarence S. (Cleveland) to Hank

P., 4 June 1939; (2) These hospitalizations (at Evangelical Deaconess Hospital) involved Dr. Smith and were exceptional — most were still sent to Akron — Edna M. (n.p.) to Wilson, 5 February 1957; Dorothy M. (n.p.) to Wilson, 30 March 1957; (3) Clarence himself stressed that his claim to priority in hospitalization rested on his use of St. Vincent's Charity Hospital; yet according to his own detailed history of this, his entree followed the Hemsley publicity of April 1940 by at least four months. Further, Clarence's sometime claim that St. John's Hospital admitted alcoholics before St. Vincent's is belied by the testimony of Sr. Victorine, whose first Cleveland assignment was to St. Vincent's and who went to St. John's only after Sr. Ignatia replaced her at St. Vincent's (interviews of 8 September and 23 December 1977).

Any interested in trying further to unravel the detailed sequence here will find the raw materials for such an effort, beyond the sources thusfar cited, in Clarence S. (St. Petersburg, FL) to Wilson, 20 February and 14 April 1957, and Wilson to Clarence S., 20 March 1957; also, Clarence S. to writer, 13 and 29 September 1978.

Wilson's own final mollifying conclusion was that St. Thomas Hospital in Akron had been "the first to give *permanent* haven" to alcoholics and to A.A. — Wilson to Clarence S., 20 March 1957 (emphasis Wilson's).

62 Sr. Ignatia, tr.; Dr. Russell Smith, interviews cited; *cf.* also Smith (Akron) to Hank P., 15 September 1939. Wilson may be heard chortling over the same images, beyond *AACA*, p. 7, in, e.g., Wilson to Dorothy M., 22 March 1957.

63 [Sr. Ignatia], "St. Thomas Hospital"; Father Vincent Haas, tr.

64 Father Vincent Haas, tr.; *cf.* note #61 above. It may have been only in 1941 that St. Thomas Hospital *formalized* its admission and treatment procedures for alcoholics, but the Haas tr. makes clear that administrative approbation was obtained no later than March 1940.

65 Bob E., tr., pp. 21–22. This point is complex: some who visited Akron in 1939 — e.g., Marty Mann — claimed that there were few alcoholics at the meeting attended and that the meetings were very Oxford Group. Others (interviews reported by Niles P.) claim that Akron meetings in this period were very much A.A. and very little OG. I hypothesize that both versions are true: the memories are simply of different perceptions of different meetings as this problem ebbed and flowed to resolution through the late summer and early fall of 1939. I offer Bob E.'s version in the text here because it seems to me that he best captures the process and its confusions. Clarence S., interview of 6 October 1978 supported this interpretation.

66 Bob E., tr., pp. 23–24; interview with Henrietta Seiberling, 6 April 1977.

67 Bob E., tr., p. 24; Smith (Akron) to Hank P., 1 January 1940; "Dr. Bob," 26–27; William V., tr; Sue G., tr.

68 T. Henry and Clarace Williams (Akron) to Bill and Lois Wilson, 29 February 1940; a letter from Clarence S. (Cleveland) to Ruth H., 5 January 1940, comments on "how much better Smith looks since he pulled his gang out of Williams" and reports Cleveland joy over the development.

69 "Landmarks in A.A. History," *AACA*, p. viii records: "1939, Summer: Midwest A.A.'s withdraw from Oxford Groups; A.A. fully on its own." Wilson's narration of this history is very subdued — *AACA*, p. 76.

IV 1939–1941

1 Clarence S., tr.; Dorothy M., tr.; Virginia M., tr.; Abby G., tr.; Wilson, "Review"; also Clarence S. (Cleveland) to Wilson, 4 March 1941, and Abby G. (Cleveland) to Wilson, 28 June 1956; Clarence S. to writer, 9 September 1977; interviews with Warren C. and Dick P., 7 and 8 September 1977. "relative calm": the OG harassment noted in Chapter Three, note #59, continued but diminished in intensity over this period. Despite the overt claim that the splitting off to be treated just below was due to this "bother," the over-all weight of even Clarence's evidence is that the Davis episode was the proximately precipitating factor; *cf.* Clarence S., (Cleveland) to Hank P., 4 June 1939; also, Clarence confirmed this in response to my direct question, interview of 17 December 1977. Dr. Smith traveled to Cleveland to participate in these meetings at least once a month until the split to be treated below (and less regularly thereafter): Smith (Akron) to Hank P., 15 September 1939; Sue G., tr.

2 *Cf.* sources cited in note #1 above; also, Lloyd T., tr. The *Plain Dealer* articles appeared on scattered dates between 21 October and 4 November 1939.

3 Dorothy M., tr., pp. 1, 8.

4 *Ibid.*, pp. 9–10. According to Dorothy M., Davis had a drinking problem; according to Warren C., Clarence sought him out expressly for publicity.

5 *AACA*, pp. 20f; Thomsen, pp. 291–292, 321; Clarence S., tr.; the Lupton sermon was reported in the *Plain Dealer* of 27 November 1939 and reprinted as a pamphlet titled, "Mr. Anonymous": basically, it told Clarence's story.

My interpretation is based not only on the founding date and locations of the first twenty-nine Cleveland groups (as "listed by Clarence [S] according to Harry [S]" — in Cleveland A.A. District Office archives), but also on my interviews with Warren C. who joined A.A. before the Davis publicity and with Dick P. who joined as a result of the Hemsley publicity to be described next. I suspect that because of the Hemsley publicity tie with the OG, to be detailed in notes #6 and 9 below, the newly self-conscious fellowship of Alcoholics Anonymous unconsciously minimized its impact. This suspicion was confirmed not only by the interviews cited, but by the tone as well as the details in the letter of Clarence S. to writer, 9 September 1977. *Cf.* also Clarence S. (Cleveland) to Wilson, 4 March 1941 and 28 February 1943; also Abby G. (Cleveland) to Wilson, 28 June 1956. Clarence S. (Cleveland) to Ruth H., 21 April 1940, testified: "There is renewed activity starting already from the Hemsley articles."

This is not to deny that "rapid growth" followed the Davis series: the approximately twenty A.A.s received over a hundred inquiries (interviews by Niles P.). But membership growth from about 120 to close to 1,000 seems more a "breakthrough" than the Davis-inspired growth from a score to just over one hundred.

6 Cleveland *Plain Dealer*, 27 November 1939; for the Hemsley press conference, see front page of virtually any American newspaper for 17 or 18 April 1940, also the sports columnists over the next week. The flavor of the following paragraphs derives from the total newspaper coverage. The specific quotation at paragraph-end may be found in the *Plain Dealer* (18), the Cleveland *Press* (17), and the Chicago *Tribune* (17).

As evidence for the OG complication, note from the *Press* story of 17

April: "C.C. Slapnicka, vice-president of the Indians, said that it was the 'Oxford Movement,' and not 'Alcoholics Anonymous,' which had worked the reformation. Hemsley informed of this, insisted that his contacts were with Alcoholics Anonymous."

According to Clarence S., letters to writer of 25 August and 9 September 1977, "the inquiries resulting from the Hemsley publicity were turned over to the Oxford Group rather than Alcoholics Anonymous." No doubt some were, but the memories of Warren C. and Dick P. (interviews cited) make clear that a substantial number of inquirers found their way into A.A. rather than the OG. Part of the problem here, even according to Clarence's own detailing of the situation, is that many in Cleveland were members of *both* the OG and A.A.: the distinction was just not that clear, *even to Clarence*, who in early 1941 was still working hand-in-hand with some Groupers in arranging "dryout houses" (letters cited).

7   *Cf.* the sports pages of virtually every American newspaper for early April 1940; beyond the Cleveland *Press* and *Plain Dealer*, I have checked the *New York Times* and *Boston Globe*. The interpretation and details in this and the following paragraphs were discussed and verified through the Sports Desk of the *Boston Globe* from that newspaper's morgue, baseball record-books, and the desk-man's memory — interview of 28 December 1976.

8   *Ibid.*, especially the *Globe* Sports Desk for memory and verification of details.

9   Bob E., tr., p. 20; according to Clarence S. (letter to writer of 9 September 1977), "thru the auspices of [two Oxford Group members of A.A.] the Cleveland Baseball Club was approached *re* Hemsley."; for the final sentence, notes #7 and 8 above.

10   For the Oxford Group concern, *cf.* notes #5 and 6 above; also trs. of Dorothy M., Lloyd T., Bob E., Dave T.

11   For the "erroneous mention of the Oxford Group," *cf.* note #6, above; for Father N.'s role, interview with Warren C., 8 September 1977, Clarence S. to writer, 9 September 1977, and interview with Sister Victorine, 23 December 1977;

for pictures in the Alexander article, *cf. AACA*, p. 191;

for anonymity, *cf.* below, pp. 104–105; for the Mary Mann incident, below. Chapter Five, pp. 117ff.

12   For the significance of the geography of Cleveland, a city divided by a winding river valley and the eastern extremities of which are the precipitous slopes of "the Heights," *cf.* U.S. Coast and Geodetic Survey topographical maps. The best interpretation of the impact of this geography, although dated, is Agnes Dureau, *Cleveland: Etude de Geographie Urbaine* (Paris: Jouve, 1925); George Condon, *Cleveland, The Best Kept Secret* (New York: Doubleday, 1967), may also prove helpful, although less directly — *cf.* his Index listing.

For particular causes as "veiled," *cf.*, e.g., the contradictions between and even the changes within the transcripts cited, especially that of Dorothy M., p. 12, where she remarks on her yet largely unconscious, lingering "dishonesty."

On Clarence S. as himself welcoming the splits at the time, Clarence S. (Cleveland) to Ruth H., ? November 1939, makes this perhaps surprising point clear. It was further attested to by Warren C., interview of 8 September 1977. That Clarence felt differently as early as 1941 is clear from Clarence S. (Cleveland) to Wilson, 4 March 1941. The relationship at this time between Clarence, Cleveland A.A., and Wilson in New York may best be grasped from a letter of Clarence to the *Cleveland Press*, published on 21 February 1941, Ruth H., (New York) to Clarence, 25 February 1941, Clarence S. (Cleveland) to Wilson, 4 March 1941, and Wilson's reply of 11 March 1941.

13   This paragraph perhaps makes informal practice sound too planned and precise, yet it is what happened — *cf.* group records in Cleveland A.A. District Office; also the structure witnessed by Warren C. and Dick P. even as they denied such explicit formalization (interviews cited).

The practice of rotation apparently antedated the splits: *cf.* Dorothy S. (Cleveland) to Ruth H., 7 October 1939. This letter contains a solid hint that even at this point, Clarence's personality and specifically his argumentativeness over his introduction of Elrick Davis into the group had led to this practice; *cf.* also Abby G., tr., where Abby claimed that this practice was formalized under his leadership after the November 1939 splits.

On Wilson realizing that Cleveland had set an important precedent for no central A.A. authority in any city (and implicitly acknowledging that such could not have happened in New York or Akron given the presence of himself and Dr. Bob Smith, and might not have happened in Cleveland but for the personality of Clarence), Wilson to Ed. M., 6 April 1942. The precise context in which this two-level localism (groups independent in any city; any city independent of New York) was based seems the matter raised by the March 1941 letters cited at the end of the preceding note; *cf.* also Ruth H., tr.

14   Interviews of 7 and 8 September 1977 with Warren C. and Dick P.; On sponsorship as from Cleveland, a strangely underplayed facet in A.A.'s self-consciousness of its own history, *cf.* Dorothy M., tr., p. 8, where Wilson affirms the fact; Thomsen continues the underplaying, *cf.* p. 321, where it is a parenthesized aside.

15   Pamphlet "Questions and Answers on Sponsorship," rev. ed. (New York: A.A. World Services, 1976), p. 5; *cf.* also the earlier edition of this pamphlet: "Sponsorship" (New York: A.A. Publishing, Inc., 1953), which better reflects the early Cleveland practice (explicitly denied in the revised edition) in which the sponsor vouched for the serious intent of his "pigeon" — *cf.* interviews cited with Warren C. and Dick P.; "The Operation of the A.A. Ward," where this practice and responsibility are heavily reflected — document in files of Rosary Hall, St. Vincent's Charity Hospital, Cleveland, Ohio. Also informative is a tr. of Clarence S. describing sponsorship, 5 October 1978, in the writer's possession.

16   Bob E., tr., Clarence S., tr., Dorothy M., tr.; *cf.* Wilson to Clarence S., 6 June 1940; Ruth H. (New York) to Clarence S., 8 July 1940.

The perennial problem with "clubhouses" was their "mis-use"; in 1954, the General Service Conference of Alcoholics Anonymous finessed it, declaring: "the problem is local rather than general"; Final Report of the Fourth General Service Conference, p. 25.

17   Morris Markey, "Alcoholics and God," *Liberty* 16: 6–7 (30 September 1939); *cf. AACA*, p. 178. The *Liberty* piece did attract about 800 inquiries. These were disproportionately (1) from the South and (2) overtly religious: *AACA*, p. 178; Ruth H., tr.; Wilson to Jack Alexander, 13 December 1949.

18   Markey, 6–7.

19   *AACA*, p. 174; *cf.* Thomsen, p. 288.

20   *AACA*, pp. 174–176; *cf.*, Thomsen, pp. 288–289.

21   *Ibid.*; the direct quotations are from *AACA*, p. 174.

22   *Ibid.*; the direct quotations are from *AACA*, pp. 175–176.

23   The *Herald-Tribune*: Wilson to Irita VanDoren, 17 July 1939;

Percy Hutchison, "Alcoholic Experience," *NYT*, 25 June 1939; unsigned rev. in *The Washington Post*, 13 November 1939; the *NYT* review may have been preceded by Dr. Silkworth's, *The Journal Lancet* 59: 312–314 (1939);

The Fosdick review, which is reprinted in *AACA*, pp. 322–323, appeared first in *The Christian Leader*, 7 November 1939, 20; it was also carried in: *The American Friend*, 12 December 1939, 437; and the *Friends Intelligencer*, 18th day of the Eleventh Month 1939, 751;

Other reviews appeared in: *Christian Science Monitor*, 17 August 1939; *Zion's Herald*, 15 November 1939 (this review seems to incorporate part of Fosdick's — without attribution); *The Baptist Record*, 23 December 1939; and *The Baptist Leader*, January, 1940;

24   *AACA*, p. 182; *cf.* p. 15; Thomsen, pp. 294–295.

Two letters from Wilson to Dr. Bob Smith open the question as to whence had come the impetus to this — or such a — dinner: 9 November 1939: "Chipman and Richardson and some others of still more importance are planning a dinner to be held in two weeks or so with invitations to some of our prominent local capitalists"; 4 December 1939 gives the date of the proposed dinner, still not mentioning Rockefeller's name, as 17 January 1940.

Many possible hypotheses could reconcile these data: most probably, the problem again lies in Wilson's deficient memory for dates, "the February, 1940, meeting" of *AACA*, p. 182, the likeliest inaccuracy. Carlton S. (New York) to Wilson, 6 March 1957, casts minor new light on the impetus to the dinner and supports this hypothesis.

25   *AACA*, p. 182.

26   *AACA*, pp. 182–183; *cf.* Thomsen, pp. 294–297.

27   *Ibid.*

28   *AACA*, p. 184.

29   *AACA*, p. 185.

30   *Ibid.*

31   *AACA*, pp. 185–186; *cf.* Thomsen, pp. 297–298, who says: "*Daily News*"; the *News* headline of 9 February 1940 read, "Rockefeller Dines Ex-Sots, Now Rum Foes"; the *Mirror* for this date was not directly available, so I here rely on the memory of NW.

"marked by the Ivy Lee touch": many papers carried verbatim the Lee press release: "John D. Rockefeller, Jr., who has tried to hide many of his philanthropies and social reform activities under the bushel of anonymity, was revealed today as interested in a 'secret' organization aimed at regenerating alcoholics. The organization is 'Alcoholics Anonymous' which started when three men who overcame their craving for whiskey and wanted to help others in the same plight began the movement that today numbers one hundred." (Quoted from copy in A.A. archives). The "three men" seems a tribute to Hank P.'s continuing promotional ability as well as to New York provincialism — meant are Wilson, Hank, and Fitz M. (NW replying to my question with information derived from Ruth H., tr.; *cf.* also Jim B., "Evolution.")

32 "Alcoholic grandiosity" does not appear in the literature but is an A.A. catch-phrase which derives from this time: Ruth H., tr.; interview with Lois Wilson, 16 November 1976. For "dry drunk," *cf.* Thomsen, pp. 301–302; for this understanding of this period, Thomsen, pp. 299–302. Wilson does not treat it directly in *AACA*, but the basis for this interpretation is clear in his later correspondence looking back on the period: *cf.*, e.g., to Dick F., 30 November 1954; to Oliver J., 15 December 1950.

    Yet: two of Wilson's letters from the period itself — to Ted E., 20 May 1940, and to Ned F., 11 July 1940 — would seem to belie this interpretation, as does Lois's admittedly sketchy memory of it; interview of 7 April 1977. For present purposes, I have chosen to accept Wilson's later memory and Thomsen who relied solely on this and here transmits it well. Even if this memory be didactic distortion, my point remains valid — indeed, is perhaps strengthened by the very didacticism in the distortion. *Cf.* also, below, Chapter Five, note #18.

33 *AACA*, pp. 172–173, 179.

34 *AACA*, p. 190, for the allusion; I here follow Thomsen, p. 300, but *cf.* note #32 above. "1955": although *AACA* was published only in 1957, the section here cited substantially replicates Wilson's oral presentation at the 1955 "Coming of Age" convention.

35 Thomsen, pp. 300–301. This is not verified by A.A.'s scrapbooks of the period; indeed, more such clippings appear in the 1946 scrapbook. Unless the 1940 scrapbooks were pasted up later, which is indeterminable, this supports my point in note #32 above, and Chapter Five, note #18.

36 Thomsen, pp. 301–302 (italics Thomsen's).

37 Thomsen, p. 301.

38 *Ibid.*; Clarence S. interview of 6 October 1978; the "resentment" quotation is from *AA*, p. 66. "How It Works" is the title of the key Chapter Five of *AA*.

39 Thomsen, pp. 304–306. The description of the clubhouse and rooms is from Lois Wilson, interview of 7 April 1977. The "financial trickery" reference here is not to be confused with Wilson's 1942 problems with Clarence and Cleveland, also instigated by Hank P. (concerning which, *cf.* Thomsen, pp. 321–322). The 1940 misunderstanding concerned the Alcoholic Foundation's taking over of Bill's and Hank's shares in the Big Book: the stock scheme alluded to above, p. 68, *cf.* p. 91.

40 The future writing would be in *12&12*, to be treated in Chapter Five. The story of Father Dowling, which begins here, does not appear in *AACA*, but was told by Wilson in loving detail at/in *LM*. The details of content and description here and in the following paragraphs are drawn from *LM*, Thomsen (who here captures well the tone of Wilson, tr.), many scattered references to the scene in Wilson's letters, the interviews previously cited with Lois Wilson and Nell Wing, who described Bill's oral tellings of the incident, and the interviews cited in the following note.

41   The description of Dowling, the man and his style, is taken from the just cited sources and also from John C. Ford, S.J., interview of 12 April 1977, who offered his memory of Dowling's memory of this meeting, and interview of 23 February 1979 with Joseph F. MacFarlane, S.J., who succeeded Dowling as editor of *The Queen's Work*. Father Ford, incidentally, is one of many who find difficulty intuiting the parallel which Dowling discerned. As editor of *The Queen's Work*, Dowling eventually published a pamphlet tracing the parallel: Ford had seen it, but I have been unable to locate a copy.

42   Thomsen, p. 309. Wilson's consciousness of "taking his Fifth" with Dowling perdured: he presented this as "a second conversion experience" in a letter to Pat M., 24 May 1969. Through the years, Wilson often sought Dowling's advice on troublesome matters; e.g., a proposed movie on A.A., Wilson to Dowling, 16 March 1944; proposed changes in the Foundation, Wilson to Dowling 5 November 1945.

43   Thomsen, pp. 308–310, 367; Wilson to Dowling, 24 September 1947 (quoted in note #46 to Chapter Two, above).

44   Interview with John C. Ford, S.J., 12 April 1977; Thomsen, pp. 309–310; on "demand," Wilson, *LM; cf.* also the discussion of *12;12,* below, pp. 125–126.

45   *AACA*, p. 190; Wilson to Clarence S., 23 April 1940; trs. of Clarence S., Bob E., Marty Mann, Norm Y., Oscar W. Clarence S., letter to writer of 25 August 1977 and interview of 6 October 1978; Warren C., interview of 7 September 1977.

46   Thomsen, p. 311, refers in passing to Alexander's initial cynicism. Wilson treated it deeply at *LM*, but generally deleted this stress in *AACA* — yet *cf.* p. 35.

47   *AACA*, p. 35, 190–191.

48   *Ibid.*, Wilson to Clarence S., 22 January 1941.

49   Alexander (Philadelphia) to Wilson, 14 December 1949; telegram covering article manuscript, 12 January 1950; Wilson to Alexander, 13 December 1949; Wilson to Alexander, 24 January 1950. Alexander served as a trustee of Alcoholics Anonymous from 1951 to 1956.

50   *AACA*, pp. viii, 190–192.

51   *AACA*, p. 26; Wilson to Jack Alexander, 13 December 1949; Wilson to Lewis C., 25 May 1967; to Ed. M., 4 April 1942; Earl T., tr.

52   *AACA*, pp. 192, 196–198.

53   The social and economic background of these early members of A.A. has been treated above, pp. 73–74: the stories especially in the first edition of *AA* make clear their treatment history and fascination with "how it worked." A.A.'s early members had experience especially with the "Keely Cure"; some had also read Richard R. Peabody's *The Common Sense of Drinking; cf.* interview with Ruth

H., 30 September 1978, with Lois Wilson, 2 October 1978. The significance of this contact will be evaluated in Part Two of the present study.

54 To grasp this at depth, the reader may wish to read the whole of Chapter Five of *AA*, "How It Works," pp. 58–71; if so, be sure to go on to read at least the opening sentences of Chapters 6 and 7: ". . . what shall we do about it?" followed by four "we have" sentences (p. 72); "Practical experience shows" as the opening words, p. 89.

55 *12&12*, p. 97; *cf.* Wilson to Harry M., 21 January 1942.

56 Wilson to Al C., 6 May 1942; to E.D.K., 27 June 1961: two letters revealing this especially clearly over a two decade span. For Wilson's self-consciousness over thus proceeding, *cf.* Wilson, "Alcoholics Anonymous Tradition: Twelve Points to Assure Our Future," *AAGV* 2:10 (April 1946), 7–9, the first public presentation of the Twelve Traditions, which opens: "Nobody invented Alcoholics Anonymous. It grew. Trial and error has produced a rich experience." *Cf.* also Ruth H., tr., for Wilson's first secretary's consciousness of this style.

57 The clearest statement of the early motive for anonymity being protection occurs *AA*, p. xiii; that this is not mere window-dressing for the book is clear in a letter from the director of Works Publishing at the time, Robert M. (New York) to J.R.B., 4 May 1939.

58 For this understanding of Alexander, *AACA*, p. 35; the first perception of anonymity's spiritual value apparently came from outside A.A.: J.E.M. (Summit, NJ) to The Alcoholic Foundation, 20 August 1939; Wilson's clearest pre-Traditions exploration of the developing concept of anonymity appears in two articles: "A Tradition Born of Our Anonymity — by Bill," *AAGV* 2:8 (January 1946), 2, 10; "Our Anonymity is Both Inspiration and Safety — by Bill," *AAGV* 2:10 (March 1946), 1, 5.

    The best brief history of A.A.'s evolving understanding of anonymity is "Why Alcoholics Anonymous is Anonymous — by Bill," reprinted in *AACA*, pp. 286–294. Even briefer is an aside of Wilson in a letter to Robert B., 6 February 1963: "Anonymity was first conceived for A.A. as a mere protection; but unconsciously we made a spiritual ten-strike of large dimensions, too — something that more and more appears as time passes."

59 J.E.M. (Summit, NJ) to The Alcoholic Foundation, 20 and 31 August 1939, might have made this paradox available to A.A.'s consciousness, but it slipped by Wilson in his reading of M. as a militant "dry" — an inaccurate reading, by the way. Wilson to J.E.M., 11 March 1940, nevertheless testifies well to the point here: "Perhaps we carry the principle of tolerance too far, and if we find that to be true I am sure we shall be willing to readjust our viewpoints."

60 *Cf.*, e.g., Wilson to Ed. B., 13 September 1949: "Most people feel more secure on the twenty-four hour basis than they do in the resolution they will never drink again. Most of them have broken too many resolutions."

    Leach and Norris, "Factors," in Kissin and Begleiter, p. 458, review briefly some of the literature examining this key A.A. idea.

    Informal A.A. lore attributes this emphasis to early Akron: This has been reflected with appropriate citations in Chapter Two, above. The affinity to "primitive Christianity" lies, of course, in the parallel to the Lord's Prayer petition: "Give us this day our daily bread."

61   *AA*, pp. 95, xxi.

62   *AA*, p. xiv; for the discussion of as Tradition Three, *AACA*. pp. 102–103; *cf.* also: "Who Is a Member of Alcoholics Anonymous — by Bill," *AAGV* 3:3 (August 1946), 3, 7. According to A.A. lore, although Wilson was never troubled by an overwhelming desire to drink after his spiritual experience, Dr. Smith was consistently tortured by such periodic craving for many years: *cf.* Smith, "Last Major Talk," and Virginia M., tr.; also Smith's own telling of his story in *AA*, p. 181.

63   "Final Report of the 8th General Service Conference of Alcoholics Anonymous, 1958," p. 20.

64   *AACA*, pp. 103–104.

65   *AACA*, p. 104. The tendency of some groups to impose special rules or practices before the publication of the Twelve Traditions is clear from: "Educational Plan," *AAGV* 2:1 (June 1945), 4, describing "The Wilson Club" of St. Louis; also "Rochester Group Prepares Novices for Group Participation," *AAGV* 2:4 (September 1945), 6. That the practice continued, in places, even after 1946, is witnessed by G.H.B. (Little Rock, AR) to Bobbie B. [A.A.'s secretary], 20 May 1947.

66   The Tiebout correspondence will be treated in detail in Chapters Five and Six: for citations, *cf.* especially note #51 to Chapter Five (p. 354, below) and notes #12-16 to Chapter Six (p. 359, below). For Ford, *cf.* Ford (Weston, MA) to Wilson, 13 February 1953 and 6 July 1957; also Wilson to Ford 14 May 1957, 8 July 1957, 15 July 1957, and 1 August 1962. Father Ford, interview of 12 April 1977, said that he had been arguing from a "theoretical philosophical understanding" of "the need for visible authority in any human society"; he indicated ultimate acceptance that "for A.A., Bill's ideas seem to work."

67   The reply quoted here is from Wilson to John M., 18 July 1962; the same idea infuses all the Wilson letters cited in the preceding note.

68   The quotation beginning the paragraph is from the Second Tradition of Alcoholics Anonymous, *cf. AACA*, p. 78; the two following quotations are from Wilson to Ford, 15 July 1957; and *12&12*, p. 178.

69   For Shoemaker leaving the OG, *cf.* Clark, *The Oxford Group*, pp. 54, 80; Shoemaker (New York) to Wilson, 27 June 1949: "God has saved you from the love of the spotlight, Bill, at least if not from the love of it — from getting too much into it, and it is one of the biggest things about you. . . . If dear Frank could have learned the same lesson long ago MRA might have changed the face of the earth."

70   The evidence for this will unfold in the following two chapters. The best citation here is Wilson's plea, in his own and Dr. Bob Smith's name, "Why Can't We Join A.A. Too!" *AAGV* 4:5 (October 1947), 3, 7; for Wilson's later understanding of this history, Wilson to John M., 18 July 1962; Wilson to Jerry E., 28 April 1965.

V   1941–1955

1   Wilson's 1957 published history, *AACA*, which contains the historical presentations made at the 1955 "Alcoholics Anonymous Comes of Age" convention, treats of this period directly on pp. 198–221 and indirectly on pp. 1–48, *passim*, beyond itself being a part of this history. The sixth printing of *AACA* (1975) carries the schematic "Landmarks in A.A. History" forward to 1975, pp. ix–xi. Thomsen treats the period from the *SEP* story of 1941 to the 1955 convention on pp. 313–354.

2   Reprinted in *AACA*, p. 301; Dr. Robert Holbrook Smith died on 16 November 1950: "Dr. Bob" [eulogy by Wilson], *AAGV*, 7:8 (January 1951), 3, says "nineteenth": no doubt the most egregious example of Wilson's lack of memory for dates.

3   *AACA*, pp. 198–199; for color and detail, Ruth H., tr.

4   A.A. General Service Office figures, compiled by Jim H. The best evaluative analysis of A.A. membership figures is offered by Leach and Norris, "Factors," pp. 443–450.
   "The first non-American branch [of A.A.] was formed in Sydney [Australia] in October, 1944": S. J. Minogue, "Alcoholics Anonymous," *Medical Journal of Australia* 35 (1st): 586 (1948).
   The *AAGV* in almost every issue through the final year of World War II carried letters from servicemen that taken together confirm the point in the final sentence; *cf.* also *AACA*, p. 200.

5   *AACA*, p. 203; the *AAGV* also of course dates from this period, partially as a partial response to the same problem: *cf. AACA*, pp. 201–202; also Wilson's lead editorial, "The Shape of Things to Come," *AAGV* 1:1 (June 1944), 1; the purpose noted here is more clear in [Wilson], "The Grapevine: Past, Present, and Future," *AAGV* 2:2 (July 1945), 1.
   Wilson's letter style has been treated above, pp. 103–104.

6   *AACA*, p. 203; "Twelve Suggested Points for A.A. Tradition," *AAGV*, 2:11 (April 1946), 2–3; "Tradition Week Issue," *AAGV* 6:6 (November 1949), 1–15; pamphlet "A.A. Tradition: How It Developed — by Bill W." (New York: A.A. World Services, 1955), pp. 3–6; *cf.* also Wilson, *LM*; "Fellowship," p. 467; and as especially revealing of the problems, the correspondence between Wilson and Carl K. — e.g., Carl K. (Chattanooga, TN) to Wilson, 9 October 1945; Wilson to Carl K., 23 October 1945 and 14 November 1945.
   For Wilson's application of these developing principles to another area at this time, *cf.* Wilson to Royal S., 12 March 1946, *re* the organization of the *AAGV* and A.A. as "a new form of society." This letter makes especially clear that Bill's fear of "centralized authority" was rooted in his understanding of "the history of religions."

7   The "short form" of the Twelve Traditions may be found in *AACA*, p. 78, or *AA*, p. 564. The "long form" is reprinted in *AA*, pp. 565–568, and discussed in *AACA*, pp. 97–137. The long form was originally published in *AAGV* 2:11 (April 1946), 2–3; the short form, in *AAGV* 6:6 (November 1949), 16–17. The Traditions were officially adopted by the fellowship in June 1950: *AACA*, pp. viii, 212–213. On the omission of "honest" or "sincere" in Tradition Three, *cf.* above, p. 106. *AAGV* 6:6 was the first publication without the qualification.
   An intriguing summary note on the Traditions was offered by Wilson to Jack Alexander, 31 March 1954: "The whole A.A. Tradition is, in a sense, a result of my gradual adjustment to reality."

8   The early understanding of "bottom" and the backgrounds of the early members of A.A. have been treated in the first three chapters, above.

9   *AACA*, p. 199, especially for the timing, which is less clear in the other sources.

10   The best written example of the "conscious technique" occurs in the treatment of Step One in *12&12*, pp. 21–24; the deepest discussion of it appears in [Wilson], "A.A. Communication Can Cross All Barriers," *AAGV* 16:5 (October 1959), 2–5. The foundation for the understanding of "progression" was already present in *AA*, p. 30 (1st ed., p. 41): "We are convinced to a man that alcoholics of our type are in the grip of a progressive illness. Over any considerable period we get worse, never better."

11   "Evidence on the Sleeping Pill Menace," *AAGV* 2:5 (October 1945), 1, 8; "Those 'Goof Balls' — Then a Miracle," *AAGV* 2:6 (November 1945), 2, 8.
     The tug to expansion may be seen beginning on the same page of the same issue (2:5) where Wilson first noted the problem. In "Pills and Twelfth Step Work . . . by an M.D. who is also an A.A.," the theme was laid down that "The problems of the pill taker are the same as those of the alcoholic . . ."; *cf.* also the discussion in Wilson, "Fellowship," p. 472. The developing and later concern over this problem will be treated in Chapter Six. Its complications were witnessed by such recurrent *AAGV* articles as "Does a Pill Jag Count as a Slip?" *AAGV* 4:9 (February 1948), 3. That Wilson himself from even the earliest moment of this concern was single-minded *re* alcoholism is witnessed by Wilson to Carl K., 9 October 1945: "It is also a powerful tradition [note lower case] that A.A. groups have but one aim only 'to help the sick alcoholic.'"

12   "Chewing your booze" does not appear in the literature but was an expression commonly heard at A.A. meetings during this writer's research. Oldtimers Ed. J. and Chuck C., interviews of 26 March 1976, testified that it was in use as long as they could remember (mid-1940's). They, as counselors at Hazelden in Center City, MN, witness to how the idea was transmitted — by individual A.A.s who worked as treatment center counselors. Hazelden is perhaps the premier A.A.-oriented treatment center and pioneered the concept of "chemical dependency" — interview with Dr. Dan Anderson, director of Hazelden, 11 June 1977.

13   "Conference Highlights," "4th General Service Conference of Alcoholics Anonymous" (1954), p. 3: "[A.A.] declines with thanks a proposal that A.A. become publisher and derive royalties from sales of 'Twenty-Four Hours a Day' book on grounds that it might set a precedent." *Twenty-Four Hours a Day* is a black-bound, prayerbook sized manual in perhaps greater use among members of A.A. than *AA* itself.
     This theme and history will be tied together at the end of Chapter Six, below.

14   "Modesty One Plank for Good Public Relations — by Bill W.," *AAGV* 2:3 (August 1945), 1, 4; C.H.K., "History Offers Good Lessons for A.A.," *AAGV* 2:2 (July 1945), 3. Between 1945 and 1976, the *AAGV* carried twelve different articles (and several reprints of these) on the Washingtonians. Further, the Washingtonians have been kept before A.A.'s attention over these years by Professor Milton Maxwell, currently an A.A. trustee, whose deepest scholarly treatment appeared as "The Washingtonian Movement," *QJSA* 11: 410–451 (1950).

15 "Modesty One Plank," 1, 4.

16 *Ibid.*; in some later A.A. literature, the concept here well-conveyed by the term *single-purposed* became obfuscated by substitution of the term *unity* as its too exact equivalent. After Wilson's death, A.A. itself seemed at times to fall into this trap. The historical narration to follow in this and the next chapter should make clear both how the change in term occurred and the validity of the understanding proposed here. The shift in terms is best clarified by reading with an awareness of this history Wilson's discussion of A.A.'s First Tradition in *AACA*, pp. 97–98. That this understanding is Wilson's own is perhaps clearest from "Review," where Bill treats of "unity" as a "legacy . . . in my own life" in the context of discussing A.A.'s singleness of purpose.

17 Wilson's Baltimore talk is unpublished, and as closely paralleling the Yale presentation noted below, I have not specifically cited it. It was delivered on 11 February 1943, the invitation from Dr. George P., (Baltimore) to Wilson, 11 December 1942, and Wilson's acceptance in a letter to Dr. P., 9 January 1943;

The New York presentation was published as W. G. Wilson [the only occasion on which Wilson's full name was published crediting any of his writings], "Basic Concepts of Alcoholics Anonymous," *N.Y. State Journal of Medicine* 44: 1805–1810 (1944);

Wilson first spoke at the Yale Summer School of Alcohol Studies on 12 August 1943, the School's first year: Jellinek (New Haven) to Wilson, 22 March 1943; Dr. Paul D. (New Haven) to Wilson, 13 July 1943; Wilson to Dr. Paul D., 4 August 1943 — this letter contains an outline of his proposed talk; the Yale presentation published as "Fellowship" is from a 1944 transcript, but seems very much the same presentation outlined by Wilson to Dr. Paul D. for 1943.

Wilson's and A.A.'s involvement at Rockland State Hospital from 1939 is passed over in this paragraph as exceptional and so not a witness to acceptance "by the medical profession"; likewise, a similar A.A. involvement at Philadelphia General Hospital from 1940.

18 "pride": I strongly suspect that Wilson's memory of his 1940 period of "inflation-deflation" was strongly colored by his parallel experiences here in 1944–1946: *cf.* discussion above, Chapter Four, note #32. I am led to this surmise by the credited article cited in the preceding note as well as by what will be discussed and cited just below of the N.C.E.A. episode.

Towns Hospital advertising brochure in A.A. archives: Wilson to Dr. John B., 30 March 1944; notation of Dr. B.'s response [by telephone?] attached.

19 The "Yale Plan" endeavors were adumbrated in a news story of 14 May 1943 (New York *Herald-Tribune*) — *cf.* clipping sent to Wilson by L.W. [New York], 14 May 1943). They were formally announced in a news-release dated 6 January 1944; *cf. New York Times*, 7 January 1944. The N.C.E.A. was in the process of becoming from mid-1943 to its formal inception on 1 October 1944. Essentially, its impetus derived from the Women's Club Movement. In most of its early literature, a third concept was added to the two cited here: "[Alcoholism] is a public health problem and therefore a public responsibility." The final quotation is from an open letter from the N.C.E.A., signed by David F. Houston, Jr., as Chairman of its Finance Committee, 4 September 1946 (italics Houston's). Wilson had been invited to comment on the letter before its mailing — Marty Mann (New York) to Wilson, 27 August 1946, but Bill was at the time vacationing in western Canada. It is not clear whether or not he saw the letter before its distribution.

The history of the National Committee for Education on Alcoholism (now the National Council on Alcoholism) is a separate research topic. The organization's papers — and many of Marty Mann's personal papers from the period — are on deposit at the George Arents Research Library at Syracuse University, Syracuse, NY., and I have researched in them as well as interviewed Ms. Mann *re* the history that follows. In the citations that follow here, I generally use only materials available in the A.A. archives as furnishing evidence of A.A.'s awareness. The fuller documentation available at Syracuse supports at depth the interpretation offered, and scholars interested specifically in this facet of A.A. history will surely wish to examine it also.

20   For the funding concern in the N.C.A. papers, *cf.* especially newspaper clippings from June through August 1946; for the tightrope: *Beverage Retail Weekly*, 8 January 1945, and *Mid-West Hotel Reporter*, 15 January 1945. The early funding concern is reflected in Harry S. (Detroit) to Wilson, 7 February 1945, and Wilson's response of 9 February 1945. A hint of its perdurance in memory may be found in the jacket blurb to Dr. Jellinek's classic study, *The Disease Concept of Alcoholism*: "'An honest publisher,' Professor Jellinek remarked one day, 'would warn on the jacket of this book that temperance societies and the alcoholic beverage industry should not read it. It will not make them happy.'"

21   Thomsen, p. 211; Marty Mann, tr. and interview of 15 November 1977; the point in the final sentence, if not sufficiently clear already, should become so as this study continues.

22   The Marty Mann publicity first appeared in the Pittsburgh, PA. newspapers: *cf.* both the *Post-Gazette* and the *Press* for 28 and 29 April 1944. The most extensive New York City coverage appeared in the *Herald-Tribune* of 9 October 1944; Ms. Mann was featured in a *TIME* story of 23 October 1944. That all this publicity did not at this point harm Mann's role within A.A. is clear, e.g., from a request for her help with a special *AAGV* issue on women: Maeve S. [*AAGV* staff member] (New York) to Mann, 29 March 1945. Also, the *AAGV* devoted its cover story and two other feature articles to Mann and the N.C.E.A. at the time of the Committee's formal founding: *AAGV* 1:5 (October 1944), 1–4, 8. This coverage was unequivocally favorable.

In 1944, visits by Wilson were given extensive coverage (without his last name) in the Dayton, Ohio *Journal*, 6 March, and the Parkersburg, WV *News*, 14 March; his full name identified as "co-founder of Alcoholics Anonymous" appeared in the Daytona Beach, FL *Journal* of 19 March.

The letterhead referred to was used for the crisis-provoking letter of 4 September 1946, cited above, note #19.

The phrase quoted at paragraph-end is from the Pittsburgh newspapers cited above. The whole point may be clearer from a *Herald-Tribune* quotation of Mann: "'To do this job . . . I had to discard anonymity, for I realized I could be more convincing if people could view me as living proof that an alcoholic can get well.'"

23   Tiebout's concern is clear from Wilson to Tiebout, 9 February 1945.

The appeal: Mann (New York) to Wilson, 27 August 1946, and the N.C.E.A. open letter of 4 September 1946, cited in note #19. The 27 August letter mentions a campaign of 11,000 letters, which it seems clear from context must have made some use of A.A. group listings.

The final citation is from Dick S. (New York) to Wilson, 4 September 1946.

24 Telegrams: Margaret B. (New York) to Wilson, 6 September 1946; Wilson (Victoria, BC) to Margaret B. and to Dr. Smith, both 6 September 1946.

The furor is described in a letter, Margaret B. (New York) to Bill and Lois Wilson, 16 September 1946. The A.A. press release, dated 12 September 1946, refers to "a special meeting [of] the Trustees of the Alcoholic Foundation on 10 September 1946."

Wilson never tried to deny or minimize his support of Mann and her efforts. He saw his mistake as allowing the use of his own name; *cf.*, e.g., Wilson to Abbo T., 22 November 1946: "I went along with Marty in dropping her anonymity and on everything else she has done to date."

The Mann episode is treated by Thomsen, pp. 331–332. My interpretation differs, but is supported by the documentation cited, as well as by my interview with Ms. Mann. Thomsen, I suspect, confused the N.C.E.A. flaps of 1946 and 1949, perhaps because apparently Wilson's memory did the same.

25 As vacation and the Hal Wallis meeting, the 16 and 17 September exchange of letters between Margaret B. and Wilson cited above; *re* his depression, among many citations in Wilson's later correspondence, Wilson to Jack Alexander, 31 March 1954, stresses its acuteness at this point; Margaret B. (New York) to Dr. Smith, 26 April 1946, expresses deep concern over its severity. Three of Wilson's letters from the period offer glimpses into its progress and relationship to occurrences within A.A.: Wilson to Dick S., 18 February 1946, to Royal S., 12 March 1946, and (Kaslo, BC), to Dick S., 1 September 1946; *cf.* also interviews of 16 November 1976 with Lois Wilson and of 15 November 1977 with Marty Mann. Thomsen, in his compression of Wilson's depression to 1940, finesses the matter here and thus makes little sense of Wilson's therapy with Tiebout: *cf.* pp. 334–337; for this connection, *cf.* especially Wilson to M.J.M., 3 March 1947.

26 Ted L. (?) to Wilson, 15 January 1944; *re The Lost Weekend*, Stanley M. Rinehart (New York) to Wilson, 20 December 1943, announced its publication on 27 January 1944 and asked A.A.'s help in promoting the book; Billy Wilder (Hollywood, CA) to Alcoholics Anonymous, 3 July 1944, asked for literature to assist in the movie production; Charles Jackson's name appears on the N.C.E.A. letterhead cited previously.

Newsreel coverage: *March of Time*, 26 April 1945, following up *September Remember*, best-selling novel by two pseudonymous A.A.s writing as "Eliot Taintor"; *R.K.O. Pathe*, "This Is America: Alcoholics Anonymous," feature by Ardis Smith, 3 July 1945; Margaret B. (New York) to Robert W. of *March of Time*, 20 June 1946, thanking for a second coverage; among radio stations broadcastings continuing A.A. series in 1945 were WWJ in Detroit and WTIC in Hartford — the latter, according to V.M.M. (East Hartford, CT) to Alcoholic Foundation, 3 January 1945, at the behest of the Travellers' Insurance Company which owned the station; the *Fortune* article, "A.A.," appeared in *Fortune* 43:2 (1 February 1951), 99–100, 138–144; no publisher is credited for the pamphlet, but it was distributed from A.A.'s General Service Office.

27   Nina Wilcox Putnam, "Let Me Tell You About the Miraculous Redemption of a Confirmed Drunkard," *True Confessions* 39: 52–57 (January 1946); on 1 June 1949, Walter S., editor of *True Confessions*, wrote Austin M. Davies, executive president of the American Psychological Association, asking his help in obtaining Wilson's own story for the magazine; there is no record of further correspondence, and the story did not appear;

Homer H. Shannon, "Alcoholics Anonymous: No Booze, BUT PLENTY OF BABES," *Confidential* 35: 54–56 (June 1954); the A.A. response is clear from Wilson to Betty E., ? June 1954, although the quotation is my paraphase from this plus John C. Ford, S. J. (Weston, MA) to Wilson, 17 May 1961 (on a different but similar matter), and Wilson's response, 6 September 1961.

28   Wilson (Victoria, BC) to Margaret B., 17 September 1946 (italics Wilson's).

29   Wilson to Mildred O., 14 November 1946; "We're Not Perfect Yet, Bill Cautions at Banquet," *AAGV* 2:7 (December 1945), 3; *cf.* Wilson to secretary of Richmond, VA, group, ? August 1949; "We Approach Maturity — by Bill," *AAGV* 6:5 (October 1949), 4–5.

30   Wilson, "To the Trustees: Concerning the Future of the Alcoholic Foundation," 1 November 1945; the quotations are from pp. 8, 7, and 9. Wilson's sense of his own "withdrawal" from A.A. is clear in Wilson to Royal S., 12 March 1946.

31   [Wilson], "Why Can't We Join A.A. Too!" *AAGV* 4:5 (October 1947), 3; Dowling (St. Louis) to Wilson, 5 November 1945; "Memorandum Concerning an A.A. General Service Office — by Bill," ? February 1949; the trustee letters of resignation are in the 1948 Alcoholic Foundation folder; Wilson to Smith, 17 February 1949; Smith (Akron) to Wilson, 14 March 1949, refused on the basis; "Do not have the feeling that this is a particularly guided thing to do now."

Anne C., interview of 7 September 1977, strongly stressed "Dr. Bob's coming to agree with Bill in the year before he died." In the early 1950's, she had privately published a pamphlet containing her evidence: I have been unable to locate a copy, but I found Anne's oral memories and evidence convincing. *Cf.* also tr. of wire recording of George H. to Wilson *re* Dr. Bob and the pressures on him in this matter (undated, but from context from 1948).

32   The reference to "writing out" is to *12&12*, to be treated just below.

33   Wilson's 1949 talk before the A.P.A. was published as "Society." The outline history of official medical attitudes to alcoholism can best be followed in the "Digest of Positions of the American Medical Association," no publisher, place, nor date given, but internally datable with each appropriate heading: 1956, pp. 12–18, "Alcohol — Consumption"; 1971, p. 38, "Alcohol and Alcoholism"; 1973, unpaged, "Alcoholism." "Illness" first appears in 1956; "complex disease" in 1967.

34   At depth, this whole monograph in its treatment of A.A. as an expression of *religious* ideas speaks to this point; for the meaning(s) of alcoholism as disease, *cf.* Chapter One, note #49.

35   Jellinek, *Disease Concept*, p. 157; the work quoted by Jellinek is A.D. Ullman, "The Psychological Mechanism of Alcohol Addiction," *QJSA* 13: 602–608 (1952); the post-Prohibition re-opening of the question within the A.M.A. occurred in 1950 — *cf.* p. 16 of the 1956 "Digest" cited above, note #33.

36 The A.A. understanding is that alcoholism is a condition that continues in its victims, albeit in a "state of remission" so long as they do not drink alcohol. My understanding of the "change" treated here was explored in depth with Lois Wilson, interview of 16 November 1976. At first — verbal — level, it had been an unwelcome idea to most A.A. oldtimers interviewed, yet it did seem they were objecting more to the word than to the concept explicated here and in the next paragraph. Lois, after discussion, confirmed the accuracy of this as Bill's point of view, especially after his experiences of 1940 and 1946: the phrase "state of remission" is from her and at her insistence — it seems to have been the key for Bill to the new distinction explored below.

37 *Living Sober* is the title of the second of the books added to the A.A. canon since Wilson's death (New York: Alcoholics Anonymous World Services, Inc., 1975). Its implications were discussed with Lois Wilson, interview of 16 November 1976, and with its anonymous author, Barry L., interview of 18 November 1976. The evolving distinction was also discussed with and confirmed by A.A. oldtimers interviewed, especially Chuck C., Ed. J., and Joe M. Chuck C. was at the time of the interview Hazelden's counselor-specialist in "relapses": this distinction was the essential foundation of his philosophical and therapeutic approach.

38 *Cf.* Harry M. Tiebout, "Direct Treatment of a Symptom," pamphlet published and distributed by the National Council on Alcoholism (New York, 1958); also Charles W. Crewe, "A Look at Relapse" (Center City, MN: Hazelden, 1974); and especially three volumes in the Hazelden "Caring Community" series, all anonymously authored and all (Center City, MN: Hazelden, 1975): "The New Awareness," "The New Understanding," and "Challenges to the New Way of Life."

39 *Cf.* citations in notes #37 and 38; *The A.A. Way of Life – a Reader by Bill* (New York: Alcoholics Anonymous World Services, Inc., 1967), published since 1972 as *As Bill Sees It*;
   The phrase "a way of life" appears in the "Foreword" to *12&12*, p. 15, without emphasis but clearly as theme.

40 "Report on the General Service Conference," *AAGV* 9:1 (June 1952), 3; full citation for *12&12* appears in the Bibliography, p. 416.

41 *12&12*: "a way of life," p. 15;
   the necessity of total deflation, pp. 21–24;
   "childish" traits, pp. 126–127;
   "humility" as foundation, p. 71.
   On the concept and term "recovering alcoholic," the best explicit treatment is Kenneth Anonymn (pseud.), *Understanding the Recovering Alcoholic* (Canfield, OH: Alba House, 1974). As early as April 1939, in the script for Morgan's presentation on Gabriel Heatter's "We The People," reference to "way to cure themselves" was crossed out and replaced by "method of recovery" in the opening description (by Heatter) of A.A. (Copy of script in A.A. archives.)

42 *12&12*, pp. 64, 59–60; *cf.* "This Matter of Humility — by Bill," *AAGV* 17:1 (June 1961).

43 *12&12*, p. 71; *cf.* p. 30; for the "strength out of weakness" theme: pp. 21, 22, 37, 63, 76, 96, 129; *cf.* also *AACA*, p. 46: "Such is the paradox of A.A.

regeneration: strength arising out of complete defeat and weakness, the loss of one's old life as a condition for finding a new one" — reprinted, *ABSI*, p. 49; also the following themes in the Wilson correspondence:
"pain is merely the touchstone of growth": to Adam C., 16 December 1957, to George ?, 3 April 1958; to Lisa N., 25 July 1960;
"A.A. is nothing but capitalized grief": to Ethel B., 5 January 1950;
"A.A. is not grounded so much on success as upon failure": to Raylene C., 17 October 1949, to Charles H., 17 November 1955.
A fascinating personal sense of this appears in Wilson to Sam Shoemaker, 3 January 1950: "To be entirely truthful, my attitude on anonymity and the like is far more a necessity than a virtue. Despite some spiritual progress, most of us A.A.'s are still so confoundedly egocentric that we cannot endure the thought of permanent leadership. You see there are so many runners-up that one gets knocked down if he doesn't stand out of the way. In this respect, our vices actually conspire to make us a quite perfect society composed nonetheless of very imperfect and misshapen people. My own rating in this regard is still very high."

44   Wilson to Mary B., 26 August 1957; *12&12*, pp. 43, 50, 65, 72, 118.
"Acceptance" as a key theme in Alcoholics Anonymous is best witnessed to by "The Serenity Prayer," often referred to (outside of A.A.) as "The A.A. Prayer": "God grant me the serenity to accept the things I cannot change, the courage to change the things I can, and the wisdom to know the difference." For the story of its adoption by A.A., *cf. AACA*, p. 196. Further, "Acceptance" is the heading for fourteen passages in *ABSI*, dating from 1940 to 1966; *cf.* also "What Is Acceptance? — by Bill," *AAGV* 18:10 (March 1962).

45   *12&12*, pp. 77, 54, 119; *cf.* p. 95; also "The Next Frontier: Emotional Sobriety — by Bill," *AAGV* 14:8 (January 1958); Wilson to Mary P., 14 April 1954; Wilson to Jack Alexander, 31 March 1954; Wilson to Caryl Chessman, 3 May 1954: the correspondence between Wilson and the condemned Chessman was instituted at the urging of Jack Alexander; the common theme underlying it implicitly accepted by all three was the similarity between the alcoholic and the criminal psychopath/sociopath in this matter of "demand";
for Wilson feeling such demands were made on him by others, *cf.*, e.g., Wilson to Bob H., 14 April 1959, where he blames this as keeping him from participating in A.A. meetings "as others do."

46   *12&12*, pp. 37, 61, 63, 108 (italics Wilson's); *cf.* p. 84; the "going it alone" reference furnishes the clearest intrusion of specifically Oxford Group thought and experience in *12&12*, and it is an intriguing one, given the history we have seen. The passage continues: "It is worth noting that people of very high spiritual development almost always insist on *checking* with friends or spiritual advisors the *guidance* they feel they have received from God," pp. 61–62, italics added.

47   *12&12*, pp. 109–110; *cf.* also "The Greatest Gift of All — by Bill," *AAGV* 14:7 (December 1957), in which "spiritual awakening" so appreciated is the topic; also [Wilson], "'The Spiritual Experience': It's [*sic*] Therapeutic Value to A.A.," prepared for and published as "The Fellowship of Alcoholics Anonymous," in R. J. Catanzaro (ed.), *Alcoholism* (Springfield, IL: Chas. C. Thomas, 1968), pp. 116–124.

48   *Cf.*, e.g., Wilson to Dorothy M., 1 April 1952; to Charles W., 3 June 1952;

to Jeff K., 1 April 1953; to Gladys B., 6 April 1953; to Al S., 13 May 1953. The "experience" to which Wilson most explicitly adverted in these letters was that of his 1946 depression — one reason for the slight bending of strict chronology here.

Although from later, the whole matter is most clearly and expansively explained in a five-page letter, complete with diagram, Wilson to Mary B., 26 August 1957.

49 The "immaturity" critique will be treated in Chapter Nine, pp. 215–219, with full citations.

50 Thomsen, pp. 334–337, the direct phrase from p. 337; the theme recurs throughout Wilson's correspondence, *cf.*, e.g., letters cited in note #48 above;

The Freudian understanding will be explained and explored below in Chapter Nine.

The best source for Tiebout's referral of Marty Mann is her tr.; this point is recalled in repetitive asides because the circumstance is so significant to the sense of "being different" as this came to be understood by both A.A. and Tiebout.

51 *Cf.* especially *12&12*, pp. 126–127; the correspondence on which I draw especially here is Tiebout (Greenwich, CT) to Wilson, 13 October 1950, 3 November 1950, and 12 July 1951; Wilson to Tiebout of 18 October 1950, 9 November 1950, and 23 July 1951; the unsent Wilson to Tiebout is dated 1 July 1951, but clearly from context is in response to Tiebout's of 12 July: it is thus clear that a digit has been dropped, and that the eventually sent letter of 23 July is Wilson's more considered response.

52 The cultural context from plays such as *The Moon Is Blue* and movies such as *The Outlaw* to the whole atmosphere of "the Eisenhower decade," from lowered hemlines to the dressing of even very young boys in long pants. The message as conveyed in advertisements for alcoholic beverages is my subjective impression from immersion in newspapers and magazines of the period. There is no direct evidence that A.A. explicitly adverted to all this, yet such ads adjoin many clippings in the A.A. scrapbooks, and the perception seems clearly behind the 1949 renewed N.C.E.A. push — *cf.*, Marty Mann, tr. as reported by Professor George Gordon who found this interpretation congenial — Prof. Gordon was at the time chairman of the Department of Communication Sciences at Hofstra University.

53 The earliest foreshadowing of this turn, revealing Wilson's ambivalence here about the responsibility of A.A. as A.A., occurs in Wilson to Mildred O., 14 November 1946.

54 The Alcoholic Foundation in 1938: *AACA.* p. 151; *cf.* above, pp. 66–67, the "no outside contributions" decisions: *AACA*, pp. 203–204; Tradition Seven is discussed in its historical development in *AACA*, pp. 110–114; the function of the trustees is clear from the "Alcoholic Foundation" documents of these years. Wilson's friendship with the trustees does not seem to require specific citation: *cf.* correspondence in "Alcoholic Foundation" files, recall Dr. Strong as his brother-in-law, and note also trustee selection by internal choice and A.A.'s financial support of A. LeRoy Chipman, in his declining years — the last and the whole point confirmed by NW, interview, 5 April 1977.

"Gratitude" as an obligation of the "Responsibility" of "Maturity" begins as an A.A. theme that will increase in importance through the 1950s with the *AAGV* "Tradition Week Issue," 6:6 (November 1949), in which the short-form of the Traditions was first published. Its tie with American Thanksgiving Day has continued each year in November, which is traditionally "Tradition Month" in Alcoholics Anonymous.

55 "Cleveland, Here We Come!" *AAGV* 6:12 (May 1950), 3; *cf.* Wilson to Trustees of the Alcoholic Foundation, 11 February 1950, explaining his intention; "May Humility Be the Keynote," *AAGV* 7:2 (July 1950), 3 (italics Wilson's); "We Come of Age — by Bill," *AAGV* 7:4 (September 1950), 3–11; "Joe Goes to the Conference," *ibid.*, 12–15.

"Hardly settled": the howl that went up from the Akronites and especially from Henrietta Seiberling still echoes: *cf.* letter of HS (New York) to Al ?, dated only "Saturday 1950" but clearly from late in the year. The kindest interpretation of its contents would be "serenely vicious," as HS equates Wilson with "the devil" come to "destroy" A.A.; also the somewhat more restrained open letter of HS, "A Message to A.A.'s," dated only "1950"; Roy S., (Glen Ridge, NJ) [A.A. trustee], to Leonard Harrison [chairman of the trustees], 28 December 1950; supporting Wilson are many letters: worthy of note are those from Dorothy G. [group secretary] (Chicago) to Leonard V. Strong, 15 January 1951; Leila P. [g.s.] (Frankfort, KY) to Strong, 17 January 1951; Harry S. [g.s.] (Decatur, IL) to Strong, 26 January 1951.

56 Tiebout to Wilson, 13 October 1950; Wilson to Tiebout, 18 October 1950.

57 "Your Third Legacy — by Dr. Bob and Bill," *AAGV* 7:7 (December 1950), 6–9; the direct quotation is from 8–9. Wilson's use of the imminently dying Smith's name should be noted, and the deep student may wish to compare this proposal with "What Is the Third Legacy — by Bill," *AAGV* 12:2 (July 1955), 5–11; *cf.* also the testimony of Anne C. and George H., reported in note #31 above.

58 Tiebout to Wilson, 3 November 1950.

59 Wilson to Tiebout, 9 November 1950.

60 "To Serve Is To Live — by Bill," and "Conference Report," *AAGV* 8:1 (June 1951), 3–5 and 6–11; the direct quotations are from 6–7.

61 Tiebout to Wilson, 12 July 1951.

62 Wilson to Tiebout, 23 July 1951; the final quotation, directly from the unsent letter misdated 1 July, was muted in the letter actually sent.

63 General Service Conference themes from each year's "Final Report"; the Bernard B. Smith quotation from "Report: A.A. General Service Conference," *AAGV* 9:1 (June 1952), 4; the Wilson quotation from "Third G.S.C.: Final Report," p. 1. "Themes" of the G.S.C. were formally denominated as such only from 1962, and "keynote addresses" since 1968. Prior to these dates, the terms were applied informally by "Final Report" editor Ralph B. (NW, interview of 5 January 1978). My use of the terms in this paragraph is thus informal but appropriately accurate as far as the meanings conveyed and significance inferred.

64 Conference theme from "Final Report," p. 1; Jack G., (Santa Monica, CA) to Wilson, 9 July 1954; Wilson to Jack G., 20 December 1954 — this response directly to a Jack G. letter of 23 November: the dialogue had continued through the last half of 1954.

For the formalization of the General Service Board, *cf.* "Landmarks in A.A. History," *AACA*, p. ix; also "Our Final Great Decision — by Bill," *AAGV* 11:1 (June 1954), 10–11; the actual minutes of the General Service Board are closed to citation.

Re-naming the Foundation had been considered, by some, for at least a decade.

65   *Cf.* "Our Final Great Decision," *ut supra*; also the whole of *AACA*.

66   *Cf.* above, pp. 46–47.

67   Wilson to Scott B., 4 December 1950, and perhaps most clearly to Charles W., 3 June 1952: "As to changing the Steps themselves, or even the text of the A.A. book, I am assured by many that I could certainly be excommunicated if a word were touched. It is a strange fact of human nature that when a spiritually centered movement starts and finally adopts certain principles, these finally freeze absolutely solid. But what can't be done respecting the Steps themselves — or any part of the A.A. book — I can make a shift by writing these pieces which I hope folks will like."

Wilson eventually felt that the same had happened to *12&12*; *cf.* Wilson to Howard E., 6 February 1961: "As time passes, our book literature has a tendency to get more and more frozen — a tendency for conversion into something like dogma. This is a trait of human nature which I'm afraid we can do little about. We may as well face the fact that A.A. will always have its fundamentalists, its absolutists, and its relativists."

Some of these changes took place slowly, through the sixteen printings of the 1st edition of *AA*; e.g., "ex-alcoholic" to "ex-problem drinker" first appeared in the 11th printing, June 1947, *cf.* p. 28 (1st ed.).

68   Memorandum, undated, "Revision of 'Big Book': points for Consideration," in A.A. archives: *AA* (2nd ed.), pp. v–x; *cf.* also Wilson to Ralph B., 29 July 1953, where in listing "five faults" of the first batch of stories collected for this purpose, a problem noted in our Chapter Three discussion of the aims of the book may be seen rising to haunt: "The hard core of A.A., maybe 50%, consists of people coming from substantial backgrounds. . . . A.A. experience shows that we have to identify with people on the basis of *where they think they are* — not where *we think* they *ought* to be." (italics Wilson's). It seems in response to this perception that the "High Bottom" section was specifically included.

69   Memoranda in A.A. archives: "Geographical Breakdown of the 37 Stories in the Second Edition" and "Breakdown of Stories in 2nd edition by Sex and Occupation": "1 Doctor, 2 Lawyers, 6 Housewives, 1 Patent Expert, 2 Organizational Executives, 1 Upholsterer, 2 Journalists, 1 Sculptor, 1 Accountant, 1 Promoter, 1 Real Estate, 1 Salesman, 1 Insurance Investigator, 1 Truck Driver, 1 Charwoman, 1 Beautician, 1 Stock Farmer, 1 Furniture Dealer, 1 Advertising Executive, 1 Insurance, 1 Soldier, 1 Educator, 2 Writers, 1 Banker, 1 Surgeon, 1 Industrial Executive, 1 Buyer." The additional information on the "patent expert," "upholsterer," and "accountant" cannot be cited more specifically without jeopardizing the anonymity of living persons.

Some further information is available from a number of the stories not used. The ten points considered were: "1. Title Impression, 2. Drinking Pattern,

3. Personality Type, 4. Family Status, 5. Education, 6. Social Status, 7. Employment, 8. Story Tone, 9. Length of Sobriety, 10. Spiritual result." The stories unused do not reveal a profile different from that of the stories used: rejection seems due mainly to (1) too close parallel to another story that was used; (2) failure of the story to meet the "Audience" criteria set down in "Points for Consideration": "Since the audience for the book is likely to be newcomers, anything — from point of view of content or style — that might offend or alienate those who are not familiar with the program should be carefully eliminated."

Some information in this paragraph and this note is also based on a letter from Tom P. (New York) to writer, 15 December 1976. Mr. P., an editor for the second edition, was too ill to be interviewed, but his son (also Tom P.) kindly took my questions, asked them of his father, and wrote up his responses.

70   *AACA*, p. 102; *cf. ABSI*, p. 175; the more telling sociological studies have been cited above, Chapter Three, note #41. This point was also discussed with Professor Milton Maxwell, A.A. trustee and sociologist.

71   Interviews with Chuck C. and Ed. J., 27 March 1976; with Lois Wilson, 16 November 1976; with Joe M., 13 May 1977; letter of Tom P., 15 December 1976. A significant point made vividly clear in most of these (and other) interviews was that degree of "bottom" was judged more by whence one had fallen to it than by what happened *at* it. This understanding of course conformed well with "bottom" as primarily *internal, cf.* above, pp. 60–61.

The most perceptive summary by an oldtimer seems Tom P.'s from the letter cited: "A.A. certainly has turned out to be a middle-class, largely white phenomenon. But at the time we were selecting our stories we were not enough aware of this trend to be concerned with it as a problem. I think in those days we felt that our spread was pretty broad and democratic."

How A.A. has tried to correct for this in the 1976 third edition of *AA*, and the fellowship's current membership profile, are matters beyond the scope of this monograph.

For recent sociological opinion on the social class of alcoholics, *cf.* M. B. Jones and B. L. Borland, "Social Mobility and Alcoholism: A Comparison of Alcoholics with their Fathers and Brothers," *JSA* 36: 62-68 (1975); David Robinson, *From Drinking to Alcoholism: A Sociological Commentary* (London: John Wiley & Sons, 1976); also the citations in note #41 to Chapter Three, above, p. 332.

72   *Cf.* especially "Our Final Great Decision — by Bill," *AAGV* 11:1 (June 1954), 10–11; "The Significance of St. Louis: A.A. Comes of Age — by Bill," *AAGV* 11:11 (April 1955), 6–7;

The direct quotations are from Wilson to David H., 16 May 1955, as aptly summarizing "Four O'Clock Sunday Afternoon," *AACA*, pp. 223–234; *cf.* also "What Is the Third Legacy? — by Bill," *AAGV* 12:2 (July 1955), 11: "Alcoholics Anonymous was at last safe — even from me." The theme was significant enough for Thomsen to pick up *verbatim* as the climactic convention theme, pp. 353–354: perhaps the best witness to its importance in Wilson's memory.

VI   1955–1971

1   This history is of course beyond the scope of *AACA*; Thomsen gives it scant attention, pp. 354–368.

2   The opening quotation is from Wilson to John M., 3 September 1958.
It is under this sensitivity that the only archive restriction beyond the obvious one of anonymity was imposed by A.A. on this research, and it is a restriction this book shall respect. An evaluation of this restriction and more detailed citation for many points to follow appear in the dissertation from which this book is derived.

3   The distinction is clearer in Wilson to Pat B., ? December 1957: ". . . how can I presume to say that my detailed theological convictions are correct? In this search I've had the advantage of what seems to have been a very genuine and illuminating spiritual experience, together with many later encounters with the psychic realm, both personal and by observation."
There is significant Wilson-Heard correspondence from 1948 through 1954, and a telling Wilson-Huxley correspondence through the philosopher's death in 1964; citable is Laura Huxley (Los Angeles, CA) to Wilson, 26 February 1964, replying to Wilson's note of condolence at Aldous's death: "Do you know the profound admiration and affection that Aldous had for you? When he described you, he would say 'a modern saint.'"

4   The act of faith as an intellectual "bottom experience" will be clarified in Chapter Eight's analysis of the "anti-intellectualism" of Alcoholics Anonymous, *cf*. pp. 188–191.

5   *Cf*: J.A.M. Meerloo, "Artificial Ecstasy: A Study of the Psychosomatic Aspects of Drug Addiction," *Journal of Nervous and Mental Disease* 115: 246–266 (1952);
E. S. Carpenter, "Alcohol in the Iroquois Dream Quest," *American Journal of Psychiatry* 116: 148–151 (1959);
C. Savage, "LSD, Alcoholism and Transcendence," *Journal of Nervous and Mental Disease* 135: 429–435 (1962);
K. E. Godfrey, "LSD Therapy," in Catanzaro (ed.), *Alcoholism*, pp. 237–252, with complete (to 1968) bibliography;
J. O. Cole and R. S. Ryback, "Pharmacological Therapy," in Tarter and Sugerman (eds.), *Alcoholism*, pp. 721–724, offer the most recent brief report on this research and its literature.

6   The correspondences between Wilson and Drs. Abram Hoffer and Humphrey Osmond make clear this concern as basic; the Hoffer and Osmond correspondences are closed to citation; *cf*. also the treatment, below, of "responsibility."

7   A parallel and earlier Wilson interest, again guided by Hoffer and Osmond, was with leuco-adrenochrome. Most adequate and complete on the B-3 point, which is mentioned (barely) by Thomsen, p. 359, are three "Communication[s] to A.A.'s Physicians: *The Vitamin B-3 Therapy* (privately printed, 1965, 1968, 1971), available to anyone with a serious medical interest from P. O. Box 125, Oyster Bay, NY 11771. The 1971 "Communication" contains a letter from Lois Wilson to the three doctors especially promoting this research with B-3. The whole merits reading for several of the points here, but I quote only the final paragraph: "Bill's great hope was that continued research would find a means whereby those thousands of alcoholics who want to stop drinking but are too ill to grasp the A.A. program could be released from their bondage and enabled to join A.A." (p. 4).

"reputed to have said": according to Dr. Russell Smith, interviews of 12 and 13 June 1977; Wilson himself said virtually this in 1967, at Lake Orion, MI — a tape of this presentation is in the writer's possession.

8   "Final Report of the 18th General Service Conference of Alcoholics Anonymous" (1968), p. 18; Wilson's concurrence is clear, e.g., from Wilson to Helen F., 11 July 1966; *cf*. also Minutes of the General Service Board for July 1966: "The Board recognized the need for keeping Bill's identification with B-3 separate from the business of the G.S.O. and that the office continue to refer inquiries *re* B-3 to Bill's upstate address and that no A.A.W.S. employees should be identified with Bill's correspondence and Bill's letterheads. . . ." (Extracted from closed "Minutes" by NW to explain closure).

9   The immaturity critique as applied to A.A. as well as to alcoholics is discussed with citations in Chapter Nine; it is reflected in Tiebout (Greenwich, CT) to Wilson, 28 December 1961, which will be quoted shortly.

The consistency of Wilson's theme in pushing for the trustee ratio-change as an expression of the "maturity" of "responsibility" is especially clear from letters to Jack T., 2 May 1958; to Jim S., 9 June 1959; to Dave B., 14 July 1965; to Nancy O., 18 October 1965.

10   *Cf*. correspondence cited in the preceding note; G.S.C. themes from each year's "Final Report"; the final quotation is from Wilson to Jack T., 2 May 1958. On "themes," *cf*. note #63 to Chapter Five, above.

11   Wilson to Jim S., 9 June 1959.

12   Tiebout (Greenwich, CT) to Wilson, 28 December 1961.

13   Wilson to Tiebout, 4 November 1964; Wilson to Jim M., 23 November 1964.

14   Tiebout (Greenwich, CT) to Wilson, 11 January 1965.

15   Wilson to Tiebout, 19 January 1965 (italics Wilson's).

16   "Landmarks in A.A. History," *AACA*, p. x; "Final Report of the 15th G.S.C." (1965), p. 10; in his Conference presentation, Wilson reviewed the "history of fear" he had outlined for Tiebout in his 19 January letter: *cf*. pp. 8–9; the complete 25-page text of Wilson's convention talk: "In A.A.'s Thirtieth Year: Responsibility Is Our Theme," is available in the A.A. archives. Its style as well as its content make very clear the depth of Wilson's feeling about this theme and point. Most noteworthy is his foundation of the responsibility for responsibility in "gratitude" — *cf*. especially p. 12.

The shift in stress from the percentage who eventually "got the program" to the number who "walked into our midst and then out again" is clear from the publication of "The Dilemma of No Faith — by Bill," *AAGV* 17:11 (April 1961), 4; the first hint of the shift in Wilson's correspondence occurred in Wilson to Howard E., 12 August 1958, which fits the timing and linkage noted in note #9 above.

17   "Landmarks in A.A. History," *AACA*, p. x.

18   Arthur H. Cain, "Alcoholics Anonymous: cult or cure?" *Harper's* 226:48–52 (February 1963);

Jerome Ellison, "Alcoholics Anonymous: Dangers of Success," *The Nation* 198: 212–214 (1964);

Arthur H. Cain, "Alcoholics *Can* Be Cured — Despite A.A.," *Saturday Evening Post* 237: 6, 8 (19 September 1965).

19   Wilson to Betty R., 11 February 1963.

20   Morris E. Chafetz and Harold W. Demone, Jr., *Alcoholism and Society* (New York: Oxford University Press, 1962), pp. 146–165; direct quotations from pp. 161–162.

21   Chafetz and Demone, pp. 163, 165.

22   Cain, "Cult or Cure," 48, 51, 49, 50, 52.

Cain's initial impetus and expanded critique are available in book form: Arthur King (pseud.), *Seven Sinners* (New York: Harcourt, Brace and World, 1961) is a novelization of his Columbia dissertation, otherwise unpublished;

Arthur H. Cain, *The CURED Alcoholic* (New York: John Day, 1964) expands the critique on the basis of response to his first article.

23   Wilson to Betty R., 11 February 1963; Cain, "Despite A.A.," 6.

24   Ellison, *op. cit.*, 212–214; Cain, "Despite A.A.," 8.

25   Interviews with Nell Wing, 6 April 1977; with Lois Wilson, 7 April 1977; with John C. Ford, S. J., 12 April 1977; "How It Seemed to One Biased Alcoholic Observer," *AAGV*, 27:5 (October 1970), 16; *AACA*, p. xi.

26   *AA*, p. 62; on this deeper meaning of "unity," *cf.* Chapter Five, note #16; the ensuing discussion should also make clearer that point.

27   "Do You Think You're *Different?*" (New York: Alcoholics Anonymous World Services, Inc., 1976); for a history of the "special group" concern in the Wilson correspondence, *cf.* Wilson to Larry J., 9 June 1942; to Frank L., 24 June 1949; to Mary H., 3 March 1960; to Rose ?, 23 April 1962. The importance of this principle to others is witnessed by a letter from John C. Ford, S. J. (Weston, MA) to Wilson, 8 June 1957.

28   The "common reminder" appears nowhere in print; in my research experience, its use is less common in the Boston area than in New York City and the mid-West.

29   There is extensive but closed correspondence on this topic in the A.A. archives; John C. Ford, S.J., has given permission to cite his letter to Wilson of 8 June 1957. The Roman Catholic "Calix Society" is one expression of the phenomenon here described; it is explained in William J. Conroy, "Calix — What and Why," *Columbia* 57:4 (April 1977), 30–33.

30   The direct quotation is from the pamphlet, "Meeting List (January 1977), Central Service Committee, Boston, MA," p. 2. It is often read at the beginning of meetings of Alcoholics Anonymous.

31   Based on diverse observations and interviews.

32   This criticism was a major point of Ellison, "Dangers of Success"; the "legend" is hearsay, and no available documentation supports it, but *cf.* note #33 below.

33   Deeper appreciation of the point may be aided by the following documentation:

Wilson to Dr. Conrad S., 18 July 1943: "I am astonished at the apparent prevalence of alcoholism among the colored people as you report it. While race prejudice will be an obstacle, I think you can depend on most A.A. groups doing their best for these people."

Wilson to Joe D., 22 October 1943, repeats this perception, noting of the "stark fact" that "whites refuse to mingle with blacks socially": "Nor can they be coerced or persuaded to do so, even alcoholics! I know, because I once tried here in New York and got so much slapped down that I realized no amount of insistence would do any good."

The first "Negro" A.A. group was organized in St. Louis on 24 January 1945; others followed in Washington, DC, and Valdosta, GA, in September 1945 — Torrence S. (St. Louis) to Secretary, Alcoholic Foundation, 20 October 1945; Margaret B. (New York) to Torrence S., 25 October 1945.

At the Third General Service Conference of A.A. in 1953, Wilson answered a question concerning "interracial groups": "With whatever personal persuasions we have, each of us wants these good people to have, as far as possible, exactly the same opportunity we had. But we do have a lot of different customs and situations in different parts of this country, and this is no place to get up and tell ourselves how broadminded we are. The sole question is this: How can each locality, from the point of view of its own customs, afford a better opportunity to colored people to get well?" ("Final Report," p. 22).

In a 1959 letter, Wilson to Bob P., 24 April 1959, Wilson used the example of "the race question" to illustrate his point that "While A.A. affects [*sic*] spectacular transformations in the lives of all of us, it by no means makes us perfectly attuned human beings."

34 *Cf.* above, pp. 115–116. The internal development may be traced in the following Wilson correspondence: to Larry J., 9 June 1942; to Frank L., 24 June 1949; to Mrs. J. M., 8 December 1959; to Sue K., 19 September 1960; to Lib S., 7 November 1968; to Katie W., 10 April 1969. The concern quieted for a time after the 1952 G.S.C. theme, "Our Primary Purpose," only to reawaken in late 1957 when intensive correspondence with Betty and Larry T., of Santa Monica, CA, led Wilson to publish "Problems Other Than Alcohol," *AAGV* 14:8 (February 1958), 1–5, since distributed in pamphlet form by A.A.; its theme is well set forth in Wilson to Jack T., 3 December 1957: "In the case of narcotics, I think the issue is confused because of the kinship that to a certain extent there is in the problems. Individuals having a double problem ought to do what they can for the narcotic [*sic*], there is no doubt about that. But some of these folks fail to realize that the simon-pure addict is only a 1st cousin of a drunk — not his brother." The concern re-opened under the impact of increasing drug use in the early 1960s, as questions in the G.S.C. "Conference Reports" of especially 1963 and 1964 make clear. In response, "A Group of Doctors in A.A." published through A.A. the pamphlet, "Sedatives, Stimulants, and the Alcoholic" (New York: A.A. Publishing, 1964), since 1976 published in the same form as "The A.A. Member and Drug Abuse." This pamphlet opens: "Alcoholics Anonymous is a program for alcoholics who seek freedom from alcohol. It is not a program against drugs."

35 This was the specific concern of Betty and Larry T.: *cf.* Wilson to Betty T., 20 October 1957; to Betty and Larry T., 25 November 1957.

"many letters and one key article": *cf.* note #34 above.

In perusing the Conference minutes through the early 1960s, the readiness with which the delegates followed Wilson on this point while resisting him on the trustee ratio-change is striking.

36 "Problems Other Than Alcohol," 2 (italics Wilson's); Wilson to Betty and Larry T., 25 November 1957; Wilson to Betty T., 20 October 1957; Wilson to T.s, 25 November 1957 (italics Wilson's).

37 *Cf.* correspondence cited in notes #34 and 35 above; the *name* concern is also especially clear in Wilson to Paul ?, 8 October 1957; to Rose R., 23 April 1962.

Final resolution was sought at the 1969 General Service Conference: *cf.* "Final Report," pp. 16–17: "Problem of A.A. Member and Pills: Strength of A.A. is Single-Mindedness." Yet the 1976 change of pamphlet title cited at the end of note #34 above, seems to testify that the matter had not yet been settled. Note that the change is in both its terms to more restriction: from "Sedatives and Stimulants" to "Drug Abuse," and from "the Alcoholic" to "the A.A. Member."

38 Many who recognize that the *program* of Alcoholics Anonymous affords the best hope of recovery to those addicted to drugs other than alcohol have argued that A.A. should therefore open the doors of *fellowship* membership to non-alcoholics so addicted. This is a difficult and emotional point, as discussion in which the author participated at the Rutgers University Summer School of Alcohol Studies in July 1978 amply attested. Cogent arguments may be offered on each side of the question. Yet awareness of A.A.'s history conjoined with awareness of the histories of other such endeavors (the Washingtonians, for example) raises the deeper question: would Alcoholics Anonymous *still be* "Alcoholics Anonymous" if it did not set this example of accepting limitation? Could the program itself survive if the fellowship ceased itself to live its program?

39 *AACA*, p. 127.

40 The theme of "strength from weakness" was examined above, p. 125 and especially note #43 to it; the point will be further explored in Chapter Nine.

41 The best single citation for this understanding of life in community is Roberto Mangabeira Unger, *Knowledge and Politics* (New York: Free Press, 1975), here truly the work as a whole, but *cf.* especially pp. 215–222 on "the paradox of sociability" and the final chapter, "The Theory of Organic Groups," pp. 236–295, and most especially within this large segment pp. 259–262. "Joyous pluralism" will be treated further in Chapter Nine.

42 Bill D. and the sense of "being different" as "denial" have been explored above, *cf.* pp. 38, 59–60; on Wilson's attitude to how his own sense of "being different" was related to his alcoholism, *cf.* in Chapter One, p. 18, and especially note #36 to that quotation.

43 The literature here is immense: to cite only the most telling of the sociological (the psychiatric and psychological, as extensive, will be treated in Chapter Nine):

R. F. Bales, "The Therapeutic Role of Alcoholics Anonymous as seen by a Sociologist," *QJSA* 5: 267–278 (1944):

M. A. Maxwell, "Interpersonal Factors in the Genesis and Treatment of Alcohol Addiction," *Social Forces* 29: 443–448 (1951);

R. L. Hoggson, *Alcoholics Anonymous: A Study in Solidarity*, unpublished dissertation, sociology, Fordham University, 1952;
William Madsen, *The American Alcoholic* (Springfield, IL: C. C. Thomas, 1974); ch. 9, "A.A.: Birds of a Feather," pp. 154–197, explores much of the literature on "community" in relation to A.A. — *cf.* especially pp. 167 ff.

44 The quotation is directly from Anne C., interview of 7 September 1977; it was also implicit in the interview of Henrietta Seiberling of 6 April 1977; Wilson marveling over the theme of this paragraph is a constant thread in his correspondence.

45 These two images recur with striking frequency in the Wilson correspondence; they were confirmed as "favorites" of Wilson by Nell Wing, interview, 16 July 1976, and Lois Wilson, interview, 16 November 1976;
the direct quotations are from Wilson to Stephen S., ? ? 1957, and Wilson to Venn V., 16 June 1952 (italics Wilson's).

46 Wilson to Mary M., 24 August 1964; Wilson to Eleanor D., 1 July 1966 (italics Wilson's).

47 "Who Is A Member of Alcoholics Anonymous — by Bill," *AAGV* 3:3 (August 1946), 3; Wilson to John G., 9 October 1967 (italics Wilson's); Wilson, "Fellowship," p. 468. Lois Wilson, interview of 16 November 1976, opined that Bill might here have been quoting himself. "Tolerance" as a special theme of Dr. Bob Smith, perhaps in self-conscious compensation for the rigidities in his own personality, is well attested to in all the literature, especially "Last Major Talk" and A.A.'s obituary pamphlet on its co-founders: "The Co-Founders of Alcoholics Anonymous" (New York: A.A.W.S., 1972). Anne C., interview of 7 September 1977, identified this expression as "Dr. Bob's second-favorite saying." (The first, of course, was "Keep It Simple.")
Further, *AAGV* 34:6 (November 1977), an issue designated "Classic Grapevine," chose to reproduce as most representative of Dr. Bob his brief article from its July 1944 issue: "On Cultivating Tolerance."

48 Wilson to Frank S., 11 March 1963.

NOTES TO PART TWO: THE INTRODUCTION

1 *Cf.* Richard R. Peabody, *The Common Sense of Drinking* (Boston: Little, Brown, 1931); and Edward A. Strecker and Francis T. Chambers, Jr., *Alcohol: One Man's Meat* (New York: Macmillan, 1938). Jim Bishop, *The Glass Crutch* (New York: Doubleday, Doran, 1945), is a biography of William Wynne Wister, a non-A.A. lay therapist whose personal history will make clear some of the unique strengths of A.A. Strecker (a psychiatrist) and Chambers (a non-A.A. lay therapist) will be cited as appropriate in Chapters Eight and Nine. The "acceptability" point will also be well covered by the citations in those chapters. The reference in the preceding paragraph to "passing mention" is to note #53 to Chapter Four, p. 343, above.
I have not made the virtually impossible attempt to analyze herein all twentieth-century approaches to the treatment of alcoholism. The insights of those that I have examined, both religious and secular, seem well-presented — as do many of the insights of A.A. — in one short book that is no doubt too often overlooked because of its dated rhetoric: Charles Follen Parker, *Inebriety: Its*

Source, Prevention, and Cure (Philadelphia: Union Press, 189 [8?]). Any interested in exploring further the specific uniqueness of Alcoholics Anonymous might well begin by reading this book and investigating the history of the Washingtonians, concerning whom I treat in Chapter Five, above, pp. 115–117.

2   The history narrated in Part One as well as the volume and diversity of the correspondence on which it is to a large part based well attests to this point. For treatment and evaluation of the other main expressions of "the ideas that are Alcoholics Anonymous," *cf.* Appendix A, following Chapter Nine.

ALCOHOLICS ANONYMOUS AND AMERICAN CULTURE

1   The "long form" of A.A.s Third Tradition reads: "Our membership ought to include all who suffer from alcoholism. Hence we may refuse none who wish to recover. Nor ought A.A. membership ever depend upon money or conformity. Any two or three alcoholics gathered together for sobriety may call themselves an A.A. Group, provided that, as a group, they have no other affiliation." (*AA*, p. 565). For "other problems" and "special groups," cf. above, pp. 146–150.

2   The significance of A.A.'s 1955 "Coming of Age" convention is treated above, pp. 131–134. Membership figures are drawn from an A.A. General Service Office document drawn up by Jim H. Their derivation and validity are discussed by Leach and Norris, "Factors," in Kissin and Begleiter, pp. 443–449; in *AACA*, pp. ix and 31, the 1957 membership was put at 200,000, following a substantially justified practice of adjusting individual group listings.

   On A.A.'s international diffusion, beyond Leach and Norris, *op. cit.*, pp. 449–451, cf. *AACA* pp. 26–31, 83–86.

3   The generalizations in the paragraphs that follow may be checked in two kinds of sources: retrospectives and text-books. Of the former, I have used especially the appropriate volumes of *This Fabulous Century*, by the editors of TIME-LIFE books (New York: Time, Inc., 1969); of the latter, especially Oscar Handlin, *The History of the United States* (New York: Holt, Rinehart & Winston, 1968), vol. II, p. 354–591, hereinafter cited "Handlin, *HUS*." The responsibility for interpretations, however, is my own.

4   *Cf.* Frederick Lewis Allen, *Only Yesterday* (New York: Harper & Row, 1931), especially Chapters 12 and 13; Broadus Mitchell, *Depression Decade* (New York: Harper & Row, 1947), pp. 3–49; John Kenneth Galbraith, *The Great Crash* (Boston: Houghton Mifflin, 1955), Chapters 8 and 9; Caroline Bird, *The Invisible Scar* (New York: McKay, 1965); also, for flavor, the selections in Louis Filler (ed.), *The Anxious Years* (New York: Capricorn, 1964); Daniel Aaron and Robert Bendiner (eds.), *The Strenuous Decade* (New York: Doubleday-Anchor, 1970); for the final phrase, *cf.* William Appleman Williams, *The Tragedy of American Diplomacy* (New York: Delta, 1961), especially Chapter 4, "The Legend of Isolationism."

   Wilson's sense of a parallel between his alcoholic "high" and the "high" of the twenties is reflected in *AACA*, p. 55; it is much more clear in Wilson, tr., and Thomsen, pp. 148–165, captures this well.

5   *Cf.* Handlin, *HUS*, pp. 456–563.

6   *Cf.* Eric F. Goldman, *The Crucial Decade — And After* (New York: Random

House-Vintage, 1960), rev. ed.; Daniel Bell, *The End of Ideology* (New York: Free Press, 1962); Will Herberg, *Protestant-Catholic-Jew* (New York: Doubleday-Anchor, 1960), rev. ed.

7   Although the emphasis here on "limits" is my own, for a good sense of the Korean War Years, *cf.*: Handlin, *HUS*, pp. 565–576; Samuel Eliot Morison, Frederick Merk, Frank Freidel, *Dissent in Three American Wars* (Cambridge, MA: Harvard, 1970). *Cf.* also Handlin, *HUS*, pp. 577–591.

8   For the role of Jung, *cf.* above, pp. 8–9 and 34–35, with citations.

9   For Buchman and the Oxford Group, *cf.* above, pp. 48–50, with citations; for Moody, *cf.* William G. McLoughlin, Jr., *Modern Revivalism* (New York: Ronald Press, 1959), pp. 166–281; for Mencken, *cf.* William Manchester, *H. L. Mencken: Disturber of the Peace* (New York: Collier, 1962), especially Chapter 6, "The Infidel Scopes."

10   For the role of William James, *cf.* above, pp. 23–24, and 34–35, with citations.

11   For John D. Rockefeller, Jr., *cf.* above, pp. 65–66, and 92–94, for the *Saturday Evening Post* and Jack Alexander, above, pp. 100–101, "Philip Wylie Jabs a Little Needle Into Complacency," *AAGV* 1:4 (September 1944), 1; "Bill's Comments on Wylie Ideas, Hunches," *ibid.*; Paul deKruif, "God Is Not Yourself," *AAGV* 8:2 (July 1951), 3–11.

12   The literature on "America" is immense; perhaps especially applicable here are: Louis Hartz, *The Liberal Tradition in America* (New York: Harcourt, Brace & World, 1955) and *The Founding of New Societies* (New York: Harcourt, Brace & World, 1964); also Seymour Martin Lipset, *The First New Nation* (New York: Basic Books, 1963); Yehoshua Arieli, *Individualism and Nationalism in American Ideology* (Baltimore: Penguin, 1966); on America as "modern," *cf.* first C. E. Black, *The Dynamics of Modernization* (New York: Harper & Row, 1967).

13   *Cf.* Lipset and Black, *op. cits.*; Henry F. May, *The Enlightenment in America* (New York: Oxford, 1976); Garry Wills, *Inventing America* (New York: Doubleday, 1978); Scavan Bercovitch, *The Puritan Origins of the American Self* (New Haven: Yale, 1975), ch. 5, "The Myth of America"; Allen Wheelis, *The End of the Modern Age* (New York: Basic Books, 1971); Adrienne Koch, *Power, Morals, and the Founding Fathers* (Ithaca: Cornell, 1961), ch. 2, "The Idea of America"; Crane Brinton, *The Shaping of Modern Thought* (Englewood Cliffs, NJ: Prentice-Hall, 1963); Peter Gay, *The Enlightenment: An Interpretation*, vol. 2 (New York: Knopf, 1969); E. A. Burtt, *The Metaphysical Foundations of Modern Science* (New York: Doubleday-Anchor, 1954), rev. ed.; Carl Becker, *The Heavenly City of the Eighteenth-Century Philosophers* (New Haven: Yale, 1932).

The date 1609 refers to Galileo's first telescope: *cf.* Herbert Butterfield, *The Origins of Modern Science* (New York: Free Press, 1965), p. 78.

14   *Cf.* from the preceding note May, Brinton, Gay, Becker; also Ernst Cassirer, *The Philosophy of the Enlightenment*, tr. F.C.A. Koelln and J. P. Pettegrove (Boston: Beacon, 1955); Reuben Abel, *Man is the Measure* (New York: Free Press, 1976; Beryl Harold Levy, "From Protagoras to Abel: The Humanist Tradition," *The Humanist* 36:5 (September-October 1976), 48; Raymond C. Cochrane, "Francis Bacon and the Architect of Fortune," in *Studies in the Renaissance* 5:

176–195 (1958); Norman Suckling, "The Enlightenment and the Idea of Progress," in *Studies on Voltaire and the Eighteenth Century* (ed., Theodore Besterman), 58: 1461–1480 (1967); Arthur M. Wilson, "The *Philosophes* in the light of present-day theories of Modernization," in *eodem*, 1893–1913; Carl Becker, "The Dilemma of Diderot," in *Everyman His Own Historian* (Chicago; Quadrangle, 1966), pp. 262–283; Carol Blum, *Diderot: The Virtue of a Philosopher* (New York: Viking, 1974); Richard Sennett, *The Fall of Public Man* (New York: Knopf, 1977); Michel Foucault, *Madness and Civilization: A History of Insanity in the Age of Reason* (New York: Pantheon-Random House, 1965); and especially Immanuel Kant, "An Answer to the Question: 'What is Enlightenment?'" in Hans Reiss (ed.) and H. B. Nisbet (trans.), *Kant's Political Writings* (Cambridge: The University Press, 1970), pp. 54–60, and "What Does It Mean: To Orientate Oneself in Thinking?" in *eodem*, pp. 168–170.

15   *Cf.* works listed in the two preceding notes; also Frank Manuel (ed.), *The Enlightenment* (Englewood Cliffs, NJ: Prentice-Hall, 1965), especially Part II: "Religion and Superstition"; and Peter Gay, *The Enlightenment: An Interpretation*, vol. 1, "The Rise of Modern Paganism" (New York: Knopf, 1966); Also well worth study for context are two works of Leszek Kolakowski: *The Alienation of Reason*, tr. Norbert Guterman (New York: Doubleday, 1968) and *Husserl and the Search for Certitude* (New Haven: Yale, 1975).

16   The final quotation is from Arthur O. Lovejoy, *The Great Chain of Being* (Cambridge, MA: Harvard, 1936), p. 250; related is the understanding of the key to the 20th century offered by Philip Rieff, *The Triumph of the Therapeutic* (New York: Harper Torchbook, 1968), p. 65: "Quantity has become quality. The answer to all questions of 'what for?' is 'more.'"

17   Although the phrasing and sense of the final sentence is my own, I am aware of debts to the thought of Weber and Durkheim and commentators on them. *Cf.* Max Weber, *The Sociology of Religion*, tr., Ephraim Fischoff (Boston: Beacon, 1963), ch. 1; Anthony Giddens (ed.), *Emile Durkheim: Selected Writings* (Cambridge: University Press, 1972), especially chs. 11, 12, & 13; also Geoffrey Hawthorn, *Enlightenment and Despair: A History of Sociology* (Cambridge: University Press, 1976), especially chs. 6 & 7; David Bakan, *The Duality of Human Existence* (Boston: Beacon, 1966); Jan deVries, *Perspectives in the History of Religion*, tr., K. W. Bolle (Berkeley: Univ. of California, 1977), introduction and ch. 1; Walter Houston Clark, *The Psychology of Religion* (New York: Macmillan, 1958), especially ch. 4, "The Psychological Sources of Religion."

18   *Cf.*: Richard H. Shryock, *The Development of Modern Medicine* (Philadelphia: Univ. of Pennsylvania, 1936). Barbara Sicherman, *The Quest for Mental Health in America*: 1880–1917 (unpublished dissertation, Columbia University, 1967), was also helpful in shaping the interpretation here. I am grateful to Ms. Sicherman for discussing with me her research and further thought, and also to Dr. Sarah E. Williams for the opportunity to discuss her yet unpublished research into the history of medicine in nineteenth-century America. A sustained critique of the assumptions underlying modern Western medicine is only now developing: *cf.* the works of Michel Foucault and Erving Goffman; most direct although probably overstated is the presentation of Robert S. Mendelsohn, M.D., in Michio Kushi, *The Macrobiotic Way of Natural Healing* (Boston: East-West Publications, 1978), pp. vii–xv.

19   For the dating, *cf.* any encyclopedia under Roentgen and Freud; for depth, Shryock, *op. cit.* and Nathan G. Hale, Jr., *Freud and the Americans* (New York: Oxford, 1971); for Descartes, Planck, and Heisenberg, any encyclopedia should again be sufficient.

20   For the pre-Freudian background, Hale, *op. cit.*; a difficult but informative book indirectly treating the point is Patrick Mullahy, *Psychoanalysis and Interpersonal Psychiatry* (New York: Science House, 1970); this emphasis on identity may be seen from two very different points of view in Louis Berger, *From Instinct to Identity* (Englewood Cliffs, NJ: Prentice-Hall, 1974) and William Kilpatrick, *Identity and Intimacy* (New York: Dell, 1975); its results are clear in David W. Johnson, *Reaching Out* (Englewood Cliffs, NJ: Prentice-Hall, 1972). The history of Behaviorism has yet to be written, but the development of ideas from Watson to Skinner seems enough a part of general knowledge to be mentioned without specific citation. For the general framework, *cf.* Duane Schultz, *A History of Modern Psychology* (New York: Academic Press, 1975).

21   This perception, somewhat overstated, is the theme of Kilpatrick, *Identity and Intimacy*; more balanced but also more theoretical is Roberto Mangabeira Unger, *Knowledge and Politics* (New York: Free Press, 1975), especially chs. 2 & 3. On the metaphor of growth as implying a goal, *cf.* Robert A. Nisbet, *Social Change and History* (New York: Oxford, 1969), an excellent critical treatment that importantly updates Bury's classic work. The literature on the "stages" and process of personal growth is rapidly becoming overwhelming: beyond the popular bestseller by Gail Sheehy, *Passages* (New York: E. P. Dutton, 1976), *cf.* especially Daniel J. Levinson, *et. al.*, *The Seasons of a Man's Life* (New York: Knopf, 1978).

22   I find the best single work explaining and analyzing the Marxist critique to be Shlomo Avineri, *The Social and Political Thought of Karl Marx* (Cambridge: University Press, 1968).

23   I find the best explanation and critique of existentialism to be William Barrett, *Irrational Man* (New York: Doubleday-Anchor, 1962); I am also indebted for perspective on this point to Thomas M. King, *Sartre and the Sacred* (Chicago: Univ. Press, 1974). For Sartre himself, nothing can improve on *Being and Nothingness*, although *St. Genet, Actor and Martyr* may make the point more clearly and concisely. Heidegger's own writings are very difficult, but the first reference is of course to *Being and Time*, tr. John Macquarrie and Edward Robinson (New York: Harper & Row, 1962). For an understanding of Heidegger, I have found most helpful Michael Gelven, *A Commentary on Heidegger's "Being and Time"* (New York: Harper Torchbook, 1970). A further and deeper interpretation of Heidegger is offered by William Barrett in *The Illusion of Technique* (New York: Doubleday-Anchor, 1978).

24   Generically, *cf.* Robert A. Harper, *The New Psychotherapies* (Englewood Cliffs, NJ: Prentice-Hall, 1975); also Virginia Binder, Arnold Binder, and Bernard Rimland (eds.), *Modern Therapies* (Englewood Cliffs, NJ: Prentice-Hall, 1976) and Otto and Miriam Ehrenberg, *The Psychotherapeutic Maze* (New York: Holt, Rinehart & Winston, 1977); for depth, *cf.* Philip Rieff, *The Triumph of the Therapeutic*; Rieff, p. 34, quotes a private letter of Freud: "The moment a man questions the meaning and value of life, he is sick, since objectively neither has any existence."

25   Rieff, *op. cit.*, p. 176; also stimulating is Rieff's discussion of "commitment" or "community" as *vs.* "analytic" therapies, outlined on pp. 71–77, but permeating this whole book.

26   The historiography of Progressivism is overwhelming. Three works that have been central to my own thinking are Richard Hofstadter, *The Age of Reform* (New York: Knopf-Vintage, 1955), especially the "Introduction"; Morton White, *Social Thought in America: The Revolt Against Formalism* (Boston: Beacon, 1957, 2nd ed.); and David Noble, *The Paradox of Progressive Thought* (Minneapolis: Univ. of Mn. Press, 1958). More recent works illuminate, specify, and qualify rather than challenge the key point in this paragraph: *cf.*, e.g., Otis Pease (ed.), *The Progressive Years* (New York: George Braziller, 1962), the editor's introduction; Allen F. Davis, *Spearheads for Reform* (New York: Oxford University Press, 1967) especially Chapters 1 and 10; John Tipple *The Capitalist Revolution* (New York: Pegasus, 1970), especially the "Prologue." For the historiographic problems, *cf.* D. M. Kennedy (ed.), *Progressivism: The Critical Issues* (Boston: Little Brown, 1971); Robert H. Wiebe, "The Progressive Years: 1900–1917," in W. H. Cartwright and Richard L. Watson, Jr. (eds.), (Washington: National Council for the Social Studies, 1973), Arthur Mann (ed.), *The Progressive Era* (Hinsdale, IL: Dryden Press, 1975). From the period itself, *cf.* Herbert Croly, *The Promise of American Life* (New York: MacMillan, 1909); later evaluations of the period by those active in it feature: Frederick Howe, *The Confessions of a Reformer* (New York: Chas. Scribner's Sons, 1925); Joseph Wood Krutch, *The Modern Temper* (New York: Harcourt, Brace & World, 1929); and John Chamberlain, *Farewell to Reform: The Rise, Life and Decay of the Progressive Mind in America* (New York: John Day, 1932).

On Americanization, *cf.* especially Edward G. Hartmann, *The Movement to Americanize the Immigrant* (New York: Columbia Univ. Press, 1948), and John Higham, *Strangers in the Land* (New York: Atheneum, 1966) especially Chapters 7, 8, and 9. A work from the period that in some ways tried to counter the trend is John Palmer Gavit, *Americans By Choice* (New York: Harper & Bros., 1922).

On the continuity of Progressivism, *cf.* Clarke Chambers, *Seedtime of Reform* (Ann Arbor: Univ. of Michigan, 1967); Otis L. Graham, Jr., *An Encore for Reform* (New York: Oxford, 1967); also, differently but very significantly, Roy Lubove, *The Professional Altruist* (New York: Atheneum, 1969), especially chs. 2, 3, & 6.

27   The understanding of the 1920's reflected here and in the following two paragraphs is the standard one. Significant in the formation of my ideas have been: William Leuchtenburg, *The Perils of Prosperity* (Chicago: University of Chicago Press, 1958); Frederick J. Hoffman, *The '20's: American Writing in the Post-war Decade* (New York: MacMillan-Free Press, 1962); Henry F. May, "Shifting Perspectives on the 1920's," reprinted in Carl Degler (ed.), *Pivotal Interpretations of American History* (New York: Harper & Row, 1966), vol. 2, pp. 210–232; Stanley Coben (ed.) *Reform, War and Reaction: 1912–1932* (New York: Harper & Row, 1972); Paul A. Carter, *The Twenties in America* (New York: Thomas Y. Crowell, 1975, 2nd ed.,).

For the income detail, *cf.* Irving Bernstein, *The Lean Years* (Baltimore: Penguin, 1966), pp. 64–66; also, for perspective, Daniel M. Fox, *The Discovery of Abundance* (Ithaca, N.Y.: Cornell Univ. Press, 1967) and Daniel M. Fox, Introduction" to Simon N. Patten, *The New Basis of Civilization* (Cambridge, MA: Harvard-Belknap, 1968) — Patten's book was first published in 1907.

28   *Cf.* notes #3 through 7, above; for the 1960s, Handlin, *HUS*, pp. 592–666.

29   *Cf.* note #7, above; also Donella H. Meadows, Dennis L. Meadows, Jurgen Randers, and William W. Behrens, III, *The Limits to Growth: A Report for the Club of Rome's Project on the Predicament of Mankind* (London: Earth Island, Ltd., 1972); Fred Hirsch, *Social Limits to Growth* (Cambridge, MA: Harvard, 1976); Barry Commoner, *The Closing Circle* (New York: Knopf, 1971); E. F. Schumacher, *Small Is Beautiful* (New York: Harper & Row, 1973); and especially Willard Gaylin, Ira Glasser, Steven Marcus, and David Rothman, *Doing Good: The Limits of Benevolence* (New York: Pantheon, 1978).

30   *Cf.* notes #20 and 24, above.

31   *Cf.* note #29, above, especially Gaylin, *et al.*

32   In addition to the works cited in note #29, above, *cf.* Milton Mayeroff, *On Caring* (New York: Harper & Row—Perennial, 1972) and Willard Gaylin, *Caring* (New York: Knopf, 1976); also, for the literature on "narcissism," note #34 to Chapter Nine, p. 385, below, offers the citations in context.

33   *Cf.* note #26, above.

VIII ALCOHOLICS ANONYMOUS AND RELIGIOUS IDEAS

1   For this and the preceding paragraph, *cf.* C. E. Black, *The Dynamics of Modernization*; Paul Tillich, *Perspectives on 19th and 20th Century Protestant Theology* (New York: Harper & Row, 1967), especially chs. 2 & 3; Jan deVries, *Perspectives in the History of Religion*, tr. K. W. Bolle (Berkeley: Univ. of California, 1977), especially Part Two. Also, on "the pragmatic criterion of truth," *cf.* John E. Smith, *Purpose and Thought: The Meaning of Pragmatism* (New Haven: Yale, 1978), especially the discussion of the differences between James and Dewey in Chapters 1, 2, and 6; and William Barrett, *The Illusion of Technique* (New York: Doubleday-Anchor, 1978), *cf.* the index listings under "James" and "Pragmatism," especially in Chapters 13 and 14.

2   For the Oxford Group, *cf.* above, pp. 46–50.

3   *Cf.* analysis of the stories in the 1st edition of *AA*, above, pp. 73–74, also, Bruce Holley Johnson, *The Alcoholism Movement in America: A Study in Cultural Innovation*, unpublished Ph.D. dissertation, University of Illinois at Urbana-Champaign, 1973, University Microfilms #74-5603. On the role of the churches in Prohibition and the "Temperance Movement," *cf.* Andrew Sinclair, *Era of Excess* (New York: Harper & Row, 1962), Chapters 1–4 and later index listings; also, with caution, Joseph R. Gusfield, *Symbolic Crusade* (Urbana, Ill.: Univ. of Ill. Press, 1963), Chapters 2 & 3; for the remote background, *cf.* Alice Felt Tyler, *Freedom's Ferment* (New York: Harper & Row, 1962), pp. 308–350.

4   Amos, "History," especially pp. 2–3;
   early, significant perceptions were those of W. H. Thompson, "The Treatment of Chronic Alcoholism," *American Journal of Psychiatry*, 98: 846–856 (1942); and W. L. Voegtlin and F. Lemere, "The Treatment of Alcohol Addiction: A Review of the Literature," *QJSA* 2: 717–803 (1942);
   George A. Little, "The God Concept in Alcoholics Anonymous," *Religion in Life* 18: 25–33 (1948);

G. Aiken Taylor, *A Sober Faith* (New York: MacMillan, 1953);

A. H. Cain, *Philosophical Psychology of the Socially Estranged Alcoholic*, unpublished dissertation, Columbia University, 1960;

G. Mouchot, "Alcoholics Anonymous. Lettre d'Angleterre," *Concurs medical* 76: 1863–1864 (1954);

R. K. Jones, "Sectarian Characteristics of Alcoholics Anonymous," *Sociology* (Oxford) 4: 181–195 (1970);

P. M. Sessions, "Ego Religion and Supergo Religion in Alcoholics," *QJSA* 18: 121–125 (1957);

H. S. Ripley and J. K. Jackson, "Therapeutic Factors in Alcoholics Anonymous," *American Journal of Psychiatry* 116: 44–55 (1959);

H. M. Trice and P. M. Roman, "Sociopsychological Predictors of Affiliation with Alcoholics Anonymous: A Longitudinal Study of Treatment Success," *Social Psychology* 5: 51–59 (1970;

I. P. Gellman, *The Sober Alcoholic* (New Haven: College and University Press, 1964);

R. F. Bales, "The Therapeutic Role of Alcoholics Anonymous," *QJSA* 5: 267–278 (1944);

G. E. Metcalfe, "Alcoholics Anonymous." *Journal of Indiana Medical Association* 37: 684-686 (1944);

R. M. Holmes, "Alcoholics Anonymous as Group Logotherapy," *Pastoral Psychology* 21: 30–36 (1970);

D. A. Stewart, "The Problem of Value in the Study of Alcoholism," *QJSA* 12: 489–494 (1951);

D. A. Stewart, "The Dynamics of Fellowship as Illustrated in Alcoholics Anonymous, *QJSA* 16: 251–262 (1955);

S. D. Bacon, "A Sociologist Looks at A.A.," *Minnesota Welfare* 10: 35–44 (1957);

W. G. Madsen, "A.A.: Birds of a Feather," in *The American Alcoholic* (Springfield, IL: C. C. Thomas, 1974); pp. 154–197;

O. R. Whitley, "Life With Alcoholics Anonymous: The Methodist Class Meeting as a Paradigm," *JSA* 38: 831–848 (1977);

R. L. Hoggson, *Alcoholics Anonymous: A Study in Solidarity*, unpublished Ph.D. dissertation, Fordham University, 1952, is especially revealing;

M. A. Maxwell, "Interpersonal Factors in the Genesis and Treatment of Alcohol Addiction," *Social Forces* 29: 443–448 (1951), the heavily condensed version of an unpublished report in the A.A. archives, is the most profound treatment carefully avoiding explicit "religion."

5 Beyond the whole tenor of the "We Agnostics" chapter of *AA*, this distinction is especially clear in Wilson to C.R.L., 1 April 1953; to Bill L., 9 November 1955; to Ed. K., 27 June 1961; to Paul H., 28 October 1964.

The "spiritual kindergarten" quotation used here is from Wilson to Caryl Chessman, 3 May 1954; other significant Wilson letters using the phrase in a clarifying way are to Dr. Tom P., 4 April 1955; to Walter B., 1 July 1958; to Father K., 28 July 1958; to Betty L., 8 December 1967;

the quotations on "theology" are from Wilson to Dr. Tom P., 4 April 1955.

6 Wilson, to Russ J., 23 June 1959; to Al ?, 22 May 1942; *cf.* also to Ted ?, 25 March 1940; to Dr. Humphrey O., 17 April 1961; to Stuart S., 8 February 1963; to Frank S., 11 March 1963.

7   Smith, "Last Major Talk," p. 19; "The Co-Founders of Alcoholics Anonymous"; *AA*, p. 570 (italics Wilson's); *cf.* also "Take Step Eleven: One Man's View — by Bill W.," *AAGV* 15:1 (June 1958), 3; Wilson to Bill F., 2 September 1966; to Jim C., 11 January 1961. The concern may be followed most easily by examining materials in the archive folder of "The Humanist Group," a New York City A.A. group which flourished under this name in the mid-1940's; also in the correspondence of Denys W. (Cambridge, England) to Wilson, 31 July, 2 October, and 12 October 1963.

Often, within Alcoholics Anonymous as elsewhere, "open-mindedness" seems valued only to the point where the one on whom it is urged begins to think as does the one doing the urging. This appears to be a function of individual temperament rather than inherent in A.A. itself, but on the possible affinity of "the closed mind" for Alcoholics Anonymous, *cf.* Milton Rokeach, *The Open and Closed Mind* (New York: Basic Books, 1960), as stimulating.

8   Wilson to Fred W., 5 March 1960; Mr. W. had been a patient of Dr. Jung and was interviewed by this writer on this point. Wilson to Helen C., 9 April 1962: "[Jung] portrays the drinker as one who is seeking a spiritual release through alcohol. . . . deeply convinced that this is a part of the motivation that most heavy drinkers have. Therefore alcohol is not always taken for escape or obliteration — rather it is an attempt, very often at least, to reach higher values. . . . Aldous Huxley . . . held to this identical view." On A.A.'s mindfulness of the Washingtonians, *cf.* above, pp. 116–117.

9   Augustine, *Confessions*, Book One, Chapter One: ". . . fecisti nos ad te et inquietum est cor nostrum, donec requiescat in te."

10   Philip Rieff, *The Triumph of the Therapeutic*, can also be read as "The End of Tragedy"; *cf.* also E. M. Cioran, and especially, Henry Alonzo Myers, *Tragedy: A View of Life* (Ithaca, NY: Cornell, 1956); and *A Short History of Decay*, tr., Richard Howard (New York: Viking, 1975), especially p. 83, "Conditions of Tragedy."

11   On the Humanistic and Liberal tradition, *cf.* William R. Hutchison (ed.), *The Liberal Tradition in America* (New York: Harper Torchbook, 1968); for Evangelicalism, especially the Introduction to William G. McLoughlin (ed.), *The American Evangelicals: 1800–1900* (New York: Harper Torchbook, 1968), pp. 1–27. For an avowedly liberal but honest evaluation, *cf.* William R. Hutchison, *The Modernist Impulse in American Protestantism* (Cambridge, MA: Harvard, 1976).

On the Oxford Group, and especially how it may have mediated this insight to Alcoholics Anonymous, *cf.* above, pp. 46–50, especially the examination of Buchman's background, p. 48.

12   The broad diffusion of the "Return to Orthodoxy" may be glimpsed in Handlin, HUS, pp. 509–510. Sidney Ahlstrom (whose phrase is *"annus mirabilis"*) offers the best brief description of neo-orthodoxy: *cf.* "Theology in America: A Historical Survey," in James Ward Smith and A. Leland Jamison (eds.)., *The Shaping of American Religion* (Princeton, NJ: University Press, 1961), pp. 312–316, and *A Religious History of the American People* (Garden City, NY: Doubleday-Image, 1975), vol. 2, pp. 434–438. The best and briefest primary source from the phenomenon's own point of view is H. Richard Niebuhr, *The Kingdom of God in America* (New York: Harper & Row, 1937). The ideas outlined in this paragraph are drawn from Ahlstrom, *locs. cits.*, and William R. Hutchison, *The Modernist*

Impulse in American Protestantism (Cambridge, MA: Harvard University Press, 1976), p. 195.

13   On the transformation of the Oxford Group into Moral Re-Armament, *cf.* especially Walter Houston Clark, as cited above, p. 324.

14   The representative literature that justifies the point here includes:
R. V. Seliger and V. Cranford, "The Rorschach Analysis in the Treatment of Alcoholism," *Medical Record of New York* 158: 32–38 (1945);
E. Bergler, "Personality Traits of Alcohol Addicts," *QJSA* 7: 356–359 (1946);
M. Werner, "Der Alkoholismus als ethisches Problem (Alcoholism as an Ethical Problem)" *Fursorger* 23: 1–14 (1955);
R. G. Bell, "Alcohol and Loneliness," *Journal of Social Theory* 2: 171–181 (1956);
J. D. Armstrong, "The Search for the Alcoholic Personality," *The Annals of the American Academy of Political and Social Science* 135: 40–47 (1958);
R. R. Rudie and L. S. McGaughran, "Differences in Developmental Experience, Defensiveness, and Personality Organization between Two Classes of Problem Drinkers," *Journal of Abnormal Psychology* 62: 659–665 (1961);
P. M. Sands, P. G. Hanson, and R. B. Sheldon, "Recurring Themes in Group Psychotherapy with Alcoholics," *Psychiatric Quarterly* 41: 474–482 (1967);
E. S. Lisansky-Gomberg, "Etiology of Alcoholism," *Journal of Consulting Clinical Psychology* 32: 18–20 (1968);
A. I. Malcolm, "On the Psychotherapy of Alcoholism," *Addiction* (Toronto) 15 (No. 1): 25–40 (1968);
J. L. Carroll and G. B. Fuller, "The Self and Ideal-Self Concept of the Alcoholic as Influenced by Length of Sobriety and/or Participation in Alcoholics Anonymous," *Journal of Clinical Psychology* 25: 363–364 (1969);
W. A. White, "Alcoholism, A Symptom," *Interstate Medical Journal* 23: 404–407 (1916);
H. H. Hart, "Personality Factors in Alcoholism," *Archives of Neurological Psychiatry* (Chicago), 24: 116–134 (1930);
R. P. Knight, "The Psychodynamics of Alcoholism," *Journal of Nervous and Mental Disease* 86: 538–548 (1937);
R. P. Knight, "The Dynamics and Treatment of Chronic Alcohol Addiction," *Bulletin of the Menninger Clinic* 1: 233–251 (1937);
M. E. Bonney, "Parents as the Makers of Social Deviants," *Social Forces* 20: 77–87 (1942);
D. Anderson, "The Process of Recovery from Alcoholism," *Federal Probation* 8 (No. 4), 14–19 (1944);
C. Landis, "Theories of the Alcoholic Personality," in *Alcohol, Science and Society*: Twenty-nine Lectures with Discussions as Given at the Yale School of Alcohol Studies (New Haven, CT: Quarterly Journal of Studies on Alcohol, 1945), pp. 129–142;
R. E. Mogar, W. M. Wilson, and S. T. Helm, "Personality Subtypes of Male and Female Alcoholic Patients," *International Journal of Addictions* 5: 99–113 (1970);
S. M. L. Kammeier, H. Hoffmann, and R. G. Loper, "Personality Characteristics of Alcoholics as College Freshmen and at Time of Treatment," *QJSA* 34: 390–399 (1973);

A. F. Fontana, B. N. Dowds, and M. H. Bethel, "A.A. and Group Therapy for Alcoholics: An Application of the World Hypothesis Scale," *JSA* 37: 675–682 (1976);

M. Keller, "Alcoholism: the Image of Reality," *Alcoholism* (Zagreb) 11: 18–27 (1975);

M. Keller, "The Nature of Addiction: Some Second Thoughts," *Alcoholism* (Zagreb) 11: 28–32 (1975);

J. Westermeyer and V. Walzer, "Drug Usage: An Alternative to Religion?" *Diseases of the Nervous System* 36: 492–495 (1975);

M. Tomsovic, "Group Therapy and Changes in the Self-Concept of Alcoholics," *JSA* 37: 53–57 (1976);

C. E. Thune, "Alcoholism and the Archetypal Past: A Phenomenological Perspective on Alcoholics Anonymous," *JSA* 38: 75–88 (1977);

E. M. Jellinek, "The Symbolism of Drinking: A Culture-Historical Approach," *JSA* 38: 849–866 (1977).

15 *Cf.* Hutchison and McLoughlin as cited in note #11, above, and especially the McLoughlin "Introduction"; on William James, *cf.* above, pp. 34–35 and 164.

16 On the neo-orthodox rejection of "psychologism," *cf.* sources cited in note #12, above, especially Ahlstrom in Smith and Jamison; "pluralism" will be treated in greater depth in Chapter Nine, *cf.* pp. 220–221, below, with citations.

17 Among the wealth of literature on "mind-cure," *cf.* especially Donald Meyer, *The Postive Thinkers* (New York: Doubleday, 1965); Meyer's treatment of specifically the role of William James, pp. 315–324, should be supplemented by the insights in Cushing Strout, "The Pluralistic Identity of William James," *American Quarterly* 23: 135–152 (1971); David W. Marcell, *Progress and Pragmatism* (Westport, CT: Greenwood Press, 1974); James B. Gilbert, *Work Without Salvation* (Baltimore: Johns Hopkins, 1977), especially pp. 181–210; and especially William Barrett, *The Illusion of Technique.*

18 The Biblical reference is to "the tree of the knowledge of good and evil," Genesis 2: 16–17 and 3: 1–23. Many thinkers through the ages have explored the implications of this mythic story; a recent and stimulating effort, on other levels also provocative of thought *re* Alcoholics Anonymous, is Thomas Szasz, *The Second Sin* (New York: Doubleday, 1973); *cf.* also Leslie H. Farber, "Thinking About Will" and 'Our Kindly Family Physician, Chief Crazy Horse," in *Lying, Despair, Jealousy, Envy, Suicide, Sex, Drugs, and the Good Life* (New York: Basic Books, 1976), pp. 3–12 and 106–119.

19 J. Clancy, "The Use of Intellectual Processes in Group Psycho-Therapy with Alcoholics," *QJSA* 23: 432–441 (1962): the direct quotation is *via* CAAAL #9456;

H. M. Tiebout, "Conversion as a Psychological Phenomenon," paper read before the New York Psychiatric Society, 11 April 1944, most easily available in pamphlet form from the National Council on Alcoholism, 733 Park Avenue, New York 10017.

20 Charles G. Finney, "What a Revival of Religion Is," reprinted in William G. McLoughlin, *The American Evangelicals: 1800–1900* (New York: Harper Torchbook, 1968), pp 87–100: the passage here is from pp. 92–94; the timing is given by McLoughlin in his introductory note, p. 86;

Harry M. Tiebout, "Alcoholics Anonymous — An Experiment of Nature," *QJSA* 22: 52–68 (1961); for clarity as well as brevity, the quotation is directly from the CAAAL abstract, #9449;

H. M. Tiebout, "The Act of Surrender in the Therapeutic Process," *QJSA* 10: 48–58 (1959); *cf.* also Tiebout, "The Ego Factor in Surrender in Alcoholism," *QJSA* 15:610–621 (1954), and Tiebout, "Psychological Factors Operating in Alcoholics Anonymous," in B. Glueck (ed.), *Current Therapies of Personality Disorders* (New York: Grune & Stratton, 1946), especially p. 165;

for this intuition by others, coming from very different directions, *cf.* D. Anderson, "The Process of Recovery from Alcoholism," *Federal Probation* 8 (#4): 14–19 (1944), and C. L. Brown, "A Transference Phenomenon in Alcoholics," *QJSA* 11: 403–409 (1950);

also suggestive although hardly profound is C. R. Woodruff, *Christian Conversion of the Alcoholic in the Context of the Protestant Parish Fellowship*, unpublished dissertation, Southern Baptist Seminary, 1966, reported by CAAAL #12235;

on larger implications of the parallel intuited here, *cf.* Gerald Heard, "The Ad Hoc Religions," *Fortnight*, 15 December 1954 (vol. and pp. unavailable); O. Hobart Mowrer, "Alcoholics Anonymous and the 'Third' Reformation," *Religion in Life* 34: 383–397 (1965); Thomas C. Oden, "The New Pietism," *Journal of Humanistic Psychotherapy* 12: 24–41 (1972); O. R. Whitley, "Life With Alcoholics Anonymous: The Methodist Class Meeting as a Paradigm," *JSA* 38: 831–848 (1977).

21   Wilson to Oliver J., 13 June 1956: "The Catholics call it salvation, the psychiatrists call it integration, and I call it growth. . . ."; *cf.* the discussion of *12&12* in Chapter Five, above; for the briefest summary statement, "The Next Frontier: Emotional Sobriety — by Bill," *AAGV* 14:8 (January 1958).

For the focus on *faith* in the alcoholism literature, *cf.*:

A. E. Carver, "The Psychology of the Alcoholist," *British Journal of Medical Psychology* 11: 117–124 (1931);

E. B. Allen, "Alcoholism as a Psychiatric Medical Problem," *New York State Journal of Medicine* 38: 1492–1505 (1938);

R. G. Heath, "Group Psychotherapy of Alcohol Addiction," *QJSA* 5: 555–562 (1945);

R. V. Seliger, "About Alcoholism," *Industrial Medicine* 18: 481–482 (1949);

A. D. Button, "The Psychodynamics of Alcoholism," *QJSA* 17: 443–460 (1956);

P. A. Bensoussan, "L'abord psychologique de l'alcoholique (Psychological Approach to the Alcoholic)," *Vie Medical* 38: 442–444 (1957);

E. S. Lisansky, "The Etiology of Alcoholism: The Role of Psychological Predisposition," *QJSA* 21: 314–343 (1960);

D. B. Wine and A. E. Edwards, "Intemperance: Psychological and Sociological Concomitants," *QJSA* 25: 77–84 (1964);

J. I. Hurwitz and D. A. Lelos, "A Multilevel Interpersonal Profile of Employed Alcohlics," *QJSA* 29: 64–76 (1968);

M. Tremper, "Dependency in Alcoholics; A Sociological View," *QJSA* 33: 186–190 (1973);

these of course do not speak explicitly to the A.A. Steps, but the historical development of this perception to explicitness may readily be traced in them.

For one specific application of the alcoholism literature to the A.A. Steps, *cf.* Leach and Norris, "Factors," in Kissin and Begleiter, pp 458–463.

22 That most in time "came to believe," *cf.* Wilson, *12&12*, p. 112: "From great numbers of such experiences [with early doubters], we could predict that the doubter who still claimed that he hadn't got the 'spiritual angle,' and who still considered his well-loved A.A. group the higher Power, would presently love God and call Him by name." The main "experience" offered is the story of "Ed" (almost certainly Jim B. of Big Book "radical" notoriety), in the Tradition Three discussion in *12&12*, pp. 147–149.

On Wilson's fascination with Buddhist success in A.A., his many references in passing to the phenomenon led me to confirm it with NW, interview of 16 November 1976; *cf. AACA*, p. 81; for Dr. Tiebout, *cf.* "When the Big 'I' Becomes Nobody," *AAGV* 26:1 (June 1969), 37–38 — a reprint of an earlier published article which is unavailable. One significance of the affinity of A.A. thought for Buddhism is treated near the end of Chapter Nine, below, p. 227. On "those unconventional in belief," *cf.* Milton A. Maxwell, "Alcoholics Anonymous: An Interpretation," in David J. Pittman (ed.), *Alcoholism* (New York: Harper & Row, 1967), pp. 211–222; and Jon R. Weinberg, *A.A.: An Interpretation for the Non-believer* (Center City, MN: Hazelden, 1975).

23 *Cf.* Lewis Yablonsky, *The Tunnel Back: Synanon* (New York: MacMillan, 1965); Steven I. Simon, *The Synanon Game*, unpublished dissertation, Harvard University, 1974; John Burns (pseud.) *et al.*, *The Answer to Addiction* (New York: Harper & Row, 1975); also the citations in the final paragraph to note #20 above, to which add: Nathan Hurwitz, "Peer Self-Help Psychotherapy Groups: Psychotherapy Without Psychotherapists," in P. M. Roman and H. M. Trice, *The Sociology of Psychotherapy* (New York: Jason Aronson, 1974), pp. 84–138; Matthew P. Dumont, "Self-Help Treatment Programs," *American Journal of Psychiatry* 131: 631–635 (1974).

The affinity of this understanding of "reality" for many modern "therapies" may also be intuited in a vast variety of approaches, ranging from the aggressively "religious" to the expressly "irreligious." Among the former: Anna A. Terruwe and Conrad W. Baars, *Loving and Curing the Neurotic* (New Rochelle, NY: Arlington House, 1972) and O. Hobart Mowrer, *The New Group Therapy* (New York: Van Hostrand, 1964); among the latter: Albert Ellis and Robert A. Harper, *A Guide to Rational Living* (North Hollywood, CA: Wilshire, 1961), and Albert Ellis, *Humanistic Psychotherapy* (New York: McGraw-Hill, 1974). It may be understood as basic to the therapeutic style of Carl Rogers: *cf.* Richard I. Evans, *Carl Rogers: The Man and His Ideas* (New York: Dutton, 1975), as well, of course, as Rogers himself — *cf.* "Some Hypotheses Regarding the Facilitation of Personal Growth," "What We Know About Psychotherapy," and "A Process Conception of Psychiatry," in Carl R. Rogers, *On Becoming a Person* (Boston: Houghton Mifflin, 1961). For a scholarly analysis of this psychiatric approach as especially American: Patrick Mullahy, *The Beginnings of Modern American Psychiatry: The Ideas of Harry Stack Sullivan* (Boston: Houghton Mifflin, 1973); for perhaps its clearest statement, William Glasser, *Reality Therapy* (New York: Harper & Row, 1965).

For one awareness of this point giving rise to a criticism of Alcoholics Anonymous, from within A.A. itself, *cf.* Appendix A.

24 For James, these ideas are most accessible in Carl Georg Lange and William James, *The Emotions* (Baltimore: Williams and Wilkins, 1922).

25 For the first Wilson-Smith meeting, *cf.* above, pp. 28–32, for the "story section" of *AA*, above, pp. 71–73, for the direct treatment of "limited control," above, pp. 105–106.

In its earliest years, based on a survey taken in Philadelphia, A.A. claimed that "50% who come in never take another drink, 25% stumble, but then pick themselves up and make good and the other 25% never make it." (Wilson to Howard B., 12 August 1958). Wilson's concern from the late 1950s over "What happened to the 600,000 who approached and left?" has been treated above, as the theme of Chapter Six. The 20% estimate is based on this figure of Wilson's compared to A.A.'s claimed membership of 151,606 at the time (1960) — "A.A. Growth: Active Membership," document compiled by Jim H., in A.A. archives. Yet if the correction factor referred to above, note #2 to Chapter Seven, be applied, the estimate would rise to about 33%. Warren C., who entered A.A. in 1939 and in later years worked administering an alcoholism treatment program for hard-core alcoholics, estimated that "not even one in ten even begin to take the [A.A.] program seriously." — interview, 8 September 1977.

26 Beecher is the only figure to appear in both McLoughlin, *The American Evangelicals* (pp. 128–140) *and* William R. Hutchison (ed.), *American Protestant Thought: The Liberal Era* (New York: Harper Torchbook, 1968), pp. 37–45. The McLoughlin selection, "Preaching Christ," is used here: pp. 129 (italics Beecher's), 130–131. The Hutchison selection, as significant, was "The Study of Human Nature."

27 "What booze did to me": *cf.* Wilson to Ted S., 25 March 1940; also an unattributed, mimeograph schema, "A.A. Talks," found in use in various alcoholism treatment centers. The tradition goes back to First Corinthians, Chapter One, verses 18–25. The resurrection parallel may be found in First Corinthians, Ch. 15, verse 14.

28 This sense on occasion came perilously close to surfacing; *cf.*, e.g., Wilson to Russ J., 6 May 1950: "Whenever 'two or three are gathered together,' an A.A. group is the inevitable result." The proximity of Wilson's apodosis to that of Jesus — "there am I in their midst" — is striking (Mt. 18:20); *cf.* also the echo of this in the final sentence of the "long form" of A.A.'s Third Tradition, *AA*, p. 565, where an additional parallel may be noted: that between Jesus's "in my name" and A.A.'s "for sobriety."

29 The "witness" is inherent in A.A.'s understanding of alcoholism as permanent condition: identification within the group remains on the basis "I am an alcoholic" rather than "I am sober." The religious intuition is perhaps clearest in Willard L. Sperry, "A Modern Doctrine of Original Sin," in *The Disciplines of Liberty* (New Haven, CT: Yale University Press, 1921), pp. 59–80. A point inviting exploratory thought, but not here, is the distinction between "'shame" and "guilt": the classic treatment is Helen Lewis, *Shame and Guilt in Neurosis* (New York: International Universities Press, 1971); it should be supplemented with Helen Lynd, *On Shame and the Search for Identity* (New York: Harcourt, Brace, Jovanovich, 1958); briefer but stimulating is David G. Edwards, "Shame and Pain and 'Shut Up or I'll Really Give You Something to Cry About,'" *Clinical Social Work Journal* 4: 3–13 (1976).

"Alcoholic" as identity or label may be thoughtfully explored *via*: Kai T. Erikson, *Wayward Puritans* (New York: Wiley, 1966); Edward Sagarin, *Deviants and Deviance* (New York: Praeger, 1975); P. M. Roman and H. M. Trice, "The Sick Role, Labeling Theory, and the Deviant Drinker," *Int. Journal of Social Psychotherapy* 14: 245–251 (1968); H. M. Trice and P. M. Roman, "Delabeling, Relabeling, and Alcoholics Anonymous," *Social Problems* 17: 538–546 (1970); E. Sagarin, "The High Personal Cost of Wearing a Label," *Psychology Today* 9:10 (April 1976), 25–31. For the sense of "identity": *cf.* D. A. Stewart, *Thirst for Freedom* (Center City, MN: Hazelden, 1960); R. G. Bell, *Escape from Addiction* (New York: McGraw-Hill, 1970); and especially "A.A. Communication Can Cross All Barriers — by Bill," *AAGV* 16:5 (October 1959), 2–4.

On the relationship between "the disease of alcoholism" and "identity," *cf.* J. H. McNamara, "The Disease Conception of Alcoholism: Its Therapeutic Value for the Alcoholic and His Wife," *Social Casework* 41: 460–465 (1969); H. L. Hershon, "Alcoholism and the Concept of Disease," *British Journal of Addiction* 69: 123–131 (1974).

30 "To Serve Is To Live — by Bill," *AAGV* 8:1 (June 1951), 3 (italics Wilson's); Wilson to Jim W., ? September 1960: "Give these people a good exposure to A.A. if they will stand still long enough, and then let it go at that. . . . You simply do as well as you can, offering the A.A. message where it will be received. If there are little or no results, that is not your fault. It is the quality of your own attitude and your willingness to try, where trying is wise, that counts. Again, I repeat, it isn't the quantity of your successful effort, it is the quality of your trying."

31 For American missionary endeavor, *cf.* William R. Hutchison, *The Modernist Impulse in American Protestantism* (Cambridge, MA: Harvard, 1976), especially the treatment of George Gordon and the ABCFM, pp. 136 ff.; for this as an aspect of pragmatism, *cf.* David W. Marcell and James B. Gilbert, as cited in note #17, above, and John E. Smith as cited in note #1, above — the point at issue here is treated well but unfortunately in scattered places in these three books.

32 Beyond Hofstadter, as cited in the footnote to the preceding paragraph, *cf.* for depth Morton White, *Science and Sentiment in America* (New York: Oxford, 1972). Although my thought here follows that of Hofstadter more closely than that of White, significant aspects of it have been profoundly influenced by Professor White's lectures on the history of philosophy in America and also by conversations with him during the anti-intellectual and anti-professional campus turmoils of 1969–1970.

33 The Eighth Tradition as "hard but healthy doctrine," from the 1937 experience, and the quotation: *AACA*, pp. 99–101, *cf.* also, in *eodem*, pp. 114–117, and *12&12*, pp. 170–175. The incident has been treated above, pp. 63–64.

". . . the ancient and consistent Pietist rejection of 'bought grace' as 'cheap grace'" has surfaced in modern times in places perhaps surprising to some: it was an impetus to Bishop John T. Robinson's *Honest to God* and underlay the "Radical Theology" of the 1960's adoption of Dietrich Bonhoeffer; *cf*, William Hamilton, "Dietrich Bonhoeffer" in Hamilton and T.J.J. Altizer, *Radical Theology and the Death of God* (Indianapolis: Bobbs-Merrill, 1966), pp. 113–118. This particular line is well traced by Richard P. McBrien, "Radical Theology," *Commonweal* 84: 605–608 (23 September 1966).

34 The earliest surfacing of this side of the "problem of professionalism" came at almost the same moment as the other side was laid to rest by A.A.'s decision to reject outside funding: "Dr. Sam Parker of Kings County Suggests 'Criteria for A.A. Work in Hospitals,'" *AAGV* 1:10 (March 1945), 1, 8; "Let's Be Friendly With Our Friends . . . The Psychiatrists — by Bill W., Co-founder," [note that final fillip] *AAGV* 14:2 (July 1957); " . . . The Physicians . . . ," 14:3 (August 1957); " . . . The Clergymen . . . ," 14:4 (September 1957);" . . . On the Alcoholism Front — by Bill," *AAGV* 14:10 (March 1958); for the context, Chapter Six, above; also Wilson to Dick S., 28 June 1949: "Your article carries the impression that we, Alcoholics Anonymous, have done wonders for the alcoholic in sharp contrast with zero performance by the doctors and, inferentially I should think, the clergy. While the substance of what you say may approximate the truth for the moment, I think it would be very unsound policy were you to present A.A. to the public in this light." Tiebout's sensitivity to precisely this is clear in Tiebout (Greenwich, CT) to Wilson, 26 June 1953.

On the deep psychological danger of such "resentments," *cf. AA*, pp. 64, 66, 128; e.g., (p. 64): "Resentment is the 'number one' offender. It destroys more alcoholics than anything else."

35 The immediate context — the thrust to "responsibility" and the Chafetz, Cain, and Ellison criticisms — has been treated in Chapter Six, above; Milton A. Maxwell, "An Exploratory Study: Alcoholics Anonymous and Professional Relations," unpublished in this form, but presented at the A.A. convention of 1964, and available in the archives; Charles H. Aharan, "A.A. and Other Treatment Programs: Problems in Cooperation," *Addictions* (Toronto) 17: 25–32 (1970); Aharan, "Problems of Cooperation Between A.A. and Other Treatment Programs," *AAGV* 27:11 (April 1971), 17–23, is substantially the same paper.

The "unofficial" lamentation was Wayne Goethe. "The Death of a Philosophy," unpublished, but available from the Association of Halfway House Alcoholism Programs of North America, Inc., 786 East Seventh St., St. Paul, MN. Mr. Goethe of course did not speak for A.A. (any more than did Maxwell and Aharan); both points of view were often expressed at meetings attended in the course of this research, albeit rarely with such lucid passion.

36 Goethe, *op. cit..* pp. 1, 3, 5, 8, 11.

37 The early perception of one aspect of the depth of this concern may be intuited from Wilson to Ned F., 11 July 1940: "Now it is an undoubted fact that professionalism in spiritual matters has too often limited the spread of real understanding and practical application. The modern world has little time for paid emissaries of God. . . ."

On this deep sense as derived precisely from the Oxford Group, Clarence S., interviews of 5 and 6 October 1978, was most illuminating. On the complexities of this for Wilson's continuing role within A.A., *cf.* pp. 42 and 76, above, with citations; also, and specifically for the Clarence S. point of view, *cf.* the Appendix, below. Concerning this as a problem of specifically Evangelically Pietist religion, *cf.* the book by G. H. Williams cited in the following note. This monumental study treats the vision well, although indirectly and in scattered places.

38 For anti-intellectualism as characteristic of Evangelical religions, *cf.* Hofstadter, as cited above in the footnote to p. 188, for "the doctrine of the priesthood of all believers," *cf.* George Huntston Williams, *The Radical Reformation* (Philadelphia: Westminster, 1962), pp. xxix f. and 845.

39   The clearest treatment of this point as inherent in "Evangelical religion" is Hofstadter, *ibid.*; for A.A., *cf.* the theme of the 1967 General Service Conference of A.A. on "Sponsorship": "That which we give away we keep. That which we keep we lose. Such is the basis of our responsibility. . . ." (Final Report, p. 9).

40   On "rationalization": *12 & 12*, pp. 97, 98; *cf. AACA*, pp. 292–293, *12 & 12*, pp. 48–49; *ABSI*, pp. 64, 279; *cf.* also the footnote to p. 188.

41   For a challenging treatment of one expression of these intuitions and insights, *cf.* Williams, *The Radical Reformation*, as cited in note #38, above, especially the final two chapters.

42   Clearer awareness of this precise danger and its corollaries could helpfully enhance much of the analysis, popularly offered, of "deviance" and "labeling": *cf.* citations in note #29, above.

43   For "denial" as central and characteristic, *cf.* above, pp. 59–60; such concern over "the clever use of language" has been best expressed within 20th century American Intellectual History by one who well fits the understanding of "pietism" proposed earlier in this chapter: *cf.* J. Gresham Machen, *Christianity and Liberalism* (Grand Rapids: Wm. B. Eerdmans, 1923), especially pp. 109–112. On modernity's "not dissimilar problem," *cf.* Thomas Szasz, *The Second Sin* (New York: Doubleday-Anchor, 1973). The substance of the point will also be explored throughout Chapter Nine, below.

44   On "alcoholic grandiosity," *cf.* above, pp. 94–95.

45   On the shift in terms in the sixteen printings of the 1st ed. of AA, *cf.* note #67 to Chapter Five, above, p. 356. The most significant sociological study of the shifts in cultural understanding of the term "alcoholic" is Bruce Holley Johnson, *The Alcoholism Movement in America: A Study in Cultural Innovation* (unpublished dissertation, Univ. of Illinois at Urbana-Champaign, 1973): *cf.* p. 57 for a summary statement of his thesis. My interpretation in this paragraph derives from my own knowledge of A.A. history and reading of the popular sources rather than from Johnson's more technically sociological and far less shaded interpretation. *Cf.* also p. 181 and note #14, above.

46   On the N.C.E.A., *cf.* above, pp. 117-119, on the first negative attitude noted, *cf.* the review by Wolcott Gibbs of Jim Bishop's *The Glass Crutch, NYT* book review section, 18 November 1945, 4; on "the alcoholic personality," *cf.* note #14, above; and on the alcoholic as specifically "immaturely dependent deficient personality," note #31 to Chapter Nine, below, p. 384.

47   For the formulation of the "Twelve Traditions of Alcoholics Anonymous," *cf.* pp. 113-114, above; for A.A.'s developing understanding of anonymity, pp. 104-105, above; citations for anonymity appear in notes #56-58 to Chapter Four, p. 344, above.

48   *Cf.* note #14, above; also, for popularization and diffusion, Albert L. Ayars and Gail Gleason Milgram, *The Teenager and Alcohol* (New York: Richards Rosen Press, 1970), a book called to my attention by Dr. Sarah Williams as available in high-school libraries; e.g., p. 57: "Major personality characteristics of alcoholics are a dependent nature, emotional immaturity, a low tolerance for frustration, and a rebellious character. . . . [Alcoholics] are regressive or infantile in their approach to problems. A lack of true identification with a well-identified masculine or feminine role is often present." Ayars and Milgram do not distinguish here between drinking and sober alcoholics, although noting, this distinction earlier. On the "shared honesty of mutual vulnerability openly acknowledged" as characteristic of A.A., *cf.* below, pp. 214–215 and 221–223.

49 On the history of the name "Alcoholics Anonymous," *cf.* pp. 74–75, above, also p. 78.

50 *Cf.* The Gospel according to John, Chapter 8, verse 32, and Chapter 15, verse 13.

IX ALCOHOLICS ANONYMOUS — MEANING AND SIGNIFICANCE

1 On medicine as a source of A.A., *cf.* above, pp. 33–34, with citations; on Wilson's and A.A.'s wariness of the term "disease," above, p. 22, for more detail on "three-fold," note #11, below.

2 E. M. Jellinek, *The Disease Concept of Alcoholism* (New Haven: College and University Press, 1960), p. 11.

3 For reviews of the literature on alcoholism as a disease, *cf.* note #49 to Chapter One, above, p. 312. The continuing and increasing complexity of the question may be well grasped from the two most recent comprehensive overviews of the subject: in R. E. Tarter and A. A. Sugerman (eds.), *Alcoholism: Interdisciplinary Approaches to an Enduring Problem* (Reading, MA: Addison Wesley, 1976) *cf.* especially A. Paredes, "The History of the Concept of Alcoholism"; R. E. Tarter and D. U. Schneider, "Models and Theories of Alcoholism"; D. L. Davies, "Definitional Issues in Alcoholism"; R. J. Cadoret, "Genetic Determinants of Alcoholism." *Cf.* also even merely the Table of Contents in each of the five volumes of the Kissin and Begleiter series cited in note #3 to Chapter One.

4 *Cf.*, for an example, Michel Foucault, *Madness and Civilization*, tr. Richard Howard (New York: Vintage, 1973); *cf.* also and especially the deep, direct treatment of the concept by Susan Sontag, *Illness as Metaphor* (New York: Farrar, Straus & Giroux, 1978).

5 *Cf.*, e.g., Paul Heinisch, *The Theology of the Old Testament*, tr. William G. Heidt (Collegeville, MN: Liturgical Press, 1955), pp. 250–264.

6 For the literature on Progressivism, *cf.* note #26 to Chapter Seven, p. 368, above. The quotation is from Robert Hunter, *Poverty*, ed. Peter d'A. James (New York: Harper Torchbook, 1965), p. 178. This book was first published in 1904.

7 It is the complaint against this cost of cancer understood as metaphor that inspires Susan Sontag's *Illness as Metaphor*.

8 On alcoholism as "real disease," *cf.* note #3, above; on "alcoholism is a disease" as cliché and A.A. as the source of this idea's diffusion, *cf.* Jellinek, *Disease Concept*, Wilkerson and Keller as cited in note #49 to Chapter One, and especially Johnson, as cited in note #3 to Chapter Eight.

9 The intuition that A.A.'s understanding of alcoholism may be understood as a metaphor for the subjective dis-ease of modernity is reflected in the primary sources. In the Wilson correspondence, *cf.*: to his Jungian friend Margarita L., 14 January 1946, where Wilson explains his preference for Jung over Freud; to Caryl Chessman, 31 March 1954: ". . . society . . . has become just as sick as we are. . . . People of all kinds and of every class, collectively and individually, are hipped on the pursuit of money, prestige and power as never before. The demand for these things is utter and terrifyingly absolute. . . . what once were normal instincts are now keyed up to such a compulsive and consuming pitch that they have become juggernauts in collision — man vs. man, society vs. society." Wilson to Dr. Albert L., 4 May 1959: "How long will it be before the world becomes willing to look at the *whole* man? . . . In the world today we seem to be confronted by myriads of specialists who would relate all learning and human experience into their several fields. Never, it appears, was there such a tremendous need for . . . a sane synthesis out of which new and better values could arise." Wilson to Purnell Handy Benson (author of *Religion in Contemporary Culture* [New York: Harper Brothers, 1960] which offers A.A. as an example of "The Functioning of Religion," Chapter 8), 25 April 1961: "As we A.A.'s say, 'The whole world is on a terrific dry bender!' In our society [A.A.], we are fortunate, of course, to have suffered a malady that has not only threatened us with extinction, but which makes it possible [should read: impossible] to pass the blame on to other people. Being thus forced to 'hit bottom,' as we say, the way to spiritual experience is opened. A.A. is simply a way of capitalizing on this inherent situation. In the world around us, however, the bottom is being hit all right, but this is always somebody else's fault."

Hints of a similar perception may be found in the alcoholism literature: *cf.*, for example:

J. L. Henderson, "Alcoholism: Its Psychiatric Treatment," *California Western Medicine* 52: 11–15 (1940) — CAAAL #789: "Alcoholism seems to be an effect of the progress of civilization dependent upon the inability of certain persons to meet its requirements."

D. A. Barbara, "The Neurotic Character Structure of the Alcoholic Personality," *Psychiatric Quarterly* 19: 503–515 (1945) — CAAAL #4237: "The alcoholic is the result of a faulty childhood and an ever-pressing and conflicting civilization. He wants to be both dependent and free."

A. E. M. van der Does de Willebois, "Alienation and Addiction," *Excerpta Criminologica* 6, #852, 1966 — CAAAL #11619: "[Alcoholics are] sensitive indicators of the kind of pathogenic trends which influence western society today, leading . . . to a kind of neurosis definable as "identity-diffusion.'"

M. Brunner-Orne and M. T. Orne, "Directive Group-Therapy in the Treatment of Alcoholics," *Int. Journal of Group Psychotherapy* 4: 293–302 (1954) — CAAAL #7060: "Alcoholism cannot be explained solely on the basis of individual psychology; it is also a manifestation of general social maladjustment."

S. D. Bacon, "Alcohol and Complex Society," in D. J. Pittman and C. R. Snyder (eds.), *Society, Culture, and Drinking Patterns* (New York: Wiley, 1962), Chapter 5, pp. 78–93, which explores alcohol as a means of dealing with the "social complexity in Western civilization."

10   For discussion of this point, *cf.* pp. 34–35 and 59, above.

11   On "three-fold disease," the first printed use and explanation that I could find was Dr. Clarence P., "The Medical Approach to Alcoholism," paper presented at the First National and International Meeting of Physicians in Alcoholics Anonymous, held at Cape Vincent, NY, 19–21 August 1949: Conference Record in A.A. archives. The context of its use makes it clear that the physicians present were all familiar with both the term and concept. More obvious, of course, is the concept without the term in *AA*: cf. first "The Doctor's Opinion"; then, p. 30: alcoholics are "bodily and mentally different"; p. 23: "the problem is first mental"; p. 44 "an illness only a spiritual experience will conquer." Within the Wilson correspondence, cf. especially with Dr. S. J. Minogue, 2 December 1957, 17 January and 6 June 1958; also Wilson to B.W.B., 19 October 1965; cf. also "Alcoholism is a Disease," *AAGV* 27:5 (October 1970), 13–15.

The most recent description of a treatment that makes central use of this concept is James R. Milam, *The Emergent Comprehensive Concept of Alcoholism* (Kirkland, WA: Alcoholism Center Associates, 1974).

12   "Alienation" and *"anomie"* as the perceived hallmarks of modernity do not seem to require specific citation. Beyond Marx and Durkheim themselves, I have found useful Shlomo Avineri, *The Social and Political Thought of Karl Marx* (Cambridge: University Press, 1968), "Homo Faber," pp. 65–95; and the "Introduction" in Anthony Giddens (ed.), *Emile Durkheim: Selected Writings* (Cambridge: University Press, 1972), pp. 12–29. A challenging review and interpretation of research that might suggest some connection between these concepts and the understanding of the word "alcoholic" explored at the conclusion of Chapter Eight is M. Clinard (ed.), *Anomie and Deviant Behavior* (New York: Free Press, 1964), see especially the final "Review of the Literature" abstracts.

On the twentieth century as the "Age of Psychology," cf. especially Philip Rieff, *The Triumph of the Therapeutic* (New York: Harper & Row, 1968).

13   The literature that details the damage that alcoholism does to the alcoholic drinker is so vast as utterly to defy citation; cf. especially for the most recent thinking the diverse selections in Tarter and Sugerman (eds.) and Kissin and Begleiter (eds.), both previously cited. For a sociological interpretation of the earlier shift in understanding alcoholism, from "moral degradation" to "spiritual disease," cf. Bruce Holley Johnson, as cited in note #3 to Chapter Eight, p. 369, above.

14   Silkworth's contribution has been described on pp. 15–16 and analyzed on pp. 21–22, above.

15   Cf. note #9 to Chapter Eight, p. 371, above, for the Latin quotation and specific citation.

16   Cf. Wilson's correspondence with Fred W., partially quoted on p. 178, above, and cited in note #8 to Chapter Eight. The Helen C. to whom Wilson is writing in the letter quoted in that note was one person who commented on the dual sense of "spirit."

17   This response is the main thrust of Wilson's treatment of Step Two in *12&12*, pp. 25-34. For a more objective treatment of the A.A. program as Higher Power, cf. the items by Milton Maxwell and Jon Weinberg cited in note #22 to Chapter Eight, p. 375, above.

18   A more direct treatment of the problem that Alcoholics Anonymous found in "Absolutes" is offered in Appendix A, below.

19   Specific quotations and citations for the ideas described in this paragraph may be found in the Appendix, where they are treated at greater depth.

20   A perception, not related to A.A., that the "addiction to addiction" treated here and in the preceding paragraph is a function of the understanding of modernity may be found in Leslie H. Farber, "Thinking About Will" and "Will and Anxiety" in Farber, *Lying, Despair, Jealousy, Envy, Sex, Suicide, Drugs, and the Good Life* (New York: Basic Books, 1976), pp. 3–34. The relationship between Farber's thought and A.A.'s insight is most clear in "Our Kindly Family Physician, Chief Crazy Horse," pp. 106–119, *ibid.*

21   The special need of the alcoholic *to control* is well although largely only indirectly treated in the literature review offered by Helmut Hoffman, "Personality Measurement for the Evaluation and Prediction of Alcoholism," in Tarter and Sugerman (eds.), pp. 309–358. It is further illuminated by *in eodem*, R. E. Tarter, "Empirical Investigations of Psychological Deficit," pp. 359–394; and P. E. Nathan and S. A. Lisman, "Behavioral and Motivational Patterns Chronic Alcoholism," pp. 479–522. The "need to control" is also related to "the narcissistic personality": *cf.* the citations of Kohut and especially Kernberg in note #34, below; the treatment in the text to which that note offers citation should also clarify my own understanding of one aspect of this connection.

22   On A.A.'s perception of the centrality of denial and the specific denial to which its program is directed, *cf.* above, p. 60.

23   *Cf. Al-Anon Faces Alcoholism* (New York: Al-Anon Family Group Headquarters, Inc., 1973), pp. 223–267; also Lois [Wilson], *Lois Remembers* (New York: Al-Anon. . . , 1979), which was available only in galleys at the time the present book went to press.

24   In recent years, there has developed an emphasis on "early intervention" in the treatment of the alcoholic. *Cf.* especially the writings of Vernon E. Johnson, *e.g., I'll Quit Tomorrow* (New York: Harper & Row, 1973), Chapter 5; but also such authors as David A. Stewart, *Thirst for Freedom* (Center City, MN: Hazelden, 1960), Chapter 6; and Roque Fajardo, *Helping Your Alcoholic Before He or She Hits Bottom* (New York: Crown, 1976). All of these approaches make significant use of Alcoholics Anonymous.

25   For the Oxford Group "Four Absolutes," *cf.* pp. 50-51, above, as well as Appendix A, below, pp. 231-247. The quotations are from Wilson to Howard C., 15 November 1960, to be quoted in context in the Appendix.

26   *AA*, pp. 60, 58; Wilson to Les V., 25 May 1961 (to be quoted in context in Appendix A). For the anti-professionalism and anti-intellectualism of A.A., *cf.* above pp. 188-191.

27   Wilson to Margarita L., 14 July 1947.

28   Wilson to Marion L., 31 March 1953.

29   Wilson to Jeff K., 1 April 1953.

30   On the "shared honesty of mutual vulnerability openly acknowledged, *cf.* above, pp. 61 and 197 and below, pp. 221–223; on "the only requirement for membership," *cf.* above, p. 106.

31 The literature on the essence of alcoholism as "dependency" is immense. A sampling of significant observers:

for the evolving consistency of the Freudian understanding:

S. Rado, "Die psychischen Wirkungen der Rauschgifte. Versuch einer psychoanalytischen Theorie der Suchte (The Psychic Effects of Intoxicants. A Psychoanalytic Theory of Addiction)," *Int. Z. Psychoanal.* 12: 540–556 (1926), CAAAL #3594;

E. A. Strecker, "Some Thoughts Concerning the Psychology and Therapy of Alcoholism," *Journal of Nervous and Mental Disease* 86: 191–205 (1937);

E. Simmel, "Alcoholism and Addiction," *Psychoanalytic Quarterly* 17: 6–31 (1948); for one interpretation of the history of this idea, *cf.* M. Tremper. "Dependency in Alcoholics: A Sociological View," *QJSA* 33: 186–190 (1972).

those who build on this a specific critique of A.A.:

F. T. Chambers, Jr., "Analysis and Comparison of Three Treatment Measures for Alcoholism: Antabuse, the Alcoholics Anonymous Approach, and Psychotherapy," *British Journal of Addiction* 50: 29–41 (1953);

J. Y. Dent in L. Williams, "An Experiment in Group Therapy," *British Journal of Addiction* 54: 109–125 (1958);

R. D. Bonacker, "Alcoholism and Alcoholics Anonymous Viewed Symptomatologically," *Mental Hygiene* 42: 562–566 (1958);

less explicit but of greater popular impact was Jim Bishop, *The Glass Crutch* (New York: Doubleday Doran, 1945), pp. 247 ff.;

those who recognize with some approval the dependence within A.A. as upon a Higher Power:

F. Cohen, "Personality Changes Among Members of Alcoholics Anonymous," *Mental Hygiene* 46: 427–437 (1962);

H. J. Clinebell, Jr., "Philosophical-Religious Factors in the Etiology and Treatment of Alcoholism," *QJSA* 24: 473–488 (1963);

those who criticize A.A. specifically for the religious nature of dependence within it:

E. A. Strecker, "Chronic Alcoholism: A Psychological Survey," *QJSA* 2: 12–17 (1941);

I. Gladston, "The Psychodynamics of the Triad, Alcoholism, Gambling, and Superstition," *Mental Hygiene* 35: 589–598 (1958);

M. Bean, "Alcoholics Anonymous," *Psychiatric Annals* 5: 16–64 (1975), is the most recent and by far the best such treatment, and is especially valuable for its extensive bibliography.

On Wilson's sensitivity to this as the psychiatric criticism of A.A., *cf.* Wilson to Oliver J., 13 June 1956: "These psychiatrists have a hell of a lot on the ball. But I sometimes wonder if many know how to pitch it. The parental relation they have with the patient is good to start treatment — but not to continue it. The normal adult relation is a participating one — not a parental one. That's where we have an advantage in A.A. that they pass up — they are trained in the doctor-patient relation primarily."

Hoggson, *Alcoholics Anonymous: A Study in Solidarity*, pp. 241 ff., offers indirectly a relatively early (1952) discussion of this perception, with telling citations.

On the modern mind and the Nietzschean will, *cf.* Farber, "Thinking About Will," as cited in note #20, above, and especially William Barrett, *The Illusion of Technique* (New York: Anchor-Doubleday, 1978), pp. 193–198.

32   On "the alcoholic's dependence upon the chemical alcoholic as in service to his infantile quest for grandiose omnipotence," *cf.* especially Rado, Simmel, Bonacker, and Gladston, as cited in note #31, above, for a representative sample.

33   On the psychology of infancy, *cf.* especially the writings of Margaret S. Mahler; most relevant here are *On Human Symbiosis and the Vicissitudes of Individuation* (London: The Hogarth Press and The Institute of Psychoanalysis, 1969), and with Fred Pine and Anni Bergman, *The Psychological Birth of the Human Infant: Symbiosis and Individuation* (New York: Basic Books, 1975) — in both, the first two chapters speak most directly to the point. For an earlier and more challenging interpretation, *cf.* William V. Silverberg, *Childhood Experience and Personal Destiny* (New York: Springer, 1952). Dr. Silverberg found hints of this interpretation in American psychiatric thought before Freud: *cf.* his use of Trigant Burrow's concept of "oceanic feeling," pp. 15–16.

34   For this understanding of infant psychology, *cf.* the preceding note, especially Mahler; for one expression of a similar insight into the meaning of the prevalence of addictions, *cf.* David F. Musto, *The American Disease* (New Haven: Yale Univ. Press, 1973).

For a deeper analysis of the implications of such "immaturity," the recent flurry of literature on "naricissism" is instructive; *cf.* the following:

Heinz Kohut, *The Analysis of the Self* (New York: International Universities Press, 1971), especially the Chapter 2 discussion of "The Idealizing Transference" and the Chapter 5 treatment of "Mirror Transference";

Otto Kernberg, *Borderline Conditions and Pathological Narcissism* (New York: Jason Aronson, 1975), especially Chapters 9 and 10: "Clinical Problems of the Narcissistic Personality" and "Normal and Pathological Narcissism"; also, his thoughts on "Prognosis," pp. 306 ff., as clarifying the relationship between "immaturity" and "narcissism";

Ernest Becker, *The Denial of Death* (New York, Free Press, 1973), Chapters 3, 4, 7, 10, and especially 11: "What Is the Heroic Individual?";

Heinz Kohut, *The Restoration of the Self* (New York: International Universities Press, 1977), especially Chapters 2 and 7 on the need for a "psychology of the self";

Christopher Lasch, "The Narcissist Society," *The New York Review of Books* 23 (No. 13): 5, 8–13 (30 September 1976), and *The Culture of Narcissism* (New York: W. W. Norton, 1978).

35   On Heisenberg's Principle of Indeterminacy — and Bohr's Principle of Complementarily and the impact of Gödel — *cf.* William Barrett, *Irrational Man* (New York: Doubleday-Anchor, 1962), pp. 36–41.

36   The "need others" component as the essential dynamic of why attending meetings "works" in keeping members sober has been well analyzed by M.A. Maxwell: *cf.* the final citation in note #4 to Chapter Eight, p. 370, above, and "Alcoholics Anonymous: An Interpretation" in David J. Pittman (ed.), *Alcoholism* (New York: Harper & Row, 1967), pp. 211-222. *Cf.* also E. Hanfman, "The Life History of an Ex-Alcoholic — With an Evaluation of Factors Involved in Causation and Rehabilitation," *QJSA* 12: 405-443 (1951); and especially W. Madsen, "A.A.: Birds of a Feather," in Madsen, *The American Alcoholic*, pp. 168 ff.

A.A.'s General Service Conference in 1967 devoted itself to the question of

"Sponsorship" in a way that makes clear this point: *cf.* "Final Report," especially pp. 8–12.

"do not require actual separation": on the possibility of the A.A. group or program serving as "Higher Power," *cf.* above, p. 206.

37   *Cf.* the treatment of this point in the Introduction to Part Two, p. 158, above, and the citations in note #1 to that Introduction, p. 363, above.

38   As the fundamental criticism of Alcoholics Anonymous, *cf.*, *e.g.*, Stanton Peele (with Archie Brodsky), *Love and Addiction* (New York: Taplinger-Signet, 1975), p. 232; also note #31, above. The fundamental nature of the criticism is most clear in the contribution by Margaret Bean cited *ibidem.*

39   For depth concerning the theme of this paragraph, *cf.*: M. P. Murray, *The Concepts of Self-Acceptance and Self-Respect in Karen Horney's Theory of Neurosis* (Rome: Dissertation Angelicum, 1961); Sidney Jourard, *The Transparent Self* (New York: Van Nostrand, 1971, rev. ed.); Henri J. M. Nouwen, *The Wounded Healer* (New York: Doubleday, 1972).

40   Much of what is said here and in the following paragraphs about what I have termed "joyous pluralism" may be found discussed without this specific term and from a different point of view in Roberto Mangabeira Unger, *Knowledge and Politics* (New York: Free Press, 1975) and *Law in Modern Society* (New York: Free Press, 1976). For an explicit treatment of pluralism in its historical and ideological context, *cf.* Robert Nisbet, *The Social Philosophers* (New York: Thos. Y. Crowell, 1973), pp. 385–442, and the treatment of "mutuality" on pp. 365–382.

Anyone seriously interested in thinking on the implications and possibilities of "joyous pluralism" can do no better than to begin with a careful reading of Peter Kropotkin, *Mutual Aid: A Factor in Evolution* (London: Wm. Heinemann, 1908).

Concerning the living out of "joyous pluralism" in A.A., beyond the meeting practice described above, pp. 214–215, note the way three favorite A.A. aphorisms are used: "First Things First"; "Live and Let Live"; and "Easy Does It." These may be found in *AA*, p. 135, italicized. That these "little mottoes" are meant to reach beyond life in A.A. itself is clear from their placement in the 1st edition of *AA* (p. 149): at the conclusion of the chapter on "The Family Afterwards."

41   On the centrality of "tolerance" in A.A., *cf.* Chapter Six, above, pp. 151–153, and note #47.

42   On the "shared honesty of mutual vulnerability openly acknowledged," *cf.* above pp. 61, 197–198, and 214–215.

43   That strength arises precisely from weakness is of course especially the insight of the Evangelically Pietist style of religious insight. An explanation of this, and the exploration of this vision's incorporation in A.A., have been offered in Chapter Eight; *cf.* also pp. 150–151.

44   For this understanding of anonymity, *cf.* in Chapter Eight pp. 195–197, on the age of "me" and "more," *cf.* the material on narcissism cited in note #34, above, and by Leslie H. Farber, cited in note #20, above.

45   On modernity and the problem of limiting the sense of limitation, *cf.* Chapter Seven, pp. 171-172, with the citations in note #29, p. 369.

46   For this and the following paragraphs, *cf.* the treatment of *12&12* in Chapter Five, pp. 124–126, with citations. That this understanding perdured in Wilson's thought is attested to by the fact that the direct quotations here and just below are taken, generally, from later correspondence: Wilson to Charlie B., 4 December 1961; to Eleanor R., 12 December 1961; to Fr. Dowling, 25 May 1954; to Glen W., 22 July 1960.

47   Within *12&12*, the instincts and moods are treated especially in the discussion of Step Four, pp. 43–55; *cf.* also in the discussion of Step Twelve, pp. 119–120.

48   Wilson applies his deepest analysis to domestic life, in a letter to Helen H., 24 March 1965: "Asking for love [can be] the deep clamor for a state of mutual possession."

49   On limited control and limited dependence, *cf.* above, pp. 105–106, 211.

50   *AACA*, pp. 26 ff. and 83 ff.; *cf.* note #22 to Chapter Eight, p. 375, also H. M. Tiebout, "Alcoholics Anonymous — An Experiment of Nature," *QJSA 22:* 52-68 (1961) and "Hitting Bottom: Its Therapeutic Significance," paper read before the meeting of the American Psychological Association held in Chicago, Illinois, 8 May 1961, printed in revised form as "Intervention in Psychotherapy," *American Journal of Psychoanalysis* 22: 1-7 (1963).

For a deeper grasp of Tiebout's thought as developing, *cf.* his unpublished Ph.D. dissertation: "Philosophy and Psychoanalysis: Theories of Human Nature and Conduct in Freud's Psychology," Columbia University, 1951. The thesis is especially germane to the point at hand, for it reveals Tiebout's thoughts on the meaning of religion (*cf.* especially its Chapters 5 and 6), and his understanding of "the general philosophical situation in the West," just before his interest in Buddhism was awakened by the A.A. development treated here.

51   The attractiveness of Buddhist thought is especially witnessed to by the brief popularity of E. F. Schumacher, *Small Is Beautiful* (New York: Harper & Row, 1973), *cf.* especially the essay, "Buddhist Economics," pp. 53–62.

52   "The spreading diversity of A.A.'s appeal and the increasing variety of its membership" are themselves best attested to by aspects of the "special group" phenomenon treated in Chapter Six, pp. 146–147, and by analysis of A.A.'s numerical membership increase after 1973 — a phenomenon especially interesting because the number of members seemed to have reached a plateau during the 1960s. These data are derived from A.A. General Service Office figures; so far as I know, there has been no sociological exploration of their possible interpretation.

53   The "quite necessarily" is philosophical: *cf.* the citations of David Noble and Morton White, note #26 to Chapter Seven, p. 368, above; also note #15 to Appendix A, p. 389, below. *Cf.* also William Barrett and Leslie H. Farber as previously cited in this chapter.

54   The most recent explicit exploration of the "perennial philosophy" is by E. F. Schumacher, *A Guide for the Perplexed* (New York: Harper & Row, 1977).

Fundamentally, the perennial philosophy is an extrapolation of Aristotelian thought.

55 Partially because of the philosophical point being made as well as the historical reality noted, there is little modern literature on "temperance." Helpful may be Josef Pieper, *Fortitude and Temperance*, tr. David F. Coogan (New York: Pantheon, 1954), pp. 47–53 and 115-118.

56 "all or nothing people": *cf.*, *e.g.*, Wilson to Howard C., 15 November 1960; to Patricia N., 7 January 1963; to Bob C., 23 June 1964. The final quotation is attributed to Dr. Daniel J. Anderson, director of the Hazelden treatment center.

57 The "End of Absolutes" in many ways began in America with the phenomena chronicled and analyzed in Morton White, *Social Thought in America*; its more recent meaning may perhaps best be grasped from Chapter One, "Modernization," in C. E. Black, *The Dynamics of Modernization* (New York: Harper & Row, 1966), or — more popularly — from Allen Wheelis, *The End of the Modern Age* (New York: Basic Books, 1971), especially pp. 79 ff., "Relativity of Knowledge"; Unger, *Knowledge and Politics*, offers philosophical rather than historical depth and perspective on the point. On the "Age of Limits," *cf.* in Chapter Seven, above, pp. 170–171, with notes #7 and 29.

APPENDIX A

1 *Cf.* discussion in Chapters Five and Six, pp. 116–117 and 145–146.

2 The quotations are from Denys W., (Cambridge, England) to Wilson, 31 July, 2 October, and 12 October 1963. On "responsibility" as a special concern of Wilson at this time, *cf.* the treatment in Chapter Six, pp. 139–142.

3 The draft from which the quotations are taken was an attachment to the letter of Denys to Wilson of 2 October 1963.

4 Jon R. Weinberg, "AA: An Interpretation for the Nonbeliever," published in pamphlet form (Center City, MN: Hazelden, 1975), pp. 4 and 6, italics Weinberg's.

5 Information based on interviews given only on the promise that those interviewed would remain anonymous. Although at first skeptical on hearing this tale, I became convinced of its general accuracy because of the similarities of details in its telling by different individuals who clearly were not drawing on some other single source.

6 Little more can be said about these pamphlets, or the Cleveland one on "The Four Absolutes," than is offered in the text. All are available from the Cleveland A.A. District Office, One Public Square, Cleveland, OH 44113.

7 "Manual," p. 1 (emphasis added).

8 "Spiritual Milestones," pp. 1–2.

9 "Second Reader," p. 3 (emphasis there).

10 "The Four Absolutes," pp. 1, 14.

11 These descriptions are slightly edited but basically *verbatim* from interviews with Warren C. and Dick P. on 7 and 8 September 1977.

12   Smith, "Last Major Talk," pp. 16–17 of the mis-dated private reprinting.

13   Although, as noted in the Bibliography, my contacts with Clarence S. were many and diverse and for the history recorded in Chapters Three and Four mainly by mail and telephone, what follows is based primarily on personal meeting with him over 5 and 6 October 1978. On these two days, I observed Clarence mingling with patients and staff at an alcoholism treatment facility; attended an open A.A. meeting at which he was the sole speaker, telling his story and offering his interpretation of A.A. for about two hours; interviewed him about some of the points in his presentation and his thoughts concerning the dissertation on which the present book is based, which he had at that time read through twice. I hold tapes of the meeting presentation and interview, and Clarence's story as it appears below is drawn directly from my tape of that presentation although edited for brevity. All other quotations in this and the following paragraphs are also drawn from these tapes.

14   Clarence bases his understanding of "qualifying" on the second and third paragraphs of "How It Works," *AA*, p. 58:

> . . . If you have decided you want what we have and are willing to go to any length to get it — then you are ready to take certain steps.
>
> At some of these we balked. We thought we could find an easier, softer way. But we could not. . . . Some of us tried to hold on to our old ideas and the result was nil until we let go absolutely.

On Tiebout's understanding, *cf.* above, pp. 183–184, with citations.

15   In Chapter Eight, *cf.* especially pp. 182–186. On the problems of "absolute relativism," *cf.* beyond David Noble's *The Paradox of Progressive Thought*, his *Historians Against History* (Minneapolis, Univ. of Minnesota, 1965), especially Chapter Eight on Carl Becker. Of the wealth of literature on this topic, I find most fascinating Becker's review of Maurice Mandelbaum, *Philosophical Review* 40: 363–364 (1940), and the historiographic studies of Becker offered by Burleigh Taylor Wilkins and Charlotte Watkins Smith.

16   The relationship between "The Survivors Program," "The Church of The Way," and "East Ridge" (a treatment center, but one aimed more at life-style than active addiction) may become clear in the following paragraphs. If it does not, it is because I am not clear about it in my own mind. After some correspondence and telephone conversations in late 1977 and early 1978, I visited East Ridge on 13 October 1978 to discuss with its staff their concerns over what I had written of them in an earlier version of this Appendix.

The interpretation that follows is "unofficial," and the people at East Ridge would very much prefer to offer their own, but such is unavailable. I have based what follows as scrupulously as possible on my conversations with three of the community's leaders and their literature as cited in this and note #20. What follows in the text does not attempt profound historical interpretation of East Ridge etc. themselves; yet it does offer sufficiently deep investigation of their philosophy to clarify a point about Alcoholics Anonymous.

The clearest and most easily available presentation of East Ridge may be found in a pamphlet distributed by it, available from East Ridge, Hankins, NY 12741. The most recent copy ("Ninth edition, August 1978") is titled: "East

Ridge — a laboratory for living the Survivors Program — the Way out when all other ways have failed.''

17   pp. 5 and 6 of the pamphlet cited in the preceding note.

18   Lewis Yablonsky, *The Tunnel Back: Synanon* (New York: Macmillan, 1965), pp. 52, 48. 55, 88. The passage quoted from p. 55, reproduced here in quotation marks, are the words of Dederick.

19   Interview with Thomas W., 13 October 1978.

20   John Burns (pseud.) *et al., The Answer to Addiction* (New York: Harper & Row, 1975), p. 213. Also especially revealing of The Survivors Program's criticism of A.A. are two issues of its magazine, *24*, vol. 6, no. 1 (July 1976), completely devoted to "Gresham's Law and Alcoholics Anonymous," and vol. 6, no. 3 (Sept. 1976), featuring "The Uses and Abuses of Anonymity," pp. 4–11, a more restrained criticism but one that again distorts history in its selective use of sources.

21   Two leaders of the Church of The Way, Thomas P. and Thomas W., insist that the quotation of Wilson incorporated in the previous citation was oral rather than written, and I accept without reservation the accuracy of that memory. My argument here is not that there was intentional and meretricious distortion of the specific Wilson letters that I shall cite, but that there has been unconscious forgetfulness both of the historical context that gave rise to these words whether spoken or written and of the other things that Wilson was surely saying at the same time even if not in the same conversation. Both Thomas P. and Thomas W. were in close enough contact with Wilson at the time that it seems just to refer to this lapse as "unconscious forgetfulness" rather than accidental ignorance.

22   Wilson to Howard C., 15 November 1960 (emphasis added).

23   *AA*, pp. 62; for "This is a selfish program" as a common saying in A.A., *cf.* the letter quoted in the second paragraph hence and cited in note #25.

24   For the analysis of the instincts in *12&12, cf.* pp. 125–126 in Chapter Five, above.

25   Wilson to Ollie and Ruth J., 10 February 1958; the longer quotation is from *ABSI,* p. 81 — the letter itself is from 1966.

26   Wilson to Patricia N., 7 January 1963; Harry J. (Saginaw, MI) to Dr. Karen Horney, copy sent to Wilson and in A.A. archives, undated, but internally datable to July or August 1953; *AA*, p. 60.

27   *AA,* p. 58; Wilson to Les V., 25 May 1961.

28   Wilson to Grafton G., 22 May 1963; to McGowan H., 13 December 1965 (emphasis added).

29   Wilson to Candy?, 7 June 1967; to Patricia N., 7 January 1963 (emphasis Wilson's).

30   Wilson to Barbara F., ?? 1960.

31   Wilson to Jim K., 24 October 1956 (emphasis Wilson's).

32   Wilson to Tom C., 19 September 1962.

33   Wilson to Fred L., ?? 1957.

34   The generalization proposed in the first two paragraphs of this Conclusion is so comprehensive, embracing as it does the whole history of American religious thought in the nineteenth century, that to attempt to support it by specific citation would be ridiculous. I welcome and invite discussion of it with scholars whose specialty is this era of American thought. To encourage such, the following two citations are offered as having stimulated my thought here:
   Sidney E. Mead, *The Lively Experiment* (New York: Harper & Row, 1963), "When 'Wise Men Hoped': The National Period," especially pp. 92ff: what was reversed by the "constellation of [six] images" here noted and explored?
   Whitney R. Cross, *The Burned-Over District* (New York: Harper Torchbook, 1965), especially "Book IV: Genesis of Ultraism": what preceded these "New Measures," "New Men," and "New Ideas"?

APPENDIX B

1   Some details from Nell Wing, interview of 21 April 1987.

2   Bob P., *Final Report of the 1986 General Service Conference,* pp. 6–7.

3   L.H., "How It Seemed to One Biased Alcoholic Observer," *AAGV*, October 1970, pp. 16–23.

4   Many of the details in the paragraph from conversations with Nell Wing, most directly on 21 April 1987.

5   John W. Stevens, "Bill W. of Alcoholics Anonymous Dies," *New York Times,* 26 January 1971.

6   Bob H., *Final Report of the 1971 General Service Conference,* pp. 12–13; *cf.* also the G.S.O. report by Eleanor N. of the Public Information Committee: "The P.I.C. [Public Information Committee] handled all media coverage in connection with Bill's death. Some time ago an obituary for Bill was distributed to the wire services, radio and TV networks. An accompanying letter signed by both Bill and Lois, gave permission for the disclosing of his full name at the time of his death. This obituary was updated periodically," 1971 *Final Report,* p. 22; a bit more detail is available in *Box 4-5-9* 16:2 (Memorial Issue, January 1971), 2. Nell Wing confirmed, conversation of 21 April 1987, that a primary concern in preparing and distributing the obituary had been to prevent distortion.

7   "To Honor Bill's Memory," *Box 4-5-9* 16:2 (Memorial Issue, January 1971), 1: The fund was "to be administered by the General Service Board of A.A. for some special A.A. purpose. Only contributions from A.A. members can be accepted, of course, because of the A.A. Tradition of self-support."

8   There is a scrapbook of press clippings from around the nation and the world in the A.A. archives; *cf.* also "One Worldwide Day of Memorial Meetings for Bill," *AAGV* (April 1971), p. 44.

9   Associated Press wire service story of 15 February 1971.

10   Waneta N., "Conference," *Final Report of the 1971 General Service Conference,* p. 21.

11   Although published for the membership and therefore not confined to A.A.'s archives, copies of the *Final Report* of each year's General Service Conference are preserved in the archives and like other archival material are generally open to scholarly investigators as well as to members of the fellowship. As the *Final Report of the 1976 General Service Conference,* p. 37, reaffirmed: "There are no secrets in A.A." — at least so long as the tradition of anonymity is respected.

12   *Cf. Box 4-5-9* 33:2 (April/May 1987), 2.

13   *Cf.* Beth K., "Planning for Conference," *Final Report of the 1970 General Service Conference,* p. 27.

14   "NCA To Recognize Other Drugs," *The Alcoholism Report,* 3 March 1987, p. 7.

15   *Cf. The A.A. Service Manual Combined with Twelve Concepts for World Service,* by Bill W. (New York: A.A.W.S., "1985–1986 edition"), with notation of the original copyright of the *Manual* in 1969 and of the *Concepts* in 1962.

16   *Cf. Final Report of the 1960 General Service Conference,* p. 8.

17   *Cf. Final Report of the 1971 General Service Conference,* p. 33.

18   Smith, who had substituted for Wilson at the Miami convention a scant month before, died on July 31, 1970; *cf. Box 4-5-9* 15:5 (October/November 1970), 1.

19   Bayard P., "As the Public Sees A.A.," *Final Report of the 1971 General Service Conference,* p. 12.

20   John L. Norris, M.D., "Highlights of Past Conferences," *Final Report of the 1977 General Service Conference*, p. 6.

21   *Cf.* above, pp. 118–119.

22   Hal M., "Alcoholic Counseling Program," *Final Report of the 1971 General Service Conference*, p. 10, reporting on "the Economic Opportunity Act of 1964 as amended December 31, 1969 [and in 1970] funded in the amount of $9,000,-000" with OEO budget requests totaling $13 million for this program in 1972.

23   For precedents, *cf.* above, pp. 117 ff.; but references to the "treatment industry" become appropriate — and common — only in the late seventies.

24   John R., "No Monopoly on Recovery," *Final Report of the 1971 General Service Conference*, p. 10.

25   "The spirituality of not having all the answers": I am grateful for this phrase to Bob D. of Rochester, New York, conversation of 14 May 1987.

26   This concern had also been raised the previous year; *cf. Final Report of the 1970 General Service Conference*, p. 31.

27   *Cf. Final Report of the 1971 General Service Conference*, p. 9.

28   The final observation is based on a comparison of A.A. meeting lists from the 1960s and 1970s with Narcotics Anonymous meeting lists available for 1985 and after.

29   The pamphlet "A.A. For The Woman," which first appeared in 1957, replaced 1953's "The Alcoholic Wife." It underwent substantial revision in 1968. A clear statement of the issues appeared in the January 1963 *A.A. Exchange Bulletin* 8:1, under the headline, "Attention A.A. Gals!" Six barriers to "female attendance" were listed:

(1) Feeling of non-acceptance in predominantly male groups with their participation in meetings discouraged.
(2) Difficulty in getting women newcomers to attend regular meetings of predominantly male groups.
(3) Reluctance on the part of wives of A.A. members to have women A.A. members attend closed groups which their husbands attend.
(4) Difficulty of getting new women contacts from well-known families to attend group meetings where such attendance may become known to the community.
(5) Isolation of lone women members in areas where A.A. attendance is predominantly male.
(6) Difficulty of making Twelfth-Step calls on women when there are so few women members in an area.

Impressionistic evidence, supported by A.A.'s triennial surveys, indicates that each of these barriers became less a reality as the proportion of women in any group moved over one in four and approached one in three.

1987 Advisory Action #10 signaled the continuing need and continuing effort on this topic, recommending that "The title of the pamphlet 'A Clergyman Asks' be changed to 'The Clergy Asks' when it comes up for reprint."

30   These generalizations are based on my notes and memory of conversations with diverse G.S.O. staff during my 1976–1978 research. According to the Dick P. interview tape, the Big Book had been translated into Spanish in 1963, by a Cleveland alcoholic of Mexican origin who had come into A.A. as a result of the Rollie Hemsley publicity in 1940, *cf.* above, pp. 86–87.

A.A.'s pamphlet designed to meet claims of exceptional status, first conceived in 1975 under the title "So You Think You're Different?" and finally published as "Do You Think You're Different?" in 1977, derived from this context and also from awareness of such groups as gay-lesbian, agnostic, and native American alcoholics; *cf. Final Report of the 1976 General Service Conference,* p. 43. The 1987 General Service Conference also advised efforts at new outreach to "Native North American" alcoholics, especially by *The A.A. Grapevine.*

31   *Cf.* Advisory Action of the 1966 General Service Conference, reported in *Summary of Advisory Actions, 1951–1978,* p. 33, recommending that "The idea of a cartoon format for A.A. literature be further explored and developed for the purpose of reaching alcoholics who are unable to read well, or who just don't read."

32   The suggested parallel between the 1940s and, the 1970s in A.A. history was first urged by Nell Wing, to whom I am grateful for her spirited discussion of it.

33   On the "five C's," *cf.* above, p. 49, and, for a more extended treatment from within Oxford Group assumptions but applied explicitly to alcoholics, Richmond Walker, *For Drunks Only* (Hazelden, 1986 reprint of the original 1945 edition), pp. 45–46.

34   *Cf. Final Report of the 1972 General Service Conference,* p. 14.

35   *Final Report of the 1973 General Service Conference,* p. 34; *Final Report of the 1974 General Service Conference,* p. 38.

36   *Final Report of the 1973 General Service Conference,* p. 6.

37   *Final Report of the 1974 General Service Conference,* p. 5.

38   *Final Report of the 1971 General Service Conference,* p. 36.

39   *Final Report of the 1974 General Service Conference,* p. 6.

40   *Final Report of the 1975 General Service Conference,* p. 1.

41   *Final Report of the 1975 General Service Conference,* p. 13.

42   "GSO Is No Censor," *AAGV,* November 1971, p. 44

43   *Final Report of the 1983 General Service Conference,* p. 6.

44   Bob P., "Closing Talk: Our greatest danger: rigidity," *Final Report of the 1986 General Service Conference,* pp. 6–7.

45   *Final Report of the 1986 General Service Conference,* pp. 10–11; *cf.* also *Box 4-5-9* 33:2 (April/May 1987), for the transition to 1987's Conference.

46   How Alcoholics Anonymous derives its estimates of membership was best described in a response to an Ask-It-Basket question — *cf. Final Report of the*

1975 General Service Conference, pp. 38–39: "A.A. makes no effort to keep complete membership records at either the group or international level, but in response to demand, we do make an annual estimate. This is based on the actual reported figures of groups and members. Where some of the groups in an area do not include membership figures, an average is made of the reporting groups in each state or province and this average is assigned arbitrarily to the groups which omit membership figures. The total figure for reported members obtained by this method is then factored to account for the members who do not regularly attend meetings to obtain an *estimated* membership for public release. We believe the resulting estimate of membership is an extremely conservative figure."

47 All figures are from each year's *Final Report of the General Service Conference.*

48 *Cf. Box 4-5-9* 18:3 (June/July 1973), 1: "Millionth Big Book at White House," and picture of Dr. John Norris presenting that copy to President Richard Nixon.

49 This projection does not take into account the impact of the first paperback edition of the Big Book, which sold over 81,000 copies in the less than three months after it appeared in late 1986, apparently without denting the sales of the regular edition. Early sales indicate that its availability will increase overall sales so that "every fifteen months" may prove an under-estimate.

50 *Cf. Final Report of the 1972 General Service Conference,* p. 33.

51 Reports of numbers of groups and members divided into "United States, Canada, Loners and Internationalists, Correctional Facilities and Overseas" can be found in each year's General Service Conference *Final Report; cf.* also *Box 4-5-9* 33:3 (June/July 1987), p. 2.

52 For the briefest summary of significance, *cf.* Mark Edward Lender and James Kirby Martin, *Drinking in America* (New York: Macmillan Free Press, 1982), pp. 189–195; *cf.* also Carolyn Wiener, *The Politics of Alcoholism: Building an Arena Around a Social Problem* (New Brunswick, NJ: Transaction Books, 1981), p. 28, for the context and *passim;* also *United States Code, Congressional and Administrative News,* vol. 3, 91st Cong., 2d sess. (St. Paul, MN: West Publishing, 1970), pp. 5724–5726; *Congressional Quarterly Almanac,* vol. XXIX, 1973, pp. 557–564; *idem,* vol. XXXIII, 1977, p. 483, vol. XXXIV, 1978, p. 592, and vol. XXXV, 1979, p. 512; also *United States Code, Congressional and Administrative News,* 95th Cong., 2d sess., vol. 6 (St. Paul, MN: West Publishing, 1978), p. 7413. Mark H. Moore and Dean R. Gerstein, eds., *Alcohol and Public Policy: Beyond the Shadow of Prohibition* (Washington, DC: National Academy Press, 1981), discuss public policy planning as flowing from the legislation. I am grateful to Professor Linda Farris Kurtz of Indiana University–Purdue University at Indianapolis for summarizing the research literature represented in this paragraph and note.

For a more detailed historical description of the background of this process, *cf.* Bruce Holley Johnson, *The Alcoholism Movement in America: A Study in Cultural Innovation,* unpublished dissertation, University of Illinois at Urbana-Champaign: University Microfilms # 74-5603, pp. 370–371.

53 On Alcoholics Anonymous as "way of life," *cf.* the original title of the book now distributed as *As Bill Sees It* (New York: A.A.W.S., 1967) and *Twelve Steps and Twelve Traditions,* p. 15; also *AACA,* p. 127.

54   *Cf.* Donald Meyer, *The Positive Thinkers* (New York: Doubleday, 1965).

55   Walter Houston Clark, *Chemical Ecstasy* (New York: Sheed & Ward, 1969); David Musto, *The American Disease* (New Haven: Yale, 1973); and Thomas Szasz, *Ceremonial Chemistry* (London: Routledge and Kagan Paul, 1975) — all afford good introductions to this topic. For a much larger but also very useful perspective, *cf.* Christopher Lasch, *The Culture of Narcissism* (New York: Norton, 1978) and *The Minimal Self* (New York: Norton, 1984); and Robert N. Bellah, Richard Madsen, William M. Sullivan, Ann Swidler, and Steven M. Tipton, *Habits of the Heart* (Berkeley: Univ. of California, 1985). For the final point, John Mack and Edward Khantzian in Bean and Zinberg, *Dynamic Approaches to the Understanding and Treatment of Alcoholism* (New York: Free Press, 1981).

56   Lender and Martin, *Drinking in America*, p. 189; for the N.C.A., *cf.* Bruce Holley Johnson, *The Alcoholism Movement in America: A Study in Cultural Innovation*, unpublished dissertation, University of Illinois at Urbana-Champaign: University Microfilms # 74-5603, especially the detailed and comprehensive Chapter Five.

57   *Cf.* Carolyn Wiener, *The Politics of Alcoholism: Building an Arena Around a Social Problem* (New Brunswick, NJ: Transaction Books, 1981); *cf.* also Mark H. Moore and Dean R. Gerstein, eds., *Alcohol and Public Policy: Beyond the Shadow of Prohibition* (Washington, DC: National Academy Press, 1981).

58   This impression derives from comparing over time meeting lists from all over the country. The sampling is unscientific, resulting from my own research in local archives while traveling and from those copies of meeting lists preserved in the G.S.O. archives or in other scattered places such as the *A.A. Grapevine* files.

59   *Cf. Box 4-5-9* 20:4 (August/September 1975), 4: "Share Your Detox Center Experience — It's Needed."

60   *Final Report of the 1973 General Service Conference*, p. 32.

61   *Final Report of the 1978 General Service Conference*, pp. 13–14.

62   *Final Report of the 1973 General Service Conference*, p. 10; *AAGV* 43:8 (January 1987), 26–35; *Final Report of the 1976 General Service Conference*, p. 25; *Final Report of the 1979 General Service Conference*, p. 43.

63   D. J. Armor, J. M. Polich, and H. B. Stambull, *Alcoholism and Treatment* (Santa Monica, CA: Rand Corp., 1976).

64   *Cf. Final Report of the 1977 General Service Conference*, p. 26.

65   D. L. Davies, "Normal Drinking in Recovered Alcohol Addicts," *QJSA* 23:94–104 (1962); R. G. Bell, "Normal Drinking in Recovered Alcohol Addicts"; Comment on the Article by D. L. Davies, *QJSA* 24:321–322 (1963); M. Sobell and L. Sobell, "Alternative to Abstinence," *Journal of the American Medical Association* 235:2103–2104 (1974); E. M. Pattison, M. B. Sobell, and L. C. Sobell, *Emerging Concepts of Alcohol Dependence* (New York: Springer, 1977); E. Mansell Pattison, *Selection of Treatment for Alcoholics* (Piscataway NJ: Center of Alcohol Studies, 1981).

The usual comment heard within A.A. on this topic runs, "There are people dying because they think like that"; and often a specific story is told illustrating that point and reminding of the pervasiveness of the alcoholic's pathognomonic denial.

66 Robert E. Tournier, "Alcoholics Anonymous as Treatment and as Ideology," *JSA* 40:3 (March 1979), 230–239. The commenting articles by Donald W. Goodwin, Mark B. Sobell, Linda C. Sobell, William Madsen, Robert A. Moore, Chaim M. Rosenberg, Harold W. Demone, Jr., and Gerald D. Shulman appear on pages 318–338 of the same issue. Tournier's "Reply to Comments" appeared in *JSA* 40:7 (July 1979), 743–749.

67 *Cf.* Alan C. Ogborne, Ph.D., and Frederick B. Glaser, M.D., F.R.C.P.(C), "Characteristics of Affiliates of Alcoholics Anonymous: A Review of the Literature," *JSA* 42:661–675 (July 1981); *Final Report of the 1974 General Service Conference,* p. 23; *Final Report of the 1977 General Service Conference,* p. 44.

68 "Results of Recent Survey," *Box 4-5-9* 13:5 (October/November 1968), 3.

69 *Final Report of the 1977 General Service Conference,* p. 40; *cf.* also *Box 4-5-9,* 20:1 (February/March 1975), 1: "1974 A.A. Survey Does Massive Twelfth-Step Job, Proves Again That 'A.A. Works.'"

70 *Cf. Box 4-5-9* October/November 1972, February/March 1975, October/November 1978, October/November 1981, October/November 1984.

71 Interview of John B., 22 April 1987, at which the point was also made that beginning in 1983, A.A. has hired a statistician to design the survey according to accepted standards. The scientifically chosen sample for 1986 numbered 6977.

72 *Cf.* above, p. 89; *Box 4-5-9* 20:4 (August-September 1975), "Share Your Detox Experience — It's Needed"; "Is your group doing enough about prospective new A.A. members sent to you by a detox center — in comparison to what your group does about helping an alcoholic who walks in off the street on his or her own?

"... as shown in the *Final Report* of the 1975 Silver Anniversary General Service Conference, the sponsorship needed for professionally referred problem drinkers is of increasing concern in A.A., as professional interest in helping alcoholics steps up."

Cf. also *Final Report of the 1975 General Service Conference,* pp. 19–20; *Final Report of the 1976 General Service Conference,* pp. 9–10.

73 *Cf. Box 4-5-9* 33:3 (June/July 1987), 2, and treatment below, pp.185–186.

74 *Final Report of the 1975 General Service Conference,* p. 19; *cf. Final Report of the 1970 General Service Conference,* pp. 18–19.

75 J.G., "That Fabulous Convention!" *AAGV,* 32:5 (October 1975), 20–25; and "Convention Vignettes," *idem,* 26–27; also Bill Pittman, "Sobriety Celebrations," *Alcoholism/the National Magazine* 5:5 (May/June 1985), 26–27.

76 "The Language of the Heart," *A.A. Today* (New York: A.A.W.S., 1960), pp. 7–11; "A.A. Communication Can Cross All Barriers," *AAGV,* 16:5 (October 1959), 2–5.

On Bill's intention to write a final book on "Practicing These Principles in All Our Affairs," *cf.* his late-1960 correspondence with Dr. John Norris. Bill began the project in a series of *A.A. Grapevine* articles that appeared in 1961 and 1962; *cf.* "God As We Understand Him: The Dilemma of No Faith, by Bill," *AAGV* 17:11 (April 1961), 3–7.

77   *Cf. Final Report of the 1976 General Service Conference,* p. 45; *The A.A. Service Manual Combined with Twelve Concepts for World Service,* by Bill W. (New York: A.A.W.S., "1985–1986 edition"), p. 28; also, how the 1987 General Service Conference approached its theme, "The Seventh Tradition — A Turning Point," with presentations on "Being Aware of Changes/Trends Within A.A." and "Our Primary Purpose: Is It Changing in a Changing World?"

78   *Cf. Box 4-5-9* 33:3 (June/July 1987), 1.

79   *Final Report of the 1974 General Service Conference,* p. 18.

80   *Final Report of the 1971 General Service Conference,* p. 13.

81   *Cf.* e.g., Dennis Wholey, *The Courage to Change* (Boston: Houghton Mifflin, 1984); on the "Creating a Sober World" project, *cf.* below, p. 202; *Final Report of the 1982 General Service Conference,* pp. 19–20: "Anonymity Breaks — How Are We Handling Them?" Answer: "G.S.O. Sends Friendly Reminder."

82   *Final Report of the 1972 General Service Conference,* p. 22; *Final Report of the 1978 General Service Conference,* p. 13.

83   *Cf.* the heading, "Never Received Salary" in the *Box 4-5-9* 16:2 (Memorial Issue, January 1971), 4; also the consistent publication, until 1971, of "Bill's Statement On His Finances" in each year's *Final Report of the General Service Conference,* e.g., in 1970, p. 42.

84   *Cf. Final Reports* of the years listed; *Box 4-5-9* 12:5 (October/November 1967); *A.A. Exchange Bulletin* 8:5–6 (1963).

85   John B., General Manager, G.S.O., presentation: "Problems and Solutions in A.A.'s Literature Operation," notes provided at First A.A.W.S./Intergroup Seminar, 5 September 1986, Chicago, Illinois.

86   *Final Report of the 1977 General Service Conference,* p. 26.

87   *Final Report 1978 General Service Conference,* p. 45.

88   *Cf.* John B., General Manager, G.S.O., presentation: "Problems and Solutions in A.A.'s Literature Operation," notes provided at First A.A.W.S./Intergroup Seminar, 5 September 1986, Chicago, Illinois.
   Also: "Quarterly Report From G.S.O.," December 1986; *Box 4-5-9,* "Holidays, 1986" 32:6 (December 1986), 3: "Why Worry About Self-Support?"
   Form letter from John B., General Manager of the A.A. General Service Office, dated "October, 1986" to district committee members — letter headed "A Call to Action for Self-Support."
   Further detail from an internal memo at the time of the Big Book copyright flap to be examined later: "[Hazelden] sales of A.A. literature are almost entirely to rehabs and are growing at a faster clip than our direct sales."

Some details in this paragraph also derive from a visit to south Georgia in December of 1986 and conversation with John B., 22 April 1987.

89   Joe P. (southeast regional trustee), presentation: "Trustees' Self-Support Committee Report," notes provided at First A.A.W.S./Intergroup Seminar, 5 September 1986, Chicago, Illinois.

90   "The Power of the Purse," *Box 4-5-9* 31:5 (October/November 1986), 6–7. The article notes 1985 net publishing income as $1,336,000; net group services deficit as $827,000.
    "An additional contribution of about $1.25 *per year* per A.A. member would have completely eliminated the need for outside support or excess publishing income."

91   *Box 4-5-9* 33:3 (June/July 1987), 4, 2.

92   Interview of 22 April 1987; *cf.* also Advisory Action #5 of the 1987 General Service Conference, recommending that 'Self-Support' be a presentation/discussion topic for the next five years, in keeping with the spirit of the Seventh Tradition."

93   *Cf.* above, p. 265.

94   Wilson, "A Report on the Grapevine," September 1960, otherwise unattributed, but apparently from a text presented to the A.A.W.S. board; Wilson (New York) to Dr. John Norris, 28 November and 28 December 1960.

95   *Final Report of the 1975 General Service Conference*, pp. 14–15.

96   *Final Report of the 1975 General Service Conference*, pp. 12–13.
    Some of Dr. Tiebout's articles have become classics: "Surrender *versus* Compliance in Therapy " (September 1953) abridged his *QJSA* article of that title; "Conversion as a Psychological Phenomenon" (March and April 1954) made more widely available the piece originally published in *Pastoral Psychology* in 1951; "Why Psychiatrists Fail Alcoholics" (September 1956) and "When the Big 'I' Becomes Nobody" (September 1965) have been generally recognized by A.A.s familiar with them to be vitally useful.

97   *Grapevine* circulation increased through the 1970s, although not proportionally to the growth in A.A. membership. In the 1980s, circulation has been flat, showing a general downward trend to 1984, and a sharper downward trend since then; 1980 circulation, 123,120, remained the high point until late 1986, when circulation briefly peaked over 126,000 only to fall back to about 122,000 in early 1987.

98   Advisory Action #30 on p. 4 of the mimeographed summary of "1987 General Service Conference Advisory Actions"; the final observations are based on a variety of interviews conducted between January and May of 1987.

99   *Cf.* E. M. Jellinek, *The Disease Concept of Alcoholism* (New Haven, CT: College and University Press, 1960); H. M. Trice and P. M. Roman, "Sociopsychological Predictors of Affiliation with Alcoholics Anonymous," *Social Psychiatry* 5:51–59 (1970); a fairly complete review (to 1981) may be found in A. C. Ogburne and F. B. Glaser, "Characteristics of Affiliates of Alcoholics Anonymous: A Review of the Literature," *JSA* 42:661–675 (1981).

100 On "the new profession" and much else, *cf.* James E. Royce, *Alcohol Problems and Alcoholism* (New York, 1981). Although some judges had recommended A.A. attendance as early as the late 1940s (according to Nell Wing, interview of 21 April 1987), A.A.'s attention was drawn to the practice especially in the early 1970s.

Cf. Box 4-5-9 18:6 ("Holiday Issue" 1973), 1: "A.A. Cooperation with Court and ASAP Programs Saves Lives." "GSO's Guidelines on Court Programs help, too. They were written when court 'classes' about A.A. started, over seven years ago. Such a class is usually held in the courtroom once a week and is run mostly by A.A. members. But those 'sentenced' are told they are *not* attending an A.A. meeting, just a court class about A.A. After a few weeks of this, the problem drinker can decide on his own whether or not he wants to join an A.A. group.

"Ralph F., Lincoln, Nebraska, says his community was one of the first to get an ASAP grant from the U.S. Department of Transportation. 'With our large open meetings, no problem. Court referrals come, are interested or not, as you would expect. In fact, they have stirred us old A.A.s up toward the effort to provide interesting, informative meetings that are meaningful to all' " (p. 2).

101 *Cf.* suggestions in "Public Information — Cooperation with the Professional Community Bulletin," Fall 1981.

102 *Final Report of the 1982 General Service Conference,* pp. 33–34; on the topic of women as "minority" in this sense, *cf.* above, p. 165, note #29.

103 *Box 4-5-9* 32:2 (April/May 1986).

104 *Cf.* Gerald King, Mary Altpeter, and Marie Spada, "Alcoholism and the Elderly: A Training Model," *Alcoholism Treatment Quarterly* 3:3 (Fall 1986), 81–94.

105 *Cf.* A. C. Ogburne and F. B. Glaser, "Characteristics of Affiliates of Alcoholics Anonymous: A Review of the Literature," *JSA* 42:661–675 (1981), especially 667–669.

106 *Cf.* Bruce Holley Johnson, *The Alcoholism Movement in America: A Study in Cultural Innovation,* unpublished dissertation, University of Illinois at Urbana-Champaign: University Microfilms #74-5603, pp. 370–371; the final sentence is based on impressions gained and the history told when I visited such settings in various cities.

107 *Box 4-5-9* 31:4 (August/September 1986), 10.

108 *Final Report of the 1979 General Service Conference,* p. 17; more widely, *cf.* also Advisory Action #57 of the 1987 General Service Conference, which recommended: "The 1986 Conference Action regarding the directories not listing 'Double-Trouble groups be reaffirmed,' i.e. 'Double-Trouble groups' not be listed in the A.A. Directories'; . . . (Double-Trouble groups are defined as groups with outside affiliation)." Consensus at the 1976 General Service Conference had opined that, for an A.A. member, marijuana use was not a slip but was "dangerous for an alcoholic, because it could lead to a slip."

109 *Cf. Final Report of the 1972 General Service Conference,* p. 13: "A long-time and continuing problem for many A.A. groups is that of the drug user attending A.A. meetings, participating in them, and in some cases holding office. A show of hands indicated that more than one-half the delegates are concerned with this problem in their areas."

110 Page 5, #31 and #32 of the mimeographed preliminary list of Advisory Actions:

THIS IS A CLOSED MEETING OF ALCOHOLICS ANONYMOUS

This is a closed meeting of Alcoholics Anonymous. In support of A.A.'s singleness of purpose, attendance at closed meetings is limited to persons who have a desire to stop drinking. If you think you have a problem with alcohol, you are welcome to attend this meeting. We ask that when discussing problems, we confine ourselves to those problems as they relate to alcoholism.

THIS IS AN OPEN MEETING OF ALCOHOLICS ANONYMOUS

This is an *open* meeting of Alcoholics Anonymous. We are glad you are all here — especially newcomers. In keeping with our singleness of purpose and our Third Tradition which states that "The only requirement of A.A. membership is a desire to stop drinking," we ask that all who participate confine their discussion to their problems with alcohol.

111 The most recent list of "Fellowship's Modeled on A.A." available through the A.A.W.S. office in mid-1987 listed a total of 83 such groups, noting that there were doubtless many others. Those appearing on the list probably contacted A.A. seeking permission to adapt the Steps — a courtesy not always paid, especially when the Steps are adopted without adaptation.

112 *Box 4-5-9* 17:5 (October/November 1972), 4: "What is an A.A. Group?"

"Staff members here at GSO have pooled their thoughts on this subject, and we have agreed on six points that describe what an A.A. group is. They are:

1. All members of a group are alcoholics.
2. As a group they are fully self-supporting.
3. A group's primary purpose is to help alcoholics recover through the suggested Twelve Steps.
4. As a group they have no outside affiliation.
5. As a group they have no opinion on outside issues.
6. As a group their public relations policy is based on attraction rather than promotion, and they need always maintain their personal anonymity at the level of press, radio, television and film."

The 1980 revision of the pamphlet, "The A.A. Group," p. 32, notes: "The group conscience of A.A. in the U.S. and Canada seems to have agreed upon six points that define an A.A. group." This list omits the words "need always" in #6 and the word "suggested" in #3, and adds to #1, "and all alcoholics are eligible for membership." On the use of the word "suggested," *cf.* below, p. 302, and note #162.

113 *Final Report of the 1974 General Service Conference*, pp. 12–13, 28; *Final Report of the 1977 General Service Conference*, pp. 23, 25; *Final Report of the 1979 General Service Conference*, p. 17; *Final Report of the 1981 General Service Conference*, p. 25.

Cf. also *Box 4-5-9* 17:4 (August/September 1972), 1: "Which Serves Alcoholics Better — Special 'Group,' or 'Meeting'?" The difference between groups and meetings is treated on page 2.

114 A 1987 General Service Conference Advisory Action (#40) asked the following change in "The A.A. Group" pamphlet: "The phrase on page 33 that reads: 'On the other hand, specialized *groups* — men's, women's, gay's [*sic*] . . .' be changed to read 'On the other hand, specialized *gatherings* — men's, women's, gay's . . .' because although the intent was to use the word group in a generic sense, its use confuses the issue about the difference between a meeting and a group." Given the context of the 1974 and 1977 discussions, it is unclear on what the 1987 delegates based their interpretation of "intent."

115 "Around A.A.," *AAGV*, January 1971; *Final Report of the 1972 General Service Conference*, pp. 12–13; *cf.* also *Box 4-5-9* 33:2 (April/May 1987), 7–8, where this point and reasoning were reaffirmed.

116 *Cf.* Joan Jackson, "The Adjustment of the Family to the Crisis of Alcoholism," *QJAS* 15:562–586 (1954), which remains the classic; a most useful review of the changes over time on this topic may be found in Royce, *Alcohol Problems and Alcoholism*, Chapter Eight.

117 *Cf.* Timmen Cermak, *Diagnosing and Treating Codependence* (Minneapolis: Johnson Institute, 1986); also Sharon Wegscheider-Cruse, lecture at Fairbanks Hospital, Indianapolis, IN, 19 February 1987.

118 *Cf.* Ernest Kurtz, "Alcoholics Anonymous: A Phenomenon in American Religious History," in Peter Freese, ed., *Religion and Philosophy in the United States of America:* Proceedings of the German-American Conference at Paderborn, July 29–August 1, 1986 (Essen: Verlag Die Blaue Eule, 1987), vol. 2, pp. 447–462; also Robert N. Bellah et al., *Habits of the Heart* (Berkeley: Univ. of California, 1985).

119 Margaret Bean, "Alcoholics Anonymous," *Psychiatric Annals* 5:16-64 (1975); Margaret H. Bean, Edward J. Khantzian, John E. Mack, George E. Vaillant, Norman E. Zinberg, *Dynamic Approaches to the Understanding and Treatment of Alcoholism* (New York, 1981); George E. Vaillant, *The Natural History of Alcoholism* (Cambridge, 1983); for Tournier, *cf.* above, pp. 272-273.

120 *Final Report of the 1971 General Service Conference*, pp. 11, 23; *Final Report of the 1974 General Service Conference*, p. 23.

121 *Final Report of the 1977 General Service Conference*, pp. 44, 6; according to Nell Wing, interview of 21 April 1987, the idea of "cooperation without affiliation" was rooted in the N.C.E.A flap and its outcome, thus going back to the period between 1946 and 1949.

122 Names are listed in an A.A.W.S. press release dated 16 June 1980. Note that the number of non-A.A. participants was not significantly greater than in 1975 or 1985, when twenty-one appeared: the point is the emphasis, which was greater even than the *Box 4-5-9* 19:3 (June/July 1974), General Service Conference Issue that headlined: "Conference Favors Renewed A.A. Cooperation With All Others Who Help Alcoholics." The coverage focused on non-alcoholics, featuring pictures of Dr. Silkworth, Sam Shoemaker, and Sister Ignatia, as well as of Bill Wilson and Dr. Bob Smith.

123 *Box 4-5-9* 25:4 (August/September 1980); *cf.* also J.G., "Super Meeting," *AAGV* 37:5 (October 1980), 18–23; Bill Pittman, "Sobriety Celebrations," *Alcoholism/the National Magazine* 5:5 (May/June 1985), 27.

124 *Final Report of the 1982 General Service Conference,* p. 21.

125 *Final Report of the 1986 General Service Conference,* p. 19; Advisory Action #8 of the 1987 General Service Conference, p. 2 of the mimeographed summary; "About A.A.," Spring/Summer 1987. *Box 4-5-9* 17:5 (October/November 1972), 2, reported the "new A.A. bulletin for professionals" — "About A.A.," noting that it had been "recently mailed to about 1,000 professional and semi-professional men and women who work in the field of alcoholism outside A.A."

126 On the phenomenon, *cf.* Daniel Anderson, *Perspectives on Treatment: The Minnesota Experience* (Center City, MN: Hazelden, 1981), which recounts the history, and James E. Royce, *Alcohol Problems and Alcoholism* (New York: Free Press, 1981), especially Chapter 21, "The New Profession," which offers perceptive analysis; *Final Report of the 1970 General Service Conference,* pp. 18–19; *Final Report of the 1975 General Service Conference,* pp. 19, 41.

127 *Final Report of the 1976 General Service Conference,* p. 42.

128 "A Summary of the Advisory Actions of the General Service Conference of Alcoholics Anonymous, 1951–1986" (New York: A.A.W.S., 1987), p. 26 (1965).

129 "A Summary of the Advisory Actions of the General Service Conference of Alcoholics Anonymous, 1951–1986" (New York: A.A.W.S., 1987), p. 26 (1967).

130 "A Summary: Ask-It Basket, General Service Conference: 1951–1978" (New York: A.A.W.S., 1979), p. 26 (1967).

131 Although direct, this necessarily anonymous quotation well summarizes responses to questions informally asked of long-time, knowledgeable members in the course of research for this final, updating chapter. It also adequately represents responses I have been able to sample on the question of A.A.'s 1986 appeal for "increased self-support."

132 *AA,* p. 62.

133 "The spirituality of not having all the answers": I am grateful for this phrase to Bob D. of Rochester, New York, who thus encapsulated much of the history outlined in what has preceded.

134 Paula C., "Our Magazine Both Records and Makes A.A. History," *Final Report of the 1975 General Service Conference,* p. 14.

135 *Cf.* "Bibliography," pp. 411ff, below; also the *A.A. Exchange Bulletin* 8:1 (January 1963), which introduces Nell E. Wing as "Bill's secretarial assistant and our archivist at GSO." *Box 4-5-9* 18:4 (August/September 1973), 1, announces "Archival Library to be a Reality."

136 *Final Report of the 1974 General Service Conference,* p. 24. *Box 4-5-9* 15:2 (April/May 1970), reported on "New Home for Your GSO." "A building between 31st and 32nd Street on the west side of Park Avenue South, is the new home for GSO and the *Grapevine* as of April 1, 1970." The story details the history of the move. "This will be GSO's fifth home: the first, in 1940, was at 30 Vesey Street. In 1944 we moved to 415 Lexington Avenue. In 1950, 141 East 44th Street became our third home, and in 1960 we moved to the eighteenth floor of 305 East 45th Street."

137 *Cf. Final Report of the 1986 General Service Conference*, p. 14, for more details on local archives; also *Box 4-5-9* 33:3 (June/July 1987), 4. Some detail on this topic also from interview of Frank M., current A.A. archivist, 20 and 21 April 1987.

Cf. also *Markings* 1:2 (February/March 1982). In answer to the question concerning the film *Markings on the Journey*, "Has this film increased your interest in developing an Archives for your area?: 70% said yes."

138 The cooperation was mainly informal, achieved mainly by Nell Wing's continuing visits to and conversations with Lois Wilson during the period of the book's being written.

139 Milton Maxwell, *The A.A. Experience: A Close-Up View for Professionals* (New York: McGraw-Hill, 1984);

Mary Catherine Taylor, "Alcoholics Anonymous: How It Works — Recovery Processes in a Self-Help Group," unpublished dissertation, Univ. of California at San Francisco, 1977; Univ. Microfilms #79-13241;

R. F. Bales, "The Therapeutic Role of Alcoholics Anonymous as seen by a Sociologist," *QJSA* 5:267 (1944);

Selden D. Bacon, "A Sociologist Looks at Alcoholics Anonymous," *Minnesota Welfare* 10:35 (1957);

Mark Keller, "The Oddities of Alcoholics," *QJSA* 33:1147 (1972);

William Madsen, *The American Alcoholic* (Springfield, IL: Charles C. Thomas, 1974);

Leonard U. Blumberg, "The Ideology of a Therapeutic Social Movement: Alcoholics Anonymous," *JSA* 38:2122–2143 (1977);

Barry Leach and John L. Norris, "Factors in the Development of Alcoholics Anonymous," in Benjamin Kissin and Henri Begleiter, eds., *Treatment and Rehabilitation of the Chronic Alcoholic* (New York: Plenum, 1977), pp. 441–543;

David Robinson, *Talking Out of Alcoholism* (London: Croom Helm, 1979);

David R. Rudy, *Becoming Alcoholic* (Carbondale, IL: Southern Illinois Univ., 1986);

Norman K. Denzin, *The Alcoholic Self* and *The Recovering Alcoholic* (Newbury Park, CA: Sage, 1987);

Margaret H. Bean, Edward J. Khantzian, John E. Mack, George E. Vaillant, Norman E. Zinberg, *Dynamic Approaches to the Understanding and Treatment of Alcoholism* (New York, 1981);

George E. Vaillant, *The Natural History of Alcoholism* (Cambridge, 1983);

William Pittman, *Alternative Explanations for the Beginnings of Alcoholics Anonymous: 1934-1939*, unpublished *summa cum laude* thesis, submitted in the Inter-College, University of Minnesota, February 1983.

140 The question of whether or not A.A. groups and local Central Service offices ought or ought not to sell non-Conference-approved literature is a perennial one within the fellowship and at General Service Conference meetings. A recent set of pro and con statements may be found in the notes provided at First A.A.W.S./Intergroup Seminar, 5 September 1986, Chicago, Illinois.

141 An especially interesting source of information is the budget that appears in each year's *Final Report of the General Service Conference,* which estimates antici-pated sales of each title for the current year.

142 Advisory Action #36, p. 5, on the mimeographed summary.

143 *Cf. Final Report of the 1986 General Service Conference,* p. 45. The "wariness of interpretation" applies also to the reflections book project. For background on this wariness, which, for example, many compilers of various concordances of A.A. literature over the years have experienced, *cf. Box 4-5-9* 22:4 (August/ September 1977). Headline: "Big Book Study Guides? A.A.W.S. Arrives at a Position."

"One trustee-director wrote: 'The individual A.A. member does not need another person or institution to think for him or her — in fact, this could be a very bad thing. Part of the beauty and magic of A.A. is that persons from all walks of life, with varied backgrounds, may benefit from the Big Book, the Steps, the Traditions, and the Concepts, from their own points of view. Placing guidelines on paper seems to say, "This is the way — the only way."

" 'The authors of this priceless material knew what they were doing. Their words require study, not interpretation.'

"Another trustee-director enlarged on this line of thinking as follows: 'As it is now, to the extent A.A. takes positions, it is in our literature, etc. — and if it isn't there, A.A. does not have a position. This is clear and simple, and we should keep it this way.' "

144 *Final Report of the 1986 General Service Conference,* p. 45.

145 *Cf.* Carol P. Christ, *Diving Deep and Surfacing* (Boston, 1980); Alasdair MacIntyre, *After Virtue* (Notre Dame, 1981); Andre Lacocque and P. E. La-cocque, *The Jonah Complex* (Atlanta, 1981); David Tracy, *The Analogical Imagina-tion* (New York: Crossroad, 1981) and *Pluralism and Ambiguity* (San Francisco: Harper & Row, 1987); Michael Goldberg, *Theology and Narrative* (Nashville, 1982); Donald P. Spence, *Narrative Truth and Historical Truth* (New York, 1982); Richard J. Bernstein, *Beyond Objectivism and Relativism* (Philadelphia, 1983); Ter-ry Eagleton, *Literary Theory: An Introduction* (Minneapolis, 1983); Paul Ricoeur, *Time and Narrative,* vol. 1 (Chicago, 1984), and vol. 2 (Chicago, 1986); Arthur C. Danto, *Narration and Knowledge* (New York: Columbia Univ., 1985); Paul Veyne, *Writing History* (Middletown, CT, 1985).

146 *Cf.,* e.g., *The Gazette* (Montreal), 3 July 1985, p. A-4; for another perspec-tive on the crowding, *cf.* Bill Pittman, "Sobriety Celebrations," *Alcoholism/The National Magazine* 5:5 (May/June 1985), 21–28.

147 Of the over 44,000 attending, somewhat under 35,000 were A.A. mem-bers, somewhat over 10,000 members of Al-Anon and Alateen. *"Fifty Years With Gratitude,"* p. 18; some details from "Celebration!" *AAGV* 42:5 (October 1985), 2–17; interview with Laurie Lukens, daughter of Ruth Hock Crecelius, 5 Sep-tember 1986.

148 Reported variously, but for the *ambience, cf.* especially "Celebration!" p. 15.

149 *Cf.* story in *The Gazette* (Montreal), 3 July 1985.

150 *Final Report of the Ninth World Service Meeting,* p. 42; *cf.* also *Box 4-5-9* 32:2 (April/May 1987), 1.

151 Dan Anderson, "Anderson's Travels: The Soviet Union," *Hazelden News,* December 1986, 1, 6. Some details that follow are also from interviews with Dr. Anderson, 21 March, 16 May, and 15 August 1987.

152 "Mid-Southern California Newsletter" 3:12 (December 1986); "Central News," Tulare County, Farmersville, CA, 3:2 (February 1987).

Cf. also form letter, "Dearest Friend" from Igor S., Old Lyme, CT, 3 June 1986, inviting participation in the October 1986 and January 1987 visits.

153 Interviews with Dr. Dan Anderson, as previously cited, and with others involved who spoke with me only on condition that not even initials be used.

154 Lois was informed of the difficulty on 26 June 1985; an agreement was signed on 26 August 1985. Much of the detail here and in what follows derives from participation and uncitable internal documents. Those documents will be available to scholars at some future date. Of available sources, *cf.,* e.g., First A.A.W.S./Intergroup Seminar, September 5–7, 1986, Chicago, Illinois, p. 47.

155 Tom J., "Update on A.A.'s Copyrights," *Final Report of the 1986 General Service Conference,* p. 8.

156 *Ibid.*

157 The price of literature to A.A. groups and the structure of discounts for such purchases were again under consideration for review at the time of this writing: interview with John B., 22 April 1987. A part of the longer history of this perennial concern may be traced in *Box 4-5-9* 21:5 (October/November 1976).

158 Based on conversations that included comments on the 25 July and 19 September 1985 meetings of the A.A.W.S. Board of Directors.

159 Joan Jackson, Ph.D., "Trustees' Literature Committee's Survey on Big Book Derivatives," *Final Report of the 1986 General Service Conference,* pp. 8–9.

160 *Final Report of the 1986 General Service Conference,* pp. 45–46.

161 Undated letter, "Dear Friend"; return address, a post office box in Pompano Beach, Florida. Internal evidence dates the composition of the letter in late 1984. What follows relies on the promotional material that accompanied this letter and on the story and advertisements in the "Salute to Ohio" issue (November/December 1985) of *Alcoholism and Addiction Magazine* as well as on participating in conversations on this topic at and after various A.A. meetings around the country; *cf.* also, "Extensions: A Newsletter for the Founders' Foundation," obtainable from P.O. Box 449, Akron, OH 44309.

162 On the history of the discussion surrounding the word "suggested," *cf. Box 4-5-9* 21:1 (February/March 1976), 4-5; also, on "A.A. of Akron," *cf.* above, pp. 234-236.

163 Nell Wing, interview of 21 April 1987, reported "one — no, I think two" earlier "feelers" on the Nobel Prize.

164 *Cf.* above, pp. 266-267.

165 Wilson to J.L.K., 1943.

166 *Cf.* above, p. 249.

167 Partially based on interview with John B., 22 April 1987, and conversations with other G.S.O. staff on that and the adjoining dates.

168 From the lecture presentation by the author, "Historical Sidelights on Alcoholics Anonymous."

BIBLIOGRAPHY

INTRODUCTORY NOTE

For both Alcoholics Anonymous itself and the field of alcoholism studies in general, there already exists a variety of aids to assist in exploration of the vast secondary literature. The literature supporting the Part Two presentation and interpretation of the historical contexts, both American and religious, is also so immense as to be absolutely unwieldy. For these reasons special care has been taken in indexing this study, and I have included brief bibliographical essays where appropriate in the highly detailed Notes. Further, I have deemed it preferable to assist the interested reader in locating where and how secondary literature has been used rather than merely to list works mentioned, and therefore offer at the conclusion of this bibliography a Bibliographic Index to authors cited in the Notes.

Concerning the primary sources, much complexity inheres in the history, versions, and consequent shaded status of some of them. I have therefore offered a specific description and evaluation of each primary source, detailing where appropriate my use of it. The apparatus that follows thus contains these major headings:

KEYS TO SECONDARY SOURCES
NOTES ON PRIMARY SOURCES
BIBLIOGRAPHIC INDEX
GENERAL INDEX

KEYS TO SECONDARY SOURCES

I   A very complete bibliography of literature relating in any way to Alcoholics Anonymous has been offered by Barry Leach and John L. Norris, "Factors in the Development of Alcoholics Anonymous," in

Benjamin Kissin and Henri Begleiter, (eds.), *Treatment and Rehabilitation of the Chronic Alcoholic* (New York: Plenum Press, 1977), pp. 519–543. It is pointless to replicate here this listing, which contains over seven hundred items. Further, Leach and Norris on pp. 507–519, "The Literature on A.A." offer classification of and occasional comment on the most significant literature. Other such treatment is also scattered through the substantive portion of their contribution, pp. 441–507.

For the field of alcoholism treatment and rehabilitation beyond but including Alcoholics Anonymous, no more complete bibliography could be constructed than that contained in the "References" at the conclusion of each of the other thirteen essays in this volume by Kissin and Begleiter. See especially that offered by Frederick Baekeland, "Evaluation of Treatment Methods in Chronic Alcoholism," pp. 428–440, with some evaluation of the literature within the essay itself, pp. 385–428.

II Julianne Phillips in 1973 compiled and privately published *Alcoholics Anonymous: An Annotated Bibliography, 1935–1972*. In her preface, Phillips carefully notes the methods, resources, and limitations of her study. The chief limitations are the bibliography's restriction to works published in the English language in the United States, and the concentration — imposed by her method — on the popular rather than published scholarly literature, especially when the latter treats only secondarily of A.A.

Especially useful is Phillips's listing of "Unpublished Theses and Dissertations" of "Psychological and Sociological Studies of A.A. and Its Members," pp. 36–41. Hoggson, for one example, is not included, and in conversation, Ms. Phillips appropriately lamented the impossibility of an *absolutely* perfect bibliography, given the limitations and fallibility of bibliographic resources.

Phillips's annotations are marvels of clear, succinct accuracy on the level of description she has chosen. It is her hope and plan to expand her bibliography to make it "as complete as possible" for formal publication on the occasion of A.A.'s Fiftieth Anniversary in 1985. Meanwhile, her bibliography and/or a listing of libraries holding it may be obtained directly from Ms. Phillips, The State Library of Ohio, 65 South Front Street, Columbus, OH 43215. Further, Ms. Phillips will share with scholars whatever current updating of her bibliography is available at the time of request.

III This research has been aided immeasurably by "The Classified

Abstract Archive of the Alcohol Literature" maintained at The Center of Alcohol Studies at Rutgers University, and replicated at various medical centers throughout the country. The CAAAL is "a cumulative collection of abstracts of alcohol-related scientific and scholarly literature." These abstracts, and the larger documentation of which they are a part, have been described by M. Keller and V. Efron, "Documentation of an Interdisciplinary Field of Study: Alcohol Problems," *QJSA* 14: 263–284 (1953), reprints of which are available from: Documentation Division, Rutgers Center of Alcohol Studies, New Brunswick, NJ 08903. The Center of Alcohol Studies ceased separate publication of these abstracts in April of 1977. Since then, abstracts of the literature are available in alternate-month issues of the *JSA*. In late 1978 these abstracts were in the process of being computerized.

IV   Finally among the secondary tools of research, John Cornelius Voorhees has produced and privately distributed "Where Does It Say So?" a concordance to key words and phrases in *AA, 12&12, AACA*, and *ABSI*. The A.A. World Service Board holds the copyright (1975), but has declined to publish or to approve this concordance because it "might tend to lend authoritarian force or rigidity to the A.A. program." (Letter of Robert P., [New York] to Voorhees, 5 September 1976.) There is a perhaps unavoidable degree of interpretation in some of the listings — and omissions — in Mr. Voorhees's compilation, and it therefore must be used with care. Copies of this valuable lexicon are available in the A.A. archives (under restriction), in the writer's possession, and perhaps directly from Mr. Voorhees, 645 Neil Avenue, Columbus, OH 43215.

NOTES ON PRIMARY SOURCES

I   EARLIER PUBLISHED HISTORIES OF ALCOHOLICS ANONYMOUS:

The basic public history of Alcoholics Anonymous is: [William Griffith Wilson *et al.*], *Alcoholics Anonymous Comes of Age* (New York: A.A. Publishing, Inc., 1957), also published for general distribution by Harper & Row, same place and date, cited: *AACA*. This "brief history of A.A." describes and records the events of the fellowship's 1955 "Coming of Age Convention." It includes the presentation of an "enlarged and edited" version of the history of Alcoholics Anonymous described orally by Wilson on that occasion. I use this work for the basic historical framework. Further, in view of the research that went into its preparation (*cf.* Section II below), I accept it as authoritative and present it as sole citation whenever it accurately reflects the earlier sources. In instances when other, more primary, sources seem not so accurately incorporated into *AACA*, this fact is noted — and, if possible, the discrepancies are explored — in the "Notes."

Robert Thomsen, *Bill W.* (New York: Harper & Row, 1975), cited: Thomsen, is a biography of William Griffith Wilson written with the cooperation of his widow, Lois Wilson, and of the General Service Office of Alcoholics Anonymous. This book contains neither notes, index, nor bibliography. Thomsen relied especially on Wilson's taped memories (*cf.* below) and in general scrupulously followed them. Unless otherwise indicated, citations of Thomsen accordingly reflect Wilson's recollections rather than Thomsen's research, and are offered as more readily accessible than the Wilson tapes or transcript. I offer citation beyond Thomsen only if they present differing data or interpretation, or if they furnish special depth for a particular point or event.

Lois Wilson, *Lois Remembers* (New York: Al-Anon Family Group Headquarters, Inc., 1979), is the autobiography of Bill Wilson's wife. The book is sub-titled: ''Memoirs of the co-founder of Al-Anon and wife of the co-founder of Alcoholics Anonymous.'' Based primarily on memories, Lois's own and others', and structured around at times spare diary entries, the book contains some slight errors of detail and chronology. This book was completed too late to be of direct use to the present research, but *cf.* p. 417, below, concerning my interviews with Lois. *Lois Remembers* may be of special importance to those interested in the complexities of Bill Wilson's employment history and in the Wilsons' continuing relationship with Ebby. Lois's memories offer much color and detail, although more often about places and settings than concerning people or ideas.

Other treatments of the history of Alcoholics Anonymous in general rely exclusively on *AACA* or the published versions of the sources listed below under II, and are very brief. A minor exception is Barry Leach and John L. Norris, "Factors in the Development of Alcoholics Anonymous," in Benjamin Kissin and Henri Begleiter, *Treatment and Rehabilitation of the Chronic Alcoholic* (New York: Plenum Press, 1977), pp. 441–543, which in a primarily sociological description makes use of some archival materials.

II   EARLIER SOURCES INCORPORATED INTO *AACA*:

Frank Amos, "History of the Alcoholic movement up to the formation of The Alcoholic Foundation on August 11th 1938," private, unpublished memorandum prepared for John D. Rockefeller, Jr., and for the Alcoholic Foundation, dated 19 August 1938; cited: Amos, "History."

[Wilson *et al.*]. *Alcoholics Anonymous*, 1st ed. (New York: Works Publishing, 1939), 2nd ed. (New York: A.A. Publishing, Inc., 1955), 3rd ed. (New York: A.A. World Services, 1976), cited: *AA*. The body of this work remained substantially the same between editions, the changes being in the "story section." Pagination of the substance remains the same from the second to the third editions — citations will be from this pagination as more readily available, unless otherwise noted. I also had access — during research, and with the generous trust of Warren C. — to a copy of the multilith, pre-publication draft of this work distributed to members for their comments. References are made to this document as appropriate, and it is on each such occasion cited as "multilith draft."

[Wilson], "Transcription of Presentation to Board Meeting, Rockland State Hospital, 14 December 1939"; unpublished, cited: Wilson, "Rockland."

Wilson, W. G., "Basic Concepts of Alcoholics Anonymous," talk given to the Neurology and Psychiatry Section, Medical Society of New York State, 9 May 1944, published *N.Y. State Journal of Medicine* 44: 1805–1810 (1944); cited: "Basic Concepts" with pagination from the transcript, as the published version was edited.

[Wilson] — with the one exception of the preceding citation, Wilson always wrote for attribution as "W.G.W." or "Bill W." — "The Fellowship of Alcoholics Anonymous," talk given at the Yale University Summer School of Alcohol Studies in August of 1944, published in *Alcohol, Science and Society* (New Haven: College and University Press, 1945), pp. 461–473; cited: "Fellowship" and pagination from this reprinting unless the reference appears only in the transcript.

Jim B., "Evolution of Alcoholics Anonymous," privately mimeographed, dated May 1947; cited: Jim B. "Evolution."

[Wilson], "The Society of Alcoholics Anonymous," talk given at the Annual Meeting of the American Psychiatric Association held at Montreal, PQ, in May of 1949; cited: "Society"; pagination from the transcript. Excerpts of this talk appear in the pamphlet "Alcoholism the

Illness" (since 1976: "Bill on Alcoholism"), published and distributed by A.A. World Services, Inc.

[Wilson], "Alcoholics Anonymous as Seen by W.G.W., a co-Founder," talk read before the New York City Medical Society, 9 May 1950, edited and published as "Alcoholics Anonymous" in *N.Y. State Journal of Medicine* 50: 1708–1716 (1950); cited: "Co-Founder," pagination from the transcript.

The transcripts of Wilson's own and other"oldtimers '"recollections recorded through 1954 in preparation for Bill's 1955 convention presentations and the writing of *AACA*; cited: [name], tr., page when paginated. Wilson's transcript runs well over one hundred pages. Because these pages are erratically numbered, I usually do not offer page citations: the material is presented chronologically and thus should be readily locatable by other researchers. This transcript is virtually the only source for biographical data on the details of Wilson's life before 1934. (One obvious exception: his surviving widow, Lois, for the years after their marriage in 1918; *cf.* below, under VI). Both Robert Thomsen and Nell Wing have made large efforts productive of frustratingly small results to check and verify these autobiographical reminiscences in any case where such seemed possible. I have accepted — not uncritically, as a few notes in Chapter One will testify — Thomsen's and Wing's judgment that the transcript, with Wing's marginal comments, is as accurate as it is possible to determine. The most significant point about the history recorded in the transcript is that while Wilson's memory for detail seems greater than average, his memory for exact dates was atrociously bad. The former is perhaps attributable to his experience doing economic research in the 1920s; the latter may be its correlative. Also, I have verified the internal accuracy of the transcript — with a few obvious, understandable, and insignificant exceptions — with the tape on which it is based by following the transcript while listening to the tape.

[Wilson], "Talk at LeMoyne College, Syracuse, NY," unpublished, April 1954; cited: *LM*. Apparently the raw try-out for his 1955 presentation of the history as it appears in *AACA*, *LM*'s significance derives from the fact that it preceded the Wilson research that is reflected in the following item. Two minor significances also aided some of my interpretations: First, Bill in *LM* was clearly conscious that he was speaking at a Catholic, Jesuit college. Second, it is clear that Wilson asked for and received substantial comment on his presentation — this was the first occasion on which he self-consciously told A.A.'s story rather than his own. Although these comments are not directly available, Wilson's later presentations of A.A.'s history suggest that he was encouraged to omit personal detail not directly related to his drinking; also, that he more "tell the story" than attempt interpretation. *LM* is thus the best direct source for Bill's *interpretation* of A.A. (at the time), although his self-consciousness of the Catholic setting must be taken into account.

[Wilson], "Bill's Review of the Movement," unpublished, dated 19 June 1954, and sub-headed: "Cleveland, Ohio." This document records Wilson's thoughts on A.A. history after a visit to Akron and Cleveland during which he interviewed as many of those cities' "oldtimers" as possible about their memories of early A.A. history. Its special significance derives from the fact that oldtimers in Akron and Cleveland cherished on some points differing memories from the recollections common among the New Yorkers about the earliest history of A.A. Cited: Wilson, "Review," this item did not substantially reconcile these differences, but it does offer insight into Wilson's mind at a crucial point and aids in interpreting much of his correspondence over the next three years, correspondence undertaken in an attempt to rectify the discrepancies before the publication of *AACA*.

Based on all the above, Wilson, "Memorandum to Our Writing Team, subject: Historical Time Table," unpublished and undated but clearly from late 1954; cited: "Memo."

III SOURCES LATER THAN AACA:

[Wilson], "Alcoholics Anonymous: Beginnings and Growth," talk given to the New York City Medical Society, 28 April 1958, published in its entirety in "Alcoholism the Illness: (since 1976: "Bill on Alcoholism"); cited: "Beginnings," pagination from the pamphlet.

[Wilson], "Clergy Conference," talk to the Annual Convention of the National Clergy Conference on Alcoholism, New York, 21 April 1960; cited: *NCCA*, pagination from the transcript. An edited version appears in the *NCCA Blue Book* 12: 179–205 (1960).

Henrietta Seiberling, "Origins of Alcoholics Anonymous," privately mimeographed and distributed by her son, John F. Seiberling, with a cover-letter detailing her background, dated May 1972, and based on a May 1971 telephone conversation; cited: HS, "Origins."

Nell Wing, "Pre-A.A. History," unpublished brief outline, cited: NW, "Pre-History."

Nell Wing, "Outline of A.A. History," unpublished, first draft drawn up by Wing for Thomsen in 1974; I have used an updated and corrected version of that draft; cited: NW, "Outline."

IV   OTHER PUBLISHED SOURCES:

The A.A. Grapevine, the "monthly journal of Alcoholics Anonymous," cited: *AAGV*. Volume One, Number One, was June 1944, and publication has been continuous. "A.A." was inserted into the title in early 1946, after discovery that an in-house F.B.I. organ had preempted "The Grapevine," as *AAGV* was at first titled.

"Final Reports[s] of the General Service Conference of Alcoholics Anonymous"; the first G.S.C. was held in 1951. Although "published," these are not available for distribution outside of A.A.

[Wilson], *Twelve Steps and Twelve Traditions* (New York: A.A. Publishing, Inc., 1953); cited: *12&12*. Like *AACA*, this book was also published for general distribution by Harper & Row, same date and place.

[Wilson], *As Bill Sees It* (New York: A.A. World Services, Inc., 1967), cited: *ABSI*. This was first published as *The A.A. Way of Life – A Reader by Bill*. It contains excerpts from both his published and his unpublished writings that were, at the time of publication, deemed worthy of wider diffusion among Alcoholics Anonymous. Its significance to this study lies mainly in that final fact.

V   CLOSED SOURCES AND THEIR STATUS TO SCHOLARS:

The "Minutes" of the Alcoholic Foundation and of the General Service Board of Alcoholics Anonymous are closed to specific citation. When my questions about their contents were answered with *visu* extracts, I have cited this circumstance.

The Wilson correspondence is closed under three degrees of restriction. The present research was the first scholarly access to the first two of these degrees. It is my understanding that all letters cited herein are open to serious scholars. Since almost all of the Wilson correspondence was sent from New York, the place is not cited unless other than New York. Further, out of respect for A.A. practice and the conditions of my access to the archives, names of all but prominent people —

in both cases whether members of A.A. or not — are cited by surname initial only.

Alcoholic Foundation and Alcoholics Anonymous correspondence: same as the Wilson correspondence.

In a continuing project, the Trustees' Archives Committee of Alcoholics Anonymous tape records the memories of surviving "oldtimers" and eventually produces transcripts of these tapes. The tapes may be heard with the permission of those still living; otherwise they remain restricted for twenty-five years after the individual's death. On occasion, information from those not open was reported to me by Nell Wing — when so, this is noted. I listened directly to the tapes of Clarence S. and Marty Mann. Whether my access was to the tape or to the transcript, the citation is to [name], tr.

The papers of Marty Mann and the National Council on Alcoholism are held by the George Arents Research Library at Syracuse University, under restriction. Permission to research in them may be obtained from Mrs. Mann *via* the NCA.

VI   INTERVIEWS OF HISTORICALLY SIGNIFICANT FIGURES:

Lois Wilson, widow of William Griffith Wilson. Lois's diaries and some early scrapbooks are available only through her. At the time of this research, Lois was working on an autobiography, and her materials were well-arranged for reference. The diaries were available for exact citation only with Lois's specific permission, which I rarely requested out of respect for her age, health, and time. Accordingly, the citation "Lois Wilson" covers both my interviews with her (tape recordings of which I hold), and some diary material.

Nell Wing (occasionally cited: NW) began working for Alcoholics Anonymous in March of 1947. From late 1950 to the time of his death, she was Wilson's personal secretary; during this time, she was part of the "Research and Writing Project" which produced *AACA*. From 1955 she was A.A.'s librarian, and since 1972 has been its archivist.

Marty Mann was the first woman to stay sober in Alcoholics Anonymous. (Because of a later "slip" by Marty, there was at the time of this research at least one woman claiming longer continuous sobriety in A.A.). Mrs. Mann had been a patient of Dr. Tiebout and in the early

1940s was his strongest link to A.A. Her role in the founding of the National Council on Alcoholism is treated within this study.

Henrietta Seiberling's (occasionally cited: HS) role in the founding of Alcoholics Anonymous is described within this study. Until the present research, she had declined to give interviews. She has since been interviewed for the A.A. archives, and I have had access to that tr.

Clarence S[nyder] reveals no shyness about the use of his full surname, but following A.A. practice I have retained only the initial within this study. Clarence's role in A.A. is described herein. He claims to have on tape and ready for publication his own version of the history of Alcoholics Anonymous: I have not had access to this work, but I have interviewed Clarence at length by telephone and hold two lengthy and detailed letters from him answering specific questions. Further, Clarence "annotated" for this research a copy of *AACA*, detailing his disagreements with Wilson's version of A.A. history. For a late added detail on my access to and use of Clarence, *cf.* note #13 to Appendix A.

VII THE SPECIAL PROBLEM OF DR. ROBERT HOLBROOK SMITH SOURCES:

For a time especially during the 1950s, some who were upset with developments within A.A. proclaimed Clarence S. to be the founder of Alcoholics Anonymous. According to Henrietta Seiberling, she with Wilson and Dr. Bob and Anne Smith are A.A.'s "co-founders." Alcoholics Anonymous itself accepted William Griffith Wilson and Dr. Robert Holbrook Smith as "co-founders": I accept the general accuracy of this last and delineate it herein.

A problem arises because Dr. Smith was not a writer, even of letters, so that with the exception of HS and Clarence — each of whom tends to argue a particular point of view delineated in Appendix A — Wilson is basically the sole source for the earliest history of Alcoholics Anonymous. Beyond the other sources already noted, I sought to correct for this by intensively directing research efforts at a grasp of Dr. Bob Smith.

The main written source on which I rely for information on Smith, beyond his story in *AA*, is "Last Major Talk," so titled and privately published under an incorrect date and place (Cleveland, Ohio, 1950) — delivered at Detroit, MI, in December of 1948. This has been supplemented by the interview sources cited in note #67 to Chapter

One, and by materials in the files of Rosary Hall, the alcoholic ward of St. Vincent's Charity Hospital in Cleveland, Ohio, which was modeled on Dr. Bob's St. Thomas Hospital practice in Akron and from 1952 to 1966 was under the direction of Sister Ignatia. These materials are described as cited. The name "Rosary Hall," incidentally, derived from the intention to honor Dr. Bob, but anonymously. The initials for "Rosary Hall Solarium" graced its main door: they just happened, of course, to be Dr. Bob's own initials.

VIII CLEVELAND SOURCES BEYOND CLARENCE S.:

Interviews with Warren C. and Dick P., who are identified and a portion of whose stories appear in the Appendix. Dick P., at the time director of the Cleveland A.A. District Office, also made available for research early group records and memorabilia in that office's archives.

Interviews with Sister Victorine, whose significance is explained in note #61 to Chapter Three.

BIBLIOGRAPHIC INDEX
· GENERAL INDEX

BIBLIOGRAPHIC INDEX

This Bibliographic Index to chapter and note number of this work is intended to assist the reader in locating where and how secondary and interpretive sources have been used. Full bibliographic data will be found in the first reference for each entry.

This Bibliographic Index does NOT list: works by William Griffith Wilson or Dr. Robert Holbrook Smith; references to Robert Thomsen's biography of Wilson, *Bill W.*; references to the anonymously authored pamphlet literature produced by Alcoholics Anonymous; and unpublished materials other than dissertations.

Aaron, Daniel: VII–4.
Abel, Reuben: VII–14.
Aharan, Charles H.: VIII–35.
Ahlstrom, Sidney: VIII–12.
Alexander, Jack: III–44.
Allen, E. B.: VIII–21.
Allen, Frederick Lewis: VII–4.
Altizer, T. J. J.: VIII–33.
Anderson, D.: VIII–14, 20.
Anonymn, Kenneth: V–41.
Arieli, Yehoshua: VII–12.
Armstrong, J. D.: VIII–14.
Augustine: VIII–9.
Avineri, Shlomo: VII–22; IX–12.
Ayars, Albert L.: VIII–48.

Baars, Conrad W.: VIII–23.
Bacon, Selden D.: VIII–4; IX–9.
Baekeland, F.: III–41.
Bakan, David: VII–17.
Bales, R. F.: VI–43; VIII–4.
Barbara, D. A.: IX–9.

Barrett, William: I-52; VII-23; VIII-1, 17; IX-31, 35, 53.
Bean, Margaret: IX-31.
Becker, Carl: VII-13, 14; APX A-15.
Becker, Ernest: IX-34.
Beecher, Henry Ward: VIII-26.
Begleiter, Henri: I-3, 49; IX-3, 13.
Behrens, William W.: VII-29.
Beigel, A.: III-41.
Bell, Daniel: VII-6.
Bell, R. G.: VIII-14, 29.
Bendiner, Robert: VII-4.
Benson, Purnell Handy: IX-9.
Bensoussan, P. A.: I-54; VIII-21.
Bercovitch, Scavan: VII-13.
Berger, Louis: VII-20.
Bergman, Anni: IX-33.
Bernstein, Irving: VII-27.
Bethel, M. H.: VIII-14.
Binder, Arnold and Virginia: VII-24.
Bircher, R.: I-54, 79.

Bird, Caroline: VII-4.
Bishop, Jim: Intr. Pt. Two; VIII-46; IX-31.
Black, C. E.: VII-12; VIII-1; IX-57.
Blum, Carol: VII-14.
Bonacker, R. D.: IX-21.
Bonney, M. E.: VIII-14.
Borghes, P.: I-54.
Borland, B. L.: V-71.
Braden, Charles Samuel: II-33.
Brinton, Crane: VII-13.
Brodsky, Archie: IX-38.
Brown, C. L.: VIII-20.
Brunner-Orne, M.: IX-9.
Burgler, E.: VIII-14.
Burns, John: VIII-23; APX A 20.
Burtt, E. A.: VII-13.
Butterfield, Herbert: VII-13.
Button, A. D.: VIII-21.

Cadoret, R. J.: IX-3.
Cain, Arthur H.: VI-18, 22; VIII-4.
Cantril, Hadley: II-33.
Carpenter, E. S.: VI-5.
Carroll, J. L.: VIII-14.
Carter, Paul A.: VII-27.
Carver, A. E.: VIII-21.
Cassirer, Ernst: VII-14.
Catanzaro, R. J.: V-47.
Chafetz, Morris E.: VI-20.
Chamberlain, John: VII-26.
Chambers, Clarke: VII-26.
Chambers, Francis T.: Intr. Pt. Two; IX-31.
Cioran, E. M.: VIII-10.
Clancy, J.: VIII-19.
Clark, Walter Houston: II-32, 33; IV-69; VII-17.
Clinard, M.: IX-12.
Clinebell, H. J.: IX-31.
Coben, Stanley: VII-27.
Cochrane, Raymond C.: VII-14.
Cohen, Felix: IX-31.
Cole, J. O.: VI-5.
Commoner, Barry: VII-29.
Condon, George: IV-12.
Conroy, William J.: VI-29.
Cranford, V.: VIII-14.
Crewe, Charles W.: V-38.
Croly, Herbert: VII-26.

Cross, Whitney R.: APX A-34.
Crothers, Rachel: II-33.
Davies, D. L.: IX-3.
Davis, Allen F.: VII-26.
Davis, C. N.: I-79.
Davis, Elrick: IV-2.
de Kruif, Paul: VII-11.
de Vries, Jan: VII-17; VIII-1.
Demone, Harold W.: VI-20.
Dent, J. Y.: IX-31.
Digest of Positions of the American Medical Assn.: V-33.
Doroff, D. R.: III-41.
Dowds, B. N.: VIII-14.
Dureau, Agnes: IV-12.
Durkheim, Emile: VII-17; IX-12.

Edwards, A. E.: VIII-21.
Edwards, David G.: VIII-29.
Edwards, G.: III-41.
Ehrenberg, Otto and Miriam: VII-24.
Eister, Allen W.: II-33.
Ellis, Albert: VIII-23.
Ellison, Jerome: VI-18, 32.
Erikson, Kai T.: VIII-29.
Evans, Richard I.: VIII-23.

Fajardo, Roque: IX-24.
Farber, Leslie H.: VIII-18; IX-20, 31, 44, 53.
Filler, Louis: VII-4.
Finney, Charles G.: VIII-20.
Fontana, A. F.: VIII-14.
Ford, John C.: II-31.
Fosdick, Harry Emerson: IV-23.
Foucault, Michel: VII-14, 18; IX-4.
Fox, Daniel M.: VII-27.
Freidel, Frank: VII-7.
Fuller, G. B.: VIII-14.

Galbraith, John Kenneth: VII-4.
Gavit, John Palmer: VII-26.
Gay, Peter: VII-13, 15.
Gaylin, Willard: VII-29, 32.
Gellman, Irving Peter: II-28; VIII-4.
Gelven, Michael: VII-23.
Ghertner, Stuart: III-41.
Gibbs, Wolcott: VIII-46.

Giddens, Anthony: VII–17; IX–12.
Gilbert, James B.: VIII–17, 31.
Gladston, I.: IX–31.
Glasser, Ira: VII–29.
Glasser, William: VIII–23.
Goethe, Wayne: VIII–35.
Goffman, Erving: VII–18.
Goldman, Eric F.: VII–6.
Graham, Otis L.: VII–26.
Gusfield, Joseph R.: VIII–3.

Hale, Nathan G.: VII–19.
Hamilton, William: VIII–33.
Handlin, Oscar: VII–3; VIII–12.
Hanfman, E.: IX–36.
Hanson, P. G.: VIII–14.
Harper, Robert A.: VII–24; VIII–23.
Hart, H. H.: VIII–14.
Hartmann, Edward G.: VII–26.
Hartz, Louis: VII–12.
Hawker, A.: III–41.
Hawthorn, Geoffrey: VII–17.
Heard, Gerald: VIII–20.
Heath, R. G.: VIII–21.
Heidegger, Martin: VII–23.
Heinisch, Paul: IX–5.
Helm, S. T.: VIII–14.
Henderson, J. L.: IX–9.
Hensman, C.: III–41.
Herberg, Will: VII–6.
Hershon, H. L.: VIII–29.
Higham, John: VII–26.
Hirsch, Fred: VII–29.
Hoffman, Frederick J.: VII–27.
Hoffman, Helmut: VIII–14; IX–21.
Hofstadter, Richard: VII–26; VIII–32.
Hoggson, R. L.: VI–43; VIII–4; IX–31.
Holmes, R. M.: VIII–4.
Horney, Karen: IX–39.
Howe, Frederick: VII–26.
Hunter, Robert: IX–6.
Hutchison, Percy: IV–23.
Hutchison, William R.: VIII–11, 12, 26, 31.
Hurwitz, J. I.: VIII–21.
Hurwitz, Nathan: VIII–23.

Jackson, Charles: V–26.
Jackson, J. K.: VIII–4.
James, William: I–51; VIII–24.
Jellinek, E. M.: I–49; V–20, 35; VIII–14; IX–2, 8.
Johnson, Bruce Holley: I–49; VIII–3, 45; IX–8, 13.
Johnson, David W.: VII–20.
Johnson, Vernon E.: IX–24.
Jones, M. B.: V–71.
Jones, R. K.: I–54; VIII–4.
Jourard, Sidney: IX–39.

Kammeier, M. L.: VIII–14.
Kant, Immanuel: VIII–14.
Keller, Mark: I–49, VIII–14; IX–8.
Kennedy, D. M.: VII–26.
Kernberg, Otto: IX–21, 34.
Kessel, Joseph: I–54.
Kilpatrick, William: VII–20.
King, Arthur: VI–22.
King, Thomas M.: VII–23.
Kissin, Benjamin: I–3, 49; III–41; IX–3, 13.
Knight, Robert P.: VIII–14.
Koch, Adrienne: VII–13.
Kohut, Heinz: IX–21, 34.
Kolakowski, Leszek: VII–15.
Kropotkin, Peter: IX–40.
Krutch, Joseph Wood: VII–26.
Kushi, Michio: VII–18.

Landis, C.: VIII–14.
Lange, Carl Georg: VIII–24.
Lasch, Christopher: IX–34.
Leach, Barry: I–3; III–4, 41; IV–60; V–4; VII–2; VIII–21.
Lelos, D. A.: VIII–21.
Lemere, F.: VIII–4.
Leuchtenberg, William: VII–27.
Levinson, Daniel J.: VII–21.
Levy, Beryl Harold: VII–14.
Lewis, Helen: VIII–29.
Lipset, Seymour Martin: VII–12.
Lisansky, E. S.: VIII–21.
Lisansky-Gomberg, E. S.: VIII–14.
Lisman, S. A.: IX–21.
Little, G. Aiken: VIII–4.
Loper, R. G.: VIII–14.
Lovejoy, Arthur O.: VII–16.

Lubove, Roy: VII–26.
Lunn, Arnold: II–33.
Lupton, Dilworth: IV–5.
Lynd, Helen Merrell: VIII–29.

Machen, J. Gresham: VIII-43.
Madsen, William G.: VI-43; VIII-4; IX-36.
Mahler, Margaret S.: IX-33.
Malcolm, A. I.: VIII-14.
Manchester, William: VII-9.
Mandelbaum, Maurice: APX A-15.
Mann, Arthur: VII-26.
Manuel, Frank: VII-15.
Marcell, David W.: VIII-17, 31.
Marcus, Steven: VII-29.
Markey, Morris: IV-17.
Maxwell, Milton A.: V-14; VI-43; VIII-4, 22, 35; IX-17, 36.
May, Henry F.: VII-13, 27.
Mayeroff, Milton: VII-32.
McBrien, Richard P.: VIII-33.
McGaughran, C. S.: VIII-14.
McLoughlin, William G.: VII-9; VIII-11, 20, 26.
McNamara, J. H.: VIII-29.
Mead, Sidney E.: APX A-34.
Meadows, Donnella H. and Dennis L.: VII-29.
Medaglini, E.: I-54.
Meerloo, J. A. M.: VI-5.
Mendelsohn, Robert S.: VII-18.
Merk, Frederick: VII-7.
Metcalfe, G. E.: VIII-4.
Meyer, Donald: VIII-17.
Milam, James R.: IX-11.
Milgram, Gail Gleason: VIII-48.
Minogue, S. J.: V-4.
Mitchell, Broadus: VII-4.
Mogar, R. E.: VIII-14.
Morison, Samuel Eliot: VII-7.
Mouchot, G.: I-54; VIII-4.
Mowrer, O. Hobart: VIII-20, 23.
Mullahy, Patrick: VII-20, VIII-23.
Murphy, M. M.: III-41.
Murray, M. P.: IX-39.
Musto, David F.: IX-34.
Myers, Henry Alonzo: VIII-10.

Nathan, P.E.: IX-21.

Niebuhr, H. Richard: VIII-12.
Nisbet, Robert A.: VII-21; IX-40.
Noble, David: VII-26; IX-53; APX A-15.
Norris, John L.: I-3; III-4, 41; IV-60; V-4; VII-2; VIII-21.
Nouwen, Henri J. M.: IX-39.

Oden, Thomas C.: VIII-20.
Orne, M.: IX-9.

Paredes, A.: IX-3.
Parker, Charles Follen: Intr. Pt. Two.
Patten, Simon N.: VII-27.
Peabody, Richard R.: IV-53; Intr. Pt. Two.
Pease, Otis: VII-26.
Peele, Stanton: IX-38.
Pieper, Josef: IX-55.
Pine, Fred: IX-33.
Pittman, David J.: VIII-22; IX-36.
Putnam, Nina Wilcox: V-27.

Rado, S.: IX-31.
Randers, Jurgen: VII-29.
Reiss, Hans: VII-14.
Rieff, Philip: VII-16, 24; VIII-10; IX-12.
Rimland, Bernard: VII-24.
Ripley, H. S.: VIII-4.
Robinson, David: V-71.
Robinson, John A. T.: VIII-33.
Rogers, Carl R.: VIII-23.
Rokeach, Milton: VIII-7.
Roman, Paul M.: VIII-4, 23, 29.
Roth, Robert J.: I-53.
Rothman, David: VII-29.
Rudie, R. R.: VIII-14.
Ryback, R. S.: VI-5.

Sagarin, Edward: VIII-29.
Sands, P. M.: VIII-14.
Sartre, Jean-Paul: VII-23.
Savage, C.: VI-5.
Schneider, D. U.: IX-3.
Schultz, Duane: VII-20.
Schumacher, E. F.: VII-29; IX-51, 54.
Seiden, R. H.: III-41.

Bibliographic Index

Seliger, R. V.:   VIII–14, 21.
Sennett, Richard: VII–14.
Sessions, P. M.:   VIII–4.
Shannon, Homer H.:   V–27.
Sheehy, Gail: VII–21.
Sheldon, R. B.:   VIII–14.
Shoemaker, Helen Smith: II–30, 33.
Shoemaker, Samuel M.:   I–55; II–30, 33.
Shryock, Richard H.:   VII–18.
Sicherman, Barbara: VII–18.
Silkworth, William D.:   I–48; IV–23.
Silverberg, William V.:   IX–33.
Simmel, E.:   IX–31.
Simon, Steven I.:   VIII–23.
Sinclair, Andrew: VIII–3.
Sister Ignatia: III–61.
Smith, Ardis: V–26.
Smith, John E.:   I–52; VIII–1, 31.
Sontag, Susan: IX–4, 7.
Sperry, Willard L.:   VIII–29.
Spoerri, Theophil: II–33.
Stewart, David A.:   VIII–4, 29; IX–24.
Strecker, Edward A.:   Intr. Pt. Two; IX–31.
Strout, Cushing: I–54; VIII–17.
Suckling, Norman: VII–14.
Sugerman, A. Arthur: I–3, 49; IX–3, 13.
Szasz, Thomas: VIII–18, 43.

Taintor, Eliot: V–26.
Taylor, George A.:   VIII–4.
Tarter, Ralph E.:   I–3, 49; IX–3, 13, 21.
Terruwe, Anna A.:   VIII–23.
Thompson, W. H.:   VIII–4.
Thune, C. E.:   VIII–14.
Tiebout, Harry M.:   V–38; VIII–19, 20, 22; IX–50.
Tillich, Paul: VIII–1.
Tipple, John: VII–26.
Tomsovic, M.:   VIII–14.

Tremper, M.:   VIII–21; IX–31.
Trice, Harrison M.:   III–41; VIII–4, 23, 29.
Tyler, Alice Felt: VIII–3.

Ullman, A. D.:   V–35.
Unger, Roberto Mangabeira: VI–41; VII–21; IX–40, 57.

van der Does de Willebois, A. E. M.:   IX–9.
Villiaumey, E. M.:   I–54.
Voegtlin, W. L.:   VIII–4.

Walther, H. A.:   II–33.
Walzer, V.:   VIII–14.
Weber, Max: VII–17.
Weinberg, Jon R.:   VIII–22; IX–17; APX–4.
Werner, M.:   VIII–14.
Westermeyer, J.:   VIII–14.
Wheelis, Allen: VII–13; IX–57.
White, Morton: VII–26; VIII–32; IX–53, 57.
White, William A.:   VIII–14.
Whitley, O. R.:   VIII–4, 20.
Wiebe, Robert H.:   VII–26.
Wilkerson, A. E.:   I–49; IX–8.
Williams, George Huntston: VIII–38, 41.
Williams, L.:   IX–31.
Williams, William Appleman: VII–4.
Williamson, V.:   III–41.
Wills, Garry: VII–13.
Wilson, Arthur M.:   VII–14.
Wilson, Lois: I–62; II–15; III–10; IX–23.
Wilson, W. M.:   VIII–14.
Wine, D. B.:   VIII–21.
Woodruff, C. R.:   VIII–20.
Wylie, Philip: VII–11.

Yablonsky, Lewis: VIII–23; APX A-18.

General Index

A.A. *Grapevine, The*, 113, 128, 130, 190; on "Pill Problem," 115; on Washingtonian movement, 116
Absolutes, 24; rejection of, by A.A., 50-51, 239, 240, 247. *See also* "Four Absolutes"
Acceptance, 297
Active alcoholism, defined, 123
Akron, A.A. of, 234-235
Al-Anon, 191n, 210n, 295
Alcoholic: A.A.'s concern with, over alcoholism, 34, 59, 202; shifts in meaning of term, 194-196; "sober," concept of, 296
Alcoholic Foundation (later General Service Board of Alcoholics Anonymous), 68, 119, 121, 127-128; creation of, 67; transformation of, into General Service Board, 131. *See also* General Service Board
Alcoholics Anonymous, 34, 47, 52, 97, 109, 124; "The Doctor's Opinion," 22, 72; "Bill's Story," 67; "There Is A Solution," 67; writing of, 67-72, 275; "How It Works," 73, 96, 103, 213, 244-245; inclusion of "story section" in, 73-74, 186; choosing title for, 74-75; reviews of, 75-76, 91-92, 92n; publication of, 76-77, 78, 81, 82, 161; orders for, 94; on limited control, 105-106; revision of, 132, 194; sales of, 267-268; use of ordinary words in, 192

Alcoholics Anonymous Comes of Age (Bill Wilson), 52, 226, 266, 277, 280
"Alcoholics Anonymous Comes of Age" Convention (1955), 19, 46
Alcoholism Rehabilitation Act of 1968, 268
Alexander, Jack, 130, 152, 164; his story on A.A. in *Saturday Evening Post*, 87, 100-101, 102, 104-105
Alienation and anomie, 202-203
Allergy, physical, alcoholism as, 15, 22, 29, 34
Americanization, 170
American Medical Association, House of Delegates of, 129. *See also Journal of the American Medical Association*
"Americanness" of A.A., 24, 163-165, 182
American Psychiatric Association, 122 and n
American Public Health Association, 112
Amos, Frank, 65, 66, 67, 68, 176
Anonymity, A.A.'s principle of, 50, 51, 86-88, 95, 196-197; as two-sided protection, 102, 104; Bill Wilson on, 297
Answer to Addiction, The, 234
Anti-professionalism and anti-intellectualism, A.A.'s, 186, 188-192, 213
Authority: dangers inherent in exercise of, 102, 106-108; A.A.'s attitude toward, 121
Autonomy, 165-166, 167, 219

"Babies," defined, 39n
Bacon, Dr. Selden D., 118
Baltimore City Medical Society,
   Neuropsychiatric Section of, 117
Banford, Bertha, 12, 16
Beecher, Henry Ward, 186-187
Bell, Griffin, 268
Bill D., 37-39, 41, 74
Bishop, Jim, 158
Bob E., 53-55, 60-61, 62, 80-81, 86
Bok, Curtis, 100
Bradley, Alva, 86
Buchman, Frank, 9n, 48, 49, 164
Buddhists, success of A.A. among, 185,
   226-227
Bullard, Dr. John, 117
Burnham, Dr. Clark, 14, 25

Cain, Arthur, 143, 144-145
Calvary Episcopal Church (New York),
   9, 18, 24, 25, 43
Cancer and alcoholism, exploring rela-
   tionship between metaphors of,
   201-202
Capone, Al, 133
Catholic membership in A.A., 47-48,
   52
Chafetz, Dr. Morris E., *Alcoholism and
   Society* (with H. W. Demone, Jr.),
   143-144
Chambers, Francis, 158
Chemical Dependency, 347
Chessman, Caryl, 353, 381
Chipman, A. LeRoy, 65, 67
Church of the Way, The, 234, 240-241
C.I.O., 162
Civilian Conservation Corps, 162
Clarence S., 78, 83-85, 234, 236, 237;
   his interpretation of A.A., 238-240
Clark, Walter Houston, 50n
Cleveland *Plain Dealer*, 91; articles on
   A.A. in, 84, 85, 90
Cleveland Press, 128
Comprehensive Alcohol Abuse and
   Alcoholism Prevention, Treatment
   and Rehabilitation Act, 268
Compulsion, *see* Obsession-compulsion
Concepts, A.A.'s rescuing of ancient,
   192-194
Confidential magazine, 120

Control: limited, 102, 105-106, 109,
   115, 211-213; rationalization and,
   165, 166, 169-171, 180, 211, 217
Conversion, 9-10, 23, 62, 182-183,
   192; necessity of experience of, 21,
   25, 34; from self-centeredness to
   interaction with others, 34
Copernicus, Nicolaus, 165
Criticism and religion, relating of, to
   their culture, 193-194
Critiques, implicit, within A.A.,
   231-232; by those emphasizing "the
   spiritual," 232, 234-247 *passim*, 249;
   by those wary of religion, 232-234,
   249

Davis, Elrick B., 87, 88; articles on
   A.A. in Cleveland *Plain Dealer* by,
   84, 85
Daytop, 241
Dederick, Charles E., 241
Deflation at depth, 21, 23, 34, 67, 238
deKruif, Paul, 164
Demand, danger in, 125. *See also*
   Dependence; Dominance over others
Demone, Harold W., Jr., *Alcoholism and
   Society* (with M. E. Chafetz),
   143-144
Denial of being "an alcoholic," 60,
   193; antidote for, 61
Dependence: upon others, 123, 125;
   proper, 125-126; limited, 210-217
   passim; as Key to A.A.'s specificity,
   219
Dependency, alcoholism as distorted,
   202, 209-213
Depression, Great, 162, 170, 229
Descartes, René, 165, 167
Difference, value of, 152, 153, 220-221
Different, sense of being, 60, 146, 151
Disease: wariness of referring to alcoholism as, 22 and n, 34; understanding alcoholism as, rather than symptom,
   122-123; alcoholism as threefold,
   199, 202-204; use of, as metaphor,
   200-202
Dominance over others, 123, 125
Dowling, Father Edward, 46-48, 121,
   130, 152; Bill Wilson's important
   visit from, 98-100

Drugs: increasing use of psychoactive, other than alcohol, 111, 135; question of expanding A.A. program to include dependency on, 115-116, 149-150, 287

"Dry drunk," 94, 96, 123, 208

Ebby T., 9, 17-21, 17n, 24, 35, 89; his 1934 visit with Bill Wilson, 7-8, 10, 16, 33; return to drinking of, 76-77, 95

Eckhart, Meister, 180

Edwards, Jonathan, 180n

Eighteenth Amendment, 30, 229

Ellison, Jerome, 143, 144, 145, 193n

Enlightenment, age of, 165-169, 175

Ernie G., 321

Evangelical Liberalism, 247

Evangelical style of religious insight, 179-182, 184, 185, 191, 247

Evangelism, 49, 51; A.A. rejection of aggressive, 50-51

Existentialist philosophers, 168-169

Exman, Eugene, 68

Experience, primacy of, 102-104, 191

Feller, Bob, 86

Fellowship and program, 33, 104, 121-122, 159, 204; distinction between, 24 and n

Fifty Years with Gratitude, 297

Finney, Charles Grandison, 183

Firestone, Harvey, 27, 31

"Five Procedures," 49

Ford, Father John, 107

Fortune magazine, 120

Fosdick, Dr. Harry Emerson, 75, 91, 93, 130, 164

"Four Absolutes," Oxford Group's, 25, 26, 28n, 44, 102; A.A.'s rejection of, 51, 207, 212-213, 247; Bill Wilson on, 242-243

"Four Absolutes, The," pamphlet, 235

Four "founding moments" of A.A., 7-8, 9, 19-21, 28-33

Freud, Sigmund, 167

"Fundamentalist A.A.," 234

Galileo, Galilei, 165

General Service Board of A.A., 131, 133-134; and Vitamin B-3 therapy, 138; and question of incorporation, 150. *See also* Alcoholic Foundation

General Service Conference of A.A., 131, 133-134, 252-254, 258-263; proposal to form, 128-129; formation of, 129-130; acceptance of "Legacies" by, 135; and trustee ratio-change, 138-142

General Service Office of A.A., 158

Grandiosity, alcoholic, 94-95, 104, 105, 123

Gratitude, 303

Griffith, Ella, 10

Griffith, Fayette, 10-11, 16

Group conscience, A.A.'s, 64, 68

Group dynamics, 191n

"Guidance," 27-28, 31; definition of term, 28n; implicit reference to in *12&12*, 353

"Guide to the Twelve Steps of Alcoholics Anonymous," pamphlet, 234-235

Haas, Father Vincent, 80

Haggard, Dr. Howard W., 118

Hank P., 43-44, 63, 75-76, 91, 342; return to drinking of, 95, 96

Harper Brothers publishers, 68

Harper's, 142, 144

Heard, Gerald, 136

Heart disease, comparison of alcoholism to, 22 and n

Heatter, Gabriel, 90, 352

Heidegger, Martin, 168, 169

Heisenberg, Werner, 167, 218

Hemsley, Rollie, 85, 86, 87, 88, 92, 95-96

"Hitting bottom," 33, 60-61, 62, 211; development of A.A. understanding of concept of, 111, 115

Hoffer, Dr. Abram, 137

Hofstadter, Richard, *Anti-Intellectualism in American Life*, 188n-189n

"Honest," dropping of word, from "Honest desire to stop drinking," 106

Honesty, shared, *see* Shared honesty of mutual vulnerability

Hopelessness of the alcoholic, 8, 15-16, 21, 34

Howard, Dr. (psychiatrist), 75, 76
"Humanist Group, The," 371, *See also*
  "Scientific Humanists"
Humanist style of religious insight,
  179, 181, 184
Humility, 124, 128, 304
Hunter, Robert, 200
Hurwitz, Nathan, "Peer Self-Help
  Psychotherapy Groups," 192n
Hutchison, Percy, 91
Huxley, Aldous, 136, 177, 371

Identification, 60, 62, 89; as antidote
  for denial, 61
Identity, 168, 171
Ignatia, Sister, 79-80, 336
Independence, 125. *See also* Dependence
Infinity, concept of, 205
Instincts; character and role of, 125,
  126, 243; and moods, 192, 225-226
Inter-racial A.A. groups, 361
Isolation and loneliness of the alcoholic,
  19, 61
Ivy Lee, 94, 164

Jack M., 283
Jackson, Charles, 350; *The Lost
  Weekend*, 120
James, William, 26, 157, 184, 185-186;
  The Varieties of Religious Experience,
  20-21, 23, 24, 164; his influence on
  Bill Wilson, 20-21, 23-24, 33, 59,
  164; his influence on A.A., 34, 35,
  158, 181, 182; and pluralism, 151
Jellinek, Dr. E. M., 117-118, 199-200
Jim B., 63, 75, 375
John B., 282
Johns Hopkins University, 117
Journal of the American Medical Association,
  review of *Alcoholics Anonymous* in, 92n
Journal of Nervous and Mental Diseases,
  review of *Alcoholics Anonymous* in,
  92n
Journal of Studies on Alcohol, 272
Jung, Dr. Carl Gustav, 23, 26, 35,
  151, 157, 177; his contribution to
  A.A., 8-9, 21, 33-34, 59, 158, 163,
  164; and LSD experimentation, 137;
  Bill Wilson's interest in thought of,
  213

Kant, Immanuel, 165
Keely Cure, 343
"Keep It Simple" stress in A.A., 67,
  103, 193 and n
Kennedy, Dr. Foster, 93, 117
Khantzian, Edward, 289
Korean War, 163, 170

Larry J., 320
Lasker Award (1951), presentation of,
  to A.A., 112
Legacies of Recovery, Unity, and
  Service, 131, 133, 135, 138, 257
Leprosy, use of, as metaphor, 200, 201
Leuco-adrenochrome, 358
Liberal style of religious insight, 179,
  181, 184
Liberty magazine, 90, 102
"Life-changing" program, emphasis on
  A.A. as, 48 and n
Limitation: acceptance of, 3-4, 36, 109,
  122, 228; wholeness of, 57, 126, 212,
  228
Limited control, 102, 105-106, 109,
  115, 211-213
Limited dependence, 210-217 *passim*
Living Sober, 352
Locke, John, 165
Lois Remembers, 295
Loneliness, *see* Isolation and loneliness
Lost Weekend, The, 120
LSD, Bill Wilson's experientation with,
  136-137
Luddites, 172
Lupton, Rev. Dr. Dilworth, 84-85, 87

Mack, John 289
Mann, Marty, 87, 117, 126, 128; her
  public declaration of alcoholism,
  118-119, 119n, 120
"Manual for Alcoholics Anonymous,"
  234-235
Markey, Morris, 90, 102
Marxist thought, 168, 169
Massachusetts Institute of Technology,
  310
Maturity, A.A.'s, 106, 121, 126-134
  passim, 140
Maxwell, Milton, 274, 295
McCarthy, Sen. Joseph, 98n

McLuhan, Marshall, 277
Medical profession, acceptance of A.A.
by, 117, 122
Medical Society of the State of New
York, Section on Neurology and
Psychiatry of, 117
Medicine, as source of A.A., 33,
199-202
Meetings, attendance at A.A., 186,
187; format of, 332
Mencken, H. L., 164
Metaphor, use of disease as, 200-202
Moody, Dwight Lyman, 49, 164
Moral Re-Armament, *see* Oxford
Group
Morgan R., 47, 76, 90-91, 93
Mothers Against Drunk Driving
(MADD), 285
Mutual vulnerability, *see* Shared
honesty of mutual responsibility

Narcissism, 172, 385
Nation, The, 142, 145
National Committee for Education on
Alcoholism (later National Council
on Alcoholism) (N.C.E.A.), 118-119,
120, 128, 195, 270, 272
Neo-orthodoxy, 180, 181
Newman, John Henry, 9n
New York Archdiocesan Committee on
Publications, 75
New York *Daily Mirror*, 94
New York Herald-Tribune, 91
New York Times, 91
Nobel Peace Prize committee 302
Norris, John L., 259, 272-273, 281, 290
Not-God and not God, 35-36, 109,
205-207, 228, 303, 306; discussion of
terms, 3-4, 57, 173

Obsession-compulsion, 12, 15, 22, 29,
34; alcoholism as, 202, 204-209
Oden, Thomas C., "The New
Pietism," 192n
Open-mindedness, 177, 181, 371
Osmond, Dr. Humphrey, 137
"Other problems," 115, 135, 149, 161,
287. *See also* Drugs
Others, needing, 35-36, 37, 82, 178;
discussion of, 218-221

Oursler, Fulton, 52, 90
Oursler, Grace, 52
Oxford Group (later Moral Re-
Armament), 9n-10, 39-40, 41, 157;
characteristics of, 17, 164; Bill
Wilson's association with, 24-26,
43-44; "Four Absolutes" of, 25, 26,
28n, 44, 51, 102, 207, 212-213, 234,
235, 242-243, and "guidance,"
27-28, 28n; Dr. Bob Smith's association with, 28-32, 33, 53-56, 77;
problems encountered with alcoholics
at, 44-46; A.A.'s break with, 46-47;
contributions of, to A.A., 48-52, 59,
68, 158, 176; Akron A.A.'s separation from, 77, 81-82; Cleveland
A.A.'s rejection of connection with,
83-89 *passim*; Evangelical Pietist insight of, 179; its second re-
incarnation as Moral Re-Armament,
180; perdurance of ideas in *12&12*, 353
Oxford Movement, 9n

Pass It On, 295
Peabody, Richard R., 158
Pietist style of religious insight,
179-182, 184, 185, 191, 247-248
"Pigeon," 39, 205; defined, 39n
"Pill problem," 115-116, 149. *See also*
Drugs
Planck, Max, 167
Pluralism, 24, 164, 256-257; joyous,
151-152, 219, 220-221, 227
Pragmatism, 24, 104, 164, 188
"Principles before personalities," ideal
of, 88 and n, 114
Program and fellowship, 33, 104,
121-122, 159, 204; distinction be-
tween, 24 and n
Progression, 152
Progressives, Progressivism, 169-170,
172, 229
Prohibition, failure of, 30, 183, 229
Psychological approach, vs. a spiritual,
289

Quality and Quantity, 377

Racial segregation, *see* Segregation by
color

Rationalization: and control, 165, 166, 169-171, 180, 211, 217; defined, 191
Reader's Digest, The, 76, 164
Rehabilitation Act of 1973, 268
Relativism, 165, 167-168
Religion: A.A.'s wariness of, 7-8, 16n-18, 90, 194; as source of A.A., 33; and criticism, relating of, to their culture, 193-194
Religious and spiritual, distinction between, 175-178, 187, 194
Religious insights, 178; two styles of, 179-182, 184
Resentment, 54, 96, 97, 123
Responsibility, 126, 140-143, 145; as chief characteristic of maturity, 127, 139. *See also* Maturity
Restitution, necessity of, 25
Richardson, Willard, 65, 66, 67, 92, 130
Rieff, Philip, 169
Rockefeller, John D., Jr., 65, 95, 101, 130, 164, 176; his gifts of money to A.A., 66-67, 94, 280; dinner given by, to encourage A.A., 92, 93, 102
Rockefeller, Nelson, 93
Roentgen, Wilhelm, 167
Roman, P. M., ed., *The Sociology of Psychotherapy* (with H. M. Trice, ed.), 192n
Rowland, H., 8-9, 26, 33
"Rule Number 62," 107
Rutgers University Summer School of Alcohol Studies, 362

St. Augustine, 178, 205
St. Thomas Hospital (Akron), 79-80, 84
Salvation, 152-153, 178, 179, 191-192; through moral regeneration, 180-181; discussion of, 182-184; sobriety viewed as, 183-184, 185
Sartre, Jean-Paul, 168, 169
Saturday Evening Post, 106, 113, 115, 164; Alexander's story on A.A. in, 87, 100-101, 102, 104-105; criticism of A.A. in, 142, 144
"Scientific Humanists," 232-233
Scott, Albert, 65-66, 176
"Second Reader for Alcoholics Anonymous," pamphlet, 235

Segregation by color, 148n-149
Seiberling, Mrs. Henrietta, 27-28, 29, 31, 40; and controversy over Rockefeller funds for A.A., 66; and separation of Akron A.A. from Oxford Group, 81; spiritual dedication of, 152; and idea of General Service Conference, 355
Self-centeredness, 59, 95, 222-224; conversion from, 34-35; distinguished from self-esteem, 243-244
Selfishness, 34-35, 59, 243-244
Self-pity, 54, 61
Selzer, Louis, 128
Serenity Prayer, The, 297
Shared honesty of mutual vulnerability, 61, 214-215, 219, 221-224, 249, 256, 304
Sheen, Monsignor Fulton, 52
Sheppard, Norman, 27
Shoemaker, Rev. Dr. Samuel, 9, 43, 45, 283; Bill Wilson's friendship with, 24, 27; and A.A.'s break with Oxford Group, 46, 47
Silkworth, Dr. William Duncan, 21, 23, 25-26, 43, 60, 105, 151; on physical allergy and mental obsession, 15, 26, 34; his care and treatment of Bill Wilson's alcoholism, 15-16, 19, 20, 204-205; special talent of, with alcoholics, 21-22; "The Doctor's Opinion," 22, 72; and efforts to obtain funding for A.A., 65
Singleness of purpose, A.A.'s, 117, 146, 231. *See also* Unity of A.A.
Smith, Anne, 27, 28, 31-33, 69; and early years of A.A., 40, 41, 42, 55; and separation of Akron A.A. from Oxford Group, 81
Smith, Bernard B., 130, 251
Smith, Dr. Robert Holbrook (Dr. Bob), 27-28, 32-33; first interaction between Bill Wilson and, 28-32, 33, 35-36, 151-152; and first growth of A.A. (1935-1937), 37-42, 53-57; and later growth of A.A. (1937-1939), 59-63, 77; efforts of, to obtain funding for A.A., 65-67; and *Alcoholics Anonymous*, 67, 68, 69; "Keep It Simple" stress of, 67, 103, 193n;

and separation of Akron A.A. from Oxford Group, 77, 81-82, 84; his treatment of alcoholics at St. Thomas Hospital (Akron), 79-80; Wilson's respect for, 83; and Rockefeller dinner to encourage A.A., 93-94; and primacy of experience, 103, 105; and limited control, 105; and N.C.E.A., 118; position of, on A.A. maturity, 121; his stress on tolerance, 177; and "the four absolutes," 237; and Clarence S.'s initial lack of faith. 239-240

Sobriety: true, defined, 123; viewed as salvation, 183-184, 185

Socialization, 151

Sontag, Susan, 201

Special groups, 146n-149, 147n, 161, 287-288

Spiritual and religious, distinction between, 175-178, 194, 198

Spiritual: approach, 289; awakening and spiritual experience, 19-21, 34, 39, 99 and n

"Spiritual Milestones in Alcoholics Anonymous," pamphlet, 235

Spiritualism, Bill Wilson's interest in, 136

Sponsorship, 89

Sponsorship, phenomenon of, 89

Story-telling, 71-74, 186, 296

Strong, Dorothy Wilson, 10, 14

Strong, Dr. Leonard, 14, 65, 67

Surrender, act of, 54-55, 56, 61-62, 191-192; discussion of, 182-184; and Hispanic attitudes, 262

Surveys, 273-274

Survivors Program, The, 234, 240-241

Synanon, 234, 240-241

Taylor, Mary Catherine, 295

Temperance, 228-230

Therapies for alcoholism other than Alcoholics Anonymous, 158, 219

Thomsen, Robert, 13, 295

Tiebout, Dr. Harry M., 107, 119, 122n, 238, 283, 399; Bill Wilson's psychotherapy with, 126-127, 213; and General Service Conference, 128-129, 130; and trustee ratio-

change, 140-141; on conversion and surrender, 183; and success of A.A. among Buddhists, 185, 227

Tolerance, need for, stressed in A.A., 51-52, 177, 181

Tournier, Robert E., 272, 289

Towns (Charles B.) Hospital (New York), 15, 19, 22, 43; job offered to Bill Wilson at, 63-64, 189; publicity for A.A. by, 117

Towns, Charlie, 63-64

Townsend Clubs, 162

Transcendence, 136-137, 205; defined, 137n

Trice, H. M., ed., *The Sociology of Psychotherapy* (with P. M. Roman, ed.), 192n

True Confessions, 120

"Trusted servants," ideal of, 88 and n, 114

Trustee ratio-change, A.A.'s, 138-142, 145

Tuberculosis, use of, as metaphor, 200, 201

Tunks, Rev. Dr. Walter, 27

Twelfth Step work, 186, 187, 190-191

Twelve Concepts, 258, 305

Twelve Steps, 3, 70, 72, 75-76, 123, 161; parallels between Exercises of St. Ignatius and, 98-99; analysis of, 182-185; proposed revision of, 232, 233; writing of, 331

Twelve Steps and Twelve Traditions, 124-127, 132, 161, 208, 214, 280, 294; use of ordinary words in, 192; analysis of instincts in, 243

Twelve Traditions, 102, 115, 161, 189, 199 and n; formulation of, 100n, 111, 195; listing of, 113-114

Twenty-Four Hours a Day, 347

Union Club (New York City), 93

Unity of A.A., 64, 146, 231. *See also* Singleness of purpose

Vitamin B-3 therapy, Bill Wilson's promotion of, 136, 137-138

Vitt, Oscar, 86

Volstead Act, 229

Vulnerability, mutual, *see* Shared honesty of mutual vulnerability

Wallis, Hal, 120
Washingtonian movement, 116-117, 306
Washington Post, 91
"Way, The," 240-241
Webber, Delphine, 31
Weinberg, Jon R., 233
Whalon, Mark, 11, 16
Williams, T. Henry and Clarace, 81-82, 152; meetings of alcoholics at home of, 40, 56, 78, 79, 80
Wilson, Dorothy, *see* Strong, Dorothy Wilson
Wilson, Emily Griffith, 10, 11
Wilson, Gilman, 10
Wilson, Lois Burnham, 15, 19, 25, 81, 300; marriage of, to William Griffith Wilson, 13, 14; importance of her husband's sobriety to, 26, 41-42; on use of term "pigeon," 39n; and early years of A.A., 42-43; financial burdens of, 63, 64, 76, 97; founding of Al-Anon by, 210n
Wilson, William Griffith (Bill W.); Ebby T.'s 1934 visit with, 7-8, 10, 16, 33; and birth of A.A., 8-9, 27, 33, 163; and Oxford Group, 9-10, 24-26; early life of, 10-13; his first drink of alcohol, 13-14; marriage of, to Lois Burnham, 13, 14; his understanding of alcoholism, 15-16; his wariness of religion, 16-18, 24, 237; spiritual experience of, 19-21, 33; his wariness of referring to alcoholism as "disease," 22n, 34, 199; influence of William James on, 23-24, 33, 164; efforts of, to remain sober, 26-27; first interaction between Dr. Bob Smith and, 28-32, 33, 35-36, 151-152; and first growth of A.A. (1935-1937), 37-45, 56-57; and A.A.'s break with Oxford Group, 45-47; and Father Dowling, 47-48, 98-100; on contributions of Oxford Group to A.A., 48-52; his instructions in Catholic faith, 52; and later growth of A.A. (1937-1939), 59-65; job offer made to, at Towns Hospital, 63-64, 189; efforts of, to obtain funding for A.A., 65-67; and

Alexander's *Saturday Evening Post* story, 87, 101, 104-105; and sponsorship, 89; and Rockefeller dinner to encourage A.A., 92-94; and era of publicity, 95-96; depression of, 96-97; and primacy of experience, 102-104; and limited control, 105, 109; and dangers inherent in exercise of authority, 106-108; and limitations of A.A., 111-112; and "Twelve Traditions," 113-114; on "hitting bottom," 115; and "Pill problem," 115-116, 149; on Washingtonian movement, 116-117; addresses given by, 117; and N.C.E.A., 118-119; personal maturation of, 120-122; his psychotherapy with Dr. Harry M. Tiebout, 126-127; and maturity of A.A., 126-128, 130-134; and General Service Conference, 128-130; death of, 135; withdrawal of his formal leadership from A.A., 135, 138; his interest in spiritualism, 136; his experimentation with LSD, 136-137; his promotion of Vitamin B-3 therapy, 137-138; and ratio-change in A.A. trustees, 138-141, 142, 145; and A.A. responsibility, 140-143, 145; last years of, 145; death of, 135, 251-255, 293; and drugs other than alcohol, 149-150; and distinction between spiritual and religious, 177-178; and success of A.A. among Buddhists, 185, 227; and A.A.'s anti-professionalism, 189-190; and alcoholism as obsession-compulsion, 204-205; psychological thinking of, 225; on alcoholics, 229, 243; his "deflation at depth," 238; on absolutes, 242-243; on selfishness, 243-244; on perfectionism, 245-247; as "professional" 321, 334. *See also Alcoholics Anonymous; Alcoholics Anonymous Comes of Age; Twelve Steps and Twelve Traditions*
Wing, Nell, 294
Wister, William Wynne, 363
Women in A.A., 132, 393
Word and Witness, transmission of A.A.'s message by, 186-188, 192

Works Publishing, Inc. (later A.A.
World Services, Inc.) 68-69, 130
World Health Organization, 232
World War I, 170
World War II, 162, 170, 229
Wylie, Philip, 164

Yale University Summer School of
Alcohol Studies at, 117; alcohol
research, treatment, and public education programs at, 118

Other titles that will interest you. . .

The Soul of Sponsorship
The Friendship of Fr. Ed Dowling, S.J. and Bill Wilson
    by Robert Fitzgerald, S.J.
    The Soul of Sponsorship explores the relationship between Bill Wilson, cofounder of A.A., and his spiritual advisor, Father Ed Dowling. This book chronicles their unlikely friendship in an exchange of illuminating letters that spans twenty years. 141 pp. Order No. 1130

Hazelden—A Spiritual Odyssey
    by Damian McElrath
    This is the definitive history of Hazelden, both the idea and the physical reality. Using documentation, photographs, and personal remembrances, this book follows the historic revolution in the treatment of alcoholism, the tensions among Hazelden pioneers, and the debates that accompanied development. Hardcover, 174 pp.
Order No. 5004

For price and order information, or a free catalog, please call our Telephone Representatives.

HAZELDEN

1-800-328-9000
(Toll Free. U.S.,
Canada, and the
Virgin Islands)

1-651-213-4000
(Outside the U.S.
and Canada)

1-651-257-1331
(24-Hour FAX)

http://www.Hazelden.org
(World Wide Web site on Internet)

Pleasant Valley Road • P.O. Box 176 • Center City, MN 55012-0176